A Chorus Line
FAQ

A Chorus Line FAQ

All That's Left to Know About Broadway's Singular Sensation

Tom Rowan

APPLAUSE
THEATRE & CINEMA BOOKS
An Imprint of Hal Leonard Corporation

Published in 2015 by Applause Theatre and Cinema Books
An Imprint of Hal Leonard Corporation
7777 West Bluemound Road
Milwaukee, WI 53213

Trade Book Division Editorial Offices
33 Plymouth St., Montclair, NJ 07042

All photos are from the author's collection unless otherwise noted.
Every reasonable effort has been made to contact copyright holders and secure permission. Omissions can be remedied in future editions.

Songs from the musical "A Chorus Line"
Lyrics by Edward Kleban
Music by Marvin Hamlisch
©1975(Renewed)Marvin Hamlisch and Edward Kleban
All rights controlled by Wren Music Co., a division of MPL Music Publishing, Inc. and Sony/ATV Harmony
Lyrics used by permission of Flora Roberts, Inc. a/a/f the Estate of Edward Kleban

The FAQ series was conceived by Robert Rodriguez and developed with Stuart Shea.

Printed in the United States of America

Book design by Snow Creative Services

Library of Congress Cataloging-in-Publication Data

Rowan, Tom, author.
  A chorus line FAQ : all that's left to know about Broadway's singular sensation / Tom Rowan.
    pages cm
  Includes bibliographical references and index.
  ISBN 978-1-4803-6754-8 (pbk.)
1. Hamlisch, Marvin. Chorus line. 2. Kleban, Edward. Chorus line. 3. Bennett, Michael, 1943–1987. I. Title.
  ML410.H1745R69 2015
  792.6'42—dc23
                                                                          2015016063

www.applausebooks.com

For my mother, Marian Lawrence Rowan,
and the memory of my father, Thomas J. Rowan

Contents

Acknowledgments

Sargent Aborn, Bob Avian, Michael Blevins, John Breglio, Diane Buglewicz-Foote, John Cerullo, Jerry Dalia, Kurt Domoney, Vanessa Erlichson, Laurie Gamache, Penni Gladstone, Michael Gorman, Tyler Hanes, Sara Hanson, Manuel Harlan, Lisa Howe-Ebright, David Hsieh, Ken Huth, Angelique Ilo, Ken Jacques, Bradley Jones, Marybeth Keating, Paul Kolnik, Baayork Lee, Kerry Long, Ron Mandelbaum, Sonie Mathew, Stephen Nachamie, Roni Page, Joseph Patton, Robert Reagle, Rita Rehn, Angela Richardson, Justin "Squigs" Robertson, Richard Rowan, Kyle Schliefer, Melissa Scopelitis, Charlie Siedenburg, Brandon Snook, Martha Swope, Will Taylor, Scott Thompson, Alec Timerman, Robert Tunstall, Kerianne Tupac, Amanda Watkins

Preface

I was twelve years old when *A Chorus Line* opened on Broadway and already a confirmed musical theatre maven. That was the year my family moved west from upstate New York to Colorado; there was no opportunity to see the show, but we were certainly aware of the excitement it was generating. We had the cast album (on LP) in the house the next Christmas, and, though we loved the songs, we could only imagine the dancing.

I didn't actually see the show until August 1981, the summer after I graduated from high school, when the International Company made one of its visits to Denver; my parents, my younger brother, and I sat in an upper balcony at the old Denver Auditorium Theatre. We felt like we were watching the show through the wrong end of a telescope, but even from that distance the power and energy of it were unmistakable. David Thomé was Zach and Thia Fadel was Cassie in that cast; I still have the program. When I started college in Texas the next month, I bought another copy of the original cast album (this time on cassette) so I could listen to it at school; I remember it drove my roommate, who preferred Boston and Lynyrd Skynyrd, to distraction.

A Chorus Line came back into my life in a big way in the late eighties, when I was applying to graduate programs in directing. Not having been to New York City since childhood, I found myself making several trips there in 1987 and 1988 for grad school interviews. The show was still playing at the Shubert, and when my Aunt Kay, who had always lived in Queens, asked what Broadway show I wanted to see while I was in town, I said *A Chorus Line*—mainly because I knew Donna McKechnie was back in the show as Cassie. We saw her (a never-to-be-forgotten thrill) and somehow she, the show, and its message managed to help carry me through the high-pressure rounds of interviews. Seeing those hopeful characters, so highly trained and disciplined, putting it all on the line for their big chance, was inspiring; they gave me hope that the choice I was making, to pursue a risky but to me inevitable educational and career path, was valid and maybe even honorable. Each time I came to the city for more interviews I saw the show again. On some level I identified with the vulnerable dancers peering out into the dark at the unseen director, as I waited for the equally inscrutable Powers That Be to decide my fate. "I hope I get it." "I would think that by now I'm allowed."

Finally in 1990 I got into grad school and had my choice of three. I chose to enter the MFA Directing program at the University of Washington School of Drama. I said good-bye to my parents and my Denver friends and headed off to Seattle, where I had never been, and—lo and behold!—the very week I arrived, I discovered that the Visa tour of *A Chorus Line* was opening there at the Paramount Theatre. Of course I went; it was a great cast, with Randy Clements as Zach and the lovely Laurie Gamache, whom I had seen as Cassie on my last visit to the show on the other coast, again in that role. (Yes, I still have that program, too.) I felt right at home.

From that point on I continued to see the show every chance I got. I saw not only touring versions but regional theatre, university, and dinner theatre productions; I read all the books about the show as soon as they came out and collected trivia about who had done it, where, and when. People laughed at me. One day in a graduate seminar in Seattle, we were discussing Ibsen's *Rosmersholm*, a play whose heroine, the tragic Rebecca West, is facing her thirtieth birthday. Our professor, M. Burke Walker, asked us to name as many other well-known female characters from world drama as we could think of who were twenty-nine-going-on-thirty and to consider the cultural significance of that milestone birthday. Of course, one of my classmates immediately mentioned Hedda Gabler, while everyone's memory banks whirred, searching for the names of characters from Shaw and Chekhov. I jumped in enthusiastically and said: "Sheila, in *A Chorus Line*. 'I'm going to be thirty real soon. And I'm real glad.'" They looked at me like I was from another planet.

I got my degree (my directing projects including a Shaw play—and one musical!), went back to Denver for a few more years to direct Shakespeare, and finally took the plunge: I moved to New York City in 1999, after winning a Drama League Directing Fellowship. Now I could see Broadway shows whenever I wanted!—provided someone gave me a ticket, which they often did, or I could get a good discount, which I also often did. I was finally going to "make it" in the big city, as the *Chorus Line* kids dreamed of doing.

Well, I'm no longer a kid, and I haven't officially "made it" yet, though I have managed to stay pretty busy with interesting plays to direct, plus work as a literary manager, casting director, acting teacher . . . office temp, bookstore clerk—and even as a produced playwright, thank you very much. I remember I was beside myself when I heard in 2005 that my beloved *Chorus Line* would be coming back the next year in a full-scale Broadway revival! Of course I went to see it during the first week of previews—and returned nine more times over the next two years, up to and including the closing week of the run in 2008. The show had lost none of its magic, and I grew to love it more and more as I gradually came to know it by heart. Like so many other fans, I never get tired of it. Sitting (or standing) in a theatre experiencing that show is like nothing else: there's something about the way it draws you in with its unique energy and honesty. It's an inspiration and a reminder of how thrilling live theatre can be when it really connects with its audience.

Fast forward. When Applause Theatre & Cinema Books announced online that they were sponsoring a contest for writers, for the purpose of selecting a winner to author one of their projected series of FAQ books on popular musicals—and when I saw that one of the titles on the list of six you could choose from was *A Chorus Line*—I knew I had to enter. And though I had by that point grown used to the endless grind of script rejections one endures as a playwright, I somehow felt that I would win: I'd been focusing more and more on writing, hadn't I? And the trove of information and trivia about *A Chorus Line* I had been accumulating for over thirty years, until then just a private obsession, might actually turn out to be useful and lead to something real: what a concept! Fortunately I was right: I submitted my sample chapter and outline, and soon afterwards was offered the book contract. It has led to a delightful and exciting year of learning everything I didn't already know about *A Chorus Line* and, better yet, the thrill of meeting some of the fantastic and inspiring people who have worked on it over the years.

So now I am a published author. Who would have thought it? Will I ever write another book? I don't know; maybe! Will I continue to write plays, and direct, and work in the theatre? Absolutely, "as much as I can and as long as I can," as Cassie says. And as I travel on, it will be comforting to remember Cassie and Sheila and Bobby and Paul and Maggie and Mike and Diana and all the rest—still out there somewhere, standing on line in the dark, waiting for their chance, reminding us that "we're all special." Once *A Chorus Line* has become a part of your life, it stays there: a ray of hope that there might still be a place for those of us who do what we do for love.

Introduction

A Chorus Line is, arguably, the most popular and successful American musical of all time. It opened in 1975 and won nine Tony Awards, the Pulitzer Prize for Drama, and a slew of other awards. In 1983, it broke the record as the longest-running show in Broadway history: a distinction it held for fourteen years. Ten different touring companies have crisscrossed the nation, and the show has been translated into over twenty languages and produced all over the world. A hit Broadway revival in 2006, which ran for two years, and its subsequent tours revived interest in the show, and today it is nearly always onstage somewhere, in regional theatres, summer stock venues, dinner theatres, community theatres, high schools, and colleges.

What is the appeal of this unique musical, and how has it so thoroughly captured, and held, the imagination of the American public?

The show plays directly into dreams and values that are deeply rooted in the American psyche. The idea of an audition, a competition, a group of people risking it all for a job—to prove they're the best—has long been a central trope in our culture. It's one of the reasons Americans are so obsessed with sports, or beauty pageants. Baayork Lee has referred to *A Chorus Line* as "the first reality show," and indeed, the explosion in the 1990s and 2000s of competition-based reality TV programs fed into that same American obsession with Cinderella stories: the everyman putting himself on the line for a chance at a dream, being judged a winner or a loser. Anyone who's ever gone on a job interview can identify with the auditionees fighting for an opportunity to do what they love—and let's admit it, once in a while we all like, if only vicariously, to be the judge as well, the one actually making the selections. *A Chorus Line* gave us a chance to root for the underdog, to choose our favorites, and then hold our breath till we found out who got the job—and weep for those who didn't. Current television shows like *American Idol, The Voice, America's Got Talent, Dancing with the Stars*, and so forth satisfy those same deep-seated needs. There have even been a few (such as the British *How Do You Solve a Problem Like Maria?* and the American *Grease: You're the One That I Want!*) where the prize was an actual role in a West End or Broadway musical!

A closer look, though, reveals that *A Chorus Line* is something subtler, something deeper than this, perhaps even slyly subversive. Dancers in the show have expressed indignation at the existence of programs like *You're the One That I Want!*; the implication that anybody off the street could be a Broadway star seems to negate the years of discipline and self-sacrifice and grueling, expensive training real dancers commit to in pursuit of their goals. And after all, the seventeen auditionees standing on that white line are *not* competing for a shot at stardom or celebrity; as the show's finale makes startlingly clear, they are asking for a chance to dance in a uniform, anonymous kick line *behind* a star. It's love of the work itself that drives them, not any misplaced desire for wealth (which won't be forthcoming in any case) or the proverbial fifteen minutes of fame. Somewhere in there can perhaps be seen a metaphorical critique of the American dream: do we chase success by competing to be as much like everybody else as possible?

The show is a product of the mid-seventies, and creator Michael Bennett said he was partially inspired by the negative example of the Watergate scandal. Americans had discovered lying and corruption at the highest levels of government; what they were hungry for was truth and honesty. What made *A Chorus Line* unique in its time were the openness and integrity the young dancers brought to the game; called on to reveal their hopes and dreams, the traumas and disappointments and struggles they had experienced growing up, they did so with what was then, especially for a Broadway musical, unprecedented honesty and stark frankness (not to mention an engaging humor; it's a very funny show as well).

Just as importantly, it's all done with remarkable economy of means. As original cast member Priscilla Lopez expressed in the book *On the Line*: "People talk about how powerful the childhood stories are, but what registers with me is how it *looks*. You're in blackness, in a black hole standing on a very narrow white line talking into nothingness, to this anonymous voice. There's nothing to hold on to. How much more vulnerable can one be? The show hits the vulnerability in everyone." Indeed, the uniquely stripped-down style of the show, its elegantly streamlined look, the sleek power of the choreography, and the driving, almost nonstop musical score all combined to express those universal themes through a uniquely thrilling aesthetic experience.

Michael Kantor and Laurence Maslon, in their comprehensive 2004 study of the history of the Broadway musical, eloquently expressed the paradoxes that give the show its unique power: "It is an anti-musical or, perhaps more accurately, the first counterintuitive musical. It had no scenery beyond some mirrors, no costumes but leotards except for a few spangles for the finale, no setting other than a non-descript theater, no intermission, and no star. Its very ethos was contrary to every convention the American musical had carefully built up over a century. As far back as *Sally* in 1920, musicals were about girls getting out of the chorus line to become stars; here, Cassie, Donna McKechnie's character, is a star *manqué* who is desperate to get *back* into the chorus line. . . . The fact that (Bennett) achieved his goal by introducing the world to the anonymity of the chorus line he so desperately sought to escape is but one of *A Chorus Line*'s many ironies."

Part of what made the show unique was the innovative workshopping process, pioneered by Bennett and producer Joseph Papp, that allowed it to develop organically through a months-long collaboration between the cast and the creative team. Due to the unique nature of its development and its enormous success with the public, *A Chorus Line* has already been the subject of more books than probably any other single musical. The purpose of this new volume is to consolidate much of the historical information while bringing the still ongoing story of the show into the twenty-first century, with chapters about more recent developments like the controversial film version, the Broadway revival, touring companies, and the plethora of regional productions all over the country.

This book is designed not necessarily to be read through cover to cover (though you are welcome to do that if so inclined!) but more as a reference book on anything you could think of to ask about the show. If you're a novice going to see *A Chorus Line* for the first time (and if so, I'm jealous!), there is plenty of information here to give you the context and the background to appreciate it. If you're an actor hoping to be cast in a production, you'll find in-depth analysis of the characters and the score that may help you prepare your audition; and if you're a producer or director considering putting on your own production, the historical and technical information here should help get you started. There's a chapter on the other books available on the topic, as well as a compendium of data on regional, local, and notable school productions, and an archive of cast lists for the major Broadway, West End, and American touring productions.

Most of all, our hope is that this book will entertain and inform you as it accompanies you on your own personal journey into the fascinating and wonderful world of *A Chorus Line*. For fifteen years, the Playbill for the Broadway production carried the following note: "The characters portrayed in A CHORUS LINE are, for the most part, based upon the lives and experiences of Broadway dancers. This show is dedicated to anyone who has ever danced in a chorus or marched in step . . . anywhere." When the show first opened downtown, the creative team wondered if it might prove to be an insider show, so specialized that only theatre people would be able to appreciate it. Obviously, they needn't have worried. By sharing their own specific struggles and dreams with such rare authenticity, they created an experience that's universal. And that more than anything else is what makes great theatre.

"It Would Be Better if I Knew Something About You"

How the Idea for *A Chorus Line* Was Born

Most musical theatre fans know that *A Chorus Line* grew out of a tape recording of a late-night rap session Michael Bennett had with a group of Broadway dancers, in which they talked about their lives, their dreams, and their hopes for the future. They also know that some of the stories told that night ended up in the script of the musical and that many of the dancers who took part in the tape session were cast in the show, some playing characters based on themselves.

Less well known are the names of the two dancers who conceived of the rap session with Bennett and were instrumental in making it happen: Michon Peacock and Tony Stevens. Both were experienced Broadway chorus dancers whose careers had started in the 1960s.

Two Dancers with an Idea

Hailing from the Midwest, Tony Stevens made his Broadway debut in a 1969 flop called *The Fig Leaves Are Falling*. In what sounds like a joke, his next three Broadway shows were entitled *Billy*, *Jimmy*, and *Georgy*—all flops that opened and closed within a year of each other. Then he went on to the Broadway revivals of *The Boy Friend*, *On the Town* (with Donna McKechnie), and *Irene*. Though he was a key player in getting *A Chorus Line* off the ground and took part in the first workshop, he ended up leaving to assist Bob Fosse on the choreography for *Chicago*, which turned out to be *ACL*'s main competition during the 1975–76 Broadway season. Stevens went on to an illustrious career as a director, working extensively in musical theatre and in films: movies he choreographed include *The Best Little Whorehouse in Texas*, *She's Having a Baby*, and *Johnny Dangerously*. He also choreographed nightclub and television appearances for such stars as Liza Minnelli, Bette Midler, Mary Tyler Moore, Dolly Parton, and Bernadette Peters. On Broadway he provided choreography for *Rockabye Hamlet* and *Perfectly Frank* and directed *The Wind in the Willows*. Ten years after Michael Bennett's death, Stevens directed and choreographed the 1997 touring production of his hit *Dreamgirls*. His last Broadway credit was reproducing

Bob Fosse numbers for the musical revue *Chita Rivera: The Dancer's Life* in 2005; he died in 2011.

Michon Peacock hails from St. Paul, Minnesota. She had made her Broadway debut with Stevens in *Georgy* in 1970 and went on to appear in a revival of the play *Beggar on Horseback* and in the musical revue *That's Entertainment*, which was choreographed by Larry Fuller, an early boyfriend of Michael Bennett's. After working with both Bennett and Stevens on the revamp of *Seesaw* and helping to launch the project that would become *A Chorus Line*, she moved on, like Stevens, to *Chicago*, in which she created the role of Annie, one of the merry murderesses, and understudied Chita Rivera as Velma Kelly. She last worked on Broadway in 1981, when she stood by once again for Ms. Rivera in *Bring Back Birdie*, the sequel to *Bye Bye Birdie*; she remained active in the industry for many years as the conservatory director of CAP 21, a major training institution for young musical theatre performers in New York.

The Legacy of *Rachael*

In a sense, the basic idea for *A Chorus Line* originated with Peacock and Stevens as surely as it did with Michael Bennett. In early 1974, both of them had recently worked on one of Broadway's most legendary flop musicals, the infamous *Rachael Lily Rosenbloom and Don't You Ever Forget It*. Peacock was in the cast and Stevens was the choreographer for this campy show about a wannabe Hollywood actress; the ensemble also included Carole (later known as Kelly) Bishop, Wayne Cilento, and Thommie Walsh, all of whom would be in the original cast of *ACL*; and Jane Robertson, who would take part in the workshop at the Public Theater. The dancers in *Rachael Lily Rosenbloom* considered it a low point in their careers, partly because of the poor quality of the material itself and partly because of the insulting way they were treated during the process by the directors. The original director was Ron Link, and he was replaced by Tom Eyen, one of the musical's authors. Stevens, who was choreographing his first Broadway musical, saw much of his work cut and replaced by new numbers choreographed by Grover Dale (who happened to be the choreographer Bennett had effectively replaced earlier that year on *Seesaw*). Stevens and Peacock had long conversations about how tired they were of seeing people treat dancers as if they were scenery, not giving them credit for any intelligence whatsoever. As Broadway dancers (known as "gypsies") move from show to show, they learn a lot about how the business works, both as art and as commerce, and many of them also develop interests and skills in acting, singing, directing, choreography, design, etc. Stevens and Peacock felt sure that if a group of Broadway's best dancers pooled their talents to create their own show from scratch, they could come up with something much better than *Rachael Lily Rosenbloom* or any number of other misbegotten projects in which they had been stuck performing. As Stevens later put it, after that experience "it became clear that most of us—the dancers in the show, the chorus people—knew more about how to put a show together than many of the producers we had worked for. That

The original cast onstage at the Public Theater, 1975.   *Photo by Martha Swope; Photofest*

we approached the work with much more discipline, and with a sense of movement and freedom that other people didn't have" (quoted in Denny Martin Flinn's 1989 book *What They Did for Love: The Untold Story Behind the Making of A CHORUS LINE*).

Broadway in the early to mid-1970s appeared to be dying. Shows were getting much more expensive to produce, and the number of musicals opening on Broadway each year had dwindled alarmingly. This meant that there were more dancers, and more talented dancers, out of work than ever before. Peacock and several of her dancer friends were Buddhists. The N.S.A. Buddhist sect that she was involved with—along with Nicholas Dante, who would be one of the book writers of *A Chorus Line*—had a philosophy of "creating value," giving back to society, taking initiative, and making positive things happen. So Peacock and Stevens decided to try to create a project that would utilize the unappreciated talents of their dancer friends, create art with merit, and better the lot of the Broadway dancer.

The idea they came up with was to start a dance/theatre company made up completely of Broadway dancers. They knew they had friends who were talented enough to make it work creatively; what they needed was someone with influence who could give the project legitimacy and help raise the needed funding. One of the first people they thought of was Michael Bennett, with whom they had both recently worked on the musical *Seesaw*. So they approached him with their idea and asked for advice.

A Musical About Dancers

Synchronicity was at work here, because Bennett had been thinking of a project somewhat along the same lines for years: a show by and about dancers, though he didn't know what form it would take or how to go about putting it together. He never forgot his own roots as a performer, and sometimes felt that the position of power and authority he had gained as a director and choreographer put unwelcome distance between him and the people he most identified with—the gypsies. He wanted to reconnect with that group, celebrate them, and give them something back.

Bennett, Stevens, and Peacock decided to start by getting together a group of the best and most interesting dancers they knew: dancers with minds of their own, with special talents, hidden or otherwise, who would be honest and open and willing to share and talk. Peacock immediately decided to include Nicholas Dante, because she knew he wanted to be a writer and thought he was talented; once on board, he helped make some of the decisions about whom else to invite. Many in the group would be people Bennett had worked with on other shows, but he made a point of saying he didn't want it to be just "his" dancers and included some performers he didn't already know. He also stipulated that it shouldn't be just a cozy group of friends; he wanted some enemies there as well, dancers who had established rivalries and felt competitive with each other, to see what that energy would bring to the group.

A Snowy Saturday Night

The now-legendary all-night session took place on a Saturday night in January 1974. It was scheduled to begin at midnight, because some of the dancers were working in shows that didn't end till around eleven. The location was the Nickolaus Exercise Center at 297 Third Avenue, near 23rd Street; it was made available free of charge because one of the owners, a former dancer named Bill Thompson, was a member of the same Buddhist group as Peacock. Though Bennett had to approve each of the dancers selected, Peacock contacted most of them herself via phone. She was sometimes hesitant to mention Bennett's involvement, as she thought some people might be intimidated if they knew he was planning to attend, though it turned out that his name helped attract some of the key players. Not everyone Peacock called agreed to come; some were wary, or scared. (There are probably some who still kick themselves over turning down the invitation, wondering whether they might have become cast members or even characters in *A Chorus Line* if they had only agreed to go!) Ironically, two who declined to attend were Bob Avian, already firmly established as Bennett's collaborator and right-hand man on all of his projects, and Baayork Lee, who had also known Bennett for years and assisted him. Lee later stated that she felt offended that Peacock rather than Bennett had been the one to call her, since she and Bennett were so close, and that she was also reluctant to talk about private and personal things in front of a group. Avian had a similar negative reaction to what sounded to him like a group therapy session. (Of course, the two of them were both soon brought on board for the project anyway, Avian as associate choreographer and Lee assisting as well as creating the role of Connie.)

The tape session is chronicled in some detail in several different books, including Flinn's mentioned above, as well as Ken Mandelbaum's *A Chorus Line and the Musicals of Michael Bennett* (1989), Kevin Kelly's *One Singular Sensation: The Michael Bennett Story* (1990), Donna McKechnie's memoir *Time Steps: My Musical Comedy Life*, and *On the Line: The Creation of A Chorus Line*, the chronicle of the show's history by Baayork Lee, Thommie Walsh, and Robert Viagas (referred to hereafter for simplicity's sake as "Viagas"). The entire original cast of the show was interviewed for that publication, and all of the books make extensive use of interviews with dancers who were present that night, so it's worth noting that there are subtle but substantial inconsistencies among the various accounts. Some of the dancers don't recall the date accurately or the number of dancers present. Though both Flinn and Mandelbaum's books specify the exact date as January 18, 1974, Viagas, whose coauthor Thommie Walsh was there, lists it as January 26. It's tempting to give Flinn and Mandelbaum the benefit of the doubt because they agree—until one discovers that the 18th was a Friday, and all accounts specify that the event was held on a Saturday night. The location of the studio space gets erroneously moved uptown five blocks to "28th Street" in two versions, as far up as "The East Thirties" in another, and down to "the Lower East Side" in yet another. The number of dancers who took part is remembered as "about twenty-two" in Kelly's book, "two dozen" in Flinn's. Mandelbaum and Viagas put the number at eighteen or nineteen and provide what appears to be a reasonably complete and comprehensive list of the participants. In addition to Bennett, Peacock, Stevens, and Dante, they included eight dancers who would eventually be part of the original cast of *A Chorus Line*: Renee Baughman, Carole Bishop, Wayne Cilento, Patricia Garland, Priscilla Lopez, Donna McKechnie, Thommie Walsh, and Sammy Williams. There was also a married couple there, Steve Boockvor and Denise Pence. The others were Steve Anthony, Candy Brown, Christopher Chadman, and Jacki Garland (sister of Patricia). Mandelbaum states that Mitzi Hamilton was there, although Flinn reports very specifically that she had been invited but had to decline because she was still recovering from breast augmentation surgery. Thompson, the studio owner, was also there and occasionally took part. Dancer Andy Bew was left off Mandelbaum's list but included in Viagas's, and Flinn quotes him, so it seems definite that he was there as well. Viagas also mentions Crissy Wilzak, who would be an understudy in the original cast.

Taking Class

The midnight session started with a dance class taught by Tony Stevens. Some of the dancers enjoyed this and felt it helped them loosen up and begin to feel comfortable together as a group, while others—especially if they had already done two performances on Broadway that day—were a bit impatient with it. The tension in the room rose when Bennett (clad in a fur coat) and McKechnie arrived, after the class was well under way; at that point, the dancers started competing for Bennett's attention and approval. After the class, there was a meal: Bennett provided huge sandwiches from the Stage Deli and a jug of red wine. Curiously, Kevin Kelly quotes Michon Peacock as saying: "Michael provided the food, the booze, the joints, the drug of your choice, whatever." (Other than a mention in Viagas that a few of the dancers smoked pot during the taping, there's no other indication that drugs were involved.)

Forming a Circle

After they ate, the dancers went into another room, where they sat on the floor, which was carpeted and equipped with pillows. Peacock remembers them sitting in a rectangular configuration. Bennett asked if it was okay with everyone if he recorded the conversation, then turned on a large, old-fashioned reel-to-reel tape recorder (It was a Sony, owned by Tony Stevens). He and Peacock and Stevens had written out a long list of questions for the dancers. Bennett began—much like Zach in *A Chorus Line*—by asking each dancer to state his or her name, stage name if it was different, and where and when they were born. Then he quickly modified that, saying the women didn't have to tell their ages if they didn't want to. Kelly Bishop— already the assertive and opinionated voice in the room like the character Sheila she would later play in the show—said she felt that was a double standard and, if openness was the goal, there was no reason why the women shouldn't give their ages just like the men. (This is an interesting detail, because Bishop herself was about to turn thirty at the time; she reported later that she had felt pleased to be entering that more adult phase of her life and was happy to advertise it. This found its way into the show: when Sheila introduces herself, she states wryly that she's "real glad" she's turning thirty—but that line has usually been read with a sarcastic edge by actresses who take a less positive view of the situation.) Bennett agreed, and also assented to Bishop's other suggestion, which was that everyone should tell their astrological sign (remember this was the seventies). In order to help break the ice, Bennett went first in answering each question, and then they would go around the circle, each dancer responding in turn and ending with McKechnie, since she was sitting next to Bennett. Bennett had already spent substantial time in analysis, as had McKechnie, who noted how that experience informed his lead-ing of the session. After the general intros, the questions moved chronologically through the dancers' lives, from early childhood and first dance classes through the traumatic teen years and their first jobs. Bennett didn't want anyone to feel pressured, so he said any dancer could choose to pass on any question he or she wasn't comfortable answering.

As it happened, though, they found they grew more and more secure opening up to each other, partly because of how frank Bennett himself was in responding to each question. Normally a private person, he revealed things that night that he generally didn't discuss in public, like his confusion over his sexuality and his relationships with both men and women—including two dance teachers who had taken advantage of him when he was very young. He talked about a dancer he toured with in *West Side Story* whom he admitted to having

Sherisse Springer as Sheila recalls a painful childhood at Musical
Theatre West, 2012. Behind her are Chryssie Whitehead as Cassie and
Matthew Williams as Bobby.   *Photo by Ken Jacques*

gotten pregnant (an episode generally not mentioned elsewhere, even in Kevin
Kelly's biography of Bennett). As he was already known to his intimates as something of a manipulator, Bennett's stories that night might have elicited skepticism
in the minds of some of those present: was he embellishing for "shock value" or
to encourage the others to open up? But McKechnie, who probably knew him
best, said later that most of what he shared that night rang true, and she ended up
feeling closer to him than ever before. She herself initially felt that Bennett didn't
necessarily want her to take part in the conversation. To some degree, it was already
an audition of sorts in his mind, and he knew from the start that whatever show or
project grew out of the session would include her; he had invited her mainly as a
friend, and for moral support. She also later wondered if he was afraid her honest
answers to some of the questions would tarnish his idealized image of her. But as
the night wore on she found herself participating more than she had expected she

would; hearing other dancers' stories inspired her, and when it came her turn to talk at the end of each round she opened up.

Dancers are performers who by nature love to be onstage, and there was at first some competition lingering beneath the surface; a few of the participants worried about how interesting their own stories would be or plotted ways to try to top the others. Thommie Walsh attempted to lighten the tone by being funny (as his character Bobby would later do in the show, before Zach asks him not to "do a routine"). But any sense of one-upmanship was soon dissipated in a growing sea of empathy as the dancers discovered how much they had in common. The more they listened, the more they wanted to share, and the prepared list of questions soon became unnecessary as the conversation took on a life of its own.

Sammy Williams's self-esteem was very low at the time, and he felt embarrassed and reluctant to talk about himself; he made Walsh, who was his friend, promise to sit next to him throughout the night for moral support. But he forced himself to answer each question and gradually opened up more and more, ultimately finding it a liberating experience.

Some of the dancers shared painful and personal memories they had seldom if ever talked about before—in particular Andy Bew, who spoke movingly about his mother's death in a boating accident, a traumatic experience he had been keeping bottled up inside him for years.

Jacki and Trish Garland each spoke of the difficulties of having a sister who was also a dancer and the competition they felt for their mother's affection; Trish later admitted she'd been less than forthcoming during that part of the discussion, for fear of hurting her sister's feelings. Steve Boockvor and Denise Pence, who had only been married for a year, talked about the challenges of being a couple in the business, sometimes auditioning for the same shows. Christopher Chadman, who was in *Pippin* at the time and lived on the East Side (unusual for a Broadway dancer), talked about his love of clothes, which he used to mask his insecurities and which some misinterpreted as snobbery. (Though he wouldn't be in the original cast of *A Chorus Line*, Chadman would become the second actor to play Bobby on Broadway, and his reminiscences were used as part of the basis for the character of Greg, played by Michel Stuart, as well.) Thommie Walsh was irritated that a few of the dancers dozed off briefly at times during the course of the night, apparently not quite as consistently excited by the conversation as he was.

A Story to Remember

One story that had a profound effect on all present was that of Nicholas Dante. He told of being asked to leave his Catholic high school at sixteen when he came out as gay, then dancing for three years in a drag revue, a job he managed to keep secret from his family—until they happened to come backstage to drop off his luggage before the show was to leave on tour. He was mortified when they discovered his secret, then deeply moved when they proved able to accept him; accepting himself and discovering pride in who he was took longer. This personal and moving account found its way into the script of *A Chorus Line* (for which Dante was to serve as co-librettist) almost unchanged from how he told it that first night. It was to become the play's longest monologue and an indelible moment in the show; as the first honest exploration of a gay man's story in a mainstream Broadway musical, it would be a pivotal moment in the history of the American theatre as well.

Another story that found its way into the show largely intact was Priscilla Lopez's account of being belittled by an insensitive acting teacher at the High School of Performing Arts—though the song "Nothing" would protect the guilty by changing the teacher's name.

All of the dancers who were present at that tape session later recalled having come to the end of it with a deep sense of camaraderie, born out of mutual compassion and understanding. Though some of them had first entered the room as rivals and competitors, even enemies, they discovered common ground they hadn't known they'd shared. Many of them grew up in broken homes or had alcoholic parents; many had felt like outsiders, even misfits, in high school. They opened up with private stories of sexual confusions and awakenings that they hadn't often been able to talk about; they found many of them shared similar reasons for falling in love with dance—and now faced the same fears about their uncertain futures. The talk lasted all through the snowy night; when the sun came up, they did another dance warm-up to reenergize themselves and stay focused, and then continued to share stories until noon. Finally, after twelve hours, the talk drew to a close, and the dancers all stood in a circle. They held hands, closing their eyes and sharing the energy they had generated as a group, passing it around and around the room until most of them were crying. They heard the noon bells from a nearby church chiming as they left the building and headed for their individual homes. They knew in their hearts and in their bones that they had experienced something unique, an experience that had changed their lives and would bond them together as a group from that day forward. As Trish Garland told Robert Viagas: "Something had been born that night." But none of them knew what it was or what it might become.

Next Steps

Bennett, Peacock, and Stevens were excited about how well the session had gone and about the quality of what they had captured on the tapes. Even though the event had lasted twelve hours, they hadn't had time to get to all the questions they wanted to ask; basically, they had progressed to the point where each dancer had arrived in New York. So they decided to schedule another session to pick up where they had left off.

Though Bennett's goal was to get the exact same group of people together for the second session, the realities of life in the business made this impossible. Some people were unavailable, and a few new ones took their places. One of the newcomers was Jane Robertson, who would develop the role of Bebe in the forthcoming workshop but depart for another project. Another was Mitzi Hamilton, born Carol Patricie, now recovered from the breast augmentation surgery that had kept her from accepting her invitation to the first session. She told the story of the how and the why of her decision to transform her body, which was to become the basis for the song "Dance: Ten; Looks: Three"—more commonly referred to as "Tits and Ass."

This second session was held at the same location, again at midnight. The different accounts place it two or three weeks after the first; Mandelbaum specifies February 8, 1974, as the date. This time, Wayne Cilento taught the dance class that got things started, rather than Tony Stevens. He came in with a long and very ambitious jazz combination for the others to learn. Though several of them grumbled about how hard it was, Cilento was gratified when Bennett, who had been watching from the sidelines, decided he wanted to learn it too and joined in with the group.

Though copious new material was recorded that night, and much of it ultimately proved useful, most of those present seem to agree that the second event, almost inevitably, failed to recapture the magic of the first. The format was somewhat different. The new dancers spoke first, filling the others in about their childhoods, in order to catch up to the point where the first session had left off. The original plan of having each person answer each question in turn was discarded. This time, Bennett would throw out a question to the whole group, and rather than progressing methodically around the circle, the discussion was open to whomever wanted to speak first. The conversation thus developed in more of a free-form fashion.

Priscilla Lopez, who had likened the first session to group therapy only more successful, said the addition of newcomers into what had become a close and insular group felt somewhat invasive. There was also a magnified sense (also present to some degree in the first session) that many of the dancers were telling their stories specifically to Michael Bennett. Of course, it was also about sharing with each other, but Bennett, by virtue of his personality, his charisma and the power they all knew he wielded, became the father-confessor figure—which would later translate into the commanding but often invisible character of Zach, the director, in the show. The participants knew that on some level they were already auditioning for something.

They were all eager to find out what was going to happen next—especially Stevens, Peacock, and Dante. But for a while Bennett kept any plans he might have been making quite close to the vest. He did have a follow-up meeting in his home office with the three of them, at which he said he didn't really think there was necessarily a stage show in the material, but that maybe it could become a book. Peacock was particularly frustrated by this, as she felt there was so much life and theatricality in the stories. Dante later realized Bennett was stalling partly in order to distance the rest of them from the project; although Peacock and Stevens had been involved with hatching the original plan, Bennett wasn't at all sure he wanted to work with them on the show.

For a while the parties went their separate ways. Stevens and Peacock attempted to continue on their original path: establishing a dance theatre company made up entirely of dancers who would generate and produce their own projects. They chose a name for their group: the Broadway Creative Commune (did we mention it was the seventies?), then changed it to the Ensemble Theatre. They took steps to apply for nonprofit status and continued to have meetings with some of the dancers. Enthusiasm soon started to fizzle. Several people were outspoken about their reluctance to work and share their training and skill without remuneration. Others felt that Peacock and Stevens, however much they liked them, didn't have the clout to make the project a reality on a business level. They had come to the tape sessions because of Bennett's involvement, and the consensus was that, if anything real were to grow out of them, he was the one who could make it happen.

Bennett meanwhile had already committed to directing a new play, Herb Gardner's *Thieves*. He cast it, rehearsed it, and went to New Haven, then Boston for the out-of-town tryouts. But the experience on *Thieves* was not a happy one, and Bennett was not able to convince Gardner to provide the rewrites he thought were needed. Both he and actress Valerie Harper departed the project (they were replaced by Charles Grodin as director and Marlo Thomas as leading lady). With its new team, the play went on to a substantial run on Broadway, but a frustrated Bennett returned to New York more determined than ever to create something of his own.

He called another meeting with Peacock, Stevens, and Dante—this time admitting that he felt the tapes had theatrical potential and that he was talking to Joseph Papp of the New York Shakespeare Festival about producing a workshop at his Public Theater. He produced release forms for the three to sign, granting him rights to the material on the tapes, and paid each of them a dollar to make it official. Peacock and Stevens were uneasy, feeling so close to the material and protective of it, but after some months of trying unsuccessfully to get their production company off the ground, they had to admit that Bennett was probably the one who had the energy and the influence to turn the tapes into a real show.

Bennett told them he wasn't at all sure what form the piece would take, though Peacock has said she's quite sure it was already taking shape in his mind as a musical. He knew in his guts that, given the chance to conceive his own show and mastermind its development from the ground up, he could build something extraordinary—perhaps even something that would change the face of the American musical. And he was determined to do just that.

The Title

Though it was a long time before the show had an official title, and it was often referred to simply as "the dancer project" during the workshops, an excerpt from the original tape session that is heard in the film *Every Little Step* reveals that Bennett at that time was already thinking of the show as being called *A Chorus Line*. Though some people tried to get him to change it to simply "Chorus Line" before starting previews at the Public, and he famously claimed the "A" had to be included because it would put them first in the newspapers' ABC listings, the indefinite article was already part of the title he mentioned that very first night.

"I Can Do That"

The Story of Michael Bennett

Any in-depth discussion of *A Chorus Line* must of course begin with the enigmatic man who created it: the director/choreographer Michael Bennett (1943–1987). Most Broadway musicals are known as the creations of their composers or composer/lyricist teams: "Stephen Sondheim's *Sweeney Todd*"; "Rodgers and Hammerstein's *South Pacific*"; "Lerner and Loewe's *My Fair Lady*." It's rare indeed for a musical's tagline to feature the director's name, but *ACL* has been known for decades all over the world as "Michael Bennett's *A Chorus Line*." Even Bennett's role model Jerome Robbins wasn't granted such auteur status, and the more recent examples of the phenomenon (for example, "Bob Fosse's *Dancin'*"; "Susan Stroman's *Contact*"; "Twyla Tharp's *Movin' Out*") have generally been dance musicals without original scores or much dialogue. In Bennett's case, the lion's share of acclaim he received was not without controversy: book writers James Kirkwood and Nicholas Dante both publicly expressed frustration with what they felt was a lack of credit due, and many of the dancers whose life stories were used eventually felt pushed aside. But few would question that *A Chorus Line* is Michael Bennett's baby: his conception, his vision, and in many respects an expression both of his life experiences and his strongly held convictions about dancers and show business.

Childhood

He was born in cold and snowy Buffalo, New York (like the character Bobby in the show), the son of Salvatore DiFiglia (known to his friends as Sam) and his wife Helen Ternoff DiFiglia. He was baptized Michael Bennett DiFiglia, and that middle name was perhaps a tribute by his mother to her Jewish heritage. The baby had been conceived before the couple's marriage, and she may have felt she had to raise him Catholic in order to stay on good terms with DiFiglia and his Italian American family. As a child, he was soon known as "Mickey."

Restless and lively even before he could walk, Mickey quickly impressed his very attentive mother, who had a strong feeling that he was going to grow up to achieve special things. At the age of two, he was dancing around their Buffalo apartment to music on the radio (much like *A Chorus Line*'s Judy and Maggie), and his Aunt Mimi offered to put him into class at Miss Betty Rogers's School of Dance before he turned three. At four, he won a prize for singing on *The Uncle Jerry Show*—a local radio program.

Bennett's father, Sam, worked for years as a machinist for General Motors and had a big gambling problem; his mother was a receptionist for Sears Roebuck, and the family never had much money. When Mickey was four, his parents had a second son, Frank. Because Helen had to work full time, much of the responsibility for taking care of Frank fell on Mickey, who would fix meals for his brother and take care of numerous other household chores until their mother got home. (He also took little Frank down to the basement and taught him tap routines.)

Helen DiFiglia wanted her sons to grow up with culture, so she took them to the movies frequently—often choosing a musical—and Michael saw his first Broadway show, *The Pajama Game* (1954), on a trip into New York City when he was eleven years old. The excitement of the show increased his appetite for

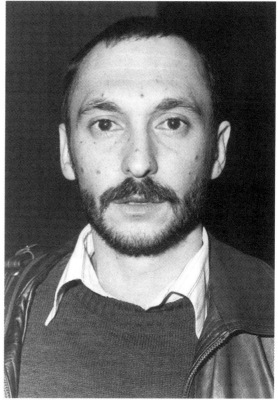

Michael Bennett

dancing. After preliminary training with Betty Rogers and further studies with local dance teachers Norma Ferrara Gelose and Beverly Fletcher, at age nine he joined a local group called Mrs. John Dunn's Little Stars of Tomorrow, which performed at hospitals and orphanages. More performing opportunities followed at weddings and parties, and soon the pint-sized song-and-dance man was appearing on the radio and on a local television show called *TV Party Time*. As a teenager, he taught dance classes himself and started his own company. He put together ambitious stage shows for his high school—and soon began, despite his youth, to perform in nightclubs (like the character Don in *ACL*).

Though Sam DiFiglia wasn't delighted to see Michael pursuing "sissy" activities, he was smarting under gambling debts and soon started to speculate about his talented son's earning potential. This led to one of the most notorious episodes in Bennett's life story: his father tried to sell a part interest in young Mickey's career to one of his Mafia friends, in exchange for having his current debts paid off. (Claiming the story has been exaggerated, Frank has said he believes their father actually needed the money to pay for Mickey's dental work.) The friend brought another associate over for an impromptu audition: they watched Mickey dance, but they weren't impressed enough to buy into the deal. (Looking at the amount of money Bennett eventually made from *A Chorus Line*, one wonders if these small-time gangsters were still around to kick themselves over their poor judgment!) Young Mickey was scarred by the experience, especially after being told that the Mafia was also responsible for the murder of his uncle Michael. He later admitted that his paranoia and fear of the mob was a psychological struggle he dealt with on and off for the rest of his life; it only intensified as he grew older.

Bennett was too talented and ambitious to be satisfied for long with life in isolated Buffalo. Longing for the bright lights of show business, he got his first extended taste of that life as early as the age of twelve, when his mother arranged for him to spend the summer studying dance at a studio in the middle of the Theatre District in New York City.

Learning the Ropes

Michael made his professional acting debut in his mid-teens, playing Puck in Shakespeare's *A Midsummer Night's Dream* at the Studio Arena Theatre, Buffalo's major regional house. During his high school years, he spent more time in New York in the summers studying dance. He got his first summer stock gig in 1959 as an apprentice with the Melody Fair Theatre in Buffalo. This three-thousand–seat theatre was part of a chain of similar venues, which was in turn part of the Straw Hat circuit, a loose network of professional summer stock theatres. Many of them were actually huge tents, where full seasons of hastily rehearsed, professionally cast revivals (often featuring big stars) of popular Broadway fare were churned out every summer. It was a bustling, colorful world that has mostly vanished. Being immersed in that kind of work was great training for a young dancer who wanted to choreograph and was eager to learn every aspect of the craft of the theatre. The teenaged Bennett bonded with Jack Lenny, manager of the theatre chain, who sensed the young man's potential and became a mentor. Michael asked Lenny to be his agent, which led to a business relationship and friendship that would last for decades.

The next year, Bennett returned to the Melody Fair as a fully professional cast member, having auditioned in New York for a stock revival of *West Side Story* set to tour the circuit. Diminutive and baby-faced at seventeen, he was cast as Baby John, one of the Jets. With a book by Arthur Laurents, lyrics by a young Stephen Sondheim, and music by Leonard Bernstein, *West Side Story* was largely the brainchild of its original director/choreographer, Jerome Robbins. Michael had seen the show on Broadway during one of his summers studying in the city, and it inspired him deeply, especially its demonstration of how powerfully a director/choreographer's vision could unify a production. Although the 1960 summer stock tour of the show in which he performed was directed by Gerald Freedman, it utilized most of the original choreography, giving the young dancer a chance to experience Robbins's thrilling work from the inside.

West Side Story was also the reason Michael Bennett never finished high school—something he regretted in later years. His high school career had not been a smooth one. He had originally attended Hutchinson Technical High School, where he didn't much care for the mechanical engineering curriculum but excelled in extracurricular activities. Like the character Richie in *A Chorus Line*, he was into everything, including the Newspaper Club, Student Council, and even the cheerleading squad. Inevitably, he began to put together musical shows at the school, producing two impressive variety revues, but he spent so much time rehearsing them (not to mention his own performing dates around town) that he ended up flunking four classes. Not wanting to repeat his sophomore year as the school required, he transferred instead to the coincidentally named Bennett High School, where he continued with his producing and directing enterprises—and incurred the jealousy of one Dan Kublitz, an English teacher, who was in charge of the school's drama productions. Years later in an interview, Kublitz claimed the teenaged Bennett hadn't been a standout performer (shades of "Mr. Karp," the unsupportive, ego-crushing high school acting teacher who temporarily stymied *A Chorus Line*'s Diana Morales!); he was also envious of the attention Michael's productions drew away from the school's official musical and dramatic offerings, which he himself directed. When Michael announced he was dropping out of school to play Baby John again on a tour headed for Europe, the teacher cautioned him against it, but to no avail. Kublitz later told Bennett's biographer, Kevin Kelly, that Michael took the school's name along with him when he left. That sounds like an egocentric misapprehension on the teacher's part, since "Bennett" was the middle name on Michael's baptism certificate, dated 1943. (Curiously, though, Donna McKechnie later wrote in her own memoirs that Michael had told her his choice of a stage name came from "Bennett High.")

Preparing for the European tour of *West Side Story*, Michael had an opportunity, however brief, to work with Jerome Robbins himself. The legendary director came in to rehearse the newly hired dancers, who were joining a cast that had already performed the show on tour throughout the United States and in a return engagement on Broadway. These returning cast members included Bob Avian, who soon became Michael's best friend and confidant and would later serve as an assistant or associate on all of his productions.

Making It in New York

After completing the tour, Michael, still only eighteen years old, got an apartment in New York City and began to pursue his Broadway dreams. He also had his first serious girlfriend: Audrey Hays, a dancer from the tour (she had played Velma), who was approximately ten years his senior. They lived together for two years in New York and seemed happy enough, but Michael, even at that age, had problems with intimacy. He convinced himself that Audrey needed too much from him and that the relationship would get in the way of his fast-developing career, so he decided to end it. Unable to face her directly, he asked Avian to tell her it was over, after which he and Avian became roommates, renting an apartment in Chelsea for seventy-four dollars a month.

By that point Michael's New York career was off and running. During his first years in the city, he was cast as a dancer in three Broadway musicals. These were:

Subways Are for Sleeping

This 1961 show had a book and lyrics by Betty Comden and Adolph Green and a score by Jule Styne, all major figures in musical theatre history. Far from their best-remembered work, it ran just long enough at the St. James Theatre to earn a profit. The story was "suggested" by a nonfiction book by Edmund G. Love about his experiences sleeping on New York City trains and the eccentric people he met and observed there. The show starred Sydney Chaplin (son of silent film great Charlie Chaplin), who would have his most memorable Broadway assignment a couple of years later as Nicky Arnstein in the original cast of *Funny Girl*, and Carol Lawrence, who had been the original Maria in *West Side Story*; Orson Bean and Phyllis Newman (wife of lyricist Green) also had roles. The director/choreographer was Michael Kidd, known for his high-flying choreography for Hollywood films like *Seven Brides for Seven Brothers* and *The Band Wagon* as well as several previous Broadway musicals. Bennett was recommended for the job when the show was already in rehearsal; the stage manager knew him from *West Side Story* and suggested him to Kidd as a replacement for a dancer who had been fired. Kidd's choreography was considered one of the show's greatest assets, and he was willing to incorporate input from his dancers. Bennett brought his own personal style and knowledge of contemporary social dance forms to a trio he and dance captain John Sharpe performed with Lawrence at the top of the second act, and he was also featured in a number called "Be a Santa," about a group of sidewalk Santa Clauses who break into a dance routine done in a faux-Russian balletic style. In addition to the young Bennett, the dance ensemble included Sandra (sometimes known as Sandy) Roveta, who years later would be chosen by him to play Cassie in the first International Company of *A Chorus Line*.

Here's Love

Santa Claus figured again in Bennett's second Broadway musical, *Here's Love* (1963), with book, music, and lyrics by Meredith Willson (*The Music Man, The Unsinkable Molly Brown*). This was the first of several musicals Bennett worked on that played the Shubert Theatre, which twelve years later would become the Broadway home of *A Chorus Line*. It was based on the classic holiday film *Miracle on 34th Street*, about a Macy's Santa Claus trying to prove that he is the real thing and the little girl whose life he changes. Michael Kidd was on board once again, but this time only as choreographer; the direction was by Stuart Ostrow, also the show's producer, who took the reins from the original director, Norman Jewison, during rehearsals. As on *Subways*, Kidd made use of some of Bennett's choreographic ideas, especially in a dream ballet where he danced the part of a rag doll. Laurence Naismith played Santa, with Valerie Lee as the little girl and Janis Paige (who had starred in *The Pajama Game*, the first show Bennett ever saw on Broadway) as her mother; Craig Stevens was the leading man. Along with Bennett, the dance ensemble included Sandy Roveta once again, as well as Baayork Lee, who would become one of Bennett's closest associates. In addition, *Here's Love*'s lighting designer was Tharon Musser, who would go on to light *ACL* and other Bennett shows; one can see how, even at this very early stage, Bennett was making note of outstanding talents and beginning to assemble his own team.

Bajour

Bennett's third and final Broadway gig as a performer, *Bajour* also opened at the Shubert, but moved shortly thereafter to the Lunt-Fontanne. The 1964 show had songs by Walter Marks and a book by Ernest Kinoy; it was based on a couple of *New Yorker* short stories about life among New York City's gypsy clans and starred Chita Rivera, one of the all-time great Broadway dancers. On this show, Bennett got to work with another major choreographer, Peter Gennaro, perhaps best remembered today as the choreographer of the original production of *Annie* (1977).

Those three shows represent the sum total of Michael Bennett's appearances onstage as a Broadway dancer. No sooner had he started his New York performing career than he began to look for opportunities to do what he really wanted to do: choreography. He began by staging dances for summer stock revivals of recent hits like *The Pajama Game* and *West Side Story*. His personal life was developing as well: during his run in *Bajour*, he met Larry Fuller, a handsome red-headed chorus boy who was performing on Broadway in *Funny Girl* at the time. The two fell in love and were soon living together in an apartment on West End Avenue. The relationship lasted for about three years, until Fuller discovered that Bennett was engaging in simultaneous affairs with several other people, both male and female. The two split up over Bennett's relationship with another chorus dancer, Scott Pearson—the man many have said was the great love of his life. (Years later, after Fuller had seen *A Chorus Line*, Bennett told him their breakup had suggested some of the lines in Zach and Cassie's confrontation scene; he also said Fuller had been the inspiration for the character of Zach's assistant, named Larry in his honor.) But it was in 1962 that Bennett got his next major career opportunity.

Nowhere to Go but Up

Bennett had only danced in one Broadway show when he was hired as assistant choreographer for this musical, a flop that ran for only nine performances in November 1962. It had music by Sol Berkowitz and a book and lyrics by James Lipton. Helmed by Sidney Lumet, better known as a film director, and choreographed by Ron Field in his first Broadway assignment, the show was about Prohibition agents in the 1920s. Its stars were Tom Bosley, Martin Balsam, and Dorothy Loudon. Loudon praised Bennett in later years for working with her extensively not only on her tapping but on her stage movement, and gave him substantial credit for the good reviews she received in a show that was otherwise mostly panned by critics.

Hullabaloo

Bennett's Broadway career as an assistant choreographer began and ended with that one show. But he was already making a name for himself with TV work, most notably the NBC series *Hullabaloo* (1964–66). This was a musical variety show on which pop and rock musicians performed their hit singles, backed by an ensemble of eight top-notch dancers. Bennett danced on the show and also found himself contributing choreography—much of it inspired by one of the girl dancers, an extraordinary talent named Donna McKechnie. The two found they had complementary dance styles and were able to bring out the best in each other, and they quickly became fast friends. Speaking years later to Rose Eichenbaum in an interview for the book *The Dancer Within: Intimate Conversations with Great Dancers*, McKechnie said of Bennett: "He loved my dancing, my line, my dynamic, but more than that, it was the emotional connection and power I could bring to his choreography." The two connected on many levels, having both started dancing early as an escape from the emotional pressures of living in troubled families. Like Michael, Donna had dropped out of high school to take a job dancing in a tour; both of them had danced on Broadway before landing on *Hullabaloo*. McKechnie would be involved with Bennett's next big stage project: a new Broadway-bound musical which he was hired to choreograph, at the age of just twenty-three.

A Joyful Noise

This musical was based on a novel by Borden Deal called *The Insolent Breed*. Edward Padula, who had been one of the producers on *Bajour* (as well as the earlier hit *Bye Bye Birdie*), conceived the idea for a musical adaptation and wrote the book; the songs were by Oscar Brand and Paul Nassau. Padula had sensed Bennett's enormous potential during *Bajour* and offered him the choreographer job. Rather than playing an out-of-town engagement in one of the traditional big tryout cities, the producers took the unusual route of developing their show on a tour of the summer stock circuit—a world Bennett, of course, was very familiar with. McKechnie was cast to play the leading ingénue role of Jenny Lee, an innocent Tennessee girl who has a romance with an aspiring country singer (played by Broadway legend John Raitt) that leads to his being driven out of town by her angry father. Dancers Bennett hired for the show included favorites Leland Palmer (one of Bennett's assistants, who was also romantically linked with him at the time), Baayork Lee, and Tommy Tune, as well as Scott Pearson. Lee later told Peter Filichia (in his book on *Broadway Musical MVPs*) how hard the dancers worked: "Giving Michael what he wanted was very hard. Every step he ever saw was in that show. He had us do so much clog dancing that we got shin splints, and we couldn't move our thighs because he was having us dance so close to the ground."

Though the show was initially well received in some of its summer tent engagements, big problems arose on the way to Broadway. Directorial duties were credited to Padula, the producer and book writer, but Raitt and several others were unhappy with the script, and at one point late in the process Padula brought in Dore Schary, a writer/director/producer with substantial Hollywood credits, to try to improve both the book and the staging. McKechnie grappled with a role that made no use of her dancing talent; at one point, Bennett tried to help by adding a small dance for her, but to no avail: Schary's innovations included several cast firings, including McKechnie, who was replaced for Broadway by Susan Watson. Ultimately, however, Schary found he couldn't do much with the show and left the project shortly before the Broadway opening; he was not credited in the Playbill. Padula found himself turning more and more to Bennett; he was so impressed with the young man's choreography, as well as the energy and style he brought to the work, that he came to rely on him for substantial help with the direction. Bennett probably could have had a codirector credit, but his agent, Jack Lenny, advised him against it because he could tell the show was unlikely to be favorably reviewed. As it turned out, Bennett's choreography was one of the only aspects of the show the New York critics liked. *A Joyful Noise* opened on December 15, 1966, at the Mark Hellinger Theatre (which was where the movie of *A Chorus Line* would be filmed almost twenty years later). The show lasted only twelve performances and closed on Christmas Eve, but Bennett emerged from the experience with his first Tony nomination.

Henry, Sweet Henry

Often a choreographer won't get a second chance on Broadway if his first effort turns out to be a big flop, but since Bennett's dances were considered some of the few praiseworthy elements of *A Joyful Noise*, he was shortly offered another show. *Henry, Sweet Henry* was based on a novel by Nora Johnson called *The World of Henry Orient*. The musical adaptation had a score by Bob Merrill and a book by Johnson's father, Nunnally Johnson, known primarily for his work as a screenwriter, producer, and director of films. He had already adapted *The World of Henry Orient* as a screenplay for a 1965 film version that starred Peter Sellers; the film's director, George Roy Hill, was also slated to direct the stage musical version. The protagonist's unusual last name was a play on words, as Nora Johnson had based the character on the concert pianist Oscar Levant, and "Levant" is a French word for Orient. Though the film had been very successful, the musical was not well reviewed. Some later blamed this on the fact that it opened right after the revolutionary rock musical *Hair*, beside which it seemed a bit old-fashioned and conventional (this despite the fact that it did contain one hippie-inspired production number, called "Weary Near to Dyin'," set in Washington Square Park). Don Ameche played the title role, in a cast that also included Bob Avian (also second assistant to Bennett) as well as Priscilla Lopez, Baayork Lee, and John Mineo (who would all be in the original Broadway company of *A Chorus Line*). The dance arrangements were done by two composers who would later write shows for Bennett: Marvin Hamlisch (*A Chorus Line*) and William Goldenberg (*Ballroom*). Though the show didn't run that much longer than *A Joyful Noise*, it did get Bennett a second Tony nomination.

Neva Small, a member of the cast, reminisced about Bennett in an interview for the 1993 book *Sing Out, Louise! 150 Stars of the Musical Theatre Remember 50 Years on Broadway*. "I was a teenager, and it was only his second show, and I had a crush on him. He couldn't do anything wrong, as far as I was concerned. I wasn't a great dancer, to say the least, and I remember he taught me the steps for 'I Wonder How It Is to Dance with a Boy' and I was very tentative, and he said, 'That's it! It's perfect! I want it just the way it is now.' I used to wander up West End Avenue and just stand outside his building and just look, because he lived there."

Broadway Milestones

In the late sixties, Bennett embarked on a series of projects that would consolidate his aesthetic ideas and seal his reputation as a major director/choreographer, paving the way to *A Chorus Line*. They followed one on another quite quickly, making this seven-year period a particular fertile time in his career.

Promises, Promises

In 1968, Bennett the choreographer finally had his first genuine Broadway hit with *Promises, Promises*, the musical adaptation of the Billy Wilder/I. A. L. Diamond film classic *The Apartment*. This show boasted the first, and only, original Broadway score penned by hit songwriters Burt Bacharach and Hal David. David Merrick was the producer and Neil Simon the book writer. The director was Robert Moore, fresh from his Off-Broadway success with the groundbreaking gay play *The Boys in the Band*, and since Moore had never before done a musical, Bennett had a lot of freedom and responsibility for staging not just dances but songs and scene transitions. This was the last Broadway musical on which Bob Avian was billed as Bennett's assistant choreographer; his credit was elevated to associate or co-choreographer on their subsequent collaborations. The cast was led by Jerry Orbach and Jill O'Hara, and the dance ensemble included future *ACL* cast members Kelly Bishop and Baayork Lee. Donna McKechnie, playing a secretary, established herself definitively as Bennett's star dancer by leading the show-stopping production number "Turkey Lurkey Time," an exuberant and intricately choreographed depiction of an office Christmas party. Other cast members included Marian Mercer, Ken Howard, future director/choreographer Graciela Daniele, and Rita O'Connor, who would be a replacement Sheila in *A Chorus Line*. *Promises, Promises* ran for over three years at the Shubert Theatre and was also produced in London and as a U.S. tour (both featuring McKechnie in her original role). The show won Tony Awards for Orbach and Mercer; Bennett's choreography was nominated, but he lost the award to Joe Layton, who won for the tap dance–heavy *George M!*

Coco

Bennett's next outing as a Broadway choreographer was a less satisfying and more trouble-plagued project. The 1969 musical *Coco* was based on the life of the legendary French fashion designer Coco Chanel; it had a book and lyrics by Alan Jay Lerner (famed for his classic collaborations with composer Frederick Loewe on *My Fair Lady* and *Camelot*) and music by André Previn (highly regarded as a versatile pianist, conductor, and composer). Though Previn has won four Academy Awards for film scores, and would later write the opera version of *A Streetcar Named Desire*, *Coco* was his only score for a Broadway musical. It was also the only musical that the great stage and film star Katharine Hepburn ever appeared in. The cast also included George Rose, both Graciela Daniele and Rita O'Connor from *Promises, Promises*, and several more future *ACL* cast members: Don Percassi, Carolyn Kirsch, Ann Reinking, and Charlene Ryan. Bennett did copious research for the project, even spending a couple weeks in Paris at the real Coco Chanel's studio. She was an octogenarian at the time but still designing clothes, and so taken with Bennett that she tried to persuade him to give up theatre in favor of the fashion industry! Bennett and Hepburn did not get along quite as well; the formidable star was highly opinionated and slow to realize that, as a nonsinger and nondancer, she needed all the help she could get from her choreographer. At Hepburn's request, Michael Benthall, a British director with many Shakespearean productions but no musicals to his credit, was hired to direct; he floundered in the unfamiliar territory of musical theatre and proved to have a serious drinking problem as well. By default, Bennett found himself taking on more and more of the directing responsibilities. He and Avian came up with some stylish production numbers for the elegant dancers who played fashion models in the show and, once Hepburn recognized her limitations, were able to tailor the staging as much as possible to what she could do. Though Bennett wasn't thrilled with Lerner's decision to use film footage in the staging (an early example of projection design, which has become much more prevalent and sophisticated in recent years), he used the show as an opportunity to continue to develop a personal staging style that was in fact cinematic, featuring fluid use of turntables and other devices designed to overlap scenes and facilitate seamless segues. By critical consensus, *Coco* was generally deemed to be more style than substance. However, Hepburn's superstar status guaranteed sellouts, and because she agreed to do the national tour as well, the show ultimately turned a profit. In the end, Hepburn and Bennett came to a place of mutual respect, but the whole rocky experience took a serious toll on the choreographer's nerves. There was no out-of-town tryout, and the first preview audience was basically a who's who of New York show business; Bennett found the stress unbearable since the production was hardly ready to be seen by so critical an audience. Demoralized over the quality of the show, he missed rehearsals during the last week of previews and, immediately following the opening, retreated to London to have a breakdown.

Company

Bennett's next Broadway show marked the beginning of an extremely important phase in the development of his art: his collaboration with legendary director/producer Harold Prince, which began with *Company* and continued with *Follies* the next season. Both musicals have scores by the great Stephen Sondheim. Prince had expressed an interest in working with Bennett as early as 1967, when Bennett had just choreographed *A Joyful Noise* and Prince had opened one of his finest creations as a director, the musical *Cabaret*. The two took a meeting at that time, but it wasn't until a couple of years later that they found a vehicle on which to collaborate. Prince was directing *Company*, based on a series of one-act plays by George Furth about marriage in contemporary New York. Furth adapted and combined the vignettes into a book for the musical; Sondheim supplied both music and lyrics. The show followed Robert (often called Bobby), an attractive but enigmatic bachelor, through various interactions with five married couples as well as dates with three different girlfriends. Although the resulting portrait of married life is ambivalent and even caustic, Bobby seems to have decided by the end that he wants to commit to a relationship, as expressed in the great song "Being Alive."

The musical was not conceived as a particularly dance-heavy show, but Prince very much wanted Bennett for the musical staging, and he sweetened the deal by casting Donna McKechnie in the show; she became Kathy, one of Bobby's three love interests, and Bennett built "Tick Tock," a spectacular dance solo, around her talents. The number was a sensation, a rare moment of unleashed passion and sensuality in a show that was largely about alienation and ambivalence. But it was the subject of some controversy during the tryout period, as neither Sondheim nor Prince was fully convinced the dance belonged in the show and at one point threatened to cut it. McKechnie fought for it, and it was saved and emerged as a highlight, but Sondheim was to rethink the scene once again over twenty-five years later for a London revival; the number was cut from that production and most subsequent versions. Happily, though, the dance was restored for the New York Philharmonic's 2011 production of *Company* at Lincoln Center, with Neil Patrick Harris, Patti LuPone, and an all-star cast directed by Lonny Price. In this version, later shown in movie theatres and issued on DVD, a new version of "Tick Tock," choreographed by Josh Rhodes, was performed by Chryssie Whitehead as Kathy, supported by four backup dancers.

Company is considered a groundbreaking show in Broadway musical history, one of the first "concept" musicals, structured as a collage of scenes and songs exploring variations on a central theme rather than a linear storyline. As such, it influenced Bennett's developing aesthetic—and the direction he would pursue with *A Chorus Line*. (Fun esoteric trivia: Both *Company* and *A Chorus Line* have characters named Bobby, Paul, and Larry.)

Follies

The next season Sondheim, Prince, and Bennett collaborated again, and this time Prince called on Bennett not only to choreograph but to be his codirector. The property was a piece that Sondheim and James Goldman had been working on for years. Under an earlier title, "The Girls Upstairs," it had been slated for Broadway production twice since 1966, but in both cases the producers failed to come through. The first script Bennett was shown was a murder mystery, and Bob Avian told him he couldn't make any sense out of it, but Prince was already in the process of working with Sondheim and Goldman to refashion the material and refocus the story. Inspired by a famous 1960 *Life* magazine photo of film star Gloria Swanson standing in the rubble of the Roxy, a demolished movie palace, the musical *Follies* took shape as a surreal depiction of a reunion of former Broadway showgirls in a theatre about to be torn down; gradually, the disappointments of their careers and their marriages come into focus. From the vantage point of the bleak and cynical 1970s, *Follies* looks back with ironic affection at an earlier Broadway, a more innocent and optimistic time in the history of American popular culture. The title plays on the double meaning of the word: a Broadway extravaganza like the *Ziegfeld Follies*, or acts of naïveté and foolishness. Sondheim's dazzling score featured pastiche numbers that skillfully evoked the earlier era while exposing the characters' fears and neuroses with enormous insight and specificity; by contrast, Goldman's book can strike audiences as fragmented and sometimes simplistic and artificial. Nevertheless, the hugely ambitious and stylish show was another step forward in the development of the concept musical, and the degree to which the story and structure were shaped by the entire creative team, including Prince and Bennett, was unusual if not unique. This doubtless planted in Bennett's mind the idea that an entire musical could be generated and shaped primarily by a director/choreographer—if that individual had a powerful enough vision to become the primary engine behind its creation, rather than functioning mainly as an interpreter of the work of the show's writers. If, as Bennett stated, *Coco* had in some ways prepared him for *Follies*, it's also true that *Follies* helped pave the way toward *A Chorus Line*.

Harold Prince was the prime visionary behind the shaping of the script and directed the dramatic scenes, but the overall physicalization of the show, including the staging of most of the musical numbers and transitions, fell to Bennett. With Avian's close collaboration, he did some of his finest work ("Who's That Woman?," for example, has been called the best number ever staged on Broadway). Still, it's rare for a Broadway musical to have two directors, and there was often tension between the members of the team. Bennett began to grow disenchanted with the show's dark, jaundiced tone and attempted without much success to persuade Sondheim, Goldman, and Prince that an added dose of hopefulness could be beneficial. At one point, he fought to have Neil Simon brought in to improve the book—something he would later do on both *Seesaw* and *A Chorus Line*. But codirector Prince was also the show's producer, and he finally pulled rank: the book stayed basically as it was. Ultimately, the critical and audience response backed Bennett up to some degree in his reservations about the script: the musical was highly respected in some quarters but never became a commercial hit or turned a profit. It has developed a cult following over the years, however, and is a favorite of many Sondheim devotees; there were Broadway revivals in 2001 and 2011.

Follies played a particularly important role in the development of Bennett's aesthetic, and Ken Mandelbaum in his book on Bennett's work makes some interesting points: "As in *Follies*, *A Chorus Line* takes place in an empty theatre, and both deal in character revelation and the past. Both deal simultaneously on levels of reality and nonreality. In *Follies*, we are simultaneously at a reunion of showgirls and on a metaphorical plane where the central characters review their lives and attempt to come to terms with disillusionment. In *A Chorus Line*, we are at an audition, but one that becomes everybody's audition for acceptance and love."

Bennett as Show Doctor

With two Tony nominations to his credit, and a growing reputation as a brilliant young choreographer with a great eye, Bennett found himself being called upon to act as a "show doctor," meaning someone who is called in to observe and suggest improvements to a show already in rehearsal. Sometimes the show doctor receives credit in the program; other times, he or she remains anonymous. Bennett helped out a good many people in this capacity over the years, and two of the first projects he contributed to were the Off-Broadway musical *Your Own Thing* and the Broadway show *How Now, Dow Jones*. Though he never asked for credit and did it out of friendship and a love of theatre, Bennett's behind-the-scenes contributions helped numerous productions find success.

Skipping ahead: Bennett briefly helped director A. J. Antoon with Neil Simon's *The Good Doctor* in 1973; this led to the offer to direct the same playwright's *God's Favorite*. And he would continue to work as a show doctor on and off for the rest of his career, seldom receiving official credit. One of the last times he did so was not a particularly happy experience for anyone. Though he had counted Tommy Tune as a close friend and collaborator for years, Bennett began to think of him as something of a competitor once Tune started directing and choreographing his own musicals. The rivalry came to a head during Tony Awards season in 1982, when Bennett was nominated for directing *Dreamgirls* but Tune won for his production of *Nine*, much to Bennett's chagrin. The next year, Bennett made a misguided attempt to revive the friendship by offering his services as a show doctor for *My One and Only*, a musical that Tune was starring in as well as directing and choreographing with his frequent collaborator, Thommie Walsh (who had been the original Bobby in *A Chorus Line*; Ronald Dennis, the original Richie, was in the cast, and Baayork Lee was associate choreographer). Bennett made aggressive changes to the show during its out-of-town tryout, but Tune and others felt his modifications were out of keeping with the delicate and whimsical tone of the show. One of the producers finally asked Bennett to leave, and Tune later said all of his work was discarded before the opening on Broadway; the relationship between the two was further strained by the experience.

Still, Bennett had not completely lost his touch as a show doctor. The next year he was called in to help with Stephen Sondheim and James Lapine's *Sunday in the Park with George*. In an interview with the *New York Times*, book-writer and director Lapine said: "'I think he's the best. In a sea of adverse opinion, Michael was a voice of reason and support. He has that real knowledge and sense of detail."

Twigs

The year after *Company*, Bennett worked with George Furth again as director of the latter's comedy *Twigs*. This was the first nonmusical play that Bennett had directed, and as such he saw it as a major career step. (The show can be seen as the real-life counterpart of the play Zach was directing when Cassie left him, as recalled in their argument in *A Chorus Line*: "If I could direct a straight play and pull it off, it meant I wasn't going to be stuck just making up dance steps the rest of my life.") A bittersweet series of related one-acts about four women and their troubled relationships, all taking place over Thanksgiving weekend, the production starred

Sada Thompson. She played all four of the central women (the old lady in the last scene is revealed to be the mother of the other three) and credited Bennett with seeing her potential and shepherding her to a breakout performance. Produced by Frederick Brisson in association with Plum Productions Inc. (the name Bennett had given his own production company), the play opened at the Broadhurst Theatre on November 14, 1971. Notably, Furth's original title for the play had been *A Chorus Line*—though it's hard to see how that name relates to the material. Obviously it was changed, but Bennett would call Furth several years later to ask permission to use the original title for another project. . . .

Seesaw

Bennett soon found himself merging his by now frequent endeavors as a show doctor with his primary career as a director/choreographer. He was called on to rescue a show struggling in its out-of-town tryout and ended up not only taking over the direction but even being credited as having written the show's book. The property was *Seesaw*, a musical version of a popular two-character play by William Gibson (best known for *The Miracle Worker*) called *Two for the Seesaw*, which is a New York love story about the unlikely pairing of Gittel Mosca, a kooky aspiring dancer, and Jerry Ryan, a conservative Midwestern lawyer in the midst of a divorce. The score was by Cy Coleman and Dorothy Fields (*Sweet Charity*), and the book, at least originally, was by Michael Stewart (*Bye Bye Birdie, Hello, Dolly!*). The lead producers were Joseph Kipness, known as a restaurateur, and Lawrence Kasha; together they had produced the 1970 musical *Applause*. They asked Bennett to direct *Seesaw* when they were first putting together their team, and he turned the project down, but Kipness called him again months later after the show, as directed by Edwin Sherin, had started previews at the Fisher Theatre in Detroit. Not much about the production was working, and Bennett had acquired such a strong reputation as a show doctor that Kipness thought he was the only person who could fix it. Bennett and Avian went to Detroit to see the show and politely declined to get involved, but Kipness, who had earned the nickname "Cryin' Joe" for his emotional outbursts, wept and begged until they relented.

Though Bennett thought *Seesaw* was a mess, he believed in the touching central love story and thought the score had merit, so there seemed to be something there worth saving. The clincher was that Kipness said he would do whatever Bennett asked; he gave his new director carte blanche, agreeing that he could change anything he wanted to change without having to get the approval of anyone—even the authors. Still smarting a bit from his failure to get all the changes he wanted made on *Follies*, Bennett was aware of the pitfalls of theatre by committee; he was now stepping into the auteur-director role he would occupy for the rest of his career. Sherin was soon out of a job. Choreographer Grover Dale, who had known Bennett since they had performed together in *West Side Story*, was kept around, but only one of his numbers was retained in the show; he was ultimately billed as co-choreographer, and Bennett brought in both Avian and Tommy Tune as associates. Grover Dale's main job as the work progressed was to inform various ensemble members one by one that their contracts were being terminated before Broadway, in essence doing Bennett's dirty work for him. Tune was originally asked to choreograph two numbers for Bill Starr, an actor in the show who was his friend, but after observing his work Bennett decided to fire Starr and asked Tune to join the cast and perform the numbers himself; the results would lead to a Tony Award and a huge boost for Tune's career.

The most dramatic cast change was the firing of the actress playing the leading role of Gittel: Lainie Kazan. Bennett knew immediately he wanted to replace her but needed her to finish the Detroit run of the original version of the show, which continued to be performed each night as he worked on the new one during the day. She could tell something was up when he came to see the show every night but never gave her notes or wanted to work with her on her songs. When her manager broke the bad news, she agreed to finish the Detroit run but asked to speak with Bennett to find out what the problem was; she later claimed that he would barely talk to her and that she took years to recover emotionally from the traumatic experience. Kazan also felt her career suffered—though she was able to bounce back to substantial successes on TV and in the movies as well as on Broadway in *My Favorite Year* (1993), in which she recreated a role she had played on film. Her replacement in *Seesaw* was Michele Lee, ironically a friend of hers.

Bennett had felt that Kazan, overweight at the time, wasn't believable in the role of a dancer, and though Lee wasn't really a dancer either, she looked more like one. She also brought to the show a polish and a sophistication that represented the qualities Bennett wanted to impart to the production as a whole. The Detroit version, set in Spanish Harlem, had a grittiness to it that Bennett replaced with a sleek, chic veneer, refashioning the show as something of a love letter to the glamour and excitement of New York City itself.

This time, Bennett was able to bring Neil Simon in to doctor the book; the playwright reportedly suggested cuts and wrote a few one-liners. Original librettist Stewart, however, was so unhappy about the new direction the show was taking that he asked to have his name removed from the program; when lyricist Dorothy Fields, who had written the book for *Annie Get Your Gun*, also declined credit for the libretto, Bennett became the author of record—though much of the dialogue came more or less directly from Gibson's original play and contributions were made by countless people including some of the actors. Bennett reshaped the whole piece and molded it into something workable and entertaining; the show that opened at the Uris Theatre (Broadway's largest, since renamed the Gershwin) on March 18, 1973, received generally favorable reviews. The revisions had been costly, though, and the producers had little money left for advertising, so the show was threatened with closing immediately; it was saved partly by a publicity gimmick that brought John Lindsay, then the mayor of New York, onstage as a guest in one number. Bennett also helped out financially: his lawyer, John Breglio, revealed years later that the director himself had paid the actors' salaries for a week when the production was in danger of closing. Business picked up somewhat, and the show ended up running till December. Because the sweeping changes Bennett and Avian made had to be implemented so quickly, there were things they still wanted to fix, and additional revisions were made for the subsequent tour, which starred

Lucie Arnaz and John Gavin as Gittel and Jerry. That version was generally found to be superior to the Broadway production.

Though *Seesaw* enjoyed a modest success at the time (artistically more than financially), it didn't become a classic and is seldom revived. Still, the challenge of revamping a huge production and turning a potential flop around in only eight weeks had become a triumph for Bennett on many levels; it sealed his reputation as a genius who could mastermind an entire show. He was also continuing to build his team: the *Seesaw* design staff included set designer Robin Wagner, who had also done *Promises, Promises*, and some of the dance arrangements were provided by Marvin Hamlisch. The role of Jerry was played on Broadway by Ken Howard (also from *Promises, Promises*), who by then was having an on-again, off-again relationship with Donna McKechnie. The ensemble included dance captain Michon Peacock, who would be one of the instigators of the project that developed into *A Chorus Line*, as well as four members of what would be that show's original cast: Baayork Lee, Thommie Walsh, Wayne Cilento, and Cris (later Crissy) Wilzak.

God's Favorite

The last show Bennett staged before *A Chorus Line* was the second, and last, full-length straight play he ever directed. Having by now established a good relationship with Neil Simon, with whom he had worked in various official and unofficial capacities on *How Now, Dow Jones*, *Promises, Promises*, *The Good Doctor*, and *Seesaw*, it was probably inevitable that Bennett would be asked to direct one of the very popular writer's plays. *God's Favorite* came at an awkward time, right between the first and second workshops for *A Chorus Line*, and it proved not to be one of Simon's—or Bennett's—more successful Broadway outings. Starring Vincent Gardenia (a Tony winner for Simon's *The Prisoner of Second Avenue*), it was a modern retelling of the biblical Book of Job, set on Long Island. The play opened at Broadway's Eugene O'Neill Theatre on December 11, 1974, and closed on March 23 of the next year.

Michael and Zach

This brings us up to *A Chorus Line* in the chronology of Bennett's career, and since that show is the subject of this entire book, we won't consider it in all its particulars here. But because it represents the high point of his career and a turning point in his life, it may be useful now to look at his personal connection to the show and the ways in which it affected him on a human level.

For years, Bennett had been nurturing a notion to do a show about dancers. He considered himself a dancer first, and even as he became more and more powerful in the Broadway community and increasingly respected as a choreographer and director, he continued to identify himself on a very basic level with the world of the Broadway gypsy. He wanted to give something back to that community and to show the world that the chorus dancer, so often overlooked by the public and even by others in the industry, had more to offer than was generally recognized. So he was in a very receptive frame of mind when Michon Peacock and Tony

Zach (played by Robert LuPone) comforts Paul (Sammy Williams) after the latter's monologue in the original production.   *Photofest*

Stevens came to him with the idea of starting a theatre company made up entirely of dancers and asked for his help and advice (see Chapter 1); he made himself instrumental in setting up the tape-recorded rap sessions that would lead directly to the genesis of the musical, and almost immediately began steering the project away from Peacock and Stevens and taking the reins himself.

That very act of taking control raises the question of an essential dichotomy that was to characterize his work on the musical, and his life from that point forward. Though *A Chorus Line* was created out of the true stories dancers told about their lives, at the tape sessions and afterwards, and was developed through a long collaborative process with the cast and a highly talented team of writers and designers, there was never much of a question in anyone's mind that it was Michael Bennett's show. Never before had a musical grown so organically out of such an effective collaboration—but, paradoxically, there had also never been a musical that was more thoroughly conceived and shaped by one individual. The writers sometimes felt like hired scribes; though Bennett never took a cowriting credit, he shaped the script aggressively, often telling Nick Dante and later James Kirkwood exactly what he needed them to write and, when they didn't provide enough humor, turning again to Neil Simon to fill the gaps. Bennett also yelled at and browbeat the songwriters to get what he wanted out of them: Avian told Kevin Kelly that Bennett would "sing/scream lyrics right into Marvin's ear, then shout 'Ya got it? That's what I want!' . . . I hate to say these things, but that's the way it happened, the way the show was put together. He'd scream right in their faces and say, 'Now THIS is what I want!'"

The dancers gave freely of their life stories and poured their hearts and guts out daily in the workshop sessions, contributing choreography as well as script material—but they always knew they could be replaced at any time, and that who and what would remain in the finished show depended completely on Bennett's decisions. He knew that the excitement and energy of the show would depend on the authentic re-creation of the tension of a real audition, so he didn't hesitate to play mind games to keep them on their toes, even if it sometimes involved pitting them against one another. Even in early previews at the Public Theater, he allowed Robert LuPone as Zach to make a different decision each night about who got the job—until the wardrobe department told him they really needed to know what order the cast would be coming offstage in to get changed for the finale! (In order to put this in perspective, though, it's interesting to note that, though Bennett declined to cast some of the actors who had contributed their life stories at the tape sessions, he never fired a single actor from the beginning of the workshops to opening night on Broadway. Barry Bostwick's relinquishing of the role of Zach during the second workshop was a mutual decision, and several dancers left of their own volition to pursue other projects. One actor who was struggling with the dancing was asked to switch places with his understudy. But no one from the original workshop group was dismissed.)

The opposite side of that coin was Bennett's role as father figure to the group. Even while they remained on edge trying to please him, they became dependent on him for emotional support, which he could offer lavishly and then withdraw at will. He knew he was asking dancers, some of whom had little or no acting experience, to open up onstage with rare honesty and emotional bravery, and he encouraged them and coddled them accordingly. All through the workshop period, he would call up various dancers on the phone, often in the middle of the night, and talk for hours about the show, the previous day's rehearsal, and so forth—sometimes making it obvious that he needed support and reinforcement from them as much as they needed validation from him. Little by little, elaborately codependent relationships were formed, and when disputes later arose at the theatre—about business matters, extra rehearsal time, or the like—Bennett didn't hesitate to play the loyalty card. The dancers loved him, hated him at times, but always respected him. They knew they were in a great show, a once-in-a-lifetime opportunity, and for that they were grateful. When interviewed for the documentary *A Chorus Line: Final Stage* in 1990—the year the show finally closed on Broadway—original cast member Priscilla Lopez acknowledged that many of the dancers had felt manipulated by Bennett during the rehearsal process, but said she herself didn't really resent the manipulation, because she understood the creativity behind it.

How much of Michael Bennett's own life story found its way into *A Chorus Line*? More than some people realize, as many of the elements of the stories told by Don (his early nightclub experiences), Bobby (growing up "strange" in Buffalo), Mark (the mistaken "gonorrhea" diagnosis), and others came from his own personal history. Starting at the tape sessions, he was reportedly open with the other dancers about his bisexuality. His honesty and willingness to share encouraged the other dancers to reciprocate by opening up even more themselves. But the sticking point came with the development of the character of Zach, the director of the show and the role ostensibly most closely modeled on Bennett himself.

As he put the show together, Bennett knew he was putting his life and his dreams and everything that was most important to him up on that stage. That's the passion that propels *A Chorus Line*; it's a celebration of dancers and their hopes and their sacrifices and everything they go through from childhood on that fuels their need to dance. Bennett had been one of them, and at heart he still was. But he knew that in creating Zach, the director/choreographer, a character many in the audience would see as at least a partial self-portrait, he was opening himself to public scrutiny. And the first to scrutinize him would be the actors playing the role: both Barry Bostwick—the only "name" in the second workshop, who withdrew once he realized he and Bennett were never going to see eye to eye on what Zach should be—and Robert LuPone, who took over the part and struggled through the final stages of bringing it to life. Both actors later spoke freely of their frustrations trying to understand the man they were trying to portray (see Chapter 7). It was bad enough to be playing the lead male role in a musical and not have even one song to sing, but where was the emotional core of the character? Where was Zach's moment of epiphany, the scene where he really opened up and let the audience see what was behind that cool veneer?

Some people have seen Zach's one real moment of tenderness in the show, which occurs with the weeping Paul after the latter's monologue, as a possible indication of sexual attraction, but that's debatable. (According to Robert Viagas in his book *I'm the Greatest Star*, "The bisexual aspect of the relationship was glossed over, though Zach appeared far more sympathetic to the character of former Jewel Box transvestite dancer Paul San Marco than to Cassie, and, in Bennett's own staging, Zach put an arm around Paul to give physical comfort, something that does not occur with Cassie—though he does finally agree to hire her.") An earlier version of the script had Cassie confronting Zach about a prior relationship he had had with a man, but by that point the scene had been cut; Bennett seemed to have become determined to present the character as heterosexual. In daily life, he didn't try to hide his attraction to men or his relationships, so why did he feel threatened by the idea of allowing that side of himself to be expressed through the character?

It's important to remember that this was the seventies. The gay rights movement, if it began at Stonewall, was still in its first decade. Though gay men were much more accepted in the dance world and the Broadway community than they were in other walks of life, there was at that time a stigma that has since largely faded away. Today, many of Broadway's most powerful directors and choreographers, not to mention some of the producers, are very openly gay. But in the seventies, homosexual artists were tolerated but still looked down on to some degree by the powerful straight men they worked for. Gay males were often thought of as kids: a real man was expected to grow up, get married, and start a family. (Producer Bernard Jacobs of the Shubert Organization admitted to Kevin Kelly that, shortly after *A Chorus Line* opened, he had actually said to Bennett: "Why don't you straighten out and marry Donna?") And Michael Bennett, son of a very traditionally minded Italian American father, didn't want to be condescended to; he didn't want to be humored as the wunderkind director who was still a child on some level. He had ambitions to be a producer himself, having already started Plum Productions, his own company; he wanted to be able to walk into a room with the Harold Princes and the Joseph Papps and the Bernard Jacobses and the Bob Fosses of the world and be accepted as their equal. And Zach gave him the opportunity to create an image of himself as he wished to be perceived.

It wasn't that he was smoothing out all the rough edges or painting himself in any way as a saint. Zach clearly has issues, as Cassie points out. And some of them are problems Bennett had struggled with and would struggle with even more after the show opened. He admitted that much of the argument Zach has with Cassie in the show, about how his obsessive drive to be the best in his work gets in the way of emotional intimacy, came from his own, ultimately failed, relationship with the dancer Larry Fuller, whom he had lived with for several years in the sixties. Both Michael and Zach had problems with commitment. But if Bennett was alternately indulgent and abusive in rehearsals with his dancers, the doting father confessor one day and the ruthless taskmaster the next, Zach by comparison remains enviably controlled: coolly blunt when he needs to be but not mean, never unfair, never—except briefly with Cassie—overtly angry. The role can still frustrate actors who look for something more to sink their teeth into, much as it frustrated Bostwick and LuPone. Donna McKechnie has said (in an interview for the documentary *A Chorus Line: Final Stage*) that Bennett never got along with the various actors who played Zach and "felt competitive" with them—but strangely, he would often cast actors in the role with whom he had intense personal relationships. His sometime lover Scott Pearson started as Bobby in San Francisco but later played Zach in the Australian company and on Broadway; Tim Millett, who played Don on tour and then Zach on Broadway, was also linked to Bennett romantically. Jean-Pierre Cassel, the French actor who played the role in the London production, was singularly unqualified for it, but he and Bennett were friends and the director cast him anyway—and later had a long-term affair with the actor's wife, Sabine. (Ironically, the Cassels had been the witnesses at Bennett's Paris wedding to Donna McKechnie.)

As Kevin Kelly wrote: "There is a lot of Michael Bennett in Zach, including sexual ambiguity, but it's a fantasized silhouette rather than a mug shot." And if Bennett created Zach as an image of the controlled, powerful director he wanted to be, after the show opened he began refashioning himself to some degree in the image of the character he had created. Life imitated art imitating life, and not all of the changes were voluntary. Audiences often take the Zach/Cassie relationship as a mirror of Bennett's with McKechnie, but it must be remembered that their marriage (and, according to McKechnie, the romantic side of their relationship) did not begin until after the show was up and running. Cassie accuses Zach of shutting her out when her career didn't take off the way his did, and in reality this is close to what would soon happen between the two of them. *A Chorus Line* didn't lead to immediate offers of other roles for her, and he wanted the two of them to ride the crest of success together. She, on the other hand, wanted children—and was told by his father, rightly or wrongly, that having his child would probably be the only way she could hold onto him. He later told her that her crime had been "making him feel"—something he never allowed Zach to do. When she returned to the Broadway cast in 1986, ten years older and wiser than when she first left it, she had more emotional history than ever before to draw on for the role: Donna and Cassie had become one in ways that Zach and Michael never would.

Their 1976 marriage shocked their friends and colleagues—many of whom couldn't imagine what she was thinking. Even putting the question of his sexual preference aside, they thought, wasn't she aware of his volatility and emotional instability? Why he married her has also been the subject of much conjecture over the years. Clearly they loved each other. As artists they had connected through dance on a very deep level. They brought out the best in each other, and each contributed to the success the other achieved. They were close friends and confidants for years, and they shared *A Chorus Line*, their greatest triumph. Their fondest dreams, nurtured for so many years, had come true, and everybody knows how a fairy tale is supposed to end: Happily Ever After seemed almost inevitable.

The marriage lasted less than a year. Although McKechnie said she would have tried anything to help work through the problems, Bennett pushed her away. Needing space, he went to Australia, where a new company of *A Chorus Line* was being rehearsed. The mostly Aussie cast included two Americans: Cheryl Clark as Cassie and Scott Pearson as Zach. As quoted in the book *The Longest Line*, Pearson said: "Michael showed up in Australia to direct us after his divorce from Donna. He needed some time to himself, and he chose to take it in Australia with us."

In California

Retreating to his position that any kind of personal intimacy was a threat to his creative work, Bennett threw himself into the next phase of his artistic life: a three-picture deal with Universal Studios. By this time, the national and international touring companies of *A Chorus Line* were both up and running, and foreign versions were starting to multiply. Casting, rehearsing, and maintaining the many companies was a demanding and time-consuming endeavor, and Bennett remained involved, though he began delegating more and more of the responsibility to Avian and various assistants, stage managers, and dance captains. Having first fallen in love with dance watching musical movies with his mother, and having been praised for the innovative "cinematic" techniques he employed in his stage productions, it was inevitable that he would want to try his hand at directing films, and the gigantic success of *ACL* provided him with the opportunity. He and Bob Avian went out to Hollywood to learn about the process of making movies and were provided with luxurious offices at Universal. The studio was very interested in having them get started on the film version of *A Chorus Line*, but Bennett wanted to tackle at least one other project first, to get his feet wet and learn the ropes of making movies. He proposed a film version of *Pin-Ups*, a stage project he had been developing for some time, and also worked with writer Jerome Kass on a screenplay called *Roadshow*.

With no connection to the later Stephen Sondheim musical by that same title, Bennett's *Roadshow* was to be a movie about a touring production of the William Gibson play *Two for the Seesaw* (or Bennett's musical version of it, *Seesaw*), mixing scenes from the show with a backstage story about the performers involved. The script focused on a young woman unexpectedly called upon to take over the leading role of Gittel Mosca—much as Michele Lee had done when hired to replace Lainie Kazan in the stage musical. Bennett wanted Bette Midler, at that point a successful recording artist but not yet a film star, to play the role opposite Robert Redford, but Universal told him they needed a more bankable name and suggested Goldie Hawn, Liza Minnelli, or Barbra Streisand. They began to push quite hard for Streisand, as did David Merrick, the Broadway producer, who was also involved. Bennett refused to be pressured, and the film was never made. (A few of the studio execs may have wanted to kick themselves a couple years later, when Midler emerged as a huge Hollywood star with *The Rose*.)

Dissatisfied with his Hollywood experience and what he had observed of the studio system, Bennett left a note on his desk that said "Gone fishing"; after a brief sojourn in San Francisco doctoring *The Act*, a Liza Minnelli vehicle headed for Broadway, he and Avian headed back to New York. Bennett's lawyer, John Breglio, who had brokered the deal with Universal in the first place, was able to get him out of the contract. Some thought the studio was happy to see him go, but the head of production, Ned Tanen, told Breglio they loved Bennett and would welcome him back anytime. He never went back.

Avian later said he believed Bennett's talent actually belonged in Hollywood; he regretted the lost opportunity to make what could have been some brilliant movies, but felt that unfortunately they had made a deal with the wrong studio. By that point in his career, though, Bennett had grown accustomed to the autonomy he had worked so hard to win for himself as a producer/director on Broadway, and it's doubtful whether he would ever have felt comfortable as part of the Hollywood machine.

890 Broadway

Back in New York, he pursued a different dream: his very own complex of rehearsal studios, offices, and performance space, where he and his colleagues could develop and produce new musicals through the kind of workshop process they had pioneered with *A Chorus Line*. According to Ken Mandelbaum, the project was born in 1978, when Bennett's friend Eliot Feld introduced him to an old loft building at 890 Broadway, between 19th and 20th Streets, that had been a department store decades earlier. A former *West Side Story* dancer who now had his own ballet company, Feld was using one of the floors as a rehearsal studio; he had discovered that the eight-story brick structure, unlike most New York buildings, was mostly free of supporting columns, so that if one were to knock down the right walls he could create large, obstruction-free studios and performance spaces. Bennett remembered Harold Prince talking about how great it would be to have one building where all the component departments needed for putting together a new show could live under one roof: offices, design studios and shops, rehearsal halls, quiet rooms for writers, even a small theatre. Initially only looking for office space for himself and one or two rehearsal studios, Bennett began negotiating for a lease on the fourth floor; before long, he ended up buying the whole building for $750,000. He made studio and shop space available for his favorite designers and other top theatrical craftspeople, including the costumer Barbara Matera. His earnings from *ACL* had by now enabled him to buy a Rolls-Royce and a luxurious home in the Hamptons, and he poured much of his remaining income from the show into renovating the old building. His plan was to host four extended workshops each year, developing new musicals away from the commercial pressures of uptown. By

Debra Pigliavento as Bebe leads the line in the "One" rehearsal scene, International Company, circa 1980.

1983, the renovations were largely complete and included a three hundred-seat theatre space used for workshops and auditions; in 1985, under the name Theatre 890, it was made available for full commercial productions as well. The beautiful, spacious rehearsal studios became some of the most sought after in town, giving birth to over a hundred Broadway and Off-Broadway productions. Notable events held there included two fully staged readings of Stephen Sondheim and James Lapine's classic *Into the Woods*, then in development, in June 1986.

Even as he worked on developing the space, Bennett looked for a new musical into which he could pour his own creative energies. He knew *A Chorus Line* would be a tough, almost impossible, act to follow, but he was determined not to let the fear of failure—and the intense critical scrutiny that would inevitably be focused on his next project—keep him from taking on new challenges.

Ballroom

The first Broadway show Bennett took on following *A Chorus Line* was to be a collaboration with one of the few people he had really hit it off with in Hollywood. Although the screenplay called *Roadshow* had never been filmed (various parties continued to fight over the rights for years after Bennett walked away from it), both Bennett and Avian had grown particularly fond of the screenwriter Jerome Kass. He was the author of *Queen of the Stardust Ballroom*, an acclaimed 1975 TV movie that had starred Maureen Stapleton as Bea Asher, a lonely widow and junk shop owner who finds a new lease on life—and a new love—at an old-fashioned dance hall in her Bronx neighborhood. Charles Durning played her love interest, a mailman who was married to another. Bob Avian was an admirer of the film and became supportive of Kass's plan to turn the property into a stage musical. Though Bennett wasn't immediately sold on the idea, he had developed a strong enough relationship with the writer that he ultimately agreed to direct. (He may have also been atoning for a certain amount of guilt over *Roadshow*, which he had abandoned after prevailing upon Kass to write it.)

With the title shortened to *Ballroom*, the musical had a score by Billy Goldenberg with lyrics by Alan and Marilyn Bergman (Marvin Hamlisch's collaborators on *The Way We Were*). The same team had contributed incidental music and lyrics to the original TV version as well.

There was much speculation as to the casting of the central role of Bea, a character inspired by Jerome Kass's own mother. Bennett initially wanted Beverly Sills, whose opera career was starting to wind down, but she was still scheduled so far in advance with international appearances that she couldn't commit the time. Sada Thompson was considered, as was Allyn Ann McLerie. Dolores Gray took part in the first workshop but was let go, and then Dorothy Loudon auditioned for the role, which she dearly coveted. After some complications Bennett was able to get Loudon out of her contract for the Broadway musical *Annie* (the still-running hit in which she had created the role of Miss Hannigan). Though she was herself a recent widow, and Bennett worried that the role might prove so close to home as to be emotionally dangerous, Loudon thrived in it. To play opposite her, Bennett cast Vincent Gardenia, who had starred for him in *God's Favorite*.

One of Bennett's main reasons for taking on the property, and for his sustained commitment to it, was the rare opportunity to cast an ensemble of mature dancers in the chorus. As the middle-aged patrons of the Stardust Ballroom, he cast some of the dancers he had worked with at the beginning of his career—many of whom had retired from performing or left the industry entirely—and was thrilled to be able to offer them the opportunity to get back onstage where they belonged. The chance to see a bunch of hoofers from the *West Side Story*/*Sweet Charity* generation dancing on Broadway once again would become one of the show's key attractions for musical theatre aficionados—although, ironically, some people would claim the old pros had worked so hard to get back in shape, and looked so sharp and classy executing Bennett and Avian's complex choreography, that they ended up evincing a glamour that was at odds with the ordinary, dumpy Bronx denizens they were supposedly playing.

From the beginning, the process on *Ballroom* was plagued by conflict. Having created the biggest hit in the history of the New York Shakespeare Festival, Bennett assumed he would be developing his next musical in partnership with the festival and probably opening it at the Public Theater, where some of the workshop sessions were held. As it turned out, though, Joe Papp didn't wish to stay involved. The theatres at the Public were not large enough to accommodate the grand physical production Bennett had planned (the whole design team from *A Chorus Line* was working on *Ballroom*), and Papp didn't think it was within the Public's mission to coproduce a Broadway show that hadn't really been developed there.

Also, some people close to the project felt Papp never really liked the material. Somewhat ironically, *Ballroom* ended up playing its tryout run in the home of another Shakespeare Festival: the American Shakespeare Theatre in Stratford, Connecticut, which had begun operations around the same time as Papp's institution but by this time was struggling to stay afloat.

The show wasn't coming together to anyone's satisfaction. There was internal strife on the creative team and a sense that the opulent production was at odds with the simplicity of the story. Bennett was such a hot property following *A Chorus Line* that investors were offering him money left and right, but he turned all of it down, preferring to finance the entire production himself under the name of a new entity he had incorporated: Quadrille Productions. Remarkably, he confided to his agent, Jack Lenny, that he had made this decision based on his suspicion that the show, being his first follow-up to *A Chorus Line*, would be a box-office flop; he preferred to risk his own money rather than throw away other people's. Unfortunately, his prediction proved to be correct.

During the preview period in Stratford, Bennett decided—as he had with *Follies* and *Seesaw* and *A Chorus Line*—that the show wasn't funny enough and that he needed to try to get another writer in to fix the book. He had Jerome Kass meet with Norman Lear first and then brought in Larry Gelbart to doctor the script. Kass was heartbroken when he heard a performance with Gelbart's jokes added, and his friendship with Bennett, which had been the impetus for getting the show off the ground in the first place, fell apart. As the show struggled to find its feet, Tommy Tune, Ron Field, and representatives of the Shubert Organization all came to Connecticut to offer advice—some of it helpful, some not.

Riding on high expectations from *A Chorus Line*'s legions of fans, *Ballroom* enjoyed substantial advance sales in New York, but the numbers started to drop off dramatically after the reviews came out. Not all of them were negative, and some critics were perceptive enough to praise the originality of the designs and the choreography, the unique ways Bennett was able to define individual characters through movement, and the sophisticated use of dance as metaphor. The characters found their humdrum lives transformed by the magic of the ballroom, much as the troubled kids of *A Chorus Line* had found escape at the ballet. But while many people remember the show as a breathtaking theatrical experience, negative notices from Richard Eder in the *New York Times* and several others did their damage.

Bennett and Robin Wagner had been invited as delegates to an international arts exchange; wishing to escape the wreckage, they embarked for China, leaving the cast of *Ballroom* feeling rather abandoned. Whether Bennett could have saved the show by staying in New York and working on public relations strategies as he had with *Seesaw* remains debatable, as there have been many theories put forth for *Ballroom*'s failure. The most bizarre of these, long circulated in the Broadway community, is that there was a conspiracy among the box-office staff at the Majestic Theatre, where the show was playing. The musical version of *I Remember Mama*, with a score by the legendary Richard Rodgers, was looking for a Broadway home, with a keen eye on the Majestic. If *Ballroom* limped along for too long, *I Remember Mama* would have to go into a different house. The Rodgers show was viewed as a likely hit with the potential to keep the theatre's staff employed for years, so the gossip held that, dreading the prospect of unemployment, the ticket window clerks were turning customers away, falsely telling them *Ballroom* was sold out weeks in advance. The show closed on March 24, 1979, after a run of 116 performances, in plenty of time for the theatre to accommodate the Rodgers musical, which opened on May 31. If the box-office workers had in fact plotted this (and many people consider the theory too outrageous to be true), it backfired on them: *I Remember Mama* closed after one performance.

At the 1979 Tony Awards, Bennett and Avian won for their choreography of *Ballroom*, which was also nominated for seven other awards. (Jerome Kass was nominated for Best Book of a Musical, though he had wanted to take his name off the show after the script had been altered by Gelbart.) Loudon was nominated for Best Actress in a Musical but lost to Angela Lansbury, who won for creating the role of Mrs. Lovett in *Sweeney Todd*. (In an odd twist of fate, when Lansbury left that show, Loudon succeeded her in the role.)

New People; New Problems

It was during the painful process on *Ballroom* that some of Bennett's close associates became increasingly aware of his dependence on drugs. He had long been devoted to vodka, and during *A Chorus Line* he was observed to be taking both Valium and Quaaludes; he also smoked pot regularly, especially at night as an aid to falling asleep. He had seemed to be keeping it under control while working on the show, but by the end of the seventies he was using cocaine regularly as well, and it had begun to affect his relationships.

In California, with his movie career and his marriage to McKechnie both hitting the rocks before they even got off the ground, he had begun to escape periodically up to San Francisco. He found he enjoyed the city and began to spend more and more time there with a new group of male friends. Chief among these was James Georgedes, who was working for the prestigious men's clothing store Wilkes-Bashford. Bennett had an affair with Georgedes and helped him out by staging an elaborate musical fashion show for the store. Georgedes introduced him to a friend of his, Gene Pruit, who coincidentally was involved with a man named Robert Herr, who had known Bennett in New York in the sixties. No longer really a couple, Pruit and Herr were living together as friends, and Bennett began to transfer his attentions from Georgedes to Pruit, who would become his last long-term male lover. He also hired Herr to be his chief secretary at 890 Broadway.

Back in New York, Bennett was an emotional wreck. He had bought a Park Avenue penthouse for himself and McKechnie, but after their marriage ended he couldn't bear to spend time there, so he moved back in with Bob Avian for a while. This was about the time he began his affair with Sabine Cassel, who ironically had been McKechnie's matron of honor at their wedding; she later claimed that Bennett had told her the night before the wedding that he was actually in love with her, but couldn't have her because she was married to another. The spark of chemistry between them was reignited after McKechnie moved out, and Sabine finally decided to leave her husband and come to New York to live with Bennett. He moved back into the penthouse with her and they even discussed marriage, but, true to form, he began to feel suffocated by the relationship. In an attempt to keep her at arm's length, he bought her a townhouse on East 64th Street, where she lived with a housekeeper and he would visit her whenever he wanted to.

One day the townhouse was burglarized while Cassel and the housekeeper were at home: a young man broke in, tied them up, and proceeded to steal whatever he could carry. The man was never apprehended, but though Cassel described him as a young Puerto Rican, Bennett's paranoid fears of the Mafia immediately kicked back in. Convinced the mob was out to kill him, he moved Sabine back into the penthouse. Though she was by this time fighting for custody of her children (Jean-Pierre initiated proceedings to keep them away from Bennett, whom he described in legal documents as a notorious homosexual), the relationship soon fell apart. Bernard Jacobs later told Kevin Kelly he thought Bennett had "paid off" Sabine Cassel for close to $100,000.

Dreamgirls

The property that would become Michael Bennett's last Broadway hit came from an unlikely source: the writer/director Tom Eyen. Though he probably didn't know it, Eyen had been an indirect part of the original impetus behind *A Chorus Line*, and not in a positive way. He was the director whose shabby treatment of the dancers in the notorious musical *Rachael Lily Rosenbloom and Don't You Ever Forget It* had so enraged Michon Peacock and Tony Stevens that it had inspired them to approach Michael Bennett with the idea of a new company run entirely by dancers (see Chapter 1). Their meeting led to the January 1974 tape session that evolved into *A Chorus Line*.

Six years later, though, Eyen and Bennett apparently still didn't really know each other, for when Eyen ran into Bob Avian one day on a Manhattan street, he mistook him for Bennett. Eyen pitched a property to Avian, a show that he was writing with songwriter Henry Krieger and had already directed in a workshop at, coincidentally, the Public Theater. He asked if they could audition it at 890 Broadway, and Avian told him that, even though he wasn't in fact Michael Bennett, he could indeed set that up. (Another version of the story has the connection originating through set designer Robin Wagner, who had already suggested Eyen to Bennett as a director for another musical they had in development, entitled *Battle of the Giants*.)

At the subsequent meeting, Avian was excited by the material: a piece then called *One Night Only* (the title of a song that remains in the finished show) that Eyen and Krieger presented with the help of three African American singers: Loretta Devine and Sheryl Lee Ralph (both of whom would ultimately open in the show) and Ramona Brooks. (Brooks's role was originally written for Nell Carter, but she had left the project after the workshop at the Public to go to Hollywood in search of TV stardom, which she would shortly achieve.) Bennett wasn't immediately sold, but he had been looking for developing musicals to bring under his umbrella at 890; fancying himself the Joe Papp of musical theatre, he wanted his new facility to be an incubator for a variety of new projects, not all of which he would direct. So at Avian's suggestion, Eyen and Krieger were offered a workshop, with Bennett and Avian initially involved only as producers.

Many fans have always assumed that the show that became *Dreamgirls* was inspired by the story of Diana Ross and the Supremes, but Eyen and Krieger vehemently denied that. The version of the script they rehearsed during that first workshop seems to have been less reminiscent of Ross's story than the finished show, which grew to resemble it more and more. Bennett would poke his head in from time to time to listen and offer advice, but by the end of the six-week session he wasn't sure there was a show there. One thing he liked was the song "And I Am Telling You I'm Not Going," a gut-wrenching, vocal cord–ripping solo sung by the character Effie. This role was being excitingly played by a very young gospel singer from Texas named Jennifer Holliday, who at the time was performing each evening in the Broadway show *Your Arms Too Short to Box with God*. Bennett and Avian gave notes on how to restructure the story, and Krieger and Eyen tried to implement some of them during a second workshop (this time without Holliday), but Bennett saw little improvement. At that point, Bob Avian made a suggestion he didn't think Eyen and Krieger would go for: having Bennett take over as director. Aware that the challenge of directing the show was keeping Eyen from focusing on improving the script, they agreed. Bennett came on board, but he and Eyen didn't always see eye to eye. With Bennett in the director's chair, though, the design team from *A Chorus Line* and *Ballroom* also agreed to join the project.

Things didn't always progress smoothly even from there. Unlike *A Chorus Line*, which was a labor of love from the very beginning, the new show (it went through several titles before becoming *Dreamgirls*) was a problem child. Bennett went back and forth on it; he wasn't always sure he loved it or that he was the right director for it. He wasn't clicking with the cast, and after the third workshop he offered to give the show back to Tom Eyen. By that point, Eyen knew the success of the undertaking depended on Bennett—and on Jennifer Holliday, who was finally persuaded to return for a fourth workshop. Like the three earlier ones, this session lasted approximately six weeks; Bennett insisted that they focus on the book and used his dramaturgical acumen to whip the story into shape.

Finally they were ready to showcase the work for potential coproducers, but at the last minute new trouble erupted. With the script focusing more on the character of Deena Jones (Sheryl Lee Ralph) and resembling more and more the Diana Ross story, with Effie mostly removed from Act Two, Jennifer Holliday felt she no longer had the leading role she'd been promised. Bennett angered her further by cutting a song called "Faith in Myself" at the last minute, at which point she told him she was willing to follow through with the backers' audition but, as she was mainly interested in pursuing a career as a recording artist anyway, she had no intention of going with the show to Broadway. A big argument between the two of them ended in her either walking out or being fired (depending on whom you ask).

The all-important presentation had already been scheduled and went ahead anyway, with Alaina Reed jumping in to learn the role of Effie quickly. The Shuberts, led by Bennett's close friend Bernard Jacobs, and record producer David Geffen were impressed; with these powerful coproducers on board, the show was scheduled to go into rehearsal for an opening at the Imperial, a Shubert house. Additional backing was promised from ABC and Metromedia. Everything had to be put on hold, however, when Bennett came down with hepatitis.

Although the backers' audition had gone well without Holliday, Bennett and the rest of the creative team had come to feel her participation was essential, so once he had recovered, Bennett went about wooing her back. The show had been on hiatus for three months when he persuaded her to return to the city to talk it over. He proceeded to wine and dine her, taking her to two Broadway shows in one day. They spent hours together and began to feel they were really communicating for the first time; he talked to her about his belief in the power and traditions of the theatre, an art form she had never been all that interested in. The result was that she came back to the show and began rehearsals for the Broadway opening. But from that point on the relationship between director and star took on a dangerously ambiguous appearance; in order to keep her where he wanted her, Bennett bought her gifts and took her out on the town repeatedly, often appearing with her at high-profile events. Before long, she was reportedly telling castmates they were in love. How much of this was deliberate on Bennett's part is hard to say; Bob Avian (always Bennett's staunchest supporter) told Kevin Kelly he didn't believe Bennett "led her on," but other associates—including Pamela Blair, Nick Dante, and other participants in *A Chorus Line*—had long noted Bennett's ability to "make people fall in love with him" in order to get what he wanted out of them creatively and professionally. If that was what he was trying to do with Jennifer Holliday, he was apparently successful: she stayed with the show—which opened on December 20, 1981—and performed her role brilliantly. Whether or not lasting emotional damage was done, she seems to have forgiven Bennett; in later years she spoke fondly of all she had learned from him about acting and theatre, and of the magic he created with the show.

Reviews for *Dreamgirls* were mixed, but Holliday's performance as Effie caused a sensation, and she won a Tony Award. Bennett shared the Tony for Best Choreography with his collaborator on the show, Michael Peters. Always the fierce competitor, however, he openly coveted the Tonys for Best Musical and Best Direction—both of which *Dreamgirls* was nominated for—but lost them to the musical *Nine* and that show's director, Tommy Tune. Even without those major awards, though, *Dreamgirls* emerged a hit—Bennett's first since *A Chorus Line*—and ended up running for over three and a half years on Broadway.

Final Years

It was during 1983, when *Dreamgirls* and *A Chorus Line* were both running on Broadway, that Michael Bennett lost his father. Their relationship had always been a complicated and conflicted one. Never the biggest supporter of his oldest son's theatrical ambitions, Sam DiFiglia had come around when Michael became a celebrity; the money the newly wealthy director/choreographer began sending home once *A Chorus Line* was an established smash hit finally put an end to his parents' lifelong financial struggles. Still, on the same day *ACL* was announced as the winner of the Pulitzer Prize for Drama, Sam was indicted on gambling charges—and his wife was convinced the authorities planned it that way.

Salvatore DiFiglia's death occasioned much domestic drama, with Michael confusing his family by showing up in Buffalo for the funeral—which he himself planned and orchestrated—elaborately dressed as a stereotypical mafioso. His father had been known for his philandering, and Bennett knew that in the early seventies he had been involved for several years with a single woman named Mary Coniglio; she had borne him a son, named Salvatore after his father, in 1974. So at the time of Sam's death, Michael had a nine-year-old half brother whom he decided he wanted to get to know. He also felt that young Sal had a right to know about his father, his family, and his heritage—and therefore he arranged for a second funeral service, scheduled the same day as the first but later in the afternoon, specifically for the boy and his mother. Bennett was by then living on an estate in East Hampton that he had purchased from David Geffen; he invited Sal to spend time with him there but found the boy to be a handful. Though the two did not develop a close relationship, Bennett provided for his half-brother in his will.

In September 1983, Bennett staged the spectacular gala 3,389th performance of *A Chorus Line* in New York, marking its new status as the longest-running show in Broadway history (see Chapter 18). But tragically, this would prove to be the last new example of his artistry that Broadway would ever see. He spent years developing a new musical called *Scandal* at 890 Broadway with collaborators Treva Silverman and Jimmy Webb, but the planned full production was abruptly cancelled. In 1986, Bennett also withdrew from the London production of *Chess* after beginning rehearsals and was replaced by Trevor Nunn. The theatre community was rocked by the news in both cases, and though very few people knew the real reason, rumors were circulating that Bennett was ill.

When he was diagnosed with AIDS, he kept it a secret, shared with only a very few trusted individuals. He was well enough in the fall of 1986 to attend a performance of *A Chorus Line* at the Shubert, to see Donna McKechnie in her return engagement as Cassie; the two had lunch and made an effort to repair their friendship, but he did not level with her about his condition. In an interview in the February 1987 edition of *Playbill*, McKechnie told Rebecca Morehouse that "he's had open-heart surgery. . . and it was very successful. It'll be a while before he works again, but he's aware he's been given a second chance." The angina story was the one Bennett's camp chose to share publicly.

In reality, he was fighting the AIDS virus with all the resources his substantial wealth made available; while living in the Hamptons, he flew every other week from New York to the National Health Institute in Washington, D.C., where he received treatments. After a while he bought a house in Tucson, Arizona, where the dry climate was salubrious, and moved there with Gene Pruit, Bob Herr, and Victoria Allen, a nurse from Washington he bonded with and hired as a personal caretaker. He never even told his mother he had AIDS, though she and his brother Frank came to see him in his last days. He accepted visits from only a very few people. Bob Avian was there, and Marvin Hamlisch, who used connections in the medical world to try to get him experimental drugs. Bennett was one of the first recipients of AZT, which at first seemed to be helping. But at that time, there was little doctors could do to slow the disease, and his condition deteriorated quickly.

Michael Bennett passed away on July 2, 1987, just four days after the openings of his final two productions. One was the return of *Dreamgirls*, which completed a Bus & Truck tour with a triumphant reopening at the Ambassador Theatre on Broadway on June 28. The other took place on the same day: a beautifully planned outdoor party at his Tucson home. The guests of honor were not theatre celebrities but approximately fifty doctors, nurses, and staff members who had been caring for him at the Arizona Medical Center Hospital. They had done the best anyone could do, and he wanted to thank them.

Remembering Michael

One of the memorial tributes staged in Bennett's honor was a special segment on the 1988 Tony Awards telecast, nearly a year after his death. Introduced by Angela Lansbury, a group of dancers performed the opening jazz combination from *A Chorus Line*, following which the original Broadway Dreamgirls sang a medley of two songs from that show. Then the dancers appeared again, and Donna McKechnie came out dressed as Cassie to perform a shortened but exciting version of "The Music and the Mirror," joined by the ensemble for a big finish.

Though her relationship with the volatile Bennett caused her substantial pain over the years, McKechnie has been able to put the positive and negative aspects of it into perspective and speaks of him with love. In a 2008 interview with Eddie Shapiro that was published in his book *Nothing Like a Dame: Conversations with the Great Women of Musical Theater*, she summed it up like this: "We loved each other. And the work. While, at that time in our lives, we both had problems with trust and the emotional intimacy that we needed desperately, there was love and respect and the work. So that was where the real intimacy was. You don't lose it. We love someone, it doesn't go away really. There was no bitterness. There were a lot of hurt feelings for both of us, but there was no bitterness. . . . I owe him so much and there've been only a few people in my life who really see me. That was something that I really appreciated him for. I was auditioning here and there and people always liked my work, but he went out of his way to create for me. That's really something to be proud of and to love."

3

"We Did What We Had to Do"

The History of the Creative Team Behind *A Chorus Line*

M r. Bennett has taken the microcosm of a chorus line and made it into the macrocosm of a generation, and this is one hell of an achievement. He has not just been helped by all of his collaborators, he has also been lifted aloft by them—no musical, essentially the work of one man, has come out as such a team effort."—Clive Barnes, reviewing the Broadway opening of *A Chorus Line.*

Though *A Chorus Line* is legendary as the brainchild of Michael Bennett, and as the show that was built out of the life stories and even the words of real Broadway dancers, it was brilliantly crafted by a top-notch creative team of professionals who worked together with remarkable effectiveness. In the process, they established an innovative new method for developing a show through collaboration. Over the years it has frequently been said that the songwriters and, in particular, the book writers did not receive quite the credit they deserved for the success of the musical—and some of them have publicly admitted to having at times felt pushed aside or unacknowledged. The show should have been a watershed in all of their careers, but each found himself to some degree stymied by its enormous success, and only Marvin Hamlisch subsequently sustained an active career in musical theatre. But none of this negates the brilliance of their work on *A Chorus Line* or the importance of their contribution to the history of musical theatre. This chapter details the individual stories of the creative team behind one of the best-integrated and most successful collaborations of all time.

Nicholas Dante

Dante was born in New York in 1941 to Puerto Rican parents; his real name was Conrado Morales. He was thirty-two years old when he attended the first of the two tape sessions that led to *A Chorus Line.*

Much of what we know of Dante's early years can be gleaned from Paul's monologue. He loved movie musicals as a child and taught himself to dance by imitating Cyd Charisse; though he liked school, he was so ostracized and tormented by the other students for his effeminacy that he dropped out at age sixteen. He started dancing with the Jewel Box Revue in his mid-teens and toured for three years before quitting and beginning to study dance seriously. In 1965, he was hired for his first summer stock job, and three years later he made his Broadway debut in *I'm Solomon*. Other Broadway shows he danced in included *Ambassador* and *Applause*. He won a chorus job in the latter by narrowly edging out Sammy Williams—who would later play the character based on him in *A Chorus Line*. (Williams ended up being hired for *Applause* as well, though as a swing.)

Dante said he always wanted to be a writer and wrote even as a child, mainly fantasies. He had thought about majoring in journalism in college, but, since he didn't finish high school, that wasn't an option. After quitting school he didn't write for close to ten years, but after his first season of stock in 1965, he found he was frustrated with the quality of the scripts; feeling he could do better, he decided to try his hand at writing musicals. His first was an adaptation of *Dr. Jekyll and Mr. Hyde* (not related to the later Broadway version by Frank Wildhorn); he also collaborated with a friend on an original musical called *The Orphanage*. He had fantasized about working with Michael Bennett, whom he knew casually; feeling they were destined to work together, he sent Bennett a copy of *The Orphanage*, but unfortunately the director wasn't interested.

In the original souvenir program for *ACL*, Dante was quoted about the original tape session: "I'd been a dancer for ten years, but the first time I'd ever auditioned for Michael Bennett was the night of the tape sessions. Now I know that he came there as a dancer—just to talk with, and about dancers. But in my mind he was the director, and I was a dancer on that line. I didn't know if I would be able to tell about my life. But as the evening wore on, slowly—it all came out. By the time I'd finished talking, Michael knew that above all I was a survivor, and he admires that in people. So when he called and asked me if I'd like to write a show about the sessions we had, I was overwhelmed."

Following the tape sessions, Dante for a time had little contact with Bennett, but he continued to meet with Michon Peacock and Tony Stevens and a few other dancers who were still hoping to get a new company, which they were calling Ensemble Theatre Inc., off the ground. When Bennett asked Dante to write the show with him, he added the proviso that, if they couldn't pull it off, he might have to bring in one or more other writers. Dante later admitted he felt Bennett was never terribly interested in his writing talent but thought he had to offer him the job in order to get the use of his monologue.

Throughout the first workshop, Dante was the book writer, though Bennett took a very active role in structuring the story. But during the hiatus between the first and second workshops, Bennett decided Dante wasn't up to completing the task on his own and decided to bring James Kirkwood on board. As a fan of Kirkwood's work, Dante welcomed the opportunity and was by all accounts a very good sport about the situation. According to Bob Avian: "Nick Dante was a wonderful guy. He was thrilled that this was happening in his life. He never objected to Jim Kirkwood being brought in, and he was always enthusiastic." He remained a team player throughout the process, attacking the work with great passion and making a point of maintaining a positive energy in the collaboration. (This is important to remember in light of the considerable venting he did in publications that came out years later, in which he revealed that he felt he never got the credit or even the remuneration that should have been his due.)

Sadly, Dante never followed *A Chorus Line* up with any additional success as a writer. Ten years after the show opened, however, he finally did get the opportunity to play the character based on him, when Baayork Lee asked him to perform Paul in a new touring company she was putting together, which was also to star Donna McKechnie in her first return to the show. At first Bennett objected and told Lee she would never work with him again unless she rescinded the offer. But an angry Dante called Bennett and challenged him, convincing him he could do it—later admitting he thought Bennett was jealous because he himself would have loved a chance to play Zach but felt his elevated stature in the business precluded it. According to recent accounts by two other dancers who were in that cast, Dante gave the lie to Bennett's fears that he couldn't play the role; he gave an honest and moving performance, and even at forty-three did not seem too old for the part. His interpretation of the monologue was rich in nuance and surprising humor, which made the emotional breakdown at the end that much more moving; he brought out poignant subtext in it that other actors hadn't been aware of. For example, he revealed in rehearsal that his mother's exclamation of "My God" when she first saw Paul at the theatre was not really a reaction to his being in drag: it was because he looked so much like his sister, who had died at fourteen. And though the line in the script is "Oh, my God," Dante when he performed it said it in Spanish: "Dios mio."

Unfortunately, the tour ended unhappily for him. The show was booked into the Valley Forge Music Fair in Pennsylvania, a three-thousand–seat theatre-in-the-round. No tour of the show had ever played in the round before, and Baayork Lee was faced with the daunting task of restaging it quickly—and without mirrors. Tensions were running high during the brief rehearsal they had to figure it all out. There was a line in the show that didn't make sense in the new configuration, and Dante, attempting to be helpful, suggested a change. Other cast members objected, claiming the book to *A Chorus Line* was sacrosanct and couldn't be tampered with; when Dante reminded them that he had in fact written it in the first place, that didn't seem to make any difference. Faced again with evidence that his contribution to the show was not respected or even recognized, he quit the tour at that point.

In retrospect, some of his castmates realized he may already have been ill at the time. He died of AIDS-related causes in May 1991, just over a year after *A Chorus Line* closed on Broadway.

James Kirkwood

Kirkwood came to *A Chorus Line* with plenty of firsthand knowledge of life in "the industry." He was the son of two stars of the silent screen. James Kirkwood Sr. began as a stage actor, attained fame working on numerous films with legendary director D. W. Griffith, and branched out into directing and writing; actress Lila Lee was thirty years his junior. Their son James was born in 1924 (though he later often

Jason Tam played Paul, the character based on book writer Nick Dante, in the Broadway revival. Behind him are Jessica Lee Goldyn (Val), Paul McGill (Mark), and Natalie Cortez (Diana).   *Photo by Paul Kolnik*

claimed it was 1930, and at the time of his death close friends were surprised to learn his real age). He had a rocky family life and peripatetic childhood, attending no fewer than eighteen different high schools—ranging from a rural one-room schoolhouse to six months at Beverly Hills High.

Both of his parents' acting careers declined in the early days of the talkies; though his father had a fine voice and was able to make the transition artistically, his temper and volatile personality became a liability. His parents divorced and each remarried twice; his mother had a series of relationships with caddish men who often mistreated both her and her son. There were long periods of time when she had to send him to live with her sister's family as she moved around in pursuit of various lovers and acting jobs; it was at his aunt and uncle's home in Elyria, Ohio, where young James felt most stable and tended to be happiest.

When he was twelve years old, he had an experience that would haunt him for the rest of his life. His mother Lila had finally begun a relationship with a decent man whom James liked: one Reid Russell, a car salesman who was only twenty-eight years old. He was married at the time, but planned a divorce so he could marry Lila. Lila and James were living on an estate in Manhattan Beach, California, that was the home of her novelist friend Gouverneur Morris and his wife Ruth. One day when James let his three dogs out for their afternoon run, one of them failed to come back up to the house; James followed him down to a hammock near the barbecue pit at the end of the large lawn, where he discovered Reid Russell's fly-covered, decomposing body; the man had been shot to death two days earlier. The local police, who were friends of the family, botched the investigation, assuming immediately that the death was a suicide; several people claimed Russell had of late been despondent, partly over the loss of his job, and had even threatened to do away with himself on more than one occasion. There were also rumors, repeated by Russell's mother, that in addition to Lila her son had been having an affair with a wealthy married woman; she said she had received a phone call from an anonymous female demanding that all investigation of the case be terminated. Because of the high-profile entertainment figures involved, the story became a scandal much anatomized in the press; there were also conflicting accounts regarding a suicide note, which Russell's mother allegedly burned and Lila, improbably, never read. The case was never solved, and ultimately there were some who suspected Lila was involved, or even that young James, distraught at seeing the man's relationship with his mother falling apart, may have had something to do with it. Though Kirkwood would speak of the event periodically over the years, and it inspired one of his best novels, he became uncomfortable answering questions about it, and the sordid mystery remains part of his mystique to this day.

There were several other morbid and macabre stories circulated about his teen and early adult years. He developed a reputation as a "body finder." In addition to Russell, he related having discovered a friend's mother after she hanged herself in her garage, as well as a boy who had drowned in a river near his home. As with other events, some of his intimates later questioned the veracity of these disturbing anecdotes, as Kirkwood was suspected more and more of exaggeration and even confusing life with fiction. There was also much speculation about whether he truly had a close friend at Brewster Academy who met a premature end—an event fictionalized in his novel *Good Times/Bad Times*, though the real-life antecedent remains murky.

Kirkwood was only seventeen when he made his Broadway acting debut, taking over a role in the long-running hit *Junior Miss*, directed by Moss Hart. The professional gig gave him a respite from an unhappy period at Brewster Academy, a boarding school in New Hampshire; though he returned there briefly following the end of his contract with the play, he kept running away and finally moved back in with his uncle and aunt. He finished his high school career with a happy year at Elyria High School, where his life briefly took on a degree of normalcy.

After graduation he decided to pursue his nascent acting career and headed for California, a state where he later said he never felt comfortable. He took a survival job as a doorman at Grauman's Chinese Theatre; gossip columnist Louella Parsons wrote in her column that Lila Lee's son had come to Hollywood to be an actor, and when she mentioned that he was working at Grauman's, producers Bill Pine and Bill Thomas went over to the theatre to see him. They cast him in several films, beginning with *You Can't Live Forever* in 1943 and including the famous *Hollywood Canteen*, in which he played a serviceman, the next year. But the roles were small, and he had to take another job working the graveyard shift in an aircraft factory; he became so exhausted that he had a nervous breakdown and was sent to a mental hospital in Arizona for several months.

Shortly after his release, he enlisted in the Navy and joined the Coast Guard. He was spotted by a morale officer named Lomax Study who had been an actor and recognized Kirkwood's name; on discovering he was the son of James Kirkwood Sr., whom he had seen in a touring stage production of *Tobacco Road*, he befriended the young man and got him assigned to the morale office on their ship; Kirkwood put out a daily newspaper on board the vessel, which marked the first time his talent as a writer was appreciated.

Following his honorable discharge from the Navy, Kirkwood proposed marriage to his high school sweetheart, Esther Hamula, but she turned him down; there may also have been another broken engagement around this time, but the girl's identity remains hazy, and some friends later suspected this story was one of his fabrications. He decided to return to pursuing his acting career, this time in New York, and went through some very lean times; at one point, he was desperate enough for cash that he bought a realistic-looking toy gun at FAO Schwarz and used it to rob a lingerie store! He was so nervous he bungled the job badly but somehow got away with it, and felt guilty about it for years afterwards. Somehow he scraped together the cash to study with the legendary acting teacher Sanford Meisner, and he eventually found work in summer stock.

He also worked with a voice teacher who introduced him to another of his students, a talented actor/singer named Lee Goodman. Goodman and Kirkwood hit it off and soon became roommates, renting an apartment in Hell's Kitchen; they also joined forces as a comedy team and began to play gigs in nightclubs. They developed a bit of a following and were hired to perform together in a Broadway revue called *Dance Me a Song*, then appeared on the first-ever episode of *Toast of the Town*—the TV series that would evolve into *The Ed Sullivan Show*. The evening was built around the theme of show business partnerships, and the young pair shared the bill with Dean Martin and Jerry Lewis, another new comedy team to which they were sometimes compared, though Kirkwood and Goodman's act was considered more intellectually sophisticated. Richard Rodgers and Oscar Hammerstein II also appeared on the show, though no one suspected at the time that Kirkwood would one day write a musical that would surpass even that team's legendary hits in popularity.

Though the two men were discreet about it—given the conservative mores of the era—Kirkwood's friends knew that he and Goodman were involved in a sexual relationship as well as a friendship and a working partnership. This lasted a couple of years, until they decided it was interfering with their work together; it was Kirkwood's first sustained relationship with a male, though he had had encounters at boarding school. For a while he lived a bisexual lifestyle, also pursuing relations with several women; these included the noted ballet dancer Muriel Bentley and the actress Elaine Stritch (who years later would work with Michael Bennett and Donna McKechnie on the Broadway musical *Company*). By the time he reached the end of his twenties, though, Kirkwood's sexual interests were by all accounts focused primarily on men.

Some higher-profile acting jobs started coming his way as well. He appeared on Broadway in a revue entitled *Small Wonder*, and in 1953 was cast in the role of the teenaged son in the first television incarnation of the radio soap opera *Valiant Lady*.

The producers had not yet cast the leading female role (his character's mother), and it so happened that his own mother, Lila Lee, recently released from a sanatorium where she had been recovering from a bout with tuberculosis, auditioned for the part. Ironically, the producers were unaware of the relationship and turned her down, claiming there was not a believable family resemblance!

The soap opera aired daily, though as with many other early TV shows each episode was only fifteen minutes long. Still, the strain of rehearsing and broadcasting a live episode every day while also performing with Goodman in clubs late at night began to take a toll: Kirkwood was sleep deprived and emotionally stressed, and would sometimes take out his anger on Goodman physically. Eventually the conflict became too great, and Goodman decided to break up the partnership. Though the act was discontinued, they were eventually able to salvage their friendship and remained close for the rest of their lives.

Other acting assignments at this time included an episode of the morning religious series *Lamp Unto My Feet*, on which he had a unique opportunity to act with both of his parents. He was also chosen by Tallulah Bankhead to be a comedian/master of ceremonies for her touring revue *Welcome Darlings*. Shortly thereafter, he came close to a big break, being cast as the adult Patrick Dennis in the Broadway production of Jerome Lawrence and Robert E. Lee's play *Auntie Mame* (the property that was later adapted as the musical *Mame*). But whether it was due to scheduling conflicts with his other acting gigs or a reported displeasure with his work on the part of the play's star, Rosalind Russell, Kirkwood was unexpectedly fired. He found this out by returning to the theatre after rehearsal one day and discovering a long line of young men waiting to audition for his role! This combined with a ridiculous and embarrassing experience auditioning for a soft drink commercial (which involved being asked to "swim" across a carpeted office floor) contributed to his growing sense of auditions as absurd and humiliating—which he would later draw on productively in writing *A Chorus Line*. (The story of the commercial audition would also show up in his play *P.S. Your Cat Is Dead!*) Shortly following these unfortunate experiences, *Valiant Lady* was finally cancelled by the network. It was 1957; his prospects in New York seeming to have dried up, Kirkwood resolved to try his luck again on the West Coast.

Los Angeles proved not to be receptive to his attempt. He struggled for months to land an acting job but had trouble even securing an agent. Finally, a reputable agent agreed to take him on and invited him to dinner at his home. But when Kirkwood called the agent's house the morning of the proposed dinner to confirm, he was told that the man had just killed himself. If this story is true (and it may be another example of Kirkwood's personal mythmaking), it marked another example of the bizarre pattern of dead bodies dropping into his life at the most unexpected and unfortunate moments. In a later interview in *Playbill*, Kirkwood said: "Now, when your agent kills himself—are they trying to tell you something?" (His fruitless struggles to establish an acting career in California must have given him personal material to draw on in developing the character of Cassie, whose scenes with Zach have been considered his major contribution to the script of *A Chorus Line*.)

At any rate, he was coming to the conclusion that he might want to switch his focus to writing. He had never attended college (partly because neither he nor his parents could have afforded it) and sometimes suffered from feelings of inferiority as a result (something he shared, incidentally, with Michael Bennett). He signed up for an extension course in writing at UCLA, taught by a novelist and critic named Robert Kirsch. Kirsch was impressed by the work Kirkwood submitted: a novel about an adolescent boy who—what else?—discovers the dead body of his mother's lover. The teacher used his influence to get him a literary agent and an introduction to a major publishing house: Little, Brown. Ultimately they did publish *There Must be a Pony!*, but only after a certain amount of wrangling over its length. Kirkwood eventually decided he was trying to do too much for one novel and got it down to size by omitting a substantial portion of the plot—which he would end up recycling for his second book, *Good Times/Bad Times*.

There Must Be a Pony! was enthusiastically received by critics, who felt a very promising new literary novelist had arrived on the scene. Galley proofs of the novel were submitted to movie studios before the book was even published, and director Alan J. Pakula immediately expressed strong interest in making it into a movie. Pakula and Kirkwood spent an evening together discussing the project, during which the director persuaded Kirkwood to adapt the novel as a stage play as a preliminary to the planned film; Kirkwood trusted him and turned down a lucrative offer from MGM for the film rights in order to keep working with Pakula. He wrote the stage version, which Pakula produced on the summer stock circuit in 1962, starring Myrna Loy as the mother. (It opened at the Ogunquit Playhouse in Maine, where a revival of *A Chorus Line* would be staged almost fifty years later.) The play received mixed to positive reviews, but there were some who felt Kirkwood's rewrites along the course of the tour weakened the script rather than improving it. Loy decided not to go to Broadway with the show, and Pakula abandoned the project as well; no film was made until 1986, when the novel was finally adapted as a TV movie starring Chad Lowe and Kirkwood's friend Elizabeth Taylor.

Meanwhile, in an ironic turn of events, now that Kirkwood had turned his career focus decisively to writing and away from performing, he suddenly began to be offered acting work. In the early sixties he appeared in mostly nonsinging roles in revivals of several stage musicals, including *Brigadoon*, *Wonderful Town*, and *Call Me Madam*. It was during the run of the last that he learned of the death, in August 1963, of his eighty-eight-year-old actor father, with whom he had always had a volatile if still loving relationship.

In 1966, Kirkwood finally succeeded in getting a play of his to Broadway, though the run would be very brief. This was a satirical farce entitled *UTBU* (an acronym for "Unhealthy to be Unpleasant"), which he wrote in collaboration with his best friend, James Leo Herlihy, another youngish actor-turned-novelist whose career started taking off around the same time as Kirkwood's (his best-known novel, *Midnight Cowboy*, was published in 1965 and adapted as a hit movie in 1969). Unfortunately, the production period for *UTBU* was quite troubled. Another friend of Kirkwood's, the popular comedic actress Nancy Walker, was hired as director—a position for which she had few qualifications. She reportedly laid on unnecessary sight gags and had trouble controlling the high-powered cast, which was led by

Alan Webb and Tony Randall; she also brought in a writer friend to doctor the script. This didn't sit well with Herlihy, who withdrew from the fray and had his name taken off the play, leaving Kirkwood as the sole credited author. The production struggled through out-of-town tryouts in Boston and Philadelphia, and right before the start of New York previews the producer felt desperate enough to bring in a much more experienced director, Jack Sydow. Sydow asked for a percentage of the gross but remained uncredited, and to his frustration Walker stayed around, continuing to give notes to the actors. Sydow suggested rewrites, which Kirkwood produced, and did what he could with a week and a half's rehearsal time. Reviews were mixed, and the show ran only seven performances; the premature closing was blamed partly on an unfortunately timed transit strike, which made it very difficult for patrons to get to the theatre. (*A Chorus Line* connection: the costumes were designed by Theoni V. Aldredge, who would later design that show, and her husband Tom Aldredge was in the cast.)

On the fiction front, Kirkwood wrote a second novel, entitled *The Angels or Whoever*, but despite the success of his first, he was unable to secure a publisher for it. He did better with his next attempt, *Good Times/Bad Times*, which was made up largely of plot material excised from the overlong early drafts of *There Must Be a Pony!* Inspired by his time at Brewster Academy, the new book focused on a teenage boy's close friendship with a sickly classmate and the damage wrought by a sexually predatory headmaster, whom the protagonist later kills in self-defense. (Kirkwood changed the characters' names and made certain plot adjustments, so technically it is not a sequel.)

During the sixties, Kirkwood flirted with the counterculture; he joined forces with a group of writers publicly denouncing the Vietnam War and was also arrested for possession of marijuana and narrowly avoided doing time in prison, getting off with a fine and a suspended sentence. At a dinner party at Herlihy's New York home, he was introduced to Clay Shaw, an urbane resident of Louisiana who had recently been charged by New Orleans District Attorney Jim Garrison with being part of a conspiracy to murder President John F. Kennedy. Taken with Shaw and intrigued by the case, Kirkwood asked his agent to obtain him a commission to write about it. What began as an article for *Esquire* magazine soon escalated to a book deal, and Kirkwood went to New Orleans to cover the entire trial, which he wrote about in a book entitled *American Grotesque* (1969). (The case later gained greater public notoriety through Oliver Stone's film *JFK*, which was sympathetic to Garrison and the theory of a CIA-instigated conspiracy.) Shaw was acquitted, but even among the many people who believed he was not guilty were some who felt Kirkwood's book was unconscionably biased in Shaw's favor; some have attributed this to a solidarity Kirkwood might have felt with Shaw, who was a fellow homosexual—despite the fact that the book makes no direct reference to Shaw's sexuality. Others found *American Grotesque* to be a well-considered and important contribution to the raging controversy over the assassination, which of course continues to this day.

It was also in the late 1960s that Kirkwood met Arthur Beckenstein, a photographer and graphic artist. They met at the Millstone, a gay bar in the Hamptons, and began a complicated relationship that would continue for the rest of Kirkwood's life. Though they had separate homes in New York, where they pursued their careers (Beckenstein became an art director for Dow Jones and later for *People* magazine), they shared a house in East Hampton and were together every weekend. The handsome Beckenstein was twenty-six, nineteen years younger than the perennially youthful-looking Kirkwood, when the relationship began; though he was from a wealthy family, he initially felt shy and painfully inexperienced among Kirkwood's celebrity friends. But he gradually grew to enjoy the social and cultural opportunities Kirkwood introduced him to, and his gentle personality—combined with the fact that he was not in show business—made him a source of stability that helped keep Kirkwood grounded. (Beckenstein's last name would find its way into the text of *A Chorus Line* as the "real name" of one of the characters, who goes by the stage name Gregory Gardner.)

Kirkwood followed up *Good Times/Bad Times* with a work that many consider his finest: *P.S. Your Cat Is Dead!* The story of an unlikely but life-changing encounter between a frustrated actor and a streetwise burglar who has broken into his apartment several times, it was published first as a novel, and the stage version that was later produced on Broadway has often been referred to as an "adaptation" of the book. However, Kirkwood wrote the story first as a play and only decided to adapt it as fiction when he began to fear it might not be produced.

Continuing in his semiautobiographical vein, Kirkwood decided his next novel would focus on the tumultuous period directly following his discharge from the Navy—a time when his desperate straits had resulted in such embarrassing episodes as the squirt-gun store robbery. But he wanted the story to be contemporary, and he was always wary of dating himself, so he decided to make the central character a veteran of Vietnam rather than the Second World War. To ensure authenticity, he conducted extensive interviews with a recently released POW named Arthur Cormier, whom he met through a librarian in East Hampton. The novel that resulted was called *Some Kind of Hero*, and it was published in August 1975—a very eventful year in the author's career.

Kirkwood first met Michael Bennett when he was looking for a director for the stage version of *P.S. Your Cat Is Dead!* He had initially approached Mike Nichols to direct it; when that didn't work out, he gave the script to Bennett. They had several conversations, and for a while it seemed like Michael was going to sign on, but he eventually passed on the project. Kirkwood was still smarting a bit from this when he ran into Bennett in the lobby during the intermission of a performance of Neil Simon's play *God's Favorite*, which Bennett directed following the first workshop of *A Chorus Line*. When told by Jack Lenny (Bennett's longtime agent) that Bennett was there, Kirkwood famously replied, "Say hello to the little bastard for me." But Bennett approached him and told him he'd been trying to get in touch about a new project. He said he had "an idea" for a musical (neglecting to mention that he already had one book writer and had completed an initial workshop) and asked Kirkwood to have lunch with him the next day to discuss it. Kirkwood replied that he didn't know how to write a musical, but Bennett said nobody really does—otherwise there would be a lot more good musicals! Bennett had a hunch that Kirkwood's background as an actor would make him a good fit for the project, and he was right: when Bennett told him the show was to be about dancers competing against each other at an audition for a Broadway show, Kirkwood was immediately excited. He was quoted in Kenneth Turan's history of the Public Theater: "Right away I was hooked because I think the audition system, especially for musicals, is the closest thing to the Romans throwing the Christians to the lions. It really is brutal."

Though Kirkwood was surprised to learn he had a collaborator on the show, he and Nick Dante found they got along. The cast of *A Chorus Line* also found Kirkwood to be a genial and sympathetic presence, one who showed great respect for their work and also considerable humility, staying quietly in the background much of the time but always offering support when it was needed. He also looked out for Dante and did his best to make sure the younger man did not feel pushed aside.

That season was a busy one for Kirkwood, because at the same time he was involved with putting the finishing touches to *A Chorus Line*, the play version of *P.S. Your Cat Is Dead!* was finally opening on Broadway as well. Following a successful run at the Studio Arena Theatre in Buffalo, directed by Vivian Matalon, the show came in with high expectations, but unfortunately the critical response was not what Kirkwood—or the producers—were hoping for. Some were offended by the raunchy gay content of the play, in which the actor character (played by Keir Dullea) has the burglar (Tony Musante) tied up in his apartment for a long period of time and is later propositioned by him; there was a sense that Kirkwood was either "proselytizing" for homosexuality or else being coy and essentially dishonest in his handling of the subject. As in his novels, Kirkwood sprinkles in tantalizingly suggestive gay situations and undercurrents, but like the teenage heroes of his first couple of books, the play's (otherwise quite autobiographical) leading male character is presented as straight. The resultant impression of ambivalence about homosexuality can be off-putting to both straights and gays; it's an issue that comes up frequently in criticism of Kirkwood's body of work. Still, some of his homosexual readers have said they appreciated the subtle ways he managed to work gay subtext into his novels while staying ambiguous enough to satisfy a mainstream audience; otherwise, they realized, he might never have been published at all. But his latest play was not a work that many would describe as subtle. When juxtaposed with the ecstatic response to *A Chorus Line*—which pioneered the inclusion of gay themes in a mainstream musical, at no expense to its popularity—the chilly reception accorded to *P.S. Your Cat Is Dead!* rankled Kirkwood to some extent. Though he was proud of his contribution to the musical, the play was all his, and more personal. It played just five previews and sixteen regular performances at the John Golden Theatre, closing on April 20, 1975—just days after *A Chorus Line* began performances at the Newman.

Believing *P.S. Your Cat Is Dead!* hadn't received its due, Kirkwood wouldn't give up on it. He followed up the disappointing run with a California production. Directed by Milton Katselas, it opened in San Francisco and did so well that it was scheduled to move to Los Angeles. But a curse seemed to hang over the play. Shortly before the move, a new actor took over the role of Vito, the burglar. Sal Mineo (famed for film roles in *Rebel Without a Cause*, *East of Eden*, and *Exodus*) was considered perfect in the role, but shortly after a brilliant rehearsal in Los Angeles on February 12, 1976, the actor, shockingly, was fatally stabbed on the street outside his home. The company was devastated, but the show went on, with Jeff Druce (an actor who had been fired to make way for Mineo) agreeing to return to the role. Once again, a grisly death had intruded into Kirkwood's life.

The play, however, refused to die and, in a revised version with several characters deleted, returned to New York for an Off-Broadway run in 1978. Opening at the Promenade Theatre on the Upper West Side, this new production, directed by Robert Nigro, later transferred to the Circle in the Square downtown, racking up an impressive three hundred performances. The play remained popular for many years in regional theatres and even internationally, though the general consensus is that neither of the stage versions is quite as effective as the novel, widely considered Kirkwood's finest.

Following the Tony Award and Pulitzer Prize he received for *A Chorus Line*, Kirkwood found himself much requested as a book writer for musicals, but, like the other members of *ACL*'s creative team, he had difficulty finding one he felt confident could live up to its predecessor. The one that got the furthest was *Murder at the Vanities*, which he and his collaborators auditioned for Michael Bennett. The director agreed to option it, but then according to Kirkwood proceeded to sabotage the deal by making impossible contractual demands: overly high percentages, the option of taking a coauthor credit any time he might choose to, etc. The project fell apart and left Kirkwood feeling betrayed.

He continued to take on film projects, including several in collaboration with Jerry Paonessa, who became a friend after obtaining the film rights to *Some Kind of Hero*. He assisted Kirkwood through writing a screenplay adaptation, though the project got bogged down at Paramount and no movie was made for several years. A hurried adaptation of *Good Times/Bad Times* for producer Jim Bradley resulted in no movie at all. He was also asked to adapt Christina Crawford's book *Mommie Dearest* for the screen, and though he passed on that, he did end up playing a small role in the film; this was part of an unexpected revival of his screen acting career that also included appearances with George Burns in *Oh God! Part II* (1980) and in *The Supernaturals* (1986).

His post-*Chorus Line* playwriting career included two comedies about show business, both of which turned into extremely rocky production experiences. The better known of these is the play *Legends!*, about two aging Hollywood stars, never the best of friends, considering making a comeback together in a Broadway show. It was produced by Kevin Eggers, Robert Regester, Cheryl Crawford, and record mogul Ahmet Ertegun; after much wooing on Kirkwood's part, they managed to sign Carol Channing and Mary Martin, two of the musical theatre's most revered and, yes, legendary divas to play the roles. The play opened in Dallas on January 7, 1986, and visited over twenty major American cities before closing in Palm Beach, Florida, just over a year later. Kirkwood later wrote a book about the experience called *Diary of a Mad Playwright*, a detailed and often witty account of what turned out to be quite a wild ride. Channing clashed with director Clifford Williams and sometimes with Martin, who, at seventy-three and nearly ten years past her retirement from the stage, found she simply could not remember her lines. Finally they resorted to an earpiece that allowed her to be fed lines continually throughout the show by an offstage prompter—a procedure that was relatively untried at the time but has since been used in several other high-profile productions; of course, it hinders the timing and pacing of a show and the actors' ability to listen to and play off one another. At a June performance in Phoenix, the earpiece started picking up dispatch signals from a taxicab company; frustrated, Martin had to pull it out and finish the show without it, discovering in the process that she actually remembered all her lines! She was device-free for the second half of the tour, which went substantially better, and Kirkwood was finally able to work on some rewrites to improve the script. A new comedic solo scene for the producer character, played by the resourceful comic actor Gary Beach, was inserted into the show in Philadelphia, and the producers ultimately persuaded Kirkwood to add a musical number at the end, since nothing else in the show gave the two ladies any opportunity to show off their fabled musical comedy chops. There was also an energetic striptease number for a male dancer delivering a strip-o-gram; this was choreographed by Trish Garland. In the *Diary*, Kirkwood mentions how Garland's makeover, including cosmetic surgery, had resulted in a much more glamorous persona than she had sported when she created the role of "Bebe" in *A Chorus Line* (as the musical's co-librettist, he should have remembered that she actually played Judy).

Though the show did good business on the road and audiences were eager to cheer the two beloved stars, reviews for the play itself were mostly lukewarm to negative. A turning point was reached in Boston, when producer Eggers announced the decision to cut a serious monologue that Martin's character had about her experiences following a mastectomy: one of her finest acting moments in the show. She was so offended that she not only refused to take the speech out, she decided on the spot not to renew her contract for a New York run; claiming solidarity with her costar, Channing followed suit. Though there were some half-hearted discussions about bringing in a new cast, the result was that the show was never produced on Broadway. Though Kirkwood's *Diary* expresses his flabbergasted reaction to the two stars' having given up what he thought was a golden opportunity for a Broadway comeback, the unspoken reality, which both ladies were certainly very conscious of by that point, is that the play itself simply wasn't very good.

Twenty years later (and long after Kirkwood's death), producer Ben Sprecher decided to give *Legends!* another chance and mounted a new tour with Joan Collins and Linda Evans, respectively, in the Channing and Martin roles. This could have been inspiring casting, but the two actresses—who had played opposite each other for years on the prime-time soap opera *Dynasty*—reportedly feuded for real during the tour. Reviews were disappointing, and the show again failed to come in to New York.

Kirkwood's last play, the backstage farce *Stage-Stuck*, was a collaboration with a young writer named Jim Piazza, with whom he was also involved personally (the relationship with Beckenstein had by this point evolved into a close but no longer physical friendship). Piazza reported later that he had also contributed, uncredited, to the script of *Legends!*, writing several laugh lines and collaborating with Kirkwood on the solo subway station scene for Gary Beach. The two took a long time to find a producer for *Stage-Stuck* that met Kirkwood's standards;

finally he agreed to a production at the Burt Reynolds Dinner Theatre in Jupiter, Florida, where Charles Nelson Reilly directed a production starring the outrageous comedian Rip Taylor. The play is a backstage story about a bunch of egotistical, bellicose theatre people attempting to salvage a production of a terrible French play. It includes lots of theatrical in-jokes, some at the expense of former colleagues of Kirkwood's like Michael Bennett and Mary Martin; it concluded with a parody of the finale to *A Chorus Line*.

The production was plagued by problems. Taylor failed to learn his lines and on opening night wrote them on pieces of paper which he taped to various pieces of furniture on the set—only to discover there was not enough light onstage to enable him to read them. The second night the show was stopped and the second act cancelled when the dinner theatre had to be evacuated due to a gas leak in the kitchen. Piazza was there working on the script and trying to improve the situation, and though Kirkwood kept telling him he'd be coming down, he was by that point too ill to leave home; he never saw the production. Burt Reynolds was disturbed that some of the theatre's patrons were walking out mid-show, and others wrote angry letters complaining about the play's vulgarity and obscene language. The producers decided to close the production three weeks earlier than planned—and later blamed the show when the theatre filed for bankruptcy. (It was later reorganized and is successful today under the name Maltz Jupiter Theatre.)

In addition to the 1986 TV movie of *There Must Be a Pony!* with Elizabeth Taylor, there were two more late film adaptations of Kirkwood novels. *Some Kind of Hero* made it to the screen in 1982, but instead of using Kirkwood's screenplay, the producers adapted the book—which had been a serious story about a Caucasian war veteran—as a comedic vehicle for the African American actor Richard Pryor; though reviews were mixed, Pryor's following ensured a decent box-office success. The more faithful film version of *P.S. Your Cat Is Dead!* was a labor of love by the actor Steve Guttenberg, who not only starred in the film but also produced, directed, and collaborated (with Jeff Korn) on the screenplay; it didn't appear until 2002, thirteen years after Kirkwood's death.

Though Kirkwood's last published novel, *Hit Me with a Rainbow* (1980), is considered one of his weakest efforts, he was working at the time of his death on a major book called *I Teach Flying*, a fictionalization of his relationship with his father. The few people who have read the unfinished six-hundred-page manuscript found much to admire, and have said it offers evidence that at that point in his career, Kirkwood still had a substantial talent that is seldom evident in his other post-*A Chorus Line* output. On his deathbed he outlined his plans for the rest of the story to Jerry Paonessa and expressed his wish that his lifelong friend James Leo Herlihy be asked to finish the novel. Herlihy declined, as did a couple of other authors who were later asked to consider it, and the work remains unpublished.

Though Kirkwood's lifestyle and personal relationships were well known to his friends and theatrical colleagues, he never came out publicly, and the cause of his death at age sixty-four was officially listed as cancer; it wasn't until several years later that the fact that he had suffered from AIDS became public knowledge.

A Chorus Line was the property that brought James Kirkwood his most lasting and widespread acclaim, including a Tony Award and a Pulitzer Prize, and the most money, earning him over a million dollars. But his feelings about the musical and his involvement in it were ambivalent. On the one hand, as he often expressed publicly, he had enjoyed working on it and loved being a part of the magic and success it engendered—while on the other he resented the way it eclipsed his other plays and novels in the eyes of the public. He was heard to say he didn't want *A Chorus Line* mentioned if there was ever a memorial service in his honor. There was also the nagging issue, which also dogged cowriter Nick Dante, of the lack of recognition given to the book writers of the show; there was a widespread perception, right or wrong, that their contribution was relatively minor and that they didn't actually deserve much of the credit for its huge success. Since much of the show was taken more or less directly from the tape sessions and interviews with the dancers, the development of the script was guided so firmly by director Bennett, and Neil Simon was famously brought in during previews to add laugh lines, many have questioned just how much Kirkwood and Dante actually contributed. Arthur Laurents, one of the musical theatre's most esteemed librettists and a friend of Kirkwood's for many years, summed up that point of view himself with savage succinctness when he told Kirkwood's biographer, Sean Egan: "In the end it was Michael Bennett who did it all and Jimmy and Nick Dante were really serving what Michael Bennett wanted. He was the be-all-and-end-all. . . . Jimmy and Nick Dante were sort of glorified secretaries for Michael Bennett. Ed Kleban—I once said to him about my friend Jimmy Kirkwood. He said, 'Who's he?'" But original cast member Trish Garland had a different view. When asked whether Kirkwood's contribution had been limited to the scenes between Cassie and Zach, she said: "I think that whoever said that, that's totally inaccurate. . . . A lot of people aren't on board from the very initial [moment] but what they bring to the table is so wonderful that it just brings everything up. I think that's what Jimmy had." (Quoted in *Ponies and Rainbows: The Life of James Kirkwood*, by Sean Egan.)

For Kirkwood's own part, despite the ambivalence he sometimes privately admitted to, he was asked in a *Playbill* interview how it had felt to see various companies open the musical in different cities and responded: "I don't think there has ever been a time when, during the opening dance combinations, the tiny hairs on my arms and along my spine haven't stood erect in honor of the pure raw energy of the actor-dancers upholding the tradition and discipline of the theatre. . . God Bless the living theatre and a million thanks for the great luck to have been a part of *A Chorus Line*."

Marvin Hamlisch

Hamlisch was born in Manhattan on June 2, 1944, the son of Jewish parents from Vienna, Austria. It was a musical family; his father Max, who was a bandleader and played the accordion, felt he could have had a substantial career in music if he hadn't been forced to move his family to America in the 1930s to escape the Nazis.

Marvin's musical talents became apparent early. His sister was taking piano lessons, and he would listen, later sitting down at the piano and playing her selections by ear (a story eerily similar to that of how the character Mike in *A Chorus Line* discovered his aptitude for dance, which Hamlisch would one day musicalize in the song "I Can Do That"). Taking note, Max Hamlisch pinned his hopes on his son, whom he groomed for a career as a concert pianist. Marvin was considered a child prodigy, earning a scholarship to the prestigious Juilliard School Preparatory Division when he was only six years old!—the youngest student ever admitted. Though the audition panel requested Mozart, young Marvin claimed he didn't know any, but passed the audition by playing "Goodnight Irene"—in every key they requested. The program wasn't full-time; he attended public school on a regular schedule, but studied piano with his assigned Juilliard teacher once a week and attended a full day of music classes every Saturday at the Juilliard campus—which, in those pre-Lincoln Center days, was located at 122nd Street and Broadway.

Marvin secretly longed to write songs, specifically Broadway musicals, but was afraid to tell his father he didn't want to be a classical pianist. He was temperamentally unsuited for it and became terrified and even physically ill every time he had to play before a jury of faculty members; the pressure was particularly great because the family couldn't have afforded tuition, so he had to pass the exam each year to remain at the school.

When it came time for Marvin to enter junior high, his father looked for a school whose curriculum would leave him plenty of time for his Juilliard studies and two hours a day of piano practice, and settled on the Professional Children's School. This was an all-academics school for youngsters who were already working professionally in the business, mostly as actors, dancers, or models. To allow time for their work schedules, the school was in session only from 10 a.m. to 2 p.m. each day. Many of the students were making a lot of money, which made Marvin feel a bit out of place at first, but his charm and his ability to play the piano and write songs soon helped him make friends. His fellow students included Leslie Uggams, Christopher Walken, and his best friend, Bobby Mariano. Mariano was a dancer in the Broadway production of *The Music Man*, and he came up with the idea of putting together an original show with a cast of students from the school. Of course he enlisted Marvin to write the songs, and the show became *All of Us*, a musical revue they presented to delighted audiences for three nights in a movie theatre called the Little Carnegie. Marvin's main songwriting partner at the time was Howard Liebling, a distant relative who was also engaged to his sister, Terry.

As a teenager, Marvin attended Broadway shows whenever he could afford a standing-room ticket. He cited *Bye Bye Birdie* and *My Fair Lady* as favorites, as well as the two classics Stephen Sondheim wrote lyrics for before he began his celebrated career as a composer: *Gypsy* and *West Side Story*.

Bobby Mariano was dating the teenage Liza Minnelli at the time. She wanted to record a demo as a Christmas gift for her mother, Judy Garland, who was an idol of Marvin's. Minnelli's plan was to use the record as a way of proving to her mother that she had the drive and talent to be a singer in her own right. Mariano suggested that Marvin and Liebling write some songs for her to sing on the demo, an assignment they completed with alacrity. Marvin was quite starstruck when Liza invited him to Garland's lavish Christmas party at their home in Scarsdale, where she presented her mother with the record. Garland was moved to tears by the gift, thanked Marvin for the songs he had provided, and then asked him and Liza to perform them live for the guests. Marvin was astonished and delighted to oblige—after which the night got even more thrilling when Garland asked him to accompany her as she sang several of her great hits, songs he had adored for years. Marvin was invited to stay the night, and in the morning Judy sent him back to Manhattan in a limousine. He later claimed that it was that party that sealed once and for all his decision to forsake classical music for show business, a world he was falling in love with, and where he felt he belonged.

He formulated a list of goals for himself. Foreshadowing Sheila and the list of "deadlines" she remembers giving herself in the "Alternatives" scene of *ACL*, he resolved to write his first #1 hit song before he turned twenty-five. He would win an Oscar before he hit thirty. And he was determined to write the music for a hit Broadway musical before he was thirty-five. All of these things, amazingly, were to come true.

First things first: encouraged by the success of *All of Us*, Marvin and Howard Liebling were determined to find a way to make some money from their songwriting. But though Marvin was still a teenager, he found his style was a bit retro for the early 1960s; music producers didn't want anything that sounded like a traditional show tune, they wanted rock 'n' roll. So Hamlisch and Liebling did their best to adjust their style and plied their wares to producer after producer in the legendary Brill Building, without success. Not only were they faced with continual rejection, an unethical producer even stole one of their song ideas.

Finally they had a breakthrough when Quincy Jones, then running Mercury Records, bought Marvin and Howard's song "Sunshine, Lollipops and Rainbows" and turned it into a hit record for Lesley Gore; it rose to #13 on the *Billboard* Hot 100, and they followed it up with a second Gore record, "California Nights," which also became a hit and would later be performed by Gore on, of all things, an episode of the TV series *Batman*.

It was thanks to Minnelli that, at age twenty, Marvin got an audition for his first Broadway job. Liza was starring Off Broadway in *Best Foot Forward* and recommended Marvin to that show's musical director, Buster Davis. Auditioning at Davis's apartment, Marvin played the whole overture to *Gypsy* on the piano. Davis was impressed and hired him to be his assistant on the upcoming Broadway musical *Fade Out—Fade In*. Marvin was ecstatic, but the excitement changed to heartbreak when the show was postponed due to the unexpected pregnancy of its star, Carol Burnett. Davis remembered the talented young musician, though, and soon hired him as rehearsal pianist for the original Broadway production of *Funny Girl*, where he got a whirlwind education on the trials and tribulations a creative team goes through putting a new musical together. His ability to play any song in any key on demand, which he had demonstrated in his Juilliard audition at age six, came in very handy, and he ended up providing many of the show's vocal arrangements. He learned an enormous amount not only from Davis but from the show's composer, the great Jule Styne, and considered them two of his most important mentors. And although he still viewed himself as something of a shy and nerdy kid, he was already developing a healthy ego. He was in awe of the show's star—the very young

Barbra Streisand—but stood up to her one night after she played fast and loose with the melody to "Sadie, Sadie, Married Lady," telling her she was throwing the chorus off. She replied by saying "Marvin, what are these people paying money to hear—your vocal arrangements?" Having learned a lesson in humility and flexibility, he rewrote the chorus part.

Once *Funny Girl* was up and running, Buster Davis hired Marvin to be the assistant vocal arranger on *The Bell Telephone Hour*, a prestigious television series featuring a variety of musical guests, from jazz musicians to Broadway stars to opera singers. The problem was that Marvin had promised his father that he would get a college degree. The original plan was to attend Queens College, but Marvin didn't want to turn down the TV job, so after intensive research into the offerings of various area institutions, he pieced together a schedule whereby he could work most of the day at the TV studio but take early morning and evening classes at Hofstra University and the RCA School of Television in addition to Queens College. He was soon working himself too hard, and his health started to suffer, but he honored his word to his father and ended up graduating with a degree from Queens College in 1967.

Though he was frustrated that he wasn't getting any opportunities as a songwriter, Hamlisch stayed with *The Bell Telephone Hour* until the series was cancelled. After that, he suddenly had more time on his hands and was free to accept an invitation to attend a run-through rehearsal of a new Broadway-bound musical called *A Joyful Noise*. He found himself so impressed with the show's dance numbers that he made a point of going backstage afterwards to meet the choreographer, who turned out to be a diminutive dancer about his own age. He recalls telling the young man: "You don't know me, but I'm telling you, you're a genius. You may not believe this, but someday I'm going to work with you. I'm writing your name in my address book under 'G' for genius." That name turned out to be Michael Bennett.

Their collaboration was still a ways off, but the next year Marvin wrote his first film score. He had received a phone call from a woman offering him a gig playing piano for a party, which he almost turned down, replying indignantly that he was a composer, but when he learned the party's host was Sam Spiegel, he immediately relented. Spiegel, a Hollywood producer, was famous for throwing terrific parties for the showbiz crowd, and this one was no exception. At one point he asked Marvin what else he did. On being told he was a songwriter, Spiegel offered him the chance to come to his office and play some of his songs as an audition for a job scoring his next movie, *The Swimmer*. Marvin was shrewd enough to know that playing "Sunshine, Lollipops and Rainbows" might not demonstrate what Spiegel needed to hear, so he read the John Cheever short story the film was based on and quickly came up with a musical theme. Spiegel liked it and hired him to write what turned out to be a quite extensive score for the film. He wrote in his parents' apartment, where he was still living, and which was made to seem even tinier by the addition of a Moviola, a large machine that enabled him to watch the film at home while he was working (this was long before the days of DVD players or even VCRs). He tended to work late, and the machine and the piano could be so loud that one night a neighbor called the police to complain! But by once again burning the candle at both ends he was able to meet his deadline.

Hamlisch continued his film career with music for the Woody Allen films *Take the Money and Run* (1969) and *Bananas* (1971), both featuring Allen with the actress Louise Lasser.

Though his career as a composer of film music was off to a good start, there was a bit of a lull in the early seventies that gave him time for other projects. These included serving as arranger, music director, and/or accompanist for a variety of nightclub acts and concert tours by two very different artists, both of whom became close friends of his: Ann-Margret and Groucho Marx. Then came a call from producer Ray Stark, whom he knew from *Funny Girl*, with an offer to write, on spec, a theme song for a new movie Sydney Pollack was directing. This turned out to be the Barbra Streisand/Robert Redford vehicle *The Way We Were*.

Marvin knew what a huge opportunity that could turn out to be, and having been a Streisand devotee since *Funny Girl*, he was inspired by the idea of writing a song for her voice. Working from the film's script and title, he came up with one melody after another until he hit on one he felt was right, and then the prestigious team of Alan and Marilyn Bergman was hired to supply lyrics. Though Streisand loved the song (she suggested a slight revision to a line of the melody, which Hamlisch agreed with), the team still thought they could maybe do even better, so they wrote a second song with the same title. Pollack experimented with both, and the first version was ultimately chosen for use in the movie. Streisand remembered both, though, and years later recorded the alternate version on her album *For the Record*.

It was also on *The Way We Were* that Marvin had a chance to demonstrate the perfectionism he would become known for. By this time, he was well aware of how much the background music can contribute to the emotional impact of a film. He had backed off from bringing the main theme music of *The Way We Were* back during the film's final sequence, thinking that would be overkill, but when he saw an early preview of the film and the audience remained dry-eyed during that scene, he realized he had made a mistake. He implored the studio to let him rerecord the music for that sequence, but was told the film was finished and that another session would be too expensive. Determined to fix it, he offered to pay the musicians out of his own pocket. The audience response at screenings of the rescored version proved he had been right—as did the subsequent acclaim bestowed on the film and, specifically, his music for it.

Hamlisch's career was suddenly in high gear, and his next big movie project came along immediately. *The Sting* was directed by George Roy Hill, who had also directed the 1967 Broadway musical *Henry, Sweet Henry*, on which Hamlisch worked as a dance arranger—and which was choreographed by Michael Bennett (see Chapter 2). Now considered one of the all-time great Hollywood films, *The Sting* was a caper movie about charismatic con artists, played by Paul Newman and Robert Redford; Hamlisch wrote a couple of jazz age–style songs for the film, which took place in 1936, but the musical compositions most memorably associated with it are by Scott Joplin. Not strictly appropriate to the period (Joplin's pieces were written thirty years before the time in which the film was set), they proved aptly evocative and contributed to a major revival of public interest in ragtime. Hamlisch adapted and arranged Joplin's works for the film—including an especially catchy piano rag called "The Entertainer" that became extraordinarily popular; a memorable highlight of the movie as well as the soundtrack album, it was issued as a single and reached #1 on the *Billboard* easy listening chart and #3 on the pop chart.

Hamlisch's theme for *The Way We Were* also became a hit record, as well as the title song of Streisand's next solo album; it won him the Academy Award for Best Original Song—the same night he also won Best Original Dramatic Score for that film and Best Original Song Score and/or Adaptation for *The Sting*. This notable feat made Hamlisch only the second person in history to win three Academy Awards in one night, the first having been Billy Wilder thirteen years earlier. (A less known fact is that Hamlisch had also received a Best Original Song nomination the previous year, for the song "Life Is What You Make It," written with Johnny Mercer for *Kotch*, the only movie ever directed by the actor Jack Lemmon. Though it lost the Oscar to the theme from *Shaft*, the song did win a Golden Globe Award. And although Hamlisch never won another Oscar after his three in 1974, he received eight more nominations between 1977 and 1997, including one for Best Original Song in 1986 for "Surprise, Surprise," a new number he and Ed Kleban wrote for the movie of *ACL*.)

His well-known later film scores included *Ordinary People* and *Sophie's Choice* in the 1980s. Two of his last projects were scores for films directed by Steven Soderbergh and starring Matt Damon: *The Informant* (2009) and *Behind the Candelabra* (HBO; 2013). This last, not premiered till after Hamlisch's death, was the story of Liberace—played by Michael Douglas, who had also starred as Zach in the film version of *A Chorus Line*.

It was on May 3, 1974, shortly after Hamlisch's triple Oscar win, that Michael Bennett called him about collaborating on a project. According to Hamlisch, he didn't tell him anything about the show on the phone, just that he wanted him to drop everything and fly back to New York right away. Amazingly, Hamlisch agreed. This was a time when his Hollywood potential seemed limitless. Most musicians in his position (and few had ever been in that position!) would have stayed in Los Angeles to pursue some of the lucrative film contracts that would be pouring in. But Hamlisch's roots were on Broadway, and his most cherished dream had always been to write the score for a musical. He still remembered *A Joyful Noise* and *Henry, Sweet Henry*, and he thought Bennett was a genius. Plus, he was still something of a mama's boy at heart: he considered New York his home, and he missed his family when he was in Hollywood; a part of him was glad to have a reason to come back.

The meeting with Michael Bennett took place at the director's apartment on West 55th Street. On hearing Bennett's brief description of the musical he had in mind, Hamlisch wasn't immediately excited, and wondered if he had made a mistake coming back to town; the idea of a musical based on tape-recorded group therapy–like sessions with a bunch of dancers didn't sound all that promising to him, despite Bennett's charisma and the conviction with which he pitched the project. Marvin worried that it sounded like there was no story. But Bennett was persuasive, and before long the composer decided this wasn't something he should miss out on; he would sign up now and, if necessary, ask questions later. His Los Angeles agent tried to talk him out of it, but Hamlisch felt his dream was about to come true, and it's a tribute to his instincts that he turned his back on all that Hollywood had to offer and agreed to take part in the workshop for the new show at a pay rate of only one hundred dollars a week—the same amount the dancers, and all other participants in the project, were making. And in another important step, he moved out of his parents' apartment and got his own place for the first time—at age twenty-nine. Flush with his earnings from the hit films, he got a designer-furnished one-bedroom on East 79th Street and Park Avenue. When his new neighbors complained about the noise from his piano, he hired a carpenter to build a box around the instrument to soundproof it.

By the end of May, Marvin had been introduced to collaborators Ed Kleban (lyrics) and Nicholas Dante (book). He had great respect for Kleban's work and liked him, though it naturally took some time for the two of them to develop a rapport. They ended up winning the Tony Award for Best Score for a Musical and, as a member of the writing team, shared the Pulitzer Prize for Drama. Hamlisch became one of only two people in history (the other being Richard Rodgers, grand-daddy of all musical theatre composers) to win both of those honors in addition to Emmy, Oscar, and Grammy awards.

Around this time, Hamlisch began a romantic relationship with another songwriter: Carole Bayer Sager, also a singer and painter. The two of them cowrote "Nobody Does It Better," the theme song for the 1977 James Bond movie *The Spy Who Loved Me*. Performed on the soundtrack by Carly Simon, the song became a hit; it has often been covered by other singers and found its way into several later films as well.

Hamlisch and Sager's relationship, substantially fictionalized, became the basis for the first musical Hamlisch wrote after *A Chorus Line*: *They're Playing Our Song*, in which Vernon Gersch and Sonia Walsk, the characters based on him and Sager, were played by Robert Klein and Lucie Arnaz. Hamlisch wrote the music for the show, to lyrics by Sager, and the book was by Neil Simon, who had recently also adapted elements of his own love life for his play *Chapter Two* (1977). (Simon, of course, had also been involved with *ACL* as an uncredited script doctor). *They're Playing Our Song* was a hit on Broadway, on the road, and in London. Although it chronicles the bumps on the road to romance for the two appealingly quirky characters, it ends with their finding true love. In real life, Hamlisch and Sager's relationship did not last much longer, though they continued to write songs together. She ended up marrying another of her songwriting partners, Burt Bacharach, whose one Broadway show, *Promises, Promises* (1968), had coincidentally been choreographed by Michael Bennett.

Along with his record-breaking award wins, Hamlisch probably also holds the distinction of being the only Broadway composer to appear as a character in not one but two Broadway musicals. In addition to his fictionalized portrait in *They're Playing Our Song*, there was a more factually based Marvin Hamlisch onstage in the musical *A Class Act*, which Lonny Price and Linda Kline wrote about the life of Ed Kleban. With a score comprised of many of Kleban's own songs, the show of course included a sequence about the writing and production of *A Chorus Line*, in which both Michael Bennett and Hamlisch appeared as characters. Bennett was portrayed by the actor David Hibbard; Hamlisch was played Off Broadway by Ray Wills and on Broadway by Jeff Blumenkrantz—a singer-actor who also happens to be an accomplished songwriter in his own right.

They're Playing Our Song would prove to be Hamlisch's last hit as a Broadway composer. The musical *Jean Seberg*, a property he was quite passionate about, had a troubled production in London in 1983 and never made it to Broadway. Following that, however, he provided the scores for three more large-scale musicals that did. First came *Smile* (1986), a collaboration with book writer/lyricist Howard Ashman, loosely based on the 1975 film of the same title (screenplay by Jerry Belson) about the backstage tribulations surrounding a fictitious California beauty pageant. Ashman also directed, and the production stumbled in its attempt to define a consistent tone; the run lasted only forty-eight performances. *The Goodbye Girl* (1993) was a musical version of the popular movie Neil Simon had written for his then-wife Marsha Mason—both of whom had contributed substantially to the development of *A Chorus Line* (see Chapter 12). With lyrics by David Zippel and a book by Simon himself, the musical version starred Bernadette Peters in the Mason role, with a cast that included Dennis Daniels, Cynthia Onrubia, and Scott Wise, all of whom had danced in *ACL* as replacements. It lasted six months in 1993 at the Marquis Theatre; a revised version starring Donna McKechnie played the Walnut Street Theatre in Philadelphia four years later. Hamlisch's next and last full Broadway score was for *The Sweet Smell of Success*, which played the Martin Beck Theatre (now the Al Hirschfeld) for less than four months in 2002. With a book by the distinguished playwright John Guare and lyrics by Craig Carnelia, the musical was based on the 1957 Ernest Lehman/Clifford Odets film about an unscrupulous gossip columnist and an ambitious press agent. Directed by Nicholas Hytner, it starred John Lithgow (who won a Tony Award for his role) and Brian d'Arcy James; the cast also included Jack Noseworthy, who had been the last Mark in *ACL* on Broadway, as well as Michael Paternostro and Eric Sciotto, both of whom would appear in the Broadway revival four years later. (Hamlisch and Carnelia later provided a few songs for Nora Ephron's play *Imaginary Friends*, which had a brief Broadway run in 2002–03.)

Hamlisch proved a late bloomer in the romance department. His relationship with Carole Bayer Sager, when he was already in his mid-thirties, seems to have been his first serious one, and it proved short-lived. It was several more years before he found true and lasting love with Terre Blair, a broadcast journalist he first telephoned on the advice of his lifelong friend Richard Kagan, who had tried to set him up on more than one previous occasion. After a round of phone tag, Hamlisch and Blair finally had a conversation and found they hit it off immediately; though he was living in New York and she in Los Angeles, they carried on a long-distance friendship that seemed to be blossoming into something much more even though they had never met face to face. She finally came to New York to meet him and was on the verge of calling it off when, according to his memoirs, he proposed marriage to her through the door of her hotel room; she accepted, and they then saw each other face to face for the first time. They were married on

Donna McKechnie, backed by the student cast from Staples High School, performs at a benefit tribute to Marvin Hamlisch at the Hudson Theatre in New York, 2013.

Photo by Kerry Long

March 6, 1989, at a small temple in downtown Manhattan, and repeated their vows on May 29 for friends and family in a second ceremony held on a yacht.

Though Hamlisch's last few Broadway shows failed to live up to the legendary precedent set by *A Chorus Line*, he found that love and his newly expanded view of the world were inspiring him to broaden his musical horizons. Branching out in unexpected directions, he produced two unusual compositions that had great personal and political resonance both for him and for audiences. The first was an orchestral piece for the Dallas Symphony Orchestra, inspired by the themes of *The Anatomy of Peace*, a book by Emery Reves, and commissioned by the writer's widow, Wendy Reves. Hamlisch spent eight months on the assignment, which emerged as a twenty-eight-minute symphony for orchestra and child vocalist; the premiere in Dallas was conducted by Maestro Edoardo Mata.

Inspired partly by that experience, Terre Blair Hamlisch then suggested that her husband write an anthem for the world. This was a time shortly after the collapse of the Berlin Wall and the fall of communism in Russia; Marvin and Terre as well as many others were feeling a rare degree of hope that the nations of the world, so long divided by ideologies, were starting to come together in harmony, and the idea of an anthem that celebrated not one nation but all the peoples of the world was enormously appealing. Hamlisch persuaded his old colleagues Alan and Marilyn Bergman to write the lyrics, and they came up with the line "Imagine what tomorrow would bring if we all sing One Song." Entitled "One Song," the piece was first performed in 1990 at Carnegie Hall by the United Nations Children's Chorus, with the great soprano Barbara Cook as vocal soloist. It was also heard at the 1992 Olympic Games in Barcelona, Spain, from which it reached an audience of over a billion people.

Though the script and score of *A Chorus Line* were the work of a group of young men, Marvin Hamlisch was the only one of the original creative team to outlive the original Broadway production by much more than a year. It closed on April 28, 1990; Michael Bennett and Edward Kleban had both passed away in 1987, James Kirkwood in 1989. Nicholas Dante died in May 1991. Hamlisch, though, was still around for the Broadway revival in 2006, and he worked with Jonathan Tunick on a revised orchestration, contributing a new arrangement of "What I Did for Love"; he took great joy in working on the show again. Beloved for his humor, kindness, and humanity as well as for his prodigious musical gifts, Hamlisch passed away on August 6, 2012, in Los Angeles. Two months later, several generations of *Chorus Line* dancers honored his memory in a tribute following the opening night performance of a revival of the show at the Paper Mill Playhouse in New Jersey.

Edward Kleban

Kleban was a native New Yorker, born in the Bronx on April 30, 1939. He attended the High School of Music and Art, and, because he lived near Yankee Stadium, he was made sports editor of the school newspaper. One of his schoolmates was Jonathan Tunick, who would later have a career as a leading Broadway orchestrator, and would in fact do many of the orchestrations for *A Chorus Line*; the two teens played in bands together, and Kleban very early developed something of a reputation as an excellent modern jazz pianist. He went on to Columbia University, where future playwright Terrence McNally was a classmate.

For a time, he worked as an album producer and executive at Columbia Records, where his projects ranged from classical to pop, as well as the cast album of one musical, *Now Is the Time for All Good Men*. But he resigned from his position there in 1968, determined to forge a career as a songwriter. He wrote material for musical revues that were performed at the Manhattan Theatre Club (not yet the huge organization it would later become) and Café La MaMa.

For years Kleban was a member of the BMI Workshop, led by the legendary Lehman Engel, where songwriting teams learned their craft, meeting weekly to support and critique each other's work developing new musicals. The workshop became a central focus of his life, and eventually he would teach there. In 1974–75, he would be there almost every Friday afternoon, often trying out new numbers from *A Chorus Line* on his classmates; his BMI colleagues' reactions were as important to him as those of his collaborators on the show, and if they didn't like a song, he would take it back to Hamlisch and tell him they needed to come up with a better one. Other projects he developed in the workshop included a musical called *Gallery*, a show he continued to revise throughout his life. This was a full-length evening consisting of songs inspired by various art objects in a museum. BMI sponsored a reading of the piece in 1972, which led to an attempt by lyricist Sheldon Harnick (*Fiddler on the Roof*) to help move the show forward to a full production. Around the same time, Kleban collaborated with book writer Peter Stone (*1776*) on another musical, *Subject to Change*. Based partly on Kleban's own life, the piece treated the subjects of marriage and divorce, but Kleban put it aside when, having previously auditioned one of his scores for Michael Bennett, he was asked to work on *A Chorus Line*.

He wasn't immediately sure he wanted to get involved in Bennett's project, as he was purposefully pursuing a career as both a lyricist and a composer, and Bennett approached him only about writing lyrics. Kleban called his old friend Jonathan Tunick (who wasn't yet involved with the show) and asked for advice; Tunick told him to go ahead and do it, as he needed the experience and the exposure and Bennett and Hamlisch were both extremely talented. (And after all, no less a light than Stephen Sondheim had had to be persuaded to write lyrics only for *West Side Story* and *Gypsy* before establishing his own career as a brilliant composer.)

Kleban's other credits include lyrics for songs for the films *The Hindenberg* (with music by David Shire) and *Brighton Beach Memoirs* (music by Michael Small), as well as both music and lyrics for "Let's Hear It for Babies," part of the legendary TV special *Free to Be You and Me*. He contributed songs to the 1979 Off-Broadway musical *The Madwoman of Central Park West*, which Phyllis Newman coauthored with Arthur Laurents. The show was inspired by Newman's life experiences and dealt with the challenge of balancing an acting career with marriage and family; songs were contributed by a number of pop and musical theatre composers and lyricists. However, Kleban never had another full production of a musical of his own after *A Chorus Line*. This has been attributed by some to the notion that in his mind the show had been such a spectacular success that it would be impossible to equal, let alone top, and so it somehow froze him creatively and professionally. The musical *Gallery*, which he had worked on for years, did get a workshop at the Public Theater in the summer of 1981, produced by Joseph Papp and directed by Richard Maltby Jr., himself an accomplished lyricist. But though Papp praised the score, he decided not to pursue the project further, feeling there were problems with the book that the workshop had not managed to solve.

Like both James Kirkwood and Marvin Hamlisch, Kleban hoped to work with Michael Bennett on another musical after *A Chorus Line*, and to that end he introduced the director to the writer Treva Silverman. The three of them began to work together on the musical that would be called *Scandal*, but the collaboration didn't work out. Silverman and Bennett hit it off immediately and connected on an intuitive level; with his more analytical, intellectual approach, Kleban felt like a third wheel and became frustrated with the process and unable to work. He ultimately withdrew from the project—which, as it happened, was never to be produced. As Silverman later told Ken Mandelbaum: "Ed was haunted by his success with *A Chorus Line*. His life stopped after it opened." Peter Stone approached him about going back to work on *Subject to Change*; Kleban told him he had retired from the business. He did make a couple more attempts to get back in the game, including beginning another musical called *Light on My Feet*, which was autobiographical; songs from this score and from *Subject to Change* would later form the core of the score to *A Class Act*, the musical his friend Lonny Price put together about his life.

While *A Chorus Line* was running on Broadway, Kleban generally went to see it every New Year's Eve. He wanted to see each new cast, but his perfectionism kept him from fully enjoying his most acclaimed creation; he claimed that when all was said and done he was not fully satisfied with the work and liked only about "sixty-five percent" of it. His complex and ambivalent relationship with the show was expressed in the instructions he left for his funeral. He had been presented with an urn made of Wedgwood china when *A Chorus Line* received the London Musical of the Year Award, and he asked that his ashes be placed in that urn and brought to his memorial service. But while he hoped that there would be music and singing at the service, he expressly forbade anyone to perform "What I Did for Love," a song he never liked—and which he knew they certainly would have included otherwise.

Kleban died of throat cancer on December 28, 1987, a few months after the death of Michael Bennett. Having been one of a consortium of composers who took over his beloved BMI Musical Theatre Workshop after his mentor Lehman Engel passed away, Kleban had devoted much of his time in his last years to the training and nurturing of the next generation of theatre songwriters. In his will, he established the Kleban Foundation, which each year identifies a particularly promising librettist or lyricist, working in the musical theatre, and grants him or her an award of $100,000.

Despite his one tremendous success as a lyricist, Kleban was frustrated throughout his life by his inability to get his own musicals—the ones for which he wrote music as well as lyrics—produced. In his will he gave the rights to his songs to two friends, novelist Avery Corman and playwright Wendy Wasserstein, with the instruction that they were to try to fashion a new musical from his songs and get it produced. They weren't able to do this, and the rights to the songs eventually reverted to Kleban's girlfriend, Linda Kline, herself a librettist, who had lived with him for many years. Kline was an admirer of the director Lonny Price, so she approached him about a Kleban musical project. Price was able to make it happen, working with Kline to fashion a libretto about Kleban's life around a selection of his songs from various unproduced projects. Since both *Subject to Change* and *Light on My Feet* also had autobiographical elements, there was a wealth of material to choose from. The show, which was entitled *Class Act*, opened at the Manhattan Theatre Club in 2000 and transferred to Broadway the following year, with Price himself both directing and playing the role of Kleban.

Though Kleban and Marvin Hamlisch took a while to find their stride as collaborators, Hamlisch had tremendous respect for Kleban, both as a lyricist and as a composer in his own right. In later years, he often described Kleban as the "unsung hero" of *A Chorus Line* and was grateful for his perfectionism; he said the lyricist had pushed him to do his best work. He also on more than one occasion singled out the line "Ev'ry prince has got to have his swan," which Kleban wrote for "At the Ballet," as the lyric that touched him more deeply than any other he ever heard.

Bob Avian

Donna McKechnie has said that Bob Avian deserves a 50 percent share of the credit for the direction and choreography of *A Chorus Line*, and his contributions to the show and to all of the other musicals he worked on as Michael Bennett's right-hand man are incalculable. The two men were best friends and inseparable colleagues for over twenty-five years, and their collaboration was such a close one that even they themselves admitted they often couldn't say where one's contributions ended and the other's began, so seamlessly did they work together and complement one another.

Avian was born in New York in 1937 and trained in classical ballet. He made his Broadway debut (under the name Robert Avian) as Indio, one of the Sharks, in *West Side Story*; this was a national touring company that played a New York engagement in 1960. He first met Bennett when he went into rehearsal for a subsequent tour of the same show, in which the teenage Bennett was cast as Baby John, and they quickly became friends.

Avian went on to dance in the Broadway productions of *Funny Girl*, *Café Crown*, and *Nowhere to Go but Up* (the last of which was Bennett's only outing on Broadway as an assistant choreographer); he also worked as an assistant stage manager on the Broadway production of the classic *I Do! I Do!*, a two-person musical that starred Mary Martin and Robert Preston. In 1967, he danced in *Henry, Sweet Henry*, which marked Bennett's second time on Broadway as a choreographer (following *A Joyful Noise*).

From that point on, Avian was on board as an assistant, associate, or co-choreographer (and sometimes coproducer) on each of Bennett's subsequent projects. He held the title of assistant choreographer only on *Promises, Promises*, being upped to associate on *Coco*, *Company*, *Follies*, and *Seesaw*. He also worked side by side with Bennett on the two straight plays the latter directed: Avian was billed as production assistant on *Twigs* and assistant director on *God's Favorite*.

When it came to *A Chorus Line*, Avian did not attend the initial group tape session that was the genesis of the show, but he worked with Bennett shortly thereafter on subsequent tapes, interviewing dancers individually at Bennett's home. When the show went into work-shop, it was reportedly Avian who felt most strongly that the framework of the musical should be an audition; he was involved with every aspect of the production, and Bennett always sought his opinion and trusted him as an editor. Bennett's dance background was mainly in tap and jazz, so Avian's ballet training was a crucial element in expanding their choreographic vocabulary; the synthesis of their two styles is what gives the dancing in *A Chorus Line* its memorable fluidity and eclectic energy. As quoted by Ken Mandelbaum in *A Chorus Line and the Musicals of Michael Bennett*, Bennett said: "We balance each other extremely well. Our personalities are very different. He has wonderful ballet technique, and his style of dancing is very different from mine. His perspective on dancing makes us that much more a well-rounded choreographer." The wording there is telling: he saw the two of them as one choreographer. Though it's been said that Bennett would often conceive the overall idea and arc of a number and then Avian would contribute more of the individual steps, the collaboration was more complex and seamless even than that; after a number was completed (often utilizing contributions from the dancers themselves) even the two choreographers often couldn't remember who had contributed what—and to them it didn't matter.

Bob Avian directs Scarlett Strallen (Cassie) in a rehearsal for the London revival, 2013.

Photo by Manuel Harlan

Avian has always been a private person with a kindly demeanor; his stability and gentleness helped smooth over the bumps in Bennett's volatile relations with performers and other collaborators. He helped keep Bennett centered and focused, and while Bennett had an enormous ego, loving the spotlight and needing to be in control, Avian didn't care about any of that; he was happy to be in the room sharing and contributing to the creative work, but had no need to be the center of attention. This complementary yin and yang relationship served them well through all the subsequent projects Bennett took on until his death in 1987. As Avian assumed more and more responsibilities, serving as co-choreographer on *Ballroom* and as a producer on that show and *Dreamgirls*, he remained happy to keep a low public profile and focus on the work. He shared the Tony Awards for Best Choreography for both *A Chorus Line* and *Ballroom* with Bennett.

Though the two lived together a couple times, shortly after Bennett moved to New York in the early 1960s and again for a while after his divorce from McKechnie, their relationship (despite what others wondered or suspected) was never a sexual one. This was one reason the trust between them was never eroded, as Bennett's fear of intimacy repeatedly sabotaged his romantic relationships with both women and men. He considered Avian closer than a brother, and Avian was one of the few trusted confidants who remained close to him when he went into seclusion during his final illness, concealing the truth from the public and even close friends and family. When Avian was asked to choreograph a major London production of *Follies* shortly before Bennett's death and didn't know if he should take it, Bennett gave him his blessing; he told Avian it was time for him to establish a solo career in his own right.

Avian took the job and later provided choreography and/or musical staging for several other major West End musicals including *Miss Saigon* and *Sunset Boulevard* (both of which came to Broadway and earned him Tony nominations), as well as *Martin Guerre* and *The Witches of Eastwick*. He also did the choreography for the Stephen Sondheim revue *Putting It Together*, both in its original Off-Broadway production at the Manhattan Theatre Club, starring Julie Andrews, and for the later Broadway version, starring Carol Burnett.

As Bennett's most trusted collaborator, Avian was approached by John Breglio, the trustee of Bennett's estate, when Breglio decided the time had come for a Broadway revival of *A Chorus Line*. Though Avian had been instrumental in the creation of the musical and had overseen the various tours and the original Broadway production until it closed in 1990, he had never before been the credited director on a production of the show. He directed the successful revival that opened in San Francisco and came in to Broadway in 2006, as well as the subsequent Equity national tour. He is married to Peter Pileski, an experienced television producer and director who has worked as Avian's assistant or associate director on several of his recent stage productions; they have homes in New York and in Fort Lauderdale, Florida. In 2013, Avian returned once more to *A Chorus Line*, directing the West End revival at the London Palladium.

4

"Rehearsals Begin August 4"

Joseph Papp and the New York Shakespeare Festival

T hough today it is relatively common for a new musical to be developed by a nonprofit theatre company and then—if all the stars are aligned—move to Broadway, in 1975 that was a very rare occurrence. The resources that Joseph Papp and his New York Shakespeare Festival provided Michael Bennett throughout the long process of workshopping and developing the show, and the fact that the Festival remained the primary producer through the move uptown and the subsequent fifteen-year Broadway run (with some last-minute financial input from Bennett's own company, Plum Productions) constituted what was then an unprecedented level of support from an institutional theatre for a new musical, and Papp's part in the success of the show cannot be overestimated. This chapter will look at Joe Papp's life and the story of the growth of his theatre, with an emphasis on the influences that led him to take on *A Chorus Line*, other musicals produced by the Festival and how they relate to the show, and the musical's effect on the theatre's subsequent life.

Growing Up in Brooklyn

Papp was born in Williamsburg, Brooklyn, in 1921. His father, Shmuel Papirofsky, was Polish, and his mother, Yetta Miritch, was from Lithuania. His mother had come to America as an orphan at age eleven, and most of his father's family was wiped out by the Nazis; Papp has said he was powerfully conditioned by his consciousness of being part of the tradition of the Holocaust.

At that time Williamsburg was a culturally mixed community, and Jews were not the majority they would later become; the Papirofsky family felt embattled to some degree, at odds with the Italians and other ethnic groups, many of them anti-Semitic, that dominated the neighborhood. There was a certain amount of gang violence in the area, and for protection at one point the young Joseph formed a loose gang with a handful of friends: he wanted to call them the Martyrs, but the name that stuck was the Mustangs.

There was a mentally disturbed Irish teen named Whitey, three years older than Joseph, who lived in the same building as the Papirofskys; he hated Jews and would frequently attack Joe physically, even with his parents watching, which was a humiliation to both Joe and his father. Ultimately the threat this posed caused the family to move from Williamsburg to Brownsville; Joe was fourteen. This early experience of anti-Semitism was formative; he came to believe that prejudice was always lurking somewhere below the surface in social interactions, and as a Jew he would have to stay on his toes. Though he would for several years conceal his ethnicity as a young adult, his fight against intolerance became a driving force behind the social and artistic missions that would inform his life's work.

The family moved frequently, often because they had gotten behind in the rent. His father had worked as a trunk maker, but during the depression he became unemployed; sometimes there was work shoveling snow, other times nothing. Papp later claimed he wasn't that demoralized by the poverty because the family was strong and supported each other emotionally; his mother was determined to keep a spotlessly clean house even when they had to use fruit crates instead of furniture.

From a very early age, Joseph took on various odd jobs to try to help the family get by. He worked as a barker at the amusement park at Coney Island. His family managed to come up with twelve dollars for a bicycle so he could work as a messenger for a telegraph company, and for a while he had a job as a paperboy in the days when newsboys roamed the street crying "Extra! Extra!" Already creative, he also tried his hand at publishing his own neighborhood newspaper, which he generated with the help of an old typewriter and carbon paper.

Joseph got his first taste of Shakespeare at Isaac Remsen Junior High, where he memorized passages from *Julius Caesar*. Later, at Eastern District High School, he was involved with the glee club and became president of the Dramatic Society. With his classmates he went on field trips into Manhattan, where he saw productions of *Hamlet* starring both John Gielgud and Leslie Howard. He was immediately attracted to the meatiness of the ideas in Shakespeare and the sound of the language, and found he enjoyed memorizing the poetry.

A Social Conscience

From an early age, Papirofsky was conscious of social injustice and wanted to get involved in helping people. During his teen years, he heard both Socialists and Communists speaking on the streets of Brooklyn. He was moved to get involved with the Young Communist League (YCL) by some other young men in his neighborhood. They were organizing a team to help families who had been evicted from apartment buildings because they couldn't pay the rent; after the landlords' deputies put the tenants' furniture and belongings out on the sidewalk, the youths would carry it back up to their apartments—and repeat the process if the family was kicked out again. The YCL used aggressive techniques that were sometimes frowned upon even by other leftist organizations, but Joseph, always one to look for immediate solutions, was willing to get his hands dirty, so he found himself drawn to this group that took concrete action while so many others just talked. He spoke publicly about economic inequality for the first time at age sixteen on a street corner in Brooklyn, and went into Manhattan to demonstrate with the League in Times Square. The group's meetings introduced him to Russian writers like Gogol and Gorky, as well as others, like the Irishman Sean O'Casey, who sympathized with communism.

On his graduation from high school, Joseph wanted to attend college, but couldn't even get into Brooklyn College because he didn't have the requisite grades in math and science. There had been no one at Eastern to provide adequate academic counseling. So he continued to work various odd jobs, including running deliveries for a laundry and then working for a jeweler on Lafayette Street in Manhattan's East Village—coincidentally just down the street from the later site of the Public Theater. He organized the workers there to join a union, and after quitting that job he joined the Navy; World War II was on, and he felt that by fighting the Nazis, America was finally uniting behind a right cause, so he was excited about serving.

Entertaining the Troops

Following the end of a brief marriage to one Betty Ball, with whom he had a daughter named Susan, Papirofsky joined up and headed for boot camp in Bainbridge, Maryland—which he later said was where he got three reliable square meals a day for the first time in his life. During boot camp he started to organize some of the recruits to put on vaudeville-type variety shows, and his producing efforts continued when he was made chief petty officer on an aircraft carrier and asked to devise entertainments on board the ship. This led to his running a new division called the Navy Entertainment Group, for which he put together shows to entertain servicemen on the various Pacific islands where they were stationed; most of the entertainers used in the productions were also enlisted men, and they included a seventeen-year-old Bob Fosse, to whom Joseph became something of a mentor. When the war ended, the budding impresario finished off his career as a producer of navy talent shows with a big revue at the Brooklyn Navy Yard.

California

Exhilarated by the end of the war and what seemed like endless possibilities for the future, Papirofsky decided to accept an invitation to visit a navy buddy who had become a screenwriter in California—but he couldn't afford airfare, so he put his uniform back on and snuck on board a military plane to Bakersfield. He found out there was money available through the GI Bill for veterans to attend college, and his writer friend told him about a school in Los Angeles called the Actors' Lab, which was an outgrowth of the legendary Group Theatre.

Founded in 1931, the Group Theatre had challenged Broadway, then dominated by lightweight drawing-room comedies and revivals of classics, by producing hard-hitting new work that expressed the reality of American life, including the economic and social challenges then faced by the middle and lower classes; the company fostered plays by the likes of Clifford Odets (their resident playwright), Paul Green, Sidney Kingsley, and Irwin Shaw. To bring these grittier, more realistic plays to life, Lee Strasberg, one of the Group's founders, led the development of a new American school of acting that came to be known as the Method, initially inspired by the work of Konstantin Stanislavsky and the Moscow Art Theatre. After ten exciting years, the Group Theatre disbanded in 1941 due to the war, financial woes, the defection of some members to Hollywood where work was more lucrative, and artistic and political conflicts within the company. After the war, several members of the theatre reunited in New York to form the Actors Studio, which would soon be directed by Strasberg.

Several former members of the Group Theatre, who had gone out to Hollywood to work in the film industry, missed the company dynamic and decided to start a laboratory—a place where actors and directors could gather and work on their craft while developing new material, but without the commercial pressures of production. Several of the key players in this new endeavor were Roman (Bud) Bohnen, Morris Carnovsky, and Carnovsky's wife, Phoebe Brand. They offered classes that quickly developed an excellent reputation, so the film studios started sending their budding stars there to train. This was the environment that Joseph Papirofsky wandered into having just gotten out of the Navy. He asked about admissions and was told he had just missed the open auditions, but he hung around the building for a while anyway and was shortly asked to step in as a scene partner for an actress who was about to give her final reading for the selection committee. They did a scene from a Eugene O'Neill play for an audience that included Phoebe Brand, and though the young actress was not admitted, Brand and the other members of the committee decided to offer a spot to Joseph. He was surprised, as he'd been told they'd only be taking a tiny percentage of the hundreds of hopefuls who had applied, and he hadn't even auditioned officially—nor did he consider himself a particularly talented actor. But after a conversation with the renowned actor Anthony Quinn, who was in charge of admissions in those days, he was offered a spot. He thought it was probably less his audition than his interview that piqued their interest, as he was eager to talk about social justice, theatre for the masses, democracy, and socialism. These ideals were close to the principles that had united the Group Theatre in the first place, and the members decided—most presciently as it turned out—that this eager but untrained young man, whether or not he was cut out to be an actor, had something genuine to contribute to the theatre.

Even with money from the GI Bill, he couldn't afford the full tuition, so he was offered a job cleaning the studios before classes started in the mornings. During his time at the Lab, he rubbed shoulders with a wide variety of theatrical and film talents, from Bertolt Brecht and Charles Laughton to John Garfield and Lee J. Cobb, not to mention young starlets like Shelley Winters and Marilyn Monroe. He took a course in theatre history, which he found inspiring, and worked with a voice teacher to lose his Brooklyn accent. The naturalistic school of Method Acting advanced by the Group did not necessarily lend itself to Shakespeare, so many of the teachers and actors at the Lab avoided the classics. But Joseph found a mentor in Phoebe Brand, who cast him as Romeo in a workshop and fostered his love for Shakespeare's works. His natural leadership qualities and ability to get things done were soon recognized, and he became the first student at the Lab asked to serve on the organization's board; he was then hired as managing director, where he got a real taste of producing. But due to the competing interests of the professional actors in the group and the school, and especially the political pressure being put on various members of the organization over their left-wing associations (these were the early days of the Red Scare), the Lab began to fall apart. Joseph attributed it to two other factors as well: the fact that the board of directors consisted mainly of actors, rather than businesspeople who knew anything about fund-raising, and the lack of a strong, visionary leader. Though always a believer in democracy, he could already see it wasn't a viable model for running a theatre company—a lesson he wouldn't forget when he had his own theatre.

Two Marriages

While working at the Lab, Joseph married for the second time. His new wife was Sylvia Ostroff, a pianist who worked there as the receptionist. She was four years older than he and later admitted she had been something of a mother figure, and knew he was fooling around with other women at the time. During this period of his life, Joseph did not generally tell people he was Jewish, mainly because he could see how discrimination sometimes hindered a Jew's career or even his ability to get a job. He told Sylvia his mother was British. He also did not tell her he had been married before, though she found that out when he had to start sending Betty Ball child support checks. Sylvia and Joseph had a son, Michael, and in fact by this time Joseph also had another child, whose mother was Irene Ball, a woman he never married and who, by a weird coincidence, had the same last name as his first wife; it's unclear whether Sylvia knew about this daughter, whose name was Barbara.

After the Lab closed down, Joseph found himself unemployed and took a job working in a sheet metal factory. But he soon got a call to go to Pasadena to take over as assistant stage manager on the national tour of Arthur Miller's *Death of a Salesman*, a position that also involved understudying the roles of Biff and Happy. There was a young aspiring actress named Peggy Bennion playing a small role in the production; she and Joseph fell in love. When the tour ended, he had to make a choice between returning to Sylvia and Michael and starting a new life with Peggy. He chose Peggy, and divorce proceedings were initiated. For a while, both Joseph and Peggy were unemployed; they planned to marry, and the price of a wedding ring seemed prohibitive. But one evening as they were walking down the street in New York City, Joe spotted something gleaming in a gutter and picked it up: it turned out to be a wedding ring! Eventually, Peggy came to view this as a metaphor for Joseph's charmed life: his ability to find what he needed, even in times of adversity.

Manhattan at Midcentury

For a brief time, Joseph sought work as an actor, attending auditions in the very competitive New York market, but discovered he wasn't really cut out for it.

Instead, he got a job as a social director at an upstate hotel, where he persuaded an elderly lady patron to put up the money to put on some one-act plays for the entertainment of the hotel's mainly Jewish clientele. With Peggy and a few actor friends from the city, he formed a small theatre company; taking the name the Ulster County Players, they did several shows on a shoestring budget, with Joseph acting as well as building sets and producing.

Back in Manhattan, he finally got a job as a "floor manager" with CBS. These were the early days of network TV, and the company was hiring theatrical stage managers for such positions; there was no official training, so he was thrown into the deep end and had to learn the job by doing it. He worked with Ernie Kovacs, Mike Wallace, and other celebrities, and he got to work on some Shakespeare when Orson Welles came in to do a TV version of *King Lear*; the stage manager was a young Peter Brook.

Because of limited space on the assignment sheets, his name would be abbreviated to "J. Pap," and he decided to start using that as a professional name, simply adding a second "p." (Later on, he sometimes regretted the decision, because he was always proud of his family's Polish heritage.) Still passionate about workers' rights, he became active in the Radio and Television Directors Guild and served on negotiating committees. Though the network was pleased with his work and offered him opportunities to move up the ladder to directing, he found that television was not his calling; he was still drawn to the theatre, where he could have more autonomy and the freedom to pursue his own vision and goals.

Therefore, while working full time for the network, he continued to pursue theatre. He was attracted to the work of Sean O'Casey, an Irish playwright who identified as a Communist, and obtained the rights to put on a triple bill of his one-acts; this became his first Off-Broadway venture as a producer/director. Along with Bernard Gersten, a friend from his Actors' Lab days, and a couple of other partners, he rented performance space at the Yugoslav-American Hall on 41st Street, directing two of the plays himself. Unfortunately, his inexperience and that of several of the cast members showed, and the production received a negative review from Brooks Atkinson in the *New York Times*.

Papp refused to be daunted, however, and forged ahead. He was asked by a friend from his high school days to direct a play for an amateur group that was performing in a run-down building on the Lower East Side of Manhattan: the Emmanuel Presbyterian Church. After that group disbanded, he went back down to talk to the church's priest, asking if he could use the space to produce some Shakespeare plays. The man was supportive and offered him use of the venue for free, charging just ten dollars a week to pay the heating bill, so suddenly Joe Papp had a theatre space to call his own.

Birth of a Shakespeare Company

Papp had two main goals: to start a theatre group along the lines of the Actors' Lab, where artists would work together over an extended period to develop their craft, and to bring Shakespeare's plays to the masses—most specifically, the working-class people he had always cared about and identified with. And in order to make it possible for everyone to attend, the tickets had to be free.

Adventuresome out-of-work actors from around the city started coming downtown to meet Papp and find out more about his new venture, christened the Shakespearean Theater Workshop, even though the Alphabet City location was considered extremely out of the way at the time. One of the first members was actress Sylvia Gassell, who heard about the group while she was working on the role of the Nurse in *Romeo and Juliet* for Harold Clurman's acting class. Since Papp was looking for someone to play the Nurse, she went downtown to meet him and audition for the prospective production—an endeavor that was eventually plagued by the defection of eight successive Romeos, several of whom quit to take paying work elsewhere. At one point, Papp hired a fat actor to play the role, deciding there was nothing in the script that required Romeo to be handsome! Ultimately they couldn't keep enough actors together to do the whole play, so they opened with a couple evenings of Shakespearean scenes; Colleen Dewhurst and Gloria Foster, two actresses who went on to big careers and long-term relationships with Papp's theatres, took part in these early presentations.

Sylvia Gassell then introduced Papp to her husband, Joel Friedman. An aspiring director with a strong knowledge of Shakespeare, he impressed Papp and was brought on board to lead the workshop and direct several plays for the growing company. Friedman and Gassell brought in some actors they knew, and Friedman came up with a concept for "black and white Shakespeare," which made the costuming affordable: the men wore simple black pants and white shirts, and the women wore dresses made from unused but slightly defective bridal gowns that a department store was getting rid of for five dollars apiece.

Audiences at the church were often small, and everyone was working for free; occasionally Papp would provide sandwiches, or a little bit of money for carfare if the actor couldn't afford it, but that was it. The entire budget for each production was about twenty-five dollars! With no one on salary, the actors weren't always reliable, and one of Papp's many duties was going on in place of people who quit or missed performances. He aggressively courted the press, and the small company finally received several reviews for its production of *As You Like It* starring Peggy Bennion Papp, but the *New York Times* stayed away.

Papp took steps to get the fledgling company chartered as a tax-exempt educational organization, which was rare in those days: most theatre was done commercially, for profit. After that, it was easier to approach people for donations. He also tried his hand at directing, with productions of Shakespeare's *Cymbeline* and Thomas Middleton's *The Changeling*, but left most of the directing during the first two years at the church to Friedman. That relationship ended when Friedman and Gassell got tired of working for free and started to express ideas about how the group should be run. Having seen at the Actors' Lab what could happen to a company without strong leadership, Papp was determined to hold the reins by himself—and he was intent on reaching a larger audience.

To that end, he moved the base of operations to the East River Park Amphitheatre, at the end of Grand Street at the FDR Drive on the Lower East Side. This was a little-known space that had been built fifteen years earlier by the Works Project Administration, with seating for sixteen hundred people on wooden benches. (After the Festival moved to the Delacorte, the amphitheater gradually fell into disuse and disrepair, but it has recently been rehabilitated and is now used for summer concerts by local bands.) Papp got permission from the Department of Parks to use the space; still earning his living working at CBS, he used his connections there to obtain equipment. For his new director, Papp enlisted Stuart Vaughan, after being impressed with his Off-Broadway production of—of all things—a play by Sean O'Casey. Unlike Papp's production of the same writer's works, Vaughan's had received a positive review from Brooks Atkinson.

They did outdoor productions of *Julius Caesar* and *The Taming of the Shrew* that first summer. The neighborhood was a dangerous one, and for a while the local teenagers, some of whom were gang members, heckled the actors during rehearsals and even threw things at the stage. But Papp and Vaughan managed to make friends with them, and as they watched the energetic, passionate work that was happening on their turf, many of them found they were intrigued by it; after a while some of them were even helping with the shows. Papp's dream of going into disadvantaged neighborhoods and making a difference in people's lives through theatre was starting to become a reality.

A *New York Times* writer named Meyer Berger heard about the new endeavor at the amphitheater and wrote about it in his column. With this, and the fact that many denizens of the neighborhood had been seeing the company come and go for weeks and sometimes watching them rehearse, there was a certain amount of excitement and expectation building; on opening night of the first show, the space was packed, and word started to spread.

Papp had picked the summer's second play, *The Taming of the Shrew*, with an eye to providing his wife, Peggy, with the opportunity to play Kate, but Stuart Vaughan didn't think she was right for the role and insisted on using the young Colleen Dewhurst. Papp finally relented, and Bennion decamped for a summer vacation with her family in Utah. Dewhurst came through with a breakout performance, and the audiences were large and appreciative. But since all the tickets were free, even with full attendance the company was running out of money. Papp managed to get a grant from the American National Theatre and Academy (ANTA) so he wouldn't have to cancel the second production, and then he went uptown to the offices of the *New York Times* and spoke to an editor and sometime theatre reviewer, Arthur Gelb, who was holding down the fort in the absence of Brooks Atkinson. Papp knew he needed a review in the *Times* if he was going to attract any donors, so he threatened to camp out in the office until Gelb finally agreed to go see the show that night. The performance was rained out after the first couple of scenes, but Gelb had seen enough of Dewhurst and her costar, J. D. Cannon, as well as the enraptured neighborhood audience, to give it a good write-up. A commercial producer, Herman Levin (*My Fair Lady*), came up with the money Papp needed to keep going. At Gelb's urging, Atkinson himself attended a later performance, and a rave review followed in his Sunday column. Papp took Atkinson's column with him on visits to potential donors: the first result was a $10,000 grant from the Doris Duke Foundation.

The last few performances in the amphitheater that summer filled up, with moneyed patrons beginning to fill the stands alongside the neighborhood people. But Papp felt it was his mission to reach out more deeply into disadvantaged areas, by touring Shakespeare around the boroughs to people who would never get out of their own neighborhoods. So he conceived the idea of the Mobile Unit, and with the Festival's growing reputation, foundation support proved available. It took a while to work through the red tape of approvals from the Department of Parks, but finally the group was ready to begin a tour, on a wooden stage that Stuart Vaughan designed to unfold over the back of a decrepit flatbed truck. The first play done by the Mobile Unit was *Romeo and Juliet*, directed by Vaughan, and the first performance was in Central Park, near the Belvedere Tower. They then toured to parks in all four of the other boroughs. Stanley Lowell, a deputy mayor at the time, was the first city official to become an enthusiastic supporter, and he was able to get the Mayor, Robert F. Wagner, excited about the project as well.

The company soon discovered that neighborhood audiences, even gang members, became enormously involved emotionally in the play's story, yelling out four-letter words as the tragic events multiplied, and even crying out to Romeo not to kill himself because Juliet wasn't really dead. (Coincidentally, this was 1957, the same year *West Side Story* was first done on Broadway, translating the Romeo and Juliet story to the world of contemporary New York street gangs—but Papp's company proved that teens could respond to the original Shakespeare text as well.) The famously demanding critic Walter Kerr of the *Herald Tribune* declared it the best production he had ever seen of the classic play.

Though the work was sophisticated enough to please demanding New York critics, Vaughan's storytelling was straightforward and clear enough that even audience members who didn't speak English could follow what was happening. Not everyone welcomed the truck; sometimes people threw rocks or bottles at the stage. At one point some Brooklyn gang leaders told Papp to get off their turf, but when Papp informed them he had been born and raised in the neighborhood, their attitude changed, and they were recruited to help with security for the performance.

By the end of the tour, Papp realized the cast and crew were exhausted; setting up the stage and the lighting equipment in each park was a huge and grueling job, and the truck was on the verge of collapse. Though the Mobile Unit would be revived for six summers starting in 1964, when the Festival had greater financial resources, at the end of the *Romeo and Juliet* tour in 1957 they decided it would be better to settle down in Central Park. They performed a run of *The Two Gentlemen of Verona* there, featuring married couple Jerry Stiller and Anne Meara, and followed that with *Macbeth*, starring Roy Poole and Colleen Dewhurst.

New Venues

In order to establish greater continuity and increase funding, Papp and Vaughan decided they needed a winter home for indoor work. The company having outgrown the church, Papp found an unused 650-seat space called the Heckscher Theater, which was located in a Children's Center on 104th Street just east of Central Park. The Department of Welfare offered its use rent free. Vaughan directed *Richard III* there, starring George C. Scott in the first of what would be many major roles at the Festival. An unknown twenty-nine-year-old actor who was working as a truck driver at the time, Scott gave a mesmerizing performance that proved a breakthrough in his career. Future productions at the Heckscher included *Antony and Cleopatra* starring Scott and Colleen Dewhurst, which she would later repeat at the Delacorte.

Around this time, Papp's wife, Peggy, gave birth to their daughter, Miranda (the name of Prospero's daughter in Shakespeare's *The Tempest*). Facing the financial pressures of a growing family, Papp found himself fearing for his job at CBS. Like many others, he was under pressure to testify before the House Un-American Activities Committee (HUAC), and as he was determined not to name names as some of his colleagues had done, he feared he might go to jail. Unsure whether the Festival could survive that, he approached Stuart Vaughan, who was still directing most of the plays, about being there to take over the reins in the event that he could not continue. But Vaughan had been approached by the founders of the Phoenix Theatre, a larger professional company in town that had been around for several years; after seeing his production of *Macbeth* in Central Park, they offered him the position of artistic director. Vaughan accepted the job, which involved more money than Papp could offer and the chance to direct a variety of material. Though the Phoenix ran a winter season and Vaughan would still have been available to direct for Papp in the summers, Papp felt the director had been disloyal, and they drifted apart. Vaughan's former wife, Gladys Vaughan, then began to direct some of the Festival's productions.

It was also during that year at the Heckscher that Bernard Gersten, who had been a close friend of Papp's since their Actors' Lab days, came on board as production manager; he was hired originally for only $125 a week, but stayed with the Festival for many years and became Papp's right-hand man for all financial and administrative matters. Merle Debuskey, a press agent who later joined the company's board of directors, joined the team during this period as well. (Both men would be instrumental in the success of *A Chorus Line*.)

Facing HUAC

In the late 1950s, the New York Shakespeare Festival seemed to be taking off. They had the indoor space at the Heckscher and had settled fairly comfortably into what felt like a more or less permanent location for the outdoor stage in Central Park. Donations and financial support were increasing. But Papp knew that all of that, and the very existence of the Festival, was being jeopardized by HUAC. FBI men were waiting for him when he came out of work at CBS on certain days; they followed him down the street asking him questions about former colleagues, and sometimes they even came to his home. They were trying to scare him into cooperating with the committee. As a former member of the Communist Party, which he had not left till Peggy persuaded him it was foolish to remain in the organization, he was an obvious target for Senator Joe McCarthy and his followers. He knew he was going to be subpoenaed to testify, but turned down an offer to appear in a closed hearing instead, aware that it was intended as an opportunity to incriminate others. He felt the worst that could happen if he was charged with contempt of court would be that he would spend a year in jail, and he said he was willing to do that rather than compromise his principles—but the potential consequences for the Festival looked dire. His lawyer instructed him to take the Fifth Amendment. Papp agreed to answer any questions about his own past, but refused to be what he called a "stool pigeon" and name others. One of the committee members questioned him about his Shakespeare productions and whether he was using them as leftist propaganda; Papp showed the panel a copy of a magazine called *Amerika*, published by the U.S. State Department and sent to Russia, which cited Papp and his Festival as a shining example of what can be achieved in a democratic society. He was not sent to prison, but the blacklisting did cost him his job at CBS, and he worried that the fallout would impact funding for the Festival. He asked the Radio and Television Directors Guild to intercede on his behalf with the network, and though they were at first reluctant to get involved, ultimately the layoff was deemed inappropriate and CBS was forced to rehire him, with back pay. Once back on the job, however, he felt he was being ostracized, so he quit. Still, the decision had left him feeling vindicated, and confident enough to devote all his time to the growing Shakespeare Festival.

Battling Moses

Having confronted HUAC and come out relatively unscathed, Papp was then faced with another formidable opponent: Robert Moses, the New York Parks Commissioner, who at the time held several other titles and offices as well and was one of the most powerful figures in city government. For several years, Moses was a vocal proponent of Shakespeare in Central Park and even helped the Festival raise money, but in 1959 he decided to revoke the company's license to perform in the park. He wrote Papp a letter claiming the landscape was being damaged by his audiences and that costly work by the city would be required to bring the electric and sanitary systems up to a reasonable level to continue productions. He offered one solution: The Festival could stay if Papp agreed to charge for tickets and channel some of the earnings into the needed improvements.

Papp could easily have agreed to this, and perhaps the Festival would have survived or even thrived on the revenue. But Papp was adamant that his theatre's mission was to provide Shakespeare productions absolutely free of charge, making them accessible to New Yorkers of all economic backgrounds, and he refused the suggestion. A shrewd businessman, he knew that the free ticket policy was attractive to donors and other funders—and it also enabled him to get around dealing with labor unions—but the main reason he refused to charge was his deep, lifelong belief that the arts should be available to everyone. He viewed the Shakespeare Festival as a civic institution on the level of a public library, with an equal potential to enrich and transform lives. He remembered patronizing the Williamsburg Public Library as a youngster and claimed that if he had had to pay to check out books, he might never have discovered Shakespeare.

The Festival gradually gathered support in the press, which began to paint Moses as the bad guy for wanting to take away the public's access to free theatre. Moses invoked Papp's Communist Party past in an attempt to turn public sentiment against him. When Mayor Wagner, apparently intimidated by Moses's power and influence, failed to back Papp up, the producer had to go to court. He got a law firm to agree to represent the Festival on a pro bono basis. They lost the first round but won on appeal, with the judge stating that Moses's instructing the Festival to charge admission was "arbitrary, capricious and unreasonable." The city could have appealed in turn, but didn't—suggesting that several key officials were secretly on Papp's side but had felt they couldn't openly oppose Moses. City assistance with funding for the Festival actually increased after the dispute.

The long, drawn-out dispute with Moses had been front-page news, and ultimately it provided invaluable free publicity: Papp was viewed as a David figure, defending the people's interests against Moses's Goliath, and he came out of it a hero, with greater public support than ever before. The audience felt he had won an important battle on their behalf; the Festival was welcomed back to Central Park with open arms, and donations increased dramatically.

Not only did Robert Moses accept the court's decision and back off from his original position, he then suggested building a permanent outdoor theatre in Central Park for the Festival. He got the Board of Estimate to approve $225,000 for the building of the new theatre, but Papp needed almost $150,000 more to make it happen. Newbold Morris, who succeeded Moses as Parks Commissioner, happened to bring up the project in a conversation with George Delacorte, president of Dell Publishing. Delacorte lived near Central Park on Fifth Avenue. He had already been a generous supporter of the park, known for providing the charming Delacorte Clock at the zoo, and when Morris described the theatre project, he agreed to put up the needed $150,000. At Morris's instigation, the theatre was named for him—although the publisher didn't ask for this or make it a condition of his gift. The Delacorte Theatre, a lovely two-thousand-seat outdoor structure overlooking the lake, opened on June 18, 1962, and as of this writing is heading into its fifty-fifth summer of free outdoor theatre in Central Park.

Growing Pains

The very first production in the new theatre occasioned a controversy. Papp chose to put on *The Merchant of Venice*, because by then George C. Scott had established himself as one of the company's leading actors, and Papp felt he would be a great Shylock. The production was codirected by Papp and Gladys Vaughan. The New York Board of Rabbis protested the selection of the play, claiming the portrayal of Shylock in Shakespeare's text was anti-Semitic; the objection came when it was announced that the production would be telecast on the local CBS affiliate station. Though George C. Scott wasn't Jewish, Papp of course was, and he had some lingering resentments from his childhood about the way lower-income Jews like his family were kept out of the more exclusive New York synagogues. He had little sympathy for the rabbis' point of view and wouldn't back down. The Board of Rabbis tried to get the mayor to take their side, but he refused to interfere with Papp, and both play and telecast went on as scheduled.

Papp had a productive creative relationship with Gladys Vaughan for a while. The productions she staged included a notable 1964 *Othello* starring James Earl Jones; as a director she was particularly admired and respected by actors. But as usual Papp wanted to remain captain of the ship, and when Vaughan proved to have too many ideas about how things should be run, she ended up going the way of her husband and Joel Friedman. This left an opening for a new principal director, and that place was soon filled by a young man named Gerald Freedman. Audaciously, Freedman first got Papp's attention by criticizing a Festival production of *As You Like It*, put on while they were still producing shows uptown at the Heckscher Theatre. Freedman told Papp he thought he could do a better job as director, and rather than being offended, Papp decided he sounded like he knew what he was talking about—though a couple of years would go by before he actually offered him a directing job. Freedman's many contributions to the Festival included introducing Papp to set designer Ming Cho Lee and costume designer Theoni V. Aldredge. Both quickly proved indispensable to the Festival's work—and Aldredge (whom Freedman had first met at Harvard University when he was directing one of the famous Hasty Pudding shows) became, in Papp's words, "the first lady of the Shakespeare Festival." (She would of course be the costume designer of *A Chorus Line*.)

The Great Years

In collaboration with Lee and Aldredge, Freedman and Papp began to develop a distinctively American approach to Shakespeare, one that was conditioned by the large outdoor space and the necessity of connecting to a broad social spectrum of audience. In Shakespeare's day, everyone attended the theatre together, from the Queen and her nobles seated in the galleries to the impoverished groundlings crowding the edge of the stage; with Papp's dedication to continuing to offer all the tickets for free, he established a similar egalitarianism in his theatre, restoring Shakespeare's plays to something more like their original audience after long decades during which classical theatre, at least in New York, had come to be thought of as a largely elitist pursuit. To bring the plays to life for these diverse crowds, the Festival developed a direct, muscular approach that carried through to both the design elements and the acting. The performers they hired brought gutsy, vivid personalities to bear on the work, bringing Shakespeare's characters to life with boldness, individuality, and great energy. In addition to Jones, Dewhurst, and Scott, a new generation of actors like Michael Moriarty, Martin Sheen, Sam Waterston, Kathleen Widdoes, Kevin Kline, Raul Julia, Richard Dreyfuss, and Meryl Streep contributed their charisma, passion, and honesty to many memorable seasons of Shakespeare in the Park. Papp and Freedman proved to have powerful instincts for identifying new talent, as many of these performers proved their mettle at the Festival very early in their careers, before becoming well known. It was a clear tribute to the creative atmosphere Papp maintained that they often made time to return to the Delacorte after finding fame on Broadway, on television, and in the movies.

The outdoor summer Shakespeare productions became so popular that people would camp out in the park all day waiting for tickets. The lines became unreasonably long, and then when the gates finally opened there would be a stampede as people raced each other for seats. After a few years of this, a more organized system had to be implemented; people were given tickets with seat numbers on them, and eventually the tickets were handed out earlier in the day.

Lafayette Street

In the mid-1960s, having been focusing almost exclusively on Shakespeare, Papp was once again in expansion mode; he wanted his company to have a space to develop new plays. Inspired by the example of European repertory companies, he felt Shakespeare and new work flourished more powerfully when engaged with in tandem: The work on one enriched understanding of the other. So the search began for a new indoor space.

After several other options failed to pan out, the Festival settled on a building on Lafayette Street in Manhattan's East Village. Built in 1854, it had originally been known as the Astor Library, New York City's first free public library. In the 1920s it had been taken over by an organization called the Hebrew Immigrant Aid Society (HIAS), which processed European immigrants and gave them temporary shelter on their arrival in the city. The building had been mostly unused for decades and had fallen into extreme disrepair, but Papp appreciated the scale and grandeur of it and could see signs of the original beauty of the architecture. Though a real estate developer had offered to buy it with plans to tear it down, the Festival was able to intervene because of the efforts being made by New York's newly formed Landmark Preservation Commission to have it declared a historic landmark—which they would be able to do if the festival bought the building. The other developer tried to fight the decision, but Papp went to see the man in his office and, after appealing passionately to everything from his pride in Jewish history to his civic responsibility to the difficulty of challenging the building's new Landmark status, ultimately carried the day and purchased the building, which was to become the Public Theater. A generous donor named Florence Anspacher donated a quarter of a million dollars to the Festival to help with the purchase.

The original renovation plans called for tearing down many of the building's walls and creating a single 850-seat theatre space. But as the debris was cleared away and the beauty of the old building was slowly revealed, Papp realized he didn't want to sacrifice that much of the original architecture. He had new plans drawn up, this time for a complex of several smaller theaters occupying different floors and rooms in the building. The largest theatre, on the upper floor, was named after Mrs. Anspacher, who contributed even more money toward its completion. The second-largest space (where *A Chorus Line* would eventually premiere), on the first floor, would be called the Newman Theatre. (It did not open until 1970, when Dennis Reardon's play *The Happiness Cage* was presented there.) Because raising the money to finish the building's renovations was an ongoing problem over a prolonged period, Papp and his crew worked on one theatre at a time and began to produce plays before the whole planned complex of four auditoriums was finished.

With space now available to do new plays, Papp began to seek out writers, revealing a specific taste for honest, cutting-edge work, often with social or political themes. Playwrights who had works produced at the Public Theater early in their careers included Charles Gordone, Dennis Reardon, Jason Miller, Miguel Piñero, Sam Shepard, Thomas Babe, and David Rabe. Rabe became Papp's favorite playwright, and they would have a long and complex artistic relationship over the course of numerous productions, some successful and some not. Financial success was secondary to Papp; if he believed in a writer, he would give that person room to experiment, to grow, and to make mistakes. Even if a play or two fell flat, the playwright had a creative home at the Public he could return to again and again.

Beginning in 1966, Papp took on another job: teaching at Yale. Though he himself had never been to college, his track record, aesthetics, and values appealed to the Yale School of Drama's new dean, Robert Brustein, who invited him to join the faculty, at first teaching only on Thursdays. Papp mentored a group of young directors, including Ted Cornell and Jeff Bleckner, whom he would later invite to work for him at the Public. He also met a young actor named Gerome Ragni, who was performing at Yale with the Open Theatre; Ragni gave him a script that would change both of their lives.

A New Kind of Musical Theatre

Though musical theatre had never played a part in Papp's career up to that point, and he shared Robert Brustein's disdain for what they both perceived as the shallowness of Broadway, Papp was looking for work that reflected the political and social turmoil he saw escalating all around him. Though the counterculture of the 1960s belonged to a generation younger than his, he empathized with the civil rights movement, the antiwar movement, and the student protests of the day, and he could see that the East Village, where his Public Theater was about to open, had become a locus of this burgeoning youth culture. So when the script of *Hair*, rough and unformed as it was, fell into his hands, he was—to the surprise and dismay of several of his key staff members—very receptive to its point of view and immediately saw its theatrical potential.

Beginning with that seminal show, it's useful here to consider the histories of three different musicals Papp produced before and shortly after *A Chorus Line*, with an eye to how each experience contributed to or was influenced by the show that would ultimately become the Festival's biggest-ever commercial success.

Hair

Though Papp had never specifically nurtured any ambition to produce musicals, *Hair* somehow became the show that opened the Public Theater. The script was unfinished when it was shown to him by Gerome Ragni, who was writing it in collaboration with another actor Papp knew, James Rado. Rado had long had an ambition to write Broadway musicals, while Ragni came out of a more experimental theatre background. Papp was immediately intrigued and showed some of the script to Gerald Freedman, who by this time had been named artistic director of the Festival, and who had a strong interest and background in musical theatre. Freedman thought the material was promising but felt that the lyrics were much stronger than the music, and suggested that the pair bring in a more experienced composer. A music producer and publisher named Nat Shapiro introduced them to Galt MacDermot, a young songwriter who had never done a musical but was eager to try his hand at one. The Vietnam War was escalating, and the protest movement inspired the creators, and Papp as well, with a certain sense of political urgency toward getting the play on. MacDermot took only three weeks to provide tunes for most of the team's existing lyrics, and after hearing how much his music enhanced Ragni and Rado's material, Papp shelved several other plays he had been working on and announced his commitment to opening the Public Theater with *Hair*—even though Bernard Gersten and several of his other associates remained opposed to the idea.

Ragni and Rado wanted Tom O'Horgan, another product of the downtown experimental theatre scene, to direct, but as he was in Europe and unavailable, Papp hired Freedman. The book and lyrics were something of a shambles at that point, barely organized into a coherent structure, so Freedman, who had worked with Jerome Robbins on *West Side Story*, became instrumental in shaping it, struggling to define a narrative backbone for the piece. Many considered his contribution invaluable, but there was friction, partly because the genuine hippie element that made up much of the cast was inexperienced and undisciplined; the sense of freedom and improvisation they wanted in the rehearsal hall clashed with Freedman's more organized and rigorous approach. Ragni and Rado kept bringing in new material all through the rehearsal period, which made it very difficult for Freedman to solidify the book. Also, having based the leading characters on themselves, they both wanted to be in the show, with Rado playing the role of Claude and Ragni as Berger. Fearing they were too old to be believable as teenagers, Freedman agreed to cast Ragni but not Rado; he chose an actor named Walker Daniels for Claude, and this became a source of continuing tension. Freedman also brought in Anna Sokolow, a modern dance choreographer, to stage production numbers. She had a different, more improvisatory way of working that appealed to the writers, who began to rely on her and to shut Freedman out, to the point where he felt he was losing control of the show. Finally, shortly before the start of previews, Freedman quit—though he later admitted he had been hoping Papp wouldn't accept his resignation, but rather use the crisis as an excuse to restore order and return the reins to him. Sokolow took over, but once the show began previews, it became clear it was in trouble. Papp called Freedman, who had escaped to Washington, D.C., and asked him to come back. He agreed, Sokolow withdrew, and with just a couple days left before the opening, Freedman restored most of his original staging.

Despite all the conflict and chaos of the development and rehearsal period, the opening of the show in the Anspacher Theatre, on October 17, 1967, was a resounding success. Though critics were divided and some of the Festival's regular audience members were offended, the innovative piece quickly found its audience.

It could have run at the Anspacher for a long time, but Papp was planning a new version of *Hamlet*, starring Martin Sheen, which he was directing himself, so he held *Hair* to its planned limited run of eight weeks. That might have been the end of it—until Michael Butler appeared on the scene unexpectedly. A Chicago businessman with political aspirations and a strong commitment to the antiwar movement, he saw the show several times and called Papp to talk about it, ultimately coming on board as coproducer. Butler told Papp and Gersten he wanted to move the show to Broadway, and they considered the Henry Miller Theatre on 43rd Street (now the Stephen Sondheim). But Papp didn't believe in Broadway in those days; he felt it was all about commercialism, and he thought *Hair* belonged in a space where it would be more affordable and accessible to young people. So he and Butler finally decided to move the musical to Cheetah, a dance club on Broadway and 53rd Street. Alas, this proved not to be the right venue, and the show closed there after only forty-five more performances.

Sensing that Papp's focus had moved on to other projects, Butler was not ready to give up on bringing *Hair* to a wide audience. He bought the Festival out and mounted a new production of the show at the Biltmore Theatre on Broadway. This time Rado and Ragni got their original director of choice, Tom O'Horgan, and Rado finally got his chance to play Claude. Many who saw both productions later said they preferred Freedman's version, but O'Horgan's proved enormously successful, and the show ran on Broadway for over four years. (The brief group nude scene that became a hallmark of the show was added for this new version; nobody had disrobed completely at the Public, and there has been speculation over how much the publicity attending that one scene might have helped trigger the box-office success of the new production.)

As the original producer, the Festival got a royalty percentage of the gross, which amounted to close to $2 million in revenue that helped support the Public's programming for the next five years. Though this was by no means inconsiderable, it was far less than the Festival could have made if it had stayed on board as coproducer with Butler. Papp learned a valuable lesson from that mistake, one he was not to repeat with *A Chorus Line*.

Now that Papp had produced a musical, the door through which Michael Bennett would walk six years later had been opened. Though *Hair* and *ACL* might seem on the surface to have little in common, there are key parallels. Both are early examples of what came to be known as the "concept musical," a piece driven more by theme and character than traditional linear storytelling. Both grew out of real-life experiences of the participants and were developed at least to some degree through improvisation and experimentation in the rehearsal hall. Each was an attempt to put before a mass audience the concerns and lifestyles of a particular youth subculture of the time, though the freewheeling hippies of *Hair* might seem a far cry from the ultra-disciplined professional dancers of *A Chorus Line*. In addition, there were some connections in terms of personnel. Theoni V. Aldredge, by then firmly ensconced as the Festival's resident costume designer, did the clothes for both shows. Robin Wagner, who would design the set for *A Chorus Line*, did the Broadway version of *Hair*. And the Broadway cast of *Hair* included (as a replacement in the roles of both Crissy and Jeannie) a young Kay Cole, who would create the role of Maggie in *A Chorus Line.*

Two Gentlemen of Verona

The second hit musical to come out of the Festival had its origins with Shakespeare in the Park. Papp invited Mel Shapiro, who had recently directed the Broadway production of John Guare's play *The House of Blue Leaves*, to direct *The Two Gentlemen of Verona* for the summer of 1971—first at the Delacorte, then on a tour of the boroughs on the Mobile Stage. On reading the play, Shapiro was less than thrilled. It's a very early Shakespeare comedy and historically has often been considered one of the Bard's weakest; the director was afraid that such light romantic comedy would not go over on a parks tour in that era of racial tension and street violence. How to present the play in a way that the intended audience could relate to?

Shapiro decided to ask John Guare to adapt the play as a musical, and Papp suggested Galt MacDermot, whose *Hair* was still running on Broadway, to write the music. They kept Shakespeare's original title, shorn of its definite article. There wasn't time to write a whole polished script and score before the show had to go into rehearsal, so of necessity the developmental process again bore some resemblance to a workshop, though happier and more harmonious than that of *Hair*, and much shorter and less rigorously structured than that of *A Chorus Line.* Guare and MacDermot attended rehearsals and would pick up on zany ideas the cast came up with on their feet, so the whole thing took on a playful sense of improvisation and surprise, with everyone gleefully contributing. (The score consisted of nine songs when they went into rehearsal; the number was ultimately increased to thirty-five, many of them very short.) Both script and score grew organically as a crazy-quilt of styles, combining much of the original Shakespearean verse with contemporary rock lyrics and music that celebrated summer life in New York City. Though the set and costumes were a mix of Renaissance and modern styles, the overall conceit was that Verona was San Juan, Puerto Rico, and Milan, to which the titular boys journey to start their adult lives, was New York. Partly as an attempt to make sure neighborhood audiences for the tour would see themselves reflected in the show, the casting was completely multiracial—a practice that would become a hallmark of the Festival's approach to Shakespeare. Proteus and Julia were played by Latino actors (Raul Julia and Carla Pinza), and the other central couple, Valentine and Silvia, were African American (Clifton Davis and Jonelle Allen). MacDermot's music proved effective at evoking various ethnic styles. The war in Vietnam was still going on, and contemporary Washington politics were satirized in the depiction of the Duke, played as a warmongering despot.

When the show opened in Central Park, it was ecstatically received by both critics and audiences, and the Mobile Unit tour was just as successful. A transfer to Broadway seemed inevitable, and Papp was approached by everyone from Sol Hurok to David Merrick. But Papp and Gersten had learned their lesson well from *Hair* and determined to keep control of the property so that its Broadway profits could all be funneled back into future productions at the Public. To this end, they enlisted LuEsther Mertz, a very wealthy board member and one of the Festival's

Marvin Hamlisch and Joseph Papp celebrate *A Chorus Line* becoming the longest-running show in Broadway history, 1983.

biggest supporters, to donate the whole (tax-deductible) $250,000 needed for the move. This approach was similar to that which the Festival would take with most of its Broadway transfers over the next few years, including *A Chorus Line*.

Surprisingly for a show that had seemed charmed from the very beginning, *Two Gentlemen* almost fell apart on its way to Broadway. Now freed of the Mobile Unit's ninety-minute running-time limit, the show could get longer; new songs were tried, discarded, and replaced. A new choreographer was hired and then fired. The initial previews were dispiriting, with the magical ambience of the Park sorely missed in the St. James Theatre. The first few scenes especially were a shambles, and audiences walked out in droves, many not even waiting till intermission. But Guare and Shapiro focused on revamping the opening of the show, experimenting until they found a sequence of numbers establishing the right irreverent comic tone while also engaging the audience in Julia's experience of falling in love. Almost at the last minute, the show came back to life; it opened to strong reviews and went on to win numerous awards. Its snagging of the 1972 Tony Award for Best Musical causes Broadway aficionados to shake their heads to this day, as it beat out not only Sondheim's *Follies* (codirected by Michael Bennett), a flawed masterpiece now considered a landmark in musical theatre history, but also *Grease*, which would go on to break the record as the longest-running musical in Broadway history (a distinction it would hold only until 1983, when its run was surpassed by that of *A Chorus Line*). The original Broadway production of *Jesus Christ Superstar*, which opened that same season, was not even nominated for the award.

In the space of just a few years, Broadway transfers had become almost routine for the New York Shakespeare Festival. The same season that *Two Gentlemen of Verona* won the Tony Award for Best Musical (1972), the Festival was also awarded the Tony for Best Play, for David Rabe's *Sticks and Bones*, which had transferred from the Public to the John Golden Theatre. The very next season, the Public Theater production of Jason Miller's *That Championship Season* moved to the Booth Theatre; it too won the Tony Award for Best Play, in addition to the Pulitzer Prize for Drama (which would also be won three years later by *A Chorus Line*). Even one of the summer outdoor Shakespeare productions, an A. J. Antoon staging of *Much Ado About Nothing* starring Sam Waterston and Kathleen Widdoes, was moved to Broadway. In 1978, another interesting new musical begun at the Public Theater found itself headed there as well.

Runaways

Runaways was the brainchild of Elizabeth Swados, a composer/playwright/director who was a product of New York's downtown avant-garde theatre community. She had been writing music for productions of classic plays directed by Andre Serban, first at La MaMa, a downtown venue known for experimental work, and then uptown at Lincoln Center, where Joe Papp presented Serban productions of *Agamemnon* and *The Cherry Orchard*. Swados's initial meeting with Papp was similar to Michael Bennett's, in that Papp approached her with a specific project in mind, asking her to write music for Tina Howe's play *Museum*; Swados wasn't any more interested in that than Bennett had been in directing *Knickerbocker Holiday*, but like him she took the opportunity of a meeting with Papp to pitch a project of her own. She began by talking to Papp about her unique adaptation of *Alice in Wonderland*, but before that project got off the ground, she changed her mind and told him she wanted instead to develop a new theatre piece about something that had been haunting her: the plight of runaway children and teenagers in the nation's cities. Though she was only twenty-six years old at the time and largely untried as a director, Papp agreed to fund a workshop. Swados would interview runaway youngsters and build a script and score in workshop, with a cast made up of a few professional juvenile actors and a number of kids she met on the streets and in the neighborhoods, some of whom came from very rough backgrounds or had been actual runaways. Papp was attracted not only to Swados's talent but to her humanitarian mission: She was grappling with a real social issue, and that appealed to the political conscience that had always informed his artistic decision making. (Though Papp's mission from the start had included multiculturalism and giving voice to artists from underrepresented groups, he had been surprisingly slow to extend major opportunities to woman playwrights; his partnership with Swados was a major step.)

In a sense, *Runaways* can be seen as a direct descendant of both *Hair* and *A Chorus Line*, once again giving onstage life to a particular sector of youth culture in a show developed organically with input from the participants. Like *ACL*, its script was built from stories shared with the director in interviews, some of the subjects of which would appear in the musical itself. Most of the youngsters cast in the show were novice actors. Though this had of course also been true of some of the original cast members of *ACL*, the big difference was that they were professional dancers schooled in the discipline of the theatre; Swados wanted to work with real kids from disadvantaged neighborhoods, with stories to tell of their own struggles, and many of them had never even seen a play.

Papp provided rehearsal space in the Annex, an auxiliary space the Festival was then renting across the street from the Public Theater. Swados worked with her young company six hours a day for five months, developing the script and songs from improvisations and stories they told about their own lives. They also took a field trip to the Kennedy Home, an institution for runaways in the Bronx, where they interacted with kids who had lived on the streets.

Swados did hire a couple of young actors with professional experience and relied on them to some degree to anchor the group and set an example. One of these was Diane Lane, then thirteen, who has gone on to a major Hollywood career; her casting by director George Roy Hill in the film *A Little Romance* with Laurence Olivier precluded her moving with the show to Broadway. (The original cast album of *Runaways*, like that of *ACL*, was recorded while the show was still running at the Public, so Lane is heard on the album even though she was not a part of the Broadway cast.) Many of the ensemble did not continue to pursue acting careers, but there were several others who did go on to further success, including Trini Alvarado, Toby Parker (now known as Timothy Britten Parker), Josie de Guzman, and Carlo Imperato, best known for the role of Danny Amatullo on the long-running TV series version of *Fame*.

The Broadway production of *Runaways* ran from May to December 1978 at the Plymouth Theatre (later renamed the Schoenfeld, where the revival of *A Chorus Line* would open in 2006). Papp kept it running for several months at a financial loss, because it was a project he believed in and he wanted it to be seen by a large audience. The show was nominated for Best Musical and for four other Tony Awards: Best Original Score, Best Book, Best Direction, and Best Choreography—all Swados, who even played guitar in the show's band. Though *Runaways* didn't win any Tonys, Swados did win an Obie Award for her direction of the original Off-Broadway production.

The *Chorus Line* Years, and After

The success of *ACL* made it possible for the Festival to support and develop more new plays than ever before, and the theatre added a Play Development Department to read submissions, scout new writing talent, and provide dramaturgical support to writers. The enormous responsibility for heading this department went to Gail Merrifield, who had been working for the theatre as Papp's assistant. Papp came to rely more and more on Merrifield's taste, integrity, and dramaturgical acumen, and a powerful personal connection developed between them as well. Though Papp had long delayed getting an official divorce from Peggy Bennion, even when their marriage had effectively disintegrated, his relationship with Merrifield pushed him finally to make that move. Merrifield had worked for the Festival for ten years by the time she and Papp were married in January 1976. His fourth wife, she was his true soul mate, and the marriage lasted the rest of his life.

Though the Festival's own funds were running dangerously low at the time, Papp and Gersten had resisted any temptation to bring additional coproducers or investors into *A Chorus Line*. Having learned a hard lesson from *Hair*, they wished to retain sole ownership of the production so that the profits would not have to be split: this was only made possible by board chair LuEsther Mertz, who opened her own pocketbook, as she had before with *Two Gentlemen of Verona*, to make possible the move to Broadway.

For a while in the 1970s, Joseph Papp was the apparent king of theatre in New York. Still producing annual outdoor Shakespeare in Central Park as well as whole seasons of new works in the Public Theater's multiple indoor spaces, with frequent Broadway transfers, he was also asked to take over the Vivian Beaumont Theatre, the large Lincoln Center venue that had struggled for several years (and with a succession of producers) to find its identity and audience base. As if all this weren't enough, at around the same time, he signed a deal with CBS-TV to produce thirteen stage productions for television over the course of the next several seasons. The new ventures got off to rocky starts, and Papp ended up abandoning both prematurely; he felt that he was expending resources on Lincoln Center that he needed to be devoting to his own core projects, and the TV deal fell apart after an ugly dispute involving censorship of the film version of David Rabe's *Sticks and Bones*. Still, *A Chorus Line* having by that point become established as a box-office phenomenon that would surely run for years, the New York Shakespeare Festival began to enjoy a revenue stream unlike anything it had ever experienced before. Of course, producing and developing more new works was high on Papp's priority list, but some of the decisions he made surprised even those closest to him.

Papp announced a subscription series of new plays at the Booth Theatre, a relatively small Broadway house that backs up against the Shubert Theatre at the other end of Shubert Alley. He planned a season of five productions, with tickets priced at $2.50, or $10.00 for the whole series. (These prices were extremely low for Broadway even in 1975; the top ticket price for *A Chorus Line* at the time was $15.00). The Booth Theatre Series was to include plays by some of Papp's favorite writers: Thomas Babe, John Ford Noonan, Miguel Piñero, Michael Weller, and, in the first slot, Dennis Reardon.

Reardon's play, which opened at the Booth the night after *A Chorus Line* opened at the Shubert, was called *The Leaf People*. A wildly ambitious "fantasia on the theme of genocide," set in the Amazon rain forest, it was largely written in an original language that Reardon himself had created, which became a unique challenge for the actors. To direct the play, Papp chose Tom O'Horgan, who had staged the Broadway versions of *Hair* and *Jesus Christ Superstar*; he didn't click with Reardon and ended up requesting an hour's worth of cuts right before the opening. Though many insiders who had followed the play since its first reading felt it was uniquely

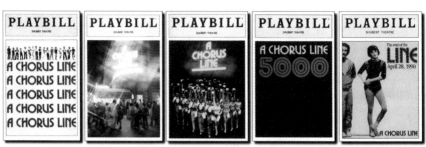

Playbill covers from various periods of the show's long Broadway run.   *Courtesy* Playbill

beautiful, it was trashed by the critics and ran only twenty-four performances. Papp announced the cancellation of the Booth Theatre Series; the other four plays would be staged at the Public. Reasons cited included the Broadway musicians' strike, which had shut down previews of *A Chorus Line* next door for almost a month, delaying the official opening and costing the Festival an estimated $200,000 in ticket revenues. (Papp announced the decision right before the opening of *The Leaf People* instead of right after, thus avoiding the appearance of scrapping the season due to the bad reviews, though he was already aware that the production had let the play down.)

When PBS announced in the late 1970s that it would be broadcasting nationwide, over a six-year period, the complete plays of Shakespeare, Papp protested publicly—because the productions would all be British-made versions that originated with the BBC. He tried to get the network to reconsider and offered his assistance if they would commission American productions of at least half of the plays, but to no avail. Looking for an alternative way to make a powerful, highly visible commitment to American Shakespeare, he decided to start a new resident classical repertory company—something certain critics and patrons had been encouraging him to do for years—to present Shakespeare in New York. Underlining the sociopolitical statement he intended to make, he announced the formation of an ensemble made up entirely of African American actors, to prove that Americans could do Shakespeare as well as anyone; it could be argued that he contradicted his own thesis by hiring a British director, Michael Langham, to come to New York to train the actors and direct the productions. Morgan Freeman and Denzel Washington were among the company. Papp and Langham decided to add Hispanic actors to the mix and opened with productions of *Julius Caesar* and *Coriolanus* that received mixed reviews. Papp remained enthusiastic about the endeavor and decided to present two more productions the following year, opening the group to Asian actors. However, Langham declined to extend his contract, and grant money proved not to be forthcoming, so the idea of a resident company was put aside.

"Surprise, Surprise"

Around this time, a rift was starting to grow between Papp and his right-hand man, Bernard Gersten. Gersten, also credited as associate producer on *A Chorus Line*, had been on staff with the Festival for eighteen years; his role as facilitator and supporter of all of Papp's projects, and his ability to play good cop to Papp's bad cop in dealings with artists and funders, had made him indispensable. Gersten had strong ideas and contributed creative solutions without demanding credit; he did much of the detailed day-to-day work that brought Papp's visions to fruition, but was generally happy to stay in the background. It wasn't that they never had arguments, but in the end Gersten would generally accede to Papp's decisions and work to realize them. In 1978, though, the two had their first major disagreement, and it was over Michael Bennett. Bennett wanted to workshop his next project, the musical *Ballroom*, at the Public, as he had *A Chorus Line*. Since *ACL* was by this point raking in the profits and had transformed the Festival's finances and creative scope like nothing before, Gersten felt there was no way they could in good conscience turn away Bennett's new project—but Papp didn't like the material. He thought it was sentimental; it didn't fit within the aesthetic parameters of the Public Theater, and it didn't seem to require his developmental acumen. Simply presenting a commercial production that was clearly intended for Broadway was not part of the Festival's mission as a nonprofit theatre. Also, Bennett was by now a very wealthy man with his own production company; he was building his own theatre and had powerful allies in the commercial Broadway community. Some observers felt that Papp was rankled by Bennett's newfound independence: the director wanted to work at the Public, but he didn't really need Papp anymore, and Papp didn't want to be perceived as needing Bennett. Gersten, uncharacteristically, would not let go, and wanted to work on *Ballroom* as associate producer whether or not Papp was involved.

The problems came into sharp relief following Papp's fifty-seventh birthday on June 22, 1978. Believing it to be a shame that most great men's lives are not truly celebrated until their memorial services, Gersten decided to present a living tribute to Papp in the form of a birthday party of unprecedented scope and style. He orchestrated a surprise party in the Delacorte Theatre for a select group of two thousand of Papp's closest friends and artistic collaborators, with live performances of excerpts from musicals the Festival had developed (including *ACL*), speeches by no less than three present and past New York mayors, and a short play satirizing backstage life at the Public, written for the occasion by John Guare.

Gersten made Gail Merrifield Papp very uncomfortable by asking her to lie to Joe to get him to the party; they had already arrived at their country house in Katonah, where he had hoped to spend a very quiet birthday, when Gail got the phone call informing her that the party was happening and soliciting her assistance in somehow getting Papp back into the city. She made up a story about a surprise dinner at a fancy Manhattan restaurant, and the family piled into the car over Papp's protests; he was still disgruntled when a cast member from the Festival's production of *All's Well That Ends Well* called him at the restaurant to tell him about a crisis at the theatre: leading lady Pamela Reed was allegedly threatening to quit! Papp hurried over to the Delacorte to try to defuse the situation and was greeted by one of the biggest surprises of his life.

The party was by all accounts a stunning tribute—though some people found Guare's skit mean-spirited and tacky, and it reportedly hurt Gail Merrifield Papp's feelings. But there was a tremendous outpouring of love, and when he finally spoke, Papp was clearly moved. He offered Gersten his profound thanks for conceiving the plan and having the wherewithal to pull it off so beautifully. But as most people by then were aware, Papp liked to be in control, and in the days following, his perspective on the party changed somewhat. He wasn't thrilled about having been lied to, even in the interests of a surprise birthday party, and he was very aware that substantial financial resources—paid for, as the press pointed out, by *A Chorus Line*—had been expended on the event without his knowledge or approval. Gersten was pushing against some long-established boundaries. So when he informed Papp soon afterwards that he intended to work with Bennett's team as associate producer of *Ballroom* for four months, Papp told him that would mean he would have to resign his position with the Festival. Gersten dug in his heels, and after consulting with the executive committee of the Festival's board of directors, Papp fired him.

This move shocked not only Gersten but many on the staff and others close to the two men. For a time, it put Papp in the position of running the huge operation primarily by himself, but as time went on, many of Gersten's duties were assumed by the general manager, Robert Kamlot, and, later, by Papp's new assistant Jason Steven Cohen. More internal strife would follow: when Papp decided to give Gersten's old title of associate producer to Cohen, Kamlot resigned.

Though Gersten was devastated by his firing and the loss of his lifelong friendship with Papp, his career recovered powerfully. After stints working with producers Francis Ford Coppola and Alexander H. Cohen and a two-year period as executive producer for Radio City Music Hall, he returned to Lincoln Center Theater, the institution that he and Papp had struggled to make work years earlier. As executive producer alongside Gregory Mosher and later André Bishop, Gersten was finally able to establish LCT as a vital and healthy institution; it remains a leading force in the theatre world today.

New Artists, New Projects

As long as *A Chorus Line* was running, Papp made good use of the revenues it provided to the Festival, which would eventually total at more than $38 million. The summer Shakespeare offerings in Central Park were by then a well-established tradition with a large and loyal audience, and Papp was able to invest resources in more new works and new artists than ever before. While continuing to produce plays by some of his favorite writers like David Rabe, John Guare, and Thomas Babe, Papp also nurtured important new voices like David Mamet, Christopher Durang, Ed Bullins, and Sam Shepard. Though the focus had always been on new American plays, a production exchange arrangement with London's Royal Court Theatre led to relationships with several British writers as well, notably Caryl Churchill and David Hare. Though male playwrights continued to dominate the schedule, the theatre began to produce more works by women, including Tina Howe, Adrienne Kennedy, and the poet/performer Ntozake Shange, who made a major impact with her innovative play *for colored girls who have considered suicide/ when the rainbow is enuf.* Directed by Oz Scott, it made its way from the Public Theater to Broadway in 1976; it toured nationally and has been revived many times regionally over the years, and was adapted as a film by Tyler Perry in 2010.

I'm Getting My Act Together and Taking It on the Road

Two other female artists who impressed Papp in the late 1970s were the songwriting team of Gretchen Cryer and Nancy Ford. Craig Zadan introduced them to the producer, and brought them to the Public to audition their musical *I'm Getting My Act Together and Taking It on the Road* (1978). Papp immediately offered to produce the show—but only if book writer/lyricist Cryer would agree to play the leading role of Heather, a former pop star putting together a new club act. Though the character was largely based on her, Cryer had not thought of wanting to perform it, but Papp loved the way she sang and knew her personal connection to the material and natural charisma would be key to making the show work. Though the musical was not well received by critics, it became a word-of-mouth phenomenon with audiences, who found it both captivating and provocative; they would stay for lively post-show discussions about the changing nature of male/female dynamics, and were often inspired to address problems in their own relationships. The show proved so popular that after it completed its extended run at the Anspacher, Papp moved it to the Circle in the Square Downtown, a three-hundred-seat commercial venue; it ended up running for close to three years and turned a healthy profit. After Cryer left the cast, Heather was played by a succession of well-known singing actresses, including Betty Buckley, Virginia Vestoff, Betty Aberlin, Phyllis Newman, and the show's composer, Nancy Ford. With its story of a singer trying to redefine herself and her image with a new show—and fighting resistance and manipulation by her manager, who is also her former boyfriend—the show has certain parallels to the Cassie/Zach scenario in *A Chorus Line*; it seems appropriate that Donna McKechnie eventually played Heather in the Chicago production.

Expanded Horizons

In 1979, Papp and Gail made a trip to the Soviet Union, where they had meetings with the leaders of numerous Russian theatres and arts organizations; they toured Moscow and Leningrad and saw two, sometimes three plays every day for a week and a half. They met with the Minister of Culture and planned an ambitious theatre exchange, whereby they would send a production of *A Chorus Line* to the USSR and in turn host New York performances by the Moscow Art Theater, a legendary company Papp revered. After a discussion of whether the gay storylines in *ACL* made it too "eccentric" for Russian audiences or censors, the Soviet government was prepared to cover the costs on their end, but though Papp appealed to numerous big corporations, foundations, and government officials for financial support, no American sponsor came forward, and the project never materialized. Papp said he was embarrassed by the failure of the attempt—though in retrospect one can see how by that point *A Chorus Line*, a worldwide box-office sensation, might have been seen as a commercial enterprise more than capable of paying its own way, and not in need of subsidy for a Russian tour.

More Musicals

Though other musicals were developed at the Public in the years directly following *A Chorus Line*, the primary focus remained plays. There were a couple of highly successful musical projects helmed by Wilford Leach, who was becoming Papp's most trusted director at the time. In the summer of 1980, Papp was disgruntled because he hadn't received any grant money from the city for Shakespeare in the Park; he decided if the city didn't want to fund it, he wouldn't do it. But this was at the height of the *Chorus Line* phenomenon, so the money was streaming in. He decided he wanted to present a Gilbert and Sullivan operetta and asked Leach, who thought he had no interest in the genre, to direct *The Mikado*. The director listened to *The Pirates of Penzance* instead and found he liked it, then embarked on a mission to blow the cobwebs of tradition off the piece and present it as if it were a new play. To help it connect with a contemporary audience, he decided to cast pop stars in the romantic leads, eventually choosing Linda Ronstadt and Rex Smith, and he surrounded them with classically trained comic actors like George

Rose, Kevin Kline, and Estelle Parsons. The results proved magical; the show enchanted audiences in the Park and moved on to a successful Broadway run at the Uris and then the Minskoff Theatre. It was later made into a movie.

Emboldened by the success of *Pirates* and Linda Ronstadt's longtime ambition to sing the role of Mimi in Giacomo Puccini's classic opera *La Bohème*, the Public staged an adaptation for her in 1984, again directed by Leach and costarring country singer Gary Morris. Though it wasn't a bomb, the magic of *Pirates* was not repeated. But Leach remained busy at the Festival, where he became artistic director; after directing several Shakespeare productions, he helmed another major musical success for the theatre: Rupert Holmes's *The Mystery of Edwin Drood*. The 1985 work is

Joseph Papp in 1985, ten years into the run of *A Chorus Line*. He is shown in his office, surrounded by posters for other New York Shakespeare Festival productions.

based on an unfinished Charles Dickens novel; because the book has no ending, the musical is written with a variety of possible conclusions, and the audience in the theatre gets to vote on the outcome. In a production starring Betty Buckley, George Rose, Howard McGillin, Cleo Laine, and Patti Cohenour, the show began at the Delacorte and moved to Broadway's Imperial Theatre, where it ran almost a year and a half. Partway through the run, the musical's name was shortened to *Drood*, but the longer title was restored when the show was revived in 2012 by the Roundabout Theatre Company at Studio 54.

At one point, Papp was courted by Hollywood. Like Michael Bennett, he was offered a three-picture deal by one of the major studios. Also like Bennett, he found he was a creature of the live theatre and couldn't stomach the Hollywood system; in a *London Times* interview, he referred to the city as "antiseptic," and said, "After a couple of days there, my stomach started heaving and I came straight back to New York. The deal was off."

Entering his sixties, Papp, who had often avoided foreign travel in the past, found himself seeking new vistas. He visited the Soviet Union, Israel, Egypt, and Poland, where he saw new kinds of theatre and met with artists who were often laboring under oppressive and dangerous political conditions. These experiences moved him further and further away from the world of Michael Bennett and *A Chorus Line*. When he returned to the United States on December 13, 1981, he and Gail went to the Broadway opening night of Bennett's latest musical, *Dreamgirls*. Gail told Helen Epstein that Papp had trouble sitting through it and that they found it represented "such a depressing frame of reference—so narcissistic and banal after the people and situations we had seen abroad."

Final Years

In the early 1980s, Papp began to suffer from various vexing health issues. He had severe chronic stomach problems, high blood pressure, and a bout with Bell's Palsy, plus a torn ligament in his leg that necessitated months of physical therapy. He was also dealing with transitions in his family life: these included finally meeting Barbara Mosser, his daughter by Irene Ball, the nurse with whom he had had an affair during World War II. He had not received the letter Ball sent him at the time telling him he had a daughter, finding out only years later, when the young woman had a medical crisis that required Ball to track him down to find out his blood type. When Ball learned that she herself had cancer, she decided it was time to tell Barbara who her father was, and they came to New York to see him. Papp and Barbara bonded immediately, and he also reached out to her two children. There was now a third grandchild in the picture as well: the son of his legitimate daughter Susan.

Papp's daughter by Peggy Bennion, Miranda, was attending Barnard College, and their son, Tony, moved back home with his father and Gail after graduating from boarding school. When Tony came out as a gay man, the usually liberal-minded Papp had surprising trouble accepting the fact, though his love for his son eventually prevailed. Tony seemed aimless, with few ideas about college or a career; he waited tables for a while and began an affair with a male dancer from the cast of *A Chorus Line*. Hoping to help him find some direction, Papp and Gail asked Elizabeth Swados to use him on the crew of *Runaways*; she recognized that the young man was struggling with depression and doing drugs, but found she got along well with him, and he worked on several of her subsequent productions as well. Tony eventually found his calling as a jewelry designer and studied at the Parsons School of Design; he moved into his own apartment, but his father continued to pay his rent.

One of the Public Theater's most notable productions of the mid-eighties was Larry Kramer's *The Normal Heart*, a largely autobiographical piece about the birth of the Gay Men's Health Crisis and the struggles of early AIDS activists to wake up an apathetic government to the magnitude of the epidemic. The script had been rejected by numerous agents, directors, and theatres before Gail Merrifield Papp took an interest in it. She worked with Kramer over an extended period to improve the piece's structure and dramaturgy before she finally showed the script to Papp; though he had reservations about the writing, he found the play moved him to tears and agreed to produce it. It opened in April 1985, almost exactly ten years after the premiere of *A Chorus Line*—which had lost, and would lose, many of its key players and creators to the disease. Papp believed so strongly in the play and its message that he kept it running even through weeks when it was losing money; though not financially profitable, it became the longest-running play in the history of the Public Theater and was revived there in 2004, long after Papp's death. With hundreds of productions worldwide, a Broadway revival in 2011, and a well-received TV-movie version in 2014, the play has endured and continued to gain in reputation as a defining statement on its era; along with Tony Kushner's *Angels in America*, it is probably one of the two most important plays to come out of the AIDS crisis. The disease continued to cast a pall over the Festival, taking the lives of many of its artists including Michael Bennett and artistic director Wilford Leach, both of whom died in 1987, the same year Papp was diagnosed with prostate cancer. Most devastating for Papp was the AIDS diagnosis of his own son, Tony, who passed away in 1991, only months before his father.

Joseph Papp's death came just a year and a half after the closing of *A Chorus Line* on Broadway. Gary Stevens and Alan George, longtime fans of the show, had initiated an effort to raise funds for a cast bronze plaque commemorating its fifteen-year run, which was officially unveiled at a ceremony in the lobby of the Shubert Theatre on October 30, 1991. Papp was too ill to attend; he died the next day.

The Public Theater Faces Life Without Its Founder

Without the steady income the musical had provided, the New York Shakespeare Festival entered a period of financial uncertainty for the first time since the mid-1970s. Papp's chosen successor was JoAnne Akalaitis, a founder of the highly respected experimental theatre company Mabou Mines. She clashed with the board and the staff and was not able to get the theatre back on a secure footing. She was succeeded by playwright/director George C. Wolfe, who ran the institution from 1993 to 2004. In addition to Shakespeare and new plays, Wolfe had a serious interest in musical theatre and helmed the Public Theater's acclaimed premiere productions of *Bring in 'da Noise, Bring in 'da Funk* (1995) and *Caroline, or Change* (2003), both of which transferred to Broadway. New initiatives during his tenure included the 1998 opening of Joe's Pub, a cabaret space named after Papp, which presents a wide variety of innovative programming throughout the year.

In 2005, Oskar Eustis was named the artistic director of the Public Theater/New York Shakespeare Festival, a post he still holds as of this writing. Eustis formerly ran the Eureka Theatre Company in San Francisco and the Trinity Repertory

The exterior of the Public Theatre today.

Company in Providence, Rhode Island. Under his leadership, the Public has thrived and expanded, and the building underwent a substantial renovation in 2009–10. Shakespeare in the Park continues as a beloved New York institution, with two productions a year, and the Public Theater presents a diverse season of new works on all its stages. Recent initiatives include the Public Lab, begun in cooperation with LAByrinth Theatre Company, which offers low-priced, scaled-down productions of Shakespeare and other works; Under the Radar, an annual festival of experimental theatre from around the world; New Works Now, a series of play readings; the Emerging Writers Group for up-and-coming playwrights; and A Midsummer Day's Camp, which trains teenagers in Shakespeare. Even the Mobile Shakespeare Unit, so dear to Joe Papp's heart, has been revived in recent years. And continuing the legacy of *A Chorus Line*, the Public Theater has demonstrated a renewed focus on new musicals in the past few years, producing a plethora of innovative and provocative works like *Passing Strange* (2007), *Bloody Bloody Andrew Jackson* (2010), *Fun Home* (2013), and *Hamilton* (2015).

Joseph Papp's biographer, Helen Epstein, saved a note in which he had written: "What is consistent in my work is that I have always wanted to provide access to the best human endeavor to the greatest number of people." *A Chorus Line* honored that ambition handsomely, and its success enabled Papp to continue to pursue his mission with countless other projects for the rest of his life. Even today, over twenty years after his passing, the great and active institution that is the Public Theater owes much of its vitality, and maybe even its continued existence, to the little musical about dancers that Joe Papp took a chance on back in 1975, before it even had a title.

5

"You Want This Job, Don't You?"

Auditions, Summer 1974

A *Chorus Line* might never have embarked on its unique journey of development if Michael Bennett hadn't met Joseph Papp of the New York Shakespeare Festival. Their first meeting was brought about through the offices of Bernard Gersten, who at that time was associate producer at the Festival and Papp's right-hand man. Unlike Papp himself, Gersten had a serious interest in musical theatre, and he had been very impressed witnessing the turnaround Bennett had recently engineered when he took over the direction of the musical *Seesaw*, transforming it from something that looked like a certain failure in Detroit into a respectable Broadway musical.

In the spring of 1974, the Festival was rehearsing a musical in its downtown Public Theater complex: *More Than You Deserve*, by Michael Weller and Jim Steinman, directed by Kim Friedman. The show wasn't quite coming together, and, aware of Bennett's reputation as a show doctor, Gersten recommended that Papp call him and ask him to look at a rehearsal and give some advice. Papp didn't think that was necessary, but he did remember being impressed by Bennett's choreography for *Follies*—a show he otherwise hadn't much liked—and he thought of his name again a few days later.

This was during the period when Papp was programming the two performance spaces at Lincoln Center Theater: the Vivian Beaumont and the Mitzi Newhouse. He was looking for a big musical about New York to produce at the Beaumont and, unable to find a new one he liked, had hit on the idea of a revival of Kurt Weill and Maxwell Anderson's *Knickerbocker Holiday*. This was a 1938 show about Peter Stuyvesant, the first governor of New York; it is best remembered today for the ballad "September Song." Papp called Bennett about directing it, and after looking at the script, Bennett declined—but he did ask to meet with Papp to pitch another project.

At their meeting, Bennett played an edited selection of highlights from the tape sessions for Papp, who found it refreshing and compelling. As quoted later by Kenneth Turan in *Free for All: Joe Papp, the Public, and the Greatest Theater Story Ever Told*, he said: "It was the most moving story; it all had to do with parents and children . . . said in the most non-sentimental way, no self-pity, not a touch of it, which made it the more unbearable, frankly. After that I said, 'Fine, let's do something with this,' and I put some money into a workshop."

The documentary aspect of the project appealed to Papp, who was also intrigued by the novel concept of developing a musical through extended workshops, something he considered a worthy experiment in itself. Some people felt he had more pragmatic motivations for taking on the project as well. Donna McKechnie later said she understood that the Festival was experiencing major financial difficulties at the time and its future seemed to be in some jeopardy; Papp may have felt the connection to Bennett's world could open doors to commercial theatre producers and partnerships that might help sustain the theatre. Most importantly, though, he believed in the idea and believed in Bennett, and thus agreed to take a chance. He would ultimately come to view his role in the process, in which he stayed largely hands-off, as that of a "watchdog": making sure the show never lost the integrity that stemmed from its initial basis in truth and authentic oral history.

What Papp initially promised was a workshop period of approximately six weeks, during which he would pay each of the participants one hundred dollars a week and provide rehearsal space. In exchange, the Shakespeare Festival would be granted the rights to produce the show that might result. If it went on to a full production, Michael Bennett would get 5 percent of the gross as director and also 15 percent of the operating profits, with the other 85 percent going to the Festival. Agreements in place, the first task facing Bennett was to put together a creative team to begin shaping the material on the tapes into a script.

"If they asked me I could write a book"

Meanwhile Bennett, with Bob Avian's help, was expanding the tape project to include interviews with close to thirty additional dancers; most of these sessions were conducted in his apartment, singly or in small groups. These included the interviews with Pamela Blair, who would be cast as Val in the show, and Baayork Lee, who would play Connie. Having gathered a trove of useful material, Bennett asked Nicholas Dante to work with him on the script. He was aware that Dante was looking to transition out of his dancing career into a new life as a writer; he also knew that the moving story the young man had told at the first tape session was something very special. Still, given Dante's inexperience, Bennett wasn't sure he would be able to go the distance, so he told him in their initial conversation that if necessary they could later bring in one or more additional writers—something that indeed would eventually happen. But throughout the first workshop, Dante and Bennett would work together on the script.

At this early stage, Bennett wasn't even sure that the show was going to develop into a full-fledged musical; he said he thought it might end up being more of a play, with dances and incidental music. But he did engage a songwriting team at the very beginning. For the music, he selected Marvin Hamlisch, with whom he had worked twice: Hamlisch had been a rehearsal pianist on *Henry, Sweet Henry* and done dance arrangements for *Seesaw*, and Bennett felt he had an unusually strong

Bob Avian and Baayork Lee in rehearsal for the London revival, 2013.

Photo by Manuel Harlan

understanding of dance and dancers. Hamlisch was a little surprised when he learned Edward Kleban was Bennett's choice to do the lyrics, because though Kleban hadn't yet proven himself with a produced show, he was a gifted composer as well as a lyricist. And having heard Barbra Streisand sing Kleban's song "Better," Hamlisch knew Kleban was a talent to be reckoned with. He had a sense that Bennett might be hedging his bets: if it didn't work out with Hamlisch, Kleban would be able to take over and write the music himself.

Next came casting. After the second tape session, the dancers were eager to hear what might happen next. Most of them were by then convinced the material could be turned into a show, and they wanted to be involved. Meanwhile, though, life went on, and they looked for work on other productions. Several of them worked together on a show called *Music! Music!*, which opened at the City Center in August 1974. This was a revue surveying the history of popular music in America over the previous eight decades, directed by Martin Charnin. Tony Stevens was the choreographer; the cast included Renee Baughman, Trish Garland, Donna McKechnie, Michon Peacock, and Thommie Walsh. (Coincidentally, the costume designer was Theoni V. Aldredge.)

"How many people does he need?"

Since Bennett was planning to develop a script from the material on the tapes, he might well have been expected to invite the dancers from the tape sessions, or at least most of them, to join him in workshopping the show. Instead, he made them all audition—and considered numerous other dancers as well. This had a strong psychological impact, establishing immediately who was boss. According to dancer Wayne Cilento, many of the dancers were "pissed" about having to audition for their own stories. But Bennett had legitimate reasons for requiring this. Now that there was a writing team in place, they were entitled to an opportunity to see the actors and have input in the selection process. And it was important that each performer selected have a distinct personality and something special to offer; no two of them could be too much alike. Most of the dancers had a sense that the project might really develop into something, so they dutifully trouped down to the Public Theater to audition.

The two sisters who had taken part in the tape sessions, Patricia and Jacki Garland, both auditioned. Jacki came into New York from the road, where she was doing a tour of *Anything Goes*, just for the day. She sang a song, but Bennett didn't give her anything to read; she sensed right away that he was not interested. Patricia (known as Trish) was very nervous, especially when Marvin Hamlisch asked her to repeat her song, a ballad, but to try it as an up-tempo number. She was also visibly shaking when she read a monologue—which was probably the first step to her being cast as the nervous, scatterbrained Judy Turner. With the sides quivering noisily in her hand, she made a joke about how it would be helpful if they could get heavier paper; the creative team laughed, and she felt that was the moment that broke the ice. She was hired, but Jacki was not. And as if that situation weren't difficult enough for the two sisters to deal with, the monologue Trish was initially given was based on the stories *Jacki* had told on the tapes!—though that wasn't the way her role in the show would eventually develop.

Kelly Bishop was also handed a monologue, which turned out to be a transcript of her own words from the tape session. She relaxed and enjoyed the reading, and Bennett told her on the spot she had the job—but said not to tell anyone yet. Still, when she went back out into the waiting area, she was irritated to see that several other women had been invited in to audition for her role.

Donna McKechnie, Bennett's close friend and favorite dancer, went to the audition because everybody was expected to go. She decided to take the opportunity to do a song she would never ordinarily get to sing, so she picked "Musetta's Waltz" from Puccini's opera *La Bohème* and sang it holding a rose. (Years later, she said making the panel listen to her sing this had been something of a joke on her part, but since she went in knowing she would be cast, she had wanted to approach it as a "celebration" rather than an audition.)

Priscilla Lopez also felt confident that Bennett wanted her in the workshop. He had taken to calling her on the phone occasionally to tell her about the progress he was making in putting the project together, and he invited her to go with him to a Tony Awards party. She had already sung at his apartment for him and Hamlisch and Kleban before attending the auditions at the Public Theater, which Bennett assured her "wasn't really an audition." She sang there as well but didn't have to read anything.

When Wayne Cilento tried to read his monologue, he found he couldn't get through it. He was self-conscious about his Bronx accent. Bennett wasn't worried; he told the dancer to put the script down and just to tell the story again in his own words. It happened to be about his own experiences in the musical *Seesaw*, which Bennett had directed.

Sammy Williams was still on the road with that show when he received a middle-of-the-night call from Bennett, asking him to come back to New York for an audition. He thought the director probably wanted him to audition for David, the Tommy Tune role in *Seesaw*, as he was looking for someone who could take it over after Tune left the cast. But instead of going straight to an audition, Williams was invited by Bennett to have brunch with him and some of his friends. Then they went to Lincoln Center to see a matinee performance of a Jerome Robbins program by the New York City Ballet. Throughout the day, Michael occasionally asked Sammy questions about his life.

When they finally got around to the audition, Sammy was given a copy of the story Nicholas Dante had related at the tape session, about his experiences in high school and as a teenage drag performer in the Jewel Box Revue. An almost completely inexperienced actor, he found he couldn't read the monologue effectively; his reading was flat, without inflection. Bennett had him try again, without much more success. So he left the room for a few minutes, telling Sammy to look over the piece a few more times, just to remember the story. When he returned, as he had with Cilento, he asked Sammy to begin telling the story in his own words—the young man did so, and when he got to the part about how Dante had been tormented by classmates in high school because he was gay, he broke down crying. Though the story was Dante's, it resonated with Sammy's own life; he became so emotional he could barely get through it. Michael put his arm around him and offered him a tissue—much the way Zach comforts Paul after he finishes telling the story in the show. Then they went over to Marvin Hamlisch's apartment where Hamlisch gave Sammy something to sing. They also tried the monologue again as an improvisation, and once again Sammy became extremely emotional.

After this whirlwind audition day, Williams went back to touring in *Seesaw*; it was weeks before he heard anything from Bennett. But the director showed up at a party one night, following the tour's opening in a new city, and told him he had been chosen to join the company of the workshop.

Married couple Steve Boockvor and Denise Pence Boockvor had attended the first tape session together and were, in part, the inspiration for the characters that would become Al and Kristine. Boockvor auditioned for the workshop but wasn't cast; he later said he felt sure it was Marvin Hamlisch who kept him out. (Years later he would do a stint as Zach in the Broadway company.) His wife Denise was acting in regional theatre at the time and couldn't make the audition.

Mitzi Hamilton, who had told the story of her recent breast augmentation surgery at the second tape session, was not offered a spot in the workshop, though she did audition. She was in *Pippin* at the time and preoccupied with a new boyfriend; she also felt she was out of shape, and had not been taking dance classes as regularly as she should. Though her audition did not go well, her story was used in the script. (Hamilton would get her first chance to play Val, the character partially based on her, when the International Company was formed over a year later. She subsequently joined the Broadway company for a long run and has been involved with the show ever since.)

John Partridge, center, as Zach leads the hopefuls in the opening number, London, 2013.

Photo by Manuel Harlan

Renee Baughman had a traumatic audition due to her lack of confidence as a singer. Very nervous, she alternately laughed and cried as she struggled to get through it. (She had cried through much of the tape session as well.) Understandably, Hamlisch and Kleban were reluctant to hire so weak a vocalist, and her spot in the workshop almost went to Victoria Mallory. (Mallory, who had created ingénue roles in Sondheim's *Follies* and *A Little Night Music*, was known primarily for her beautiful, legitimate soprano voice.) But Michael Bennett liked Baughman's dancing, her vivid stage presence, and her vulnerable, overtly emotional personality; he and Nicholas Dante told the songwriters they wanted to hire her but would reconsider after the workshop if her singing proved an insoluble problem. Ultimately, they wrote the number called "Sing!" just for her, and her hyper, nervous personality became the basis for the Kristine character.

Thommie Walsh's audition was something of a trial, for himself and everyone. The monologue they handed him to read was his own, and he found himself getting so angry about having to compete with other performers for his role that he went overboard, imitating movie stars and generally overacting (in short, "doing a routine"—which is exactly what Zach reproaches Bobby with in the finished show). He sang "Get Happy" and could tell Marvin Hamlisch was not excited about using him, but as usual Bennett prevailed.

Some of the dancers from the original tape sessions had recently auditioned for another show: John Kander and Fred Ebb's *Chicago*, which, as directed by Bob Fosse, was poised to be the big musical of the coming season. Michon Peacock, one of the instigators of the tape sessions, had already been offered a role in *Chicago* when she came in to audition for Bennett's workshop. She read her own monologue from the tape session, but didn't feel she did terribly well. Though she was an admirably good sport about auditioning for a project she could justifiably have felt she herself had initiated, others have speculated that Bennett had already decided he didn't want her to remain involved: he intended to assume full leadership of the enterprise and wanted full control, so he may have been wary of working with anyone he thought might have felt entitled to share in the decision making.

Christopher Chadman was also close to accepting a role in *Chicago*—as well as being quite ill with hepatitis—when Bennett phoned him and pressured him to come to the auditions. He got out of bed and dragged himself downtown to the Public. For reasons known only to himself, Bennett had him sing "Santa Claus Is Coming to Town" as a striptease. (Though parts of Chadman's story were used in the show, he chose to do *Chicago*; much later, he would join the Broadway cast of *A Chorus Line* as the first replacement for Walsh as Bobby.)

Baayork Lee, a close friend of Bennett's, had already worked with him on several shows. She came in, but left feeling her singing audition hadn't gone particularly well. She did the song he requested of her: "Put On a Happy Face," from the musical *Bye Bye Birdie*, but forgot some of the words and felt like she had let him down. Years later she told Peter Filichia, for his book *Broadway Musical MVPs 1960–2010*: "I wasn't counting on being in his new show, so I auditioned for Bob Fosse for *Chicago*. When I got home that day, the phone was ringing. It was Michael, who said, 'I heard you were at the Fosse auditions. You start rehearsals with me tomorrow.'"

Ron Kuhlman, who considered himself primarily an actor, had not been at the tape sessions. He went in with some trepidation, afraid that Bennett would remember him from his audition for *Follies*: dancing in his stocking feet on a raked stage, he had slipped and fallen on a double pirouette. But he read Andy Bew's monologue from the tapes and did well enough to be cast.

Cameron (generally called Rick) Mason also hadn't taken part in the tape sessions. A handsome young dancer, he was known by Bennett for his work in the *Milliken Breakfast Show* (an industrial) and was invited to the auditions for that reason. His repertoire as a singer at that time consisted of exactly one song: he sang it and waited while the team conferred, then Bennett said "You'll do." He was hired on the spot.

Robert LuPone, an experienced ballet dancer intent on achieving the transition to an acting career, was sent in by his agent and sang a nervous rendition of "Once in Love with Amy," from the old musical *Where's Charley?* He didn't even attend the dance audition because he had decided he was through with chorus roles. He was called back for an acting audition and showed up to read—but when he arrived at the studio on August 4, 1974, he found he already had the job. He was surrounded by a newly assembled company of dancer/actors who were about to set off on the adventure of their lives.

6

"There's a Lot I Am Not Certain Of"

The First Workshop

It was like group therapy. They were fifteen weeks of everyone at some point having his nervous breakdown or her nervous breakdown. I'm talking about really falling apart."—Kelly Bishop, looking back on the workshop and rehearsal period on the NBC Nightly News, April 1990.

As the first workshop began, Michael Bennett's plan was to develop the new show through improvisation, experimentation, and further interviews and conversations with the dancers over the course of the next five or six weeks. Each of them would be paid only a hundred dollars a week, which even then wasn't enough to live on in New York; they were making an investment in their futures and putting their faith in Bennett, who many of them believed was a genius. Plus, they knew Bennett himself and the writers were getting the same amount of money; they were all in it together.

Somehow, there was a shared sense from the beginning that the project could really develop into something and a pronounced if cautious excitement in the room. The workshop sessions would be held six days a week, both at the Public Theater and at the American Theatre Lab (now known as Dance Theatre Workshop) on West 19th Street in Manhattan, a complex of studios that the New York City Ballet used for rehearsals.

To begin with, there was a preliminary working script, which had been developed by Bennett and Nicholas Dante during the few months that had elapsed since the second tape session. It read at about an hour and a half long and consisted mainly of monologues culled from the tape sessions and the subsequent individual interviews that Bennett and Avian had recorded at Bennett's apartment. There were as yet no songs.

The Company

Since most of the characters had not yet been named, there was no "cast list"; the dancers chosen for the workshop, in alphabetical order, were: Renee Baughman, Kelly Bishop, Pamela Blair, Candy Brown, Wayne Cilento, Trish Garland, Ron Kuhlman, Baayork Lee, Priscilla Lopez, Robert LuPone, Cameron Mason, Donna McKechnie, Michael Misita, Jane Robertson, Thommie Walsh, and Sammy

Williams. (The attrition rate would prove to be surprisingly low, as all but three of these people would ultimately go on to open the show on Broadway.) Misita was the first to leave, having signed on with the understanding that he would have to go if an Off-Broadway show he was associated with got picked up. He was replaced by Tony Stevens, who, it will be recalled, was one of the original initiators of the tape sessions, along with Bennett and Michon Peacock. Stevens had begun to work as a choreographer and was mostly interested in exploring that career path; a dancing role seemed like a step back. But when Misita left and Bennett contacted him a second time, Stevens finally agreed to come on board, partly for the chance to help Bennett and Avian with the choreography.

Early Experiments

Each dancer was given typed pages from the rough script and assigned specific material to work on. Some had their own words from the tape sessions, transcribed and handed back to them, while some were given other people's stories to interpret. The idea was never for the actors to "play themselves" in strict documentary style, but rather for the company and writers to begin to develop a set of characters. The stories would be mixed and matched and embellished until distinct personalities began to emerge. Even Kelly Bishop, whose "Sheila" role was founded very specifically on her own personality and the stories she had shared on the tapes, later said she drew on four other women she had worked with as well in developing the character. (One of them, Charlene Ryan, would eventually play Sheila in the first National Company.)

Besides Sheila, the characters who were most clearly defined right from the beginning were Paul, Connie, and Diana. Bennett had chosen Sammy Williams specifically to play a character based on Nicholas Dante, knowing the latter's monologue was likely to be a centerpiece of the project. The role of Connie is based very closely on Baayork Lee's life and personality, though what exactly she would do in the show, and how much, remained unclear for quite some time. (Lee was also working as Bennett's assistant, and to her this was a more important contribution than her own performance, so she didn't obsess over the size of her role the way some of the others did.) In addition, Diana Morales was a clear avatar of actress Priscilla Lopez, complete with her experiences at the High School of Performing Arts, and the character was always positioned to be a linchpin of the show.

Because they were also there from the beginning, many people have assumed that Wayne Cilento and Thommie Walsh were playing themselves, but this is not quite the case. Cilento was already married, had children, and lived in the suburbs at the time, and none of this was reflected in the character of Mike. He later admitted it made him angry when Bennett told him he didn't think the audience would buy him as a husband and father; those aspects of his own story were passed on to Ron Kuhlman in the role of Don. Though Cilento and Walsh were friends, Bennett was fond of pitting them against one another in the workshop and would often have each of them try the same material in turn; Cilento knew he was probably the best male dancer in the group, but he often worried that Bennett thought Walsh

Tiffany Chalothorn as Connie looks on from left as David Grindrod (Bobby), Tyler Jent (Mark), and Alex Puette (Greg) dance in the opening number at the Weston Playhouse, 2014.   *Photo by Hubert Schriebl*

the better actor. And though the character of Bobby would take on much of Walsh's personality and offbeat sense of humor, the character's stories, even including being from Buffalo, came in part from Bennett's own childhood.

Dante's initial working script had a surreal tone and an almost existentialist setup that recalled writers like Pirandello and Beckett; the dancers entered a mysterious empty space through a doorway, as if they had been summoned there for some unknown reason to answer questions posed by a disembodied, godlike Voice. It was Bob Avian, the co-choreographer and Bennett's right-hand man, who persisted in suggesting that the frame should be an audition and the voice a director; eventually Bennett and Dante came to agree. No actor had yet been cast in the role of the Voice, which Bennett himself usually played at that point.

First Steps

Though work on the script was important, many of the earliest workshop sessions were devoted to dancing. The show, whatever final form it would take, was already definitely, in Bennett's mind, a show about dance and about dancers, so it was crucial that the choreography develop and grow along with the script; there was no way to separate the two. As quoted in Ken Mandelbaum's book, Bennett said: "It wasn't improvising, it was sketching out. . . . The dancing in this particular musical needed to come first, because the dancing was the plot of the musical; it wasn't something that could be done after the fact."

A very important figure in this part of the process was Robert (Bobby) Thomas, a drummer Bennett had worked with on various projects over a period of fifteen years, including the Broadway production of *Promises, Promises*. Thomas had been thinking of getting out of the theatre, so frustrated was he with the creative compromises inherent to working on Broadway; when Bennett told him there was no other director or producer they would have to answer to, Thomas, who had great faith in Bennett's artistry, got excited about the creative possibilities and agreed to join the team (he was eventually billed as the show's music coordinator). He would sit in rehearsals with his drums, providing and developing purely rhythmic accompaniments to the dances that Bennett and Avian were building with the cast. Sometimes Thomas would come up with a rhythmic pattern that inspired the steps; often the dancers themselves had choreographic ideas, and Bennett listened to everybody. Thus the various dance combinations developed from the very beginning of the process alongside the characters and the script. Marvin Hamlisch was often in the room; he would watch and listen to the work and begin to fashion music out of Thomas's rhythms and the dancers' movements.

Ideas for Songs

Edward Kleban was also in rehearsal almost every day, and he spent time conducting his own side interviews with the dancers. Learning about their lives and their dreams provided invaluable inspiration for the lyrics he would soon begin to write—as did simply having the time to soak up the atmosphere and the unique world of the professional dancer. Hamlisch knew early on that a traditional series of self-contained songs was not what this project required; he wrote in his production journal, later excerpted in his memoirs, that he knew he wanted "it all to sound as if the music and the stories are totally 'seamless.' . . . I have been struck with the spontaneity of the kids. The songs must be absolutely lifelike. They must sound like true stores, as if they're coming from the dancers' hearts and minds. But how?" When they weren't watching Bennett rehearse with the dancers, Hamlisch and Kleban worked on the score either in Hamlisch's Park Avenue apartment (where Hamlisch was irritated by Kleban's smoking) or in a music studio uptown at Lincoln Center. Sometimes the individual actors would be sent up there to work with them on the new songs.

Though Bennett did not devote much time to rehearsing songs during the first workshop, Hamlisch and Kleban presented some of their work to the production team and the cast. "I Can Do That" was one of the first songs they wrote, and several cast members later recalled as a milestone the day they first heard "At the Ballet." The group was very much moved by that song, which so simply and beautifully expresses the yearning of a young dancer; it set the tone for the full score that was to come. Bennett declared it perfect, and Hamlisch was so pleased he rewarded himself with a coffee ice cream sundae!

Nevertheless, the collaboration did not always progress smoothly; Bennett reportedly yelled at the songwriters and all but banged them over their heads to get the kind of material he wanted. At one point, Bennett even fired Hamlisch; in

Mitzi Hamilton and Gary Griffin codirected the 1996 Chicago production at Drury Lane Oakbrook Terrace. Shown here are Mary Beth Dolan (Maggie), Andrea Sabesin (Sheila), and Sloan Just (Bebe), performing "At the Ballet." *Photo by Greg Kolack*

his memoirs, the latter claimed it was because he was being asked to keep writing more dance numbers and instead tried to impress on the director the importance of what he called "character songs," which he felt were needed to bring out the humanity of the characters and make them easier for the audience to relate to. Hamlisch and Kleban had been getting along well most of the time, so Hamlisch understandably hoped that his partner would show solidarity with him during the crisis—but since Kleban was also pursuing a composing career, he instead let Bennett know he could finish the score on his own if he had to. Thankfully, Hamlisch's manager, Allan Carr, flew in from California to help smooth over the blowup, and soon all parties were friends again.

Though the number known today as "One" did not appear until right before previews started months later, it was during the first workshop that Bennett began to experiment with ideas for a finale. He knew early on that he wanted a big production number in a classic 1930s style, and that on some level it would evoke the title songs from Jerry Herman's *Hello, Dolly!* and *Mame*, with the full chorus line celebrating the charisma of a female star. For a while, he and Avian played with a concept that involved the dancers pulling a woman out of the audience and serenading her, dancing around her and making her look like a star as she was led around the stage by Wayne Cilento, Tony Stevens, and Sammy Williams. The idea was to demonstrate the point, dear to Bennett's heart, that the chorus dancers are the ones with all the skills—not to mention the ones who do most of the work. They're so good they can make anyone look like a star, and then she gets all the credit. The concept of using an audience member understandably proved unworkable, but the germ of the idea remains in the song "One," in which the mysterious star never appears.

Getting at the Truth

Day after day, Bennett and Avian would ask the dancers questions, often similar to the ones many of them had already answered at the tape sessions. "What made you start dancing?" "What would you do if you couldn't dance anymore?" Already exhilarated by the dancing they were doing in rehearsal, the performers grew even more excited about being active participants in creating a show. More than singers and actors, dancers are used to keeping their mouths shut and being told exactly what to do. So the feeling that they would finally have a voice, would finally get to express who they were and what was important to them, gave them a heady sense of empowerment; as Donna McKechnie has put it, they were finally going to "stand up and be counted."

This aspect of the process led to an unprecedented level of openness and honesty in the room. The dancers could tell that Bennett wouldn't tolerate "bullshit," so they made sure not to generate any. But there was a less positive side effect as well. A sense of competition started to emerge, as the actors found themselves trying to outdo each other in efforts to earn the director's approval and, thus, get better material in the show that was developing. It soon became clear that a few of the more outgoing, confident dancers, who had a tendency to be "on" most of the time, were getting the lion's share of Bennett's attention and being given more to do. This proved frustrating for some of the less aggressive people in the cast, like Rick Mason and Trish Garland, who saw their roles taking longer to come into focus, or even shrinking. Significantly, in the finished script of the show Zach cautions Bobby not to "do a routine" and warns Sheila not to "perform." So it was clear that Bennett demanded and expected honesty and realness. The dancers who could provide this and continue to deliver energy and ideas day after day inevitably started to move to the forefront. And far from discouraging competitive behavior, Bennett encouraged it, in ways both subtle and otherwise. For a while, once the audition framework of the musical had been established, he would end each day's rehearsal by acting out the final eliminations scene—as an improvisation. Each day he chose different dancers—rewarding, most thought, the actors he felt had done the best work that day by "casting" them in the show. In short, he made sure that, on some level, they all felt like they were auditioning every day, and at times they literally feared for their jobs. If this wasn't always healthy for their cast morale or self-esteem, it did ensure that the developing show sustained the necessary tension and undercurrent of desperation.

Staying Afloat

There was another kind of pressure weighing on the dancers as well: financial. Unable to make ends meet on a hundred dollars a week, some of them squeezed in work on industrial shows or commercials—if they were lucky enough to book any. A few were in other shows at the time: Wayne Cilento was performing on Broadway eight times a week in *Irene*, and Priscilla Lopez stayed with the hit *Pippin* for a while; Ron Kuhlman was acting in an Off-Off-Broadway play called *It Pays to Advertise*. If these projects helped pay the bills, they also added to the increasing level of exhaustion the dancers experienced. But they were young and excited about what they were doing, so they mostly managed to stick it out and even thrive under the pressure.

Making Scenes

Though working with their actors mostly on monologues or question-and-answer sessions with "the Voice," Bennett, Avian, and Dante also explored the possibility of interactive scenes between sets of two or three characters. Most of these were eventually cut. But in the earliest scripts there were brief exchanges between Donna McKechnie and Kelly Bishop, sitting on folding chairs and commenting, sometimes caustically, on the overly enthusiastic younger dancers. There was also a fight scene that broke out between a very masculine, married character they had begun calling Al and the openly gay Greg, based on a story from Christopher Chadman's experience at the High School of Performing Arts. This was certainly nothing like anything in the final script. But the point is that there was plenty of time to explore, and finding out what didn't work was just as important as discovering what did. Always in search of honesty and verisimilitude, Bennett felt the writers couldn't approach the scenes until he had experimented with them in rehearsal; Ken Mandelbaum quotes him as having said: "I had to 'dummy' chunks of the show on people before the writers could write it."

"Eliminating down"

Some of the performers had a lot more material than they ultimately ended up with. Ron Kuhlman, whose role of Don Kerr is one of the smallest in the finished show, was one of the few cast members who thought of himself primarily as an actor. Like the others in the cast who hadn't taken part in the tape sessions, he was asked to stand up on the first day and talk about his life. Though he had enjoyed ballroom dancing in high school, he hadn't started studying dance seriously until college, and even then hadn't really thought of it as a career. So he was a bit intimidated by the much more accomplished dancers in the group and had to work extra hard to keep up; he later said that Robert LuPone reached out to him and helped him with his turns, and the two soon bonded as friends. As an actor, though, Kuhlman was much more confident. He was given a long monologue that was culled mainly from the stories dancer Andy Bew had told at the tape sessions (Bew wasn't cast in the workshop), and since the two had similar backgrounds, Kuhlman found it easy to relate to. It included the harrowing story of Bew's mother's death by drowning in a boating accident, which for a while was a dramatic sequence that rivaled Sammy Williams's monologue in intensity.

In addition, there was an early attempt to pair Kuhlman's Don with Kelly Bishop's Sheila as a sexy, comic couple. The writing team was aware of the often successful device, employed in many musicals, of having two central couples: one romantic and one comic. At this point in the development of the show, the characters of Cassie and Zach had not been defined, so quite a bit of time was spent on Al and Kristine (at that point a relatively serious pair) and the more comedic Sheila and Don. Don was supposed to have previously had an affair with Sheila; much sexy byplay ensued when, now married to someone else, he found himself unexpectedly reunited with her at the audition. Kuhlman and Bishop enjoyed the interaction, and Kuhlman was disappointed later when this relationship and much of his other material was cut. However, he proved a good sport who understood the needs of the developing show and was able to see the big picture; he made himself focus on the dancing, which he came to enjoy more and more, and ultimately felt thankful to be part of a great show, however small his own role may have become.

"Oh, and send Paul in . . ."

Sammy Williams experienced frustration of a different sort. He had left the road company of Bennett's *Seesaw* to take part in the workshop, but had danced so enthusiastically in his last performance of that show that he had seriously injured his back. To his great dismay, he was unable to dance at all during the workshop. He had Nick Dante's powerful monologue to work on, but Bennett kept that on the back burner for a long time; as he waited for his chance to rehearse, Williams felt a mounting pressure and apprehension similar to what Paul goes through in the first half of the show ("What am I gonna say when he calls on me?").

On one of the last days of the workshop, Bennett did something that has come to be known as one of the quintessential legends in the saga of *A Chorus Line*. After confiding his intentions only to Avian and the stage manager, he began rehearsing a choreographic routine with the cast, dancing full out. After a few minutes, he twisted his leg and went down to the floor, howling in pain. Because an injury can be devastating to a dancer, the cast immediately panicked, and a variety of different reactions ensued. A few of the more experienced gypsies moved in to help; the younger and less confident ones backed away in fear. Some froze in confusion, others made suggestions or offered to call doctors. After a few minutes, Bennett stood up, unharmed, and asked all of them to remember exactly how they had felt and what they had done at the moment of crisis. He was planning a scene where a dancer would be injured (eventually it was decided that it would be Paul), and he had felt this was the only way to get his cast of mostly inexperienced actors to play the moment believably. Some of the dancers cried in relief, others were furious; Baayork Lee, usually one of the director's staunchest supporters, screamed at him and sobbed, feeling manipulated and betrayed by the deception. But, as with so

Paul's accident at the Olney Theatre, 2013, with Bryan Knowlton as Paul and
Carl Randolph as Zach.   *Photo by Sonie Mathew*

many of the other tactics he had used throughout the workshop, Bennett had
gotten the artistic result he wanted and seemed never to question whether the end
justified the means. (Years later, Ron Kuhlman admitted with some irony that he
had suspected almost immediately that the injury was a ruse, since Bennett was no
great shakes as an actor.)

A Visit from the Producer

Throughout the first workshop period, which lasted over six weeks, producer
Joseph Papp had given Bennett and his team complete freedom, never interfering with the work and seldom watching. But as Papp was the one providing the
resources, Bennett knew he would eventually have to show him some results. On
the last day, the company ran through all the material they had developed so
far, which included only a couple of songs, an extensive "Dance Combination"
sequence with group and solo sections, a few short scenes, and an endless series
of mostly serious, angst-ridden monologues. Bennett jokingly referred to this
run-through as "The Towering Inferno"—a reference to a popular disaster movie
of the time—because all the characters seemed to be trying desperately to escape
from the turmoil of their lives. Nevertheless, even in this early, inchoate form, the
honesty and energy of the work were compelling; something fresh and original
was happening. Papp told Bennett it was "interesting," and gave him the green
light to continue. Another workshop would probably be scheduled, but Bennett
had other commitments, and the work-in-progress would go on hiatus for several
months. Whether the performers could all stay committed to the project remained
to be seen.

7

"Changes, Oh!"

The Second Workshop

A fter the first workshop ended in late September 1974, the project went on hiatus for over three months. Michael Bennett and his creative team, as well as most of the dancers, were eager to continue the work they had found so exciting, but there were several reasons to take a break.

The Hiatus

First, Bennett was committed to a completely separate project: directing Neil Simon's play *God's Favorite* on Broadway. Second, the creative team needed some time to digest what had been learned in the first workshop and use it to generate more songs and a new script. The run-through of the piece at the end of September had been mostly monologues, short scenes, and dances, with minimal music: there was an early version of the opening number, originally called "Résumé," plus "I Can Do That" and "At the Ballet"—but the piece as it then stood was far from a full-fledged musical, and many more songs would have to be written.

In addition, Bennett decided he needed to bring in another book writer—something he had initially warned Nicholas Dante of as a possibility. Though the "Paul" monologue, based closely on Dante's life and enacted by Sammy Williams, was already seen as an emotional cornerstone of the developing show, and Dante had worked hard transcribing the tapes and attempting to distill the material, he was not an experienced enough writer to shape a libretto on his own. Marvin Hamlisch reportedly pushed to have a more experienced writer brought on board. After the first workshop ended, Dante took a performing job as a backup dancer in Cyd Charisse's nightclub act in Las Vegas. (Paul's monologue includes a line about how, as a young fan of movie musicals who would imitate the choreography, he was "always being Cyd Charisse.") He tried to work on the script while he was in Vegas, but feared he wasn't accomplishing much.

A New Collaborator

The writer Bennett chose to join the team was James Kirkwood, whom he ran into at a preview performance of *God's Favorite*. Kirkwood was initially apprehensive about working with a collaborator, and Dante didn't appreciate the way Bennett told him Kirkwood would be joining the team: he informed him bluntly over the phone and then immediately hung up. Some people thought Bennett would have been happy to replace Dante entirely, but kept him on the team because he didn't want to lose the Paul monologue or some of the other ideas Dante had already contributed. (It's probably significant that the program credits would ultimately say "Book by James Kirkwood and Nicholas Dante," with Kirkwood billed first; alphabetically, it would have been the other way around. Kirkwood, like Hamlisch, also asked for a percentage point on the royalties; Dante later claimed Kirkwood made twice the money that he himself made on the show.)

Despite their initial apprehensions, the two writers ended up hitting it off immediately. This was in large part due to the fact that Dante was already a fan of Kirkwood's work; at their first meeting, he told him his novel *Good Times/Bad Times* was one of his favorite books. Dante was later quoted in Kenneth Turan's history of the Public Theater: "Actually, I think I was sort of relieved that they had brought in Jimmy. It did me a big favor because it took all the pressure off me. In the whole month's hiatus, I was so stuck, I didn't write a word, and I was just terrified that I had let Michael down." The two writers found they enjoyed working together. As quoted in Ken Mandelbaum's book, Kirkwood said: "Nick and I worked separately and together. Sometimes he would do a draft and I would go over it. Sometimes the two of us would sit in a room, and one would pace, the other type, then we'd reverse positions. We played 'What if?' a lot . . . . The only arguments we ever had were about punctuation." Kirkwood said he never listened to the famous tapes and found the transcripts he was given hard to read, as they didn't include names or even identify the sex of each speaker. After the second workshop got underway, he conducted his own informal interviews with some of the cast members.

"I Need a Job"

Dante was not the only member of the team who had taken out-of-town work over the hiatus. Though the dancers were eager for the next phase in the development of their project, they had been working for only a hundred dollars a week, and most of them needed immediate income. Pamela Blair did the best, getting the part of Curly's Wife in a major revival of the John Steinbeck classic *Of Mice and Men*; it marked her debut on Broadway as a serious actress and substantially raised her profile in the industry. Cameron Mason also did a show in New York, playing Bobby in a revival of the musical *The Boy Friend* at the Equity Library Theatre. Baayork Lee had apparently made a strong impression on producer Joseph Papp during the first workshop, as he hired her to choreograph two shows during the hiatus: a revival of David Rabe's play *In the Boom Boom Room*, which was about a go-go dancer, and a new musical entitled *Apple Pie*. Like Dante, Marvin Hamlisch and Thommie Walsh traveled to Las Vegas, where both worked on Ann-Margret's show at the Hilton Hotel, Hamlisch as music director and Walsh as a lead dancer. Donna McKechnie and Robert LuPone both acted in plays at regional theatres, and Ron Kuhlman did several shows at a dinner theatre in Pennsylvania.

The most problematic of the dancers' new jobs turned out to be Kelly Bishop's. She had felt very much committed to the project during the first workshop and

Pamela Blair (Val) demonstrates her assets in "Dance: Ten; Looks: Three"; original Broadway cast, 1975.   *Photo by Martha Swope; Photofest*

hoped it would continue. Attempting to stay available, she remained in New York and did industrial shows for a while. But her bank account was dwindling by the time she was offered the role of Helen in the national tour of the musical *Irene*. It was a show she admittedly disliked, but because she had no idea when Bennett's workshop would start up again, or whether the money needed for it would be raised, she accepted the role and signed a contract for the tour. This resulted in her spending Christmas alone with her dog in a hotel in Denver. When Bennett chose a date to begin the second workshop, he called the producers of the tour and ultimately managed to buy her out of her contract. Bishop happily returned to New York.

During the break, Hamlisch and Kleban accomplished substantial work on the score, turning out early versions of both "Nothing" and "Dance: Ten; Looks: Three." And on New Year's Eve, Renee Baughman, who was feeling frustrated working as an office temp, called Bennett: she was desperate to find out when the project might resume. To assure her that all would be well, he played her, over the phone, a tape of the two songwriters performing "Sing!"—the number they had written for her. This gave her confidence that the show was really going to happen and that her place in it was secure.

Finally, Bennett was able to announce that the second workshop would begin in late January 1975 and began the task of tracking down all of the cast members. (Not as easy as it sounds, since this was before the days of cell phones and e-mail, and some of them were far afield.) Most were eager to drop whatever it was they were doing and return to the Public Theater. However, there would be a couple of defections, and once again this was due partly to another show that was shaping up as the big musical of the coming Broadway season: Bob Fosse's production of *Chicago*. Candy Brown, who had been playing a character named Angel in Bennett's workshop, accepted a role when Fosse offered it.

In order to replace her, and add some new dancers to the lineup, Bennett held auditions in January. Word of the excitement generated by the first workshop had traveled fast, and hundreds of dancers showed up, hoping to get involved in the developing project.

Adding to the Cast

Bennett used these auditions for another purpose as well. During the first workshop, several people had questioned whether it was believable that a director at an audition would ask dancers such personal questions, and how they would really respond if he did. (This is a criticism that is occasionally leveled at *A Chorus Line* even today.) So Bennett decided to experiment by running this new round of auditions much like the one in the show, asking the dancers questions similar to those the original group had answered on the tapes. The results reassured him that the scenario was plausible. Also, the writers were present at these auditions and took copious notes, both on the overall atmosphere and energy in the room and the behavior of the participants, which were later useful in developing the script and score.

As Angel, Candy Brown had been the only African American performer in the first workshop, and Bennett hoped to find another to take her place. What he hadn't expected was that the one to capture his attention would be Ronald Dennis; he had auditioned for Bennett before, but they had never worked together. Bennett saw in him the key qualities of the character Brown had been developing: an upbeat, high-energy dancer from a happy, middle-class background. He decided there was no reason the role couldn't be changed to a male one: thus, Angel became Richie. Dennis had an attitude about his life and work that set him apart from most of the other dancers; as he later said to Denny Martin Flinn: "Some of the people at that last callback really laid out some heavy stories about the hurt of studying dance and all that, and I felt too much joy dancing to care about all that other bullshit."

Bennett decided he also wanted to add a more mature dancer to the lineup and called a performer he had known for many years: Michel Stuart. Stuart hadn't been on Broadway for nine years and considered himself retired as a dancer; he was switching his focus to writing and producing. But he later recalled his response when Bennett phoned him about the auditions, as quoted in *On the Line*: "Michael, we both did West Side Story in the fifties, we both turned down Hair in the sixties. I know this is going to be the show of the seventies and I will be there tomorrow morning." (It's a great quote, whether or not he was being precisely accurate.) Stuart would create the role of Gregory Gardner.

Because it was clear by the end of the first workshop that "At the Ballet" was going to be a highlight of the show, finding a new actress to sing that song with Kelly Bishop and Jane Robertson was important. The recollections sung by the character Maggie were based on the childhood of Donna McKechnie, but now

Bennett was thinking in terms of a new character for her to play, and Maggie was to be passed on to another performer. Bennett remembered seeing Kay Cole, a petite dancer with a large, wide-ranging voice, in a Broadway revue called *Words and Music*; he requested an audition through her agent. In a show cast primarily with dancers who had some singing ability, Cole's superb voice stood out; Hamlisch would tailor the song to highlight her individual range and talents.

The role of the director was still very nebulous at this point. During the first workshop, there was no one cast in the part; the team had experimented with a concept whereby "the Voice" was unheard by the audience; only the dancers could hear him, and only their responses would help the audience understand what he had supposedly said. They would wait a few beats in silence between their lines, imagining what he was saying and then responding—but this soon proved awkward. At other times, Bennett himself had been playing the part, which came naturally since he was the actual director of the show. But now he knew it was time to bring in an actor. The choice would be a key one, as the director would be the prime authority figure in the show; his energy would have to drive it and keep it focused.

Robert LuPone, who had been playing the role of the married dancer Al in the workshop, coveted the part of the director and was frustrated when he learned that Bennett would be hiring an outsider to take on the role. For a while, the young Christopher Walken was the front-runner. Unbeknownst to many of his fans, the actor, who later became a major film star, had been trained as a dancer; he had also been friends with Marvin Hamlisch since high school. Actor Chris Sarandon was also considered seriously, but ultimately the team felt he didn't have enough of a dance background. They offered the role to Barry Bostwick, a tall and charismatic actor who was being touted as an up-and-coming star after recent acclaimed appearances as Danny Zuko in the original Broadway cast of *Grease* and Brad Majors in the cult film *The Rocky Horror Picture Show*. He was in enough demand that his agreeing to do a workshop for a hundred dollars a week was perhaps unexpected, but he was highly intrigued by the project. He did, however, enter into it with two provisos: He had to be free to leave if the part didn't develop into a large one, and he wanted to be in on all of the production meetings. There were two reasons for this second request. First, he had an interest in becoming a producer and had a couple projects he was already developing, so he was eager to learn about the process of putting a show together. Second, he knew the role of the director was to be to some extent based on Michael Bennett himself, and he thought observing the director/choreographer at work would give him valuable clues for use in building the character.

With Bostwick in place as the director, now being called "Zach," and Ronald Dennis, Kay Cole, and Michel Stuart joining the line as Richie, Maggie, and Greg, Bennett still had a few more spots to fill. With the prospect of an actual production now looming, he realized he would need a small group of dancers who, between them, could understudy all the characters. And because the show was about an audition, certain dancers would have to be eliminated early in the evening. To fulfill both of these needs, he hired a group that included Michael Serrecchia, Chuck Cissel, Crissy Wilzak, Carolyn Kirsch, Nancy Lane, Donna Drake, and Don Percassi (a couple more would be added by the time the show opened).

After the workshop had gotten under way, Percassi found himself playing the role of Larry, the assistant choreographer, in addition to understudying a couple of the dancers on the line. This was because of one final defection to *Chicago*. Tony Stevens, who with Bennett and Michon Peacock had initiated the original tape sessions, had been a part of the first workshop, playing the small role of Larry. He began the second workshop but soon received a call from Bob Fosse, offering him a job as his assistant on *Chicago*. Serious about pursuing a career as a choreographer, Stevens decided he would rather be an assistant choreographer on a Broadway show than play one in an Off-Broadway show, so he departed with Bennett's blessing.

It's natural to wonder whether any of the dancers who left the project had second thoughts, given the tremendous success the show went on to achieve—particularly in Stevens's case, as he had been one of the originators of the whole undertaking. Years later, he told Denny Martin Flinn: "I knew that whether I was there or not it didn't make much of a difference. I knew I would share in the experience whether I was onstage or not, because it was my life. I don't have any regrets about leaving." A dancer named Leland Schwantes was hired as his replacement, but only briefly, as unexpected developments would soon lead to more shuffling of the cast.

Back to Work

On the first day of the second workshop, in the last week of January 1975, the cast assembled to read the revised script. Dante and Kirkwood had done some good work, and a couple of new songs had been added, but the reading lasted four hours. Because the material was drawn from their own lives, the dancers took it very seriously, and the play was sorely lacking in humor. It was clear the team members had their work cut out for them.

In keeping with the structure of the show and the precedent set by the original tape sessions, this first rehearsal continued with the actors getting up one by one and speaking to the group. The new cast members and understudies introduced themselves and talked about their lives and why they had become dancers. And those returning from the hiatus were asked to speak about what they had done with their time off. This resulted in an important breakthrough for Trish Garland. Garland had almost not returned to the project; during the first workshop, she had felt intimidated and overshadowed by the more aggressive personalities in the group, and her character had not gelled. Though Bennett had invited her back, he had told her that her role was likely to be small and that the choice of whether or not to return was hers. As compared to Kelly Bishop, for example, for whom Bennett had gone to the trouble and expense of buying out a contract in order to keep her in the show, Garland did not feel particularly wanted, and she wasn't sure how much she was contributing to the project. Still a devoted Buddhist, however, she had once again turned to chanting and meditation to regain her focus, supported by fellow Buddhist friends like Baughman, Dante, and Michon Peacock, and she credits this with the ability she found to turn her situation around. When she spoke to the group that first day back, she told a story about the holiday trip she and her boyfriend had taken to Morocco. They had come up with the idea of making some money by selling American blue jeans, which were a scarce commodity over there. But she had been unaware of the strict codes of conduct followed by women in that culture, and her aggressive salesmanship and relatively immodest attire resulted in some comically awkward encounters with Moroccan men, including one who seemed to be mistaking her for a prostitute. Garland had a great time telling the outrageous story, and the group laughed uproariously. When she finished, Bennett was grinning broadly; he could tell Garland had found her voice and established her unique place in the cast. From that point on, the role of Judy Turner began to grow, and Bennett would sometimes assign her comedic lines the other actors had failed to make work, confident that she could bring out the humor.

"Jane Robertson Out; Nancy Lane In"

Work seemed to be progressing well when Jane Robertson made a surprise announcement: she was leaving the cast. She wasn't happy with the way her character, Bebe Nichols, was developing. Resenting the fact that some of the other performers were continually being given more to do, Robertson believed that she could have done just as well with their material but that Bennett wasn't giving her a chance. She later said it might have been different if she had been able to leave the stage and go to her dressing room during their scenes, but found the developing structure of the show, which had the whole group standing on line most of the night listening to each other's stories, was oppressive and added to her frustration. She might have stuck it out, though, except for the fact that an Off-Broadway musical she had been developing for a while with a group of her friends, entitled *A Matter of Time*, was finally going into production. Bennett was angry, as he had so carefully been grooming the mosaic of personalities that made up the line and hated to lose one of them. Leland Schwantes, who had only recently been asked to take over the role of Larry, also left to take part in *A Matter of Time*; Bennett took his defection better, since Schwantes, unlike Robertson, had warned him of the possibility when he first came on board, and because Larry is not part of the line and would not be as tricky to replace.

To fill the newly available roles, Bennett turned to two of the understudies, giving Don Percassi the Larry part and assenting to Nancy Lane's request that she be allowed to audition for Bebe, one of the two roles she had been hired to understudy. Lane had an appealing, self-effacing sense of humor and managed to win Bennett over. The youngest person in the cast at twenty-four, she became the new Bebe, and the character's last name was changed from Nichols to Benzenheimer. She was soon providing some of the humor the show had been lacking so far. Carole Schweid, who like Lane was a brunette from New Jersey, replaced her as the understudy for Bebe and Diana.

The returning cast members had grown insular to some degree, and the newcomers didn't all find it easy to fit in. There were two main cliques in the group.

One was the Buddhist group, led by Garland, Baughman, and Dante. Then there was an in-group of experienced gypsies who all lived on the Upper West Side and would hang out together after rehearsal at a 76th Street restaurant called Dobson's: the mainstays were Priscilla Lopez, Kelly Bishop, and Thommie Walsh. They were outspoken and opinionated, which made some of the other dancers feel intimidated. Cameron Mason and Nancy Lane, playing Mark and Bebe—the two youngest characters in the show—felt like outsiders at times, with Lane especially disappointed that her attempts at befriending some of the other women were not reciprocated. She also knew that some of this was Bennett's doing. He wanted Bebe, the newcomer to Broadway, to feel like an outsider eager to fit in, so he used his influence to keep her separate from the group.

"Too Good for the Chorus"

Another cast member who felt isolated to some degree was Donna McKechnie, Bennett's favorite, who was now incurring the kind of resentment that is often directed at teacher's pets. The other dancers knew Bennett was grooming her for special things and that she would ultimately have a solo dance number. They also knew that, as a spectacular dancer and singular talent, she deserved it. But her new character of Cassie, the formerly featured performer trying to return to the chorus after a failed attempt at an acting career in California, was slow to come together—both in the writing and in the choreography. For some time, Kirkwood and Dante struggled with the parameters of her relationship with director Zach. Though Bennett and McKechnie often spent time together socially, he made sure they did so alone or with Avian and not in company with the other dancers. Moreover, he did nothing to dispel the others' resentments of her, determined as he was to establish and maintain Cassie's identity as a figure apart from the group.

The Director and His Alter Ego

Though Bennett could at times be a benevolent father figure, nurturing his actors and encouraging them to open up more and more, he could also turn on a dime and become a dictator, sometimes blowing up unexpectedly. So the dancers felt continually on edge, as if they were being judged and could at any moment be found wanting. Unbeknownst to them, however, there was someone who was making Bennett feel the same way, and that person was Barry Bostwick. In attempting to understand the character of Zach, Bostwick observed his real director closely. Before long, this started to make Bennett uncomfortable, as he felt Bostwick was second guessing his directing and judging his methods. (To some extent, this was true: Bostwick later said he thought a great deal of time was being wasted in the sessions.) But the actor's real reason for scrutinizing Bennett so intently, as he later told Denny Martin Flinn, was to "fathom out the heart of that character." He also understandably expected that, as the leading male character in a musical, he would get at least one song to sing, and for a while he waited patiently for it to materialize. Marvin Hamlisch told him he was working on it and that Zach would eventually have a moment alone on stage, a soul-searching number following the scene of Paul's accident. But the song never appeared. Still, the actor longed for a chance to give the audience a glimpse of Zach's humanity and inner life. He himself was naturally empathetic, and there were times in rehearsal when he would tear up in response to one or another of the dancers' gut-wrenching revelations. Whenever this happened, Bennett would impatiently shut him down. His position was that Zach needed to remain detached and objective at all times, serving as a catalyst for the emotional epiphanies of the others but never allowing himself to lose his icy self-control. If Zach got emotional, Bennett reasoned, his manipulation of the dancers would start to seem sadistic rather than professional.

After a month of this, it became clear that the role wasn't working out for Bostwick. Neither of his original two conditions for staying with the project had been met, and his relationship with Bennett, despite the efforts of both men to make it work, had become something of a clash of egos. They mutually and amicably decided that it was time for Bostwick to leave the company.

For a few days, Bennett played the role, as he had during the first workshop, but clearly a replacement had to be engaged. Robert LuPone, who had coveted the role in the first place, saw a possible chance and asked Bennett for an audition, which took place at the director's apartment on 55th Street. Bennett agreed to let him try the role, but continued to play it himself for a couple more days, with LuPone watching. When the actor finally began to rehearse the part, he was frustrated by the lack of feedback he received from the director. Bennett's silence was probably part of the same issue that had troubled Bostwick: his fundamental unwillingness to grapple with some of the darker parts of his own character as he saw them reflected in the character of Zach—and, now, in LuPone's performance.

At the time, LuPone wasn't really aware of this, or of how much his performance was thus discomfiting Bennett. But the two of them had enjoyed a warm relationship when LuPone was playing Al, and now it started to sour. The tension continued throughout the workshop and the rehearsal process, and erupted most vehemently after one preview performance at the Public at which LuPone had decided to try playing Zach with overtly gay mannerisms. Bennett was so angry that he nearly attacked the actor physically after the show, and might have had Bob Avian not intervened; he barely spoke to LuPone for a couple of weeks after that. The actor has since referred to his and Bennett's relationship as "absolute war."

Final Additions to the Cast

Scott Allen, a young actor who was a good friend of Nick Dante's, was invited in to audition to be the new Al. As he was the first to admit, he was more a singer than a dancer, but Bennett liked his audition and hired him. After about a week of work, though, it became clear that he was having serious trouble keeping up with the other dancers. The solution Bennett came up with was to have him switch places with his cover: Allen would join the ranks of the understudies who danced in the opening number, and his place as Al would be taken by Don Percassi. Percassi was a very experienced hoofer with a strong voice and a great laugh; his good humor and the joy he felt in being part of the show were infectious, and he became a morale booster whose energy proved very welcome. He later said he was glad he had joined the cast so late in the process and thus wasn't called on to bare his soul in interviews as the other dancers had done; he claimed he had had a very happy childhood and had no sob stories to tell. His easygoing persona was a far cry from the angry, macho character LuPone had been developing as Al. The first time Percassi attempted the fight scene between Al and Greg, the rest of the dancers laughed, and it was clear the scene had to be cut. But Percassi brought his own brand of charm and charisma to the role, and Al began to reemerge as a different but very effective character.

One more piece of recasting remained. With Percassi now playing Al, the small role of Larry, the assistant choreographer, was available yet again. Unexpectedly, Bennett ran into Clive Clerk at a party at James Kirkwood's home, celebrating the out-of-town opening of the latter's play *P.S. Your Cat is Dead!* (which was soon to move to Broadway). Clerk and Bennett had worked together

It was during the second workshop that "Sing!" became a duet for Al and Kristine. Shown here in the roles are Venny Carranza and Theresa Murray at Musical Theatre West, 2012. Tory Trowbridge as Val is at right.

Photo by Ken Jacques

in Toronto as teenagers, after which Clerk had moved to Los Angeles and given up dancing for an acting career, finding some success on TV and in the movies. Ultimately disillusioned with that world, he had recently decided to return to New York and attend art school. But he had already heard about Bennett's dancer project and thought it sounded intriguing, so when Bennett invited him to attend a rehearsal, he jumped at the chance.

Clerk came down to the studio and watched the cast work on the opening number. He found the dancing and the music and the energy of it thrilling and began to realize how much he missed dancing. The show was clearly something he would love to be a part of—and since it was in New York, he thought he wouldn't have to quit art school to do it. Bennett offered him the role without an audition, and Clerk happily accepted, though not without surprise that Bennett assumed he could still dance. But he was a gym regular, and it was obvious he was in great shape. In fact, his exceptional beauty of face and body became a source of consternation and envy from several of the other cast members; that and the fact that he was not part of the dance world led to a few of them giving him the cold shoulder for a while. But others welcomed him, and he was soon a well-liked presence in the group. He had long ago given up any ambition for a Broadway career, so he didn't mind the small size of the role; just being a part of the extraordinary project felt like a gift to him, and like Percassi, he became a source of positive energy.

The open male understudy position was given to Brandt Edwards, who would cover the roles of Don and Mark. He turned out to be the last hire: the cast that would open *A Chorus Line* at the Public Theater had now been fully assembled. When the workshop was extended another few weeks, Bennett knew that any more changes in personnel could be damaging, so the dancers were all put on contract. If anyone still doubted it, this made it clear that the project was really headed for an opening and an audience.

"Think about your life, Pippin"

Two more key members of the music team came on board during this workshop as well: Don Pippin and Fran Liebergall. Pippin was hired as music director/vocal arranger and Liebergall at first as rehearsal pianist; she would later take on the titles of dance arranger (along with Robert Thomas) and musical supervisor. Pippin and Liebergall ended up making important contributions to the show and would be instrumental in maintaining it over the years.

"Time to doubt, to break out"

By now, Hamlisch and Kleban had hit their stride, and the score was coming together more quickly. The single biggest musical sequence in the show was the Montage, now entitled "Hello Twelve, Hello Thirteen, Hello Love." It took a long time to develop, but the idea for it was originally suggested by Nick Dante; in retrospect, many consider it to be his most valuable contribution to the show, outside of Paul's story. The line now comprised seventeen dancers, and the team was becoming aware that the show would take on an oppressively monotonous rhythm if each of them had a self-contained monologue. As Dante later told Ken Mandelbaum: "I said, 'Remember at the tapes, how when somebody would start talking, it would trigger you off on a whole train of thought? Suppose we have a scene where people are talking, then we go into pantomime as others start associating.'" He knew the lighting would be key to making it work, and Tharon Musser would prove more than up to the challenge.

For a while, Baayork Lee and Ronald Dennis, as Connie and Richie, had a duet called "Confidence," about the unique experience of minority performers auditioning for a predominantly white musical. Though it included some clever and perceptive lyrics, the song was ultimately deemed too cute for the show and was cut. For a while the two performers didn't know what the writers would come up with to replace it and had little to do in the show; Lee was philosophical about it, as she still believed her contribution as assistant choreographer was more important than her onstage role, but Dennis was more worried. Finally, he got the "Gimme the Ball" section of the Montage. In an interview much later, Dennis revealed that the short number isn't really Hamlisch's: Bennett and drummer Robert Thomas came up with a general concept and rhythm, and then gave it to Dennis himself to take home; he came up with the melody, in an Aretha Franklin–type vocal style. Combined with his high-energy, athletic dancing, it emerged as the climax of the whole Montage and remains Richie's big moment in the show.

The song "Nothing" was a favorite of Ed Kleban's and initially seemed to be working well. It was taken very directly from Priscilla Lopez's experience at the High School of Performing Arts, as she had related it at the first tape session. But somehow, during the second workshop, the number started to flounder, and was threatened with being cut. Kleban believed that the theme of the song, about the way an insensitive teacher can damage a vulnerable young performer, was an important part of the show's message—and he thought the bluntly honest ending, where Diana says she felt nothing when she heard of the teacher's death, was devastatingly true. Bennett had come up with a rather elaborate staging for the song, with the other dancers playing students in the acting class, imitating bobsledders, sports cars, and so forth, and Lopez's performance had grown proportionately bigger as well. Intent on saving the number, Kleban asked for a session alone with Lopez. They went into a room, and he worked with her on simplifying it and getting back to the honest impulse that had inspired the song in the first place. Bennett was pleased with the result, and after Don Pippin convinced him to axe the cute choreography and give Lopez the stage to herself, the effective solo number we know today came together.

"Gimme the ball. Yeah!" American actor James T. Lane played Richie in both the 2006 Broadway revival and the London production (shown here) seven years later.   *Photo by Manuel Harlan*

Money Matters

Behind the scenes and on the financial end, serious obstacles were presenting themselves. About halfway through the workshop, Joseph Papp announced that he had no more resources to put behind the project. He went so far as to give Michael Bennett his blessing to take it elsewhere. But the Shakespeare Festival's press agent, Merle Debuskey, and associate producer, Bernard Gersten, were very excited about the show by this point; they believed strongly in it, and they persuaded Papp to stick it out. At one point, Gersten had a meeting with Bennett's agent, Jack Lenny, to try to find a solution to the financial problem. Lenny said he thought he and Bennett could put together $150,000 to keep the production afloat, in exchange for a 50 percent interest in the show. Gersten took the offer back to Papp but advised against taking it, and Papp agreed to come up with the needed cash in order to avoid taking on partners. Given the enormous profits that the musical ended up feeding into the Shakespeare Festival over the next fifteen years, this proved to be a very wise decision indeed. (As the opening approached, Bennett ultimately did end up putting some of his own money into the show; this was a result of a brouhaha that resulted when the mirrors were first delivered to the Newman Theatre. They had been made of inexpensive mylar and distorted the dancers' reflections; Papp wouldn't come up with the money to have them redone in a higher-quality material, so Bennett stepped in. Afterwards, his own company, Plum Productions, was credited as coproducer, and therefore Bennett would earn a larger percentage of the box office.)

Tensions rose again between Bennett and Papp toward the end of the workshop period, when Papp decided he wanted to open the show in the Vivian Beaumont Theatre at Lincoln Center. This was partly a financial decision, as the season's budget for shows in the Public Theater's spaces was tapped out; since Papp was at that time also running the Lincoln Center Theater and finding it much harder to come up with productions that would sell to that audience, he saw an opportunity. This also proved he was feeling a lot of confidence in the project, since the Beaumont's seating capacity is more than three times as large as that at the Newman. However, Bennett was strongly opposed to the move. He described the musical as the quintessential proscenium show; not only had he staged the whole thing with the traditional proscenium stage of the Newman in mind, but *A Chorus Line* actually takes place in a Broadway theatre. The Beaumont had a modified thrust stage that was embraced by a wide, curving audience, sort of halfway between a proscenium and a three-quarter arena configuration. Its sightlines were tricky. (Although subsequent renovations have made it a more hospitable space in the years since, its wide-open configuration remains an unusual challenge for a director.)

Papp was adamant, however, with the result that Bennett took a meeting with Bernard B. Jacobs and Gerald Schoenfeld at the Shubert Organization: the largest producing office on Broadway and one that owns numerous major theatres. He auditioned the show in their office, with Hamlisch and Kleban singing the songs. It proved an awkward affair: Hamlisch later recalled playing the score on an office piano that seemed ancient enough to have been used by Rudolph Friml; it was propped up on broken legs and collapsed the moment he began playing. But the song then entitled "Tits and Ass" was apparently a big hit. Both Jacobs and Schoenfeld were interested enough to promise $50,000 to keep the project alive at the Newman. This was only half of the amount needed, however, so Bennett audaciously took another meeting, this time with James M. Nederlander, who was the Shuberts' main rival as a producing organization on Broadway. Nederlander was prepared to make up the difference, but when the Shuberts found out about this, they came up with the whole $100,000, which they put up in the form of a grant to the New York Shakespeare Festival. This enabled the show to go on at the Newman as Bennett wanted—and also established a relationship with the Shubert Organization that would prove very useful a few months later when it came time to move the show to Broadway.

"The Papp Test"

As the second workshop drew to a close in late February 1975, it was time for Joe Papp and Bernard Gersten to take another look at the show and evaluate what had been accomplished. The company jokingly referred to this run-through as "The Papp Test." Other people were also invited, not just friends but some high-profile people in the industry. Though the show had obviously grown and developed substantially since the end of the first workshop, and had new scenes as well as a lot more songs, it still ran over four hours—twice as long as it needed to be. So much of the company's anxiety was over which sections Papp might tell Bennett to cut. After the run-through, the producer spoke to the cast only briefly and praised their work. In private with Bennett, however, he broke some very bad news: He didn't feel he could put any more money into the project.

No one can say for sure what the precise reasons were for the decision. At that point, the Shakespeare Festival didn't have a cash cow running on Broadway, and its crop of new plays presented downtown at the Public that season had been disappointing. Fund-raising was an ongoing problem, and Papp had already put an unusually large amount of money into the dancer project—which still didn't have an official title. Some people have said they suspected Papp was never really in love with the show: it wasn't really his kind of theatre, and though the raw honesty of the initial tapes had excited him, the developing musical was taking on a high-energy sheen and slickness that moved it further away from the edgy work he liked to support and more in the direction of something that, however innovative in many respects, felt like commercial Broadway.

In his 2013 book *Anything Goes: A History of American Musical Theatre*, Ethan Mordden summed up the difference quite articulately: "Despite its unorthodox incubation and the lack of apparent glamor in its nearly bare stage (there were mirrors against the back wall, used in important ways) and more or less unknown cast, *A Chorus Line* was no off-Broadway musical. Indeed, that very genre, of the campy homages and quirky subject matter, was all but over; by 1975, the 'off-Broadway musical' was simply a Broadway musical having its tryout in another part of town. More important, Michael Bennett—as he would have been quick to tell you—was not an off-Broadway talent. In MGM's *For Me and My Gal*, Judy Garland berates Gene Kelly with 'You'll never make the big time because you're small time in your heart!' Bennett reversed the image: he never did anything small time because he was Big Broadway from top to toe, with all the flash and dazzle that the term 'Broadway musical' conveys."

Despite Papp's wavering, Bennett of course was not about to give up. Since the Shuberts and the Nederlanders had both expressed strong interest, there was a good chance that the musical could go directly to a commercial run. He was afraid some of the actors would jump ship; with their meager salaries discontinued and no guarantee that the show would have a life, they might have to take other jobs. But remarkably, the cast hung together; they had come so far with the show already that they were determined to see it through if humanly possible. And Bernard Gersten was still firmly on the show's side.

Ultimately it was LuEsther Mertz who came to the rescue. As chair of the Board of Directors of the New York Shakespeare Festival, she had given very generously to the theatre over the years—including funding the Broadway transfer of the musical version of *Two Gentlemen of Verona* so that all of its earnings could be used to support the Festival rather than shared with any investors or commercial entities. That strategy had paid off. Mertz had watched the run-through with Papp and Gersten and believed in the show; when Bennett said he would need an additional seven weeks to be ready for an audience, she agreed to donate the money needed to make that happen. It wasn't an investment per se, as she never expected any personal return, but it would prove to be a shrewd move as well as a generous one, with an enormous eventual benefit to the Shakespeare Festival. Throughout the Broadway run, the program said the production was "made possible by a contribution from LuEsther Mertz."

With the funds they needed to continue working, and a first preview date in sight, the cast and creative team launched into a final period of intensive, concentrated work.

8

"Your Stage Name, Real Name if It's Different"

The Characters

With a large cast of characters who are all young, attractive dancers, the original creative team was aware of the danger that they could start to blend together, so they took pains to make sure "the line" was suitably varied. Both the casting decisions and the development of the characters through the workshop process focused on identifying and defining unique personalities—no two of which could be too much alike.

Still, there are enough characters that it can be challenging to keep them all straight the first couple times you see the show; even some critics have been known to confuse the different characters' names, with occasionally embarrassing results. This chapter will take a close look at the nineteen principal characters, including background on which real-life dancers' experiences were utilized and incorporated into their stories, as well as specific requirements, both physical and vocal, for casting each role. This information is intended to be useful both in appreciating the musical and as a set of guidelines for directors casting their own productions—or actors planning to audition for the show.

Zach

Zach is the director/choreographer who drives the action, teaching the dance routine that opens the show and then conducting the auditions/interviews from the back of the theatre, his amplified voice heard through a microphone. We never learn his last name. He is based primarily on Michael Bennett, who directed and choreographed the actual show, although as we have seen, the character departs from Bennett's actual life and personality in some key respects (see Chapters 2 and 7). Zach is coolly professional, usually but not always patient, driven and demanding. As Cassie points out in their confrontation scene, he is devoted almost obsessively to his work, to the exclusion of successful personal relationships. Except for that scene, and the moment where he comforts Paul after the latter's devastating monologue, Zach generally remains emotionally detached and professional. The actor should have a commanding stage presence and a strong, impressive speaking voice, though no solo singing is required. Actors of varying heights and ages have played the role; he is usually seen as being in his thirties or early forties. The element that varies from production to production is how much of a dancer he needs to be. As a choreographer/director, it would be understood that he was once a dancer, and usually dance ability is considered strongly in the casting. Sometimes, however, because of the strong acting required, an actor with limited dance skills is cast. In those cases, the staging has been modified accordingly, even in productions that use the original choreography. If the actor is a strong dancer, he can lead off the ensemble when they do the jazz combination "facing away from the mirror" in the opening number; after that, there is also a mimed moment where he demonstrates one of the most challenging sequences of moves in that combination—the most difficult ensemble routine in the show—in response to a question from Maggie. If a Zach is not a strong dancer, he often steps downstage to watch the opening combination rather than leading it, and some of the demonstrating can be handed off to Larry. Zach also dons the top hat and "One" regalia to sing and dance with the rest of the cast in the finale, where the choreography is less athletically challenging but still demands a substantial degree of precision and control. If the actor can't even handle that, there is an alternate version where he appears only for his bowing entrance near the start of the song and then dances immediately offstage, leaving the rest of the number to the ensemble. The role was created by Robert LuPone, played in the film by Michael Douglas (who didn't dance at all) and in the Broadway revival by Michael Berresse. (When Berresse was succeeded by the popular TV personality Mario Lopez, the staging was modified somewhat to feature him more prominently in the dancing and put him onstage for the first half of the Cassie scene, where he is usually heard but not seen.)

Don Kerr

Don, who holds the position on the stage right end of the line, is the first to introduce himself. He is twenty-six years old and hails from Kansas City. Of all the men on the line, this is the smallest role. The part was originally based on the life story of dancer Andy Bew, who took part in the tape sessions but was not cast in the show, but most of his stories were cut during the workshopping process. What remains is a brief spoken/sung monologue in the Montage sequence about working in a nightclub as a teenager (based on Michael Bennett's own experience) and striking up a friendship, if not an actual affair, with a female stripper. Later in the show, Don reveals that he is married with two children—which actually comes from the life of Wayne Cilento, who played Mike in the show. Don is from the Midwest and generally has wholesome, all-American good looks; the role is usually cast with a tall, athletic dancer. The singing is not extensive, but he should have a pleasant baritone or tenor voice. The role was played originally by Ron Kuhlman, in the film by Blane Savage, and in the revival by Brad Anderson.

Diana (Natalie Cortez), Maggie (Mara Davi), Kristine (Chryssie Whitehead), and Judy (Heather Parcells) do the opening jazz combination in the Broadway revival, 2006.

Photo by Paul Kolnik

Maggie Winslow

Next in line is twenty-five-year-old Maggie, from San Mateo, California. Maggie is one of the more serious, as opposed to comic, female characters in the show. The role also requires one of the best singing voices of the women, as she sings both the gentle, lullaby-like little song about missing her mother in the Montage and the last verse of "At the Ballet," including the famous sustained E, which ideally should be belted. The actress is usually very pretty, with a girl-next-door sweetness and vulnerability. Most of her story is based on the childhood of Donna McKechnie, who played an early version of the character in the first workshop, before the role of Cassie was created. Once the decision was made to move McKechnie to the new character, Maggie was passed on to Kay Cole, who joined the company in the second workshop and originated the role. The part was played in the film by Pam Klinger and in the revival by Mara Davi.

Mike Costa

Mike is twenty-four and comes from an Italian family in Trenton, New Jersey; his real last name is Costafalone. This character has the only male solo number in the show, "I Can Do That," which includes an exuberant dance break. He has a brash, smart-alecky but likable sense of humor and a streetwise confidence, and is generally seen as heterosexual. The song, about discovering his affinity for dance while watching his older sister in class, was based on a story first told by Sammy Williams, who ended up playing the very different role of Paul in the show; Mike's personality developed as a combination of Michael Bennett himself (also from an Italian family) and the actor who originated the role, Wayne Cilento. For casting purposes, Mike should be one of the strongest male dancers in the show; actors with gymnastics skills have often added acrobatic moves to the dance solo. He is usually seen as dark-haired and often, though not always, short of stature. The role was played in the film by Charles McGowan and in the revival by Jeffrey Schecter.

Connie Wong

Connie is from New York's Chinatown, and, though she gets out of telling her age by saying she was born in the Year of the Chicken, she is eventually revealed to be a young-looking thirty-two who can still play a kid because of her diminutive size. That height is specified as "four foot ten" in the Montage, where she sings of her thwarted ambitions to be a cheerleader and a ballerina. Ideally the dancer should be that short, but since the song is a reminiscence of her teenage years, it could be believable that perhaps she ultimately did grow a couple more inches, and slightly taller actresses are sometimes cast. Though she was born in New York and doesn't have an accent, the actress should be Asian American; there are alternate lines in the script for a "Connie McKenzie," but these should only be used in the case of an understudy going on (companies of the show almost never have a second Asian actress to cover the role). The monologue is sung/spoken, so the part does not require a particularly great singer; dance and comedy skills are more important. The character was closely based on the life of the role's originator, Baayork Lee, and was played in the film by Jan Gan Boyd and in the revival by Yuka Takara.

Gregory Gardner

At thirty-two, Greg is the oldest male dancer on the line and probably the most experienced. He is Jewish, from New York, and openly gay, with a dry, jaded sense of humor. There's very little singing, but the actor should have good comic timing and a sophisticated sense of style. The original Greg, Michel Stuart, was relatively short, but very tall dancers have sometimes been cast in the role as well. The character has aspects of Stuart's personality as well as that of the show's associate choreographer, Bob Avian, and some of Christopher Chadman, who took part in the tape sessions. He was played in the film by Justin Ross and in the revival by Michael Paternostro.

Cassie Ferguson

Cassie doesn't give a full introduction like the other characters, instead asking to speak to Zach privately; he tells her he doesn't have time. So she never says her last

Tommy Berklund took over the part of Greg during the run of the Broadway revival; he is seen here in his first assumption of the role, at the University of Michigan in 2004.

Photo courtesy U-M School of Music, Theatre & Dance, Department of Musical Theatre

name, and it doesn't appear anywhere in the libretto, but show insiders know it to be Ferguson. She also doesn't tell her age, but Zach later reveals it to be thirty-two, making her one of the oldest characters on the line along with Connie and Greg. (The age reference has sometimes been deleted when a more mature actress plays the role.) Cassie broke out of the chorus as a featured dancer, stopping the show with dance solos in two previous musicals; she tried for an acting career in Hollywood and is now back in New York looking for work. The character is based partly on the story of Judy West, a dancer Bennett knew, with substantial elements inspired by the life and personality of Donna McKechnie, who originated the role. (Some of the parallels to McKechnie's story, such as Cassie's romantic relationship with the director, actually postdate the premiere of the show, as life in some respects came to imitate art.) Aspects of the troubled Zach/Cassie relationship were inspired by Bennett's past relationships with dancers Leland Palmer and Larry Fuller. Cassie is usually of average height or taller and should be an elegant beauty. The acting, singing, and dancing demands are extraordinary. The role calls for great emotional honesty and vulnerability. Her number, "The Music and the Mirror," includes one of the longest and most demanding solo dance sequences in musical theatre, requiring a dancer of enormous passion, style, star presence—and sheer stamina. The singing is also sustained and lyrical, although the song has been transposed into several different keys to suit individual actresses. Cassie was played in the film by Alyson Reed and in the revival by Charlotte d'Amboise.

Sheila Bryant

From Colorado Springs, Sheila is twenty-nine and claims she is glad to be approaching thirty, though she knows her days as a chorus dancer are numbered. (Broadway dancers have longer careers now than they did in the 1970s, when they generally weren't considered employable past their early thirties.) This is one of the great acting roles in the show, much coveted by performers, as Sheila has a caustic wit and a brazenly outspoken personality; she says things everyone wishes they could say at an audition but would never dare to. Though tough, she has a vulnerable side, and she is honest enough to let it show at key moments. The role was created by Kelly Bishop, who had a low, throaty voice; her solo in "At the Ballet" is in the alto register. The character is closely based on Bishop, though she has said she incorporated aspects of four other dancers she had worked with, and some of her best laugh lines were famously written by an uncredited Neil Simon (see Chapter 12). The role is almost always played by a relatively tall, statuesque dancer, and she needs to be quite shapely: the traditional Sheila costume, a tight, shiny flesh-colored leotard, conceals nothing, and the dialogue indicates that she is more curvaceous than Val, who had her figure surgically enhanced. The part was played in the film by Vicki Frederick who, like Bishop, was white, but occasionally has been cast with African American dancers, including Deidre Goodwin, who played it in the Broadway revival.

Bobby Mills

Like Michael Bennett, Bobby hails from Buffalo, New York—where to commit suicide "is redundant." He is twenty-five. In a comic monologue that resembles a stand-up routine more than Zach would like, Bobby tells tales of his outrageous escapades as a "strange" youngster who was a misfit in school. (Though Greg and Paul are the only characters in the show who talk about being homosexual, Bobby's story of growing up different is generally interpreted to indicate that he is gay as well.) Because much of his story is mimed while the other characters are singing "And," the actor needs to be physically inventive, with a strong sense of comic timing and a likable eccentricity. He is usually cast as tall and thin, sometimes very handsome and other times more goofy and gangly; wit and style are important. The character is understood to have a strong friendship with Sheila, whom he stands next to on line, and they frequently ad-lib to each other. The role was created by Thommie Walsh, on whose personality it is partly based, and was played on film by Matt West and in the revival by Ken Alan.

Bebe Benzenheimer

Bebe is from Boston and, at twenty-two, the youngest and least experienced of the female dancers, eager for a shot at a Broadway debut. Her story was suggested by those of Michon Peacock (who helped plan and took part in the tape sessions but wasn't in the show) and Kelly Bishop. In the first workshop she was played by Jane Robertson and the character's last name was Nichols; it was changed to Benzenheimer when Robertson departed and was replaced in the second workshop by Nancy Lane, a brunette from New Jersey. The character is generally thought of as Jewish and often cast with a dark-haired actress; she sometimes has a tomboyish quality, and the song lyrics describe her as looking "different" rather than "pretty"—which hasn't prevented a lot of very nice-looking dancers from getting the role. She should have warmth and a self-effacing sense of humor; she needs a solid belt voice for "At the Ballet," but doesn't sing as high as Maggie. She was played by Michelle Johnston in the movie (where the role was rewritten as a more fragile, emotionally troubled character) and in the Broadway revival by Alisan Porter.

Judy Turner

Judy was created by Patricia (known as Trish) Garland, who proved her comic mettle early in the second workshop and therefore inherited comic lines that some of the other actors had been struggling with. So the character is a mix of several different people—though the story she tells about shaving her bratty little sister's head is an exaggeration of one Donna McKechnie related on the tapes. The character is twenty-six years old and is supposed to have been born in El Paso, Texas, and raised in St. Louis, Missouri. She is the first of the dancers to speak in the show, frantically telling Zach she has forgotten her assigned number and revealing her kooky, somewhat ditzy but outgoing personality. She doesn't need a strong singing voice as her monologue is half-spoken recitative. The lyrics of the song "And" say that she is tall, but there is an alternative verse in the script for an actress who is thin rather than tall, and another one that makes no mention of these attributes. She is often cast tall and skinny like Garland, sometimes with a big nose or "character" face, though some very shapely and glamorous dancers have also played the role. It's a relatively small part and needs an actress with charm and a distinctive comic personality to fill it out; when well cast, the character can be refreshing and delightful. Judy was played by Janet Jones in the movie and by Heather Parcells in the revival.

Richie Walters

Hailing from Herculaneum, Missouri, Richie is the only character in the show defined as black, which he announces when he introduces himself. There is usually a second African American dancer in the show to understudy him, and the role should never be played by a white actor; on the rare occasions when it has been, they have sometimes substituted the line "and I'm straight" for "and I'm black." In the first workshop, the character was called Angel and was played by Candy Brown, who left to originate a role in *Chicago*; when she was replaced by Ronald

Dennis, the name was changed to Richie and the character became a male. He has his own solo section in the Montage called "Gimme the Ball," where he sings a melody devised by Dennis himself in a style emulating Aretha Franklin; a high falsetto range is required, as is exceptionally strong dancing for an exuberant, athletic dance solo. The character is high-spirited and loaded with energy, and is usually but not invariably played by an actor of diminutive stature; he was played on film by Gregg Burge and in the revival by James T. Lane.

Alan DeLuca

The thirty-year-old Alan, usually called Al, is from the Bronx. The dialogue implies that he knows Zach pretty well and that they have worked together before. His main goal in the show seems to be to support his new wife, Kristine, who is also auditioning and stands next to him on the line. He keeps the nervous young woman on track and sometimes finishes her sentences, as in the musical number "Sing!"—where he gets some sustained notes that can show off a strong singing voice. In what may seem like an oversight, that number is Al's only real moment in the spotlight, though the song is all about Kristine; Al is the only character never called on to tell his own story. (In regional productions on small stages that use a reduced cast, Al often gets Don's "Lola Latores" monologue, the latter character being cut. This works well; the story fits Al's character and makes up for his lack of a backstory.) Outgoing and energetic, he has a genial, easygoing charm. Usually played by a dark-haired actor, Al, like Mike, comes from an Italian family and has a scrappy city-boy confidence; many actors have played both roles. The character was originally based on Steve Boockvor, who attended the first tape session with his wife Denise but was not initially cast in the show (he later played Zach as a replacement), but his personality more closely parallels that of Don Percassi, who joined the cast in the second workshop and originated the role. Al was played in the movie by Tony Fields and in the revival by Tony Yazbeck.

Kristine Urich (DeLuca)

Al's wife is almost twenty-three and hails from St. Louis. The character was initially to be based on Denise Pence Boockvor, who attended the tape session but was out of town on an acting gig when the workshop was being cast and did not audition; ultimately it was tailored to suit the persona, and vocal limitations, of Renee Baughman, who created it. Kristine is inexperienced and very nervous; she is hyper and comically scattered, and needs her husband Al to keep her grounded and focused. She is also very open about her inability to carry a tune, which is comedically expressed in their duet "Sing!" Thus, the role obviously does not require a great singer—though an actress as tone-deaf as the character is supposed to be would have trouble negotiating the group numbers. Kristine is usually pretty, often tall, and should have a sweetly eager personality, high energy, and an inventive sense of comic timing. Nicole Fosse played the role in the film (where "Sing!" was cut), Chryssie Whitehead in the Broadway revival.

Val Clark

From Arlington, Vermont, the ambitious Val admits to being twenty-five, with the implication that she may be shaving off a year or two. She sings the famous comedy number "Dance: Ten; Looks: Three"—more popularly known as "Tits and Ass." The story of her cosmetic surgery comes from the second tape session's Mitzi Hamilton, who lost the role in the initial auditions but later played it in the International Company and on Broadway as a replacement; Pamela Blair, who originated the role, contributed most of the other aspects of the character's story as well as her famously foul mouth. Though Val is brash and brazen (and devious, as she purposely dances directly behind Sheila in the opening number so that Zach, who wants to see her better, will move her to the front), the character shouldn't come across as overly hard or tough; she has to be likable, with a refreshing humor and honesty. The song requires a confident belt voice but no extremes of range. In remembering when she first came to New York, she mentions that her blonde hair "was natural then"—though this could be interpreted to suggest that she now dyes it a different color, it is generally understood to mean rather that she enhances the blonde color artificially: 90 percent of the time, the role is played by a blonde, natural or otherwise. She should be lively and sexy and very at home in her body, as the choreography includes a certain amount of flaunting. Though she needs to have a good figure to make the song make sense, she's not supposed to be overly buxom; Sheila comments that her enhanced breasts are not all that big, and Val says she wanted them "in proportion." Audrey Landers got the role in the film version, and Jessica Lee Goldyn played it in the revival.

Mark Anthony

Mark says his real last name is Tabori, but seems to have taken his stage name from Roman history and Shakespeare. From Tempe, Arizona, he is the youngest character in the show at twenty, and some of the other dancers express irritation at his wide-eyed eagerness. Mark's big moment is the monologue that opens the Montage sequence, where he tells of his childhood fascination with a medical textbook he found in his dad's library— and which he used to diagnose his own appendicitis (correctly) and gonorrhea

Jack Bowman as Mark with the Staples Players, 2013. *Photo by Kerry Long* (incorrectly). Often cast with a tenor, he also needs to be able to fake a deep singing voice for the couple of lines where he imitates a priest. He usually wears a sleeveless leotard or tank top and should have a nice physique and a fresh-faced, boyish look. Acting-wise, the part is deceptively simple; if the actor isn't genuine and honest, what should play as earnest naïveté can easily slip into a phony cuteness. As he is one of the characters who gets the job, he should be a very strong dancer, more than holding his own with the more experienced men on the line. The stories he tells were taken primarily from the life of Michael Bennett; the role was created by Cameron (Rick) Mason, then played in the film by Michael Blevins and in the revival by Paul McGill.

Paul San Marco

This character is based very specifically on the show's coauthor, Nicholas Dante, who told his story at the first tape session; though somewhat pared down in length, the long monologue that remains in the show is very close to what he said that night. An emotional centerpiece of the show, the moving story demands an actor of unusual sensitivity and emotional openness who can command an otherwise empty stage with simplicity and honesty. He also has a brief vocal solo ("Who Am I Anyway?") at the end of the opening number. Zach singles him out as an excellent dancer, so the performer needs to be strong there as well. The part is usually

cast with a young man slight of stature; the character is Puerto Rican and should ideally be played by an actor who is Puerto Rican or at least Latino—though, like Dante, he changed his name to an Italian one and says people tell him he doesn't look Puerto Rican. (That line may have been put in to justify the casting of the role's originator, Sammy Williams, who did not share the character's ethnicity.) Paul, who is supposed to be twenty-seven and from Spanish Harlem, was played in the movie version by Cameron English and in the Broadway revival by Jason Tam.

Diana Morales

Diana holds down the end of the line on stage left. Priscilla Lopez, the experienced Broadway dancer who originated the role, attended the tape sessions, where she contributed the story of her experiences at the High School of Performing Arts that forms the basis of the song "Nothing"; the

Yamil Borges as Diana in the film of *A Chorus Line*.   *Embassy Films/PolyGram Pictures* character is based primarily on Lopez herself. Diana hails from the Bronx; like Paul, her friend who stands next to her on the line, she is twenty-seven and of Puerto Rican heritage. She is generally played by a brunette of short stature. As the only character in the show with two solo vocal numbers, she should have a very strong voice in the mezzo or belt category; the range is not extreme, but she needs to lead the lyrical anthem "What I Did for Love" with authority and vocal beauty. Though the character is initially nervous and declines to be the first to talk about herself, she proves herself a spunky optimist with a feisty determination, and emerges as something of a leader in the group. Great warmth and a sense of comedy are key. In the film, Diana was played by Yamil Borges; in the revival, by Natalie Cortez.

Larry

Larry does not stand on the line, as he is not auditioning for the show. The audience never learns his last name or age, or where he is from. As Zach's assistant choreographer, he helps teach the routines and keep the audition organized, but reveals little about himself as a person. There is no solo singing required, though he does take part in the "One" finale and sings and dances with the group in some sections of the Montage. Because he demonstrates the choreography and is the model the dancers are meant to emulate, he should be a superb technician with a terrific line and flawless jazz style. Traditionally, the role has usually been cast with exceptionally good-looking young dancers. School and community groups that are short on male dancers have often changed the character to a woman, but he is almost always a male in professional productions. Michael Bennett told Larry Fuller, a former boyfriend of his who had been a Broadway dancer and became a choreographer, that he had been the inspiration for the character, which was named after him. The part was played originally by Clive Clerk (who subsequently changed his name to Clive Wilson), and in the movie, where the role was much expanded, by Terrence Mann; Tyler Hanes played it in the Broadway revival.

In addition to these nineteen principal characters, there are an additional seven who appear only in the opening number. Three women (Tricia, Vicki, and Lois) and four men (Frank, Roy, Butch, and Tom) are eliminated from the audition after dancing the ballet and jazz combinations: for more info and fun facts on these characters, the actors who play them, and their function in the show, see Chapter 10.

9

"People That Look Terrific Together— And That Can Work Together as a Group"

The Original Cast

Thousands of performers have now appeared in *A Chorus Line* all over the world, but seldom has an entire cast been so indelibly linked to any musical as the original company is to this show. The original photo of them standing on line was adapted as the standard show graphic that is still often used today, so their visual images are fixed forever even in the minds of fans who never saw the original production. Because these nineteen actors were there when the show was being created and contributed their own life experiences and personalities to the development of the characters, it has often been said that the original company can never be equaled. The line, from left to right:

Ron Kuhlman (Don)

Kuhlman did not take part in the initial tape sessions; he joined the company for the first workshop, having been asked to audition after Bennett saw him perform in the 1974 edition of the *Milliken Breakfast Show*, a big-budget industrial that employed many *ACL* dancers over the years. Kuhlman grew up in Cleveland; his family struggled financially due to his parents' health problems, and he started performing in high school, playing in the school band as well as acting in plays. Though he developed an interest in ballroom dance early and won amateur dance contests as a teen, he didn't start training seriously until, as a student at Ohio University, he happened to take a course in Afro-Cuban dance. This inspired him to change his major from biochemistry to theatre and dance.

From the beginning he was serious about acting, alternating performances in musicals with roles in plays by Shakespeare and Arthur Miller. He had performed Off Broadway, in stock, and in dinner theatre before landing his role in *A Chorus Line*. His post-*ACL* career has been focused mainly on film and TV acting, with guest or recurring roles on popular series like *Alice*, *Dynasty*, *Melrose Place*, and *Silk*

Stalkings, as well as a regular role on the soap opera *Days of Our Lives*. He played Jan Brady's husband on *The Brady Girls Get Married*, a 1981 TV-movie sequel to the 1970s sitcom classic *The Brady Bunch*, which gave rise to the series *The Brady Brides*. He reprised the role again in a popular TV movie, *A Very Brady Christmas* (1988), and another short-lived series, *The Bradys* (1990). On the big screen, he has had roles in such films as *Splash*, *King of the City*, and *The Heartbreak Kid*. As recently as 2005, he looked fit in his Don Kerr costume, recreating scenes from *A Chorus Line* with original cast members Ronald Dennis, Sammy Williams, and Nancy Lane for an AIDS benefit in Los Angeles.

Kay Cole (Maggie)

Born in Florida and raised in California, Cole had fallen in love with acting and dancing as a young child and worked professionally from an early age; her parents did not push her to pursue performing but supported her efforts. Early accomplishments included touring in *The Music Man* and appearing as a child on classic TV shows like *Playhouse 90* and *Bachelor Father*. By the time she was cast as Maggie, she had already appeared in six musicals on Broadway, starting as a replacement in *Bye Bye Birdie* and including the original Broadway casts of *The Roar of the Greasepaint–The Smell of the Crowd* and *Jesus Christ Superstar*.

Cole had a happier experience in *ACL* than many of her castmates and later claimed she was given more to do than she had expected; while other dancers were seeing their parts shrink, she joined the process relatively late in the game and ended up with some choice vocal moments. She claimed the intensity of the experience and the way it stretched her made her a better person. Though famous for creating Maggie and her famous soaring high notes in "At the Ballet," Cole switched to the larger role of Diana Morales when she returned to the Broadway company in 1982. Her most recent Broadway venture was as a choreographer, staging dances for the play *Six Dance Lessons in Six Weeks* by Richard Alfieri in 2003; at the time of this writing she is choreographing the film version of that play.

She acted extensively in Los Angeles, playing Madame Thenardier in the LA company of *Les Misérables* as well as numerous film and television roles, before changing her focus to directing and choreography. In those capacities, she has enjoyed a very successful second career, staging productions for such venues as the Hollywood Bowl, the Pasadena Playhouse, and the Coconut Grove Playhouse, among others. In addition to many new and classic works, she has directed and choreographed regional revivals of *A Chorus Line*. She has also taught acting and musical theatre for Emerson College and UCLA.

Wayne Cilento (Mike)

Cilento had been in the original cast of *Seesaw*, which proved to be a turning point in his life for two reasons. It was the first time he worked with Michael Bennett, who later invited him to the tape session that led to *A Chorus Line*. In addition, observing the way Bennett transformed the troubled *Seesaw* into a successful property was inspiring to the young dancer, who in more recent years has pursued a career as a choreographer himself.

From the Bronx, Cilento enjoyed social dancing as a kid; a girls' phys ed teacher cast him in a high school musical, which she was choreographing, and encouraged him to study dance seriously. He resolved to pursue the career after seeing the original Broadway production of *Cabaret*. As a young man pursuing dance, he had been concerned about being stigmatized by classmates, though his fears turned out to be mostly unfounded; he tells of how he adamantly refused to wear tights in dance classes while he was a teen. He later worked with dancer Bill Glassman of American Ballet Theatre, one of his teachers at the State University of New York College at Brockport (where Cilento's "no tights" stance didn't last a week); like Cilento, Glassman was straight and of diminutive stature, and he became a role model.

In addition to *Seesaw*, Cilento's early Broadway experiences included the infamous *Rachael Lily Rosenbloom and Don't You Ever Forget It*. Post-*ACL*, he danced on Broadway in *The Act* with Liza Minnelli and appeared in Bob Fosse's *Dancin'* (for which he received a Tony nomination for Best Featured Actor in a Musical) and *Big Deal*. He was in the first movie version of *Annie* and also appeared in more than a hundred TV commercials. It was through commercials as well that he started to build his career as a choreographer. He staged concert appearances for various music industry stars, as well as videos for Billy Joel and Barry Manilow.

Cilento's very successful career as a Broadway choreographer began with *Baby* (1983 Tony nomination) and has included *Jerry's Girls* (which he also conceived with Jerry Herman and director Larry Alford), *The Who's Tommy*, Disney's *Aida*, *Wicked*, and revivals of *How to Succeed in Business Without Really Trying* and *Sweet Charity*. He married his high school sweetheart, Cathy Colety, and they have three sons.

Baayork Lee (Connie)

Lee made the earliest Broadway debut of any of the cast members, having played Princess Yaowlak in the original cast of Rodgers and Hammerstein's *The King and I* in 1951—an experience her character, Connie Wong, alludes to in the Montage sequence of *A Chorus Line*. Lee was inspired by the adult dancers who performed the Jerome Robbins ballet in *The King and I* and vowed to learn how to dance and sing. She attended the High School of Performing Arts and the School of American Ballet, and although she was not tall enough for a career as a ballerina, she found steady work in musical theatre, working with Rodgers and Hammerstein again in the original cast of *Flower Drum Song* and dancing on Broadway in *Bravo, Giovanni*; *Mr. President*; and *Golden Boy*. By the time she joined *A Chorus Line* she knew Michael Bennett very well, having worked with him in *Here's Love; A Joyful Noise; Henry, Sweet Henry; Seesaw*; and *Promises, Promises*—in which she introduced Bennett's celebrated "Turkey Lurkey Time" alongside Donna McKechnie, whose role she took over later in the run. She turned down an invitation to attend the now-legendary tape session that inspired *ACL*, but, having been dance captain on both *Promises, Promises* and

Seesaw, she was highly trusted by Bennett and Avian, so they brought her into the project early on, taping her reminiscences later in a private session.

In addition to creating Connie, she was named assistant choreographer, and has been indispensable to *A Chorus Line* ever since, recreating Bennett's direction and choreography for over forty productions of the show, including regional revivals and touring companies, both nationally and internationally. In many ways she has been the glue that holds the *Chorus Line* family together; dancer Robert Tunstall recently said "Baayork means 'Precious Jewel,' which she was/is to all of us." In 2006, she helped to spearhead the Broadway revival of the show; she choreographed that production and its touring versions, as well as the show's return to the West End in 2013.

Lee has also accumulated an extensive list of credits of her own as a director and choreographer, including tours and revivals of such musicals as *Cinderella*, *Barnum*, and *Porgy and Bess*. She has choreographed several operas for the Washington National Opera and has worked with Lotte World in Korea and Tokyo Disneyland. With Nina Zoie Lam and Steven Eng, Lee founded the National Asian Artists Project, a dynamic organization dedicated to educating youth, building theatre audiences, and creating performance opportunities for Asian and Asian American performers; the company has produced all-Asian revivals of such classic musicals as *Oklahoma!*, *Oliver!*, and *Hello, Dolly!*; among its many other programs are a Broadway Community Chorus, training and educational opportunities for both working professionals and schoolchildren, and collaborations with other companies nationally. In 2014, Lee was honored by the Actors' Equity Foundation with the Paul Robeson Citation Award, which, according to the AEA website, "honors individuals or organizations that best exemplify and practice the principles to which Mr. Robeson devoted his life: dedication to the universal brotherhood of all humankind, commitment to the freedom of conscience and of expression, belief in the artist's responsibility to society, respect for the dignity of the individual and concern for and service to all humans of any race or nationality." Lee also conceived and coauthored (with Thommie Walsh and Robert Viagas) the 1990 book *On the Line: The Creation of A Chorus Line*.

Michel Stuart (Greg)

Stuart was born in New York in 1943, the son of Jewish parents who had come to the United States to escape the Nazis during World War II. He attended the High School of Performing Arts for two years but had to transfer to the Professional Children's School when he started working regularly as a dancer. He did summer stock, appeared in the movie *Let's Rock* for choreographer Peter Gennaro, and was cast in the London production of *West Side Story* before he was fifteen. Stuart first worked with Michael Bennett on summer stock and touring productions of that same show. Early Broadway credits included *Milk and Honey*, *The Gay Life*, and *Little Me*, as well as assisting choreographer Ron Field on the original *Cabaret*; Stuart was always interested in choreography and design in addition to performing.

His next Broadway musical after *A Chorus Line* was *A Day in Hollywood/A Night in the Ukraine*, which featured Priscilla Lopez and was directed by Stuart's longtime partner, Tommy Tune; Stuart was not in the cast but designed the costumes. He then worked in the fashion industry as a sportswear designer before returning to the theatre as a producer; he produced Broadway's *Nine* and Off-Broadway's *Cloud Nine* (both directed by Tune) as well as the musical *The Tap Dance Kid*. Though "Michel Stuart" was listed as a producer, both *Nine* and *The Tap Dance Kid* also bore the credit "produced in association with Michael Kleinman Productions." Because Kleinman was Stuart's real last name, this recalled his *ACL* character, Gregory Gardner, who reveals both his real name and his "Jewish name" during the introductions scene at the top of the show. Stuart was killed in a car accident in 1997.

Donna McKechnie (Cassie)

Born in Pontiac, Michigan, in 1942, McKechnie grew up in the Detroit area. Some of her childhood memories found their way into the show as Maggie's reminiscences of her parents' troubled marriage: McKechnie's mother encouraged her daughter's passion for ballet, but her father, raised as a strict Presbyterian, saw dancing as a sin. Struggling with repressed family tensions, McKechnie quit high school and ran away to New York to join a touring dance revue.

Having already danced with the Detroit City Ballet, she auditioned for American Ballet Theatre but was told by the company's director, Lucia Chase, that she was too young to be hired; though Chase offered her a chance to study with the company for a year and then reaudition, McKechnie saw it as a rejection and deserted ballet for musical theatre—specifically a summer stock season at the Carousel Theatre in Framingham, Massachusetts, where she made her professional acting debut as Louise in *Carousel*. The production starred John Raitt in the role of Billy Bigelow, which he had originated on Broadway some fifteen years earlier, with Inga Swenson as Julie Jordan; McKechnie later said it inspired her to pursue a career in musical theatre.

She made her Broadway debut at eighteen, dancing for Bob Fosse in the original production of *How to Succeed in Business Without Really Trying*, then vowed it would be her last chorus role. A lead in the national tour of *A Funny Thing Happened on the Way to the Forum* was followed by a life-changing stint on the TV series *Hullabaloo*, where she danced to Top 40 hits—often partnered with a young dancer named Michael Bennett. The two inspired each other's best work; he choreographed a number for her on the show, and she would soon be his lead dancer in the Broadway productions of *Promises, Promises* and *Company*. She earned a cover story in *Dance Magazine*, for which Bennett was interviewed and called her the most beautiful dancer he had ever seen. He later defined the qualities that made her his muse: her unique ability to dance as strongly and athletically as a man and yet maintain a compelling feminine lyricism. She went on to star as Ivy in the 1971 Broadway revival of *On the Town*. But a move to the West Coast and an attempt to establish a Hollywood acting career proved disappointing (despite a role as the

Donna McKechnie (Cassie) in the final pose from "The Music and the Mirror." *Photofest*

Rose in the movie of *The Little Prince*), so when McKechnie returned to New York in 1974, she was, like Cassie, almost desperate to get back onstage and dance again.

A *Chorus Line* propelled both McKechnie and Bennett to the center of the theatre world, but the elation of success and creative fulfillment was accompanied by the almost unbearable pressure of enormous attention and publicity. After she recreated Cassie with the National Company in California, the two were married. She wanted a family; he wanted her career to keep pace with his. Like Zach, he proved consumed by work and incapable of emotional intimacy, and the marriage foundered within a year; he told her that her flaw was that she loved him. For McKechnie, the next few years were a low point both personally and career-wise. She began experiencing disturbing pains in her limbs and, though only in her mid-thirties, was diagnosed with rheumatoid arthritis; she was initially told that she would never dance again.

At one point she says she considered taking her own life, as there didn't seem to be a way out. Finally a friend arranged for her to see Dr. Sam Getlen, an eccentric but well-respected doctor in Trenton, New Jersey, who only saw patients at night, between 10 p.m. and 5 a.m. The ninety-five-year-old doctor immediately put her on a regimen of intensive vitamin therapy and prescribed an extremely limited and specific diet. (She spelled out the details later in her autobiography, as one of the main reasons she wrote the book was to offer encouragement to others who might be dealing with similar health issues.) There were also simple emotional prescriptions, like avoiding conflict and arguments, and saying to herself aloud "This feels good!" any time she found something physically pleasurable. The doctor told her her mobility would start to improve within about six weeks, and, when she asked if she would be able to dance again, he said possibly in about a year. Amazingly, he charged her only eighteen dollars—because in Hebrew, the number eighteen symbolizes life. McKechnie determinedly followed all his instructions; she also went to a new psychotherapist, who helped her begin to work through her emotional issues, the anger and guilt that had been exacerbated by her unhappy marriage and her grief over her father's recent death. Perhaps, she thought, her arthritis had been partly psychosomatic: a result of her suppression of these destructive feelings.

The journey back to health was gradual, but she soon found herself performing again, first in an Off-Broadway play called *Wine Untouched*. She starred in the Chicago production of *I'm Getting My Act Together and Taking It on the Road* and played Sally Bowles in *Cabaret* in summer stock with Billy Crystal. A second try at Hollywood proved much more successful than her first, with numerous TV roles including an appearance as the former wife of Ted Danson's Sam Malone character on *Cheers* and a recurring role on the TV version of *Fame*. By the time she was asked to recreate Cassie for the record-breaking 3,389th performance of *A Chorus Line* in New York, she was back in fighting trim as a dancer; she returned to the role again for a tour in 1985, followed by engagements in Japan and Paris and a triumphant eight-month return engagement in the Broadway company.

Bob Fosse came to see her as Cassie numerous times during her 1986–87 run in the show and offered her the title role in the touring version of the Broadway revival of *Sweet Charity*; McKechnie had a personal triumph in the part, though during the production period she had to cope with the deaths of both Bennett and Fosse himself, who passed away unexpectedly following a final rehearsal for the show in Washington, D.C.

Though she didn't return to Broadway until 1996 (as Emily Arden in the stage version of Rodgers and Hammerstein's film musical *State Fair*), McKechnie has maintained a very active performing career. She has taken on the leading lady roles in numerous classic musicals at theatres around the country, including Annie in *Annie Get Your Gun*, Agnes in *I Do! I Do!*, Joanne in *Company*, Desiree in *A Little Night Music*, and all three of the leading female roles (Phyllis, Sally, and Carlotta) in different revivals and concert presentations of Sondheim's *Follies*. (Writing in the *New York Times*, Ben Brantley called her interpretation of Sally in the 1998 Paper Mill Playhouse production "the performance of her career.") She also spent years developing a one-woman show about her life and career, *Inside the Music*, performing both theatrical and cabaret versions at various venues around the country and in London; she followed it up with a second installment, *Gypsy in My Soul*. When she did her show at Arci's Place on Park Avenue in 2001, Brantley wrote in the *Times* that "This winning hour of song, dance and reminiscence gives you the privileged feeling of watching a star turn from the wings of a big theater." He added that when, late in the show, she recreated "The Music and the Mirror," the number "still fits her like a spandex glove. 'Give me a chance to come through,' she sings with a fervor that sears. There is something truly touching, although nothing pathetic, in Ms. McKechnie's making this request so sincerely after so many years. So scared, so hearty, so happy to be doing what she's doing, she remains the essence of the heroic drive that 'A Chorus Line' celebrates."

Her memoir, *Time Steps: My Musical Comedy Life*, was published in 2006. In 2015, she returned to Broadway, standing by for Chita Rivera in the long-awaited musical *The Visit*.

Kelly Bishop (Sheila)

Like the character she played, Kelly Bishop was born in Colorado Springs. She grew up in Denver and became very serious about ballet at an early age. Also like Sheila, she was inspired by *The Red Shoes* and had a mother who was a frustrated dancer and pushed her to succeed, starting her in serious training by the time she was seven and taking her to see all the ballet companies that toured through town. When the ballet school Kelly was attending in Denver closed, her mother moved the family to California so she could continue to study with the same teachers, Francesca and Dmitri Romanoff of the American Ballet Theatre.

Bishop moved to New York right after high school, intending to join ABT, but, like Donna McKechnie, she was rejected by the company's director, Lucia Chase, and, also like McKechnie, immediately joined the corps de ballet at Radio City Music Hall instead. The grueling schedule of multiple performances every day *en pointe* took their toll on her body, and, looking for a change of pace, she got a job dancing for the great choreographer Michael Kidd at the 1964 World's Fair in Queens. She found she related easily to the theatre dancers she met there and took naturally to jazz dance, so she changed her career focus, moving away from classical ballet, and danced for choreographer Ron Lewis in nightclub revues in Lake Tahoe and Las Vegas. Like Gwen Verdon and Chita Rivera, Lewis had been a protégée of the legendary Broadway and Hollywood choreographer Jack Cole, and Bishop found herself inspired by his legacy. She admired Lewis's choreography and his high standards but she found he could be cruel and abusive in rehearsal, and the schedule was so grueling that one day she broke down crying in rehearsal out of sheer exhaustion. Like many of the other dancers in Vegas, she began taking amphetamines, which provided energy and caused her to lose weight, while also enabling her to dance while injured. But this, combined with the fact that there was only so far a Vegas dancer could advance in her career unless she was willing to dance topless, which she wouldn't do, ultimately led to a decision to return to New York.

Her first Broadway show was *Golden Rainbow*, a Steve Lawrence/Eydie Gormé vehicle that featured dance arrangements by a young songwriter named Marvin Hamlisch. She later worked with Bennett on *Promises, Promises*, with Michon Peacock and Tony Stevens on *Rachael Lily Rosenbloom*, and with Stevens and Donna McKechnie in the revival of *On the Town*, so she knew many of the participants and was a natural choice to join the tape sessions.

In the years following her Tony win for *A Chorus Line*, Bishop returned more than once to the Broadway company; she also took part in the workshop of Bennett's last musical, *Scandal*, which sadly was never produced. Since changing her focus from dance to acting, she has had a very successful career in films, including *An Unmarried Woman*, *Dirty Dancing*, *Queens Logic*, *Six Degrees of Separation* (also the stage version), *Private Parts*, and *Wonder Boys*. On television, she has played many guest star roles and was a regular on the series *The Gilmore Girls* and *Bunheads*. Stage acting roles have included Maxine in two productions of Tennessee Williams's *The Night of the Iguana*, the role of Vera Charles in *Mame* at New Jersey's Paper Mill Playhouse, and returns to Broadway for *The Last Night of Ballyhoo*, *Proposals*, and the Roundabout's revival of *Anything Goes*. She is married to Lee Leonard, a talk show host who was a pioneer in the field of cable television.

Thommie Walsh (Bobby)

Walsh, born Thomas Joseph Walsh III, is closely identified with the character he played in the show, Robert Joseph Henry Mills III, though some of the details of that character's story actually came from the life of Michael Bennett. Like Bobby, however, Walsh was from upstate New York (Auburn, not Buffalo) and was known as something of an eccentric and a prankster as a kid. His parents spotted his talent for dance very early and put him in class; he watched *The Ed Sullivan Show* and dreamed of performing with a top ballet company.

When Walsh came down to New York City to audition (unsuccessfully) for the dance program at the Juilliard School, he saw both *Mame* and *Hello, Dolly!* These first two musicals he saw on Broadway also coincidentally became two of the first in which he performed, shortly afterwards in summer stock. He studied at the Boston Conservatory and was in the national tour of *Applause* (understudying future *ACL* castmate Sammy Williams) and the movie of *Jesus Christ Superstar* (performing alongside Baayork Lee and Robert LuPone). Walsh was cast in the Broadway productions of *Rachael Lily Rosenbloom and Don't You Ever Forget It* and Bennett's *Seesaw*, both of which led to his being asked to participate in the tape sessions.

Seesaw was a turning point in another way as well, as it was the first time Walsh worked with castmate Tommy Tune, who was instrumental in the growth of his subsequent career as a choreographer. Walsh was associate choreographer (under Tune) for *The Best Little Whorehouse in Texas* and was Tune's co-choreographer for *A Day in Hollywood/A Night in the Ukraine*, for which they won the 1980 Tony Award for Best Choreography. On *Nine*, Walsh was credited as choreographer with Tune as director, and on *My One and Only*, the two shared the credits for both direction and choreography, sharing a second Tony Award for the latter. Walsh's other choreographic credits include the Broadway productions of *Do Black Patent Leather Shoes Really Reflect Up?* and *My Favorite Year*. He also staged commercials and nightclub acts, and directed Donna McKechnie's one-woman autobiographical show *Inside the Music*, which took its title from a cut song from *A Chorus Line*.

Walsh collaborated with Robert Viagas and castmate Baayork Lee on the book *On the Line: The Creation of A Chorus Line*, published in 1990. He attended the opening night of the revival of the show in October 2006, looking tan and fit when he was photographed at the party with Ken Alan, who played Bobby in that production; less than a year later, Walsh died of AIDS-related lymphoma. He had given a scarf he had worn as Bobby in the show to Alan as an opening night gift; at the performance the night after he died, Alan wore the scarf onstage in tribute.

Nancy Lane (Bebe)

The youngest member of the original line, Lane was only twenty-four when the show opened. She often felt ostracized by most of the cast, attributing that to the unfettered enthusiasm she demonstrated for the work in her first Broadway show, as well as the fact that they didn't see her as part of their insular world of gypsies.

Growing up in a Jewish family in New Jersey, Lane was often brought into New York City by her parents to see shows, including the Rockettes at Radio City Music Hall. She claimed she inherited her sense of humor from her parents, who were known for keeping the other guests laughing at parties, though they weren't in show business. Like Kristine in *A Chorus Line*, she was inspired by watching *The Ed Sullivan Show* and decided she wanted to be in the business; as children, she and her sister performed in charity shows. Her first chance to audition for Broadway came when she was still a child and a teacher recommended her for *Milk and Honey*, but her mother declined the opportunity; her parents never really approved of the idea of a performing career until she was cast in *A Chorus Line*, though Lane took dance and singing lessons religiously from the time she was in elementary school.

She put ballet on hold after being rejected by the New York City Ballet, and her mother insisted she go to college; she entered Virginia Commonwealth University in Richmond, Virginia, to major in recreational leadership—then outraged her parents by switching to the theatre department. At the university she won an award for acting, playing the lead in Tennessee Williams's *Suddenly Last Summer*. After moving to New York, she did some summer stock and dinner theatre before auditioning for the national tour of *Seesaw*; since she looked a bit like Michon Peacock, she thought she might be cast in Peacock's role. On the tour, she worked with Bennett, Baayork Lee, and Sammy Williams, but she wasn't part of the tape sessions and didn't become involved with *A Chorus Line* until she auditioned for the second workshop.

As a relative newcomer to the scene, Lane had a freshness and an enthusiasm that helped define Bebe, who is auditioning for her first Broadway show. Her sense of humor and desire to be the life of the party also contributed to the character's personality as the script developed. Later on, when the show had been running for months and was an established hit, Lane expressed a desire to try one of the other roles, specifically Sheila or Cassie, but Bennett refused to consider her as anyone but Bebe; she returned to the part ten years later with a touring company that went to Japan.

After leaving the show, Lane turned her newfound celebrity into success as a game show contestant, appearing on *The New $25,000 Pyramid*, *Password Plus*, *The Match Game/Hollywood Squares Hour*, and *Super Password*. She also did well as an actress in Hollywood, playing guest roles on many popular TV series and recurring or regular roles on *Angie*, *Rhoda*, and *The Duck Factory*. It was due to TV acting commitments that she was unable to participate in the record-breaking reunion performance of *A Chorus Line* in September 1983. Lane has also worked as a TV writer, including an episode of the classic sitcom *Taxi*. With her husband, Dennis Fisher, she had a son, Benjamin Fisher, who is now a working actor in New York City.

Patricia Garland (Judy)

Garland, known to her friends as Trish, attended the first tape session with her older sister, Jacki. Growing up in a poor family in Kansas and Michigan, the two girls had studied dance from an early age; before their parents could afford to send them both to lessons, Trish had contented herself with watching Jacki's classes and copying her movements. But their mother, who had failed to realize her dream of becoming a nurse, wanted better for her daughters, so she took in laundry to pay for lessons for both of them; soon the girls were helping the family by earning money dancing at county fairs. The willowy Trish had a lyrical style, while Jacki, though older, had a shorter build and was drawn to gymnastics and acrobatics. It could be tough having a sibling with the same interests, and Trish often felt she was competing with Jacki for the affections of their dance teacher and even of their mother.

By their teens, both girls were serious about ballet: Jacki studied with the New York City Ballet, while Trish apprenticed with companies in Chicago and San Francisco. While she was studying with the San Francisco Ballet, her father was killed in a car accident; her mother told her not to come home, because she was on a scholarship and she knew the opportunity could be the key to a real future as a dancer. At age seventeen, Trish moved to New York. She was offered apprenticeships but was unable to get a full-time corps position with a major ballet company, so she shifted her sights to musical theatre and was soon cast in the national company of *Cabaret*. She worked with Tony Stevens and Michon Peacock in her first Broadway show, *Georgy*, an unsuccessful 1970 musical version of the hit film *Georgy Girl*; she also got to know Michael Bennett when she took over a dance role in the Broadway production of *Follies*. Jacki, now also in New York and doing musical theatre, had worked with Bennett too, on *Promises, Promises*. So both sisters were invited to take part in the tape sessions.

After opening *ACL* on Broadway, Trish went with most of the original cast into the National Company; one night during their run in Los Angeles, she landed wrong out of a jump in the opening number and seriously damaged her knee. This effectively ended her dancing career, though she gradually rehabilitated herself through two surgeries and a course of therapy focused on Pilates. A Buddhist, she also spent time refocusing her personal outlook and trying to overcome her insecurity and shyness; this was abetted by cosmetic surgery, which replaced the angular, gawky image she had projected as Judy Turner with a much more sophisticated and glamorous persona.

She found success acting in movies, including *1941*, *Heartbreak Ridge*, and the film version of the Broadway musical *The Best Little Whorehouse in Texas*, choreographed by Tony Stevens. She also did TV commercials and guest spots on several series. Like Nancy Lane, she tried her hand at TV writing, scripting an episode of the series *Baywatch*, on which she had previously appeared as an actress. As a choreographer, she staged several productions of *A Chorus Line* for Civic Light Opera groups in California, as well as a dance number for *Legends!*, a play by *ACL* co-librettist James Kirkwood. Crediting Pilates with her recovery from her knee injury, she became well known as a trainer of Pilates instructors; she now teaches the discipline at seminars around the country and the world, as well as at her own Sherman Oaks studio, Trish Garland Pilates, which she has run since 1990. She lives in Los Angeles with her husband, George Drucker.

Ronald Dennis (Richie)

Dennis is from Dayton, Ohio. Like Trish Garland, he came from a family that struggled financially, and like her he helped pay for his dance lessons by cleaning the studio. He went on to study at Butler University in Indianapolis and later the Joffrey Ballet School in New York City.

Dennis's big break was being cast as a dancer in the Music Theatre of Lincoln Center revival of *Show Boat*, starring Barbara Cook, David Wayne, William Warfield, Constance Towers, and Stephen Douglass. He toured in *Hallelujah, Baby!* and *Hello, Dolly!*, and appeared on Broadway in the latter show and in *Don't Bother Me, I Can't Cope*. He joined *ACL* for the second workshop.

With most of the original cast, Dennis took the show to California in the hopes of establishing a television career, and landed guest roles on *Baretta*, *Chico and the Man*, and *Welcome Back, Kotter*. He toured as the Leading Player in *Pippin* and in *La Cage aux Folles* and Fosse's *Dancin'*, and returned to Broadway for *My One and Only*, which was co-choreographed by his *ACL* castmate Thommie Walsh; Baayork Lee was the associate choreographer.

Don Percassi (Al)

Percassi was an experienced gypsy by the time he was cast in *ACL*, having made his Broadway debut over ten years earlier in *High Spirits*, the musical version of Noel Coward's *Blithe Spirit*. His other Main Stem credits included *Sugar* and *Mack and Mabel*.

Percassi came from a performing family, his mother a nightclub singer and his father a marathon dancer; they put him in dance class early to remedy his flat feet, but his natural talent emerged so quickly that at thirteen he was studying at the Joffrey Ballet School—as was Ron Dennis, who would one day stand next to him on the line as Richie. Percassi first met Michael Bennett when, as very young dancers, they were both performing in separate companies of *West Side Story*; they later worked together when Bennett choreographed the Katharine Hepburn vehicle *Coco* and Percassi was in the cast. He joined the second workshop of *A Chorus Line* as an understudy, but inherited the role of Al shortly after Barry Bostwick, who had been rehearsing as Zach, left the project, and Robert LuPone was moved up from Al to replace him.

Percassi had a warmly self-effacing sense of humor. He had problems with night vision and therefore sometimes lost his bearings onstage when the lights came down; he was later able to laugh at himself and told stories of some embarrassing onstage accidents, including a night when he was in the wrong place and a curtain came down on top of him: Baayork Lee rescued him by dragging him out from under it by the feet. Though some of Al's big scenes were cut after he came on board, he never complained; he had done so many shows he thought of this one as another job, acknowledging that his role was a big step up from dancing in the chorus. He felt the show would have a healthy run and was happy to be there—even when Bennett was yelling at him—and never expected anything more than what he got. He stayed with the Broadway company longer than most; after leaving, he joined the original cast of *42nd Street*; that show also became a major hit, and Percassi stayed with it throughout its run of over eight years.

Renee Baughman (Kristine)

Like the character she played, Baughman started studying dance after a traveling salesman told her parents she had talent and sold them on lessons. Having fallen in love with dance watching Fred Astaire movies with her father, she couldn't wait to get started and progressed quickly in her studies of tap and ballet. She joined the St. Louis Civic Ballet and also danced in a nightclub chorus while still in her mid-teens. At fifteen, she lied about her age to get her Equity card dancing in *My Fair Lady* with the St. Louis Municipal Opera. She worked with the company for three seasons; Michael Bennett directed her in a small role in *West Side Story*, and Larry Fuller, after choreographing a production of *The Wizard of Oz* in which she performed, invited her to audition for him in New York. This resulted in her getting cast in *Li'l Abner* at the Paper Mill Playhouse in Milburn, New Jersey. She danced on television variety shows, and, although she hated Broadway chorus auditions because of her discomfort with her singing, she was good enough to land a Broadway debut in *Applause* and a second job in a short-lived musical called *Smith*, with a cast that also included Nicholas Dante and Trish Garland.

Baughman almost didn't attend the famous tape session because she felt she was out of shape and overweight at the time, and she didn't want Bennett to see her at less than her best; she later said Nick Dante literally had to take her by the hand and make her go.

Following her time in the show on Broadway and in California, she did some acting on television but switched her main career focus to assisting directors and choreographers. She racked up a long list of credits including the Broadway musical *Merlin*, on which she assisted choreographer Christopher Chadman. She also assisted Tony Stevens when he choreographed the movie version of *The Best Little Whorehouse in Texas*. A long-term job assisting Michael Arceneaux, a producer and director of fashion shows for the world's top designers, led her to high-profile projects at international venues. Later, she became a marketing manager for a cosmetics firm.

Pamela Blair (Val)

The character of Val was modeled partly on Blair and her famously colorful language, but the cosmetic surgery story that inspired the song "Dance: Ten; Looks: Three" was related at the second tape session by another dancer, Mitzi Hamilton. Blair herself had not taken part in the tape sessions but was hired for the first workshop and contributed her own experiences to the development of the script.

She had grown up on a horse farm in Vermont and was inspired to become a performer by her love for the Beatles. She excelled in both dance and sports, and moved to New York at sixteen to finish high school at the National Academy of Ballet. Turned down for jobs in ballet companies, she shifted her focus to jazz dance; like Val, she dreamed of becoming a Rockette, but her New York career was going nowhere, and she found herself waiting tables, tending bar, and working as an underage go-go dancer. She tried California, where she danced on TV, but came back to New York—and ended up getting involved with a pimp who almost lured her into prostitution.

Blair was finally hired as a replacement dancer on two Michael Bennett shows, *Promises, Promises* and *Seesaw*. She was also cast as Curley's Wife in the 1974 revival of John Steinbeck's *Of Mice and Men*, making her the only member of the original line who had already played a major role in a straight play on Broadway. Her other Main Stem credits before *A Chorus Line* had included the flop *Wild and Wonderful* and *Sugar*, the Jule Styne musical based on the Marilyn Monroe film *Some Like it Hot*, in which she understudied, and later replaced, Elaine Joyce in the Monroe role. The cast of that show also included Don Percassi as well as original *ACL* understudy John Mineo, future Cassie replacement Pamela Sousa, and dancer Andy Bew, who took part in the original tape sessions.

Following her success as Val, Blair created a role in the musical *The Best Little Whorehouse in Texas*, on which the associate choreographer was her *ACL* castmate Thommie Walsh (Bobby), and where she had the unenviable experience of having her song taken away from her and given to the leading lady. She also appeared in the Broadway musical version of *King of Hearts* and in the straight plays *The Nerd* and *A Few Good Men*, the latter directed by Don Scardino, to whom she was married from 1984 to 1991. She has worked extensively Off Broadway and in regional theatres, and played Hedy La Rue in the touring version of the revival of *How to Succeed in Business Without Really Trying*, opposite Ralph Macchio. Her résumé also includes a lot of TV work, including recurring roles on several soap operas and guest star appearances on numerous prime-time series. On the big screen, she was in the 1982 movie version of *Annie* as well as *Mighty Aphrodite* and *21 Grams*. More recently, she moved to Arizona and opened a therapeutic and myofascial massage studio.

Cameron Mason (Mark)

Mason's real first name was Richard, and, though he chose Cameron as a stage name, he was usually called Rick by his friends. Born in Colorado and raised in Phoenix (his character, Mark, says he's from Tempe, Arizona), he fell in love with dance watching old movies. His mother started him in classes when he was in seventh grade, though his father wasn't thrilled about it. He went to Dallas to audition for the Dallas Summer Musicals and was cast in a season of shows, starting with a revival of *Irma La Douce* starring Chita Rivera. Next he tried the West Coast, where he studied with Eugene Loring at the University of California at Irvine. He was cast as a dancer on TV and in Sylvie Vartan's nightclub revue, which took him to Paris.

On returning to the States, Mason saw the original production of *Pippin* and was inspired to move to New York and try Broadway. Before long he was dancing in his first Broadway show, a 1973 revival of *The Pajama Game* directed by George Abbott, who had staged the original production with Jerome Robbins. Mason, who had already danced Bennett's choreography in a regional revival of *Promises, Promises,* was first seen by the director at a rehearsal for the *Milliken Breakfast Show,* in which he was appearing alongside Bennett dancers Wayne Cilento and Baayork Lee. This led to an invitation to audition for the first workshop of *A Chorus Line.*

Mason was quite open in interviews over the years about his emotional struggles with the experience, having often felt overlooked by Bennett, competitive with the other dancers, and disappointed with the way his role was shrinking as the script developed. He later tried to focus on the positive aspects of what had been a life-changing experience for all of them. After outgrowing the role of twenty-year-old Mark, he returned to the Broadway cast for a while as an understudy, dancing in the opening number.

He only stayed in the business for a few years after leaving the show, working as a dancer in industrial shows and TV specials, and as a regular on *Mary,* a variety series starring Mary Tyler Moore. He worked with Rivera again on his last gig, touring with her nightclub act. After that he lived in California for a while, where he worked as a location scout for film producers; he also went to massage school and then opened his own business focused on massage, exercise, and nutrition. Despite success in this new endeavor, he left California and went back to Arizona, where he joined his mother for a time selling antiques and then started a second business of his own, cleaning houses. He also became active in the animal rights movement. Though Mason had played the youngest character in *A Chorus Line,* he was, ironically and sadly, the first member of the original cast to pass away. One of several key members of the *ACL* family to have become infected with the AIDS virus, he died in 1992, at the age of forty-two.

Sammy Williams (Paul)

Williams is from Trenton, New Jersey. He first got interested in dancing by watching his sister in dance class and thinking he could do it too—a story that found its way into *A Chorus Line* through the character Mike, played in *ACL* by his friend Wayne Cilento, rather than Williams's own character of Paul, which was based on Nicholas

The company listens to Sammy Williams (Paul), at left, sing "Who Am I Anyway?" at the recording session for the original cast album, June 3, 1975.   *Photofest*

Dante. Dancing was all he did from age eight on, performing locally for benefits, Elks Club events, hospitals, etc. Williams and his sister made their stage debuts together as Jerome and Ngana, the two children of Emile DeBecque, in a tent theatre production of *South Pacific*. He danced in more of the classic musicals in high school and summer stock, and at Ryder University.

Though Trenton is not terribly far from New York City, Williams's parents had not been able to afford to take him to see a Broadway show when he was growing up; the first one he saw turned out to be *The Roar of the Greasepaint—The Smell of the Crowd*, in which a director he was working with on a local production was understudying the lead (Anthony Newley); the day he went on for Newley, he had to cancel rehearsal and invited his cast, including Williams, to come see the show instead. It inspired Williams greatly; coincidentally, it also happened to be playing at the Shubert Theatre, the future home of *A Chorus Line*, with a cast including Kay Cole, who would originate the role of Maggie.

After being directed by Tommy Tune in a community college production of *Carousel*, Williams began to audition in New York. One of his earliest auditions was for *Henry, Sweet Henry*, choreographed by Michael Bennett. He didn't get that one, but his outstanding dancing skills got him noticed before long, and he went out on tour in both *Funny Girl* and *Hello, Dolly!* He made his Broadway debut as a swing in *The Happy Time*, following that up with both the Broadway and touring productions of *Applause*, starring Lauren Bacall. It was while doing *Applause* that he first met Nicholas Dante, whose life story he would go on to tell in *A Chorus Line*.

He took over a role in Bennett's *Seesaw* late in its Broadway run, which resulted in an invitation to the tape session.

Though Williams had very limited acting experience, Bennett saw something special and honest in him that he was determined to draw out. The emotional manipulation that the director employed during the rehearsal process took a toll on Williams, but resulted in a memorable performance and a Tony Award. Having been thus celebrated for playing the most demanding acting role in the show, Williams could well have been expected to go on to a big acting career, but this was not to be. He did a guest role on TV's *Kojak* and appeared in the film *God Told Me To*, but his acting was mostly limited to several return engagements as Paul over the next eleven years, both on Broadway and on tour. Ironically, he broke his foot dancing in the show in 1984, living out in reality the horrific scene in which Paul is injured, but in Williams's case he recovered and was soon dancing again. He felt he grew in the role over the years and wished Bennett could have seen his work in his last tour as Paul in 1986. Shortly thereafter he left the industry, and he later opened his own floral business.

Priscilla Lopez (Diana)

Like Diana Morales, the character based on her, Lopez was born in the Bronx to a Puerto Rican family, but she was raised in Brooklyn, where her family moved before she was two years old. She began studying dance at age seven, starting in Brooklyn and then switching to a dance school in Manhattan, where she took five classes a week during her junior high school years. Like several key figures in the history of *ACL*, including Michael Bennett and Bob Avian, Lopez counted *West Side Story* as an early professional credit—especially early in her case, as she was cast as an extra in the movie version when she was twelve. She was accepted to the High School of Performing Arts, a school whose recognition factor broadened substantially when she immortalized her experiences there in the song "Nothing."

Lopez's very first Broadway open audition resulted in a job: dancing in the musical adaptation of *Breakfast at Tiffany's*, which unfortunately was closed by producer David Merrick before reaching its Broadway opening night. Later she worked for Michel Stuart (her future *ACL* castmate) on a revue he produced in Florida, with choreography by Ron Field. She returned to New York, where she met Michael Bennett and worked with him on several projects, including the short-lived Broadway musical *Henry, Sweet Henry*, an edition of *The Milliken Breakfast Show*, and the Broadway production of Stephen Sondheim and George Furth's *Company*, with choreography by Bennett: she understudied Donna McKechnie in the role of Kathy and took over that role later in the run. During this busy period, Lopez also succeeded Leland Palmer in the leading role of Viola in *Your Own Thing*, a popular Off-Broadway rock musical based on Shakespeare's *Twelfth Night*. At the time of the tape sessions that led to *A Chorus Line*, she was playing Fastrada (again as a replacement for Palmer) in the Broadway production of *Pippin*.

With these major assignments already to her credit, she was one of the most experienced actors in the original cast of *ACL* and well established as a triple-threat performer. She served as the production's Equity deputy and was unafraid to speak up when she felt the cast was being treated unfairly, financially or otherwise. She was also the only cast member entrusted with two solo songs: in addition to "Nothing," based on her life, she sang the show's iconic eleven o'clock number, "What I Did for Love." Looking back on the *Chorus Line* experience for an interview on the *NBC Nightly News* in 1990, she said, "The best thing that it gave us was that it gave us a place in theatre history. You know, that's such a gift."

Her performance as Morales earned her a Tony nomination as Best Featured Actress in a Musical, but she lost the award to castmate Kelly Bishop; she did, however, win a Tony in the same category for her double role in the 1980 musical *A Day in Hollywood/A Night in the Ukraine*, which was co-choreographed by Thommie Walsh and featured costumes designed by Michel Stuart. Later Broadway credits include *Nine* (as vacation replacement for Liliane Montevecchi; she was also special assistant to the show's director, Tommy Tune) and, more recently, *Anna in the Tropics* and *In the Heights*. She has stayed very busy as an actress, with Off-Broadway appearances including the straight plays *Extremities* and *Key Exchange* and the musical revue *The New Yorkers* at the Manhattan Theatre Club. She did a one-woman play Off Broadway, *Class Mothers of '68*, in which she played six different characters, all mothers of students in the same high school graduating class. Film credits include *Revenge of the Nerds II: Nerds in Paradise*, *Center Stage*, *Maid in Manhattan*, *Musical Chairs*, and *Sleeping with the Fishes*. On television, she has guest-starred on many of the top series and played regular or recurring roles on *As the World Turns*, *In the Beginning*, *Kay O'Brien*, and *Law and Order: Special Victims Unit*. She is married to Vincent Fanuele, a Broadway conductor who worked on *ACL*, and they have two children. Her most recent projects have included *Somewhere*, a play written by her nephew Matthew Lopez, and, in the summer of 2014, a stint in director Diane Paulus's hit Broadway revival of *Pippin*. Forty years after first doing that show, she took over the role of Berthe (with Charlotte d'Amboise, who had been Cassie in the *ACL* revival, in Lopez's original role of Fastrada). In addition to singing the memorable song "No Time at All," she was required by the unusual circus-inspired staging to do an aerial trapeze stunt with a muscular partner, for which the still-disciplined former dancer got back into top physical shape and wowed her audiences eight times a week.

Robert LuPone (Zach)

Like most of the cast members, LuPone's interest in dance started in childhood. He started class early and performed as part of a trio with his twin brother, William, and their sister, Patti, who went on to become the celebrated Broadway star of *Evita*, the revivals of *Sweeney Todd* and *Gypsy*, and other musicals. They performed together on *The Ted Mack Amateur Hour*, a TV series that is mentioned in the script of *A Chorus Line* (see Chapter 14). One of the few *ACL* cast members to have a serious background in modern dance, he studied on a scholarship at the Martha Graham School of Contemporary Dance for three years while he was still in high school. He attended Alfred University and the Juilliard School, expanding his dance vocabulary to classical ballet and studying under the great Antony Tudor.

After a time performing professionally with the Harkness Ballet, LuPone decided he wanted to pursue musical theatre and started out by getting cast in the 1968 Lincoln Center production of *West Side Story*. He made his Broadway debut the same year in the revue *Noel Coward's Sweet Potato*, following that up with *Minnie's Boys*, *The Rothschilds*, and *The Magic Show*. Having appeared onstage in *Jesus Christ Superstar*, he was also cast in the film version, on which he worked with Thommie Walsh and Baayork Lee.

By the time *A Chorus Line* came into his life, LuPone had set his sights on a career as an actor, feeling that dancing was no longer fulfilling his creative aspirations. He had not been part of the tape sessions but joined the company for the first workshop. As a serious student of acting and already somewhat interested in directing, he was an opinionated collaborator, and over the years he has been vocal about the frustrations and dissatisfaction he felt at various points during the process. Later, there was the uncomfortable situation of his being put in competition with castmate Sammy Williams (Paul) when both were nominated for the Tony Award for Best Featured Actor in a Musical—an award that Williams won. When the record-breaking gala performance was being planned for September 1983, LuPone was one of the very few original cast members who chose not to participate. He did, however, play return engagements as Zach in the Broadway company in 1986 and 1988. His Cassie during the latter run was Laurie Gamache, with whom he was romantically involved at the time; he later recreated Zach once more in a production she directed for the Reagle Players in Massachusetts.

LuPone performed opposite Andrea Marcovicci in the musical *Nefertiti*, which never reached Broadway, and starred in the short-lived Broadway musical *Late Nite Comic*. He began to focus successfully on straight acting roles, playing the Dauphin in the 1977 Broadway revival of *Saint Joan*, starring Lynn Redgrave. He has appeared frequently on TV, including regular roles on several soap operas and recurring ones on *The Sopranos* and *Law and Order: Criminal Intent*, in addition to guest appearances on many other popular series. He performed in Broadway revivals of *A View from the Bridge*, *True West*, and *A Thousand Clowns* and continues to work in film, most recently in the 2013 feature *Isn't It Delicious*, which has made the rounds of numerous film festivals.

In 1986, he became a founding artistic director, along with Bernard Telsey, of Manhattan Class Company, a theatre group focused on supporting outstanding emerging artists through classes and workshops and discovering important new plays. Originally housed at the Nat Horne Theatre on West 42nd Street, the company, now known as MCC Theatre, has grown steadily and presents a season of plays each year Off Broadway at the Lucille Lortel Theatre in Manhattan's West Village. Their award-winning productions, some of which have transferred to Broadway or other commercial venues, have included *Beirut*, *Wit*, *The Glory of Living*, *The Mercy Seat*, *reasons to be pretty*, *Frozen*, *Coraline*, *The Pride*, and *The Other Place*. In addition to running the company and continuing his acting career, LuPone was head of the MFA Program at the New School for Drama from 2005 until 2011.

Clive Clerk (Larry)

Clerk was born in Trinidad to one of the only white families in his community. His mother started him in dance class when he was eight and two years later arranged for him to live in California with relatives so he could attend a better dance school. The family moved to Toronto during Trinidad's struggle for independence; Clerk got to see a few Broadway shows as a child and, like several other *ACL* dancers, was particularly inspired by *West Side Story*. He decided to pursue a career as a dancer and was immediately successful, appearing on Canadian TV frequently while he was still in high school.

Clerk first worked with Michael Bennett on a TV special while both were teenagers. He appeared in Canadian productions of *The Most Happy Fella* and *Flower Drum Song* and was offered a place in the original Broadway cast of *Little Me*—choreographed by Bob Fosse—but he had to turn the job down because he was still only fifteen and didn't yet have a work permit for the United States. Film work in Hollywood also beckoned, and after finally obtaining the work permit he danced with Doris Day in the film *Send Me No Flowers*. Other work included the 1965 movie *Billie*, starring Patty Duke (in which Donna McKechnie also served as assistant choreographer to David Winters and appeared, uncredited, as a dancer). He held a regular role on the soap opera *Days of Our Lives* and guested on such TV shows as *The Mod Squad* and *Happy Days*.

Although he enjoyed a lot of early success as a dancer and actor, he was always interested in painting as well, and pursued that career separately under the name Clive Wilson. As much of a prodigy as a painter as he was as a performer, he had a show of his artworks in Trinidad when he was eight years old. While he was acting in California, he pursued his art training at UCLA. A chance reunion with Bennett at a party led to his being invited to attend a rehearsal for *A Chorus Line*, and he was asked to join the workshop as Larry, the assistant choreographer. While still performing in the Broadway production, he opened an interior design business in New York.

After taking over as dance captain when Baayork Lee left New York to join the National Company, Clerk was promoted to the role of Zach, which he played on tour for some time and briefly on Broadway. On completing his run, he decided to put his performing career behind him—though he did return to *A Chorus Line* for the record-breaking gala in 1983, and later collaborated with Lee on staging a production of the show for the Surflight Theatre in New Jersey. He continued to paint while focusing his energies on his interior design business, Clive Wilson Design Associates, which enjoyed substantial success and public acclaim. He died in Los Angeles in 2005 at the age of fifty-nine.

10

"Who Am I Anyway?"

The Understledies

A n important, but largely unsung, component of *A Chorus Line* is the small contingent of performers who appear as "cut dancers," seen only in the opening number, and also understudy the performers "on the line." Though all Broadway musicals have understudies and swings to cover the cast—usually at least two for each role—the way these assignments have been handled in the major productions of *ACL* is atypical in several respects. You may or may not have taken notice of these individual performers as they whirl by on the crowded stage during the show's busy opening number, so this chapter provides a chance to take a closer look at this hardworking group of dancers and find out more specifics about who they are and what they do.

When the lights first come up to start the show, there's a total of twenty-six people on stage (all the numbers in this chapter refer to the official Broadway and tour staging; configurations can be different in regional productions). This includes the seventeen dancers who will make up the line, plus Zach and his assistant Larry. The other seven are the understudies, seen playing auditionees who will be cut when Zach announces eliminations near the end of the number. After this, these four men and three women are not seen again, though they are heard singing from offstage to reinforce the cast during group numbers (important in a dance musical, where the onstage performers are often singing and dancing at the same time and can get winded). They don't even get a curtain call, which is almost unheard of in a Broadway show.

In addition to the seven onstage cut dancers, there are also several swings, the number of which can vary from company to company. Like the others, these performers each understudy two or more roles on the line, but they are not seen in the opening unless one of the seven is out sick—or is going on as understudy for a role. Each of the swings, as well as the understudies, is expected to know all the cut dancer roles for his or her gender, so they can be reshuffled depending on who is out of the show on any given night.

Though the audience never hears the names of the seven cut dancer characters, they all have names that are listed in the script and in the program. Here's a rundown to aid in identifying who is who:

Tricia

The first solo voice heard singing in the show belongs to one of the soon-to-be-cut dancers, whose name is Tricia. She usually wears blue and is seen near the top of the number stretching out her leg next to the proscenium arch on stage left and belting a few high-lying phrases ("I really need this job . . ."). She is also the dancer who irritates Sheila a few moments later by dancing directly in front of her during the ballet combination. Right before announcing the eliminations, Zach asks her if she's been in any Broadway shows, and she tells him only touring companies.

The role was originated by Donna Drake, a petite brunette who bore some physical and vocal resemblance to the original Maggie, Kay Cole. Drake understudied that role as well as Connie and Kristine. She later told a story about how she mentioned one day that she found it frustrating to play Kristine, since she prided herself on her outstanding voice and hated making the audience think she couldn't sing. In typical blunt fashion, Michael Bennett snapped at her: "Then you'll never be an actress." Unlike most of the original understudies, who never got to move up onto the line, Drake played Maggie for a while in the National Company during the 1976–77 season and took over the role on Broadway the next year. She later became a successful director and has staged several regional revivals of the show.

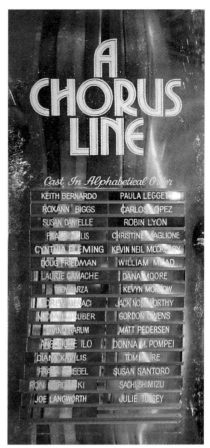

The cast board at the Shubert Theatre, with each actor's name on an individual mirrored tile; shown here are the names of the final Broadway company, 1990.

Vicki

Vicki is the other girl in the group who has a couple of lines. She is usually played by a sexy, shapely dancer and wears a green leotard. During the ballet combination, Zach asks if she has any ballet training; when she says she doesn't, he tells her to stop dancing. Later, as her group of four is beginning the jazz combination, she raises her hand to stop, then asks if someone could do the steps in front in case she forgets the sequence. Zach obliges and tells Larry to dance with the group. Before the elimination, Zach asks her if she's done any Broadway shows, and she says she hasn't.

The original Vicki was Crissy Wilzak, who may be remembered by TV audiences for her later role as Glenda Faye on *Mork and Mindy*. The role of Vicki was tailored to her, as she really wasn't a trained ballerina—though she was a strong enough jazz dancer to have been cast in the musical *Seesaw* and to have kept her job even when Michael Bennett fired and replaced fourteen members of the ensemble. Wilzak understudied the roles of Judy and Val, but the agreed-upon procedure was that even when she went on in one of those roles, she would still be the one Zach told not to dance in the ballet combination, since she really couldn't do it very well. (This may have caused some especially observant audience members to question Zach's judgment on those nights, since Judy and Val are both among the eight dancers who "get the job" at the end of the evening.) Because Pamela Blair was out sick, Wilzak has the distinction of having played Val on the last night the original cast did the show together on Broadway, before most of them departed to open the National Company in San Francisco.

Lois

The third girl in the opening is Lois. Dressed mostly in white, she is notable as the only character dancing in ballet slippers. The idea is that she's really a ballerina rather than a Broadway dancer; though technically strong, she gets cut because her style is wrong for the show. Originally the character danced beautifully, with a lovely high extension, but would stand out because of her classical line. In more recent productions, she has sometimes been treated as more of a joke, the dancers playing her exaggerating the stylistic difference to the point where the character appears to be daintily moving through a sequence of poses, with no sense of the dynamism required for show dancing; sometimes her port de bras is specifically balletic, ignoring the choreography. (This isn't particularly believable, as it's unlikely that any highly trained ballerina would be that clueless about style, but it does draw more focus from the audience during her brief moments onstage.)

The role was originally played by Carolyn Kirsch, an experienced gypsy with several Broadway shows to her credit, who had worked with Michael Bennett before. She was the understudy for Cassie and Sheila. Because Lois needs to be very accomplished technically, it quickly became a tradition that the dancer in that track would usually understudy the Cassie in any given company; new girls hired as potential Cassies would often go into the show first as Lois and then move up when there was an opening. Because Lois does not speak and is never specifically spoken to, this is the character eliminated from the show on nights when there are more female dancers out than there are swings—thus leaving a "hole" in the opening number.

Barbara

The original program also listed the fourth female understudy, Carole Schweid, as playing a character named Barbara. After the first couple of previews, however, that character didn't really exist. After it was decided that Cassie's late "diva" entrance,

Courtney Iventosch (as ballerina Lois) and Kate Levering (Cassie) in *A Chorus Line*. Sacramento Music Circus, June 2014.   *Photo by Charr Crail*

sweeping onstage in a fur and asking for money to pay a cab, was not working, Donna McKechnie was added into the opening, and from then on was seen onstage from the top of the show. She was given Schweid's spot in the number, which meant Schweid (who was the understudy for Bebe and Diana) effectively became the show's first swing. Of course, she did appear onstage any time the Tricia, Vicki, or Lois was out or went on as an understudy, in which case that character simply became "Barbara" that night: since none of their names is spoken in the show, no program change was necessary. (See below for more on the complexities of how these dancers were listed in the Playbill. . . .)

Roy

Roy is the male dancer who can't get the port de bras right in the ballet combination; Zach asks how many years of ballet he has had, to which he replies only one. Zach corrects his arm positions, but he continues to struggle, to comic effect. He generally wears a navy blue sweatshirt with red sleeves.

The role was created by and for Scott Allen, a singer who auditioned during the second workshop and was initially cast as Al, the role that had been vacated when Robert LuPone was moved up to Zach. Allen really did struggle to keep up with the other dancers, however, and Bennett shortly decided to replace him with his understudy, Don Percassi, moving Allen down to the understudy position. Several years later, Allen briefly but successfully took on the role of Zach in one of the touring companies.

Frank

Frank tends to get a couple of big laughs. He's the "boy in the headband," who can't keep from looking at his feet while he's dancing; Zach has to yell at him repeatedly to keep his head up.

This role was originated by Michael Serrecchia, who was the understudy for Larry, Greg, and Bobby. Remarkably, Serrecchia had built a career as a professional dancer despite a troubled physical history: due to a rare medical condition, he hadn't been able to walk till the age of thirteen. When he finally grew out of it, his family sent him to dance class to improve his balance and coordination, and he obviously took to it. But he really did have a bad habit of looking down while he danced; Michael Bennett picked up on that one day in rehearsal and decided to use it.

Butch

In a show where several of the characters are racially specific, the question arises as to whether there are understudies of the appropriate ethnicities to cover them. Companies of *ACL* almost never hire a second Asian actress to understudy Connie, and there are alternate lines in the acting edition of the script for nights when a Caucasian actress (usually the shortest of the understudies, since the "four foot ten" lines remain unchanged) goes on in the role; on these occasions, Connie Wong becomes "Connie MacKenzie." The idea of a white actor singing "Gimme the Ball," however, is more worrisome, and there is usually a second African American actor in the ensemble to cover Richie. He usually understudies one or two other roles as well, often Larry or Paul. In the opening number, this actor traditionally plays Butch.

Butch was originated by Chuck Cissell, the understudy for Richie and Paul. When initially cast, he was still nursing a bit of resentment left over from the auditions for *Follies* several years earlier: he had been the last male dancer eliminated, and Bennett had told him it was because that show was a period piece and a black dancer would have looked out of place. So he had a bit of an attitude, which he got to display for a brief moment nonverbally when Zach gave Butch a correction on the jazz combination. Bennett had suggested naming the character Freddy, which Cissell rejected, declaring his name would be Butch Burton. The character usually wears a physique-revealing, sheer see-through top.

Tom

The fourth and last of the cut male dancers is called Tom; he usually wears a turtleneck and a sweater. The role was played originally by Brandt Edwards, who understudied Don and Mark. Because Tom is never singled out in any way during the number, he is generally the first character deleted on nights when there are not enough male swings to go around. He's been described as an athletic performer

Deidre Goodwin (center) as Sheila in the revival at the Curran Theatre in San Francisco, 2006, prior to the opening on Broadway. Understudy Mike Cannon, playing Mike, is seen over her right shoulder.   *Photo by Paul Kolnik*

who dances like a jock, talented but still too young and inexperienced to get the job. Sometimes he can be seen counting out loud while he's dancing.

At This Performance . . .

During the initial Off-Broadway run at the Public Theater, where the small seating capacity and limited ticket revenue dictated the smallest possible cast, there were only the eight understudies, and all of them except Carole Schweid appeared in the opening. (Clive Clerk, who played Larry, understudied Zach.) That meant that any time there was a male out of the show, or more than one female, there would be a hole in the opening number. So when the show moved to Broadway, a number of swings were added, covering all the cut dancers as well as two or three line characters apiece. Each swing or understudy covered a different combination of roles, in an attempt to ensure that there would be enough people to go around no matter what combination of actors called out sick on any given night. As the run went on, this didn't always prove to be the case, and sometimes dancers who had done the show on the road or in a previous company were called in on short notice to fill in temporarily. (For example, Rita Rehn, who had played Diana and Sheila on tour, recalls jumping in as Bebe, a role she had never done, for a few performances on Broadway when they were short-handed.) As the long Broadway run

"I Hope I Get It": Matthew Johnson as Zach leads the full cast, including the seven "cut dancers," in the opening number, Gordon Crowe Tour, 1993.   *Photo courtesy Stephen Nachamie*

continued, it also became more common for actors playing characters on the line to understudy each other. Don Percassi, the original Al, understudied Mike for a while. Often a Don or a Larry would understudy Zach, or a Val or a Judy might understudy Cassie or Sheila. Sometimes this arrangement was based on the fact that a dancer had already played a certain role in another company of the show; since she knew that part, she was added to the understudy pool as extra coverage. For example, Pamela Ann Wilson played Val in the International Company, then understudied that role while she was playing Bebe on Broadway.

In some of the more recent productions, there has been yet another category of cover as well: the "standby for Cassie and Sheila." (A standby is traditionally someone who covers a major role but, unlike an understudy, does not otherwise appear in the show.) This assignment would generally be offered to a more mature, prestigious dancer, who would probably prefer not to play one of the kids cut in the opening number. During the run of the Broadway revival, both Dylis Croman and Kimberly Dawn Neumann took brief turns as the Cassie/Sheila standby.

Complications have arisen over the complex question of how substitutions were to be listed in the program. For most of the original Broadway run, all the covers were simply listed on the regular cast list; those not playing the seven named characters described above were assigned, or chose, other names, like Jarad, Kim, or Linda. This made the cast look bigger than it really was, with up to thirty-one dancers listed at any given time for a show that only uses twenty-six. However, since everyone was already listed as part of the cast, and the audience can't tell the names of the cut dancers anyway—none of which are spoken aloud—this simplified things. If, for example, the dancer who normally played Tricia went on as Maggie, this substitution was announced to the audience. But if the swing listed in the program as playing "Rosemary" stepped in as Tricia, no announcement was made; the character simply became Rosemary for that performance, and who could tell the difference?

For the record, the understudies in the first cast of the Broadway revival were Michelle Aravena as Tricia, Lorin Latarro as Vicki, Nadine Isenegger as Lois, David Baum as Roy, Grant Turner as Frank, E. Clayton Cornelious as Butch, and Mike Cannon as Tom. The swings were Lyndy Franklin (also the assistant dance captain), Pamela Fabello, and Joey Dudding.

"That Light . . . What Color Is That?"

The Designers and What They Did for *A Chorus Line*

ust as the music, dialogue, and choreography were integrated with unprecedented seamlessness, the design elements of *A Chorus Line* grew and developed through the workshop sessions and emerged as fully integral components of the finished musical, to the point where most fans can't imagine the show without them. This chapter will look at the supremely talented design team Michael Bennett and Joseph Papp put together, their backgrounds, and the innovative work they did on the show.

Robin Wagner (Set Designer)

Robin Wagner was brought into the workshop for *A Chorus Line* by Michael Bennett, having developed a strong working relationship with him through collaborations on *Promises, Promises* and *Seesaw*. If the designer had a previous connection to the Public Theater, it was a tangential one: he designed the set for the Broadway production of *Hair*, but that was a total revamping of the show, no longer under Joseph Papp's auspices. After establishing a relationship with the NYSF with *A Chorus Line*, Wagner became an integral part of the organization and eventually held a seat on the Festival's Board of Trustees.

He grew up in California, where he had something of an itinerant existence as a child. His mother was from New Zealand, where she had been a classical pianist (a career she did not pursue after moving to America), and his Danish father was a marine engineer who worked on large ships. Though Robin wasn't involved with theatre as a child, he early on demonstrated a talent for drawing, which his parents encouraged. He discovered his love of the theatre at the age of twenty; wanting to be involved as something more than an audience member, he started working as a light board operator at the Theatre Arts Colony in San Francisco, while also attending art school in that city.

The young Wagner started working with small theatre groups in the Bay Area and did a design for a production of *Waiting for Godot* that was invited to represent American regional theatre (a movement then in its infancy) at the 1958 Brussels

Theoni V. Aldredge's classic finale costumes are seen in front of Robin Wagner's mirrored periaktoi. Shown here is the London cast, 1977, with Michael Staniforth, center, as Paul.

Photo courtesy Roni Page

World's Fair. On their way home from that, the company stopped off in New York
City, which inspired Wagner to move there. The Off-Broadway scene was burgeoning at the time, and he soon found opportunities to design seventeen productions;
he also started working on Broadway as an assistant designer to such top names as
Ben Edwards and Oliver Smith. He developed an early interest in musical theatre;
the shows on which he assisted Smith included the original productions of *110 in
the Shade* and *Hello, Dolly!* His first credit as a scenic designer on Broadway was *The
Condemned of Altona*, presented at the Vivian Beaumont Theatre by the Repertory
Theatre of Lincoln Center in 1966 (this was before Joe Papp was tapped to run the
Beaumont), followed the next season by a large-scale revival of Brecht's *Galileo* in
the same space.

Still professionally active at age eighty, Wagner has had an extraordinarily long
and impressive Broadway career. He has won three Tony Awards for Best Scenic
Design: for *On the Twentieth Century* (1978), *City of Angels* (1990), and *The Producers*
(2001). His six other Tony nominations were for *Jesus Christ Superstar*, *Dreamgirls*

(directed by Michael Bennett), *Jelly's Last Jam, Angels in America Part One: Millennium Approaches*, the 2000 revival of *Kiss Me, Kate*, and *The New Mel Brooks Musical Young Frankenstein*. He became Michael Bennett's designer of choice after they worked together on *Promises, Promises* (with Bennett as choreographer) in 1968, and their collaboration continued with *Seesaw, A Chorus Line, Ballroom* and *Dreamgirls*. He worked with Bennett in London on the West End production of *Chess* and stayed with the project after Bennett departed due to his declining health, working with director Trevor Nunn first in London and then on a very different set of designs for the Broadway version. Wagner's dozens of other Broadway designs included *The Great White Hope, Lenny, Sugar, Rachael Lily Rosenbloom and Don't You Ever Forget It, Mack and Mabel, Comin' Uptown, 42nd Street, Song and Dance, Jerome Robbins' Broadway, Crazy for You, Victor/Victoria, Big, The Life, Side Show, Saturday Night Fever, The Wild Party, The Boy From Oz, Never Gonna Dance*, and *Leap of Faith*—as well as the Broadway revivals of *Hair* (1977) and *A Chorus Line* (2006). He has also designed for regional theatres and both the New York City Ballet and the Metropolitan Opera, as well as several major European opera houses. He has taught in Columbia University's graduate program in theatre arts.

Ironically, though *A Chorus Line* swept the 1976 Tony Awards, Wagner's set did not win—nor was it even one of his nine nominations. Chalk it up to a preference for elaborate, splashy spectacles on the part of the nominators; few of them are designers, and they are less likely to recognize the brilliance of a spare, elegantly simple design.

Describing his work on the show for a Playbill.com feature in 2007, Wagner told an uncredited editor the design was his personal favorite: "Because it's so simple. That was the result of two years' work, of Michael Bennett and I trying to distill things. We started with big ideas for visualizing scenes, and as we went through the show's workshop period, they got smaller and smaller. Finally, we realized we could do the whole show with nothing but a line. That was the real beginning. And then we knew we needed a black box, which represents theatre, and that we needed the mirrors, because they represent the dance studio."

Because the designers were hired early and were part of the two lengthy workshop sessions, discussion of design concepts began before there was anything resembling a finished script, and numerous ideas were considered and discarded. *A Chorus Line* could have ended up with a much bigger, more extravagant design: for a while Bennett and Wagner talked about grand pianos for the finale, or a sweeping staircase for a star entrance à la *Hello, Dolly!* But gradually all that was stripped away, leaving just the essentials. As Wagner said, the straight line of tape (in actuality it's white paint) across the full width of the stage, a few feet up from the edge, was a key focus for the show, both physically and metaphorically: it stood not only for the line the dancers stood on to be evaluated, but the idea of "putting yourself on the line," risking everything for what you most want, what you need to survive. The line and its location on the stage anchor the blocking and the choreography, and the relationship the dancers develop with it is a vital component of the evening.

Then there was the question of the mirrors. Bennett wanted a full wall of mirrors that could appear upstage whenever needed, both representing realistically the dance studio mirrors dancers use to correct themselves when they are learning choreography, and providing a reflection of the audience out front: we see ourselves reflected along with the cast and realize on some gut level that the show is about all of us, the challenges we face and the choices we make. But Bennett and Wagner also wanted the mirrors to be able to disappear at will, leaving only a black void. How to accomplish this?

Ultimately, Wagner hit on the elegant solution of the periaktoid, a simple scenic element that has been around for thousands of years, since the age of early Greek drama. This is a three-sided arrangement of flats, rotating on a center axis. By placing a row of these upstage, Wagner created a flexible backdrop: one side of each periaktoid was covered in black velour, and when all of these sides were facing forward, the audience saw a solid black wall. But the second side of each was a mirror, and when the devices were all rotated at the same time, a whole mirrored wall magically appeared. (There were eight periaktoi in all, each sixteen feet tall: their rotations were controlled by a single stagehand operating a manual crank upstage right.) And what about the third side? That was ultimately used for the art deco sunburst design, not seen until the "One" finale.

There are also additional mirrors that appear for the slow section of Cassie's dance solo. A semicircle of tall, narrow mirrors materializes around her as if by magic, and when she dances in the center, she sees multiple reflections of herself— as does the audience. During the original Off-Broadway run at the Public Theater, the mirrors were on rolling units and were pushed onstage by some of the male dancers; on Broadway, they were flown in from above. The number of mirrors was increased from five at the Public to seven on Broadway. Though they looked like real glass, the mirrors in the show were all made of Mirrex, a lightweight mylar developed for the space program. Sometimes the dancers would get too close and kick them by accident, creating creases and wrinkles that would have to be repaired—but since they weren't glass, they didn't break.

A black box stage, a colorful backdrop, and mirrors: the three key visual elements of a dancer's world, according to Wagner and Bennett. And really, along with the white line, that's the whole set. A Chorus Line is one of the only large-scale musicals ever produced with no doors, no windows, no furniture—though there is the one stool for Zach, which some people don't even notice because it's so far stage right, almost in the wings.

Because the stark simplicity of the environment feels so inevitable and so right—and has become so familiar to fans of the show—it's easy to overlook the fact that this might not have been the most obvious design solution to start with. A Chorus Line takes place, after all in "a Broadway theatre"—originally referred to in the program simply as "Here." The show's feeling of immediacy and authenticity springs partly from the fact that the audience is watching it in the very place where the story is meant to be unfolding. Thus, many designers might have thought that stripping the theatre down to its backstage essentials might have been the obvious choice: if an audition is being held on the stage of a Broadway house where no show is currently running, might we not see the backstage architecture—including stairways, catwalks, ladders, ropes, sandbags, old flats, and so forth—all the way to the bare brick wall at the back of the building? (Something like this was later done with the musical *RENT*.) And indeed, this type of approach has occasionally been tried by the designers of later productions—as well as, probably inevitably, the movie version, where the realistic medium of film demanded a more literal approach.

A consideration of why Wagner may have chosen NOT to go that way can shed some useful light on what *A Chorus Line* really is—and what it isn't. What it isn't is a realistic depiction of an audition. As critics have occasionally pointed out, it's highly unlikely that any director would ask dancers the kinds of personal questions Zach asks them in the show or devote the amount of time he does to listening to their answers. It will be recalled that the creators of the show were some days into the first workshop before they even agreed on the idea of setting the show at an audition at all: originally, characters were seen entering a mysterious, limbo-like space and answering questions from a disembodied "Voice," not yet identified as a director. The whole show, in that very early draft of the script, was more metaphoric and existential—and some of that sense of universality and symbolism survives in the finished show. By setting the musical in a streamlined, empty black box rather than a realistically appointed theatre, Wagner subtly gives us in the audience permission not to take the "audition" too literally, and to experience it as a metaphor for something bigger: the open, scary place we all enter at turning points in our lives, where we submit to evaluation by others in the hopes of being allowed to move forward, and where we are forced to reflect on our own pasts and our own choices. (It's very significant that the mirrors were meant to reflect not only the dancers but the audience beyond them as well: at many points in the evening, we are watching ourselves.) The ways in which the show departs from the actual circumstances of a Broadway audition could feel like liabilities on a more realistic stage, but in Robin Wagner's magically simple setting, which allows the imagination to take flight, this very lack of literalness becomes one of *A Chorus Line*'s greatest strengths.

Theoni V. Aldredge (Costume Designer)

Aldredge was already the resident costume designer for the Public Theater/NYSF when Joseph Papp introduced her to Michael Bennett. Though she had previously studied on scholarship at the Goodman Theatre/DePaul University in Chicago, she claimed she learned her craft working for Papp, who originally paid her only eighty dollars a week; she designed the costumes for such legendary NYSF productions as *Short Eyes*, *Sticks and Bones*, *That Championship Season* and the musical version of *Two Gentlemen of Verona*, many of which moved to Broadway. Papp called her the Queen of the Public Theater, and she worked there for over twenty years.

Born Theoni Athanasiou Vachlioti in Thessaloniki, Greece, in 1922, Aldredge attended the American School in Athens before moving to America. She met actress Geraldine Page at the Goodman Theatre: a connection that led to her first Broadway job, the premiere of Tennessee Williams's *Sweet Bird of Youth*, starring Page, in 1959. (Though the costume design for that production was credited to Anna Hill Johnstone, Aldredge designed Page's costumes; in those days, it was not unheard of for a separate designer to do the clothes for a female star, and Aldredge did the same duty for Page again for the 1963 revival of *Strange Interlude*, otherwise designed by Noel Taylor.) In her long Broadway career, Aldredge, like Robin Wagner, became especially identified with musicals, winning three Tony Awards for her designs for *Annie* (1977), *Barnum* (1980), and *La Cage aux Folles* (1984). After *A Chorus Line*, she remained a close collaborator of Michael Bennett's, designing costumes for both *Ballroom* and *Dreamgirls*, and receiving Tony nominations for both. Her other nominations were for *The Devil's Advocate*, *Two Gentlemen of Verona*, *Much Ado About Nothing*, *The Au Pair Man*, *A Chorus Line*, *The Threepenny Opera*, *42nd Street*, the 1990 revival of *Gypsy*, *The Secret Garden*, and the 2001 revival of *Follies*. She had over a hundred Broadway credits in all, ending with the 2006 revival of *A Chorus Line*, for which she recreated her original designs, with a few modifications, with major assistance from associate designer Suzy Benzinger. She also designed for film, including such notable movies as *Never on Sunday*, *Network*, *Eyes of Laura Mars*, *Ghostbusters*, and *Rich and Famous*, as well as the 1974 version of *The Great Gatsby*—for which she won the Academy Award for Best Costume Design on April 8, 1975, a week before *A Chorus Line* began previews at the Public Theater. Her 1920s-era designs for *Gatsby* were so popular that they were adapted as a clothing line, sold exclusively at Bloomingdale's. Her many other honors included the Theatre Development Fund's 2002 Irene Sharaff Lifetime Achievement Award, which is named after another legendary Broadway and Hollywood costume designer.

Costume designer Theoni V. Aldredge. *Photofest*

In 1953, she married Tom Aldredge, the respected actor perhaps best remembered for creating the roles of Norman Thayer in *On Golden Pond* and The Narrator/Mysterious Man in *Into the Woods*. They were married for almost fifty-eight years, until her death in Stamford, Connecticut, in January 2011; he passed away six months and one day later.

Though Aldredge, unlike Robin Wagner, was nominated for a Tony Award for *A Chorus Line*, she was one of the show's few nominees who didn't win. Again, this was probably due to the deceptive simplicity of the show's designs and the fact that the voters tend to be most impressed by spectacle. Although Aldredge's costumes for the finale provided a shot of glitz and glamour, for the majority of the evening the dancers are seen in simple rehearsal clothes. A great deal of art and care went into the creation of a distinctive look for each character.

Like the other designers, Aldredge spent a lot of time observing the workshop sessions, and she paid particular attention to what the dancers wore. In some cases, they came to regret careless decisions about what to throw on before a given day's rehearsal. For example, Pamela Blair sometimes wore sneakers, and Aldredge and Bennett decided the look was right for Val; Blair resented it, because dancing in the flat footwear every night is hard on the arches. By contrast, Nancy Lane as Bebe, like most of the women in the show, was asked to wear jazz shoes with heels; she said she would have preferred sneakers, as she had occasional back problems and standing on line all night in heels could be uncomfortable. Priscilla Lopez also requested sneakers, and got them, along with what she thought of as her Katharine Hepburn look: a turtleneck under a pullover, though Bennett vetoed the pants she wanted to wear because he preferred the women in tights. (He ultimately assented to pants only for his close friend Baayork Lee, who requested them.) Lopez's sneakers became a permanent part of the show when a line about them made its way into the script: she blames her shoes when Larry tells her he can't hear any taps in the Tap Combination. (Val apparently thought ahead and brought a change of shoes in her dance bag, since she has by that point changed from her sneakers into the heeled jazz shoes most of the other girls wear.)

Donna McKechnie expressed a preference for the color red and asked to wear a dance skirt—the only one in the show. She was accommodated on both counts. The original Cassie costume was fire-engine red, but over the years some of the replacements wore a darker shade, almost a maroon; it depended on the dyer, since the leotards were ordered in white and then sent out to be dyed. The skirt, which had to flow just right, was made in a fabric called Alix Jersey. Traditionally, Cassie is no longer wearing the skirt when she returns to the stage after the Paul scene; because Zach is demanding a uniform line from all the dancers in the "One" number, she has presumably removed it to conform to the group silhouette.

The now-classic Sheila costume, a low-cut, flesh-colored leotard in a shiny, reflective fabric, was the result of Aldredge and Bennett falling in love with a leotard Kelly Bishop wore to the workshop one day. She felt it was too tight for her and only wore it because all her other ones were at the laundry; the resulting costume looks great on a woman with a perfect figure, but is singularly unforgiving, and has been the bane of many a Sheila's existence over the years.

Ultimately, Aldredge came up with a distinctive look and line for each character—more challenging than it sounds, because standard dance clothes of the day didn't offer a huge array of options. The two most similar are the looks for Richie and Mark, each of whom wears stretch pants and a simple tank leotard, though the colors are different. Ron Dennis didn't like the pea-green color of his leotard; though Aldredge didn't change it for him, later generations of Richies have often worn yellow or gold.

The original look of the line was immortalized in a famous photo of the original cast that later became the official logo for the show. A close look at this very familiar image reveals some inconsistencies. Because the photo was taken before the opening of the show at the Public Theater, a couple of the characters do not look the way we are used to seeing them onstage. Mike (Wayne Cilento) is seen in the photo in a long-sleeved, collarless shirt with multicolored horizontal stripes; by the time the show opened on Broadway, it had been replaced by the simple blue, short-sleeved shirt that has become the character's trademark. It also took Aldredge a while to finalize the costume for Maggie: in the logo photo, Kay Cole is seen wearing dark pants and a wraparound crocheted top, which she later said was hard to dance in. Some of the early production photos show a different shirt, also with horizontal stripes. By the time of the cast's well-known appearance on the Tony Awards telecast, Maggie had succumbed to Bennett's dictum of tights for the women and was wearing the brown trunks and peach-colored, V-neck top that became the norm for the character—though over the years the Maggie costume has remained subject to occasional variations.

Kristine's simple brown leotard was also immortalized in the script: in the opening number, Zach, who doesn't yet know her name, refers to her as the "girl in brown." Like Bebe, Kristine originally wore black tights, but some of the replacements wore fishnets, or flesh-colored ones like most of the other girls. Bobby's distinctive sweater and neck scarf were based on Thommie Walsh's own favored look; he said he enjoyed having a bit of "armor" and would have felt too skinny in just a leotard.

Because "One" was one of the last parts of the show to come together, the classic costumes for it were a late addition to the game plan. Bennett originally requested that Aldredge design the finale costumes in red, but she felt the airy, dreamlike nature of the number required a more subtle color and came up with the pale gold, "champagne" hue that has become a classic part of the show's look. Bennett took some convincing but admitted she was right when he saw them in dress rehearsal. Recalling 1930s Busby Berkeley chorus lines or the Radio City Music Hall Rockettes, the top hats and sequined tuxes have a classic showbiz elegance. A particularly significant decision was the choice not to use the expected tailcoats. The women wear vests but no coats, and the men wear short, waist-length jackets; this saved an enormous amount of time and expense over the years, as tailcoats would have had to have been continually rebuilt to maintain a uniform length on actors of different heights. The more compact silhouette also suits the choreography.

Once the show was an established hit and indeed a cultural phenomenon, the costumes began to have an effect on fashion. This coincided with the peak of the disco era, when people would go out on the town in leotards and dance skirts. It should be noted, however, that no character in the original *Chorus Line* wore leg warmers, which would shortly become a fashion cliché.

For the next five years or so, the designs stayed pretty consistent, with occasional minor variations; there were some modifications made for the second Broadway cast. Because the temperature could be hard to predict, or control, in theatres on the road, Aldredge gave some of the characters additional layers they could wear if they were feeling chilly; this was considered important, as a cold dancer is more prone to injuries. Some of the Cassies even had a turtleneck leotard. But these new elements were not worn very often. In the early eighties, however, Bennett decided the show was starting to look dated. When a new company was assembled to begin the Bus & Truck tour, Aldredge redesigned many of the clothes to reflect current styles. Though the iconic looks on some of the characters, like Cassie, Sheila, and Diana, were too well established to be changed, some of the others got makeovers, with brighter colors, higher-cut leotards to make the women's legs look longer, and so forth. The reflective fabric known as Milliskin had recently become popular, and several of the new costumes were done in this material, giving them a shinier (and perhaps somewhat tackier) look. Mike's blue polo shirt was replaced by a tank leotard, and Mark got a new pullover sweater; at this time too, a couple of the characters got leg warmers. The updated designs were briefly incorporated into the International Company and the Broadway production as well, but they never really caught on, and before long it was decided to change the "Time" designation in the Playbill from "Now" to "1975." From that point on, the show was set in the year it was first created, and the original costumes were restored. (The exception was for Greg: Bradley Jones, who played that role in the Bus & Truck company, wore a simple black T-shirt with white and yellow piping, based on a favorite shirt of Bennett's: the new costume has remained standard for that character.)

For regional productions, many theatres have done their best to recreate Aldredge's designs for most or all of the characters. Even when this isn't the case, most costumers will at least tip the hat to a few of the iconic originals: Diana usually wears some combination of red and green, Sheila wears her sleek skintight leotard, and Val is usually dressed in pink or lavender. Iconic looks like Larry's number 17 tank top or the TKTS logo on Al's T-shirt often reappear. And even when a designer chooses to start from scratch and forego all of these, Cassie almost always wears the classic red leotard and skirt: "The Music and the Mirror" just isn't the same number without it.

Tharon Musser (Lighting Designer)

The third member of the original *ACL* design team, Musser came into the project with a long Broadway track record. She first met Michael Bennett in 1962, when he was working as an assistant to choreographer Ron Field on the Broadway musical *Nowhere to Go but Up*. Years later she told Ken Mandelbaum that Bennett would always come to the morning tech rehearsals, even when the cast wasn't present, and sit behind her watching her work; he knew lighting was an important part of any show and, already sure he wanted to be a director, was eager to learn as much as possible about it. Nine years later, Musser's stunning lighting design was a powerful component of *Follies*, which Bennett codirected with Harold Prince, and from then on she was an indispensable member of his team—though he was disappointed that she wasn't available to work on his nonmusical directing debut, *Twigs*.

Musser was born in Roanoke, Virginia, in 1925, the daughter of a preacher, and grew up in a poor family. They couldn't afford electricity, so their home was lit by candles and gas lamps in a period long after this had ceased to be the norm; perhaps this contributed to her lifelong fascination with the power and potential of light and the technology behind it. She attended Berea College in Kentucky and then, in 1951, earned a graduate degree from the Yale School of Drama. She made her Broadway debut in 1958, designing the original production of Eugene O'Neill's *Long Day's Journey into Night*, and though her work for the next several years included numerous serious works by the likes of Brecht, Cocteau, Ibsen, and O'Casey, she discovered her affinity for musical theatre almost immediately, starting with *Li'l Abner* (1958), her second Broadway show, and continuing with *Shinbone Alley* and *Once Upon a Mattress*. She had a long association with Neil Simon, designing eighteen of his plays and musicals on Broadway, including *God's Favorite* (1974, directed by Michael Bennett) and *They're Playing Our Song* (1979, music by Marvin Hamlisch). She also worked repeatedly with Stephen Sondheim and Harold Prince: in addition to *Follies*, she designed the original Broadway productions of *A Little Night Music*, *Pacific Overtures* (which opened the same season as *A Chorus Line*), and the 1974 revival of Leonard Bernstein's *Candide* (which included additional lyrics by Sondheim). Other major Broadway musicals she designed included *Applause*, *Mame*, *The Wiz*, and the 1971 revival of *On the Town* featuring Donna McKechnie. Some considered her most significant creative partnership to be that with Michael Bennett; all three of her Tony Awards were for shows they did together: *Follies* (1972), *A Chorus Line* (1976), and *Dreamgirls* (1982); she also received Tony nominations for Bennett's production of *Ballroom* and for *Applause*, *A Little Night Music*, *The Good Doctor*, *Pacific Overtures*, *The Act*, and *42nd Street*. All in all, she designed over a hundred Broadway productions; the last one she worked on was Martin McDonagh's play *The Lonesome West*, directed by Garry Hines in 1999. By 2006, she was suffering from Alzheimer's disease and no longer able to work, but her classic design for *A Chorus Line* was adapted for the Broadway revival by Natasha Katz; both designers were credited in the program. (A detailed documentation of the lighting design for the revival can be studied online at www.thelightingarchive.org.) Musser's longtime life partner Marilyn Rennagel was with her when she passed away in Newtown, Connecticut, on April 19, 2009.

Musser loved working with Michael Bennett, claiming it was the most fun she ever had in her career. The only one of *A Chorus Line*'s designers to win a Tony for her work on the musical, she used an unusually complex array of lighting effects to define space, mood, and the multiple levels of reality the show required. The stark simplicity of the set and costume designs allowed lighting to become an especially vivid and dynamic component of the production. She began with a harsh white light that suggested the work lights that would be seen in an actual audition; the show often returns to this look for the spoken sections when the dancers are all seen standing on the Line. (One criticism occasionally raised is that these flat white lights can be unflattering to the girl dancers' legs, making them appear heavier.) When the audience is meant to be hearing the characters' inner thoughts, the light shifts to a bluish "thought light," clearly delineating the transition. There are tight spotlights that can isolate individual dancers' faces and colorful geometric patterns (suggested by the artist Mondrian) that appear on the black stage floor in some scenes—particularly the Montage, where the crisp isolation of areas is crucial to the effectiveness of the number. Another visual influence was a photography book by David Duncan.

The set's use of mirrors created a particular challenge for Musser, as they can reflect light back into the audience's eyes if the angles aren't just right. (A small blue light was placed in the back of the theatre's orchestra section for the dancers to focus on when they were supposed to be looking out at Zach, but this had to be turned off when the mirrors rotated in to avoid having its reflection seen by the audience.) Brighter, glitzier lighting was used for the lavish finale.

In order to achieve all these effects, Musser used an unusually large number of lighting instruments: 312 units and footlights. When the show was in its first home at the Newman, it was run manually from a preset board, plus an additional console that Musser brought in to handle some of the special effects. When it came time to move to Broadway, Bennett and Musser wanted the show to look exactly the same, which proved a big challenge because the space at the Shubert was so different. At the Newman, footlights were used, more for their decorative effect than for the light they cast. Because the audience there is so steeply raked, they worked. The Shubert has a steeper rake than most Broadway houses, which was one reason they put the show there, but it wasn't as steep as the Newman's; Musser realized that because of the lower angle, some of the audience members in the orchestra would not be able to see the dancers' feet—they would be blocked by the footlights. But she didn't want to cut them, and finally Joe Papp suggested a workable solution: the footlights were placed on a small elevator so they could be raised and lowered, and were only brought up for the scenes in which they were actually used.

More challenging was the fact that the Shubert didn't have the lighting positions Musser needed to create the clean floor patterns she wanted without bouncing light off the mirrors, and without casting shadows on the back wall of the set; she told Bennett she needed a forty-five-degree angle to make it all work. The Shuberts tried to talk Bennett into using the balcony rails as lighting positions, but he insisted on the angle Musser asked for—which necessitated the construction of an all-new lighting bridge in the theatre. To get it in the right place, they had to cut into the ceiling of the house and build into the offices of Shubert Organization executives Bernard Jacobs and Gerald Schoenfeld on the floor above. In addition, a new light booth had to be built in the back of the balcony. In old-fashioned Broadway houses, the stage manager calls the show from the wings, but because the lights in *A Chorus Line* were so specifically cued to the music and choreography, it was important that the stage manager be able to see the whole stage as he had at the Newman.

The final and most important innovation was the introduction of a computerized light board—the first one ever used on Broadway. The extremely complex show had 280 light cues; Musser wanted a memory board, which was something very new at the time, and Four Star Stage Lighting, the company from which the equipment was being rented, didn't have what she needed. But the company's head, Frank DeVerna, found out about a board on the West Coast that he thought would fit the bill. He and Musser flew out to Hillsboro, Oregon, to look at the board, which cost $160,000; they made the decision to bring it in, which changed the face of Broadway lighting from that day forward. They named the board Sam, and it lasted the first twelve years of the run, proving a very good investment indeed.

12

"Wow, You Dance on Broadway . . . You Got Somewhere"

Rehearsals and Previews

B ecause the show was still twice as long as it needed to be at the end of the second workshop, much of the work of the rehearsal period leading up to the opening at the Public was focused on tightening the script. This was traumatic for several of the actors, because roles that had been much larger in the workshops were whittled down until they had very little left to do. Some of them took this in stride and were happy just to be part of a show they could tell was going to be extraordinary; others became frustrated or angry. But since they had all been through the workshops together, even the cut material had a beneficial effect on the finished show: the extra knowledge the actors had stored up about all the characters' stories remained, and fed the subtext and the onstage interaction. As understudy Michael Serrecchia later said: "A lot of material came and went, but everything that went flavored what stayed" (quoted in *The Longest Line*).

With regard to new material, much of the work of the seven-week rehearsal period centered on three key sequences in the show: The Montage, the Cassie/Zach confrontation, and the "One" finale—which would be one of the last sequences to be choreographed.

"There's a Lot I Am Not Certain Of"

The Montage, which had originally been Nick Dante's concept, had been developing for a while. Early in this final rehearsal stage, the creative team had the cast sit down in a circle—much as several of them had done at the original tape session over a year earlier—and talk specifically about their adolescent years. Embarrassing parents, teenage crushes, confusion about changing bodies and frustrations over perceived inadequacies of physical appearance all emerged in painful and often hilarious detail, along with very personal stories about the dancers' first sexual encounters. Hamlisch and Kleban mined this new material, combined with ideas from Kirkwood and Dante as well as stories from the original tapes, and fashioned it into a long musical number with several distinct movements. The sequence was staged and choreographed, but then Bennett decided he didn't like the music. It had an old-fashioned Charleston-type melody, and the director asked why these young dancers weren't singing in a more contemporary style. Finally, during a working session with the cast, Hamlisch pulled the tune for "Hello Twelve, Hello Thirteen, Hello Love" seemingly out of the blue, and it stuck. The number had to be substantially reconfigured and rechoreographed around this new base, but it finally started to work. A kaleidoscope of spoken lines and mini-monologues, high-energy ensemble dance sequences, and song—with one complete solo number, "Nothing," smack in the middle of it—the number wove all the elements of musical theatre into a perfectly integrated expression of the pain and exhilaration of growing up. It was funny, poignant, and thrilling. Every member of the company contributed something to it, including the dancers, who were often asked to improvise dance routines or even vocal riffs during the process. Understudy Crissy Wilzak, who was an inveterate fan of *American Bandstand* and up on the latest fads in rock dancing, contributed some of the groovy steps—as well as the idea for the "Shit, Richie!" choral underpinning.

"Cassie, stay on stage."

One of Michael Bennett's main goals for the show had always been to create something special for his muse, Donna McKechnie; at one point later, he told her he did the show for her. The other actors always knew she would have a dance solo, and it was important to Bennett that her character stand apart from the others on the line. But her number and her extended dialogue scenes with Zach were among the last parts of the show to come together. Both required much experimentation, and a certain amount of trial and error, during the rehearsals and into the preview period.

The song itself went through about five different versions before it was finalized. Hamlisch and Kleban knew McKechnie was a trained soprano, and they wanted to come up with something that capitalized on her vocal range. At one point they wrote a lyrical, introspective piece called "Inside the Music"—which McKechnie would introduce to audiences many years later as part of her autobiographical cabaret show; she even adopted the song's title as the name of the show. But it didn't quite work in *A Chorus Line*: something more desperate and propulsive, with greater theatrical energy, was needed. And the choreography for the dance solo also wasn't coming together; the passion and energy were there, but the piece stayed on one level and didn't really build.

Following substantial frustrations in rehearsal, Bennett called a meeting at his apartment one night, where he sat down with McKechnie, Marvin Hamlisch, Bob Avian, and rehearsal drummer Bobby Thomas. Taking their cues from McKechnie's instincts, they broke the sequence down into smaller sections, each with its own specific subtext and emotional color. Several distinct movements would explore different aspects of Cassie's relationship to Zach, to the music, to her reflection in the mirrors, to the line, to her passion for dance. As McKechnie later told Denny Martin Flinn: "I was portraying a character who was totally desperate and it was the last battle of her life. It was the most desperate fight imaginable for this woman." The choreography grew organically out of the scene and the song; it looks and feels like an improvisation as Cassie rediscovers herself in dance. As they worked, Bobby Thomas listened to the ideas and devised percussive rhythms for each section, providing a structure that Hamlisch then started to fill out musically.

Piece by piece, the number came together in the form we know today. There's a first dance break after which Cassie sings the final lines of the song. Then, in show parlance, it goes into the "slow section" ("the small mirrors," which descend from above), which explores the idea of narcissism, followed by "accelerando," where the mirrors rise again and the music speeds up as the movement becomes more erotic (this has also been informally known as the "bondage" section). Then there's the expansive "Swan Lake" movement, McKechnie's acknowledged favorite part, where she spins and does layouts all over the stage to the strains of a lyrical trumpet solo, exulting in the joy of movement. Next comes the "red" section, where the color of the lights changes as Cassie confronts her own anger and frustration, building into "heat wave" and then the big finish, which challenges the stamina of any dancer. The driving turn sequence along the line from stage left to stage right is followed by the manic "handshake," where the dancer appears to be propelled backwards to stage left while reaching out in desperation for what she needs, and then finally a quick run back to center on the line and the final layout pose.

(Though each Cassie has had to find her way into the psychology of the number—the joy in movement, the desperation, the challenge to Zach, the rediscovery of herself as a dancer—a fascinating alternate interpretation was shared by Anthony Inneo, a Broadway replacement Zach, in the book *The Longest Line*. He said: "Michael explained that when Cassie is in her spot and moves back toward the mirror to dance and the lights change into an 'internal,' she never really leaves that spot. The 'internal' is Zach's creation. It's not Cassie's. He imagines how she danced, he remembers her as a fabulous dancer. She's his invention, which is what made it so difficult for him to deal with her. It's almost like a flashback." Though it's doubtful that Bennett would have explained it that way to anyone playing Cassie, he was known for saying what he thought each actor needed to hear in order to stay grounded in the emotional reality of the show, and viewing the number from that perspective kept Zach invested in the scene and the relationship. It also gave him a reason to watch the number every night—instead of balancing his checkbook, which some later Zachs were reported to have done!)

With the choreography now mostly complete, there was to be one more false start, causing a backstage rift that would take a long time to heal. At the Public Theater, before the move to Broadway, the small mirrors had to be pushed onstage manually rather than flown in, and Bennett originally had four of the male dancers—Wayne Cilento, Cameron Mason, Michel Stuart, and Thommie Walsh—bring them on and stand behind them during the slow movement. They then emerged to dance the final section along with Cassie. Some of the choreographic ideas came from a number that Bennett and Avian had worked on with Lucie Arnaz for the revised touring version of *Seesaw*. It led to an exciting finish with all five dancers stretching their arms out toward the audience in an expression of the need to perform. But Bennett called McKechnie up one night after a run and asked why

Cassie (played by Jena VanElslander) confronts Zach (Grant Thomas Zabielski) during the "One" rehearsal scene in the 2014 production at the Surflight Theatre.   *Photo by Jerry Dalia*

she wasn't dancing full out. She replied that she was being careful to watch the numbers on the stage and stay in formation with the boys. In Bennett's view, this was keeping her from dancing with the needed abandon, and the next day he took the four men out of the number. From then on it would be a solo for Cassie.

Artistically, the change was right, because there was something too flashy and Las Vegas-like about seeing her dance with backup boys at that point; it had become more like a nightclub act, and Bennett understood that the piece needed to focus on Cassie's isolation and personal struggle. But the four men, especially Mason, were furious with McKechnie. The number was one of their favorite moments in the show, an opportunity to really spread their wings as dancers—and they assumed she had asked to have them taken out of it. This was of course untrue, and she knew the issues with spacing and concentration could have been resolved with one or two more rehearsals. Bennett, however—still alert for ways to maintain the backstage tension he felt fueled the show—did nothing to dispel their misconception.

"Joanne"

While Sammy Williams as Paul was playing a character based on Nick Dante, Wayne Cilento (Mike) was in a sense playing Williams, because his song was taken from a story the latter had told at the tape session about discovering his talent for dance while watching his older sister take class. But Cilento had a tough time during the final rehearsal and preview period. The song, entitled "I Can Do That," was one of the first that Hamlisch and Kleban had written. Combined with his high-energy dancing, it seemed to be working for Cilento, but as the show neared its opening night, Bennett began to fear the number was out of place. It was written in a traditional Tin Pan Alley style, and the rest of the show as it had since developed had a more contemporary beat. One day, Bennett told Cilento the song "stunk" and asked the writers to come up with a new version. They tried several variations and at one point came up with a completely new song for the character. Called "Joanne," it came from a story Cilento had told of his own childhood. Living in a neighborhood where there were no other boys his own age, he had fallen in puppy love with a little girl named Joanne, who was his best friend; they ate cookies and watched TV together, and she took him to his first dance class. Bennett wanted the song to go in immediately, and Ralph Burns, one of several uncredited orchestrators who worked on the show, was asked to do an arrangement overnight. Cilento sang it at one preview performance, after which Bennett told him it didn't work; the actor asked for another shot at it, but Bennett was adamant and put the original version of "I Can Do That" back into the show. Having been told it was no good, however, Cilento felt thrown for a loop and had to struggle to regain confidence in the song and in his performance. Of course, the number became a real crowd-pleaser, a delightful moment in the show that always works.

"Give her your attention."

The "One" finale had been on the back burner for a long time and became the last major piece added to the show. Bob Avian worked out the choreography with McKechnie and Baayork Lee; he said some of it was adapted from a number he and Bennett had previously staged for an industrial. But the long delay in getting to the number—and the various preliminary ideas they discarded along the way—meant that no decision had been made about how to design and tech it. When Bennett finally knew what he wanted, he and Theoni Aldredge came up with the concept for the glittering tuxedo-and-top-hat costumes, which would be seen only in the final minutes of the show. The last-minute addition of the costumes and backdrop for the finale added a surprise $50,000 to the show's budget.

Orchestrations

One of the last steps in preparing a new musical for its first audience is the orchestration of the score. Because numbers are often added or deleted right up until opening night, the orchestrations usually have to be done very fast and under extreme pressure. For this reason—and because it began as an Off-Broadway show with a very limited budget—*A Chorus Line* was worked on by an unusually large number of orchestrators, including some of the best in the business. Most of them knew Bennett, Hamlisch, and/or Kleban and wanted to help out their friends, but none of them could afford the time needed to orchestrate the whole show, especially for the limited pay available, so different songs were assigned to different arrangers. Hamlisch reportedly knew most of them and handed out numbers

Kyle Schliefer as Mike performs "I Can Do That" at the Olney Theatre, 2013.
Photo by Sonie Mathew

based on his perception of their individual styles and strengths. The program eventually listed three orchestrators: Bill Byers, Hershy Kay, and Jonathan Tunick—but there were at least three more who worked on the show at one point or another. Rehearsal drummer Bobby Thomas and musical director Donald Pippin, who also did many of the vocal arrangements, were also closely involved.

Jonathan Tunick is probably the best-known orchestrator in the business, still working today. By 1975, he had already done Sondheim's *Company* and *Follies* (both with Michael Bennett as choreographer) and *A Little Night Music*. For *ACL*, he did "At the Ballet," "And," and "Nothing." Bill Byers worked on "I Hope I Get It" (though the opening section of it was done by Larry Wilcox), "I Can Do That," and the "Hello Twelve, Hello Thirteen, Hello Love" montage—which also included contributions by others. Phil Lang and Ralph Burns, both uncredited, worked on "Dance: Ten; Looks: Three" and the splashy final section of the "One" finale, respectively. Burns had to keep his work on the show a secret since he was also involved with Bob Fosse's *Chicago*, which was trying out in Philadelphia at the time, and he knew Fosse and the producers of that show would not have wanted him doing double-duty. Hershy Kay, whose Broadway career extended back to the original production of *On the Town* almost thirty years earlier, worked on other sections of "One." At one point, Byers was asked to fix and polish several of the numbers the others had contributed, and ultimately there were so many hands involved that it is very difficult to apportion out who did what in the finished score. (Interestingly, this is similar to the situation with the book, where the process was so collaborative among Dante, Kirkwood, Bennett, the cast, and eventually Neil Simon that even some of the collaborators themselves eventually claimed they couldn't remember who wrote certain lines.)

A particular challenge emerged with "The Music and the Mirror," which includes not only the longest solo dance but the longest nonvocal, instrumental musical sequence in the show. As discussed above, the dance took a long time to develop, and the music was no easier. For a while they worked with versions that proved too frenetic and complicated, evoking some of the dances in *West Side Story*, and the team began to realize they needed a more flowing, melodic approach to bring out the line and lyricism of McKechnie's dancing. They finally decided that if any orchestrator could make the number work, it had to be Harold Wheeler, who had worked with Bennett as dance arranger on *Coco* and as musical director on *Promises, Promises*. He and Bennett had clashed during *Company*, a show from which Wheeler withdrew over contract issues, and hadn't spoken in a while, but Bobby Thomas asked both of them to meet him for drinks at an Eighth Avenue bar one day, each unaware that the other had been invited, and a reconciliation was achieved. Wheeler worked with Bennett, Hamlisch, Thomas, and McKechnie, along with rehearsal pianist Fran Liebergall, to come up with a new approach to the Cassie dance music, which finally came together as the number we know today. At that point in his career, however, Wheeler didn't want his name on a show unless he had been the sole orchestrator, so he chose to remain uncredited.

Getting an Audience

As the first preview (April 23, 1975) approached, the cast really didn't know what to expect. They hoped audiences would like the show, but they had been completely immersed in it for so long—and were so exhausted—that most of them didn't have any confident expectation of how it would go over. They had been working for a hundred dollars a week for so long that many were almost broke, and to make ends meet, some of them (Rick Mason, Baayork Lee, Thommie Walsh, Wayne Cilento) took jobs in that year's *Milliken Breakfast Show*, an industrial that performed in the mornings. The overwork was taking its toll. Though *A Chorus Line* was rapturously received by audiences from the very first preview, and word spread like wildfire around the theatre community, the dancers weren't able to enjoy much of the work at that stage—partly because almost all of them got sick. Marvin Hamlisch, who had until that point been diffident with the actors, now reached out to them as a nursemaid, arranging doctor visits and even delivering a humidifier to Thommie Walsh's apartment. This helped the songwriter finally bond with the cast, but there was also self-preservation involved, as he needed to ensure they would have enough voice left to sing his songs!

As much as possible, the dancers went on no matter how sick they were feeling, but sometimes there was no choice but to take a night off. At that point, there was still only one understudy for each character, and the understudies covered several roles each, so if more than one person was out, things could get tricky. The worst occurred on a preview night when both Donna McKechnie and Kelly Bishop called out sick. Carolyn Kirsch was the one understudy for both ladies; she had to go on as Cassie, so at that performance (and the next night as well) there was nobody to play Sheila. Nancy Lane and Kay Cole did "At the Ballet" as a duet, and many of Sheila's lines were hastily reassigned to Greg (Michel Stuart) and other characters. (When the show moved to Broadway, more swings were added, to avoid such calamities in the future.)

Though Stuart might have enjoyed having a bigger part, inheriting some of Sheila's choice zingers on those two nights, he had been disappointed to feel his role as Greg slowly shrinking during the workshop period. He was aware of the special position he was in playing one of the first openly gay characters in a mainstream musical, and though he felt he had more to contribute in that capacity, he had for the most part adjusted his expectations. But there was one day during previews when, during the afternoon rehearsal, Bennett did some restaging of the opening number and moved him from the front to the back. That was the last straw for Stuart, who had come out of retirement as a dancer to do the show at Bennett's invitation. He told the director he'd be departing the cast if the change wasn't reversed, and wrote his two weeks' notice on the back of a page of sheet music on his way out for the dinner break. When he returned for the performance that night, he was told that Bennett had indeed moved him back to his original downstage position in the dance—one of the few times any of the cast members went toe to toe with the director and prevailed.

"She Walks into a Room"

Previews provided an opportunity to gauge audience reactions to various plot points and to adjust the show accordingly. One of the biggest changes involved the way Cassie was introduced to the audience. At the first preview, she had something of a star entrance; she wasn't in the opening number but swept onstage during the next scene, all dressed up in a silver lamé jumpsuit and a fur. She interrupted the proceedings to ask for change to pay the cab driver waiting outside, then asked if she could crash the audition; she just happened to have a leotard in her bag. Then she went off to change and reappeared shortly to join the line.

Bennett and McKechnie went out to eat after the performance, and she told him she understood he was trying to make her a star, but that he was killing her with kindness. She could feel the audience starting to hate the character for her presumptuous behavior, and was afraid she would never be able to get them back on her side. Bennett agreed, and starting with the second or third preview, Cassie was onstage from the top of the show. Already in her red leotard and dance skirt, she was seen in the back row learning the combination with everyone else. Though she doesn't sing in "I Hope I Get It" (something audiences don't always notice, but it gives her a sense of dignity and of separateness from the eager younger dancers around her), she dances the ballet and jazz combinations alongside all the others. During the first half of the show, small hints are dropped about her past with Zach, but until her big scene, the audience doesn't learn much about her. There's a self-effacing humility and dedication to work that help define her personality; the original grand entrance would have been out of character. (Note: Ten years later the writer and director of the film version made the same mistake, giving Cassie a very similar late entrance, to detrimental effect. Both Hamlisch and Kleban worked on the movie; one wonders if they said anything.)

"Doc" Simon

Much discussion and speculation over the years have been devoted to the question of Neil Simon's uncredited contributions to the final script of *A Chorus Line*. During previews at the Newman, Michael Bennett felt that the show needed more laughs; he invited Simon to see a run, and then took him out to a restaurant in the neighborhood to get his feedback on the show—and ask him to help doctor the script.

Simon has always been called "Doc" by his friends, and though he has said that the nickname dates from his childhood, when he received a toy stethoscope as a gift, many people think of it as a reflection of his decades-long reputation as an excellent show doctor. Bennett was well aware of Simon's gifts in that area, and by 1975 the two men had worked together several times, so it was natural that the director would turn to Simon when he felt he needed help with his new show.

The exact nature and extent of Simon's contribution were a mystery for years, and even today nobody could tell you exactly which lines he wrote. Nicholas Dante remembered approximately eight new lines appearing in the show during previews, which he assumed Bennett himself wrote. Since Bennett had always been the engine guiding development of the script, Dante didn't think much of it at the time; only years later did he learn that Simon had been involved. He believed most of the lines Simon had contributed were additions to Sheila's dialogue with Zach leading into "At the Ballet," as well as Diana's line identifying the Bronx as "uptown and to the right." Bob Avian later told Ken Mandelbaum that Simon had contributed rather more, including some of the funniest lines in Bobby's monologue.

Of course, there were reasons to keep Simon's involvement quiet, including his wish to avoid stepping on Kirkwood and Dante's toes as well as concern that a Dramatists Guild rule against tampering with another writer's work was being violated. But much of the mystery was finally cleared up in 1995 (twenty years after the event), when Simon himself provided a lengthy explanation of his involvement in the show to Gary Stevens and Alan George for their book *The Longest Line*.

Simon said he could tell the show was going to be a big hit, but Bennett told him he felt it needed more laughs, so Simon returned to see it again and then asked for a copy of the script. He took it home and worked on it for about a week. He suggested a few cuts—lines that were intended to be funny but weren't working—and inserted approximately twenty-five new lines of his own, not all of which Bennett ultimately used. Many of the lines were right in character for the dancers and indeed achieved the intended laughs, but not all of them worked. One day Bennett handed Kelly Bishop a new monologue to do, and she could feel that night's preview audience turning on her. Sheila is famous for having attitude, but the new material crossed a line and made her tacky and nasty. In the dressing room after the performance, she remarked that if those lines were staying in the show, another actress was welcome to say them—but luckily Bennett agreed and they were out the next night. Most of the other lines Simon wrote for Sheila worked, though; he knew Bishop and her comic voice, and was able to contribute some of the character's most memorable moments.

Simon explained—and Bob Avian has confirmed this—that Bennett placed sheets of paper containing his new lines on the floor between his feet at rehearsal; he would look down and think, then raise his head and suggest the new lines, which most of the actors thought he was coming up with on his own. Both Bennett and Simon wanted to keep his involvement a secret, but as Simon admitted to Stevens and George: "It got around in Shubert Alley somehow. . . Reporters knew about it. They would ask me if I did help on *A Chorus Line*, and at the beginning I wanted to play it down, I didn't want to say anything because I thought it would be trouble for everybody. Later on I admitted to it. . . . In a way, I didn't want to horn in on Michael's success. I knew it was going to be huge, whether they had the extra lines or not."

Despite Simon's reticence on the matter, Nick Dante ultimately felt he took too much credit, and told Mandelbaum: "Eight lines does not a doctor make, and it disturbed me that Neil allowed that rumor to take hold. Perhaps his lines plus Marsha's involvement in the ending made him feel he was a doctor to the show."

What Dante was referring to there was an equally important contribution made by Simon's then-wife, Marsha Mason, who had attended the preview with him. At that point, Cassie was not among the eight dancers chosen by Zach to get the job at the end of the show, and Mason made an emotional appeal to Bennett to change that. Because the audience was rooting for Cassie so strongly by that point, she felt that seeing her be rejected ended the show on a downer, and that it was important for the play to end on a note of hope and convey the message that it's possible in life to get a second chance. Bennett at first resisted the idea, claiming it was unrealistic that a dancer who had done featured roles would ever again be hired for a job in the chorus, especially by the man who had tried so hard to make her a star. But he soon relented—probably partly because he still believed that *Follies* had been sabotaged by an overly depressing ending and couldn't bear the idea of *A Chorus Line* falling into the same trap. So Cassie gets the job. Nick Dante originally resisted the change and thought Bennett was selling out, but ultimately came to recognize that it had been the right thing.

Friends and Colleagues

A Chorus Line opened officially on May 21, 1975, and earned immediate and nearly unanimous rave reviews. A transfer to Broadway was inevitable, and Papp, Bennett, and Bernard Gersten wasted no time in planning their move. Even before previews had begun at the Public, the Shubert Organization had shown a strong interest in the property; now that it had proved itself with audiences and the press, they were eager to get involved. Though several Broadway theatres were considered, including the Barrymore and the Broadhurst, it wasn't long before the show was scheduled into the Shubert Theatre, the organization's flagship house, a revered 44th Street venue where Bennett had previously worked on *Here's Love*, *Bajour*, and *Promises, Promises*.

After the opening at the Public, Joe Papp famously sent Michael Bennett a letter telling him he was welcome to come back and fail at the Public Theater anytime.

"One": the finale, as performed by the cast of the 1993 tour.   *Photo courtesy Stephen Nachamie*

Though the show's status as a bona fide hit was practically a foregone conclusion at that point, the letter wasn't intended ironically: Papp's developmental theatre was conceived as a place where artists could feel free to experiment, and when he announced the workshops he had planned for his season, he told his board: "We expect to fail many more times than we succeed by the critics' yardstick, and, in fact, insist on the right to fail" (quoted in Helen Epstein's biography of Papp).

Actually, the opening night invitation to come back anytime and fail was one that Papp sent to most of his playwrights. A much more personal and individual- ized document was soon to be presented to Michael Bennett. On June 11, while *ACL* was still playing at the Newman, the producer and the director went out for dinner together in celebration of both the success of the show downtown and the impending transfer. The restaurant they chose was Orsini's, near Bennett's midtown west home. Knowing the dangers that can come with unprecedented financial success, and valuing their positive feelings for one another as artists, busi- ness associates, and friends, Papp wanted to do something to commemorate—and hopefully preserve—the bond. So when he went home that night, he typed up an agreement on his old Remington typewriter, which read in part as follows:

> Being sound in mind and body and pure in heart, we do solemnly vow, prom- ise, swear, pledge and affirm to perform all the duties, obligations, expecta- tions, as they are construed and understood to apply to the term "friendship"

such as loyalty, fealty, mutual assistance, honesty, truthfulness and trust in all dealings, arrangements, both verbal and written, both spoken and unspoken, both at home and abroad, in all companies, at all hours, for all times, to set a shining example of integrity in human affairs, in contradistinction and toward the obliteration of backbiting, undermining, innuendo, opportunism, greed, the devil's larder of subtle seductions preying on man's weakness for aggrandizement at the expense and over the corpus of his fellow.

Be it understood and acknowledged that this signature, though set down in ink, shall be as binding as the power in a blood knot, and whosoever shall attempt to sever or untie it shall suffer the penalty of the damned and remain forever in a dark and empty theater.

Despite the playful tone, it was meant in earnest. According to Epstein, Papp's future wife Gail witnessed the signing of the document by both her husband and Bennett on June 13, 1975. And in spite of various conflicts that would continue to erupt in various quarters as *A Chorus Line* became a juggernaut, the producer and the director managed to live up to the agreement.

13

"Play Me the Music"

The Score

The program for *A Chorus Line* lists thirteen musical numbers, but it's possible to consider the score to have only eleven, since the "One" reprise and the "Tap Combination," which isn't quite a full-fledged song, are both included in the tally. That's a relatively small number of songs for a contemporary musical. But this is deceptive, because it's a show in which the music almost never stops. Marvin Hamlisch and Edward Kleban fitted the sung passages seamlessly into the flow of dialogue and dance, which, along with Hamlisch's almost continuous underscoring, resulted in an all-enveloping musical texture that was unique for its time; never before had a score been so fully integrated into the structure of a musical. Though the show spawned only one or two "standards," the score is richer and greater than the sum of its parts. Still, the parts include many gems of musical theatre songwriting. This chapter will examine each of the numbers individually.

"I Hope I Get It"

One of the first songs Hamlisch and Kleban drafted for the show was called "Résumé"; it had the dancers singing about their qualifications and the past shows they had been in. But true to his solid training in the BMI workshop, Kleban pointed out that what was really needed to get the show started right was an "I Want" number. This is a classic genre of musical comedy song, where the central character sets the show in motion by expressing his or her key wishes and longings in a lyric; unforgettable examples are "Wouldn't It Be Loverly" from *My Fair Lady*, "If I Were a Rich Man" from *Fiddler on the Roof*, and "I'm the Greatest Star" from *Funny Girl*. Since the point of *A Chorus Line* is that the leading character is the whole ensemble, the number here of course needs to be a group one.

Hamlisch later said that the moment Kleban handed him the basic four lines of the lyric for "I Hope I Get It," the show started to come into focus for him. "Ed has caught the essence of what our show is about," he wrote in his show diary. "You might say the music and the lyrics were born at this moment. I had all I needed."

This number includes the most difficult piece of ensemble choreography in the show: the jazz combination that Zach is teaching as the lights first come up and that is then repeated in its entirety seven times before the end of the number (plus a couple of false starts). It's notable as the combination that "doesn't travel": other than a leap forward at the beginning, the dancer stays basically on one small patch of stage doing an intricate and high-energy sequence of kicks, turns, and back-bends. (That's why it's possible for twenty-six dancers, including Zach and Larry, to do it onstage at the same time without bumping into each other or dancing into the wings.) The combination was designed to be difficult, so that only the most technically polished dancers in any cast can make it look effortless; it's supposed to reveal the various strengths and weaknesses of the dancers auditioning, and it will do this automatically even if all the actors are trying their darnedest to do it right. Rather than being danced in perfect unison (which we will see in the "One" finale), it should look like something the dancers have just learned and that they are coming to grips with, even struggling with, in different ways.

The singing in the opening number is secondary to the dancing, but it establishes from the very start a convention that will return frequently during the evening: the sung lines are "thoughts" that the audience is allowed to hear, but are understood not to be spoken aloud or heard by the other characters onstage. Marvin Hamlisch said that he wanted the music here to have an "angular" quality and to express the frenetic energy of a real audition. A major character, Paul, is introduced vocally at the end of the number, while assistant choreographer Larry is collecting the résumés. We hear his nervous, plaintive thoughts, as he worries that his photo and résumé don't really represent him and wonders what the director is looking for.

Musically, the number is dominated by the themes accompanying the two dance combinations. The ballet theme for the women is piano based, with a delicate melody that recalls the classical music heard in ballet classes and yet drives relentlessly forward; the variation on the same theme for the men is lower and more masculine, and almost gives the impression that the melody has been turned upside down. The music for the jazz combination (nine measures plus a brief drum solo for the walk-off at the end) establishes immediately the contemporary beat of the show and its driving, pulsing energy; it's heard several times as the combination is repeated by different groups of dancers, and Hamlisch and his orchestrators provide slight variations to keep it from getting monotonous.

A curious sidebar: before the famous moment when the dancers turn away from the mirrors and dance the jazz combination all together, starting the show with the proverbial bang, Zach calls out "a-five, six, seven, eight!"—but the music is in 6/4 time, and thus would properly be counted in sixes rather than eights.

"I Can Do That"

One of the first songs Kleban and Hamlisch wrote, Mike's solo seemed to be working in rehearsal, but at one point in previews Bennett wanted to replace it because it sounded so different from the rest of the score. It has a vaudevillian flavor to it and an offhand playfulness that fits Mike's cocky, wisecracking character. The story of a boy discovering his calling while attending his older sister's dance class, it's the show's only solo number for a male character—unless you count Richie's "Gimme the Ball," which is a portion of the "Hello Twelve, Hello Thirteen, Hello Love" montage. Mike's vocal is fairly brief but leads into a snazzy, athletic dance break choreographed for Cilento, who was thought by many to be the best male dancer in the cast.

Contrary to the evidence on the original cast album, it wasn't a tap number; no character in the show wears tap shoes (even in the "Tap Combination" later on), but in an effort to help the listener visualize a dance routine, the sound of taps was added for the record. (Fun trivia point: It was actually not Cilento but Michael Bennett himself who donned tap shoes in the recording studio and provided the footwork.)

Though the show is very rigidly choreographed from beginning to end, "I Can Do That" is the number where the staging has been allowed to vary the most over the years. Different dancers playing Mike have been encouraged to bring their own personalities and specialties to the dance breaks: some have inserted acrobatic moves, like handsprings or backflips, which Cilento never did. Dancer Robert Tunstall tells a great story about a rehearsal in Albuquerque, where Thommie Walsh, the original Bobby, had come to work with the touring cast and give notes. Walsh was astonished by the tumbling pass that the Mike did at the end of the number, and Tunstall heard him say aloud, "Wayne, they're flipping!" (He was talking to his old friend Cilento. . . though the latter wasn't actually present.)

"And"

Early in the process of putting the show together, Michael Bennett decided he needed a song with several verses to intersperse with the sections of Bobby's comic monologue. The first version was called "Confidence," and it was a duet for Connie and Richie that was eventually cut. Ron Dennis as Richie got the first verse of "And," the song that replaced it. This little song is an excellent example of Marvin Hamlisch's stated goal for the score: "To marry music to the flow of thoughts." As Bobby goes through his monologue about growing up in Buffalo, he segues into pantomime; the audience can try to guess from his gestures what he's talking about as they hear instead the inner monologues of other characters on the line, picked out by the "thought light," trying to decide what they're going to say when Zach calls their names. Val and Judy sing the second two verses, and most of the other dancers chime in a couple of times in groups. The effect is something like a song with verses but no full chorus, as each time it sounds like the group is going to sing a real refrain, we're taken back to Bobby's spoken lines instead. His anecdotes take the place of the expected musical climax: an unusual idea, and one that well represents the "seamlessness" the creators aimed for, with song and speech blending naturally one into the other as we follow a "train of thought."

Because of the brief and fragmentary nature of the song, and the fact that it can't effectively be performed without the monologue it frames and punctuates, this number was not included on either of the show's two Broadway cast albums. (It was in fact recorded by the revival cast, but issued only as an iTunes supplement.) The title of the song has been known to appear in crossword puzzles with the clue "Chorus Line song." This is a trick question, and a clever one, because most people seeing a three-letter word with that clue—even if the middle letter is already filled in—would immediately assume the answer to be "One."

"At the Ballet"

The lyrics for this song were inspired mostly by the life stories of Kelly Bishop and Donna McKechnie. Bishop spoke about the film *The Red Shoes* and her difficult family life at the first tape session, and McKechnie contributed Maggie's story about her parents' troubled marriage and her fantasy of a father inviting her to dance. Kleban interviewed Bishop one-on-one to get more ideas, which included the fact that her mother was only twenty-two when her father told her he was her last chance at finding a husband. Hamlisch and Kleban wrote their initial draft of the song before the end of the first workshop, and Bennett and the dancers were immediately moved by the beautiful melody and the sentiments expressed, which so clearly encapsulate the magical allure the world of ballet can hold for a child and the escape it offers from the more painful and mundane realities of life. McKechnie didn't end up performing it in the show; when the character of Cassie was created for the second workshop, Maggie was passed on to new cast member Kay Cole, and the number was customized for her exciting, wide-ranging belt. The middle verse would be sung by Nancy Lane as Bebe.

Musically, the piece has three distinct sections: the hard-driving verse, with a propulsive, percussive accompaniment, depicting Sheila's (and later Bebe's)

Maggie (Alison McCartan) sings about her mother in the Montage, Weston Playhouse, 2014.
Photo by Tim Fort

childhood frustrations and problems with their parents; then the gentle, sweeping "everything was beautiful" chorus, with its evocation of classical ballet music; and then the "narrow stairway" bridge, which is more similar to the verse and carries a sense of the relentless drive of a student pouring all her dreams and energy into dance class. Each verse is slightly higher in range, starting with Sheila's earthy alto, then up to Bebe's more youthful, plaintive belt and finally Maggie's higher one. Her famously difficult sustained E leads the full orchestra into a soaring restatement of the main theme, as the other dancers appear and fill the stage with balletic moves: known as the "ballet blaze," this is one of the most breathtaking moments in the show.

"Sing!"

The song was written for Renee Baughman and the vocal limitations she was very open about—although it can probably be assumed that she herself wasn't quite as tone-deaf as the character Kristine, since she had already enjoyed substantial success in the choruses of musicals both regionally and on Broadway. Kristine expresses her musical challenges in short, semi-spoken phrases; the sustained note at the end of each line, which she ostensibly couldn't handle, was originally meant to be sung instead by the full line of dancers standing behind her. It was cute but it wasn't quite working—until one day in rehearsal when Bennett wanted to work on the number even though most of the cast had already left the studio. Don Percassi, playing the role of Kristine's husband Al, said he knew the chorus part and was happy to sing it by himself so Baughman could get a rehearsal in; when Bennett heard it done that way by the two of them, he knew they had stumbled on a solution that made the song absolutely work. So from that point on, that's how "Sing!" has been performed, with supportive husband Al filling in the notes for his wife, and the full chorus joining in (with Al conducting) only at the very end.

An alternative version of this story, shared by Baughman herself in the book *On the Line*, has it that the idea of doing the song as a husband/wife duet actually came from Linda Kline, the girlfriend of lyricist Ed Kleban, who happened to be watching rehearsal one day when they were working the number. Either way, the suggestion basically saved Al as a character, since much of his original material from the first workshop had by that point been cut.

"Hello Twelve, Hello Thirteen, Hello Love"

This very complex number has four distinct sections and takes up over twenty minutes in the middle of the show. It springs from Mark's embarrassing anecdote about his medical adventures, which inspires the others on the line to begin musing on their own teenage years. It includes partly spoken, partly sung mini-monologues for Connie, Don, Judy, and Greg—as well as Diana's complete song "Nothing" (see below) and elaborate choral sections that include lots of dancing as well as solo lines for all of the other characters.

Ed Kleban interviewed some of the dancers who joined the cast for the second workshop; when Kay Cole told him her mother was half Irish, he got the idea of writing a lullaby in an old-fashioned Irish mode for her to sing. This became the centerpiece of the "Mother" section, Maggie's poignant message of love to her absent mother, which she sings in counterpoint to contrasting memories of parents—some comic or even caustic—voiced by other characters. The lyrics don't define whether Maggie's mother is dead or simply far away; this in effect adds to the song's emotional impact, allowing each listener to fill in the gaps with his or her own memories and connect with it on a very personal level.

There is also a rock-flavored instrumental section that accompanies the most free-form dance sequence in the show, in which all the characters experience a group "nervous breakdown." It reaches its climax with Richie's "Gimme the Ball" and the comic refrain "Shit, Richie" as the other characters back up his high-energy dance routine.

This number was not fully represented on the original cast album, which presented a heavily cut version. "Nothing" was separated out and placed after the Montage as a separate track, whereas in the show it comes in the middle of the sequence; the solo sections for Mark, Connie, Don, Judy, and Greg were not included. Some of the deleted material was actually recorded, however, and the 1998 CD reissue rectified the situation to some degree by including more of it, adding three minutes to the Montage overall. Though Mark's "gonorrhea" monologue and Don's story of his teenage days working in a strip club are still missing, the reissue includes most of the half-sung monologues of Connie, Greg, and Judy. But the complete number, with "Nothing" in its proper position, was not available on a recording until the Broadway revival cast album was released in 2006.

"Nothing"

This number is performed in the middle of the "Hello Twelve" montage, but it's a complete song in its own right. Diana Morales's tale of life in a bad high school acting class was a story from the tapes that Kleban found particularly evocative: he knew he wanted to write about the bobsled improvisation and the damage a teacher can do to a young student. He later revealed that Priscilla Lopez's original story never once made use of the word "nothing," which is repeated so frequently in the song; this was his own contribution. Hamlisch's melody has a skipping, rollicking flavor that suggests a children's song as well as the energy of the bobsled ride described in the beginning; though it builds to suggest some of Diana's frustration and angst, the overall twinkling lightness of the music underscores the optimism of her character and leavens the meaner aspects of the text. Ethan Mordden, in his book *One More Kiss*, described the song as "one of those numbers so disarming in its helpless innocence that one cannot anticipate the wicked twist ending." The number's humor and energy have made it a perennial favorite of singing actresses, who have often used it as an audition piece.

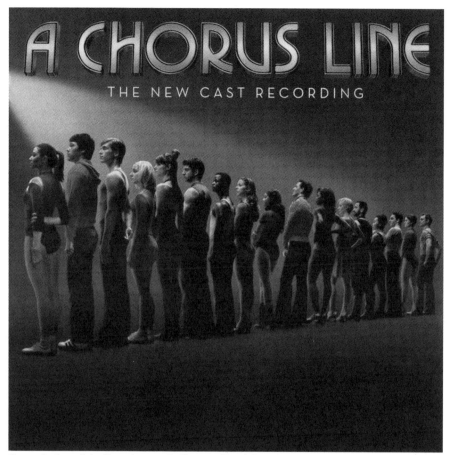

Cover design of the Broadway revival's cast album; Sony Masterworks Broadway.

"Dance: Ten; Looks: Three"

To fully appreciate this song, you really have to put it in the context of 1975, when Broadway was generally a more polite and old-fashioned place than the one it has since become. Yes, the Great White Way (and the Public Theater beforehand) had both experienced *Hair* seven years earlier, but that show was still considered an anomaly, a unique antiestablishment event that had somehow leaped successfully into the mainstream. And if Joe Papp's theatre and other Off-Broadway venues were pushing the envelope more and more, Broadway was still very much the establishment. So certain elements of *A Chorus Line* that we now take for granted, or that seem commonplace in today's cultural market, were pretty bold and risqué for their time. Certainly the honest depictions of homosexuality were unexpected in a mainstream musical, as was the liberal use of four-letter words. And a big part of the appeal of Val's brash and brassy number came from the novelty of hearing the words "tits" and "ass" belted unabashedly from a Broadway stage.

Long considered one of the sure-fire comic moments in the show, the song occasioned a great deal of concern during previews at the Public and was almost cut. This was because, even though the creative team and the company all thought it was a blast, it didn't get laughs at the first few performances. Michael Bennett told Hamlisch and Kleban that they'd have to write a new song for Pamela Blair if they couldn't figure out what the problem was. Finally, the pair decided they needed to experience the show like paying audience members if they were ever going to find out what was wrong, so one night they entered through the lobby with the ticketholders and were handed programs before taking their seats. When they looked at the program (a simple mimeographed sheet at that early stage), they quickly perceived the problem. The song at that point was called "Tits and Ass," and audience members laughed when they read the title on the song list; by the time they actually heard the words sung onstage, the joke (and the shock

value, which was a big part of it) had been spoiled. The next night the title in the program was changed to "Dance: Ten; Looks: Three" (probably the only song title in the history of the American musical that has the distinction of including two colons and a semicolon), and lo and behold, the crowd laughed their heads off when Blair first sang the naughty words.

Of course, once the show became a hit (which was immediate), and especially after the original cast album came out (which was soon), many in the audience came in knowing what to expect, and through the long run and in subsequent revivals and tours over the years, the number became a classic comedic character song. Today it rarely receives enormous laughs—a combination of familiarity and the fact that that type of language is no longer much of a novelty onstage or elsewhere. But it's still a fun part of the show. Kleban's clever lyrics and Hamlisch's jaunty melody, built on a vamp that suggests music hall or burlesque, add up to a juicy vehicle for a singing actress with comic chops. Val's unabashed honesty about something most actresses in

"The Music and the Mirror": Robyn Hurder as Cassie in the national tour, 2009.   *Photo by Paul Kolnik*

that situation would want to keep secret is disarming. Following the manic energy and exhilaration of the Montage, and preceding the intense emotions of Cassie and Paul's scenes, Val's number provides a breezy, refreshing whiff of comic insouciance at just the right time in the show.

"The Music and the Mirror"

Throughout rehearsals, Bennett and his writing team worked in tandem to explore ever more innovative ways of blending the usually separate elements of musical theatre—book scenes, songs, dance numbers—into seamlessly integrated sequences. The workshop structure gave them time to work together building numbers that mixed and combined all three, nowhere more effectively than in Cassie's big scene. Her spoken dialogue with Zach, expressing her need for a job and her hunger to express herself as a dancer, builds organically—and gradually—into the song. The scene has a gentle piano underscoring, and the first few sung lines are interspersed with the dialogue: these are the moments when we hear Cassie's inner thoughts. When the emotional intensity of what she is trying to say to Zach grows too powerful to be contained in speech, she has to sing, so the song builds and takes over. And then when even singing isn't enough to express all she has inside, she begins, inevitably, to dance. There's one more brief sung section after the first dance break, climaxing in exhilarating sustained high notes, and then she sails into one of the longest and most complex—and exciting—dance solos in musical theatre. The number was so specifically tailored to McKechnie's unique talents, both as a dancer and a soprano, that it represents a colossal challenge to other performers taking on the role. Most of her successors over the years have sung it in lower keys. And though some performers have been allowed leeway to try slight variations in the choreography, bringing their own personal styles to bear, the iconic structure of it remains sacrosanct: the supreme test of a dancer/actress.

"One"

From Hamlisch's rehearsal diary, as related in his memoirs: "Michael has new thoughts about the finale . . . The dancers are gonna go high-kicking their way through the glorious final dance combination . . . the chorus kids, who normally do a number like this behind the star, will now take center stage and become the star themselves. I love this idea. These dancers have become one."

This is an old-fashioned razzle-dazzle production number, with the dancers we have come to know so well as individuals now identically costumed and difficult to tell apart, finally blending into a perfectly synchronized unit. The irony is that these young performers have all bared their souls in pursuit of a job that has robbed them of their individuality. Bennett initially wanted the effect to be chilling, and said at one point that he hoped the audience would be too disturbed by it even to applaud. Of course, this isn't exactly how it turned out; the finished number carries an undercurrent of this notion of mechanized dehumanization, but it mainly works as a thrill-inducing production number, building and building till the audience reaches a frenzy of appreciation, finally able to release the tension the long "audition" had been building up all evening. Still, *A Chorus Line* is unique among Broadway musicals in not having a traditional curtain call: at the beginning of the number, the audience gets to applaud each dancer briefly as they enter one by one and tip their hats, but the song and the show end with the lights gradually fading out on a seemingly never-ending kick line. This unusually structured conclusion is one reason why, even in today's era of near-obligatory standing ovations, the show seldom receives one; there just isn't a moment when it feels right to stand, as you probably would if the dancers stayed onstage after the song and dancing have ended. (In the early days of the original production, ecstatic audiences stood anyway.)

The number is heard twice in the show: first in a complex rehearsal sequence that shows the dancers learning the choreography (not only singing the lyrics, but vocally repeating the names of dance steps and other instructions to themselves as "inner thoughts") and then in its fully staged and costumed version for the show's actual finale. Presumably this is a number from the finished show we saw the dancers audition for—but presented as if all seventeen of them had been cast in it.

As quoted in *On the Line*, Nancy Lane (Bebe) expressed the difficulty the dancers had in learning the "rehearsal" version of the number: "A lot of these people were just dancers. They didn't have any idea of madrigal singing or round singing, which was what it was. Kay Cole, the people with musical background, they got the hang of it. For the rest it was difficult to get the words and the rhythm and then to get to dance it—oy oy oy, that was another five hours."

Ed Kleban described to Ken Mandelbaum the challenge of the lyrics, which are supposed to have been written for a fictitious musical we never see: "It has to have a subtext about other things in the play. To get all specific meaning out of it so that it can seem to have all kinds of other meanings is one of the harder tasks. You have to prune out any possible specificity, keep it very plain, like it's almost a Jerry Herman song, but it isn't quite, or an Alan Jay Lerner patter lyric in the middle section. . . . To say nothing is always harder than to say something."

One reason the number works so well is that the opening vamp section was heard way back at the beginning of the evening, when the spotlight first followed the row of dancers' faces down the line as Zach explained what was coming; it was also heard again as the dancers slowly moved back into their line positions just prior to the final eliminations. So when the number finally erupts in all its glory at the end of the show, starting with that same vamp, it has a feeling of inevitability to it, as if this is of course what the whole evening has been building toward.

The now-classic choreography for "One" is almost always reproduced faithfully in revivals, including such iconic moments as the triangular "wedge" formation (which Bob Avian said was borrowed from a number called "Blaze On" that he and Bennett had previously choreographed for a *Milliken Breakfast Show*) and the crowd-pleasing circular grapevine. That section is sometimes called the "Circle of Death" by dancers: according to Will Taylor, who has danced in the show and also directed it, the move is quite dangerous for the cast, because "if even one person gets off on the wrong foot, you can snap somebody's ankle." According to *On the*

Line, most of the number was choreographed by Avian with input from Baayork Lee and Donna McKechnie.

The complete number received national exposure on the 1980 ABC-TV special *Baryshnikov on Broadway*, at the end of which ballet superstar Mikhail Baryshnikov danced it in full costume with the cast of the International Company.

"The Tap Combination"

This is the least talked-about number in the show and the one people tend to forget about; its main function is to lead into the climactic accident, when Paul falls and hurts his knee. The scene grew out of an improvisation one day during the workshop, when Bob Avian taught the cast a combination and Clive Clerk (Larry) took notes that he later handed off to Kirkwood and Dante so they could write the scene. The sequence is another example of the show's seamless blending of dance, music, and dialogue.

Larry divides the dancers into groups and coaches them through several repetitions of the dance combination, while "breaks" in the music give us a chance to hear some of the characters' half-spoken/half-sung thoughts, mainly dealing with how exhausted they are at this point in the grueling audition day. There are some good laughs along the way, mostly having to do with Diana's inability to make a tapping sound in her sneakers, Sheila's comic facial expressions in response to Larry's instruction to smile, and Connie—who is nervous about her borderline tapping ability—making exaggerated attempts to loosen up while dancing.

This number is one of the examples of a song where the choreography came first and the music followed. Bob Avian did most of the choreography, and since there was no music yet, he set it to the tune of "Tea for Two," a classic Broadway tap number from the musical *No, No, Nanette*. Afterwards, Hamlisch wrote a new musical theme to fit the steps; it's written in a jaunty, imitation vintage style that, like "One," suggests that the musical the dancers are auditioning for will have a 1930s setting. Because the vocal element is so minimal, "The Tap Combination" is the other number in the show (along with "And") that was not included on either one of the Broadway cast albums.

"What I Did for Love"

The team had talked about needing a song to sum up the themes of the show, and Bennett wanted it to be "haunting." He began telling Priscilla Lopez early in the workshop period that she was going to have a second song, along with "Nothing," but it took a long time for it to materialize. (Hamlisch later recalled that he came up with the idea for the melody on the 79th Street crosstown bus—between Fifth and Madison Avenues.)

There was a certain amount of disagreement over the song, as the lyrics are intentionally nonspecific; Joe Papp told Bennett at one point that he thought it was the weakest number in the show and suggested cutting it. But Hamlisch felt it was important to include one song that could stand on its own outside the show,

"What I Did for Love": Kate Loprest as Diana leads the ensemble at the University of Michigan, 2004.   *Photo courtesy U-M School of Music, Theatre & Dance, Department of Musical Theatre*

and in response to that Kleban wrote lyrics open-ended enough that they could be interpreted either as an anthem of devotion to one's art or as a simple love ballad. Though Hamlisch knew he hadn't won over everyone on the team, he was vindicated when the song did indeed become something of a standard. There have been numerous cover recordings of it, including versions by Jack Jones (who also used it as the title of his album), Cleo Laine, Elaine Paige, Aretha Franklin, Christiane Noll, opera tenor Jerry Hadley, and even Robert Goulet (whose name is mentioned in the show itself). Though the exposure contributed to the popularity of the show, Kleban always felt he had been pressured into a compromise; he was embarrassed about the generic lyrics and later admitted he thought the song was "dreadful." Whether or not it's the most effective possible summing up of the show's theme, it almost always works in the theatre, where it has been known to elicit tears from the dancers onstage as well as the audience.

The Underscoring

In its spoken dialogue scenes, *A Chorus Line* uses musical underscoring much more extensively than most musicals. There are only three times in the evening when the orchestra stops playing completely: the introductions scene, where the characters go down the line and give their names, ages, and birthplaces; Paul's monologue; and the final eliminations scene, where we learn who got the job and who didn't. Otherwise, there is nearly always music playing, and this was made possible because of Marvin Hamlisch's expertise as a film composer. Film generally makes much more use of background music than theatre, and Hamlisch was able to take his experience writing for that medium and use it to craft an almost continuous score that gives *A Chorus Line* a unique energy, tension, and theatricality. As Bob Avian has pointed out, "Marvin Hamlisch's underscoring dictates so much about what's going on in the show; it dictates the pace."

Much of the underscoring is characterized by repeated variations on the "One" vamp. But there are also numerous other themes heard subtly in the background, many of which are associated with specific characters and help define their individual energies and personalities. The eager, childlike skipping tune that introduces the opening of "Nothing" is first heard much earlier, when Zach is trying to get Diana to be the first to tell her story; it expresses both her nervousness and her spunky charm and sweetness. The jaunty, jazzy figures that accompany Mike's monologue suggest his easygoing, showbiz-loving personality as clearly as does the following "I Can Do That." Bobby's monologue has an underscoring that evokes old-school television comedians and punctuates his one-liners effectively, and the sinuous, percussive beat that accompanies Sheila's dialogue with Zach reveals her edginess as well as her sexiness. The gentle piano riffs heard under Mark's monologue segue seamlessly into the opening of "Hello Twelve," and the lovely, yearning phrases, also mainly on the piano, that underscore Cassie's scene with Zach show a sensitive, lyrical side of her nature before transforming into the more passionate, driving melody of "The Music and the Mirror." Several of the other characters have similar defining themes, and many of these resurface in the "Alternatives" scene near the end of the musical, woven into new patterns that remind us of what we've learned about these people and how well we've gotten to know them.

14

"Bob Goulet Out, Steve McQueen In!"

A Chorus Line Cultural Literacy

T he book and lyrics of *A Chorus Line* are full of names of places, people, films, and so on that would mostly have been very familiar to audiences in 1975 but in some cases are more obscure today. Whether you're doing a production of the show or just going to see one, this chapter is your handy-dandy guide to the pop-cultural references in the script.

Allyson, June (1917–2006)

In describing her arrival in New York dressed all in white, *A Chorus Line*'s Val compares herself to this popular movie star, whose career peaked in the forties and fifties. Since Val is lamenting her former naïveté, the allusion is to Allyson's well-known reputation as a wholesome girl-next-door type, an image cultivated in such films as *Two Girls and a Sailor* and *Good News*, in which she was presented as a fresh-faced newcomer. What many fans don't know is that Allyson (born Eleanor Geisman) came to Hollywood with substantial experience as a dancer in Broadway musicals, making her mention in *A Chorus Line* especially apt. Her success as a dancer was remarkable given that she had been confined to a wheelchair for an extended period after a horrific childhood accident; her doctors had believed she would never walk again. Early stage credits included *Sing Out the News* and *Very Warm for May*, as well as the Cole Porter musical *Panama Hattie* (1940), in which she not only had a chorus part but understudied Betty Hutton in the role of Florrie. George Abbott happened to catch one of her performances in that role and subsequently offered her a lead in his Broadway production of *Better Foot Forward*; it was the film version of that show that brought her to Hollywood. After dating both Peter Lawford and John F. Kennedy, she married actor Dick Powell; two more marriages followed after his death. Her many popular films included *Words and Music*, *The Glenn Miller Story*, and the 1949 version of *Little Women* (as Jo). In her later years she returned to high visibility with commercials for Depend undergarments and TV appearances on such shows as *Hart to Hart* and *Murder She Wrote*; she also made a return to Broadway in the play *Forty Carats*.

Cardinal Hayes High School

An all-boys' Catholic high school located at 650 Grand Concourse in the Bronx. It was founded by Archbishop Francis Spellman, who was the sixth archbishop of the Archdiocese of New York, and named in honor of Patrick Cardinal Hayes (1867–1938), his predecessor in that position. The school opened in 1941 and still operates in the same location. This is where *A Chorus Line*'s Paul went to high school. In his monologue, he talks about being taunted by other students for his homosexuality; when he told the principal, he was sent to a psychologist, who recommended that he quit school, which he did.

Channel 47

One of the nation's first Spanish-language TV stations. A UHF station also known as WNJU, it was founded in 1965 by Henry Becton and Fairleigh Dickinson Jr., and sold in 1970 to Screen Gems Productions, which owned it during the time of *A Chorus Line*. Though the programming was originally multicultural, by the 1970s it was primarily in Spanish, with English-language religious programs in the morning hours only. The station still exists, and the line in Paul's monologue about Channel 47 being the only reason Puerto Ricans know anything about theatre tends to get a laugh in revivals even today.

Charisse, Cyd (1922–2008)

Long-legged, elegant dancer/actress who was one of the few dancers in Hollywood to have partnered with both Fred Astaire and Gene Kelly. Born in Texas, she started out as a ballerina and toured with the celebrated Ballet Russe de Monte Carlo. She had her first speaking role in the musical *The Harvey Girls* and later starred opposite Astaire in *The Bandwagon* and *Silk Stockings* and opposite Kelly in *Singin' in the Rain*, *Brigadoon* (based on the Broadway musical), and *It's Always Fair Weather*. She had a long and happy marriage with nightclub singer Tony Martin. After retiring from dancing, Charisse continued to work in films as an actress, and she made a belated Broadway debut in 1992, taking over for Liliane Montevecchi as the aging ballerina Grushinskaya in *Grand Hotel*. The reference to Charisse in *ACL* comes in Paul's monologue, where he remembers that, when he was learning to dance by imitating Hollywood musicals, she was the star he wanted to be like.

Day, Doris (b. 1924)

A Chorus Line's Kristine says she wanted to be like Doris Day, rather than hoofer Ann Miller, when as a child she fantasized about becoming a star—which was a shame because she was a good dancer but couldn't sing. The irony is compounded when one learns that Day, as a child, wanted to be a dancer and performed as part of a team, only switching her focus to singing because of a car accident that damaged her legs when she was thirteen. She found early success as a big band singer, performing with Les Brown and His Band of Renown, and later as a solo act; she achieved Top Ten status with numerous hit songs like "Sentimental Journey," "My Dreams Are Getting Better All the Time," and "Secret Love." She made her film acting debut in *Romance on the High Seas* in 1948 and appeared in several light musicals before proving her acting chops in more demanding roles in vehicles like *Love Me or Leave Me* and *Midnight Lace*. She starred in the screen version of the Broadway musical *The Pajama Game* and was nominated for an Academy Award for the 1961 film *Pillow Talk*, one of several vehicles in which she starred opposite Rock Hudson. Day became known as the quintessential wholesome, American, blonde girl-next-door, with enormous audience appeal, and still holds the record as the top female box-office star of all time. After winding down her film career, she starred on the CBS sitcom *The Doris Day Show* (1968–73); that series's theme song was "Que Sera, Sera (Whatever Will Be Will Be)," the Oscar-winning song Day had first introduced in the Alfred Hitchcock film *The Man Who Knew Too Much*. In her later years, Day focused her attention on animal rights activism as founder of the Doris Day Animal League. (Fun trivia alert: In her 1964 film *Send Me No Flowers*, Day had a scene where her character danced with a dry cleaning man, played by a very young Clive Clerk—who eleven years later would create the role of Larry in *A Chorus Line*.)

Donahue, Troy (1936–2001)

American film and TV actor who began his career in small film roles but became a teen idol with his appearance in *A Summer Place* in 1959, opposite Sandra Dee. Other films included *Monster on the Campus, Parrish, Palm Springs Weekend, Come Spy with Me*, and *The Godfather Part II*. His numerous TV appearances include regular roles in the series *Surfside 6* and *Hawaiian Eye*. Donahue's mention during the Montage sequence of *ACL*, where Bobby sings that if Donahue could be a movie star then he could surely be one as well, is not his only appearance in the lyrics of a hit Broadway musical: His name is also heard in the song "Look at Me, I'm Sandra Dee" from *Grease* (1972).

Ed Sullivan Show, The

A television variety show that ran on CBS from 1948 to 1971, one of the longest-running entertainment programs in TV history. Originally entitled *Toast of the Town*, it was broadcast live from Studio 50 at Broadway and 53rd Street, near the north end of the Theatre District in Manhattan; the studio was renamed The Ed Sullivan Theatre and years later became the longtime home of *The David Letterman Show*. The much-imitated Sullivan (1901–1974) presented several acts each week on the hour-long show, ranging from novelty and puppet acts (including early appearances by Jim Henson and the Muppets) to classical musicians, pop singers, comedians, athletes, and rock musicians—and almost everything in between. Though Sullivan occasionally clashed with rock stars (Bob Dylan, the Doors) over conservative ideas about what was appropriate for a family television show, the program presented early-career performances by Elvis Presley and the Beatles that shattered ratings records and are still remembered as watershed moments in the history of pop culture in America. Sullivan was also a champion of African American talent and presented numerous black artists at a time when other producers were reluctant to do so; the Supremes (later fictionalized in Michael Bennett's musical *Dreamgirls*) were a personal favorite of Sullivan's and appeared on the show fifteen times. Like *A Chorus Line*'s Kristine, who claims that she watched the show religiously (though she has to be reminded of the name by her husband, Al), many American families adopted it as a Sunday night ritual; Bennett watched the show in Buffalo as a child and counted it as an early influence. He later choreographed numbers for the show, including a production number for Carol Lawrence called "I'd Rather Lead a Band." In addition to producing and hosting the show, Sullivan sustained an influential career as a writer for the *New York Daily News* whose long-running column focused on the Broadway theatre community, and *The Ed Sullivan Show* made a permanent contribution to Broadway history by featuring excerpts from numerous classic musicals during their original runs. These clips, many of which have since been issued on DVD, are often the best surviving footage of legendary stars from Broadway's golden age, in costume, performing the roles they created. Broadway returned the favor: in addition to the mention in *A Chorus Line*, Sullivan's show was immortalized in a song from the 1960 Broadway musical *Bye Bye Birdie* entitled "Hymn for a Sunday Evening (Ed Sullivan)."

Goulet, Robert (1933–2007)

American singer/actor best known to musical theatre aficionados as the original Lancelot in *Camelot* (1960). In the 1990s, he toured and returned to Broadway as King Arthur in a revival of that same show; other Broadway appearances included *The Happy Time* and the 2005 revival of *La Cage aux Folles*. Goulet also had a successful recording career ("On a Clear Day You Can See Forever," "What Kind of Fool Am I?") and appeared in nightclubs, in films, and on TV. His second wife was Carol Lawrence, the original Maria in *West Side Story*. His reference in *ACL* comes in the Montage, where he is named as one of the actors Bebe (originally played by Nancy Lane) had a crush on as a kid. After the show opened, Goulet came to see it and made a point of visiting Lane backstage following the performance.

Hamilton, George (b. 1939)

American film and TV actor who began his film career at age thirteen. Early successes came in the romantic comedy *Where the Boys Are* (1960) and the film version of Elizabeth Spencer's novel *The Light in the Piazza* (1962), in which he was seen as romantic lead Fabrizio, the role later played by Matthew Morrison in the Broadway musical version of the same novel. Other films included *The Victors, Your Cheatin' Heart, Evel Knievel,* and *The Godfather Part III*. He was still in his thirties when *A Chorus Line* opened; Bobby's mention of him comes in the Tap

Combination number, where he opines that if Hamilton could have a Hollywood career, he should have one too; it's a comical repeat of the same statement he made about Troy Donahue in the Montage. The reference could be taken as not terribly complimentary of Hamilton's acting ability; by mid-career, he was known more for his never-fading suntan and suave, man-about-town persona than for his artistic accomplishments. But Hamilton had a well-developed ability to laugh at himself and became a popular TV personality with a regular role on the nighttime soap opera *Dynasty* and countless appearances on talk shows, game shows, and reality shows. His flagging film career received a boost in the late 1970s and 1980s with tongue-in-cheek comedies like *Love at First Bite* and *Zorro, the Gay Blade*. More recently, he toured in a leading role in a revival of the Broadway musical *La Cage aux Folles*.

The High School of Performing Arts

A public alternative high school in Manhattan where talented students, selected by audition, could undertake intensive training in music, dance, or theatre in

addition to their general education requirements. The school's many famous alumni include original *A Chorus Line* cast members Baayork Lee (Connie) and Priscilla Lopez (Diana), as well as Christopher Chadman, who took part in the original tape sessions and was the first Broadway replacement in the role of Bobby. The song "Nothing," sung by Diana and based on Lopez's own experiences, gave the school an international reputation—although its comic portrayal of one of the institution's acting teachers is anything but flattering. (It's been said that anyone who attended the school during that period could easily have identified the real Mr. Karp based on the description in the song.) During the years when Lopez attended, the school was located in an 1894 building at 120 W. 46th Street in Manhattan's Theatre District, now the site of the Jacqueline Kennedy Onassis School of International Careers.

High School of Performing Arts graduate Diana Morales, here played by Victoria Hamilton-Barritt in the 2013 West End revival.   *Photo by Manuel Harlan*

Five years after *A Chorus Line* opened, the school received additional widespread attention as the subject of the movie *Fame*, conceived and produced by David De Silva and directed by Alan Parker. Due to the Board of Education's concerns over adult content in the screenplay, the producers' requests to film at the actual school were denied, so they used other Manhattan sites instead. The popular movie was the inspiration for three television series, a 2009 remake, and several stage adaptations. The school later merged with its sister school, the High School of Music and Art, and was given a new home near Lincoln Center, which opened in 1984; it is now known as the Fiorello H. LaGuardia High School of Music & Art and Performing Arts. A student production of *A Chorus Line* was presented there in 2009 (see Chapter 24).

"It Had to Be You"

Inaccurately referred to by Val as "Gee, It Had to Be You," this is a song standard that has been recorded by countless singers and featured in numerous movies. The lyrics are by Gus Kahn and the music by Isham Jones. Published in 1924, it was immediately popular, with no fewer than nine different recordings released that year, including those by Marion Harris, the Ambassadors, the California Ramblers, and the orchestras of Paul Whiteman, Stan Lanin, and Isham Jones himself. First sung on screen by Ruth Etting in the 1936 short "Melody in May," it has also been featured in such films as *The Roaring Twenties*, *Incendiary Blonde*, *Show Business*, and *I'll See You in My Dreams*, as well as the all-time classic *Casablanca*, in which it was performed by Dooley Wilson. More recent film uses include *Annie Hall*, *A League of Their Own*, and *When Harry Met Sally*; the song was even sung by the character Ginger (played by Tina Louise) on an episode of the TV sitcom *Gilligan's Island*. The list of major artists who have covered it includes Billie Holiday, Ella Fitzgerald, Frank Sinatra, Betty Hutton, Barbra Streisand, Ray Charles, Doris Day, Liza Minnelli, Tony Bennett, and Harry Connick Jr. (The song's title was borrowed for a 1981 Broadway play written by and starring Renee Taylor and Joseph Bologna.) "It Had to Be You" has a mellow, slinky melody and a playful romantic quality that has often lent itself to performance by sexy, sultry actresses and singers; thus it's appropriate that Val would have been asked to perform it after completing her physical transformation.

The Jewel Box Revue

The drag show that Paul (like his real-life counterpart, Nicholas Dante) joined as a teenager was a real one, and the script of *A Chorus Line* uses its real name. It was operated from 1939 until the late 1960s, successfully touring the United States and Canada, and is considered in retrospect an important part of the history of gay culture in America. The company was founded by Danny Brown and Doc Benner, a male couple—which was itself unusual in an era when most drag clubs were run by heterosexual producers who didn't necessarily like gay people or treat them particularly well.

Paul San Marco (here played by Michael John Hughes) remembers his time in the Jewel Box Revue. Weston Playhouse, 2014.   *Photo by Tim Fort*

For young people coming of age in the era of *RuPaul's Drag Race*, the Broadway musicals *La Cage aux Folles*, *Hairspray*, and *Kinky Boots*, and dozens of other examples of the widespread popularity of drag acts in today's mainstream pop culture, it may come as a surprise that female impersonators were once marginalized and looked down on as disreputable. Originally a part of the vaudeville circuit, they were gradually siphoned off to the less respectable burlesque theatres, and part of Brown and Benner's intention was to establish drag as a legitimate form of entertainment for mainstream audiences, both gay and straight. They reportedly ran a tight ship, insisting on discipline and professionalism from their performers, but were equally rigorous in expecting and demanding that their company be treated with dignity and respect, both by audiences and by the tough managers at the various venues where they played. If things ever got to the point where they had to defend their interests in a fistfight, they were both capable. They presented their shows, which became highly popular, as entertainment for a mainstream audience, and made a point of steering clear of any of the indecency or deviance charges often leveled at drag acts in those days. The company functioned as something of a "family," a feeling that was supported by the fact that both Brown and Benner's mothers sometimes came along on the tours. Both men functioned as surrogate parents to the young men in the show, strict but also protective—something Paul's father couldn't have known when he asked "the producer" to "take care of my son."

Advertised as a company of "Twenty-five men and one woman," the show had a multiracial cast, also unusual at the time. It featured a variety of name acts that became celebrated on the circuit, including such figures as Jan Carlove, Tony del Ray, Jean Fredricks, Bruno La Fantastique, Selina Powers, and George "Titanic" Rodgers, as well as the legendary dancer Mr. Lynne Carter. The "one woman" was usually Miss Storme Delarvarie, an African American male impersonator, who claimed her place in gay history as a key figure in the resistance against the 1969 police raid at the Stonewall Inn, a bar in Manhattan's West Village, which led to a riot still considered a key moment in the birth of the gay rights movement.

The company performed on Broadway at the Loew's State Theater in 1958, and its later engagement at the famed Apollo Theatre in Harlem (where Nicholas/Paul performed) was also considered a high point in its popularity. In *A Chorus Line*, Paul's emphasis on the "lack of dignity" he felt in the show, and among the other drag performers, should be seen in context: Brown and Benner made it part of their mission to ensure that their artists were treated with respect. In a December 2012 blog entry for the *Huffington Post*, Wayne Anderson wrote "in many ways, it was America's first gay community . . . it cannot be denied that the revue fostered one of the first gay-positive communities in America, if not *the* first. It was a place where 'gayness' was accepted before the concept of gay-identity had even been fully conceived."

The King and I

A 1951 Broadway musical with music by Richard Rodgers, book and lyrics by Oscar Hammerstein II. Based on Margaret Landon's novel *Anna and the King of Siam*, the musical tells the true story of Anna Leonowens, a young British widow who journeyed to Siam (now Thailand) in the 1860s to take a position as governess to the many children of the king. The original production starred Yul Brynner as the king and Gertrude Lawrence as Anna; a 1956 film version paired Brynner with Deborah Kerr. This is a rare example of one classic Broadway musical being mentioned in the script of another. In *ACL*, during the Montage sequence, the character Connie recalls being five years old and appearing in "King and I." Connie was played by, and based on the life of, the dancer Baayork Lee, who had in fact created the role of Princess Yin Yaowlak (the only female child with a substantial speaking part) in the original Broadway cast of *The King and I*. There is perhaps a slight error of chronology in the script, when Connie finally reveals herself to be thirty-two years old; since *A Chorus Line* takes place in 1975, this would put her birth in the year 1943. She would then have been eight by the time *The King and I* first opened. Lee herself was younger than Connie: born in 1946, she actually was five when she did the show.

McQueen, Steve (1930–1980)

American actor who trained at the Neighborhood Playhouse in New York and got his start in stage productions before going on to Hollywood stardom. He spent several years on the TV series *Wanted: Dead or Alive* and made numerous films, including *The Great Escape*, *The Magnificent Seven*, *The Sand Pebbles* (Oscar nomination), *The Reivers, Papillon,* and *The Towering Inferno.* His other pursuits included motorcycle and auto racing and martial arts. Known in the sixties and seventies as a quintessential film "antihero," an icon of the counterculture, he was christened "the King of Cool." In *ACL*'s Montage sequence, Bebe confesses that her childhood infatuation with Robert Goulet gave way to one with McQueen.

Miller, Ann (1923–2004)

American dancer/singer/actress who was considered the quintessential Hollywood hoofer during the 1940s and 50s. She lied about her age so she could dance in nightclubs as a teenager (like the character Don in *ACL*) in order to support herself and her deaf mother. She was discovered by Lucille Ball at age thirteen (pretending to be eighteen) at the Black Cat Club in San Francisco, and was signed first by RKO, then by Columbia Pictures; she later moved over to MGM, where she was featured in major movie musicals like *On the Town* and *Kiss Me, Kate* (both based on Broadway shows). Usually cast as the brassy friend rather than the leading lady, she was known for her high-speed tap dancing. Her other films included *You Can't Take It With You* (winner of the 1938 Best Picture Oscar), *Lovely to Look At, Easter Parade, Texas Carnival,* and *Hit the Deck.* In the 1960s, she changed her focus to stage musicals, starring in productions of *Mame, Anything Goes,* and *Hello, Dolly!* She had a late career success on Broadway in *Sugar Babies* opposite Mickey Rooney. Her mention in *ACL* is in the scene leading up to the number "Sing!," where Kristine claims she was inspired by movies to pursue a performing career, but emulated singer Doris Day more than dancer Ann Miller. Twenty-three years after *A Chorus Line,* Miller starred opposite the original Cassie, Donna McKechnie, in a 1998 revival of Stephen Sondheim and James Goldman's musical *Follies* at the Paper Mill Playhouse in New Jersey. Miller played Carlotta and McKechnie was Sally in the production; a cast recording was released.

Nureyev, Rudolf (1938–93)

Russian dancer who is considered one of the greatest male ballet dancers of all time. He performed as a young man with Russia's Kirov Ballet, but his outgoing and rebellious personality infuriated the Soviet-era authorities, who curtailed his touring opportunities. In 1961, he defected to the West and joined London's Royal Ballet as Principal Dancer; there, he began a now-legendary partnership with the great ballerina Dame Margot Fonteyn, though she was almost twenty years his senior. They performed together in such classic ballets as *Romeo and Juliet, Les Sylphides, Swan Lake,* and their signature piece, *Marguerite and Armand,* choreographed by Sir Frederick Ashton. In later years, Nureyev took over the artistic directorship of the Paris Opera Ballet, where he continued to dance as well as choreograph. He is credited both with expanding the role and importance of the male dancer in classical ballet and with encouraging crossover and mutual acceptance between the worlds of ballet and modern dance: Martha Graham created a piece for him. Nureyev also worked as an actor, starring in the films *Valentino* and *Exposed* and touring in a revival of the musical *The King and I* (see above). He died of AIDS-related causes at age fifty-four. In *A Chorus Line*, he is named by Bebe as the third of her childhood celebrity crushes, though the line is seldom clearly heard in performance; it tends to get buried in the cacophony of overlapping voices all singing different lines in that late section of the Montage.

Peyton Place

A 1956 novel by Grace Metalious (1924–64) that chronicled the often sordid lives of the denizens of the titular locale, which was a composite of several real-life towns in New Hampshire. Metalious had grown up in a poor family in the area, and the novel portrays the harsh divisions between the region's economic classes, as well as various unhappy romantic relationships. Some citizens of the towns were outraged by their portrayal in the book, which was unusually frank for its day in its depiction of sex, violence, incest, and murder; the novel was also denounced by religious groups and generally dismissed by critics, but it became an enormous popular success and remained on the bestseller list for fifty-nine weeks. A year later, it was made into a popular movie, directed by Mark Robson, with a cast including Lana Turner, Hope Lange, Diane Varsi, Lee Philips, Arthur Kennedy, Barry Coe, Russ Tamblyn, and Terry Moore. The Hays Code required that certain elements of the novel's story be sanitized for the film, and Metalious was unhappy with the results. The movie was nominated for nine Academy Awards, including Best Picture, but did not win any of them. Metalious's novel was also the basis for a TV series, produced by 20th Century Fox Television, that ran from 1964 to 1969 and is considered to have been the first American prime-time soap opera, a precursor to such later hits as *Dallas, Dynasty, Knots Landing*, and *Melrose Place*. Later incarnations included *Return to Peyton Place*, a daytime soap opera that ran on NBC from 1972 to 1974, and two TV movies. The mention in *A Chorus Line* is a brief one in the Montage sequence: the character Mark remembers being "locked in the bathroom with *Peyton Place*." Since *ACL* predated Netflix, DVD players, and even VCRs, one wonders if he took a portable television in there to watch the movie or the TV show; since he has already expressed his fondness for books, we can probably assume he found the novel itself sufficiently stimulating.

Radio City Music Hall

A huge and world-famous performance venue located at Rockefeller Center in the heart of New York City. The theatre opened in 1932 and was immediately celebrated for its innovative art deco interior design, enormous seating capacity (nearly six thousand), and huge pipe organ, known as the Mighty Wurlitzer. For decades, the venue's entertainment format was built on several performances a day that combined a high-profile film premiere, usually of a family-friendly, G-rated movie, with a spectacular live stage show featuring the Rockettes (see below), that iconic line of high-kicking female precision dancers. In *ACL*, Val speaks of Louella Heiner, a girl from her hometown who had become a Rockette, and her own unsuccessful audition for the group. After 1979 (four years after *A Chorus Line* opened), Radio City Music Hall ceased to be a regular venue for movies (with occasional exceptions, as when it hosted the premieres of some of the Harry Potter films); it was nearly closed down and converted into an office building in the early eighties. A public outcry and the intervention of historical preservationists kept the venue alive, however, and the interior received a major restoration in 1999. Now operated by the Madison Square Garden Company, it continues to serve as an active performance venue, with the annual Radio City Christmas Spectacular long established as a popular tourist attraction. During the rest of the year, the theatre hosts a variety of high-profile music acts and special events like awards shows: most years since 1997, it has been the home of the Tony Awards ceremony, making it a more integral part of the Broadway community than ever before. In 2007, the cast of the Broadway revival of *A Chorus Line* opened the Tony telecast by performing part of "I Hope I Get It" on the street outside the Music Hall; they were subsequently seen performing "One" (a number whose style has always recalled the Rockettes to some degree) on the venue's huge stage.

Sheila (played by Leigh Zimmerman, who won an Olivier Award for the role) talks about her love for *The Red Shoes* in the 2013 West End revival.

Photo by Manuel Harlan

The Red Shoes

A British film released in 1948 but not widely distributed in the USA until 1951. Directed by Michael Powell and Emeric Pressburger and choreographed by Robert Helpmann and Léonide Massine, the film was suggested by the Hans Christian Andersen fairy tale about a young woman who can't stop dancing after she puts on a pair of magical red shoes. It includes a ballet based on the fairy tale and a framing story that parallels its theme: the conflict between dance and love in the life of a young ballerina, played by Moira Shearer. In *A Chorus Line*, Sheila remembers seeing the film as a child and being inspired to become a ballerina— and later, Val claims she never saw it and didn't care about it. The movie is considered a landmark in film history for its extensive use of ballet and its stylish Technicolor cinematography. Besides its mentions in *ACL*, it has further Broadway connections. In 1993, it was adapted as a large-scale Broadway musical with music by Jule Styne and book and lyrics by Marsha Norman. Norman was assisted on the lyrics by Bob Merrill, writing under a pseudonym; the cast included Laurie Gamache, who had been the final Broadway Cassie. The production received harsh reviews and closed after less than a week. In 2006, the Andersen story was adapted for Broadway again as *Hot Feet*, a jukebox musical with a score made up of songs by the rock band Earth, Wind and Fire. The story was given a modern setting, with the lead character an African American girl who dreams of dancing on Broadway. Directed and choreographed by Maurice Hines, this version also received poor reviews and ran less than three months.

The Rockettes

The high-kicking all-female dance company that has performed at Radio City Music Hall (see above) since its opening night on December 27, 1932. The group is actually older than the Music Hall, having been founded in St. Louis in 1925 by an impresario named Russell Markert; they were originally known as the Missouri Rockets. Their first New York engagement was at the Roxy movie palace, where they were rechristened the Roxyettes; the group was later taken to Radio City when the Roxy's producer, Samuel Roxy Rothafel, took over that venue. The association has lasted ever since, and today the company is known primarily for their performances in the annual Radio City Christmas Spectacular. In addition to the New York group, there are touring companies that perform a similar show at other venues around the United States and Canada. The Rockettes have also performed at special events such as the halftime show at the Super Bowl and, annually, at the Christmas tree lighting ceremony in Rockefeller Center. They have also been seen on the Tony Awards telecast, since that ceremony is often held at Radio City. The rigorous auditions for the company (where, according to *ACL*, Val was unsuccessful) are held each April; dancers are required to meet a height requirement and perform in various dance styles including jazz, tap, and ballet.

Roseland

An iconic ballroom/music performance venue in New York City's Theatre District. Situated on a quarter-acre plot, with a large dance floor and stage plus a balcony, the hall was often referred to as "the World's Greatest Ballroom." Located at 239 W. 52nd Street, next door to Broadway's August Wilson Theatre (formerly known as the Virginia Theatre), it was built in 1922 as an ice skating rink. In the early 1950s, Roseland founder Louis Brecker bought the building and converted it into a roller rink; when Roseland's former home on 51st Street was torn down in 1956, Brecker moved the ballroom there. In the late fifties, Roseland was known not only for its great size (it could accommodate a dance party of 2,500 guests) but for its presentation of top-name big bands and jazz musicians, including Louis Armstrong, Tommy Dorsey, and Glenn Miller. *ACL*'s Al, in the Montage, remembers his father taking his mother dancing there. Even in the seventies, the management limited the programming to old-fashioned "cheek to cheek" dancing, though after the building was sold in the early eighties it eventually became a venue for disco parties and rock concerts. For several years after the turn of the millennium it was the home of *Broadway Bares*, a spectacular annual revue where Broadway dancers put on (and take off) outrageously fantastical costumes and perform elaborate production numbers as a benefit for Broadway Cares/Equity Fights Aids; many of the participants, including founder/choreographer Jerry Mitchell, have been *Chorus Line* alumni. The owners of the building, the Ginsberg family, had wanted to tear it down for years in order to build a large apartment building on the property, a prime piece of Manhattan real estate; the ballroom was closed down permanently in April 2014, after a final series of concerts by Lady Gaga.

St. John, Jill (b. 1940)

American film and TV actress who made her big-screen debut in *Summer Love* in 1958. Her other films include *The Remarkable Mr. Pennypacker*, *The Lost World*, *The Roman Spring of Mrs. Stone*, *Tony Rome*, *Around the World in 80 Days*, and *The Player*. A glamorous redhead, she is married to actor Robert Wagner. At the time of *A Chorus Line*, she had recently received a lot of publicity as the first American actress to play a "Bond girl," in the James Bond movie *Diamonds Are Forever* (1971), and she had also starred opposite Frank Sinatra in the movie version of *Come Blow Your Horn*, a play by *ACL* script doctor Neil Simon. In the show, Val says one of her career goals is to replace St. John in Hollywood.

St. Joseph's Hospital

The emergency room to which Paul is taken following his accident seems to be fictitious. This is surprising, because the other place references in the script are real. The closest hospitals to Manhattan with that name are in Yonkers and Bethpage, Long Island. In former years, there were also other St. Joseph's in the Bronx, Flushing, and Far Rockaway (so it's understandable if Kirkwood and Dante thought it sounded like a typical name for a hospital). But in the play, Larry speaks on the phone to a doctor who offers to meet him and Paul at the emergency entrance to St. Joseph's, claiming this is the quickest solution, and they leave in a cab, clearly indicating the hospital is meant to be near the Theatre District.

Tallchief, Maria (1925–2013)

The first prima ballerina of the New York City Ballet, Tallchief was muse, protégée, and, for a while, wife of the company's founder, George Balanchine. Her mother was of Scotch-Irish descent, and her father was a member of the Osage Nation, making her the first Native American dancer to achieve stardom in the ballet world; her sister Marjorie was also a ballerina. Tallchief's family was wealthy, and her mother was an ambitious stage mother who recognized her daughters' talents early, so the family moved from the reservation in Oklahoma to Los Angeles when

Maria was still a young child, in search of training and performance opportunities for both girls. Maria was both a piano prodigy and an exceptional dance student as a young teen, and for a while was unsure which career path she would pursue. She danced in an MGM musical (*Presenting Lily Mars*, with Judy Garland) before moving to New York and joining the Ballet Russe de Monte Carlo, where she met Balanchine; she later became his prima ballerina at the New York City Ballet. In her later career, Tallchief danced with American Ballet Theatre and the Hamburg Ballet and, after retiring from performing, moved to Chicago, where she was director of ballet for the Lyric Opera of Chicago and cofounder, with Marjorie, of the Chicago City Ballet. Her passionate dance style, as athletic and fiery as it was lyrical and technically refined, helped define both the Balanchine style and the image of the American ballerina; her many awards included a Kennedy Center Honor in 1996. At five feet nine inches, she was almost a foot taller than *A Chorus Line*'s Connie, who laments in the Montage sequence that her failure to live up to the image of Maria Tallchief kept her from a career in classical dance. Hamlisch's music for Kleban's lyric cleverly underlines the humor by emphasizing the "Tall" in her last name.

The Ted Mack Amateur Hour

A popular television program that premiered on the DuMont Television Network in 1948 and was seen at various times on all three of the other main broadcast networks (NBC, CBS, and ABC) by the time it completed its run in 1970. The show, officially known as *Ted Mack and the Original Amateur Hour*, was a successor to a radio program called *The Major Bowes Amateur Hour*, which premiered in 1934. Ted Mack (1904–1976) had worked as a director and talent scout for original host Major Bowes and revived the show on both radio and TV after Bowes's death. The format was that of a talent competition featuring vaudeville-type acts (jugglers, baton twirlers, and the like) as well as numerous singers, musicians, and dancers. Famous performers who got early exposure on the show included Frank Sinatra (on the original radio version), Gladys Knight, Pat Boone, Ann-Margret, and Irene Cara, who later starred in the film *Fame*. Auditions were held in New York City at Radio City Music Hall or at various locations around the country; Albert Fisher served as the "in-the-field" talent scout and probably would have run the St. Louis auditions that Judy laments having missed in the Montage section of *A Chorus Line*. After viewing the various acts that appeared on the show, audience members voted for the winner by calling a phone number displayed on the screen or mailing in a postcard. An early forerunner of reality TV, the *Amateur Hour* was a prototype for such popular later TV series as *Star Search*, *American Idol*, and *America's Got Talent*.

Turner, Lana (1921–1995)

Popular American film actress and sex symbol, who was famously discovered in a drug store (the Top Hat Malt Shop on Sunset Boulevard). Originally noted mainly for her beauty, she played undemanding but glamorous roles in her early films, earning the nickname "the Sweater Girl" and becoming a popular World War II-era pinup. She was paired in several films with Clark Gable, and their onscreen chemistry (along with rumors of an offscreen romance) fed her popularity. She gained more respect as an actress by taking on serious roles in such films as *The Postman Always Rings Twice*, *Green Dolphin Street*, *Peyton Place* (see above), *The Bad and the Beautiful*, and *The Sea Chase*. She was married eight times to seven different men. Turner's personal life threatened to eclipse her career in 1958 when her abusive boyfriend, Johnny Stompanato, was stabbed to death by her daughter Cheryl, then fourteen, who was acquitted of the crime on the basis that she had been defending her mother. Turner's film career had faded by the mid-1970s, but after several years in retirement, she returned briefly to the spotlight in a series of guest appearances on the CBS nighttime soap opera *Falcon Crest*. The reference in *A Chorus Line* comes in the scene where the dancers first introduce themselves: the character Judy Turner jokes that her real name is Lana Turner. (Oddly, Turner's real name was Julia and her friends called her Judy when she was a child; it's unclear whether the writers of the show knew this.)

Verdon, Gwen (1925–2000)

American actress/dancer/singer who was considered the premier Broadway dancer of her generation. Verdon began ballet studies to correct damage to her legs caused by a childhood case of rickets, and by the time she was in her teens she was performing small dance roles in Hollywood films. Early in her career, she assisted famed Broadway and Hollywood choreographer Jack Cole and coached several prominent film stars for their dance numbers in movies; she continued this type of work throughout her career as assistant/collaborator to Bob Fosse, the director/choreographer for whom she danced in numerous musicals beginning with *Damn Yankees* in 1956. Verdon won a Tony (one of her four) for the role of Lola in that musical, which she repeated in the film version. Her other collaborations with Fosse included *Redhead*, *Sweet Charity*, and *Chicago*, in which she originated the role of Roxie Hart in 1975, the year that *A Chorus Line* also premiered on Broadway. Verdon was nominated for what would have been her fifth Tony for the role, but lost the award to Donna McKechnie. The *Chorus Line* awards sweep that year kept *Chicago*, now also considered a major contribution to the history of the American musical, from winning any Tony Awards. Yet Verdon is permanently memorialized in *ACL* through her mention in the "alternatives" scene as a beloved role model to the dancers.

She married Fosse in 1960, and though they were legally separated in 1971 due to his well-documented extramarital affairs, they remained close colleagues and collaborators, and she was considered his muse; their relationship paralleled to some degree that of Bennett and McKechnie. The two women worked together, and became good friends, when Verdon coached McKechnie for the title role in the 1987 revival tour of *Sweet Charity*. Other *ACL* connections become intriguingly tangled if not incestuous. In Fosse's 1979 film *All That Jazz*, generally considered to be largely autobiographical, a character based on Verdon was played by Leland

Palmer, a dancer/actress who worked extensively with both Bennett and Fosse and had briefly played Cassie during the original Los Angeles run of *ACL*. The Fosse character's lover in that film, a role based on the real life Ann Reinking, was played by Reinking herself; she had been the first Broadway replacement Cassie and also replaced Verdon in *Chicago*, and later took over the title role in the Broadway revival of *Sweet Charity* (the production in which McKechnie toured). A final connection: The role of Kristine in the movie of *A Chorus Line* was played by Fosse and Verdon's daughter, the dancer Nicole Fosse.

Wong, Anna May (1905–1961)

Chinese American actress, born in Los Angeles, who gained fame as the first female Asian American movie star and the first Chinese American to star in her own TV series. Wong became enamored of silent films as a child and began contacting film producers to ask for casting consideration when she was only nine years old. Despite her family's ambivalence about her ambitions, she began to work in silent films as a teen and successfully made the transition to "talkies." Frustrated by the stereotypical roles available to her in the United States, she spent time in China, studying her cultural heritage and Chinese theater, and in Europe, where she appeared onstage and in more artistically ambitious films. She learned several languages and toured in a musical cabaret show. Hollywood notoriously refused to cast her in the leading female role of O-Lan in the film version of Pearl S. Buck's novel *The Good Earth*, casting instead the German American actress Luise Rainer, though Wong had campaigned actively for the role. For a time, she put her acting career on hold to focus on supporting the Chinese cause in the war against Japanese imperialism, which later escalated and became part of World War II. Her most famous films included *The Thief of Baghdad*, *Dangerous to Know* (based on a Broadway play in which she had also starred, *On the Spot*), *Daughter of the Dragon*, and *Shanghai Express*, in which she played opposite Marlene Dietrich. Rumors of a romantic relationship with Dietrich contributed to making her an icon in the gay community, which embraced her for her efforts to overcome her outsider status. Her mention in *A Chorus Line* comes in Paul's monologue: He says he looked like her in his costume for an Asian-themed number in the Jewel Box Revue.

15

"I Knew He Liked Me All the Time"

The Opening, the Critics and the Awards

N ever before had a new musical caught the public's attention and become an immediate hit in quite the same way *A Chorus Line* did. At the first preview performance, there were only 6 empty seats in the 299-seat Newman Theatre; after that, every single seat was filled every night. The extraordinary word of mouth that began to spread on the morning following that first public performance soon resulted in a sold-out run at the Public; the house staff was violating fire code rules almost every night by squeezing in as many extra bodies as they could, many of whom (even including celebrities like Liza Minnelli and Diana Ross) agreed to sit on the steps when there were no seats available. And still people were being turned away. So a move to Broadway, and to a Shubert House, was a foregone conclusion. Fortunately, one of Michael Bennett's favorite houses, the Sam S. Shubert Theatre on 44th Street, became available.

Moving the Show

Less than two weeks would elapse between the 101st and last performance at the Public on July 13, 1975, and the first Broadway preview on July 25—but the producers and the designers had weeks to plan the move and prepare the theatre while the show was still running downtown. The Shubert Theatre had been chosen partly because it had a narrow enough house with a steep enough rake to approximate the sightlines at the Newman. Michael Bennett wanted to keep the design elements as close as possible to what they had been downtown, but of course the much larger Broadway space, while opening up new possibilities, also necessitated some modifications.

At the Newman, the additional mirrors that appeared for the slow section of Cassie's dance were pushed onstage manually from the wings by a few of the male dancers. On Broadway, that would not be allowed: both the actors' and the stagehands' unions have strict rules about what their members may and may not be asked to do. There was very little else in the show that required the services of stagehands, so in order to have someone available to move each of the seven mirrors, five people would have to be added to the crew—at very substantial weekly salaries—unless another solution could be implemented. Bennett said he wanted the mirrors to pop up from under the stage—and once Michael Bennett got attached to an idea, it could be hard to talk him out of it. But that would have been an enormously expensive and impractical solution, as it would have involved tearing up the whole stage and rerouting much of the theatre's plumbing. A representative of the stagehands' union (Local 1) named Robert McDonald was invited to see the show and suggest a solution, and he came up with the idea of flying the mirrors in. Finally, with the help of the Shubert Organization's Bernard Jacobs, who was becoming a close friend and mentor figure to Bennett, the team managed to talk the director into the idea—which anyone who ever saw the show on Broadway or on tour knows was a wonderfully graceful solution. The descent was timed to the music, and the bottoms of the mirrors were weighted so they would all reach the floor at the same moment; the effect was elegant.

Other changes included the stage floor itself; the deck at the Shubert was worn, and in a dance show the floor is extremely important, so a new one was put in at a cost of $40,000. Another dance floor was installed in the basement so the dancers would have a suitable surface on which to warm up. The biggest and most expensive change was the new lighting bridge that Bennett and designer Tharon Musser insisted be installed so they could duplicate the lighting angles that had worked so beautifully at the Newman; building it involved cutting through the ceiling of the house and into the offices above, and the bridge ended up costing $43,000. (Needless to say, the show's record-breaking fifteen-year tenancy would more than justify the effort and expense of the renovations.)

There were also major decisions to be made about the orchestra. Downtown, there were just sixteen musicians, but the Shubert had a union minimum of twenty-six. Orchestrator Jonathan Tunick wanted to hire string players and write parts for them to enrich the sound of the ballads in the score, especially "At the Ballet." But Don Pippin, the musical director, was opposed to it; he thought the show as it was had a unique, contemporary sound that served the material, and didn't want it to move to a more generic, traditional Broadway style. Michael Bennett ultimately agreed with Pippin, partly because he was superstitious about changing anything that had worked so well downtown. So they stayed with the small orchestra, and *A Chorus Line* to this day is performed with no string players.

Still, according to the union rules, the production had to hire ten more players to meet the theatre's minimum. These extra musicians are called "walkers" because they are basically paid not to play, although in the case of *ACL* they sometimes subbed in for musicians who were out, and the trumpet parts were so demanding that it was decided that the extra trumpet player would sub in a couple of performances a week for each of the three in the regular band, reducing their load to six shows each.

At the Newman, the musicians were backstage, but at the Shubert, there is an orchestra pit. To preserve the feeling of an audition, Bennett wanted the musicians to be invisible and wouldn't even let them warm up after the house was open. A cover was built over the pit so they couldn't be seen, and the sound had to be mixed by the sound operator and piped back into the theatre over speakers. This made some audience members suspect that the music was all prerecorded, with the result that the producers decided to start listing the names of all of the musicians in the program—standard practice today but almost unheard of at the time—so the audience would know that they actually existed! The original plan was for the seven understudies, who became offstage singers after the opening scene, to be in the pit with the band; it turned out there wasn't room, so a special booth was built for them in the wings, and their voices were also routed through the sound system. They couldn't see the musicians or the conductor, and so got their cues by watching the dancers on the stage.

The show only encountered one unexpected speed bump on the way to its Broadway opening, but it was kind of a major one: a musician's strike that shut down all the musicals on the Great White Way on September 18. Performances could not resume until October 13, when a new agreement was finally reached by the union and the producers. This gave the dancers an unexpected, if nerve-wracking, vacation, though some rehearsals were held; the official press opening had to be pushed back three weeks, from the originally announced September 28 to Sunday, October 19.

Critical Response

The performance that night began at 6:45 p.m., to enable the TV critics to write their reviews in time to broadcast them at the end of the eleven o'clock news telecasts. The audience was filled not only with friends and family, but also many fans who had seen the show one or more times downtown and were thrilled to be part of its opening night on Broadway. As Don Percassi (Al) told Denny Martin Flinn: "After we finished each number, the warmth, the love, just came over the stage like a wave. You could feel it come and feel it go. It was unbelievable." In the last scene, each dancer received individual applause as he or she stepped back into place on the line to await Zach's decisions.

Unlike certain other groundbreaking musicals, which were so far ahead of their time that they bemused some of the critics, *A Chorus Line* was immediately appreciated. There were two rounds of reviews, one following the downtown opening in May and another for Broadway in October, and the press was as enthusiastic as the audiences.

Clive Barnes, in the all-important *New York Times*, wrote that Bennett's "choreography and direction burn up superlatives as if they were inflammable. . . . The dances have the right Broadway surge, and two numbers, the mirror-dance for Miss McKechnie and the Busby Berkeley-inspired finale, deserve to become classics of musical staging. And talking of classics, while there will be some to find fault, perhaps with a certain reason, with the hard-edged glossiness of 'A Chorus Line,' it is a show that must dance, jog and whirl its way into the history of the musical theater. 'Oklahoma!' it isn't, but no one with strength to get to the box office, should willingly miss it."

T. E. Kalem, writing in *Time* magazine, waxed almost poetic: "Michael Bennett, who may be a direct descendant of Terpsichore, has added to the dance vocabulary of the U.S. musical. He has made dance a central theme as well as a supremely exhilarating act. The chorus line is his symbol of mass anonymity. It is also his

"The Big Six": Sammy Williams (Paul), Pamela Blair (Val), Donna McKechnie (Cassie), Robert LuPone (Zach), Kelly Bishop (Sheila), and Priscilla Lopez (Diana) on Broadway in 1975.

Photo by Martha Swope; Photofest

symbol of teamwork, with the emphasis equally distributed between team and work. Bennett distills one more element. Behind the faceless mask, there is a face; behind the dazzling precision of the dance, there is a terrifying vulnerability, not the false step of a foot but the crippling fall of a psyche."

Jack Kroll of *Newsweek* was won over by the courage and excitement of the show, while declaring that "Both format and material flirt with danger. The disembodied voice of Zach interrogating the vulnerable dancers can sound like a show-biz Gestapo. The extended monologue of the homosexual boy touches the damp skirts of sentimentality. What seals things tight is the heart-gripping sincerity of the performers and the rare intensity of the entire show, which builds to an over-powering emotional climax. Formal imperfections are overridden by Bennett's tremendous musical staging, reinforced by Tharon Musser's marvelous lighting and Robin Wagner's setting, a camera obscura of black walls and shifting mirrors where reality and dreams ricochet off one another like desire and frustration."

Ethan Mordden has long been known as a historian of the musical theatre—and an expert on American theatre history in general, opera, gay history, and various other cultural topics. His book *Better Foot Forward: The History of American Musical Theatre* was published in 1976, just as *A Chorus Line* was establishing itself as a phenomenon; at that moment, the show was effectively the last chapter in said history. Referring to Bennett's work on *Company* and *Follies* as well as *ACL*, Mordden wrote eloquently of the director/choreographer's unique gift for staging: "Bennett was on his way to being the best stager of musicals there is, a man who apparently kneels at the altar of concept rather than gloss. . . . He moved his actors/singers/ dancers in the best of all possible ways, renewing musical comedy tradition by developing it. The Bennett patterns suggest the past without living in it, and they flourish, fusing bits of our experience with arrant distinction." A few pages later, he says of the show: "If its occasional hints at making a statement about anonymity versus identity didn't pan out, it was still a tremendous evening, mainly for Bennett's staging." But then he perhaps contradicts his own caveat by saying of the dancers in the finale: "Then, horrifyingly, they materialized one by one in a phosphorescent apotheosis, the dancers who were so painstakingly individualized for us now submerged in a grim, callous, defiant 'big number.' It was scary, but all the same, one was moved because the characters worked as people. And more: they had hope."

Coping with Success

After the opening and the raves, the pressure on the cast didn't really let up, but it changed. Now they were in a hit show, and they had to continue to deliver opening night–level performances eight times a week. They also had to do interviews and special appearances, and make the rounds of numerous parties, all of which wore them down and in some cases left them exhausted. But they took pride in the show and gave it everything they had, determined that each and every audience should have the full *Chorus Line* experience.

Though each of the actors received a certain amount of recognition, it soon became evident that audiences, and particularly the press, were most interested in a small number of performers who had the biggest roles. Soon known informally as the Big Six, this group included Robert LuPone (Zach), Donna McKechnie (Cassie), Kelly Bishop (Sheila), Priscilla Lopez (Diana), Sammy Williams (Paul), and Pamela Blair (Val). The others started to feel like second-class citizens at times, and the tension increased when *Newsweek* did a cover story on the show but, instead of putting a picture of the whole line on the cover, used a full-length photo of McKechnie alone. And if there was a renewed sense of competition for attention among the cast, it was to some degree exacerbated by the announcement of the nominations for the Tony Awards.

Awards Season

All of the Big Six except for Blair were nominated for Tonys, with Bishop and Lopez placed in competition with each other for Best Featured Actress in a Musical and LuPone and Williams pitted against each other for Best Featured Actor. The Best Actor and Best Actress categories were traditionally reserved for stars with their names above the title, and all the actors in *A Chorus Line* received equal, alphabetical billing. However, Bennett, still intent on making McKechnie a star, campaigned successfully to have her put in the leading actress category.

The Tony Awards Ceremony turned out to be a triumphant and memorable night for the show. As the producers of the Awards had a strong hunch *A Chorus Line* was going to sweep, the musical was put at the center of the ceremony and the telecast. The event was even held at the Shubert, so the cast was performing on its home turf, and Bennett went all out to ensure that the show was showcased to its best advantage. Much viewed and cherished by fans over the years, the Tony night performance of "I Hope I Get It," the opening number of the show (which also opened the telecast) is a unique document of the entire original cast in living color. (There is an invaluable archival video of the whole show, taped while it was still playing at the Public, but it was done with a primitive video camera and is dark, grainy, and often hard to see.) The number had to be shortened to fit the parameters of the broadcast, and Bennett did a shrewd job of tightening it up, cutting the section where the dancers are being divided into their groups and the verse of the song that goes with it; he also reconfigured the dancing so that the repeated combinations are performed by four groups of six dancers, rather than six groups of four as in the show. He has been much praised for the excellent camera work that reveals telling character details while heightening the tension of the scene; Ethan Mordden said it well in another book, *One More Kiss: The Broadway Musical in the 1970s*: "Asking for one extra camera. . . Bennett edited on the run, drinking in the action while moving from screen to screen. He jumped, pivoted, close-upped: for instance on Cassie, distractedly staring at Zach while the others sang their 'I hope I get it!' lines. Throughout the dancing audition, Bennett kept the screen feeding on character information—the different levels of talent, the worried or merely persevering looks. Again, a few stood out among the crowd—but then, that's Bennett's view of show biz/life, isn't it?" The cast reappeared at the end of the broadcast to perform the final segment of the "One" finale.

The show ended up winning nine Tony Awards out of twelve nominations. The only category it lost was Costume Design, with Theoni V. Aldredge edged out by Florence Klotz for *Pacific Overtures*. The only reason there weren't eleven wins was because the nominations were in only ten categories; only one could win in each of the featured performer categories, and Bishop and Williams were victorious, leaving Lopez and LuPone to go home empty-handed. (Coincidentally, LuPone's sister Patti was also nominated that year, for Best Featured Actress in a Musical for *The Robber Bridegroom*, and Barry Bostwick, who had left the cast of *A Chorus Line* during the second workshop, was nominated for Best Featured Actor in a Play for the revival of *They Knew What They Wanted*.) *ACL*'s other Tonys were Best Actress in a Musical for McKechnie, Best Book of a Musical for James Kirkwood and Nicholas Dante, Best Score of a Musical for Marvin Hamlisch and Edward Kleban, Best Lighting Design for Tharon Musser, Best Choreographer for Bennett and Bob Avian, Best Director of a Musical for Bennett, and of course Best Musical.

In his acceptance speech as Best Director, Michael Bennett said, "I really wanted this, and so many people did so much to help me get this. I only wanted one thing: to be a Broadway director. And I am. And I wanted one moment, and I have it."

The honors did not stop there. *A Chorus Line* also won the 1976 Drama Desk Awards for Best Book, Best Score, Best Director, Best Choreographer, and Best

Actress—which was awarded to both McKechnie and Bishop in a tie. The Obie Awards (for Off-Broadway productions) cited the creative team and the performances of Lopez and Williams, and the show won the New York Drama Critics Award for Best Musical of 1975. A special Theatre World Award was presented to the entire cast and creative team, which some people felt was the most appropriate way to honor this particular musical, given the themes of the show.

Finally, *A Chorus Line* was declared the winner of the 1976 Pulitzer Prize for Drama, a prestigious award that has only very occasionally been awarded to a musical. Its touring companies would later win several Los Angeles Drama Critics Circle Awards and the London Evening Standard Award for Best Musical.

Their triumphant Tony Awards telecast performance turned out to be the last time the entire original cast would perform together. Pamela Blair was out of the show for the rest of the week, and understudy Crissy Wilzak played Val the next Saturday night, which was the original company's final performance on Broadway. The next day, fourteen of them would leave town to open the National Company in San Francisco. A major chapter in the history of *A Chorus Line* had ended, but new adventures and new triumphs were still ahead.

"Who Wrote *A Chorus Line?*" The Royalty Issue

One of the most controversial and emotionally fraught topics surrounding *ACL* over the past forty years concerns the financial arrangements made with the original cast members and the other dancers whose stories, and in many cases words, were used in the show.

During the first workshop, all the dancers were asked to sign a short release form giving Bennett the rights to use their personal stories in the show, as well as their likenesses for marketing purposes. For this they were each compensated the sum of one dollar; most were paid in cash.

The forms were handed out during a break in rehearsal one day and presented as a routine formality; though some of the dancers briefly had misgivings, they all agreed to sign. They very much wanted to be part of the new musical that was coming together, and they suspected Bennett might drop any of them who did not agree; they thought this was the price they had to pay to stay with the show. Also, at that point there was no money involved, they were all working for a hundred dollars a week, and there was little inkling in anybody's mind of the huge moneymaker the show would eventually become.

Bennett had already had similar documents signed by Michon Peacock, Tony Stevens, and Nicholas Dante, who had initially worked with him on conceiving and organizing the tape sessions, and at this point the dancers who were on the tapes but not taking part in the show were contacted and asked to sign as well. As quoted in a 2006 *New York Times* article by Campbell Robertson, Stevens remarked: "When you ask an actor to do something, their first response is to ask 'Why?' Dancers, on the other hand, do not ask questions; they just perform." Everybody signed.

Later, as the Broadway opening loomed, Bennett called his lawyer John Breglio for help in working out an arrangement to provide royalties to the dancers: something that, since he already had the signed release forms, he was in no way legally obligated to do. According to Denny Martin Flinn's *What They Did for Love*: "Michael and Nick Dante took one half of one percent of the gross weekly box office income, as well as a prorated share of subsidiary rights, all from their own writers' royalties, and assigned it to the dancers in a complicated formula administered by the accounting firm of Lutz & Carr." According to Ken Mandelbaum, the contract was drawn up on January 1, 1976, when the show had been running on Broadway for almost six months. The performers, thirty-seven in all, were divided into three groups. Group A included the dancers who had been in at least one of the original tape sessions and/or the workshops and whose stories were used substantially in the show. Group B was dancers who were on the tapes but not cast in the production. Group C consisted of those who were not added to the cast till the second workshop and therefore had contributed less to the development of the script. The people in Group A were allotted twice the share that the others would receive. Though most of the dancers who were not actually in the show considered this almost a gift, many of those who had worked hard on it and were in the cast came to feel that the remuneration was insufficient given their contributions. (Though the dancers in Group A and Group B would continue to receive their percentages for life, those in Group C were eligible only as long as they performed in the show.) In some cases, the amount per actor added up to $10,000 a year while the show was selling well on Broadway and on tour; Pamela Blair estimated that by 1989 (the year before *ACL* closed in New York) she had made about $36,000. But this was from a show whose combined companies grossed $280 million and by 1990 had fed over $38 million into the coffers of the New York Shakespeare Festival.

Early in the Broadway run, when the atmosphere was rife with tension between Bennett and the cast for a variety of reasons, there were several disputes about money. The

Cover design of the original cast album, Columbia Records.

actors were each offered a fee of just $500 for recording the cast album (which now sounds like a ridiculously small amount considering that it has been selling well for almost forty years), but were promised a double fee if the session lasted more than eight hours. Though it ended up going all day and half the night, the checks they were given were for the original $500 only. Though they hadn't thought to get the promise in writing, they managed to get their second checks—but only by banding together and refusing to perform the next night if the money was not forthcoming.

Later, a bigger argument arose over the show's logo, the photo of the seventeen dancers standing on line, which had become so popular that it was being used not only to advertise the show but on numerous souvenir and gift items. The dancers asked for a share in the merchandising profits, but since they had already agreed on the original release form to allow their likenesses to be used for a dollar, Bennett said no—claiming he didn't want to see them hawking T-shirts outside the theatre. When the logo appeared on expensive bath towels sold at Bloomingdale's, a department store that wouldn't even issue the dancers credit cards, they decided to sue for a share in the profits. However, several of them eventually backed off, and the others ended up dropping the case. To placate them, they were eventually each given one of the towels—and one of the credit cards.

More discord followed over Broadway salaries. When the show opened at the Shubert, the dancers were each paid $650 a week; that was more than twice the Equity minimum at the time, and they mostly felt well taken care of. They had been promised they were being treated as "favored nations," all making the same amount, but then Pam Blair's agent found out that Donna McKechnie alone had been given a substantial increase, and Blair told Priscilla Lopez, who was the show's Equity deputy. Lopez stood up to Bennett on the issue, but was told that "favored nations" means everyone is guaranteed a certain salary but doesn't prohibit any individual from getting more than that, so the cast had no legal basis on which to dispute the discrepancy.

In the ensuing three decades, none of the original cast members went on to the kind of stardom the success of the show had led them to hope for, and some regretted having signed away their life stories without demanding more compensation. In 2006, when the Broadway revival of the show was announced, they thought they would once again start receiving royalties, but, according to Robertson, "When they consulted lawyers, they discovered that the royalty agreement covered the original production and that show's subsidiary rights. According to the terms of that document, the 2006 revival fits neither category." When they approached Breglio (who was not only Bennett's executor but was producing the revival), he "said the only way the arrangement could be changed is if all of the interest holders in the Bennett estate agreed to have the interviewees' royalties taken out of their shares."

In a 2009 interview with Michael Reidel on CUNY-TV's *Theater Talk*, Breglio expressed frustration that the *Times* article had appeared the week before the show opened, and without his input. He explained that after the former dancers complained to him, he approached the heirs to the Bennett estate and was eventually able to work out an agreement with them. Though the specific terms have not been publicly disclosed, according to Philip Boroff of Bloomberg.com: "The two sides agreed it 'would be fair and appropriate' to extend the existing agreement to the revival and to other productions."

16

"This Is Whatcha Call Trav'ling"

The Story of How *A Chorus Line* Toured the United States and the World

O nce the transfer to Broadway had been smoothly accomplished and *A Chorus Line* was established as the biggest phenomenon to hit the New York theatre in years, one would think that Michael Bennett and his team would have been able finally to relax, take a breath, and enjoy the sweet smell of success. But the pressure was not off. Even before the show moved out of the Public Theater, the creative team was aware that it wouldn't be long before whole new casts of dancers would have to be hired, both to replace the originals in New York and to launch the inevitable touring companies. In live theatre, every night is a new adventure, and *A Chorus Line* would only be able to coast so far on the accomplishments of its original cast; Bennett knew the show would have to prove itself, and soon, in major cities all over the United States and the world, and that continued success depended on finding the right performers to take on the roles.

The task of finding replacements was a greater challenge in the seventies than it would be today. *ACL* was really the show that created the demand for the so-called triple-threat performer, highly accomplished at acting, singing, and dancing. Although other recent shows like Bob Fosse's production of *Pippin*—and even *West Side Story* back in the fifties—had given chorus dancers the chance to be noticed as individuals and create specific characters, never before had there been a show in which everyone in the cast had to be a very highly trained dancer as well as an honest, believable actor, and in which most of them had substantial solo singing responsibilities as well. In fact, until recently, many Broadway shows had had separate singing and dancing choruses. In 1976, the new breed of triple threat was just starting to emerge, and it was largely *A Chorus Line* itself, on tour across America, that over the next few years would inspire a new generation of youngsters to pursue the kinds of training needed to succeed in such a show.

Nevertheless, there were a lot of dancers in New York who were eager to test their wings as actors, and they knew *ACL* offered a rare opportunity. They saw the show at the Public and later at the Shubert and dreamed of one day having a chance to play one of the roles. So when the auditions for the first tours were announced, the theatre community was on fire: everyone wanted to be in *A Chorus Line*.

According to Denny Martin Flinn, Bennett anticipated the need for replacement dancers to the point that he started looking for them before the show even moved to Broadway. During the first season, with the original cast performing every night, Bennett and Bob Avian flew periodically to different cities around the country to audition young hopefuls. Although no one was being hired yet, files were being built up for the moment when the new companies would need to be formed. The best candidates from various cities were flown to New York for callbacks, where they auditioned for specific characters.

Hollywood, Here We Come!

When it came time to start planning the tours in earnest, Bennett decided he wanted the entire original cast to travel to California. The first National Company would open in May 1976 at the Curran Theatre in San Francisco and then move on to Los Angeles for an open-ended run (which ended up being a year and a half) in that city's Shubert Theatre. Bennett told the cast it was important to him that the entire group stay together for this new adventure. For many of the performers, the possibility of being discovered in Los Angeles as actors was a big lure, and they hoped the attention they would receive in the highly anticipated musical would lead to opportunities in film and TV. Others were dubious about their prospects—and rightly so, as it turned out.

In the end, despite Bennett's entreaties, five of the original cast members chose to remain in New York. Kelly Bishop had toured for years and was enjoying the security of finally being in a hit Broadway show. She wanted to stay in town and told Bennett she would be willing to go to California only if she got a raise; he refused. Wayne Cilento and Cameron Mason were both skeptical about acting opportunities on the West Coast; they knew Hollywood execs had been flying into New York to see the show and felt they would have been approached already if people were really interested. Mason thought his role as Mark was so small that he was unlikely to draw major attention; he also had a new boyfriend in New York whom he did not want to leave. These three stayed in New York, along with Clive Clerk and Thommie Walsh. Walsh was enjoying being in a Broadway hit and wanted to savor it. Clerk, who had originated the role of Larry and also understudied Zach, had become involved with auditioning and training the replacements, which he enjoyed. When Baayork Lee was preparing to leave for California, she asked him to take over her position as dance captain in New York, and he accepted.

Though there had often been friction and competitiveness among various of the original cast members during the long process of developing and performing the show, the dancers who left for California made repeated efforts to talk the remaining five into changing their minds and going with them. As Trish Garland said (quoted in *On the Line*): "I thought if we could get one of them to change their mind then maybe another would, too. I just didn't want to see it come to an end. Even though there was another rebirth, it was never going to be those people. The first is always the first." Baayork Lee added: "I couldn't look at those five people.

I couldn't talk to them. I couldn't deal with them, I shut them off. They ruined my plans to go forth with *the word*." These sentiments make it clear that, whatever infighting and resentments may have divided the originals, they had by this point bonded powerfully as a family; both those who left and those who stayed felt the pain of the separation.

"Front line, thank you very much . . . I'm sorry."

The next thing that came up, naturally, was the question of the understudies. The group, which by now numbered nine, had been very loyal to the show from the beginning; they had proven themselves versatile, each covering two or three roles, so they understandably hoped and expected that when the original cast members started to move on, and when touring companies were first put together, they would each get the opportunity to move up into one of the roles they had been covering. No such luck, unfortunately. For some reason, Bennett was unwilling to give even one of them the chance to take over a role on the line. There was an infamous rehearsal where the understudies ran through the show and then Bennett sat them down and basically told them he didn't think any of them was good enough to move up to the line. They felt betrayed, and all of them refused the invitation to accompany the fourteen original cast members who were heading off to California; if they were still going to be sitting around backstage waiting to sing from the booth, they reasoned they might as well do it in New York. Besides, they knew no one was going to pay any more attention to an understudy in Los Angeles than they did on Broadway.

Auditioning to Join the Line

In addition to the cattle calls at major cities nationwide, extensive auditions were held in New York for the new companies. A routine was established that soon became standard: dancers were first asked to do a time step and a double pirouette, and if they passed that test they were taught the jazz and ballet combinations from the opening number: the most difficult ensemble choreography in the show. As in the play itself, they were asked to introduce themselves and give their ages, so the team could get a sense of their voices and personalities. (This wouldn't be allowed today, when union rules and legalities prohibit asking for a person's age at an audition, or any job interview.) The best dancers would be asked to sing, as would any whose dancing had been borderline but who seemed to have the right look or presence for one of the characters. The team preferred not to hear songs from the show until they called people back for specific roles, so the dancers sang sixteen bars of other musical theatre material or pop songs. Bennett had too much experience of seeing performers cut off in mid-song or eliminated rudely in auditions for other shows over the years, so he insisted on treating the actors with respect and letting every person complete his or her selection. Those who passed the dance

Future Broadway and television star Bebe Neuwirth (center) played Sheila on tour and on Broadway in the early 1980s. Here she is shown in the International Company, with Eric Horenstein (Greg), Deborah Henry (Cassie), Michael Gorman (Bobby), and Tracy Shayne (Bebe).   *Photo by Martha Swope; from the collection of the author*

and singing auditions would be asked to improvise and read from the script, and callbacks would be held in groups of dancers all auditioning for the same role.

In addition to the National Company and replacements for Broadway, there would be an International Company opening at the same time. The plan was for them to play an initial engagement in Toronto and then move on to London, where they would open the show in the West End and stay there for six months. After that, in compliance with British Equity rules, they would be replaced by a cast of British performers, at which point they would return to North America to continue touring.

Casts for all three companies, including understudies and swings, were chosen at the same time. Bennett held extensive callbacks and took his time making final selections, and then he began to rehearse the new dancers (there were more than sixty) all together in a huge rehearsal hall in the basement of the City Center on West 55th Street—less than a block from his own apartment building. He wanted to delay the decisions on who would join which companies as long as possible, but Actors' Equity soon insisted he make those selections official so the actors could plan ahead.

New Cassies and Zachs

Not everyone had to go through the audition process. Especially for the role of Cassie, which ideally requires a more mature dancer, negotiations were initiated with some more experienced performers. Ann Reinking, who was already something of a name in the Broadway community, was asked to take over for Donna McKechnie in the New York company; she knew she could handle the acting and the dancing but wanted to make sure Bennett was okay with lowering the key of her song. He agreed to that and also worked with her on adapting the choreography for "The Music and the Mirror" to her own specific strengths, adding more backbends, jumps, and her trademark high kicks.

For his other new Cassie, in the International Company, Bennett chose Sandy Roveta, an old friend who had danced on Broadway with him in the early sixties. She did audition, but Bennett knew that her personal circumstances would make her a natural for the part. She had stepped away from the business to focus on her role as wife to dancer-turned-TV-director Tony Mordente, but the marriage had recently fallen apart. Like Cassie, Roveta needed a fresh start and an opportunity to return to what she had always done best. Bennett not only gave her a chance to dance Cassie, he created a built-in emotional obstacle by casting Mordente's new girlfriend, Jean Fraser, as Maggie in the same company!—another example of pushing the dancers' personal buttons to get the results he wanted on stage. Roveta reportedly gave a heart-wrenchingly personal and vulnerable performance as Cassie, knocking out audiences in Toronto and then London (though she left the company when it returned to the states and was replaced by Pamela Sousa).

Lynne Taylor-Corbett had auditioned for the first workshop; she too now found herself on Bennett's short list of performers who could pull off the difficult role. She was reluctant to commit to an extended period out of town, however, because she was changing her career focus to choreography and had started her own dance company. So assistant producer Sue MacNair suggested an unusual solution: Taylor-Corbett became the "floating Cassie," who could be called upon when available to fly to a given city and jump in as needed. If a Cassie was sick or injured, the producers would have the option of bringing her in rather than relying on the touring understudies—who in most cases at that point were too young for the role.

Finding new actors to play Zach also posed specific challenges. For a while, the team was very interested in a young actor who was then starting to make a name for himself in the New York theatre and has since gone on to major stardom: Kevin Kline. At the time he was sharing an apartment with Patti LuPone (sister of Robert, the original Zach), with whom he had attended Juilliard. As an actor, he would have been perfect for Zach, and Bennett was interested in finding a way to make it work, so he asked Clive Clerk to work with him on his dancing. Bennett said that "anyone" could dance the "One" finale (a questionable statement), and in some companies, that's all the dancing that has been asked of the Zach. But in those early days, Bennett insisted that the actor also lead the cast in the very difficult jazz combination that opens the show. Clerk met with Kline in the mornings for a period of weeks to work on it, but ultimately they had to admit that it wasn't going to come together. When Robert LuPone went to San Francisco to open the National Company, Joe Bennett (no relation to Michael) succeeded him in New York. Eivind Harum, a former dancer with the Harkness Ballet, opened the International Company and went with it to London, then replaced Joe Bennett in New York; he was to play Zach on and off for the next fourteen years, up to and including the closing performance on Broadway.

Recreating his Zach in California with thirteen of his original castmates plus five newcomers, LuPone found himself in an unusual position—and he handled it in a unique way. Though he was disappointed that some of the originals hadn't come West, he is quoted in *On the Line* as saying "The people that were replaced were missed until the other people got good—and they did get good." But since he was playing the director, he decided to take responsibility for keeping the dancers on their toes and in the moment, and adopted some startling techniques for achieving this, including ad-libbing lines and once or twice even changing the show's sequence. One evening he jumped ahead to Kristine's section, infuriating Renee Baughman; not generally known for her assertiveness, on that night she took a stand and complained to the stage manager. As LuPone told the writers of *On the Line*: "It almost cost me my job. Renee was furious. But I saw the Line go from 'at-ease' to 'attention' in about three words. That's all that mattered, and that's why I kept my job." A decade later, during his return engagement in the New York company, LuPone used similar tactics with that cast.

The Battle of London

When the International Company arrived in London, they faced some unique challenges. The show was scheduled into the Drury Lane Theatre, a venerable London venue that is considered one of Britain's greatest theatres, especially for musicals. London theatres are mostly smaller than Broadway ones, and the Drury Lane was one of only three West End venues with a proscenium arch large enough to accommodate the line (the minimum width required for the original Bennett staging is forty feet). But like many English theatres, it has a raked stage; the upstage wall is sixteen inches higher than the front edge of the stage. This can cause back and knee problems in the best of circumstances, and for a dance show, it's extremely difficult. Learning to execute pirouettes on a rake can be disorienting, and the dancers commented that even the moment where the line backs up into the darkness at the top of "At the Ballet" was a challenge, as they were effectively walking backwards uphill. Still, the young American cast felt welcomed, and audiences embraced the show; theatre is a more central part of the culture in London than in the United States, and the passion the public there feels for the stage was palpable, and inspired the company.

Insiders remember this cast as an exceptionally strong group of dancers, with tremendous technique. They also did a version of the show that was somewhat different than the others in terms of choreographic detail. During rehearsals at the City Center, the three new casts had worked together during the day—but in the evening the original cast had to go to the Shubert to do the show, and since the new Broadway replacement cast and the National Company were each to include

A rare rehearsal photo of Donna McKechnie working with the first British cast in London, 1977. From left: Geraldine Gardner (who played Sheila), Petra Siniawski (Cassie), McKechnie, and Jean-Pierre Cassel (Zach).

some of the originals, those casts couldn't rehearse in the evenings. However, the International Company was an all-new cast, so Bennett continued working with them at night, and without Baayork Lee there to keep an eye on the steps, he had a tendency to get creative. There were also a few lines changed for the British audience. These were mostly American cultural references that might have been confusing, like Bobby's line about having attended "P.S. Shit"—not because the four-letter word might have offended, but because "public schools" in England are what we would refer to as private schools, and vice versa.

Though *ACL* has never been quite the smash hit in England as it is in America, it received largely positive notices from the London critics—some of whom, viewing the show from a cultural distance, perceived significant underlying themes the American press tended to pass over. Music critic Tom Sutcliffe, writing in *Time Out London*, said "*A Chorus* Line is the stripped-down no-shit musical for the new depression. . . . It turns the 'ultimate escapism' image of the musical on its head and lays waste the whole Busby Berkeley-onwards syndrome for the heartless as well as vainglorious fake it always was. . . . *Golddiggers of 1933* began with 'We're In the Money,' a brazen celebration of the all-embracing triumph of being in work. *A Chorus Line*, born of a less wide-eyed age, begins with a song called 'I Hope I Get It,' with the line 'Please God, I need this job.' And they *don't* all get it."

Harold Hobson of *The Sunday Times* had an equally erudite but more dubious response, finding the show hypocritical: "With dazzling technical skill and a clever pretence that it is doing the exact opposite, it reinforces the capitalist middle class ethic that the ordinary man or woman stands no chance against the elite. It is itself entirely elitist. The show is a glorification of absolute power."

In the *London Times*, Irving Wardle said the musical "leaves you with an enhanced respect for the dignity of professionalism, and a feeling that intelligent life still survives in the competitive society." In *The Guardian*, Michael Billington wrote: "Like all good art, 'A Chorus Line' is ambiguous, contradictory and indefinable. But not the least of its achievements is that it alters one's perspective: One will never again be able to look at any well-drilled choric lineup without speculating on the individual stories behind the sanitised ensemble perfection. You go in expecting a Broadway smash and you come out having met a group of people." He added, "Anyone who regards the musical as a serious theatrical art form should rejoice in this superb production. It has a resonance that spreads far beyond its immediate context."

The audience on opening night included the great British playwright Tom Stoppard as well as both Andrew Lloyd Webber and Michael Crawford—over a decade prior to their joint triumph with *The Phantom of the Opera*. The production won the London Evening Standard Award for Best Musical and also became the first musical to win the Society of West End Theatre Award—an honor whose name was shortly thereafter changed to the Laurence Olivier Award.

The low ticket prices in those days made it possible for fans to see the show again and again, and the company developed quite a London following. At their last performance, the audience was made up largely of hard-core devotees who had seen the show before, and they applauded throughout—even giving each individual cast member a hand in the opening scene where they first introduce themselves.

As the American cast's six-month run drew to a close and the British replacement cast was rehearsed, trouble began to brew. The casting had been a particularly long and drawn-out process, as the British musical theatre scene was very different from that in America and didn't have the same tradition of chorus gypsies. Finding a full cast of triple threats who could handle the roles took time, but interestingly, though they might not have had the chorus experience, many of the British actors chosen had far more acting experience than their American counterparts, having already played leads in other West End musicals. For example, Veronica Page (now known as Roni Page) had played the role of Liesl in the West End production of *The Sound of Music* and had recently completed her run as Anne Egerman in Hal Prince's London production of Sondheim's *A Little Night Music* when her friends told her she was perfect for *A Chorus Line* and should audition. She was at first reluctant, having looked forward to a bit of a vacation after her run in the Sondheim show, but she went to the auditions and saw a queue of actors lined up all the way around the block where the Drury Lane Theatre was situated. Eight hundred British performers auditioned for the company. Page was called back no fewer than ten times before being offered the role of Maggie.

Page recently reminisced about the day Bennett lined up his new English cast on the stage of the theatre. He went down the line congratulating each of them, and when he got to her, she said, "Thank you, Michael, but actually I'm not sure I'm going to accept the role." He asked her why not, and she replied, "I didn't want to play Maggie; I wanted to play Val, because she's the one who's gutsy and ballsy and that's what I want to do."

She continued: "He told me, 'You have to play Maggie because you're beautiful and you have a voice and that's Maggie, and you can't play Val because you don't have the tits.' And I said, 'They can be created!'"

Nevertheless, she accepted the role of Maggie, joining a cast that included Diane Langton, who had appeared with her as Petra in *A Little Night Music*, as Diana Morales. Rehearsals were going well until one afternoon when, at a dress rehearsal, Page was given the new shoes she was to wear in the show. Trying them on, she could tell they felt too big, but the cast was being called to the stage to run a number and she didn't want to hold things up, so she began to dance in them—and soon went over on an ankle, tearing a ligament quite severely. She ended up watching the opening night performance from the audience on crutches and was out of the show for six weeks. But she recovered and stayed with the production for almost two years. She said, "It was a fantastic time; I'm so very proud to have been a part of it. It was a great show; I did love every minute of it."

Enormous controversy attended the preparations for the opening of the new cast, however. Though *A Chorus Line* is a show that because of its very themes resists star casting, the British actress cast as Cassie was a name with a substantial following in London. Elizabeth Seal had starred in the French musical *Irma La Douce*, which she had played both in the West End and on Broadway; she had been away from the theatre for some time, and the London press was excited to welcome her back to the boards in *A Chorus Line*. However, Michael Bennett missed much of the rehearsal period for the new cast, as he and Donna McKechnie had just gotten married and were on their honeymoon at the time; T. Michael Reed, who had played Larry with the American cast that opened the show there, was putting in the new dancers. When Bennett returned to London, he attended a rehearsal to see how things were going—and immediately fired Seal. In a private meeting he reportedly told her the chemistry between her and the Zach was wrong, and that he had made a casting error; later, he said that if she had done it the show would have been about Elizabeth Seal returning to the stage and not about Cassie. He also revealed that he felt she was too old for the part, though this had not seemed to be an issue during the eight auditions he had put her through.

The London press, as well as the theatre community, was in an uproar, and the controversy became front page news. It got worse when Bennett announced his decision to replace Seal with McKechnie, who had not performed the show in London but had a following there from her appearances in the West End productions of *Promises, Promises* and *Company*. He auditioned more dancers but claimed no suitable British candidate for Cassie had been found, and proposed to have McKechnie play a limited run while helping to teach the role to the understudy, Petra Siniawski, who would take over when she was ready.

Initially British Equity agreed, but reversed their decision almost immediately when all hell broke loose: Vanessa Redgrave was leading the London acting community in protest and reportedly paid out-of-work British actors a pound to vote against permission for McKechnie to perform. There were marches and picket lines at the theatre. McKechnie later recalled that the ongoing controversy, which even included death threats, made the front pages of the London papers for several days, even pushing the inauguration of U.S. President Jimmy Carter back to page four! Along with Bennett and Avian and Michael White, one of the London producers, McKechnie was mobbed by reporters and paparazzi one night on exiting the theatre. Bennett went into a paranoid emotional crisis and threatened to quit the production; McKechnie later said his lack of support for her during the turmoil hastened the downward spiral of their relationship.

Petra Siniawski opened as the first British Cassie. Her reputation has been much maligned in some of the other books about *A Chorus Line*. It has been stated that she was so weak vocally that the offstage singers (the understudies) were asked to back her up in "The Music and the Mirror." She had red hair, and the production team decided that the classic red Cassie costume was not becoming on her, so she became the only Cassie to wear blue instead. Denny Martin Flinn's book states that she was "too heavy" for the red leotard—but photos of her in the role show an exceptionally svelte dancer. Kevin Kelly's book on Michael Bennett refers to her (in a quote attributed to McKechnie) as "this Lithuanian girl who spoke very little English." By contrast, Page, a lifelong friend of Siniawksi's, recently confirmed that she is of Latvian parentage but was raised in England and spoke perfect British English like the rest of the cast. Though she was young for the role and not considered an outstanding singer, she was an excellent dancer and had already played Anita in a West End run of *West Side Story* and danced in the movie of *Fiddler on the Roof*. Siniawski went on to play Lily St. Regis in a London revival of *Annie* and Velma Kelly in a regional production of *Chicago*, and has had a long and successful career in musical theatre that continues to this day; she has numerous credits as a director and choreographer and is currently the resident associate director for the London production of *Wicked*.

Once Siniawski had learned the role and the new cast opened, McKechnie and Bennett returned to the U.S. The British company was mostly favorably reviewed, though Jean-Pierre Cassel, a French actor who was a personal friend of Bennett's, was widely considered miscast in the role of Zach. The production ran for over two more years, if not quite as long as the producers had originally intended. It developed quite a following. According to Page, "People loved the show; they came back to see it again and again, especially people in the business; it sort of hit the spot."

Crisscrossing America

On returning to America, the International Company reopened in Baltimore and began a North American tour that would last close to six years; when the National Company completed extended sit-down runs in Los Angeles and Chicago, it too began to play shorter engagements in major cities, and the two companies

The first British cast at the Drury Lane Theatre in London, 1977. From left: Lance Aston (Don), Veronica Page (Maggie), Michael Howe (Mike), Cherry Gillespie (Connie), Stephen Tate (Greg), Petra Siniawski (Cassie), Geraldine Gardner (Sheila), Leslie Meadows (Bobby), and Susan Claire (Bebe). *Photo courtesy Roni Page*

coexisted for years, returning to some of the larger markets three or more times. A "convention" of all the dance captains was held at one point to standardize the choreography and clean up any minor inconsistencies among the various companies; this made it easier for performers to move from one tour to the other (or into the Broadway cast).

The two touring companies began to develop their own unique personalities. For dancers who eventually performed in both, the experiences were quite different. The National Company seems to have started out quite happily, as the original cast members who agreed to go to California were excited about it, and the five new performers who joined them were thrilled to have the opportunity. The originals were more relaxed on the road and found they were getting along better than they had been in New York. Kay Cole (Maggie) later spoke about how the new people reenergized the group, who had been together for over a year at that point, and in particular how Charlene Ryan as Sheila brought a whole new dynamic to "At the Ballet." After a while, though, the stage managers and dance captains who were maintaining that company developed something of a reputation as martinets, even going so far as to time certain scenes with a stopwatch. The International Company, on the other hand, felt they had more freedom: as the first cast of the show that didn't include any of the original cast members, they all started from the same place and were encouraged to make it their own to some degree.

As the Broadway, National, and International Companies all continued to run simultaneously, actors over the next several years were shuffled around so much that it became impossible to keep track of all the cast replacements. *Theatre World* and *The Best Plays* are hardcover books published annually as records of the theatre season around the country, and while an examination of their pages on *A Chorus Line* from 1975 through 1990 yields a reasonably complete list of the Broadway replacements over the years (there are some omissions), both publications gave up on trying to track the cast changes on the tours after about 1980.

Visits from Michael

As more and more dancers were hired, the responsibility for teaching the show and the choreography fell more and more to dance captains, stage managers, and their assistants. But Michael Bennett would check in on all the companies periodically. Rudy Hogenmiller, who in later years would go on to perform in, choreograph, and/or direct several productions in the Chicago area, began his association with the show when he attended an audition for the National Company at the Shubert Theatre in Chicago in 1977. He was only twenty-one when Baayork Lee cast him as Larry, and he went to Los Angeles to join the cast.

Hogenmiller performed the show for several weeks before Bennett made an appearance and spent a day with the company, which the dancer later described as very strange. As he told Marion E. Kabaker for a *Chicago Tribune* interview: "We weren't allowed to speak to him, even though he was standing right on stage with us. We had to talk to Bob Avian. . . who would relay our questions to him. . . . He started at the line, stage right, and he did every character's part, and then each person would have to do their lines exactly the way he did it. If he was dissatisfied, you'd have to do it over, but during all of this you weren't allowed to talk to him. He got rid of several people, including me, because he thought I was too young for the part."

Substance Abuse

During the late seventies and early eighties, drug use was quite prevalent, especially among performers, and this at times had an adverse effect on the show. It was considered more of a problem for the touring companies than in New York. Especially in the International Company, there would be times when a dancer was so out of it that he or she had to be pulled offstage mid-performance, and an understudy would be sent on to finish the show. Robin Lyon, a longtime understudy, said there were even nights when dancers would surreptitiously pull cocaine out of their dance bags and do lines while they were onstage. Some of them rationalized it; Scott Pearson was quoted in *The Longest Line*: "If you were honest to yourself, drugs did not affect the show. Michael loved us to experiment. . . 'this must be about you, this must be real.' So changes in cast, somebody with a hangover, somebody with a drug problem, it all worked for the character. It became the character was hung over, the character was on drugs. It worked for the show as long as it was real."

Pamela Sousa and Cheryl Clark, both of whom played Cassie during the height of this period, were very aware of the problem and managed to stay above it, attempting to set an example. Michael Bennett made a point of not passing judgment on what people did in their personal lives—and he himself developed a problem with cocaine in later years. But he didn't tolerate actors letting it affect their work, and some dancers were fired over it.

The Bus & Truck Company

On September 14, 1980, after touring for almost four and a half years, the National Company played its last performance, in Montreal. But it was quickly reorganized and reopened on the 18th in Schenectady, New York, as a Bus & Truck tour. This is a smaller-scale tour, on a different Equity contract, that plays shorter engagements in smaller cities, and the cast and crew literally travel on buses and trucks rather than planes. Since *A Chorus Line* had by then been seen in all the major cities in the nation, and in most of them repeatedly, it was now time to take it to smaller markets. Today, when a tour of a popular musical progresses to that stage, it is often replaced by a non-Equity company—a practice that has been controversial and is abhorred by the unions. In the early eighties that was not yet the practice, and the first Bus & Truck Company of *ACL* was an Equity cast. It was, however, the youngest group that had ever done the show. The grueling schedule, which often involved sitting on a bus all day and then giving only one or two performances in a given town before shipping out, required dancers with unusual energy and physical resilience; many of them were twenty years old or younger. In the late stages of rehearsal, Michael Bennett flew in to work with them and made some last-minute cast changes, firing a couple of the dancers who had been selected and switching a couple of others with their understudies. Eivind Harum, who had opened the International Company in 1976, provided much-needed maturity and experience in the role of Zach, and though most of the rest of the cast was extremely green, it turned out to be an unusually talented group, several of whom would eventually go on to do the show on Broadway. The Cassie was Thia Fadel, a dancer from Salt Lake City who had been living in Los Angeles. Jan Leigh Herndon played Sheila, with DeLyse Lively (who later changed the spelling of her first name to DeLee, to match the pronunciation) as Val, Wayne Meledandri as Paul, Alison Gertner as Diana, John Salvatore as Bobby, and Bradley Jones as Greg.

Laurie Gamache, who would become a major player in the history of *A Chorus Line*, first joined the show at this point. She had played a couple of performances as an understudy for Judy and Bebe with the National Company in Montreal, where the new company was in rehearsal, when Bennett unexpectedly moved her to Kristine. She remembers having to go on as Kristine the first time having had next to no rehearsal in that role, and that Jerry Colker, who was playing Al, told her there was nothing to worry about; if she got lost or was unsure of what to do next, he would simply tell her—which is exactly the way Al and Kristine relate to each other all through the show. The performance went well, launching Gamache's

The line from the 1993 non-Equity tour, produced by Gordon Crowe. Future Broadway star Amy Span

ten-year run in the show, which concluded with her playing Cassie for the last three years of the Broadway run.

The Bus & Truck was also characterized by a slightly different set design than that used in the Broadway production and the previous tours. Because the show had to be set up and struck so quickly, and flexible enough to play on stages of different shapes and sizes, the periaktoi became impractical. They were replaced by flying drops: the wall of mirrors could be covered by a descending black drape or, for the finale, a drop with the signature art deco sunburst design. The three looks were basically the same as before, but the transitions between them looked different without the famous revolving three-sided flats. The smaller theatres in which the tour often played might require last-minute staging adjustments too; sometimes there was less than ten feet of depth from the line to the mirrors, requiring reconfiguring of some of the choreography, especially in the Montage.

More significantly, this company was the one for which substantial changes were made to the show to make it more contemporary. Five years into the life of the musical, it had begun to look and sound dated in some respects, so the creative team changed some of the pop-cultural references and moved the characters' birth dates up by five years. Bebe's reference to Steve McQueen in the Montage was changed to "Roger Moore," Val's mention of June Allyson became "Sandy Duncan," and Judy's reference to wanting to be "the next Gwen Verdon" was changed to "Ann

s Me, Kate, Rock of Ages, The Wedding Singer) is seen as Cassie, sixth from left. *Photo courtesy Stephen Nachamie*

Reinking"—the name of a dancer who had actually appeared in *A Chorus Line* on Broadway! (That particular change may seem cruelly ironic to anyone who knows the history of the people involved.) Theoni V. Aldredge also modified some of the costumes to make them look more up-to-date (see Chapter 11). The changes were incorporated into the Broadway and International Companies for a short time as well, but after about a year a decision was made to put everything back the way it had been originally. At that point, *A Chorus Line* officially became a period piece, and the Place and Time notations in the program (originally "Here" and "Now") became "A Broadway Theatre" and "1975."

Later Tours

The Bus & Truck Company played ninety-three different cities and towns in its first nine months alone; it continued to tour for just over two years, closing in Pittsburgh on October 3, 1982. The International Company, which had been on the road for over seven years, went on a little longer, ending its run on August 14, 1983, in Toronto—the same city where it had originally opened. After that, for a couple of years there was only the Broadway company running—though it wasn't long before new tours were formed, beginning in 1985 when Baayork Lee put together a company that featured Donna McKechnie in her original role as Cassie and the show's coauthor, Nicholas Dante, finally getting the chance to play himself as Paul. That company eventually went to Japan. Another tour starring McKechnie went out in 1989.

During the eighties, there was also a series of short European tours with American casts, which played limited runs in such countries as Germany, the Netherlands, Italy, France, and Switzerland. Baayork Lee directed the first ones, with subsequent companies staged by Roy Smith and Mitzi Hamilton; they often cast actors who had done the American companies and knew the show. The tours tended to run ten to thirteen weeks and gave the dancers a welcome opportunity to see new parts of the world. One thing they tend to remember about the experience: they were paid in cash. (These tours were in addition to foreign productions in numerous countries, cast with local performers and translated into their native languages; many of these were also directed by Smith or Lee.)

A major new national tour opened in 1990, shortly after the closing of the Broadway production; directed by Baayork Lee, it was variously referred to as the "Farewell tour" or the "Visa tour," since Visa was the main sponsor. Gamache played Cassie, with Randy Clements as Zach, Porfirio as Paul, Michael Gorman as Bobby, Bradley Jones as Greg, Christine Gradl as Maggie, and Fosse dancer Gail Benedict as Sheila.

One memorable performance during the run of the Visa tour has become known in *ACL* lore as the "Night of a Thousand Cassies." Gamache called out sick, and standby Cheryl Clark went on in the role, but, during the opening jazz combination "facing away from the mirror," she tore something—a serious enough injury that she had to leave the stage. Dana Leigh Jackson, a new understudy, was quickly rushed into a red leotard and pushed onstage—but she had had only minimal rehearsal and did not yet know the big Cassie scene. So stage management got desperate and called Gamache at her hotel; being the trouper she has always been, she came to the theatre and suited up, and was ready to replace Jackson onstage in time for "The Music and the Mirror." Following the performance, the stage manager got on the PA system and announced the names of the three actresses who had been seen onstage as Cassie since the start of the show—hopefully clarifying things for audience members who had been confused by seeing a tall brunette Cassie, then one with long blonde hair, and then another short-haired brunette!

Since then, new Equity and non-Equity tours have sprouted up periodically, and there was a major new national tour that went out in 2008 following the Broadway revival. (For cast information on the various American tours, see Appendices Three through Five.)

Robert Tunstall, who has played Bobby in several companies of the show, recently reflected on his touring experiences, expressing the important place the show holds in the lives of many of the dancers who have done it over the years:

> Being a part of this production was incredibly special. I remember at the call-back for the audition having to do the jazz and ballet combinations alone in a room with Baayork Lee, Michael Gorman and Fran Liebergall. It was exciting and terrifying all at once. But, I thought "how special is this moment, to be

standing here in front of these amazing people and that they were taking the time to share the choreography and music with me."

Later, while we were on the road, Michael Gorman moved on to the National tour of *Chicago* and Thommie Walsh came in to be our show supervisor. I remember performing in Schenectady, New York, which was the first time he saw us in action. I felt like I "glowed" on stage. Knowing the original person was sitting in the audience that night. I'll never forget it or the kind words he had to say afterwards.

I always enjoyed learning the show from Baayork Lee. She said "Michael (Bennett) gave us a gift, with this show." Every show, I'd remind myself of this and the fact that there was going to be someone in the audience that night who had never seen *A Chorus Line* and was about to be affected by the experience we would share together. My life has been so blessed by this production and what we do for love.

17

"They're All Special"

The Ladies Who Played Cassie

A *Chorus Line* was conceived as an ensemble musical with no leading role. Actually, that's the whole point of the show. Michael Bennett's original vision was of the formerly anonymous chorus dancers taking center stage for once, rather than backing up a star as they had done for decades. Still, the character of Cassie, the one-time featured dancer who "stopped two shows cold" on Broadway and then tried for an acting career in Hollywood, has emerged as a central figure in the show and in people's memories of it. The idea of the struggling, slightly older performer returning home to New York and asking for a second chance to do what she loves to do resonates with audiences, who tend to root for her. The vision of the elegant woman in red, her trademark dance skirt swirling as she spins before the mirrors, has become an iconic image of the show. Cassie is a dynamite part for a triple-threat performer, and it was a touchstone role for each of the dancers who played the part on Broadway.

Donna McKechnie

"Vulnerable, spirited, and inexhaustible, Donna McKechnie is the finest female dancer of her generation, inspiring the finest choreographer of his generation, Michael Bennett, to create a series of spectacular set pieces for Broadway."—Ken Bloom and Frank Vlastnik in their book *Broadway Musicals: The 101 Greatest Shows of All Time.*

The creator of the role, McKechnie was a legendarily tough act to follow. This is partly because she took part in both of the workshops and contributed not only to the development of the character but to the choreography. When she danced "The Music and the Mirror," it looked like an improvisation—as it should—and it was so specifically tailored to her body and her style that it's often proven difficult for others to conquer. A big-voiced soprano, McKechnie sang the song in a high key that many dancers find difficult, with the result that it was transposed down for most of the subsequent Cassies (they have sung it in several different keys), as were the character's solo lines in the show's Montage sequence.

To be sure, McKechnie brought unique and inimitable qualities to the role, as actor, singer, and dancer. But the character's story has personal resonance for many performers, especially those who have had some success and yet still had to struggle to prove themselves in the fickle business of theatre. Though even some of the best interpreters of the role have said it's almost impossible to nail every aspect of it, at least in the same performance, the challenge of measuring themselves against its daunting but exhilarating demands is one that many dancers dream of: it provides a woman not merely with a chance to dance, but with an opportunity to express who she is and what being a dancer means to her. McKechnie was succeeded in the Broadway company by a succession of eight highly accomplished performers, and each of them brought something special to the role.

Ann Reinking

When Reinking was invited to take over the part as McKechnie's first replacement, she had already played major roles on Broadway in *Goodtime Charley*, for which she received a Tony nomination, and *Over Here!* She had worked with Bennett in the ensemble of *Coco*, her Broadway debut. Though Reinking was only in her mid-twenties when she played Cassie and young for the role, her life story already had some parallels with that of the character, as she too was involved in both a working and a romantic relationship with a Broadway director/choreographer: the legendary Bob Fosse.

Being the first replacement, Reinking got more attention from the creative team than most of the later Cassies, and the role was re-tailored for her more than for any of her successors. She was the first to sing the song in a lower key (a full third lower than McKechnie), and she also worked with Bennett on some modifications to the choreography of the dance solo, adding more of her trademark high kicks and backbends, and ending the number in a different pose. Her short-waisted, long-legged physique was different from McKechnie's, and her red leotard was cut with a V-neck rather than the scoop neck the others all wore; she even did a few performances without the trademark skirt, which she felt was unflattering to her, though it was restored when all concerned realized it had become a signature image for the character.

After leaving *ACL*, Reinking took over the role of Roxie Hart (originated by Gwen Verdon) in the Broadway production of *Chicago*, which had opened the same season as *A Chorus Line* and was famously overshadowed by the latter show. Almost twenty years later, she choreographed a concert staging of *Chicago* for City Center Encores! in New York and was unexpectedly asked to recreate the role of Roxie, though by that point she thought she had officially retired from performing. Playing opposite Bebe Neuwirth (a former Cassie understudy and Broadway Sheila) as Velma, Reinking reprised her Roxie yet again when the production moved to Broadway, where it continues to run to this day. The longest-running revival in Broadway history, *Chicago* finally got its revenge, running even longer than the original production of *A Chorus Line*.

Vicki Frederick

Even younger than Reinking when she played Cassie, Vicki Frederick was another Fosse protégée. With a more curvaceous figure than many dancers and a mane of long, luscious hair that she let down during the solo, she brought a unique and striking look to the role. She played Cassie for an extended period on an understudy contract before being signed for the role officially in 1977; shortly thereafter, she stepped aside when Bennett decided to put one of his touring Cassies, Pamela Sousa, into the Broadway cast. But if she was never one of Bennett's personal favorites, she was always one of Bob Fosse's, having already worked with him in *Pippin*. After leaving *A Chorus Line*, she went on to dance for Fosse in Broadway's *Dancin'* (in which she took over the role created by Reinking) and on screen in *All That Jazz*, and was cast in numerous acting roles on TV and film in the eighties and nineties. Though video footage of her as Cassie is not readily available (except for the 1983 gala, where she was one of seven Cassies dancing the number behind McKechnie), she became a permanent part of *Chorus Line* history when she played Sheila in the 1985 film version of the show; her subtle, authentic performance is generally considered one of the best parts of the movie.

Pamela Sousa

Pamela Sousa was another of several Cassies who had appeared in the Broadway cast of *Pippin*, as well as Fosse's *Chicago*, in which she originated the role of Mona. When *A Chorus Line* was first auditioning replacements, she came in and was asked to read for Val; since that wasn't the right role for her, she initially didn't even get a callback. But shortly thereafter Bob Avian happened to see her do a solo dance number in an industrial show, and it was immediately clear to him that she had the stuff for Cassie. She learned the role and made an early debut with the Broadway company on a night when the Cassie and both covers were unexpectedly indisposed. She stayed with the New York cast as an understudy, playing ballerina Lois in the opening number (which was how many of the Cassies started) until she took over Cassie with the International Company in Baltimore, their first stop after returning from London. She later played two substantial engagements in the role on Broadway, both times at the personal request of Michael Bennett, and was widely considered one of its finest interpreters.

Not especially known for her singing, Sousa was a lithe, striking dancer with an elegant, balletic line; a fine actress, she brought passion and vulnerability to the character. She went on to act in plays on Broadway (*The Loves of Anatol*, *Stepping Out*) and has some credits as a choreographer, including the Broadway musical *Romance, Romance*. However, she once stated ironically that she felt her identification with *A Chorus Line* had, if anything, hurt her future acting prospects, as casting directors pigeonholed her as a dancer. This raises the somewhat troubling question of why the role of Cassie, such a unique showcase for a singing, dancing actress, has generally done so little to advance the careers of the women who have played it. Of the Broadway replacement Cassies, the only one to go on to lasting fame has been Reinking—and she was already something of a "name" when she did the part.

Cheryl Clark

Yet another Cassie from the Fosse camp, Cheryl Clark had been in *Pippin* on Broadway and created the role of Liz in *Chicago*, performing the famous "Cell Block Tango" alongside Pamela Sousa. (Their cohorts in the number also included Michon Peacock and Candy Brown, both of whom had figured prominently in the genesis of *A Chorus Line*.) Clark first played Cassie in one of the show's earliest international mountings, an Australian company in which she and the Zach, Scott Pearson, were the only two American performers. Bennett coached them extensively, so Clark was well prepared, though young for the role, when she first took over Cassie on Broadway. A videotape of her rendition of the scene with Zach and "The Music and the Mirror," circulated online, reveals relatively routine acting but a strong, clear singing voice and extraordinary dancing. One of the few Cassies to challenge McKechnie in the solo, the long-legged Clark, with her phenomenally high extension, danced with passion and a majestic, catlike authority; she made the number look like it was choreographed just for her. She had one of the longest tenures in the role, as she was the Cassie/Sheila standby on the Visa tour that went out after the Broadway show closed in 1990—a gig that allowed her to bring her young daughter along with her on the road. She had the same billing in another touring company, directed by Baayork Lee, as late as 1997.

Deborah Henry

One of the only two blondes (Wanda Richert was the other) to play Cassie on Broadway, Deborah Henry had begun her career as a classical dancer with the Royal Winnipeg Ballet. She appeared in *ACL* originally as Val, a role she performed with her native Southern accent; when she played that part, a line in the script was changed to identify Val as a native of Tennessee (like Henry herself) rather than the usual Vermont. During the early days of the tours, Michael Bennett sometimes feared that Middle America might not be ready for the frankness of "Dance: Ten; Looks: Three." After seeing Henry's adorable take on the character, he felt she was perhaps the only actress who could get away with Val's foul-mouthed utterances without alienating a conservative, Bible-belt audience. This led to one of the strangest casting arrangements in the history of the show. When the National or International Company arrived in a new town, Bennett would sometimes pull Henry out of the Broadway show for a day, fly her to the city in question, and have her play Val in the opening night performance. Once the critics were safely out of the way, she flew back to New York and went back to performing Cassie on Broadway. (One wonders how the Vals in the touring companies felt about this arrangement!) Another piece of *A Chorus Line* lore revolves around the time on the road when bats got into the theatre and flew around Miss Henry's head during the Cassie dance; she finished the number, but claimed it had included more head pops than usual!

John Corry re-reviewed the Broadway production for the *New York Times* in 1981, saying: "'A Chorus Line' is a perfect ensemble show, but some of its roles are more perfect than others, and Donna McKechnie, the original Cassie, won a Tony. Now

Deborah Henry as Cassie with Scott Pearson as Zach.
Photo by Martha Swope; from the collection of the author

Miss Henry exudes star quality, which Cassie is supposed to do, while not turning our attention away from the other actors. Her long solo dance—its style so different you are not sure it belongs in the show, and perhaps it doesn't—is also extraordinarily graceful. Maybe Miss Henry would have won a Tony, too." She went on to play several roles in *Cats* on Broadway, and tragically died of ovarian cancer in 1996, when she was only forty-four years old.

Wanda Richert

Richert was the third Cassie whose life story mirrored the character's in that she had been romantically involved with a major director/choreographer (the other two such relationships being McKechnie's with Bennett and Reinking's with Fosse). Richert's principal claim to Broadway fame was her creation of the role of Peggy Sawyer, the ingénue turned star, in the wildly successful 1980 stage version of *42nd Street*, during which she had a personal relationship with that show's director, Gower Champion. Champion passed away the very day the production opened on Broadway, and Richert had the traumatic experience of learning of his death onstage, when producer David Merrick announced it to the audience and cast following the curtain calls.

Her involvement with *ACL* predated all that. She was eighteen years old and in beauty school when one of the touring companies came through and held auditions in her home town; she was cast as an understudy and promoted to Cassie by the time she was nineteen. Though she and Michael Bennett had their ups and downs over the years, he recognized her star potential and acting ability early on. After her experience with *42nd Street*, she replaced Anita Morris as Carla in the Broadway production of *Nine* and worked with Bennett again, playing a role in an early workshop of *Scandal*, a musical he was developing with Treva Silverman and Jimmy Webb (Angelique Ilo was in the workshop as well). She also returned to *A Chorus Line* for a long run on Broadway as a slightly older and wiser Cassie. Her interpretation of "The Music and the Mirror" has been widely viewed and discussed on YouTube. Though the camera caught her somewhat out of shape and not at her considerable dancing best, the verve of her acting and power of her singing voice are still much in evidence; she owned the character. She stayed with the show through the third month of her pregnancy in 1986; her maternity leave provided the opening for McKechnie's much-ballyhooed return to the Broadway company. Richert returned to the show after having her baby, this time as an understudy, and ended up giving her final Broadway performances in the role of Val; by 1992 she was back out on tour as Cassie. As she told Gary Stevens and Alan George for their book *The Longest Line*: "Cassie was fulfilling to me as an actress, a woman, and a sexual being . . . I don't think there will ever be a role like that again for a woman." In 1993, Richert appeared in a Long Beach Civic Light Opera production of *Company*, starring Patrick Cassidy and Carol Burnett. Playing Kathy (another part originated by Donna McKechnie), she gave a particularly sexy and vividly emotional performance of the "Tick Tock" dance solo. In 1999, she recreated her original role of Peggy Sawyer in a revival of *42nd Street* that she also choreographed, at the Diamond Head Theatre in Hawaii. Since 2004, she has been much involved with spiritual causes, working as a motivational speaker and Interfaith Reverend with the Rhythm of Life Mission, an organization she founded in Florida.

Angelique Ilo

The long-legged Angelique Ilo, five feet nine inches tall, was one of the most glamorous performers to play Cassie; she alternated the role with the smaller part of Judy throughout her eleven-year career with the show. Half-Japanese, Ilo grew up in California and studied at Miss Starr's Dancing School, where she took "ballet, tap, jazz and acro" all in the same hour; she remembers spending half the time changing shoes. She performed professionally with the Steven Peck Jazz Company for five years starting at age fourteen, and after moving to New York appeared in the last two editions of the legendary *Milliken Breakfast Show*. At her audition for *A Chorus Line*, she remembers, "I wore a one-shoulder, electric blue leotard designed by Rudi Gernreich, with my hair slicked straight back like David Bowie; I had the balls!" She sang "Nothing Can Stop Me Now" from *The Roar of the Greasepaint-The Smell of the Crowd*. Indeed, nothing could stop her from getting the job; within two days she was playing Vicki on Broadway, and within a week had been promoted to Judy. She brought a unique warmth and humanity to that role, and says, "I loved trying to find the fullness in Judy, getting the laughs, letting myself come through in that role—to fill out the character more than it appeared to be when I saw the show."

Angelique Ilo as Cassie. *Courtesy Angelique Ilo*

The Cassie dance, with its fast footwork, is notoriously difficult for a long-limbed dancer, and Ilo says, "Doing Cassie was gratifying but very frustrating. My stamina never seemed to hold out." Still, she was successful in the role and played it in several touring casts as well as on Broadway. She married Eivind Harum, who played Zach in the show, and they had two children; in 1987, she played Judy in New York until the fifth month of her pregnancy, adding a zippered sweatshirt to her costume to disguise the fact. She returned to the show two years later and played Judy for the last year of the Broadway run.

Ilo served as dance captain for the Broadway musicals *Crazy for You* (1992), *Steel Pier* (1997), *Contact* (2000), and *The Wedding Singer* (2006); she had a long association with director/choreographer Susan Stroman as an assistant and associate, and has recently restaged productions of *Crazy for You* in Brazil and *Contact* in Shanghai. She also returned to *A Chorus Line* for the first time in over twenty years, as associate choreographer for the 2014 production at the Fifth Avenue Theatre in Seattle. Her daughter, Sonya Harum, is an up-and-coming actress in New York.

Laurie Gamache

The final Broadway Cassie, Laurie Gamache was fresh out of Stephens College in Missouri, where she earned a degree in dance, when she was first cast in the show at the age of twenty. She joined the Bus & Truck Company as an understudy for several roles but was promoted to Kristine when Michael Bennett saw her in rehearsal; that company featured Eivind Harum as Zach and Thia Fadel as Cassie.

Gamache later joined the Broadway company, where she understudied five different roles. When Donna McKechnie returned to the cast in 1986, Gamache not only understudied her but stood beside her on the line one night in April 1987: the only time she ever went on as Sheila in the Broadway company. McKechnie was so impressed with the young dancer that she recommended her to take over as Cassie when she left the show; Gamache played that role for the last three years of the Broadway run and received her share of the limelight, including numerous TV spots and interviews, during the flurry of publicity that accompanied the landmark show's closing weeks.

A natural actress, Gamache brought an affecting simplicity and vulnerability to the role; she also danced with great passion and lyricism and was one of the few Cassies who managed to make "The Music and the Mirror" look easy. (An interesting tidbit: the final Broadway Kristine was a dancer named Cynthia Fleming, who had changed her name from Thia Fadel; ten years after first touring in the show together, the two dancers had traded roles.)

Gamache went on to perform on Broadway in the unsuccessful stage version of *The Red Shoes* (based on a film mentioned in the script of *A Chorus Line*: see Chapter 14) and toured with Tommy Tune in *Busker Alley*, which closed before reaching Broadway. She reprised Cassie for a tour of South Africa, directed by Troy Garza, and continued to play the role periodically in tours and regional productions, some of which she also directed, until 2002. She has also played roles in regional revivals of *Brigadoon*, *West Side Story*, *Bye Bye Birdie*, *Dames at Sea*, and *Gypsy*. She lives on the Upper West Side of Manhattan and has taught in the Catholic School System for the past ten years; she currently teaches drama to students aged three to thirteen at the School of the Blessed Sacrament, and directs a teen theater company at the Franciscan Community Center.

Laurie Gamache as Cassie.   *Courtesy Reagle Music Theatre*

The Revival's Cassie

Charlotte d'Amboise had appeared in no fewer than nine musicals on Broadway by the time she auditioned for the revival of *A Chorus Line*. Widely respected in the business as one of the finest Broadway dancers of her generation, she had not attained star status with the general public, partly because she had so often gone into shows as an understudy or a replacement—though she did already have one Tony nomination to her credit, for the revue *Jerome Robbins' Broadway*. The daughter of Jacques d'Amboise, a legendary star of the New York City Ballet, Charlotte got her early training through that company's School of American Ballet; she recalls having attended her first Broadway audition dressed and behaving like a "bunhead"—similar to the character Lois in *ACL*'s opening number. But she discovered she was as interested in singing and acting as she was in dancing and soon moved away from the classical ballet world to focus on musical theatre.

She was not yet twenty years old when she got her first Broadway show, Andrew Lloyd Webber's *Cats*, in which she took over the role of Cassandra, the Siamese cat; she appeared alongside her future husband, Terrence Mann, who played the Rum Tum Tugger. Subsequent Broadway appearances included Lloyd Webber's *Song and Dance* and a major supporting role in the legendary Broadway flop *Carrie*. In the 1995 Roundabout Theatre revival of Stephen Sondheim's *Company*, d'Amboise played Kathy, a role that, like Cassie, had been originated by Donna McKechnie.

She played Gwen Verdon's original role of Claudine in the City Center Encores! concert presentation of Cole Porter's *Can-Can*, and also recreated Verdon roles in no fewer than three Broadway revivals, succeeding Bebe Neuwirth as Lola in *Damn Yankees* and Ann Reinking as Roxie Hart in *Chicago*. Her third Verdon role on Broadway involved a dramatic

Charlotte d'Amboise as Cassie in the 2006 revival.

Photo by Penni Gladstone/San Francisco Chronicle/Polaris

and highly publicized story, when she understudied TV star Christina Applegate in the title role of the 2005 revival of *Sweet Charity*. Near the end of the out-of-town tryout, Applegate broke her foot during a performance; that day's show was finished by another understudy, Dylis Croman (who would later stand by for both d'Amboise and Deidre Goodwin in *ACL*). The producers asked d'Amboise to play the New York previews while Applegate was on the mend, and choreographer Wayne Cilento (*A Chorus Line's* original Mike) immediately started retooling the dances to capitalize on her superior dancing skills. She performed brilliantly for a week of Broadway previews, and there was speculation that she would finally earn the recognition she had long deserved by opening the production, as Applegate had had little time to recover. The injured star proved a determined trouper, however, and reappeared for opening night. Still, d'Amboise was honored with that season's Fred Astaire Award (her second) for her work as Charity; this award, presented each year to the best male and female dancers on Broadway, had never before been given to an understudy, and the honor proved that the industry was aware of her contribution. She handled the whole episode with grace and aplomb, but the image that remained in the public eye was that of a superb Broadway dancer who had been in the business for twenty years but somehow still couldn't catch a break; when the revival of *A Chorus Line* was cast just a few months later, the fit seemed more than perfect: she *was* Cassie.

D'Amboise brought great warmth and passion to the role and was the only member of the revival cast to receive a Tony nomination, her second. As one of the honored performers to speak at that season's Drama League luncheon, she stated that the role of Cassie was the most personal she had ever played, and the most rewarding. She later directed and choreographed a student production of the show at Western Carolina University, where Mann is on the faculty.

More recently, she has performed in a Washington, D.C., revival of the musical *Parade* and in two return engagements in her most celebrated role, Roxie in the record-breaking revival of *Chicago*, still running after seventeen years. In 2013, she played Fastrada, the scheming, high-kicking wife of Charlemagne (played by her real husband Terrence Mann) in the American Repertory Theatre's revival of the Stephen Schwartz musical *Pippin*; the production transferred to Broadway for a very successful run.

18

"Good-bye Twelve, Good-bye Thirteen, Good-bye Fourteen, Good-bye Fifteen . . . "

The Record-Breaking Run in New York

More than any other musical, *A Chorus Line* was *about* the original cast: their dreams, their lives, and their souls. Putting a first replacement cast together for a hit musical is never easy, but in this case the transition was a particularly delicate one, especially since five of the originals would be staying in New York and performing with the fourteen newcomers.

New Siblings

The new cast rehearsed at City Center along with the newly formed National and International Companies. For a while most of the dancers didn't even know which company they would end up in, and some were unsure whether they would be given roles or end up as understudies. Once Actors' Equity demanded that these decisions be finalized, the "new New York company" came together as a group.

The originals who stayed on were Wayne Cilento, Kelly Bishop, Thommie Walsh, Cameron Mason, and Clive Clerk. Some of them felt lonely and disoriented, surrounded by new faces they didn't know and who hadn't shared the complex and sometimes painful process of giving birth to the show. For their part, some of the newcomers did not feel very welcome at first, as if they had to prove themselves to become members of an exclusive fraternity, but little by little the ice began to thaw. Surprisingly, it was the understudies—all understandably disappointed about not being promoted to roles on the line—who made the biggest effort to be welcoming. Even though they were having to help teach the roles to new actors they would then be covering, they made a point of rising above any ego issues they might have been struggling with in order to be good colleagues. Michael Serrecchia, who was the understudy for Bobby and Greg, bought coffee mugs for all the new cast members and left them in their dressing rooms with notes that read "Welcome to the New Chorus Line Experience."

That experience included a unique episode: the night when Kelly Bishop walked off in the middle of the show—an event that would take its place in *A Chorus Line* lore. Shortly after beginning her dialogue with Zach, she told him she couldn't go on and simply left the stage. Thommie Walsh (Bobby) followed her, making up a line to tell Zach he wanted to see if Sheila was okay. Bishop was reportedly emotionally drained by the experience of performing with the new and unfamiliar cast, and frustrated about having been denied a raise in salary. She would return the next night, and finished out her contract, but that one night there was no Sheila—and the company scrambled to assign some of her lines to other characters in order to get through the show. (No lasting damage was done to her relationship with the production; she would return to the role twice in the 1980s.)

Some of the new cast members, like Justin Ross as Greg, Ann Reinking as Cassie, Gillian Scalici as Bebe, and Sandahl Bergman as Judy, were immediately successful and appreciated in their roles. Others struggled more. The biggest problem proved to be finding a new Diana Morales that met Bennett's expectations. The first replacement was a friend of his, Barbara Luna, a respected actress who had been a professional performer since childhood (like Baayork Lee, she played one of the children in the original cast of *The King and I*). But she reportedly wasn't used to dancing with an ensemble, and Bennett had problems with her acting and singing as well. In addition, she called out sick four times during the brief time she was in the show; she lasted less than two weeks.

Her replacement was Carole Schweid, the original understudy, who some thought should have been offered the role in the first place. As Schweid told Dennis McGovern and Deborah Grace Winer when interviewed for their book *Sing Out, Louise*: "I got a call telling me they wanted me to take over Morales, and I was a wreck. It was all very, very weird. Michael came in and said, 'Okay, we're going to change this. You're going to say, 'I have a Jewish mother and a Puerto Rican father and a lot of internal conflicts.' It was an attempt to fit the person." Finally one of the hardworking understudies had a chance to move up to the line, and as a group they felt somewhat vindicated; however, Schweid played the role for only three months before being told, incongruously, that Bennett thought she was miscast in it. Offered the option of returning to her old job as understudy, she turned it down and left the company. Diana number four, Rebecca York, was with the show for four months. Finally, the producers brought Loida Iglesias (later Santos) in from the International Company; she clicked with the part and played it on and off for the next eight years.

Clive Barnes re-reviewed the show in *The New York Times* on December 18, 1976, by which point most of the new cast members had been playing their roles for over six months. He said: "Some performances were marginally inferior to the originals, and in one case it was markedly superior." As for the new Cassie, he remembered McKechnie's Tony-winning performance and wrote that Ann Reinking "has a difficult act to follow, and sensibly follows it by being very different. She is more gauche than shy, and her dancing is a little more classically accented." The first replacement Zach, Joe Bennett, had already been succeeded by Eivind Harum, and he was the newcomer Barnes deemed "superior," adding that the character "is now made into the dominating role that Mr. Bennett and the authors presumably envisaged. Robert LuPone, the original, was fine, but perhaps a little diffident. Mr. Harum, a former dancer from the Harkness Ballet, is a giant of a man, and both in his acting and his dancing he positively gleams."

Because the two touring companies were already out and running, it became the norm for new cast members to prove themselves first on tour and then, if they were deemed outstanding, be offered a place in the New York company if an appropriate role opened up. So for the next few years, it was rare for anyone who hadn't done the show before to be hired directly into the Broadway cast, though there were exceptions. Sometimes the dancers from the road had trouble fitting in at first, because the touring companies played in much larger theatres; the actors had become used to playing on a broad scale that could look forced or phony in the more intimate confines of the Shubert. By that time the show was being taught mainly by stage managers and dance captains who weren't necessarily trained as acting coaches, so the adjustments were slow and painful at times, and the veterans sometimes lost patience with the newcomers. But standouts from the road, like Bebe Neuwirth as Sheila, Mitzi Hamilton as Val, and Pamela Sousa as Cassie, brought new vitality to the show when they joined the New York team.

As the length of the run exceeded all expectations, some people stayed longer than they should have, and many were fired once their performances were deemed stale; some were later asked back. After a few years of this, Actors' Equity established new rules that made it harder to replace an actor without "cause": this was a direct result of director Martin Charnin's mass firings of actors in the Broadway cast of another long-running hit, *Annie*. After this, some *ACL* cast members outstayed their welcome. In the mid-eighties, so many of the dancers had been with the show's various companies for years on end that a purposeful effort was made to hire people who had *not* done the show before and bring them directly into the New York company. Still, many continued to perform well and have their contracts continually renewed; some of them stayed fresh by switching characters. The cast member who gave the most performances in a single role was probably Ron Kurowski, who opened the International Company as Bobby in 1976 and subsequently played the role in the National Company and the Hawaiian Company; he joined the Broadway cast during the 1984–85 season and stayed until the show closed in 1990, racking up over 4,500 performances.

"Give him your attention."

Though most of the replacement dancers over the years did not get to know Michael Bennett as well as the original cast had, his presence would always have a galvanizing effect, and the occasions when he would show up to give notes to a company both energized and terrified the performers. Because everyone knew he was perfectly willing to fire someone whose performance he didn't consider up to par, the anxiety was palpable. He was known to enter the theatre on stage left, where the stage manager's office was, during a performance and gradually move closer to the stage. Scott Pearson has said that when he was playing Zach, he could tell by the dancers' posture when they had realized Bennett was there watching;

they straightened up and stood taller and all of a sudden the show felt like an audition again—as it was meant to.

According to Steve Boockvor, another Zach quoted in *The Longest Line*: "The musicians were playing better and the dancers jumped higher, everything was better when Michael was in the wings. . . . I'd be in my Zach chair at the back of the theatre and Michael would talk to me and give me directorial notes as the show went on. I would get crazy because I had to concentrate on lines." Donn Simione, who also played Zach, had a similar experience: he told the editors of the same volume that Bennett had stood beside him giving direction throughout most of a performance. Most actors would consider something like that a violation, but Simione seemed to appreciate it, saying, "Whatever Michael said was always correct. He had an uncanny ability to know what would work and all you had to do was listen to him." And if the fear of being fired provided an extra tension that added energy to a performance, some of the dancers who knew him better said they actually felt more relaxed and comfortable when he was there.

Alphonse Stephenson, one of the conductors, figured out a way to take advantage of the powerful effect the director had on people even on nights when he wasn't actually there. He knew what kind of cologne Bennett usually wore, a distinctive scent, and bought a supply of it; if he thought discipline was slipping, he would splash some of it around backstage so people would think Bennett was around and shape up. Apparently it worked! And sometimes the stage managers resorted to a similar tactic: enlisting a certain stagehand who looked like the director, putting a red baseball cap like Bennett's on his head, and having him watch from the wings. The change in the caliber of the performance was very noticeable.

3,389

By the summer of 1983, Joe Papp, Michael Bennett, and the rest of the staff at *A Chorus Line* had begun giving a lot of thought to a coming milestone. On September 29, the show would break the record (then held by *Grease*) as the longest-running show (play or musical) in Broadway history. Not only that, but it would be the first show in many years to earn that distinction while still doing very healthy box office, with no closing even in sight; Bennett and Papp knew they needed to do something special to celebrate the event.

Initially, Bennett considered reassembling the original company, who had not performed the show together for almost seven and a half years, to do that one performance. But that would have been disrespectful of the cast that was then doing the show eight times a week at the Shubert. So he conceived a grand and staggeringly difficult scheme: to restage the musical for a special performance that would include as many as possible of the 457 dancers who had appeared in the Broadway show and touring companies over the years—including representatives from foreign productions. In an era before Google and e-mail, just tracking them all down proved a major challenge—a task that fell to general manager Bob Kamlot, his assistant Richard Berg, and stage managers Tom Porter and Wendy Mansfield, with help from others.

The first step was to call the original cast members and invite them to take part, which Bennett did personally. Though the event he was planning was meant to be a celebration, not all of them received the news that way. In some cases the phone calls reopened old wounds or stirred simmering resentments—especially when the actors started to realize that not all of them would get to do their own monologues or numbers. Many had faced life and career struggles in the intervening years, and none had gone on to the kind of stardom that their success in the show had led them to expect or at least hope for. So there were insecurities there, and a sense that some of the same old buttons were being pushed, with Bennett once again manipulating them into doing what he wanted. But most of them soon decided to rise above any ego issues and agreed to take part in an evening they expected would prove to be quite meaningful, and bigger than any one individual.

An exception was Robert LuPone, the original Zach, who said he disapproved of the idea and thought the whole thing was going to be a circus designed to celebrate not the show or the cast but Michael Bennett himself—a person he had clashed with and whose values he questioned. Despite phone calls from several other cast members as well as Bennett and Papp urging him to reconsider, LuPone held firm. On the other hand, Thommie Walsh, though taken aback when he learned the originals would not all be doing their own scenes, soon got on board with the concept and felt it was going to be something that would be important to all of them. He called some of the others to reassure them and encouraged them to say yes.

Donna McKechnie was the last of the original cast members Bennett called. Some of her friends from the company had already let her know what was brewing, so she was prepared. She and Michael had spoken very few times since their divorce, and she could tell he was nervous on the phone, so she made a point of being encouraging and told him she would be honored to take part, also agreeing to host a party with him for all the dancers on the Sunday night before starting rehearsals.

The lighted sign outside the Shubert Theatre was programmed to flash the names of all the dancers who would be taking part. There is some disagreement over exactly how many people that was, but the figure most commonly quoted is 332. (The Playbill listed 290, but there were more who confirmed after it went to press.) Some of the dancers from the various tours and replacement casts were surprised to get the invitations, because so many of them had actually ended their association with the show by being fired. Taking part in the gala helped them put that in perspective, as they realized how many others had shared that fate; it's been said that being fired at some point (sometimes more than once) was really just part of the *Chorus Line* experience. A very small number of people who had left on especially unhappy terms were not invited, and, although foreign companies were included, the members of the original British cast, who had taken over the West End run when the American company finished their six-month engagement in 1977, suspected they were intentionally excluded—probably as a result of the turmoil over the casting scandal that had attended that production (see Chapter 16).

The event reportedly cost half a million dollars, which was covered by the New York Shakespeare Festival, the Shubert Organization, and Bennett himself. The

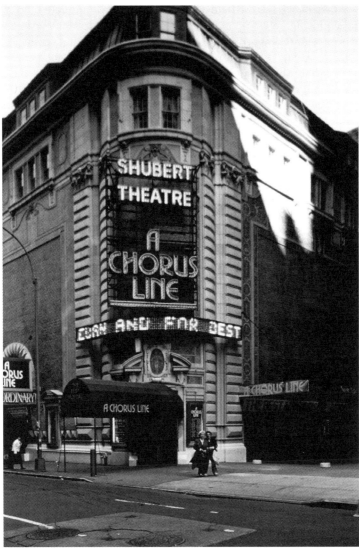

The Shubert Theatre, 225 West 44th Street, the Broadway home of *A Chorus Line* for almost fifteen years. *Photofest*

expenses included travel and accommodations (at the Milford Plaza Hotel) for the dancers who didn't live in New York, plus a lavish party in a tent set up in Shubert Alley, where patrons could mingle before the performance and again afterwards, when they would be joined by the cast. An agreement with Actors' Equity was reached whereby each performer was paid only an honorarium of fifty dollars. Many of them had to be released from performances of other Broadway musicals in which they were then appearing (these included *42nd Street, Cats, La Cage aux Folles,* and *My One and Only,* as well as the revival of *On Your Toes*), but the actual performance was to be held at 10:30 p.m. to accommodate their schedules as much as possible.

For those who took part, it often felt like a high school or college reunion, though the three days of preparation were so busy they barely got a chance to talk with one another. Rehearsals began on Monday, September 26, at the Shubert; Bennett and his assistants took the group through the restaging of the finale, which was to include all the dancers, and then divided them into separate groups to work with various dance captains on individual scenes and numbers, which were rehearsed in Bennett's studios at 890 Broadway. Many of the scenes were done by more or less complete companies who had performed the show together—and the selections were made based on who Bennett most wanted to see doing certain numbers. A particular novelty would be "Nothing," performed in Japanese by Chikae Ishikawa, who had played Diana in the Tokyo company.

Famed theatre photographer Martha Swope, who had shot the production photos of the original cast in 1975, attended some of the rehearsals and took pictures, and there is private video footage as well. Most moving is the scene of Donna McKechnie recreating "The Music and the Mirror" for the first time in almost seven years, initially referring to a script and with dance captain Troy Garza doing the steps beside her in case she needed prompting. The large studio is ringed by dozens of dancers standing or sitting on chairs or on the floor, all in hushed and rapt attention as they listen to the original Cassie sing her lines again; a shot of Michael Bennett's face, as he watches his great inspiration and onetime wife, reveals a multitude of inexpressible emotions. McKechnie soon puts the script down on the floor and belts the song with confidence, then begins the dance. Bennett had restaged it so that, at the point where the fly mirrors descend, seven other dancers who had played Cassie on Broadway and/or on tour would join her to complete the number. Cheryl Clark, Vicki Frederick, Deborah Henry, Angelique Ilo, Wanda Richert, Ann Louise Schaut, and Pamela Sousa, all exciting and highly individual dancers, took the floor with her and became reflections of the Cassie experience, each in her own way.

Sammy Williams as Paul also did his scene with numerous other Pauls, nine in all, sharing lines and sometimes speaking in unison. (They were Tommy Aguilar, Rene Clemente, Steven Crenshaw, Drew Geraci, Wayne Meledandri, Evan Pappas, George Pesaturo, Sam Viverito, and Timothy Wahrer.) The "Alternatives Scene," in which the dancers talk about what they would do if they had to stop dancing, was recreated by representatives from various foreign productions—all speaking in their own languages. Afterwards, they were joined by the originals and others who had played the same parts, and then Priscilla Lopez came forward to begin to sing "What I Did for Love." In the rehearsal footage, Lopez, choked with tears, is so moved that she can barely emit a thread of voice; when she gets to the line "Look, my eyes are dry," the whole room erupts in sympathetic laughter.

The highly emotional rehearsal days were not without tension. Unfortunately, some of the original cast members did not understand until they got there that they would not be doing their original numbers, and that caused some bruised feelings. Ron Dennis in particular felt insulted that a Richie from a touring company (who turned out to be Gordon Owens) would be doing "Gimme the Ball." He has said he attributed Bennett's choice to resentments left over from his recent unhappy stint as a show doctor on *My One and Only*, a musical in which Dennis performed. Pamela Blair, the original Val, was shooting a soap opera at the time, and the producers wouldn't let her off for all of the rehearsals. She had been pleased about the idea of sharing the Val scene with Mitzi Hamilton, as the character was based on both of them, but when she found out Bennett was staging it as a trio with a third girl involved, she felt slighted. She also said Bennett, who was irked that she was missing rehearsals, rechoreographed the number and rehearsed it when she couldn't be there, making it impossible for her to learn it. Finally she walked out. Though Bennett sent her flowers and tried to cajole her into coming back, she refused. (In the event, "Dance: Ten; Looks: Three" was performed by Hamilton with Karen Jablons—who also stood in Blair's place on line with the original cast—and DeLyse Lively.) Nancy Lane also had scheduling conflicts with a TV series, which was filming in Los Angeles, and was unable to take part—though she dearly wanted to. Terri Klausner took her place as Bebe and paid tribute to Lane by holding up her picture during the "résumé" section.

Cameron Mason (Mark), who had not always been the happiest member of the original cast, wished Lane could have been there and was disappointed in Blair and LuPone; he knew some of their resentments toward Bennett were probably justified, but later said he felt they should have been able to "swallow it" like he did and be there for the group. But like most of those who took part, Mason ultimately found the performance to be a joyous experience. Individual egos and past injuries faded in the face of the glory of the show and a shared sense of pride and love for what they had accomplished together.

Some of the performers felt the event enabled them to put the show into perspective as they never had been able to do before. As Wayne Cilento told Ken Mandelbaum: "It was so rewarding for me. Every frustration that I had doing the show came full circle. Everything I had fought in my part originally now made sense to me."

Two audiences got to see the special staging, because there was an invited black tie dress rehearsal on the Thursday afternoon—largely for people who had worked on the show backstage and offstage over the years—followed by the performance at 10:30 that night, for an invited audience studded with celebrities. (The rehearsal audience got to see the finale twice, as Bennett came onstage at the end and asked the spectators in rows J and K to vacate their seats to make room for a roving TV camera that was about to film it for broadcast that night on NBC's *Live and In Person*.)

The opening number was performed exactly as it was every night at the Shubert by the current Broadway company. This happened to be an unusually illustrious group that included Eivind Harum as Zach, Mitzi Hamilton as Val, and Jane Summerhays as Sheila—all three of whom had played the same roles with the first International Company seven years earlier. The Cassie was Pamela Sousa, who had joined that company in Baltimore on their return from London and had a long history with the show as well. Bobby and Maggie were being played by Matt West and Pam Klinger, both of whom would shortly be tapped to recreate their roles in Richard Attenborough's film version. Fraser Ellis, who was doing one of the cut dancer roles, recalled the thrill of starting the show and then turning around to see the audience already on their feet—and recognizing Ruth Gordon and Garson Kanin, Helen Hayes, Liza Minnelli, Patti LuPone (even though her brother had decided not to appear!), and Mikhail Baryshnikov. The current cast was replaced by the originals (with Terri Klausner and Karen Jablons standing in for Lane and Blair) during the blackout before the "résumé" section: when the lights came up, the originals were standing in the traditional lineup with their headshots in front of their faces, and a lit sign appeared over their heads with the words "The Original Company." The audience went through the roof.

One thrill followed another throughout the evening. The originals performed "I Can Do That," Bobby's monologue and "And," and "At the Ballet" before being replaced by the International Company for the ballet blaze and "Sing!"—which was done by the handsome Scott Plank as Al and the hilarious Kerry Casserly as Kristine. Timothy Scott of the first International Company played Mark (he had recently opened the Broadway company of *Cats* in the lead dance role of Mistoffelees). Greg's monologue was done by the second Broadway Greg, Justin Ross, who said he was thrilled to be chosen but then became a nervous wreck over having to do it (he too would later recreate his role in the film). Sandahl Bergman from the same company did Judy's section of the Montage, and David Thomé and Jennifer Ann Lee did the Don and Connie monologues. Several different casts, including the National and Bus & Truck companies, rotated in for different sections of the Montage. (In actuality there was a fair amount of shuffling, with performers being substituted in and out of the different companies, partly because not all the alumni were able to take part.)

Donna McKechnie returned to the stage to do Cassie's big scene with poignant simplicity and emotional conviction, and proved she could still dance like nobody's business. The other seven Cassies who joined her for the dance pulled off the complex number without a hitch and claimed they felt no sense of competition with each other. The Las Vegas company did the "One" rehearsal, with Ann Reinking and Joe Bennett of the first Broadway replacement cast playing Cassie and Zach in their confrontation scene.

In order to accommodate the huge number of dancers, the Booth Theatre—which backs up against the Shubert—was commandeered as a gigantic dressing room. Some of the participants felt that experiencing the show from the Booth, where it was being projected on large screens, was even more thrilling than being in the house, because they could share in the backstage adrenaline rush and the excitement of the dancers from the various companies cheering for their colleagues. The casts milled around the house at the Booth, reminiscing and congratulating each other and cheering every number—but when McKechnie began "The Music and the Mirror," she was paid the tribute of absolute quiet, as every dancer in the theatre turned to the screen to watch and listen.

Both in the dress rehearsal and at the late-night performance the frenzied response was unlike anything anyone had ever experienced—especially for the "One" finale, in which all 332 dancers gradually filed out in their identical champagne-colored, glittering Theoni V. Aldredge costumes; they filled not just the stage but also the aisles of the Shubert's orchestra section, mezzanine, and even the balcony—and then all came down and took their places on the stage, which had been specially reinforced to hold the weight of thirteen rows of dancers. At the end, each row took a final bow—and stayed down so the audience could see the faces of the row behind them; after all thirteen rows had bowed, they rose as one, to deafening applause and cheering.

Media interest in the event was tremendous; a trailer was obtained for press use outside the theatre, and the back row of orchestra seats in the Shubert was removed to make room for cameras. The post-show party continued until five o'clock on Friday morning, despite pouring rain that hammered the tent and destroyed much of the elegant décor. Press agent Merle Debuskey said very little

September 1983: Michael Bennett and Donna McKechnie at a party celebrating performance number 3,389. *Photofest*

promotional follow-up was needed, as TV stations and newspapers all over the country enthusiastically reported on the event. The result was a substantial rise in box-office receipts for the show over the next several weeks; it had been grossing about $300K per week on Broadway and spiked up to $340 or $360K several times following the gala. Company manager Bob MacDonald estimated that the half million dollars spent for that one day's events paid off in an extra three or four million eventually taken in at the box office.

Many found it to be the most thrilling and memorable night they had ever experienced in a theatre. It's impossible for anyone who wasn't there to comprehend exactly what it was that made it so special. But Michael Bennett had an acute understanding of what is unique and powerful about theatre, and the way he orchestrated that night made brilliant use of it. Because strange as it may sound, what gives live theatre its particular potency is its ephemeral nature. Each show is unique, and, as the saying goes, if you weren't there—you missed it. A production burns brightly for a short time and then dissolves forever into history, remembered or not. But somehow, on that night *A Chorus Line* had come closer than any show had ever done before to bucking that reality. It had run longer than anything else, and it seemed like it might run forever. The people onstage and in the audience were celebrating the chance to see the show they loved so much attain a measure of immortality; it felt like a miracle. And brilliantly, paradoxically, the best way that miracle could be expressed and honored was by producing an event so singular and so big it could never in a million years be repeated. All those people in one room together, the logistics, the timing: it was a once-in-a-lifetime moment if ever there was one. *A Chorus Line* flirted with permanence and immortality by giving one performance that demonstrated with unique power the very transiency and evanescence of the theatrical event. The moment it all comes together is the moment it burns itself out, gone forever. The thirty-two hundred people who were privileged to be in the room with it knew they had had an experience nobody else would ever be able to share.

Still, *A Chorus Line* had originated with the idea of sharing: twenty-four dancers sitting down in a room together to talk about their lives. That one special performance underlined with great resonance the grand theme of the show, which has always had to do with finding the commonality in our dreams. For one day and night those 332 people onstage and 3,200 in the audiences were truly "One." Don Percassi, the original Al, summed up the experience as well as anybody when he said, in *On the Line*: "The celebration was the closest thing to a religious experience I've ever had in my life. Nothing has ever moved me as much as the beauty and the truth of it. It had to do with the idea of people thinking alike and a connection between everybody. . . . We had the common memories, the common things dancers go through to become dancers, the psychological things. It's a love of what you're doing, of being a part of it; it's a family unit, all the brain cells function like one brain cell. I don't think I will ever experience anything like that again."

Back on the Line

Following a run in a touring company of the show that played across the United States and then went to Japan, Donna McKechnie returned to the Broadway cast on September 1, 1986. The original plan was for her to do an eight-week engagement, but her stay in the show was extended to eight months. She remembers it as a very happy time, and felt that, free of the tensions and pressures of the show's early days, she was able to bring more to the role—and enjoy the experience more thoroughly—than she had the first time around. Interviewed by Peter Filichia as one of the *Broadway Musical MVPs 1960–2010*, she said: "When it originally opened, we'd all been through this hard time creating it. Then we had all that attention and were asked to do a million things. The company was not happy, for there was strife and bitter jealousy. After I left, I said to myself, 'What a shame; here's the most important show in my whole career and I can't look back at it with fondness.' But when I came back, there was a very friendly cast there, almost sibling-like, who was thrilled they were getting to do it with me. How many get a second chance like that?"

She gave some pointers to the young dancers, who had been taught the steps by dance captains but didn't necessarily get all the imagery and intentions behind the choreography. As she told Eddie Shapiro in 2008 when interviewed for his book *Nothing Like a Dame*: "When I came back to the show I saw they weren't really doing

Michael's choreography. They were doing sort of a half-assed version of it. And I couldn't really blame the dancers. It's just that over time, things got diffused. I would go, 'Wait a minute, that's not the move.' Then we had a little resurgence. We cleaned it up. . . . It was not my intention to come in and shake things up, but when I saw it. . . It was great for the company because they were getting sharp instruction and clear, specific choreography with the back-story and Michael's real work."

The dancers were grateful for her guidance, and some of them were awe-struck by the chance to work with the original, now-legendary Cassie; the stage manager recorded that the week she returned was the first in years when no cast member called out sick, they were all so excited about being on stage with her. One in particular, Bradley Jones (who stood next to her on the line as Greg) was particularly self-conscious around her; he recently recalled that he was so nervous he got tongue-tied during the moments when (unheard by the audience) Greg and Cassie are supposed to ad-lib asides to one another. Finally, McKechnie told him she wanted to take him out to dinner, and they went to Orso. At dinner, she graciously told him there was no reason to be uncomfortable around her as she was just a person who was there to work and do the show; he was doing a fine job as Greg and there was nothing to worry about. He appreciated the gesture and from that point on was able to relax more and enjoy working with her—but added: "A couple weeks later I went on as Bobby and stepped on her foot! I felt terrible."

At a time when the box office had started to slow down, McKechnie's return helped boost audience interest and ticket sales. Until then, no performer in *A Chorus Line* had ever received star treatment or publicity, but now the producers took out newspaper ads featuring her picture and the slogan "Donna is Back." On her return to the show, Frank Rich wrote in *The New York Times*: "Ms. McKechnie dances as terrifically as ever—and perhaps more urgently. Here is a performer doing her job with complete conviction, for love of working, long after the parade of sold-out houses and fame has passed by. That is the spirit enshrined by *A Chorus Line*, and that's why Ms. McKechnie's 1986 Cassie induces the shiver that comes when performer, role and theatrical history all merge into a poignant one."

McKechnie was not the only original cast member to return to the show in the eighties. Kay Cole, the first Maggie, came back into the show in 1982 to play Diana—one of the only original cast members to return in a different role (Clive Clerk, who originated Larry, had done a stint as Zach). She said she enjoyed experiencing the show from the other end of the line, but turned down a later invitation to play Maggie again. Kelly Bishop (Sheila) and Sammy Williams (Paul) both returned in 1983–84, perhaps inspired by their experience doing the gala.

Since Robert LuPone had turned down his invitation to take part in that gala, some thought he had put the show permanently behind him, but he ended up accepting invitations to return in 1985 and again in 1987. His return engagements caused some controversy among the other cast members. Always outspokenly rigorous about what he felt constituted truthfulness onstage, he took it upon himself to improve the acting of the performers who were in the cast at the time. Robin Lyon, a longtime understudy who went on frequently as Bebe, Maggie, Diana, and Val, stood up to him and told him it wasn't appropriate for him to be giving her acting notes, but many of the others put up with it, whether they liked it or not. Even more controversially, LuPone would keep the dancers on their toes by occasionally ad-libbing or changing the order of things, as he had done in the National Company (see Chapter 16). Some of the cast members resented this and considered it unprofessional, but most were afraid to say anything. Bob Avian told stage manager Tom Porter to let LuPone do it because it helped keep the show fresh; Kevin Neil McCready, who played both Al and Larry at different times, later told the authors of *The Longest Line* that "it was like when someone else messes around, they're fucking around, but when Bob LuPone does it, it's acting." Some of the dancers liked it and found it stimulating; Karen Ziemba, who was playing Bebe at the time, said she looked forward to the unexpected moments LuPone would bring to the show and found it helped her feel like she was really at an audition; Laurie Gamache (Cassie) said he taught her a lot about listening and made her a better actor.

Facing Loss

Less than two months after McKechnie's last departure from the cast in May 1987, the company dealt with a blow when they learned of the death of Michael Bennett. The day he died, July 2, they had to give a performance just like any other night. Laurie Gamache, who was playing Cassie at the time, had just begun her vacation and was about to leave for the airport to attend her brother's wedding when she got a call from Tom Porter, the stage manager. He gave her the bad news and asked her not to go, because the whole cast needed to be together to cope as a group and get through it. The creative staff and many people who had worked on the show over the years found themselves drawn back to the Shubert; they wanted to be in the audience that night to experience the show and remember Michael. With no prompting from management, the cast decided to pay tribute by changing the pronoun "she" in the "One" finale to "he." That was the only change they made in the show. Some people were especially grieved because Bennett had chosen to share the truth of his illness with so few individuals; others had simply lost touch or stopped hearing from him, and missed having a chance to say good-bye.

Milestones

On August 10, 1987, *A Chorus Line* celebrated a milestone no play or musical had ever reached before: its five-thousandth performance on Broadway. Because Michael Bennett had passed away just a few weeks earlier, what should have been a joyous occasion was as bitter as it was sweet; the evening's performance was officially dedicated to Bennett's memory. It was a unique performance because it featured nineteen extra dancers who had won something called the "Chance to Dance Contest." Performers who had appeared around the nation in amateur, stock, or school productions of the show were invited to submit letters to the New York Shakespeare Festival. Once received, the letters had been sorted into piles, one for each character, which were placed in turn in a top hat from which Joe Papp drew out one dancer's name for each role; the winners, each with a chosen guest, were brought to New York, where they got to meet and rehearse with the Broadway cast. On the night of the celebration, the nineteen dancers made their collective Broadway debut in the show, appearing to stand onstage with their Broadway counterparts during "What I Did for Love," and then dancing with them in the "One" finale. It was the thrill of a lifetime for the performers, most of whom were amateurs who knew it was their one chance to appear on a Broadway stage. At the end of the show, Joseph Papp came out and said a few words to the audience about Michael Bennett and all he had accomplished with *A Chorus Line*. Then a large anniversary cake was wheeled onstage. The New York Shakespeare Festival sponsored an after-party at Palladium on East 14th Street for seven hundred and fifty guests.

What followed was one of the ugliest and most notorious episodes in the annals of *A Chorus Line* history. At the party, book writer James Kirkwood was seated at a table with several people, including his new writing partner and boyfriend Jim Piazza, his "date" for the evening Sydney Biddle Barrows (popularly known as the Mayflower Madam), and the Australian singer/songwriter/showman Peter Allen (later the subject of the musical *The Boy from Oz*). Kirkwood was venting to his friends about Papp's speech at the theatre. Though he didn't begrudge the late Bennett his tribute, the evening was meant to celebrate a major milestone in

"The Big Six" in the International Company, circa 1977. Gina Paglia (Diana), Tommy Aguilar (Paul), Jane Summerhays (Sheila), Eivind Harum (Zach), Pamela Sousa (Cassie), and Karen Jablons (Val).   *Photo by Martha Swope; from the collection of the author*

the life of the show, and Kirkwood was enraged that Papp had failed to mention not only himself but Nick Dante, Ed Kleban, or Marvin Hamlisch, giving all the credit for the musical's success to Bennett. (The show's book writers in particular had often felt underappreciated and shoved aside by a public and an industry that failed to accord them the credit generally due to the authors of a hit show, and Papp's speech that evening had reopened unhealed wounds.) Kirkwood asked his friends what they thought he should do about it, and Piazza suggested speaking to Papp or writing him a letter at some point to clear the air—but certainly with no intention of inciting Kirkwood to pick a fight with the producer that very night.

That's exactly what happened, though, as Kirkwood strode over to Papp's table and asked him to explain his "reprehensible" behavior. The producer reportedly replied "Go fuck yourself" and began to get up from the table; according to Piazza, Papp additionally remarked that he had made Kirkwood a millionaire. Kirkwood pushed Papp in the chest and knocked him down, and after someone helped him back up the two men began to scuffle on the dance floor, yelling obscenities at each other and throwing punches; they had to be pulled apart by a group of people led by Piazza and Papp's son Tony. (Both Papp and Kirkwood were in their mid-sixties at the time and neither was in good health.) Nick Dante, seated nearby, was humiliated, and Peter Allen, shaken by the events, left the club and went home. Having gotten the matter off his chest, Kirkwood stayed, and later said he thoroughly enjoyed the rest of the party.

He felt no remorse whatsoever and proudly recounted the story on several occasions afterwards. He claimed that the next day, rather than apologizing, he ordered a bouquet of black flowers to be sent to Papp with a note calling him a "megalomaniacal prick." Both Papp and the gossip columnist Liz Smith, a longtime admirer of Bennett's and self-professed friend of Kirkwood's, blamed the latter's outburst on booze and cocaine—though Kirkwood himself flatly denied that they had played any part.

The next month, a more formal and better-planned tribute to Bennett was held in the form of a memorial service, also on stage at the Shubert, at 3:00 p.m. on September 29, 1987. (Whether or not it was intentional, the date was poignantly significant: four years to the day after the triumphant gala celebrating the show's record-breaking 3,389th performance.) Writer Ken Mandelbaum attended the event, which he described in detail in the prologue to his book on Bennett. Marvin Hamlisch played "What I Did for Love" on an onstage piano, after which heartfelt testimonials were delivered by Bob Avian, Robin Wagner, General Manager Marvin Krauss, Bennett's brother Frank DiFilia, his lawyer and friend John Breglio, Donna McKechnie, and Bernard Jacobs, followed by Liz Smith and Papp. Stephen Sondheim, through tears, played and sang "Move On," from his musical *Sunday in the Park with George*—a song that Bennett had particularly loved and whose lyrics resonated with new meaning given the occasion. The current cast of *A Chorus Line* performed the "One" finale to end the program, and at the moment when the periaktoi usually revolve to reveal the art deco sunburst pattern, they displayed instead a huge photo of Bennett, arms outstretched. All the speakers were eloquent, and Wagner summed up the feelings of many when he said: "He made everyone who knew him his own. We all felt singled out. Last January, he said that whatever happened, he didn't think he missed anything. It is certain that we'll never know the full extent of his loss as an artist, and his loss as a friend is inconsolable."

That night, on the same stage, there was, as always, a performance of *A Chorus Line*. Bennett's greatest creation had outlived him. It would continue to play on Broadway for another two and a half years.

The End of the Line

As Michael Kantor and Laurence Maslon wrote in *Broadway: The American Musical*, the companion volume to Kantor's PBS documentary series: "The image of Bennett's heroic army of beautifully toned dancers, clad only in pre-spandex leotards, infiltrated nearly every aspect of pop culture. Television specials paid tribute to 'gypsies,' Hollywood rediscovered dance, producing movies such as *The Turning Point* and *All That Jazz* for the older crowd and *Staying Alive*, *Footloose*, and *Flashdance* for the younger crowd. Jane Fonda aerobicized on videotape, costumed like one of the eight dancers who get eliminated at the top of *A Chorus Line*, and became an idol to millions. Even the television exercise shows that have clogged the airwaves since the late 1970s tap in to the show's basic concept: if you work hard enough—in leotards—you too can make it."

A Chorus Line ran so much longer than any other Broadway show had ever run that by the mid-eighties people had started to feel like it might go on forever. But by the end of the decade there had been enough money-losing weeks at the box office that reality had to be faced; it was time to think about closing. Joseph Papp was initially pained by the very idea; he loved being the producer of the longest-running show ever, and he had kept it running through lean times because he felt it should always be on Broadway as a living memorial to Bennett. But by 1989, the New York Shakespeare Festival's finances were suffering; the institution had been supported by *ACL* for so long that grants from foundations and the government, as well as individual donations, had declined dangerously; people assumed the theatre didn't need the money. *ACL* wasn't pumping in the capital it once had, and the endowment the show had helped to establish was being spent at an alarming rate. So once the musical had gone a couple hundred thousand dollars into the red for the season, both Papp and the Shuberts started to read the writing on the wall.

It was clear that the show was no longer able to fill the Shubert Theatre, but no one wanted to see it end, so several options for keeping it running were considered. Jim Kirkwood suggested putting in an all-black cast, as David Merrick had done years earlier with *Hello, Dolly!*; he told Joe Papp he felt that would generate enough new public interest to keep the show running another couple of years, but the suggestion remained just an idea. The show's weekly operating costs were only $160,000, relatively small for a Broadway musical at the time. There was discussion of working out an arrangement with a large corporate sponsor to back the show, in exchange for putting its name above the title on the program and all other publicity materials, and moving it into the Music Box Theatre, a much smaller Broadway house; negotiations were begun with Actors' Equity to explore a new contract for the cast to make that feasible. But for some reason Irving Berlin, the legendary songwriter who owned the Music Box, decided not to lease it. While he was still alive, Michael Bennett had said that when the show was no longer selling out at the Shubert he would move it to his theatre at 890 Broadway—which was about the same size as the Newman, where the show had originally opened—and run it there indefinitely, so a move back to Off Broadway was considered. But *ACL* was too big for Off Broadway, where theatres have to have fewer than five hundred seats; no house that size paying union salaries could break even with a cast and orchestra as large as the show's.

So finally, press agent Merle Debuskey sent out an invitation to a mysterious press conference that Joe Papp would be holding at the Shubert on Wednesday afternoon, February 21, 1990, promising significant news about the show. At the conference, Papp announced that *A Chorus Line* would be closing on March 31. Bernard Jacobs and Phil Smith of the Shubert Organization felt he should have given more advance notice, that if the public knew the show would be closing even six months in advance, ticket sales would increase dramatically as people came back to see it again; five and a half weeks was not enough time. The rush for tickets after the closing notice was posted proved them right, as the show began to sell out again for the first time in years. Ultimately they convinced Papp to extend for one more month, and the closing was pushed back to April 28; the show continued to do so well that the Shuberts pushed for another extension, and the cast felt sure it would happen, but Papp was firm that an announcement had been made and it was time to close. People close to Papp have said they believe he made the decision partly because at that point he already knew he was dying; he wanted to be in control of how and when the show finished its run, and to write the end of that story himself, rather than leaving any loose ends for others to tie up after his passing.

The cast at the Shubert immediately felt a jolt of unexpected energy from their audiences. Many of them had joined the cast during a period when the show was playing to relatively quiet, half-empty houses, and they had never experienced the kind of excitement and electricity that had characterized audiences during the show's early years; the last two months of the run gave them more than a taste of it, as fans returned in force to see—and cheer—their favorite musical one last time. The current ensemble (including Jack Noseworthy, a very young dancer who was playing Mark and had been hired just before the closing notice was posted) began to sense the historical importance of their position as the Final Broadway Company of the show; they also experienced the play itself with a more authentic urgency than they were used to, now that they were painfully aware that they would soon be out of a job and, like the characters they played, looking for work once again.

The Final Broadway Company also got a taste of the kind of media frenzy the original cast had experienced during the show's first year. There were frequently film crews at the theatre and numerous requests for interviews on a variety of TV programs, including *Entertainment Tonight, Geraldo, Nightline* and *The Phil Donahue Show*—some of which also interviewed members of the original cast. There was even an hour-long documentary called *A Chorus Line: Final Stage* made for Japanese TV, which included substantial footage of the events leading up to the closing; interviews with Joe Papp and original cast members Donna McKechnie, Baayork

Lee, Thommie Walsh, and Priscilla Lopez; and performance clips from the final Broadway performance, including much of Laurie Gamache's spectacular rendition of the Cassie dance. (Though the narration of the film is in Japanese, the interviews are in English with Japanese subtitles, and it's eminently watchable.)

The closing cast's Bobby was Ron Kurowski, who had played the role over forty-five hundred times since opening the International Company in 1976. In an interview with *Equity News* about the imminent closing, he said: "We had an audience full of young people today, and it's amazing to see their faces. They don't even understand it, and they love it. . . . The show affects people in a way that's different from all other musicals, and you look at other musicals differently based on seeing this show. It's sad that the audiences ran out, and that financially the show can't continue, but I would think that it could run somewhere, and it's really sad to me that it's going to be gone."

As the closing approached, Baayork Lee gathered most of the original cast for a reunion on stage at the Newman Theatre, where they had first done the show fifteen years earlier. The originals also joined the current cast and crew backstage at the Shubert before the final performance, where longtime understudy Robin Lyon played and sang "We Will Remember," a song she had written in tribute to the occasion. There were two performances that Saturday, a matinee and an evening show, and before the evening performance a whole row of seats had to be taken out to make room for all the TV cameras.

After the curtain call, the original cast members were invited to come up onstage and join the dancers. As in the past, unfortunately, there were some hurt feelings involved. The understudies, as usual, felt shut out of the festivities, and there was a definite "us and them" dynamic between the final cast and the originals; the two groups occupied opposite sides of the room during the after-party at Mamma Leone's restaurant, and most of the originals made no effort to reach out to their counterparts in the closing night cast. There were a few exceptions, however, who were more gracious—including Ron Kuhlman, the original Don, who had sent Keith Bernardo a bottle of champagne with a card that said: "To Keith: It's not how you start. . . it's how you finish. Here's to Don Kerr, the first, the last, all those in between, and all those yet to come."

The Tag Sale

Three days after the show closed, the Shubert Theatre reopened for "The End of the Line Tag Sale," where enormous amounts of memorabilia and actual pieces of the show were sold off as a fund-raiser. Paradoxically, the longer a show runs, the sadder it feels when it closes, and if anyone had failed to believe the run of *A Chorus Line* had finally ended, the depressing sight of the set having been torn up and replaced by what looked like a garage sale drove the point home. Everything from costumes to photos to lobby signage to pieces of the set was available for purchase—including individual panels from the stage floor, each containing a segment of the famous white line, which were priced at $100 each. Many cast members, from originals up to and including actors from the company that had just closed the show, came to the theatre for a melancholy reunion of sorts. Priscilla Lopez bought a finale costume (priced at $200), and Laurie Gamache purchased a complete set of line costumes, one for each character, since she knew she would want to direct her own production of the show someday. On the second day there was an auction; the auctioneer was Randy Clements, who had been playing Zach on tour—and would soon go out on the road again, with Gamache, in the Visa-sponsored "Farewell tour" of the show. The Shubert Theatre may have gone dark after fifteen glorious years, but it was already clear that, somewhere or other, the line was going to keep on kicking.

The Plaque

To commemorate the run of A Chorus Line, Gary Stevens and Alan George, longtime fans of the show and authors of the book The Longest Line, initiated a nationwide fund-raiser, headed up by eight actresses who played Cassie on Broadway and supported by Joseph Papp and three critics who had reviewed the show's opening, to commission a permanent cast bronze plaque to hang in the Shubert Theatre lobby. Designed by artist Immi Storrs, the plaque features the line logo and title with the words "The Longest Running Show in Broadway History" and the dates of the run, bookended by large bas-relief figures of a male and female dancer in finale costumes. It was unveiled on October 30, 1991, at a ceremony attended by many alumni of the production. It hangs in the Shubert lobby today as a lasting tribute to the theatre's longest and most legendary tenancy.

19

"If Troy Donahue Could Be a Movie Star . . ."

A Chorus Line and Its Journey to Film

Like so many other film projects, the story of the movie of *A Chorus Line* begins with the producers: Cy Feuer and Ernest Martin. They had been around Broadway as well as the film industry for decades and could smell a hit a mile away. So they made a very early bid on the property, offering $150,000 for the film rights two days after the show started previews at the Public Theater. But Michael Bennett and Joseph Papp also believed the show was going to be really big, so they held out and turned down the offer. Little did any of them know that after ten years, and several failed attempts by other producers and studios, Feuer and Martin would actually be the ones who made the film.

Before the end of 1975, the film rights were sold to Universal for $5.5 million (then a record), and the initial plan was for Michael Bennett to direct: he was offered an office at the studio and a multipicture deal. The initial contract for the rights stipulated that no film could be released for at least five years, so as not to compete with the stage version, and Universal took out a full-page ad in *Variety* announcing that Michael Bennett was to produce and direct the film of *A Chorus Line* in 1980. Unfortunately, they were counting their proverbial chickens.

Bennett, of course, was well aware of the unique theatrical immediacy that made the stage version special. The show took place in a Broadway theatre, Here and Now, and there was a metatheatrical dimension to it: the audience felt like secret observers at a real audition happening in the actual theatre where they were watching the show, which added to their sense that anything could happen, that the outcome of the audition was up for grabs. A literal film adaptation would inevitably lose that resonance, that aura of being an Event. Wanting to find a way to translate the docudrama feel of the show, and its essential honesty, to the screen, Bennett conceived of a radical adaptation. He did a treatment for *Chorus Line II*, a film about dancers auditioning for the movie version of *A Chorus Line*; each song or monologue would be broken down and performed by several hopefuls for the same role. This innovative cinema verité approach just might have succeeded in translating the excitement of the stage version to the screen. But Bennett knew it wasn't what Universal had in mind. He also wasn't comfortable in Hollywood, or really getting along with the studio heads. Ultimately, none of the projects he proposed got made, and he ended up asking his lawyer to get him out of the film deal and leaving Hollywood before he'd really gotten started there.

Nevertheless, Universal had the screen rights to *A Chorus Line*, which by then was well on its way to becoming the longest-running musical in Broadway history. The film had to get made, with or without Bennett. So the studio approached a succession of other directors and writers, several of whom did treatments and worked on the material for a while before giving up. The legendary Mike Nichols was announced to direct at one point (though not known for musicals, his credits did include producing *Annie* and directing *The Apple Tree* on Broadway), as was Sidney Lumet. Many people have speculated on what the film of *A Chorus Line* might have been like had Bob Fosse directed it; his own film *All That Jazz*, released in 1980, also explores the world of the Broadway dancer, and its famed opening audition sequence has obvious similarities to "I Hope I Get It." Though Fosse had no connection to the stage version of *ACL* (he would get irritated when confused fans congratulated him on it, and resented its sweep of the 1976 Tony Awards, which resulted in the shutout of his show *Chicago*), he did see the show many times and had a begrudging admiration for it. He also directed the very successful 1972 movie version of *Cabaret*, a show he had not been involved with on Broadway. All this might have made him an obvious choice for the *Chorus Line* film, and years later Vicki Frederick (a Fosse dancer who played Sheila in the movie) asked him why he hadn't directed it. Ironically, he reportedly told her that he would have been happy to, but since everyone assumed he wouldn't want the job, he was never asked!

The production team that got the most traction during this period was producer Allan Carr (who had also been Marvin Hamlisch's agent) and director/writer Joel Schumacher; they got so far as hiring John Travolta to play Zach. But the script and the budget didn't come together. Ultimately the studio heads grew discouraged and ended up selling the rights to Polygram Pictures—this time for $7.8 million. Peter Guber and Jon Peters came on board as producers, and when Bennett declined to get involved again, they chose James Bridges to direct and write the screenplay, and announced that ballet and film star Mikhail Baryshnikov (a longtime devotee of the show) would be their Zach. But Polygram balked at the proposed $18 million budget. After trying to work out a deal with original producer Joseph Papp, the studio finally made one with Cy Feuer and Ernest Martin, the team who had made the very first attempt to buy the rights; they agreed that the film could be made without major stars and for a substantially smaller estimated budget of $11.5 million. As veteran Broadway producers with some film experience, they seemed qualified to take on the property, which they produced with Embassy Film Associates (owned by Norman Lear, Alan Horn, and Gerry Perenchio) along with Polygram. But Embassy was in the process of going out of business by the time the film had been completed; it was eventually released through Columbia Pictures.

Cy Feuer and Ernest H. Martin (Producers)

Cy Feuer was born in Brooklyn in 1911 and originally planned on a career as a musician. He played trumpet professionally while he was still a teenager, then dropped out of high school to work, helping to support his family. He later attended Juilliard and played in New York City orchestras (including Radio City Music Hall) before a tour with Leon Belasco and His Society Orchestra took him to California. He spent a decade working for Republic Pictures as a musical director and composer of film scores, with three years off for military service. After an affair with Hollywood star Susan Hayward, he married Posy Greenberg, and they had a son, Jed.

Despite earning five Academy Award nominations for composing film scores, Feuer decided that wasn't where his future lay, and he returned to New York. There he met Ernest H. Martin (born 1919), who worked for CBS Radio as head of comedy programming. They began a partnership as producers that would last almost forty years, beginning with the 1949 Broadway musical *Where's Charley?* This show, an adaptation of the classic stage comedy *Charley's Aunt*, had a score by the great Frank Loesser; Feuer and Martin's future projects would include Loesser's *Guys and Dolls* (1950) and *How to Succeed in Business Without Really Trying* (1961: the musical that marked the Broadway debut of Donna McKechnie). *How to Succeed* received the Pulitzer Prize for Drama, as only the fourth musical ever to earn that distinction. (There would not be a fifth until fourteen years later–when the prize was won by *A Chorus Line*.) It also won the Tony Award for Best Musical, and Feuer and Martin shared the Tony for Best Producer of a Musical (a prize no longer awarded today; the producers are presented with the Best Musical award).

Other major Broadway musicals the pair produced included *Can-Can*, *Silk Stockings*, *The Boy Friend*, and *Little Me*—which Feuer also directed, receiving a Tony nomination. On his own, Martin produced *Whoop-Up*, a musical for which he also wrote the book, as well as *Walking Happy* and the straight play *The Goodbye People*. The duo's last Broadway credit as producers was the Liza Minnelli vehicle *The Act* (1977), on which Michael Bennett did some work as a show doctor. Feuer later directed the musical version of *I Remember Mama*, which followed Bennett's *Ballroom* into the Majestic Theatre.

Though primarily associated with Broadway, Feuer produced the movie version of the musical *Cabaret* in 1972. The film won eight Oscars, at a time when interest in movie musicals was clearly waning; this triumph, combined with the team's track record producing on Broadway, would have seemed to situate Feuer and Martin for potential success with the film of *A Chorus Line*.

In addition to their producing endeavors, Feuer and Martin purchased a Broadway theatre, the Lunt-Fontanne, which they owned from 1960 to 1965. Martin passed away in 1995. Feuer became chairman, and then president, of the League of American Theatres and Producers, which he ran from 1989 until 2003— when he was ninety-two years old. That same year he published his autobiography: *I Got the Show Right Here: The Amazing, True Story of How an Obscure Brooklyn Horn Player Became the Last Great Broadway Showman*. He died in 2006.

Sir Richard Attenborough (Director)

The director was born in Cambridge, England, in 1923 and studied at the Royal Academy of Dramatic Arts. He served in the Royal Air Force during World War II and was assigned to the Film Unit, where he worked as both an actor in propaganda films and a camera operator recording missions on bomber jets.

He had acted onstage before the war and in 1942 began his film acting career as a sailor in the British film *In Which We Serve*, following that up with numerous movie roles including that of Pinkie Brown in *Brighton Rock*, a high-profile adaptation of a Graham Greene novel; he had played the same role in an earlier stage version. Other theatre credits included a part in the original cast of Agatha Christie's *The Mousetrap*, the longest-running play in history: Attenborough and his actress wife Sheila Sim created the roles of Detective Sergeant Trotter and Mollie Ralson in 1955 and used their salaries to buy shares in the production's profits. It proved a shrewd investment; the production is still running almost sixty years later. Through the fifties, sixties, and seventies, Attenborough continued to act in both British and American films, including the Hollywood hit *The Great Escape* (1963); he won the Golden Globe Award for Best Supporting Actor for both *The Sand Pebbles* (1967) and *Doctor Dolittle* (1968).

Attenborough began his producing career in the 1950s, joining with partner Bryan Forbes to start Beaver Films; the company produced *The League of Gentlemen*, *The Angry Silence*, and *Whistle Down the Wind* (which years later was turned into a stage musical by Andrew Lloyd Webber). The first of Attenborough's dozen

Sir Richard Attenborough (right) directs Blane Savage in Don's monologue, as the rest of the line looks on. In this rehearsal shot, several of the female dancers' costumes are covered by white bathrobes, which were removed before the cameras rolled.

Moviestore Collection/ Rex/ REX USA

full-length films as a director was a star-studded version of the stage musical *Oh! What a Lovely War*—his only musical before *A Chorus Line*. Other major films he helmed included the historical pictures *Young Winston*, *A Bridge Too Far*, and of course the Academy-Award winning 1982 film *Gandhi*, which he also produced, winning the Oscars for both Best Picture and Best Director. (The acclaim and awards he received for that film in the early eighties were probably the primary factors that put him into contention for *A Chorus Line*, but the producers also remembered *Oh! What a Lovely War* and felt it had demonstrated his aptitude for musicals.) After his work on *A Chorus Line* (which, it must be remembered, earned him a Golden Globe nomination for Best Director), he returned to his usual specialty of political and historical films, including *Cry Freedom*, *Chaplin*, and *Closing the Ring*. He also revived his acting career in his later years, with a cameo appearance in Kenneth Branagh's film of *Hamlet* and major roles as John Hammond in the *Jurassic Park* films and Kris Kringle in the 1994 remake of *Miracle on 34th Street* (Michael Bennett had danced in the stage version, *Here's Love*, in 1963.) A surprise late return to musical comedy was the role of Jacob in a British film version of Lloyd Webber's *Joseph and the Amazing Technicolor Dreamcoat* (1999).

Attenborough was married to Sheila Sim for almost seventy years. They had three children, one of whom (Jane Holland) perished, along with her fifteen-year-old daughter Lucy, in Thailand in the 2004 tsunami. Attenborough and Sim were both active in philanthropic causes, contributing to educational institutions as patrons of the United World Colleges movement. Attenborough also served for over thirty years as President of the United Kingdom's Muscular Dystrophy Campaign; in 2004 he was named Honorary Life President of that organization. He fought for education equality in South Africa and Swaziland, both through his work on the film *Cry Freedom* and via the establishment of the Jane Holland Creative Centre for Learning in Waterford Kamhlaba, named in honor of his late daughter. Attenborough's other children are the director Michael Attenborough, formerly artistic director of the Almeida Theatre, and the actress Charlotte Attenborough.

Attenborough's many awards and honors included the Martin Luther King Jr. Nonviolence Peace Prize in 1983, the year following the release of *Gandhi*. He also held numerous corporate positions and joined the boards of various charitable, theatrical, political, film, and educational institutions, many of which he chaired; he served as both chancellor of the University of Sussex (1998–2008) and chairman and then president of the Royal Academy of Dramatic Arts (1973–2014)—where he had originally trained as an actor. For his tremendously distinguished career in the arts and his contributions to public service, he was honored with a knighthood and later a lordship. Attenborough's autobiography, *Entirely Up to You, Darling*, written with Diana Hawkins, was released in 2008. He died on August 24, 2014, five days before his ninety-first birthday.

Arnold Schulman (Screenwriter)

Schulman was chosen for the film by the producers before they hired Attenborough. The two men were of the same generation, Schulman having been born in Philadelphia in 1925. He served in the Navy during World War II and studied writing at the University of North Carolina and with playwright Robert Anderson (author of *Tea and Sympathy* and *I Never Sang for My Father*) at the American Theatre Wing. He acted in stage productions in New York, playing small roles in two Broadway plays in 1950: the original production of William Inge's *Come Back, Little Sheba* and a revival of Arthur Miller's *An Enemy of the People*. He became an early member of both the Actors Studio and New Dramatists, and wrote TV scripts—initially for money to support his career as a playwright—working on classic anthology shows like *Omnibus* and *GE Theater*. For the stage, he wrote the 1957 Broadway play *A Hole in the Head*, which he adapted two years later as a film vehicle for Frank Sinatra. In 1968, the play was adapted again, this time as the stage musical *Golden Rainbow* by Ernest Kinoy and Walter Marks (the writers of *Bajour*, in which Michael Bennett and Bob Avian danced on Broadway); this show—like *A Chorus Line*—played the Shubert Theatre and featured Carole (later Kelly) Bishop in the cast. Schulman's other musical theatre–related projects included the screenplay for *Funny Lady*, the 1975 film sequel to *Funny Girl* (though he himself later claimed that Jay Presson Allen deserved most of the credit for that script) and the book for the 1963 Broadway musical *Jennie*, a Mary Martin vehicle based loosely on the life of actress Laurette Taylor, with a score by Howard Dietz and Arthur Schwartz. His most notable screenplays include *Love with the Proper Stranger* (1963) and *Goodbye, Columbus* (1969), both of which earned him Academy Award nominations, and *The Night They Raided Minsky's* (1968). Schulman also wrote and coproduced the 1993 docudrama *And the Band Played On*, based on Randy Shilts's book about the early days of the AIDS epidemic. The ending of the film features a montage of images of major figures in the AIDS crisis—including Michael Bennett, who had died from the disease six years earlier. For his work on that film, Schulman was honored with a Humanitas Prize.

Pat McGilligan's book *Backstory 3: Interviews with Screenwriters of the 1960s* includes a chapter on Schulman—the title of which is "Nothing but Regrets." He admits to feeling he frequently sold out and said he hated himself for the years he spent as a "writer for hire." He had this to say about his experience adapting *A Chorus Line* for film—an assignment many other screenwriters before him had attempted and failed to pull off:

> Finally, I came up with a surrealistic approach that [the producers] Norman Lear and Jerry [sic] Perenchio must have liked, because they put up twenty-four million dollars of their own money to make it. Richard Attenborough must have liked it, because he agreed to direct it; but for reasons known only to him, Attenborough threw away the script completely and tried to photograph the play.
>
> In addition to this disastrous decision was a set of circumstances nobody could have coped with. After Lear and Perenchio put up the money and the picture was being made, they sold their company to Columbia, and Columbia wanted nothing to do with *A Chorus Line*. So every single element was fighting with every other element, and all the pressure landed on Attenborough. Columbia versus Embassy versus the two producers; everybody disagreeing

with each other about the casting, this and that, about everything. How Attenborough survived it, I have no idea, but he is the most decent man in the world, a truly warm, intelligent, beautiful human being.

I'll always remember one meeting we had with the producers. . . . we were going to make the final decision as to who would be the leading lady. . . . I offered my opinion, and one of the producers said, "Who asked you? You have nothing to do with this. Go to your room!" "Go to your room"? Like a little kid. I was stunned. I said, "You're right; it's none of my business," and I left. . . .

Schulman also said Attenborough later had to intercede on his behalf to get him a ticket to the film's preview, after one of the producers claimed outright that a screenwriter wasn't entitled to an invitation.

Jeffrey Hornaday (Choreographer)

Hornaday was inspired to pursue a dance career when, as a child, he saw Bob Fosse's film version of the Broadway musical *Cabaret*—coincidentally produced by Cy Feuer. He started as a performer, centered in Los Angeles and dancing on TV specials; he played one of the dancing Aggies in the 1982 movie of *The Best Little Whorehouse in Texas*. Hornaday's interest in the creative possibilities of dance on film surfaced early, and he spent a couple of years choreographing and directing rock videos in Mexico City before he got his big break as a choreographer: the sleeper hit *Flashdance* in 1983. After that, he did a gig as a chorus dancer on a Sheena Easton TV special before being offered the daunting assignment of rethinking the dance numbers of *A Chorus Line* for film.

Unlike most film choreographers, who establish their styles initially through stage work, Hornaday was a child of the camera. He developed his aesthetic through work on TV and film, and has always been as interested in camera angles and editing techniques as he is in dance steps; he conceptualizes the movement and the cinematographic elements in tandem.

Speaking about his work on *A Chorus Line* after the film came out, he described some of the challenges he faced to Lewis Segal, the dance writer for the *Los Angeles Times*: "I didn't want just to adapt or imitate Michael Bennett's (original stage) choreography. And I had to be real rooted in my reasons for doing the film because it was so apparent up front that it was a no-win situation. Even if you did a brilliant job, people would go, 'Of course. It was a brilliant show; *you're* not responsible.' And if, God forbid, you changed it, they'd go 'How dare you touch this?'" He also explained that the film's widescreen format posed a particular challenge when it came to filming dance numbers: "The format was a decision made early on—I don't know if it was by the director of photography or Richard or who—but in order to get a head-to-toe view of anyone, you had to get so far back that it was really a passive effect to watch." Compensating for this, he sometimes chose to focus in more closely on a dancer, with the result that his or her feet were cut out of the frame—something he would later be criticized for in reviews, though he was aware of the problem.

The cast of the film poses in costume for a group portrait. Director Richard Attenborough and choreographer Jeffrey Hornaday are at left and right, respectively, in the top row.

Courtesy Michael Blevins

In another interview, this one with Bob Thomas of the *Gainesville Sun*, he revealed that *A Chorus Line* "was an intimidating assignment because I would be working so much in the shadow of the original. I decided not to listen to the recording of the original music, which would make me self-conscious. Instead, I worked with an accomplished pianist and an excellent drummer, and together we reinvented the score."

Hornaday's highest-profile assignment in the years immediately following *ACL* was *Captain EO*, the famous eleven-minute 3-D film starring Michael Jackson that played for years at the Disney theme parks in the United States, France, and Japan. The musical film was produced by George Lucas and directed by Francis Ford Coppola; Hornaday collaborated with Jackson himself on the choreography. His later film choreography credits include *Tango and Cash*, *Dick Tracy*, *Carlito's Way*, *Bird of Prey*, and *Sweet Jane*. He also directed touring stadium shows for Paul McCartney and Madonna, and special events for Presidents Clinton and Obama. In recent years, his career has been on an upswing with a couple of very successful projects: he directed the Disney Channel's cable movie *Geek Charming* in 2011 and followed that up with Disney's *Teen Beach Movie* (2013), which turned out to be the highest-rated nonsequel original movie in the history of cable television. For each of these two films, Hornaday was nominated for a Director's Guild of America Award.

Casting

Because *A Chorus Line* not only offers opportunities to a large cast of young performers, but is also actually *about* an audition, interest in any new production of the show often focuses on the casting process—and the much-anticipated movie version of course was no exception. Since the show is about unknown performers auditioning for chorus jobs, even for the film it was felt that the focus should be on finding fresh faces: with the possible exceptions of the characters of Zach and maybe Cassie, famous names and personalities would clash with the themes of the piece and inhibit verisimilitude. (The reduced budget also made casting stars impractical, and Michael Douglas, who was eventually cast as Zach, agreed to work for far less than his usual fee.) To their credit, Attenborough as well as Feuer and Martin all decided early on that they wanted to make dance ability the prime criterion: with the whole line involved in dance numbers throughout the film, nobody wanted to hire actors who couldn't dance and then deal with doubles and stand-ins. (In one case an exception to this was considered, when TV actress Audrey Landers was cast as Val. She accepted on the condition that she might have to ask for a dance double, and that position was offered to DeLyse Lively, who had played the role on stage. Lively understandably turned it down, and in the end Landers proved able to do her own dancing.)

Julie Hughes and Barry Moss, with extensive experience in New York theatre, were hired as casting directors. The search for undiscovered talent included not only casting calls for actors who were already members of the Screen Actors Guild (SAG), but open cattle calls in both New York and Los Angeles: the team, including Attenborough and Hornaday, saw over three thousand performers. In the industry, however, professional actors and dancers don't want to go to open calls, so interest focused on how to get an individual appointment. Any dancer who had ever appeared in a stage production of the show was automatically granted an audition. Otherwise, appointments were hard to come by, and dancers and agents had to use their connections to get seen.

A sadly ironic footnote to the story involves the original cast members, quite a few of whom actually auditioned for the film—for roles they had created and that were based largely on their own life stories. But the team was going for a highly contemporary, youth-oriented flavor; in the screenplay the ages of several of the characters were lowered from what they had been in the stage version. Almost ten years after the premiere of the show, most of the original cast members were considered too mature for their roles, especially on film. When Wayne Cilento went in to audition for Mike, the role he had originated, Attenborough asked him to read for Larry instead. Because that role was to be substantially expanded for the film, he was excited to be considered, but he never got to do a screen test. The original cast member who came closest to getting cast was Sammy Williams, a Tony winner for his role as Paul, but ultimately even there the decision was made to go with a younger dancer.

Michael Blevins, who was to end up with the role of Mark in the film, was an experienced Broadway dancer then appearing in *The Tap Dance Kid*. (That show's choreographer, Danny Daniels, was seriously considered as a choreographer for the film but turned it down, saying he wouldn't touch it; like many, he was reluctant to compete with Bennett's iconic work.) Blevins happened to meet Cy Feuer at the Minskoff Studios while he was working on the show, and months later his castmate Karen Curlee (who had played Bebe as a replacement in *ACL* on Broadway), knowing he was right for the role, encouraged him to audition for Mark. Blevins had never been in the show, but it was the first Broadway musical he'd ever seen and he had auditioned in Nashville for one of the national tours when he was only seventeen (the age Mark is supposed to be in the movie). He called his agent and was initially told that only dancers who had been in the stage companies were getting appointments, but shortly thereafter he heard from the casting director and was called in to dance for Jeffrey Hornaday. The whole process spread out over six months, with several dance callbacks and then a reading for Attenborough, followed by a screen test. Attenborough telephoned him personally to tell him he was being offered the role. The first time most of the cast members met each other was at a photo shoot, and Blevins recalled recently that they could all tell immediately which parts everyone would be playing.

On the Set

Though there may have been turmoil among the producers and creative team, Blevins remembers that Attenborough and Hornaday created a very positive, nurturing environment on the set. He said: "The thing that was great about Richard was he always made you feel like he believed in you. He made you feel like you were the only person and the best person walking the face of the earth to play that role." Blevins spoke of the difference between the two groups of dancers in the show: the Broadway veterans from New York and those who had come from Los Angeles with more film experience. But far from condescending to the Hollywood dancers, he was impressed with their energy and discipline: a theatre person's day seldom begins before 10 a.m., and some of the New York dancers would drag themselves in to early morning sessions to find the Californians already eager and energized. At times he felt the pressure as part of a group of superbly skilled dancers: with a background mainly in tap, he was a bit in awe of great jazz dancers like Vicki Frederick, Gregg Burge, and Blane Savage and the high standard they set. But the cast members bonded and began to feel like a family.

They cast rehearsed for eight weeks (almost unheard of for a movie) at New York's Minskoff Studios, and then began filming on October 1, 1984, in Broadway's Mark Hellinger Theatre (now the Times Square Church). The sixteen-week shoot was often grueling, but Attenborough made a point of maintaining a humorous and informal atmosphere without sacrificing focus and discipline. Admittedly not a specialist in musicals, he had his own ideas about how the process should go. Though the production mostly followed the time-honored practice of prerecording the vocal tracks to the musical numbers and then having the dancers lip-synch to them on camera, the director felt that, in the case of this particular film, that method worked against the spontaneity he was seeking, so he insisted on having a couple of the songs recorded live during filming. He claimed in the book *Richard Attenborough's Chorus Line*, edited by Diana Carter: "I can honestly say that the final result was eminently worthwhile. . . [and] has resulted, I believe, in a spontaneity of performance and a degree of passion created in front of the camera which would have been impossible in the clinical atmosphere of the recording booth."

The Film

Although the screenplay is admirably faithful to the original dramatis personae, including all seventeen of the same characters who appear on the line in the stage version, a few of them have different last names. Mike Costa becomes Mike Cass and Bebe Benzenheimer becomes simply Bebe Benson—both a little more white-bread than their Italian and Jewish stage counterparts. Judy is now Judy Monroe rather than Judy Turner, and in her introduction she jokes that her real name is Marilyn Monroe; the screenwriters presumably thought—probably correctly—that a 1985 audience would be more familiar with Monroe than with Lana Turner. Kristine's last name for no apparent reason is changed from Urich to Erlich.

The opening number is extended to a lengthy sequence, with shots of the dancers doing routines interspersed with footage of Cassie coming into Manhattan in a cab, greeting her old friend Larry, re-exploring the backstage area and dressing room, and so on, while hoping to talk to Zach. The dance sequences, with a stage full of dozens of dancers, have a propulsive energy, and the gradual winnowing down of a huge group of hopefuls is clearly delineated—though the jazz combination is unrealistically long and complicated for a cattle call. Having seen huge numbers of dancers eliminated, the audience gets perhaps a stronger sense than in the stage version that the sixteen kept onstage are a very select group indeed, having survived to near the end of a very competitive process. With the camera's freedom to roam and zero in on individuals and groups, we get to hear spoken asides and exchanges among various dancers—including a few lines Paul and Diana speak to each other in Spanish, with no subtitles. Many of the lyrics in "I Hope I Get It," sung by the whole group in the stage version, become solo lines for various characters. Some of these are presented as inner thoughts, with the dancer's lips not moving (this technique will be used periodically in place of the blue spotlight that defines "internal" thoughts in the stage version). The brief solo beginning with "I really need this job," sung in the stage show by the soon-to-be-eliminated character of Tricia, is here given to Maggie (Pam Klinger had sung it before, having toured as Tricia before taking over Maggie in the Broadway company).

Unlike the play, which is done on a streamlined black set where mirrors can be made to appear or disappear at will, the film, by virtue of the inherently more literal quality of the medium, is set in a detailed and mostly realistically appointed theatre. It's fully open to the brick wall at the far back (fronted throughout by a shallow semicircle of nine tall mirrors), creating a very deep and spacious playing area that is filled effectively by row upon row of dancers in the opening. Once the sixteen finalists are alone onstage (sixteen rather than seventeen, for Cassie is kept separate for most of the film), they line up in their traditional order; the camera can of course view them from any angle, and sometimes it effectively shows them from behind, backed by long shadows, with the empty house and Zach's desk—set far back in the orchestra section—also visible.

The "Names" sequence is very similar to that in the stage version, and when the dancers start to tell their individual stories, the realistic setting is honored at first: "I Can Do That" is shot in a fairly naturalistic mode (though how Mike and Richie, whom he gets to dance with him at one point, suddenly conveniently have tap shoes on is never explained). Mike's dance solo is extended far longer than in the original—though with some interruptions to show us what is going on with Cassie backstage; during these we can still hear what's happening onstage in the background. (This alternation is continued through much of the film and can make fans of the stage version, trying to listen to their favorite scenes, feel at times like they're missing something.)

After a while, the new Cassie scenes start to become an excuse for cutting certain sections out of the script; if the camera cuts away from a character telling his or her story, much of that story can be omitted. This happens particularly with Connie, who doesn't get the "four foot ten" ditty but only a version of the last few lines of her monologue, about her ability to play younger than her age (here reduced from thirty-two to twenty-three). Kristine also only gets to talk about how she started dancing, watching "variety shows" on TV (the references to Ed Sullivan, which by 1985 were dated, are cut); there's no "Sing!"—and Nicole Fosse actually gets to demonstrate a reasonably secure voice on a solo line in the abbreviated "Hello Twelve." In place of the song, we do get an added bit of monologue from Al, talking directly to Zach about what a reliable hard worker he is, reminding him he's straight (as if anyone needed to hear that, especially after meeting his wife) and claiming that he's "not too talented"—probably the last thing anyone would say at an audition. (It's also questionable whether a dancer—especially a straight one—would have gone through that much of an audition, even in the eighties, with his shirt completely unbuttoned. But we digress.) Reservations about the content aside, however, Al's little monologue does give him a solo moment in the spotlight, something he never quite gets in the stage version.

That spotlight first becomes a literal factor in the previous number, "At the Ballet." Prior to that, the audition had been conducted in realistic work light, but Zach specifically asks a technician to turn on a spot right before he calls on Sheila. This would seem like an awkwardly obvious way of setting up Sheila's well-known complaint about the harshness of the light, which does indeed follow a moment later, but it also opens up the possibility of more stylized lighting in the numbers that follow. Attenborough uses the spot and opens it out for effects that sometimes intentionally warp perspective, focusing in on certain dancers and disconnecting us from the physical reality of the playing area. For example, Sheila, Bebe and Maggie step *forward* to sing in individual spots during "At the Ballet," then appear in wide shot and seem to be on an empty stage—but when they are seen moving back into their places in line at the end of the number, they do so from *upstage*, behind the other dancers, which has an intentionally disorienting effect.

Mark, the youngest auditionee, is so eager that he asks to go next (a nice new touch), and his monologue about his wet dream and his visit to the priest is very similar to the stage version. We hear a very few lines of "Hello Twelve, Hello Thirteen, Hello Love" interspersed with it, presented again as inner thoughts in voice-over. An abbreviated version of Greg's monologue, nicely acted by Justin Ross, is also interwoven with this. But then instead of going into the dynamic Montage sequence, the film brings "Hello Twelve" to a very premature conclusion, following which Richie (Gregg Burge) comes forward to tell Zach all about his first sexual experience via "Surprise, Surprise," a new song written for the movie. The wide-ranging vocal, complete with falsetto, is reminiscent of the Richie of "Gimme the Ball," but "Surprise, Surprise" has quite a different tone, and includes one of the film's most extended dance sequences. This is led off by a very dynamic Burge and includes sections for the whole group as well as solos, duets, and trios that give several of the cast members individual opportunities to strut their considerable stuff as dancers. (When the movie first came out, some criticized it for its hyperactive, rock video–style editing, claiming that the frequent crosscutting detracted from enjoyment of the dance performances. In subsequent years, though, musical films directed by the likes of Baz Luhrmann and Rob Marshall have gone so much further in that direction that the camera work in *A Chorus Line* now seems almost sedate, and certainly straightforward, in comparison.)

Without the Montage, there's no "Lola Latores" sequence for Don. That character gets a monologue, but it's completely original to the film, a spoken sequence that has him sputtering disjointedly about trying to juggle a career with marriage and a day job as a waiter. Delivering it partly to Zach but largely to his colleagues onstage, actor Blane Savage struggles valiantly to make it sound natural. Diana Morales's "Nothing," about her experience at the High School of Performing Arts, though little changed from the original, is also delivered partly to the other dancers (including Connie, who says she remembers Diana from the school). This makes for quite a different effect from the stage version, in which it's one of the only numbers where a character is completely alone onstage.

Judy (the very impressive-looking, long-limbed Janet Jones) is left with only a couple of lines of her original monologue, including a version of the bit about shaving her sister's head. Val (Audrey Landers), on the other hand, gets to do most of her original monologue and song with minimal changes, though the banter with Sheila over relative bust size is cut. For some reason the reactions of the other characters here, mostly indulgent laughs, seem artificial and clumsily spliced in.

When Cassie finally takes the stage, now dressed in a purple leotard, and demands her chance to audition, we come to one of the most controversial creative decisions the team made: the replacement of the iconic "The Music and the Mirror" with the new song "Let Me Dance for You." This number, written by the original songwriting team of Hamlisch and Kleban especially for the film, contains substantial lyrical and musical echoes of the original, but whereas "The Music and the Mirror" begins in a gentle, introspective mode and gradually builds to a powerful climax, "Let Me Dance for You" is simpler and punchier: the film Cassie, having been kept off the stage by Zach for close to an hour, seizes her moment and cuts straight to the chase. This Cassie can barely contain the impulse to move, with sudden bursts of dance sprinkled in between the lyrics; when she finally takes off, she flies across the stage with abandon—plenty of high kicks and deep backbends. Alyson Reed is a powerhouse, and one longs to see her do the full original number (which she had done on tour six years earlier)—or at least watch her burn up the stage in this one rather than constantly cutting away to cheesy, self-conscious flashbacks showing her in dance studios with a younger Zach. (There's one section that she does barefoot, in a chiton, as if channeling Ruth St. Denis or Isadora

Duncan.) Finally we return to the stage and the present for her big finish, ending with a furiously belted reprise of the melody (in a movie, you never have to run out of breath. . .), which Zach angrily cuts off. But he does relent and tells her to join the others downstairs to learn a song.

The Paul scene is tenderly performed by Cameron English. He is placed on a plank spanning the orchestra pit, which effectively if a bit obviously underlines the precariousness of the character's situation and the risk he feels in finally opening up. But the famous speech is drastically condensed, and the emphasis on Zach's questions makes it seem more like a scene and less like a monologue. Though the piece as always ends with "take care of my son," there are a couple of new lines added just before that about the difficulty both of Paul's parents were having even looking at him; this makes his father's acceptance of him feel more like a way of saying good-bye, expressing love but also regret over a perhaps unbridgeable gulf that has suddenly opened between them. This bleaker version misses the point of Nick Dante's original story, where Paul was moved by his parents having accepted him before he was ready to accept himself.

The "One" rehearsal sequence follows; it begins realistically but then starts to go surreal with the addition of harsh spots and footlights. Reed effectively demonstrates the difference between ensemble and star dancing while trying to take direction from Zach. After he pulls her out of the line, they jump immediately to the "is this what you want/they're all special" dialogue, which in the stage version doesn't come till the end of their long argument. Then they backtrack and go through a heavily rewritten version of the confrontation, which adds a bit more detail to their backstory and a telling explanation of why Cassie moved out.

In the most jarring departure from the original script, Cassie then almost immediately launches into "What I Did for Love"—which is actually performed simultaneously with "The Tap Combination," the number in the film that looks most like the original choreography. Cassie belts the song while climbing the upstage stairway up to—what, a catwalk? Her mouth is moving, but it seems like it's meant as an internal monologue, certainly not something Zach or the other dancers are supposed to be hearing. The filmmakers have been widely criticized for diminishing the song, originally a paean to the dancer's commitment to art and work, by repurposing it as a ballad about Cassie and Zach's romantic relationship. (One could say that Marvin Hamlisch had it coming, as retribution for purposely conceiving the number in generic enough terms that it could be interpreted out of context as a love song—and become a hit in the process.) However, a close reviewing of the scene in the film reveals that to be an oversimplification. The staging may be ineffective, but Reed, a resourceful actress, manages to find some interesting ambivalence in the song, implying that there may indeed be some regret involved (never an option when Diana sings it); she is also very aware of the other characters tap dancing below her, and there are moments when it's clear she's not singing just about Zach.

Paul's accident follows, much like in the stage play, but Zach's instantaneous calling out of the doctor's phone number feels unrealistic—and Cassie seems to get back down all those stairs with preternatural speed. Paul is helped to a cab, and the scene between Zach and the dancers that follows is one of the film's most interesting moments. There's a fragile, hushed dramatic tension that the long "Alternatives" scene in the play, with the dancers chattering over an often jaunty instrumental underscoring, doesn't attempt. It's one of the quietest moments in the film, with Zach connecting on a more sympathetic level with the dancers—a few of whom, especially Sheila and Bebe, unexpectedly come out with new and highly personal revelations. Yet somehow the original point of the scene—the brevity of a dancer's career and the fear and uncertainty about what comes next—never quite comes into focus.

The eliminations scene, with lots of close-ups, is poignantly sustained despite some unsubtle, schmaltzy musical underscoring. The question of why Zach announces his decisions in a way that makes the eliminated dancers think at first that they are the ones chosen has always been a bit of a puzzle. Onstage, it's joltingly effective the first time you see the show, and it does underscore the cruel randomness of the game, as the first list of dancers named seems almost as reasonable a choice of cast as the ones who are actually selected. But it's hard to keep from wondering whether Zach does it that way on purpose, and if so what reason there could possibly be behind this final moment of emotional manipulation. In the film, where we can see Zach's face, the question seems even more salient, yet still remains unanswered. Seven of the eight characters who get the job are the same as in the stage version; the exception is Judy, who in the film loses her spot to Bebe. The camera reveals subtle touches in the characters' individual reactions to being eliminated or chosen, including a lovely unexpected moment where the disappointed Sheila makes a point of throwing Cassie a brief parting gesture of congratulations.

Due to the way the screenplay keeps Cassie separate from the dancers onstage for the majority of the film, she is never seen in her traditional position between Greg and Sheila on the line. When she finally does join the group at the very end to wait for Zach's choices, she stands on the stage right end next to Don. This enables hers to be the last face seen when the camera takes a long pan shot down the line, focusing in close-up on the relieved and elated faces of each of the dancers who have been chosen. There is also a bit of added dialogue at the very end, after the others leave, between Zach and Cassie, lightly hinting that perhaps their romantic relationship will be rekindled now that they will be working together again. This is the type of thing that used to be known as a "Hollywood ending" and really has nothing to do with *A Chorus Line*; the choice to focus so much attention on the history and relationship between the two characters (with its attendant implication that an audience needs to have a love interest in every story) was one of the most controversial decisions made by Attenborough and Schulman in adapting the material for the screen, and arguably the most damaging. And despite all the extra time spent on their relationship, we don't really learn much about Zach and Cassie that we didn't know in the stage version.

The "One" finale is performed in costumes similar to what was worn on stage, but done in a glitzier, reflective gold fabric. (Theoni V. Aldredge was asked for permission to use her original finale costumes but declined since she wasn't invited to design the whole movie.) Though some of the dance moves echo Bennett's originals, the choreographic style Hornaday adopts for this number is in many

This shot of the dancers in finale costumes shows the eight characters who get the job at the end of the film.   *Embassy Films/PolyGram Pictures*

ways more of an homage to Bob Fosse, complete with dramatic lighting angles and attitude-heavy Brechtian poses that recall *Cabaret* and *Chicago*. Several of the dancers get opportunities to show off specialty moves, which at first seems like a contradiction of the intention of the number, conceived as it was to demonstrate how individual personalities are subsumed into the mechanical precision of a true chorus line. But Rockettes-style unison soon takes over, and the stage gradually fills with row upon row of additional dancers (the same ones who were in the opening) doubling, tripling, and quadrupling the cast. (This may have been an intentional nod to the legendary performance in September 1983 when Bennett restaged the show to celebrate its record-breaking performance on Broadway with a cast of over three hundred present and former cast members—all of whom appeared in the finale.) The camera pulls slowly back from the shrinking image of hundreds of dancers kicking in perfect unison as the credits start to roll.

Is It Dated?

The question of dating comes up frequently when discussing *A Chorus Line* today. Though a brief attempt had been made to update cultural references (and a few costumes) in the stage version during the early eighties, by 1985 the Broadway production had been defined as a period piece, and the program notes informed audiences it was set in "a Broadway theatre" in "1975." When it came to the film, however, an all-new script made it much easier to update or delete any out-of-date references. In watching the film today, the throat catches almost at the very beginning when Cassie's cab is seen coming into the city—with a beautiful shot of the World Trade Center in the background. She later looks out the window of the theatre and sees a marquee across the street advertising *Hurlyburly*, which opened on Broadway in 1984. (The play is by David Rabe, who was Joe Papp's favorite playwright, but the coincidence may not have been intentional.) There aren't as many direct cultural references as there are in the play, mainly because most of those come in the "Hello Twelve, Hello Thirteen, Hello Love" number, which in the film is almost completely omitted. But the sleek, elegant lines of the original leotards have mostly been replaced (by costume designer Faye Poliakin) with brightly colored sweats, legwarmers, midriff-revealing tops, and an assortment of motley mix-and-match garments that suggest working Broadway gypsies less than they recall MTV and movies like *Flashdance*. Hornaday indeed choreographed that film, and his dances for *A Chorus Line*, if invigorating, are full of the kind of flashy display and sexy gyrations audiences were used to seeing in rock videos. The drum-and-synthesizer-heavy new arrangements of most of the songs complete the eighties bubblegum-pop picture. Paradoxically, the film now feels more dated than the show, whose costumes and arrangements, though of a vintage a decade older, have a sort of classic Broadway simplicity that has aged surprisingly well. Faithful revivals of the musical in the original designs don't scream "seventies" as loudly as the film screams "eighties."

The Critical Reception

The reviews that greeted the film on its initial release were largely disappointing (though by no means unanimously so). Even sympathetic reviewers addressed the seeming impossibility of translating the theatrical immediacy of the show, in which the audience almost feels like participants, to the medium of film.

The famously caustic Rex Reed, a devoted fan of the stage version, opined in *The New York Post*: "Songs have been cut for no reason. New routines have been added (also for no reason). The obnoxious 'opening up' process every play goes through on its way to the screen robs the chorus line of necessary dramatic presence by taking the audience on an unnecessary tour of the backstage dressing rooms and even the street outside the theater. . . If you are among the legions of *Chorus Line* fans, you can't escape the fact that this is a sorry disappointment, a well-intentioned but poor substitute for the real thing, a stand-in for a star."

David Denby, writing in *New York* magazine, admitted his preference for film over theatre, but wrote his review after having recently revisited the Broadway production. He pinned the movie's shortcomings on a failure to replicate Michael Bennett's dynamic choreography and ever-changing orchestration of grouped bodies and stage space, which he felt was what made the original riveting. He also wrote: "The screenwriter, Arnold Schulman, won't settle for the myriad tales of woe included in the original Kirkwood-Dante book. He adds a few of his own: Little Bebe (Michelle Johnston) comes tapping directly from her hospital bed, where she was confined after a nervous breakdown. Everyone suffers—the chorus line has become the wailing wall. . . . I enjoyed Alyson Reed's resigned, gutsy Cassie, and among the others, Gregg Burge, as Richie, brings a charge to his big number, while Charles McGowan, as Mike, looks to be an inventive comic dancer. The movie has its moments, but that's all."

Charles McGowan as Mike dances "I Can Do That.
Embassy Films/PolyGram Pictures

In the *New York Daily News*, Kathleen Carroll was more positive. Though she felt Attenborough wasn't the ideal director for the material, saying "One suspects that only [Bob] Fosse could have injected the movie with the stinging honesty and aggressive energy which made the show a legend," she found the film "extremely well cast. Alyson Reed is still too much the blushing ingénue to be able to match the mature elegance of Donna McKechnie, the original Cassie, but she has a Claudette Colbert radiance that makes you warm up to her. . . . Vicki Frederick is tartly funny as Sheila, the dancer who's bitterly aware she's past her prime. Cameron English makes Paul's painful confession of his father's reaction to his homosexuality a terribly touching scene."

Clive Barnes, who had long been a major champion of the stage version, which he wrote about several times in the *Times*, was writing for the *New York Post* by the time the film came out: he championed it too, even though he had read the first round of negative reviews before seeing the movie as a "second nighter." He said it was "pretty much infinitely better than the disaster I had been led to expect. . . . Believe me, on any count the film is nothing like so bad as most critics and word-of-mouthers, in this riotous bout of overreaction and perhaps over-expectation have painted it. . . . The performances—including the generally maligned Douglas—are terrific, and the movie is not merely wonderfully entertaining, it is, quite specifically and unexpectedly, entertaining in the grand tradition of the Hollywood musical. . . . I liked all of it, and loved some of it. It is the best dance film, and, for that matter, the best movie musical for years."

Beloved critic Roger Ebert was also quite positive, saying: "The result may not please purists who want a film record of what they saw on stage, but this is one of the most intelligent and compelling movie musicals in a long time—and the most grown up, since it isn't limited, as so many contemporary musicals are, to the celebration of the survival qualities of geriatric actresses." He did, however, confuse the characters of Cassie and Sheila, crediting Vicki Frederick with Alyson Reed's performance—an embarrassing error that was not corrected even when the review was reprinted in an anthology or years later on rogerebert.com.

The Red Carpet

The world premiere was an exciting event for the young dancers, most of whom had never before had featured roles in a major film. It was held at Radio City Music Hall, with the movie starting at 11:00 p.m. in order to accommodate Broadway schedules; the producers had invited the chorus dancers from every musical then playing on Broadway to attend as guests, along with the original cast of *A Chorus Line*. Though the general public was charged $500 for tickets to the event (a benefit), each of the film's cast members was given two complimentary seats for guests; Michael Blevins invited his parents. He recalls his excitement on realizing that Liza Minnelli (a longtime fan of the musical) was sitting behind him. Choreographer Jeffrey Hornaday was encouraged by the audience response that night; he told Bob Thomas of the *Gainesville Sun*, "I expected a reserved audience, because New Yorkers are that way. But they responded with cheers and applause. It was like a crowd at a football game!" The postscreening party was at the Waldorf Astoria Hotel.

One group that did not share in the enthusiasm was the original Broadway cast of the show. Priscilla Lopez told *Entertainment Tonight* that she thought "the dancing was hot," but that she disagreed with many of the decisions the film's creative team had made. As quoted in *On the Line*, Wayne Cilento said, "I thought the opening was pretty amazing, the auditioning. But by the time they had Mike swinging on ropes and rafters, I thought, 'Oh God, they lost it.' They were just doing things for effect. We were all auditioning for our lives. I don't think you ever felt that emotion in the movie." Kelly Bishop, who had created the role of the pushing-thirty Sheila, was quoted on Wikipedia: "It was appalling when director Richard Attenborough went on a talk show and said 'this is a story about kids trying to break into show business.' I almost tossed my TV out the window; I mean what an *idiot!* It's about veteran dancers looking for one last job before it's too late for them to dance anymore. No wonder the film sucked!" (An actor playing Mark or Bebe, both Broadway newcomers, might have been more inclined to agree with Attenborough, but the show covers a broad range of dancers' experiences.)

The gala event was shortly followed by the Los Angeles premiere, and another in Atlanta, both of which were attended by many of the cast members. The Royal Premiere in London was especially exciting, as the cast was invited to dinner with members of the Royal Family; Matt West (Bobby) later recalled waltzing with Princess Margaret. More festive openings followed in Germany and Japan; ultimately, the film was better received by critics and audiences overseas than in America.

The Future

Fans of the show often wonder if there will ever be another attempt at filming *A Chorus Line*. Such a thing would not be unheard of, especially if it were a made-for-TV version. Television productions of hit Broadway musicals were regular occurrences in the 1960s, and the vogue for TV retreads has surprisingly resurfaced in recent years, beginning with the lavish TV production of *Gypsy* starring Bette

Cover design of the DVD edition of the film.

Midler (1993), followed by full-length TV movies of such classics as *Bye Bye Birdie, Once Upon a Mattress, Annie, The Music Man,* and *South Pacific*—with widely varying degrees of success. An interesting new development came in 2013 with the live telecast of *The Sound of Music,* the great ratings for which led to the announcement of an annual series, with a new, live *Peter Pan* as the second installment. Given that the challenge of translating the unique theatrical energy of *A Chorus Line* to the screen has long been seen as a vexing conundrum, one might think a live TV treatment could be a way to preserve that elusive sense of immediacy—but the producers of the new live musicals seem focused on particularly family-friendly properties, and *ACL* has never been a children's show.

Though the movie of *A Chorus Line* was made during a twenty-five-year period when theatrical film versions of Broadway musicals were exceedingly rare, the vogue for them returned with a vengeance following Rob Marshall's phenomenally successful movie of *Chicago* (2002). After that film won the Academy Award for Best Picture, studios rushed to film the backlog of Broadway hits that had accumulated during the drought, resulting in big-budget theatrical releases of *The Phantom of the Opera, RENT, Dreamgirls, Sweeney Todd, The Producers, Hairspray, Les Misérables,* and *Into the Woods,* among others. A second cinematic version of a Broadway show that has already been filmed once for the big screen would be almost unheard of: The 1951 version of *Show Boat,* previously filmed in 1936, was the last example for over sixty years (unless you insist on counting the cartoon of *The King and I*). But the multiethnic 2014 update of *Annie,* previously filmed in 1982, and the long-discussed potential remake of *Gypsy* with Barbra Streisand (as of this writing still the subject of gossip and speculation) may have opened the door to further such projects.

Given *A Chorus Line*'s unique place in the history of American musicals, it's tempting to think a new film or video version will be attempted at some point. But until and unless that happens, fans will have to content themselves with the pleasures (guilty or otherwise) of the 1985 version, the extensive clips of stage productions on YouTube, and, of course, looking forward to their next chance to see the show live onstage—which after all is where *A Chorus Line,* itself a celebration of the unique excitement of live theatre, will always belong.

20

"Then I Could Be a Movie Star"

The Cast of the Movie

Over three thousand performers auditioned for the movie of *A Chorus Line*; the group chosen was a diverse collection of highly trained dancers, including several Broadway gypsies and others who came from film and TV backgrounds in California. Here is a rundown of who they were and what they have done since.

Blane Savage (Don)

Savage came to the film from the Broadway world, having appeared in the original cast of Bob Fosse's *Dancin'*. He also had a few prior film credits, including *New York, New York* and *Can't Stop the Music*, and had appeared in regional theatre and as a guest on various TV series. Later film credits included *Naked Gun 33⅓: The Final Insult*. Fourteen years after the filming of *A Chorus Line* he returned to the show, playing Zach in a 1999 stage production at the Sacramento Music Circus; he played the part again in 2001 at the Walnut Street Theatre in Philadelphia.

Pam Klinger (Maggie)

The beautiful actress was cast in the film based largely on having impressed Attenborough as Maggie the first time he saw the show on Broadway. A graduate of Point Park College, she had already been in *A Chorus Line* for years at that point, having started out as an understudy in the International Company. While making the film, she began a romance with Charles McGowan, who stood next to her on line in the role of Mike; after filming, she returned to the New York cast of *ACL* as Maggie, and for a while McGowan joined her in the Broadway company (though not swinging on a rope as he had in the movie). Klinger considered herself mainly a singer, but had a long career as a Broadway dancer; her post-*ACL* career included originating the role of Mrs. Simpson in *The Who's Tommy* and a long run as Babette in Disney's *Beauty and the Beast*. Her sister, Cindi Klinger, was also a Broadway dancer; she had played Bombalurina in the national company of *Cats* and later joined Pam in *ACL* on Broadway, first as an understudy for several roles and then taking over the part of Judy. Cindi also played Pam's role in *Tommy* in the national tour of that show.

Charles McGowan (Mike)

An accomplished musician as well as a dynamic dancer, McGowan had substantial television and regional theatre credits when he was cast in the movie, as well as appearances in the films *Grease II* and *Annie*. He was born without a pubic bone, among other handicaps, and didn't start walking till age four; his adoptive mother started him in dance classes to strengthen his lower body. This background makes his exciting, highly athletic dancing in the film all the more extraordinary. McGowan had auditioned unsuccessfully for the stage version of *A Chorus Line* several times before getting the movie, but he went into the Broadway cast shortly after completing the film, learning the original Bennett choreography and playing Mike briefly alongside his then-girlfriend, Pam Klinger. He appeared in later films including *Death Becomes Her* and *Beaches*, but his health issues persisted, and he passed away in September 2013, at the age of fifty-three.

Jan Gan Boyd (Connie)

Jan Gan grew up in Fremont, California, and was put into dance class early by her mother, who thought she was awkward and hoped that the classes would make her less clumsy. Her father was a dentist and wanted her to go into science, feeling that dance would not make a satisfactory career; he changed his mind when she got a good job touring with Yul Brynner in a revival of *The King and I*. She had regional theatre credits and a role in the film *Gimme an F* under her belt when she was cast in *A Chorus Line*. Jan took a weekend off from rehearsals for the film to marry veterinary student John Boyd. Her later film credits were *Assassination* and *Steele Justice*, both released in 1987.

Justin Ross (Greg)

Ross was one of the most experienced gypsies hired for the movie, having appeared on Broadway in *Pippin* and *The Magic Show* before becoming the first Broadway replacement Greg in April 1976, almost ten years before the release of the film. He stayed in the stage production for over two years then, and returned to it in the mid-eighties, which is when Attenborough saw him play the role. He was to return to the Broadway cast one more time after doing the film, and as he told Gary Stevens: "It wasn't until I went back into the show for a two-week stint before it closed that I was the right age to play Gregory Gardner. And it wasn't until that time that I truly understood who Gregory is, and could honestly say, 'Just get me through the day.'" A graduate of the High School of Performing Arts, Ross now lives in Los Angeles and has stayed active in the industry as a writer and director. He directed and choreographed the hit Off-Broadway show *I Could Go on Lip-Synching!*, was a founding member of the Lincoln Center Directors Lab, and has taught choreography at New York University.

Alyson Reed as Cassie in the film.   *Embassy Films/PolyGram Pictures*

Alyson Reed (Cassie)

One of the few cast members to have appeared in the show onstage, Reed had toured as both Cassie and Val before being chosen to play Cassie in the movie. Her first audition for the film was for Val, and Attenborough noted qualities he felt made her more right for Cassie; he reportedly went to bat for her quite force-fully over the objections of others on the production team, even to the point of threatening to leave the project if she were not cast. She had played leads in several musicals in regional theatre as well as filming a (cut) ballet number for the Blake Edwards film *10* as a dance double for Bo Derek. Most notably, she played Marilyn Monroe in the short-lived Broadway musical *Marilyn* (years before the TV series *Smash* postulated another musical on the subject). Getting the role of Cassie in the movie seemed like the break of a lifetime, but Reed felt the film's poor reception seriously damaged her career and made it hard for her even to get an audition for some time afterwards. She did make a triumphant return to Broadway in 1987, starring as Sally Bowles in the first revival of *Cabaret*; she worked with the show's original director, Harold Prince, and costar Joel Grey, recreating his legendary performance as the Emcee. She later appeared on Broadway in the Rodgers and Hammerstein revue *A Grand Night for Singing* and starred in a Pasadena Playhouse revival of the Richard Rodgers/Stephen Sondheim musical *Do I Hear a Waltz?*; cast albums of both productions were released. In recent years, she has amassed a large number of guest appearance credits on popular TV series, as well as recurring roles on *Desperate Housewives*, *Party of Five*, and others. Her most visible recent role has been as Mrs. Darbus, the haughty drama teacher, in Disney's *High School Musical* series of movies. A teacher in reality as well, Reed has an active career teaching acting and musical theatre classes and workshops around the country.

Vicki Frederick (Sheila)

Frederick was the only performer to be cast in the film after playing a different role in the Broadway production; she had been the third Cassie in New York, following Donna McKechnie and Ann Reinking. For more on her career, see the chapter on the Broadway Cassies (Chapter 17).

Matt West (Bobby)

West was the other cast member who was recreating a role he had played on Broadway; Attenborough saw him play Bobby at the Shubert in 1984, and he had previously played Don and Mark on tour. He returned to the show in 1989 (four years after completing the film), playing Bobby again on a tour directed by Baayork Lee and starring Donna McKechnie. Other credits as a performer included Uncle Willie in *High Button Shoes*, Barnaby Tucker in *Hello, Dolly!*, and Sasha in *Fiddler on the Roof*; television and club work found him dancing with the likes of Tim Conway, Ann-Margret, Liza Minnelli, Bernadette Peters, and Red Skelton. West worked with Alyson Reed when they were both thirteen years old and dancing at Disneyland; his affiliation with the Disney organization continued on and off for many years and culminated in his choreographing the Broadway and London productions of *Beauty and the Beast*. The role of the Beast was originated on Broadway by Terrence Mann, who had played Larry in the *Chorus Line* movie. West's progression from performing to choreography mirrored that of the original Bobby, Thommie Walsh; his other credits as a choreographer include the Elton John musical *Lestat*, a Broadway adaptation of Anne Rice's novel *The Vampire Lestat*. In addition to choreographing that show, West was one of its producers.

Michelle Johnston (Bebe)

Johnston had previously danced in the films *Staying Alive* (the sequel to *Saturday Night Fever*) and *One from the Heart*. Feeling like a misfit and an ugly duckling as a child, she found, like Bebe, that ballet could be an escape, but her dance teacher's insistence on an extremely low body weight led to a bulimia problem that returned to plague her briefly during the filming of *A Chorus Line*. The film's choreographer, Jeffrey Hornaday, was extremely impressed with her as a dancer and made her his assistant on the film; in subsequent years, she went on to assist him on numerous other productions including rock videos and projects for Madonna and Michael Jackson. Hornaday also hired her to choreograph the John Travolta film *Shout*, which he directed. Her later acting appearances included the movies *California Casanova* and *Showgirls*.

Janet Jones (Judy)

A former competition dancer, Jones had won the "Miss Dance of America" title as a teenager. By the time she was cast in *A Chorus Line*, she had established a film career, dancing in the 1982 screen version of the musical *Annie* and playing a major role in *The Flamingo Kid* with Matt Dillon; other screen appearances had included *Staying Alive* and *One from the Heart*, in both of which she had worked with Michelle Johnston, who stood next to her on line in the film as Bebe. Subsequent films have included *American Anthem* and *A League of Their Own*, and she has guested on various TV series. Her visibility increased with her marriage to Canadian hockey superstar Wayne Gretzky; the couple has now been married for twenty-five years and has five children.

Gregg Burge (Richie)

Burge started dancing very early and was a phenomenally successful child actor in commercials. After attending the High School of Performing Arts, he won a scholarship to Juilliard. He made his Broadway debut in *The Wiz* at a young age, ultimately taking over the role of the Scarecrow. Other Broadway credits included *Sophisticated Ladies*, the revival of *Oh, Kay!*, and Andrew Lloyd Webber's *Song and Dance*, on which he was also credited as associate tap choreographer. He twice won the Fred Astaire Award, presented annually to the outstanding male and female dancers on Broadway. While filming *A Chorus Line*, he did double-duty, assisting choreographer Hornaday along with his performing responsibilities. Like Chuck McGowan, he went into the Broadway cast of *ACL* only after having completed the film. Widely believed to have been suffering from AIDS, Gregg Burge died of a brain tumor in 1998, aged forty.

Gregg Burge as Richie performs "Surprise, Surprise," a song added for the movie. *Embassy Films/PolyGram Pictures*

Tony Fields (Al)

Fields had performed from 1980 to 1984 as one of the dance ensemble on *Solid Gold*, a popular if kitschy TV series where spandex-clad dancers gyrated to Top 10 hits. He also had experience dancing in rock videos, including Michael Jackson's "Beat It" and "Thriller." Fields had done a substantial amount of musical theatre regionally and appeared in the films *Protocol* and *Night Shift.* The year after *A Chorus Line* was released, he starred in the horror movie *Trick or Treat*; later stage credits included portraying Oberon in Shakespeare's *A Midsummer Night's Dream* at South Coast Rep in Costa Mesa, California. Fields died of AIDS-related cancer in 1995, aged thirty-six.

Nicole Fosse (Kristine)

Fosse could be considered Broadway royalty, being the daughter of two legendary figures in musical theatre history: Bob Fosse and Gwen Verdon. As a youngster, Nicole studied dance extensively and apprenticed with the Cleveland Ballet. She filmed a cameo role in her father's semiautobiographical film *All That Jazz* and a guest role on the 1980s TV series *Miami Vice.* Though she said she enjoyed making the film of *A Chorus Line*, she was at the time undecided as to whether she wanted to pursue a performing career; as it happened, her appearance in the original ballet chorus of Broadway's *The Phantom of the Opera* in 1988 turned out to be her last high-profile credit as a dancer or actress. She married Andy Greiner, and they had three children before he was killed by a drunk driver in Salt Lake City in 2000. Nicole has taught dance and been involved with projects to preserve her father's legacy, including assisting with the creation of the Broadway revue *Fosse* in 1999, though her official program credit on that show is simply a "Special Thanks." She has also served as an advisor on preparations for a Broadway revival of Fosse's *Dancin'*, originally planned for 2009, but, after repeated postponements, that project has yet to come to fruition. Fosse serves on the advisory board for the Group Theatre Too, a small New York production company founded by castmate Michael Blevins, who played Mark in the movie.

Audrey Landers (Val)

Widely known to television audiences for her role as Afton Cooper on the prime-time soap opera *Dallas*, from which she took a leave of absence to film *A Chorus Line*, Landers was the highest-profile actor cast in the movie after Michael Douglas. She was also the only member of "the line" who was not a highly accomplished dancer, and accepted the role with the condition that she could ask for a dance double if needed. She reportedly worked extremely hard with Hornaday to master the choreography and ended up doing her own dancing in the film. She began her career performing in musicals in community theatres, and by twelve was writing her own songs; she performed on daytime soaps during her teen years, appearing on *The Secret Storm, Search for Tomorrow, Somerset*, and later on *One Life to Live.* Her sister Judy is also an actress, and they have frequently performed together. Their family background is somewhat conservative, and Audrey ironically reports having been offended by Val's number, "Dance: Ten; Looks: Three" when as a child she was first taken by her mother, Ruth, to see *A Chorus Line* onstage. Audrey's recording career got a boost from her appearance in the movie, and she released several albums that became big hits in Europe. She has continued to act regularly in film and TV projects, including a reprise of her original role in the 2013 network return of *Dallas*. In addition, she and Ruth have started a successful fashion line, the Landers STAR Collection.

Michael Blevins (Mark)

Though Blevins played the youngest character in *A Chorus Line* (Mark's age was changed from twenty to seventeen for the screen version), he already had three Broadway shows to his credit: *The Tap Dance Kid*, *Bring Back Birdie*, and the 1982 revival of *Little Me*. *A Chorus Line* was made before the famous cleaning up (and Disneyfication) of the New York Theatre District, and Blevins was mugged one night after leaving the Hellinger during the filming, though thankfully not seriously injured. He recently said of the film that he "felt lucky to be part of it, just to be associated with all the other great actors and dancers who were in the movie; I just thought that was special." His only subsequent major film acting credit was in *Chaplin* with Robert Downey Jr., but he has stayed active in the New York theatre

Michael Blevins as Mark. Behind him are Nicole Fosse (Kristine), Audrey Landers (Val), Cameron English (Paul), and Yamil Borges (Diana).   *Embassy Films/PolyGram Pictures*

as an actor and director, often with a company called Group Theatre Too, which he cofounded with Justin Boccitto in 2003. He has choreographed numerous plays and musicals for New York and regional venues—most notably the Manhattan Theatre Club production of Caryl Churchill's *Mad Forest*. The multitalented Blevins is also a playwright with several published children's plays to his credit, as well as a musical called *Count to Ten* that he wrote, directed, choreographed, and performed in as part of the New York Musical Theatre Festival in 2009. He currently directs and teaches for the Young Performers Workshop at Centenary Stage, a regional theatre in New Jersey, and has staged several youth productions of *A Chorus Line*.

Cameron English (Paul)

Attenborough felt English was a natural for the role of Paul and therefore cast him in one of the most demanding roles in the movie, even though, like Sammy Williams who originated the role, he had little or no acting experience. His highest-profile job as a dancer had been as a regular member of the dance ensemble on the TV series version of *Fame*, a highly accomplished group who performed large production numbers nearly every week on the show. After *A Chorus Line*, he continued to work as a dancer into the 1990s; his only other credit in a major film was dancing in the comedy *Death Becomes Her* (1992) with Meryl Streep and Bruce Willis, though he was also hired as a dancer (uncredited) on the Coen brothers' film *Barton Fink*, released the previous year. English later went back to school, earning a degree in physical therapy from the State University of New York Downstate. He now lives in California, where he works for Precision Orthopedics in Corral de Tierra and does pro bono therapy work for the Smuin Ballet in Carmel.

Yamil Borges (Diana)

Though Borges never did *A Chorus Line* onstage, the character of Diana Morales parallels her life almost as closely as it did that of Priscilla Lopez. Borges was born in Puerto Rico and, like Morales, grew up in the Bronx and attended the High School of Performing Arts. After graduation, her stepfather (one of two) insisted that she go to college; instead, she left home on her own to pursue her dancing dreams in New York. She struggled financially until she got a job performing at a nightclub called Club Ibis, and eventually made her Broadway debut as Rosalia in Jerome Robbins's 1980 revival of *West Side Story*. Post-*ACL* credits include the Broadway musical *Roza*, which ran twelve performances in 1987, and the films *The Luckiest Man in the World* and *Four Senses*. With her dancing years behind her, Borges moved to Berlin, where she has pursued a successful career as a jazz vocalist.

Michael Douglas (Zach)

Although Attenborough and the producers had expressed an intention to hire all unknowns for the film, in keeping with the musical's themes, they ultimately settled on an established star, Michael Douglas, to play the role of the director/choreographer. Since Zach is supposed to be famous, there was a consensus that this was the one role that could justifiably be cast with a celebrity. The son of movie star Kirk Douglas, Michael had been born famous, but had earned recognition on his own terms early on through acting successes (including the hit television series *The Streets of San Francisco*) as well as high-quality forays into film producing, most notably the Oscar-winning *One Flew Over the Cuckoo's Nest*. His endeavors as a producer may have helped him identify with the character of Zach; in the years preceding *A Chorus Line*, he had produced two of his own most successful acting vehicles, *The China Syndrome* and *Romancing the Stone*. After the release of the *Chorus Line* movie, he went on to even more highly respected film performances, such as *Fatal Attraction*, *Wall Street*, *Basic Instinct*, *The War of the Roses*, and *Wonder Boys*. If musical theatre played no part in his career after he played Zach, it came back into his life following his marriage in 2000 to the Welsh actress Catherine Zeta-Jones, who had been a dancer in musicals in London prior to her movie stardom, and more recently has appeared in the film version of the musical *Chicago* (winning an Oscar) as well as a Broadway revival of *A Little Night Music* (winning a Tony Award). Publicity surrounding Douglas in recent years has often focused on their sometimes tempestuous relationship as well as his battle with cancer; he fought off a Stage IV diagnosis successfully enough to recover his acting career. Recent successes include *Wall Street: Money Never Sleeps* (a 2010 sequel to his 1987 classic), and the 2013 television film *Behind the Candelabra*, in which he gave a highly acclaimed performance as Liberace. Douglas is also known as a political activist who has campaigned tirelessly for disarmament and other antiwar causes.

Terrence Mann (Larry)

Mann earned a degree in acting from the prestigious North Carolina School of the Arts, which led to several classical leads at the North Carolina Shakespeare Festival early in his career. He played the Ringmaster in the Broadway production of *Barnum*, later moving up to the title role in the national company of that musical, and was the original Rum Tum Tugger in the Broadway cast of Andrew Lloyd Webber's *Cats*. In that show and the later *Jerome Robbins' Broadway*, he performed alongside dancer Charlotte d'Amboise, whom he married in 1996. Two years after completing the movie of *A Chorus Line*, Mann played his most iconic role, Inspector Javert in the original Broadway company of *Les Misérables* (1987); he reprised that role for a return engagement before the production closed in 2003. Later Broadway roles included the Beast in Disney's *Beauty and the Beast*, choreographed by Matt West, who played Bobby in the movie. Mann also has numerous film credits, including the *Critters* movies. *A Chorus Line* came back into his life in 2006, when d'Amboise was cast as Cassie in the Broadway revival. In 2008, he directed a production of the show for the Wake Forest School District in North Carolina; d'Amboise, who had recently finished her run in the show on Broadway, assisted him and helped to teach the choreography to the teenage cast. Now a distinguished professor of musical theatre at Western Carolina University (where d'Amboise directed another student production of *ACL*), Mann continues to have a thriving stage career. In 2013 he opened as Charlemagne, with d'Amboise playing his wife, Fastrada, in the American Repertory Theatre revival of the musical *Pippin*; they moved with the show to Broadway, where Mann was nominated for a Tony Award and the production won the Tony for Best Revival of a Musical.

21

"Starting Over"

The Broadway Revival

Because *A Chorus Line* is one of the most beloved of all musicals, it's not surprising that fans started hoping for a Broadway revival only a couple of years after the original production had closed. Of course, that would have been too soon. But by the year 2001, producers had started calling John Breglio to inquire about availability of the rights.

Breglio had been Michael Bennett's lawyer and one of his closest friends. He was also the sole executor of his estate and thus had control of the property. For several years he declined all requests, feeling the time was not right, but by 2004 he had begun considering how best to approach the show's inevitable return to Broadway. It was important to him that it be done right, so ultimately he decided to produce the revival himself; though he had never produced a show before, he was an expert on the business, having been involved as legal counsel and support on numerous plays and musicals both on and Off Broadway. And so it's with him that we begin the story of the Broadway revival.

John Breglio (Producer)

Breglio was born in 1946 and spent his early years in Astoria, Queens, and Garden City, Long Island. He first discovered theatre at the age of ten when his parents took him to see the Broadway production of *Damn Yankees*. That experience inspired him to study music and acting, and he was very active in theatre as an undergrad at Yale University. He dreamed of being a director or performer but was well aware of the competitive nature of the industry and didn't think he could necessarily make a living in it, so he went to law school at Harvard, without having a clear notion of how he wanted to use the degree.

He happened to stumble upon a *New York Times* article about John Wharton, founder of Paul, Weiss, Rifkind, Wharton & Garrison LLP, an international law firm known for its prominent entertainment practice. Breglio didn't know much about entertainment law at the time but thought it sounded like a way to combine his legal training and his love of theatre in a career, so he interviewed with the firm and began as an intern there in the summer of 1970. He eventually joined the firm and has worked there ever since. He has represented hundreds of artists including, in addition to Bennett, *A Chorus Line* composer Marvin Hamlisch, Bernadette Peters, August Wilson (who relied upon Breglio rather than using an agent), Stephen Sondheim, and Andrew Lloyd Webber. In addition to his work supporting the production of numerous Broadway and Off-Broadway shows, he has represented clients in the motion picture, music, publishing, and computer software industries. He has lectured at Yale and been an adjunct professor at Columbia University, teaching a course entitled "Theater and the Law."

Nonprofit organizations he has advised include the Actors Fund of America and the Foundation for AIDS Research, for which he served as a board member. He is also a former chair of the Theatre Development Fund (TDF), one of whose projects is managing the TKTS ticket booth in Times Square (source of the logo on the T-shirt Al wears in *ACL*). Breglio has served as a legal advisor to many of New York's largest institutional theatres, including the Manhattan Theatre Club, Roundabout Theatre Company, Second Stage, Playwrights Horizons, and the New York Shakespeare Festival—original producer of *ACL*. Over the years he has been instrumental in developing models of collaboration for nonprofit and commercial producers—once considered completely separate worlds—allowing the Broadway transfers of shows developed at institutional theatres to generate funds to keep the nonprofits in business and enable them to develop more new works. *A Chorus Line*, of course, was one of the earliest examples of this dynamic, which has continued in recent years with plays like *Doubt* and *Proof*, both of which originated at the Manhattan Theatre Club, and musicals like *Bloody Bloody Andrew Jackson*, from the Public Theater.

John Breglio first worked with Michael Bennett in the early seventies, when the director approached Wharton for help on the production of *Seesaw*; he also advised Bennett on the proposed production of *Pin-Ups* (a show that never materialized) and the two quickly became friends. As Breglio told Mervyn Rothstein in a 2007 interview for Playbill.com, Bennett "was one of the most captivating, almost mesmerizing, human beings I've ever met. He was someone who just looked right into your eyes. He had an innate sense of what made people tick, what drove them, what was interesting to them, what they loved in life. . . . With all of his incredible, innate talents, he was insecure when it came to business. And somehow or other, we just clicked from the beginning." In addition to supporting him on various productions, Breglio was instrumental in Bennett's deal to buy 890 Broadway, which became his artistic and business headquarters.

Breglio is married to the poet/playwright/lyricist Nan Knighton, who wrote the book for the stage version of *Saturday Night Fever* and the book and lyrics for the musical *The Scarlet Pimpernel*. They have two daughters.

The New Team

When he finally decided the time was right to go ahead with a revival of Bennett's most beloved show, Breglio was excited about introducing it to a new generation—and he wanted to do it while some of the key players from the original production team were still around and could take part. As he told Rothstein: "I'm Michael's executor, so he entrusted me with the show—with the admonition in his will that I should always confer with Bob Avian." Breglio engaged Avian, who had been co-choreographer of the original production, to direct, and Baayork

Lee, the original assistant choreographer who had also created the role of Connie and subsequently staged dozens of productions of the show, to choreograph. He also brought back designers Robin Wagner and Theoni V. Aldredge to recreate, and slightly modify, their original set and costume designs. Lighting designer Tharon Musser had retired, so Natasha Katz, a major Broadway talent in her own right, was engaged to adapt Musser's original design. Peter Pileski would be the assistant director, and Michael Gorman, who had played Bobby on Broadway and on tour and subsequently assisted Lee on numerous productions of the musical, was engaged as assistant stage manager/dance captain/assistant choreographer.

The choice of a theatre was of course important. There was no question of returning to the Shubert, where the hit musical *Spamalot* was in the midst of its long run. After an attempt to get the Imperial, the production settled on the Schoenfeld Theatre, a beautiful and relatively intimate Broadway house that proved a perfect fit. Built in 1917, it had been known for decades as the Plymouth Theatre, but on May 9, 2005, had been renamed the Gerald Schoenfeld Theatre, in honor of the man who had been chairman of the Shubert Organization since 1972. (On the same day, the Royale Theatre next door was renamed after Schoenfeld's business partner, Bernard Jacobs, the Organization's president.)

Nowadays the typical Broadway musical has a long list of producers' names, sometimes a dozen or more, listed at the top of the title page of the Playbill. So the revival of *ACL* was something of an anomaly, with Breglio's Vienna Waits Productions the only named producer. According to Avian, there were five investors who between them came up with the $8 million budget, but they were investors rather than producers, without any creative control—which is as it should be in a business where financiers with little or no theatrical expertise often buy into a show and then throw their weight around. Breglio trusted his creative team, and Avian and Lee, who had a deep friendship going back several decades, were thrilled to have a chance to work together again. Though Avian initially had mixed feelings about revisiting a show with so much emotional history, he quickly became excited and enthusiastic about the prospect—particularly when auditions began and he saw the level of talent that was available.

Every Little Step

Early on, Breglio was approached by TV producers about doing a reality series focused on the casting of the show, much like a British series called *How Do You Solve a Problem Like Maria?*, which had allowed the audience to vote on the choice of the leading lady for a recent West End revival of *The Sound of Music*. Breglio understandably resisted the very idea, with its "anyone can be a star" mentality that makes a mockery of the years of training, dedication, and sacrifice that go into the making of a professional dancer: the very precepts *A Chorus Line* was meant to celebrate. So he turned down the lucrative offers. (There would later be a network show called *Grease: You're the One That I Want!* that focused on the casting of the roles of Danny and Sandy for the 2007 Broadway revival of *Grease*.)

Instead, Breglio decided he wanted to make a film that, in the true spirit of *ACL*, would explore the reality of the life of the Broadway gypsy. The result was *Every Little Step*, which he produced in conjunction with documentary filmmakers Adam Del Deo and James D. Stern. These two partners had previously coproduced and directed the documentaries *The Year of the Yao* (about Chinese basketball player Yao Ming) and *So Goes the Nation* (dealing with the 2004 Presidential election).

The first challenge was getting Actors' Equity Association to permit taping of the auditions, something that had never been allowed in the past. As Breglio told Broadwayworld.com, his proposal to the union was based on the idea that "If we ever are going to do something like this, *A Chorus Line* is the show to do it with. My intent is not to demean or ridicule people. It's not Chorus Line gone reality TV. It's just the opposite—celebrating what it is to be a professional dancer and showing the journey and drama that goes with it." After six months of extensive negotiations, AEA agreed to allow cameras into the auditions and callbacks—an unprecedented move—specifying that every actor had to sign a release allowing his or her audition to be taped; only a few declined. (The performers also had the option of changing their minds within forty-eight hours after the audition, in which case that person's footage could not be used in the film.) All of the auditions (over five hundred hours) were videotaped, and one of the many conditions AEA imposed on the producers was that they were not allowed to view any of the footage until after the show had been cast; it was important that the tapes not be used as a substitute for callbacks or a shortcut to making decisions.

For a while, the creative team found the cameras made them a bit self-conscious during what would in any case have been a high-pressure situation. But after a few weeks they got used to it, and the camera reveals fascinating details of the casting process. The team was open to discovering new young talent, so an open call was held in addition to Equity Principal Auditions and invitational calls; hopeful young dancers lined up around the block, and approximately three thousand candidates were eventually seen. (Coincidentally, the same number of auditionees has been quoted as having come out for the film version twenty years earlier.)

Avian and Lee found the current crop of performers to be better trained than ever before. There have now been a couple of generations of dancers who saw *A Chorus Line* as kids and decided that was what they wanted to do, so in a way the show itself inspired the rise of a new breed of triple threats; BFA programs in musical theatre have sprouted up at colleges and universities all over the country, training more and more performers for a dwindling number of available jobs. But as Avian put it: "You still have to find that one particular person," and there were new challenges. Lee explained that the culture of Broadway has changed: Even though everyone's a triple threat now, "When we did it we were all gypsies. The biggest challenge now is that we don't have gypsies anymore; you can't do two shows a year because the shows run twenty-five years. The book is the challenge now. Before, they could play themselves. Now you have to break the character down and dig into the belly of the character and explain it to them."

The top candidates were all asked to prepare monologues and songs from the show, and it's fascinating in the film to see the familiar material being performed under the intense pressure and high stakes of a real Broadway audition; the results are often electric. Highlights include Jason Tam's take on Paul's monologue, which reduced everyone on the panel to tears. In a way, *Every Little Step* became an homage to Michael Bennett's own unrealized plan for how he had said he wanted to direct the film of *A Chorus Line*: as a cinema verité-style chronicle of the auditions for a movie of the show, with several performers sharing each role. (In addition to examining the casting process for the revival, *Every Little Step* documents the original creation of the musical and includes snippets from the 1974 tape sessions that started it all and from the grainy black-and-white videotape of the original cast performing the show at the Newman, plus interviews with Marvin Hamlisch, Donna McKechnie, and others.) The finished film premiered at the Toronto International Film Festival in September 2008; it was released in Japan under the title *Broadway Broadway* and played several other film festivals before a limited U.S. release in April 2009. It was critically acclaimed, and A. O. Scott's *New York Times* review makes it clear that Breglio's goals for the film were realized: "There is a superficial resemblance between 'Every Little Step' (and, for that matter, 'A Chorus Line' itself) and television reality shows in which ordinary people use their talents to scramble for the spotlight. But those programs are spectacles of amateurism chasing after celebrity, an impulse that could not be further from what Mr. Stern and Mr. Del Deo, taking their cues from Mr. Bennett, set out to honor. The 17 members of that chorus line. . . are professionals, and one of the names they give to the glory they seek is work. The other is love."

Tyler Hanes recently reminisced about his audition for the show; he was play-ing the lead role of Ren in the stage version of *Footloose* at the Marriott Theatre in Lincolnshire, Illinois, and flew in on his day off to attend (on no sleep) an invited call in New York. Though he had been doing musical theatre professionally since childhood and had already been in six shows on Broadway, somehow he had escaped ever having seen a production of *ACL* and didn't know the show at all. Because the musical is so beloved of performers, most dancers, if they are even decently trained, know the basic choreography for the opening number; if they haven't been in the show before, they've learned it at some point in a jazz class. So Hanes walked into his audition to discover a group of dancers already running through the combination and had to point out to Baayork Lee that he didn't actually know the steps. He must have picked them up fast, because Avian says he decided right away that he wanted him in the show. Hanes spent a full day dancing and read for both Greg and Bobby; at the final callback, he was asked to stand next to Michael Berresse (Zach) so the team could see how they looked together; he was cast as Larry in the show (also as understudy for Bobby and Zach), and the first thing they did was dye his hair blond.

The grueling casting process stretched out over eight months. There was speculation on whether the team would incorporate any nontraditional casting, which has become much more prevalent on Broadway than it was in the seventies; they did cast Deidre Goodwin, an African American dancer/actress, as Sheila. Of course, much attention in the theatre community focused on the question of who would play Cassie; noted Broadway performers like Elizabeth Parkinson (*Fosse, Movin' Out*) and Natascia Diaz (*The Capeman, Seussical*) were prominently consid-ered. Although she said she thought she had blown her callback, the role went to

Michael Berresse as Zach demonstrates a leap to the auditioning dancers in the opening number, Broadway revival, 2006.   *Photo by Paul Kolnik*

Charlotte d'Amboise, a highly respected dancer/actress whose many Broadway appearances had often been as a replacement in roles associated with Gwen Verdon and/or Donna McKechnie. The choice was announced in a *New York Times* story by Jesse McKinley, who quoted Avian: "We've been watching her for 20 years dance, but she's got this great combination of vulnerability and strength. She's had that roller-coaster career, but she's a survivor. This is her life, and this is what she does." At the end of the piece, d'Amboise revealed that she had dreamed of playing Cassie since seeing the original production as a child, adding: "When you're a dancer, and that's what you started off doing, it never gets out of you, no matter what you do. And to do this role is the epitome of dance on Broadway. There's nothing like that."

Rehearsals

The rehearsals for the revival were held at 890 Broadway, which imparted a powerful sense of history to the proceedings; this was the building that Michael Bennett had purchased with his earnings from the show and turned into a bustling hive of theatrical offices, rehearsal studios, and performance spaces. (Though Bennett sold it in 1986, it was purchased by a consortium of dance companies with the assistance of philanthropist Lawrence A. Wien and remains an active rehearsal venue today.) Tyler Hanes found that Avian and Lee created a very safe environment for the first few days of rehearsal. The cast sat in a circle and, much like the participants at that first tape session, told stories about their lives, some more personal than others. "We had to bare our souls on that first day," he said, adding that he found his lack of experience of the musical itself to be a plus. "Everything was fresh; that's what made the experience so special for me." The cast also had to learn Baayork Lee's killer *Chorus Line* workout, a forty-five-minute routine designed to whip a cast into shape, with special focus on the muscle groups used in Bennett's choreography; she had been teaching the exercises to various casts since the seventies and was still able to do them right along with the young dancers. Though Lee was used to teaching the show in just a week or two for regional productions, the much longer rehearsal period for a Broadway show, plus the out-of-town run and previews, allowed far more time for refining and perfecting every aspect of the staging and the characterizations.

Though there were a few people in the cast who had played their roles before (Michael Paternostro as Greg, Chryssie Whitehead as Kristine, Jessica Lee Goldyn as Val), many of them were new to the show. Still, it was a very accomplished group: of the nineteen principals, only five (Whitehead, Goldyn, Natalie Cortez as Diana, Mara Davi as Maggie, and James T. Lane as Richie) were making their Broadway debuts. Even Paul McGill (Mark), the youngest cast member at eighteen, had already appeared in a Main Stem revival of *La Cage aux Folles*. Unlike the original cast, which as we have seen was continually plagued by angst and bitter jealousies, the revival cast quickly bonded as a group. According to Hanes: "We worked our butts off. We were at the same point in our careers. It was a big break for a lot of us. There were no divas; there was so much excitement about the revival, there wasn't room for ego. We wanted to honor the show to the best of our ability."

Avian and Lee, both having been part of the creation of the show, knew all the lore and background and what was behind the original staging and choreography, which for the most part they reproduced very faithfully. Avian did make a few modifications. Though the original 1975 time frame was retained and no attempt was made to update the show, there was also no desire to overemphasize its period-piece qualities. Rather than stating their years of birth (and confusing an audience trying to do math in their heads), the characters just gave their ages in the opening "Names" scene. There were several cuts in Bobby's monologue—including some lines that have traditionally generated laughs—because Avian felt that it had come to seem too long and that some of the references (Elmer's Glue, Astroturf) were dated and risked confusing the audience. Jonathan Tunick adapted the original orchestrations, and Marvin Hamlisch worked on a new arrangement of "What I Did for Love." About eight bars of music were deleted from the dance section of "The Music and the Mirror" at Avian's request, to pick up the pace of the number and enhance the build toward its climax.

There were also subtle changes to the design elements. Robin Wagner devised a new look, done in purple, for the sunburst backdrop for the finale. That number also featured the addition of twinkling lights encircling the stage. The side masking flats rotated to reveal side mirrors, also used only in the finale, and the number of fly mirrors that descended for the Cassie dance was increased from seven to nine.

Though the aged Theoni V. Aldredge came to rehearsals a couple of times to take notes, most of the adaptation of the costumes was done by the associate designer, Suzy Benzinger. Here too the changes were minimal, and according to Avian they were dictated by what would be flattering on the new cast's bodies. The traditional "flesh-colored" Sheila leotard would not have been right on Deidre

Goodwin, who got one that was done in an interesting reflective fabric that could look either amber-colored or almost lilac depending on the light; unlike the long-sleeved original, it was sleeveless. Kristine also lost her sleeves, and Tony Yazbeck as Al did not wear the traditional cap, though the sleeveless TKTS T-shirt remained.

Out of Town

On July 14, 2006, the company flew to San Francisco for their out-of-town tryout; not only were they excited about opening the show, they were thrilled for cast member Heather Parcells (Judy), who had received a wedding proposal two days earlier from her boyfriend. The San Francisco run was at the Curran Theatre, which brought back memories for Avian and Lee: it had been the first stop on the show's original national tour, the theatre where most of the original cast opened it immediately following their sweep of the Tony Awards in 1976 (see Chapter 16). Misfortune struck when Jeffrey Schecter (Mike) twisted and broke an ankle rehearsing the opening number, an injury that kept him out of the majority of the San Francisco run, where the role was played by understudy Mike Cannon. But Schecter was determined to rejoin the cast and had recovered in time to begin Broadway previews.

Early Reviews

The production began previews at the Curran on July 23 and opened on Wednesday, August 2—despite an earthquake centered forty miles north of town, which caused tremors at 8:08 p.m., just minutes after the show had started. The production's first review, by the *San Francisco Chronicle*'s Robert Hurwitt, was a very positive one. He began with effusive praise for Charlotte d'Amboise: "The toss of the head, the sensuously smooth sidle, the effortless extension of a leg high above her head, the impossibly graceful elongated arch of the back—each element of Charlotte d'Amboise's 'The Music and the Mirror' solo blends with the rest in engrossing harmony. . . . D'Amboise's every move builds upon the last in a glorious tribute to dance, the musical theater and the choreographer who created the piece in the first place, Michael Bennett." He praised many of the actors individually, expressing reservations only about the Zach: "Michael Berresse nicely conveys his humanity and concern, but little sense of his power." Aware that the show was still undergoing some fine-tuning on its way to New York, he added, "But its glories far outshine its defects."

Karen D'Souza in the *San Jose Mercury News* was the principal complainer: "The creative team seems content with replicating the vintage look of this classic, right down to retro unitards and George Hamilton jokes, but not its edge. Aficionados with high expectations are likely to walk away a tad disappointed, and newbies may wonder what the fuss was about. Morales isn't the only one who feels nothing."

The *San Francisco Sentinel*'s Seán Martinfield was also much taken with the Cassie: "'Oh, The Lady In Red'—she took our breath away."

A caricature of the entire cast of the revival.   *Illustration ©2006 Justin "Squigs" Robertson*

The revival's cast album, issued by Sony Masterworks, was recorded in California during the San Francisco run. (Compared to the beloved 1975 original cast album, the new one is substantially more complete, with a much fuller version of the Montage and the songs presented in correct show order.) The production closed at the Curran on September 2 and the company came back to New York, where they began previews on September 18 and opened on October 5.

The gala opening night was an old-fashioned formal affair, complete with red carpet and tuxedos at the theatre; the audience included such celebrities as Liza Minnelli (long a devoted fan of the show), Sarah Jessica Parker, Celeste Holm, and Joan Rivers. Several members of the original cast were also in attendance and posed for photos at the party afterwards (held at the New York Palace Hotel on Madison Avenue) with their revival-cast counterparts. (All of the surviving members of the original company had sent the cast a Western Union fax/telegram with their opening night good wishes.)

Back on Broadway

The reviews that greeted the Broadway opening were largely positive, but more mixed than might have been expected. Jeremy McCarter, the youthful critic for *New York* magazine, analyzed the enduring appeal of a show he found dated in many respects, but found the production less than perfect, saying "Moments that

The Broadway revival cast, including second-year replacements, at a brush-up rehearsal.
Photo by Lee/ The Everett Collection

ought to be explosive, like Cassie's big dance break, are merely effective, and the only completely satisfying performance belongs to Michael Berresse. Unfortunately, he plays Zach, the stern choreographer, and it's hard to steal the show when you spend most of it posing questions from the back of the house. No two ways about it, this revival confirms *A Chorus Line*'s exalted spot in the Broadway canon and pride of place in the annals of the backstage confessional. If only it had found a really exciting way of doing so."

In the *New York Times*, Ben Brantley devoted a lot of space to comparing the performance, unfavorably, with the original production, which he remembered seeing as a college student. He found the opening number as thrilling as ever, but opined that the new cast mostly hadn't made the roles their own, adding, "It doesn't feel fair to the cast members to have them stand in the same poses and the same clothes as their predecessors, on whom the roles were custom-fitted." He singled out only a couple for praise: "Ken Alan achieves a winning nervous narcissism as Bobby. But the one performer who unconditionally owns her role is Jessica Lee Goldyn, who as Val sings 'Dance: Ten; Looks: Three,' an ode to the career-enhancing benefits of plastic surgery. Strutting her chassis with a breasts-forward walk, and speaking like someone who decided as a child that her role models would be Bond girls, Ms. Goldyn creates a deliciously credible study in self-invention."

Roma Torre on cable television's NY1 was much more positive about the new cast. "Incredibly, there are 17 characters and each of them springs vividly to life. The casting for the most part matches the unforgettable talents in the original company. . . . Jeff Schecter's Mike, . . . Kristine and her tenor hubby Al played by Chryssie Whitehead and Tony Yazbeck, and Natalie Cortez as Diana Morales who felt nothing in acting class, all show tremendous flair. . . . Michael Berresse is a commanding Zach. And Jason Tam, heartbreaking as Paul. The one liberty taken in this production is the casting of Sheila as a black woman. The statuesque Deidre Goodwin fits the bill quite nicely complete with tart tongue."

John Heilpern, who had worked with Michael Bennett as librettist of an unproduced musical called *The Children's Crusade*, reviewed the show for the *New York Observer* and called it a "loving revival," saying: "Has there ever been a major musical sequence that can top the sustained brilliance of. . . 'At the Ballet'? The excellent Baayork Lee. . . has restaged Bennett's choreography wonderfully. 'At the Ballet' touches greatness in a sublime synthesis of dance and music and light, as mirrors turn in space. We want to cry out at the wonder of it all: 'How beautiful! How beautiful life can be.'" He added, "What more could the wonderful Charlotte d'Amboise do as Cassie. . . ? Ms. d'Amboise all but leaves her blood on the stage in the exceptionally demanding dance sequence, 'The Music and the Mirror'—and she triumphs."

David Rooney of *Variety* succinctly summed up the central dilemma of reviving the show: "When news emerged that 'A Chorus Line' was returning to Broadway in a revival virtually identical to its 1975 debut production, the surrounding debate ranged from skepticism to cautious approval. Was it misguided to resurrect the iconic musical as a museum piece, or wise to acknowledge that Michael Bennett's superlative original staging couldn't be bettered? . . . The thrill of discovery can never be repeated, and the legendary synergy of that first cast, many of whom were part of the development process, is lost forever. But this lovingly mounted replica gives ample evidence of what makes the show such a landmark."

Meeting Eddie Murphy

One of the oddest chapters in the story of the revival is the cast's unexpected appearance in the movie *Meet Dave*, a monumentally unsuccessful comic sci-fi flick directed by Brian Robbins and released by 20th Century Fox and Regency Enterprises in the summer of 2008. The plot centers on a human-shaped alien spacecraft (played by Eddie Murphy) containing a minuscule crew; they visit Earth, where their search for a missing "orb" leads them to stumble into a Broadway theatre where guess what show is playing. We see a couple of shots of the cast onstage, in Theoni V. Aldredge's classic champagne-colored costumes, singing and dancing a bit of the "One" finale in front of the art deco backdrop. There's also a shot of Murphy watching from the back of the house, by a door with a sign bearing the information that *A Chorus Line* is performed without an intermission (the only mention in the film of the show's title). Though "Dave" (the spaceship) quickly realizes he's in the wrong place and leaves the theatre, the rest of the crew has observed the show from inside the "ship," and it proves to have a lasting effect on one of them. "Number Four," the ship's top security officer (played by Pat Kilbane), is later seen in his cabin awkwardly attempting to imitate the "One" choreography, and throughout the rest of the film it becomes clear that his first Broadway musical has awakened his inner homosexual, as he suddenly transforms into an outrageous gay stereotype, calling himself "Johnny Dazzle" and dispensing makeup and fashion advice.

The scene was shot at the Schoenfeld between shows on a matinee day. Though the excerpt from the musical in the finished movie is extremely brief, all nineteen performers seen in it are listed in the end credits as "Chorus Line dancers," and the film's title appears on most of their IMDB pages—in some cases as the only big-screen credit. Several of the cast members apparently opted out, because the filmed cast includes understudies and swings in place of five of the regular performers. One can only hope they were well compensated for their time.

Settling In for a Run

The production proved very successful financially, recouping its initial $8 million investment within nineteen weeks of opening; during its first five months at the Schoenfeld, it broke the house box-office record seven times.

The revival received two Tony nominations: Best Revival of a Musical (which it lost to the John Doyle revival of *Company*—also a show that Michael Bennett had originally choreographed) and Best Featured Actress in a Musical for Charlotte d'Amboise (she lost to Mary Louise Wilson of *Grey Gardens*).

Shortly after the show opened on Broadway, d'Amboise gave an extensive interview to Melissa Rose Bernardo of Broadway.com, in which she spoke of the challenges of playing Cassie, which she described as "A grueling role. . . . I always feel like I'm able to do two out of three—the acting, the singing or the dancing. I always feel like I sang it well and I acted it well and I didn't dance it well. Or I danced well and sang well but didn't act it well. I never feel satisfied. It is the hardest role I've ever done. There's no doubt about it. It's because you just have to blow it out—blow out the dancing to its fullest, the singing to its fullest, the acting to its fullest. Nothing is held back." When it came time for the cast to sign contracts for the second year of the run, d'Amboise requested to be allowed to do only six performances a week, partly so she could have more time to spend with her two young daughters. The other two performances were split between two understudies, with Nadine Isenegger doing the Thursday nights and Jessica Lea Patty the Sunday afternoons.

About half the cast was also replaced at that time. Notably, most of the dancers who played the characters who "get the job" at the end of the show stayed with the production, while those who played the actors who lose out moved on. (This raises the question of whether a long run of *ACL* is harder to do for the actors who have to deal with rejection at the end of every performance.) The replacements had three weeks to rehearse their roles, during which time they watched the show together most nights from the balcony, but only one or two runs with the rest of the cast before they took the stage. Michael Gruber, who took over for Michael Paternostro as Greg, had been the final Mike in the original New York run of the show in 1990; he was the only performer to appear in both Broadway productions of *A Chorus Line*. Other standouts in the new cast included Krysta Rodriguez, who would shortly go on to leads on Broadway in *The Addams Family* and *First Date* as well as the TV series *Smash*, as a compelling Bebe, and Will Taylor as an especially charming Bobby.

Taylor tells an interesting story about a rehearsal with Baayork Lee where he worked on the unspoken section of Bobby's monologue, where he pantomimes a comic story while the others are singing "And." (In a show that is very specifically choreographed almost from beginning to end, that pantomime section is one of the only scenes where the actor has leeway to improvise.) According to Taylor: "Very early in rehearsals, when I had just gotten off book, Baayork said to the cast, 'Okay everyone, sit down in the front of the room! Will, you stay on the line. Okay everyone, Will is gonna do his Bobby monologue for you all now. And he will fill in the pantomime sections verbally!' As the whole cast sat down on the floor I realized I hadn't even thought about those pantomime sections. I figured there would be plenty of time to figure all that out. But they were all staring at me waiting for me to entertain them. So I started the monologue, terrified. When I got to the part where I spray painted the kid silver all over, the first pantomime section was to follow. I kept talking. It went something like this: ' . . . so then I followed the silver-painted boy all the way to the hospital, and hid in the hallway. I crept down to where the boy was taken. I found his room, where he was lying, alone and awake. So I leaned up against the glass rectangle on the door, got his attention, then I stood on my tip toes. . . unzipped my pants. . . and flashed him!' I was on a roll all the way through to the end of the monologue, and as I remember the cast was in stitches."

Dancing with a Star

In the spring of 2008, when the production had been running for almost two years, the box office was sagging, and the management decided to take a step that had never been undertaken during the original run of the show: adding a celebrity to the cast. The choice was one that the theatre community found surprising: Mario Lopez, a TV personality who had begun as a child actor and performed on *Kids Incorporated* and *Saved by the Bell* before going on to adult celebrity as both actor and reality show host. Lopez was to take over the role of Zach. Though he was going into the Broadway company, his arrival coincided with rehearsals for the national tour that was about to go out; the opportunity to rehearse with the tour cast gave him a bit more preparation time than is customary for a replacement.

In his recent memoir, *Just Between Us*, Lopez wrote of his experience with the show:

> Why was I nervous? Because this was like nothing I'd ever attempted before and everyone in the theater world knew it. . . . Bob Avian, the show's director, had been talking to my agent about another actor who wasn't available. So my name sort of came up as an offhand possibility. Bob Avian had seen me on *Dancing with the Stars* and followed his gut instinct that, as an actor, I could pull off the intense Zach. Avian reported to all the entertainment press that he was so sure I was right for the part, he didn't even audition me. True. But everyone in the Broadway community, supposedly unbeknownst to me, was holding their breath. Was I going to be worth the risk? I had to deliver and I made a promise

to myself that I would. . . . But it was not a walk in the park. Those first few days learning the choreography, I had flashbacks to *Kids Incorporated* when the choreographer barked at me for not getting it. However, Bob Avian and the rest of the production team had complete faith in me and never once showed concern, except that only made me more nervous. And that made me work even harder. . . . There were so many highs to come from this experience, but I have to say that when some of the cast and I went for drinks at Joe Allen's to wrap up my first week with the show, I felt that I'd made the rite of passage—I belonged.

(The experience changed Lopez's life in another way as well when he met Courtney Laine Mazza. Mazza had done a stint in the production earlier and returned during Lopez's run to play Lois and understudy Bebe, Diana, Kristine, and Val. Lopez was immediately interested, and though it took him a while to get her to go out with him, she eventually agreed. The two were married in 2012 and have two children.)

Modifications to the staging were made to accommodate the new star, including keeping Zach (who spends so much of the time speaking on a microphone from the back of the house) onstage during the first half of his scene with Cassie, and putting him in a more featured spot in the "One" finale, leading the cast in the "wedge" section. Some longtime fans of the show found this offensive, as the whole point of that number is supposed to be that the dancers we have come to know so well are now blending into an anonymous, identical chorus, with no one allowed to stand out more than anyone else. There were rumors in the theatre community that Lopez or "his people" had asked for the changes. However, Bob Avian has recently confirmed that this is untrue and that he himself suggested the adjustments when they brought Lopez in, though in retrospect he doesn't feel they were necessary. A new costume was designed for Lopez; instead of the famous beige pullover sweater Zach had worn since the seventies, he was given a sleek, form-fitting, short-sleeved brown shirt, to show off his celebrated physique. Much publicity and gossip attended the concurrent change to the costume worn by Nick

Mario Lopez rehearses for his Broadway debut as Zach.
Photo by Lee/ The Everett Collection

Adams, who was playing Larry at the time and had been wearing the traditional number 17 tank top. To avoid placing him in competition with Lopez's biceps, the costumer put Adams, whose body was at least as impressive as the star's, in a sweatshirt whenever the two were onstage together. Although the chatroom community gleefully imagined a rivalry between the two actors, generating publicity that probably helped at the box office, Lopez and Adams later revealed that they had actually become good friends and enjoyed working out together—something they reportedly sometimes even did in the back of the house or in the lobby while the show was going on. Several members of the company have recently confirmed that they found Lopez to be a team player and an excellent colleague.

An added benefit to having Lopez in the show was an opportunity for the cast to appear on *Dancing with the Stars*, the popular TV series on which he had previously been seen as a contestant. Following a Sunday performance, the dancers hopped on a night flight to Los Angeles, where they quickly rehearsed and performed their number (a medley of the opening jazz combination and "One") on Monday; exhausted, they flew back to New York in time for their Tuesday night show. The whole experience was documented with additional TV coverage on *Extra*, the entertainment news show on which Lopez was moonlighting as a host; it was timed to coincide with the May 6, 2008, opening of the new national tour of *A Chorus Line* in Denver, Colorado.

The Strike

An unfortunate event during the run of the revival was the strike by Local One, the stagehands union, which shut down Broadway theatres from November 10 to November 28, 2007. (For *ACL* fans with long memories, this was a reminder of the musicians' union strike, which had delayed the official Broadway opening of the show back in 1975.) A tentative agreement between Local One and the League of American Theatres and Producers was finally signed after nineteen days, in time for most shows to reopen for the all-important holiday season. However, in the case of *A Chorus Line*, the damage seemed to have been done; although the show reopened and continued to run for almost nine more months, the box office never quite bounced back to the very healthy levels it had been enjoying before the strike, which some believe may have shortened the show's run. Though profitable, and very healthy for a revival of a musical, the almost-two-year run was a disappointment to those fans who had hoped it would, like the revival of *Chicago*, run a decade or more. Many feel that *A Chorus Line*, the quintessential musical about Broadway, deserves to be a permanent fixture there; in an era in which some shows have become like theme park attractions and seem poised to run forever, it didn't seem like an unreasonable thing to hope for.

The Tour

The success of the revival led to a new first-class Equity national tour of the show, the first in over ten years. Another round of extensive auditions yielded a new cast, and Avian and Lee repeated their directorial and choreographic duties. Because the show continued to run on Broadway, the tour cast was completely different from the New York company, though Michael Gruber, who had been playing Greg on Broadway, went into the tour as Zach (he was replaced as Greg at the Schoenfeld by Tommy Berklund). Nikki Snelson, who had been a major presence in the film *Every Little Step*, where she is memorably seen watching from the wings as Jessica Lee Goldyn narrowly steals the role of Val out from under her, was chosen to play not Val but Cassie on the tour.

The production opened at the Buell Theatre in Denver, and though *Denver Post* reviewer John Moore found it still a little rough around the edges on opening night, he singled several cast members out for praise: "There's Val (crowd favorite Natalie Hall), the homely girl who has bought herself the physical attributes nature denied her; there's father-of-two Don (Northern Colorado grad Derek Hanson. . .); there's drag-queen Paul (a wrenching Kevin Santos); there's statuesque diva Sheila (Emily Fletcher) and a dozen more. Most endearingly, there's Cassie (the intoxicating Nikki Snelson). She's the ex-girlfriend of omnipotent director Zach (Michael Gruber), a girl once considered a star but now a woman desperate for work—even 'back in the line.'"

The short engagement in Denver was followed by a seven-week run at the Ahmanson Theatre in Los Angeles and then three weeks in San Francisco at the Curran (where the revival had begun two years earlier); the tour visited thirty-five cities over the course of the next year.

At one point during the run, Snelson was offered a role in the new TV series *Valentine* on the CW Network, but she was not able to get out of her contract. She did depart when the contract came up for renewal after the first six months and was replaced as Cassie by Robyn Hurder, a dynamic, glamorous dancer who had been playing Marty in the Broadway revival of *Grease*. Hurder left that show to take the role in *A Chorus Line*, joining her husband, Clyde Alves, who had been playing Mike since the tour began. Also at this point, Gruber was replaced as Zach by Sebastian LaCause (Broadway's *Chicago* and *The Rocky Horror Show*).

When the tour completed its run, a new non-Equity company was assembled by NETworks Presentations; it went out to play shorter engagements, often in smaller cities, with Baayork Lee this time assuming directorial as well as choreographic duties. It opened in September 2010 at the Shubert Theatre in New Haven, Connecticut, and toured for nine months before spawning a new company that played a sit-down engagement in Japan.

Return to London

Having returned the show successfully to Broadway and the nation, it followed naturally that Breglio would want to take it back to London, where it had had a memorable but conflict-plagued run in the 1970s (see Chapter 16). It took some time to secure the right theatre, as there are still only three houses in London with the forty-foot-wide proscenium opening necessary to reproduce the original staging. Though Avian had hoped for the Prince of Wales Theatre, the show was

"The line" at the London Palladium, 2013.   *Photo by Manuel Harlan*

booked into the huge London Palladium. Breglio put together a group of British and Canadian investors; the credited producers were Breglio and Mark Goucher, Act Productions, Tim Lawson, Bronowski Productions, Daniel Sparrow & Mike Walsh Productions, Just for Laughs Theatricals/Tanya Link, Gale King Productions, and A Chorus Line Broadway. A February 2013 opening was announced, with Avian and Lee repeating as director and choreographer.

Avian later said "I loved the London cast; the cast just fell into place. We had the strongest talent in town." The company included three Americans. James T. Lane, who had played Richie for the entire two-year run of the Broadway revival, recreated his role, and Alexandra Sarmiento, whom Lee had cast as Connie in the recent non-Equity tour and then again at the Pittsburgh CLO, made her West End debut in that part. Leigh Zimmerman was cast as Sheila. A statuesque American dancer who had appeared on Broadway in *The Will Rogers Follies, Crazy for You,* and the revivals of *A Funny Thing Happened on the Way to the Forum* and *Chicago,* she now resides in London. Looking gorgeous and dancing superbly at forty-four, Zimmerman owned the role and was generally seen as a highlight of the production. According to Avian, "Leigh Zimmerman was a great Sheila: the epitome of having fun with the role." She was honored with a Laurence Olivier Award for her performance.

Gary Wood (Paul) and Harry Francis (Mark) were tapped to repeat roles they had recently played for Baayork Lee in a Tel Aviv company of the show. Francis, a superb dancer who also went on as an understudy for Mike, is an accomplished amateur videographer; the backstage footage and cast interviews he posted online became popular with fans and helped publicize the show.

John Partridge, a muscular British TV star who had been a professional actor since childhood and was known for his role as the Rum Tum Tugger in *Cats* (available on the official video version of that show) was cast as Zach; his diverse experience ranged from extensive ballet training to fronting his own rock band. The new Cassie was Scarlett Strallen, a well-known British musical theatre star with a powerful soprano voice as well as strong dance skills; she had been seen in West End productions of *Singin' in the Rain* and *Chitty Chitty Bang Bang*, and as a replacement in the title role of Disney's *Mary Poppins*, which she repeated for her debut on Broadway in 2008.

Following two weeks of previews, the production opened on February 19, 2013, to mostly appreciative reviews. Libby Purves, in the *London Times*, eloquently expressed the show's lasting appeal to the English audience: "Michael Bennett's show about show-dancers, in its blank mirrored space, lifts and quickens the dullest heart and triumphantly outlasts its gloomy era. The music (by Marvin Hamlisch) certainly does, but so do its people. . . . The memories and sorrows of a disparate group melt into universal human experience. Two hours straight, at headlong pace: the beautiful, racehorse effort so shines that the first-night audience, in sheer physical sympathy, rose to its feet."

Henry Hitchings in *The London Evening Standard* singled out several performers for praise: "Leigh Zimmerman's Sheila gets a lot of the funniest and sassiest lines, and Victoria Hamilton-Barritt aces the big ballad. Scarlett Strallen's Cassie is an intriguing blend of high-kicking exhibitionism and confessional despair, and John Partridge, until recently Christian Clarke in 'EastEnders,' makes a suitably imperious Zach. . . . Not everything has stood the test of time—there are moments that feel flat or contrived. . . . Still, the rhythm of the show is seductive. Its best sequences are exhilarating or raw, and the finale is majestic. Running at two hours with no interval, it's a tight and entertaining celebration of physicality—and of life."

Michael Billington in *The Guardian* called it an "excellent show that makes no claims to rework the original. Bob Avian, the director, co-choreographed the 1975 production with Bennett and has reproduced it with loving fidelity. But the current cast bring their own personalities to the roles and, in addition to Strallen, there is striking work from Leigh Zimmerman as the sassy Sheila, Victoria Hamilton-Barritt as a would-be actor, and Gary Wood as the Puerto Rican boy who always longed to be Cyd Charisse. That, in a sense, is the permanent paradox of *A Chorus Line*: it hymns the individuals who are finally turned into figures of glittering anonymity."

Despite strong reviews and a devoted fan base, the enormous Palladium (seating capacity 2,286) proved too large a space for the production to fill consistently; though originally announced to run until January 2014, it closed on August 31, 2013. An international and UK tour was announced to follow.

22

"This Fabulous Library"

The Literature on *A Chorus Line*

For the reader interested in learning more about *A Chorus Line*, there is a plethora of information available; more books have probably been written about this show than any other single musical. Though several have gone out of print, most of them can be tracked down fairly easily through used book dealers. Remarkably, the first four books on the stage production were all published within a year and a half during 1989 and 1990; this means all the authors were doing similar research concurrently, though the close publication dates make it unlikely that any of them had the benefit of access to each other's work. All of the books have been very helpful in the preparation of the present volume. The survey below is in chronological order by publication date.

Richard Attenborough's 'Chorus Line,' compiled by Diana Carter

It may come as a surprise that the first complete book about *A Chorus Line* that came out was devoted in its entirety to the movie version. This attractive volume is basically a souvenir of the film and was timed to coincide with its release in 1985; it was published by Plume/New American Library and featured as a hardcover monthly selection of the Fireside Theatre, a popular theatrical book club at the time.

The format of the book mimics the show itself, with a chapter on each of the twenty principal cast members; these include the usual seventeen dancers "on the line," along with Zach and Larry, plus Zach's secretary Kim (played by Sharon Brown), a new character added for the film. In each case there is a handsome, posed portrait (most of them full-length) of the given actor in costume, on a page with an abbreviated version of his or her résumé, followed by a brief essay written by the dancer about his or her experiences making the film; some of these also include stories from their childhoods or early careers. Each essay is followed by a page or so, in boldface type, of personal commentary and insights about that dancer written by Attenborough himself.

In keeping with the theme of the show, most of the focus is on the casting process and the director's reasons for selecting each performer, though there are anecdotes from the rehearsal period and the film shoot as well. Attenborough and the dancers shower each other with effusive praise, giving the impression that the director presided over a safe and happy set where the dancers felt loved and supported (a striking contrast to the original Broadway cast's much-circulated stories of angst and manipulation during their workshop and rehearsal process). Though one might be forgiven for suspecting a puff job, some of the cast members have more recently reinforced that their respect and affection for Attenborough was very genuine.

The director also provided opening and closing chapters on the making of the film, which include some interesting technical insights and tributes to the talents of many of the key players on the production team. In the back of the book is a reasonably full list of the film's production credits—including the names of over 130 additional dancers who appeared in the opening number and the finale. The wide-format 127-page book (long out of print) is profusely illustrated with shots from the film and additional full-color photographs by Josh Weiner and Alan Pappé.

What They Did for Love: The Untold Story Behind the Making of A Chorus Line by Denny Martin Flinn

The first of several books focusing on the creation of the show, Flinn's was released by Bantam in July 1989, two years after Michael Bennett's death and almost a year before the original production closed on Broadway. Though it has long been out of print and was eclipsed by Ken Mandelbaum's more scholarly study and by the original cast's definitive oral history of their experiences in *On the Line* (see below), Flinn's contribution holds up remarkably well against the competition.

Flinn himself had appeared in the show, not on Broadway but in the International Company, playing Greg and Zach. So he had an insider's view and understanding of the musical itself. He also seems to have gained access to the tapes from the original tape session, given the extensive quotations found in the chapter about that historic night. Throughout the book there are generous quotes from many members of the original cast, most of whom become vivid characters under Flinn's sympathetic but clear-eyed scrutiny, and he also spoke to Nicholas Dante and some of the dancers who were at the tape sessions but not in the original cast, including Michon Peacock, Tony Stevens, Candy Brown, and Chris Chadman. Of particular interest is a section about Barry Bostwick's participation in the second workshop, where he played the role of Zach for four weeks before parting company with Bennett and the project—a chapter in the show's history not dealt with in detail anywhere else. There are also unique contributions from dancers Sandy Roveta and Ron Kurowski about their experiences with the International Company that played London, as well as substantial quotes from several of the original New York understudies, offering valuable perspectives.

The brief final chapter looks back at the 3,389th performance gala in September 1983, but that event is covered in much greater detail in later books. Although Flinn provides some useful background information on the film version of *A Chorus Line*, he is scathingly dismissive about the movie itself, finishing his discussion of it with the assertion that "no film exists" of the musical. Though he gets a few details wrong (including the date and location of the initial tape session), Flinn's work is lovingly thorough; he writes gracefully, and while he doesn't back away from exploring the backstage conflicts and some of the uglier episodes, his writing is balanced and he evinces affection and respect for all the people involved. The book was published as a trade paperback, with eight pages of black-and-white photos by Martha Swope, including shots of the original cast in performance and in rehearsal with Bennett as well as pictures from the gala.

Martin's other writing credits include the Off-Broadway musical *Groucho*, which he also directed; the screenplay (with Nicholas Meyer) to *Star Trek VI: The Undiscovered Country*; as well as mysteries, a *Star Trek* novel, and how-to books on auditioning and screenwriting. In 1997, he won the ASCAP Deems Taylor Award for *Musical! A Grand Tour*, his large-scale history and analysis of the art form. He died of cancer in 2007 at the age of fifty-nine.

A Chorus Line and the Musicals of Michael Bennett by Ken Mandelbaum

Following quickly on the heels of Flinn's, Mandelbaum's book was released later the same year. An acknowledged and much respected authority on musical theatre, Mandelbaum developed a devoted following as a columnist and critic for *Show Music* magazine, *Playbill*, *TheaterWeek*, and *InTheater*, among other publications. He is best known as the author of *Not Since Carrie: Forty Years of Musical Flops*, considered the major study of that subject; it was published in 1991, two years after his book on Bennett and *A Chorus Line*.

Mandelbaum is a true scholar of the musical theatre, and his book is the most thorough analysis of the show itself, taking pains to detail not only the process behind its creation, also covered in other books, but also its historical significance and its unique place in the development of the American musical as an art form. The majority of the book is about *A Chorus Line*, but there are also chapters about Bennett's early life and the other shows he worked on as a performer, choreographer, and/or director. The chapter on *Dreamgirls*, Bennett's only hit following *ACL* and his other major opus as an auteur director, may seem surprisingly brief; it gets sixteen pages, as compared to twenty for the unproduced *Scandal*. There is a six-page chapter on the movie of *ACL*, more space than most of the other books devote, but Mandelbaum is highly critical of it.

The book as a whole is extremely thorough and full of fascinating details. There are lengthy quotes from interviews with Bob Avian as well as Marvin Hamlisch, Edward Kleban, James Kirkwood, and Nicholas Dante. Donna McKechnie is heavily quoted as well, and Mandelbaum also interviewed some of the other original cast members, though he explains that several declined to speak with him, claiming they didn't want to revisit the *Chorus Line* experience at that point in their lives. In retrospect, that may be because they had recently spoken to Denny Martin Flinn or, more likely, because they were already talking to Baayork Lee and Thommie Walsh for *On the Line* (see below), which promised to be the definitive document of the dancers' side of the story (Lee and Walsh themselves were not interviewed for Mandelbaum's book).

Though Mandelbaum does not shrink from addressing the more controversial aspects of Bennett's personality and directorial methods, the emphasis is on his generosity, creativity, and passion for the theatre. Published so soon after his death, the book at times has the tone of an elegy or a tribute; it begins with a prologue about his memorial service and includes an epilogue called "Remembering the Man." Published in hardcover by St. Martin's Press, the 335-page volume includes thirty two glossy pages of black-and-white photos. Unfortunately out of print, this book is the most exhaustive study of Michael Bennett as an artist and his unique contribution to the musical theatre.

On the Line: The Creation of A Chorus Line by Robert Viagas, Baayork Lee, and Thommie Walsh

Original cast members Baayork Lee and Thommie Walsh, who created the roles of Connie and Bobby, initiated this project: a detailed account of the creation, opening, and aftermath of the show as told by the original cast, all nineteen of whom were interviewed at length for the book. (The understudies were not included; by that point they were used to it.) The authors make a point of emphasizing, in an initial Authors' Note, that these nineteen individuals were the only people interviewed: "This book is their memoir exclusively." Aware of how much had been said and written about the show over the years, in articles and elsewhere, as well as the other books that were appearing on the subject more or less concurrently, Lee and Walsh felt it was important that the dancers have their say. They had contributed their own life stories as well as their sweat and tears to the work, but had not always been listened to or given due credit; this was to be their chance to look back, examine the experience, and express its meaning and the impact it had had on their lives, both positive and negative.

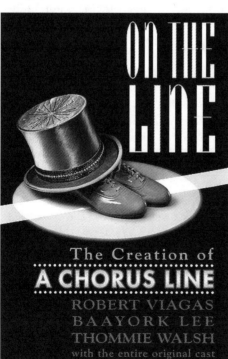

The cover of *On the Line.*   *Limelight Editions*

It was the September 1983 gala performance, where most of the original cast was reassembled along with over three hundred other performers who had done the show all over the world, that inspired the originals to conceive of the book project; they realized they were still carrying around enough unresolved baggage from the experience that it was worth revisiting, expressing, and working through. Lee and Walsh developed a list of questions to get the ball rolling with each person and conducted interviews on both coasts. Though they initially intended to publish the unedited transcript of each interview (with a history of having their words appropriated by others, their priority was giving each dancer a chance to be heard fully and uncensored), they couldn't find a publisher who was interested in that type of project. They considered self-publishing, but decided instead to collaborate with a professional writer who would weave the interview material together into a narrative text. Thommie Walsh's agency, International Creative Management, suggested the writer who eventually came on board: Robert Viagas, an experienced journalist with a strong expertise in musical theatre. The dancers were quite articulate and thoughtful in looking back at the experience, both artistic and emotional, of creating *A Chorus Line*, and the resulting narrative in rich in nuance and detail.

The original hardcover edition, published by William Morrow in 1990 (the year the show closed on Broadway), has 367 pages, plus sixteen pages of production, rehearsal, and backstage photos. There are also biographies of each dancer before and after they did the show; the latter section was revised and updated for the later paperback version, published in 2006 by Limelight Editions.

One Singular Sensation: The Michael Bennett Story by Kevin Kelly

Journalist Kevin Kelly first met Michael Bennett in 1968, during the Boston tryout of *Promises, Promises.* They became friends: if not close friends, as Kelly points out in his Preface, close enough to have been invited to numerous parties at each other's homes and dinners together at various New York restaurants; their last in-person meeting was at 890 Broadway in 1983. Kelly had interviewed Bennett for articles in the *Boston Globe* and *New York* magazine, and conducted extensive tape-recorded interviews with him in 1978 during the Stratford, Connecticut, tryout of *Ballroom.*

Kelly was apparently an interviewer who knew how to put a subject at ease and get him or her to open up; his book's strength is its many vivid and often pungent quotes not only from Bennett but from the friends, colleagues, family members, and associates he interviewed at great length. Bob Avian is more outspoken here than in other publications, and Nick Dante is especially fierce and pointed in his observations and interpretations. There are long and sometimes rambling, but revealing, quotations from Bennett's mother and his brother; personal reminiscences from Donna McKechnie and Larry Fuller; and dialogues between Bernard and Betty Jacobs. Marvin Hamlisch displays his characteristic linguistic quirks, starting numerous sentences with "you have to understand," and Sabine Cassel, with whom Bennett had one of his few extended heterosexual affairs, is colorfully candid in apparently verbatim transcriptions of her admittedly less than perfect English. Aware of the numerous maddening contradictions in Bennett's character and the paradoxical nature of many of his relationships, Kelly lets the interviewees speak for themselves and mostly leaves the reader to sort out the inconsistencies—probably a solid strategy. When he does intervene in his own voice, it is often to provide something akin to stage directions, describing the mannerisms and behavior of the speaker in terms that are not always flattering.

The structure of the book can be circuitous; the beginning of each chapter moves Bennett's life story forward, but the quotations and a sort of stream-of-consciousness approach repeatedly lead the narrative backward to his childhood or forward to his final illness. A sometimes lugubrious preoccupation with the latter can be attributed to the fact that most of the book was written in the months and years immediately following his death from AIDS in July 1987. Chapters 9 through 11 focus mainly on *A Chorus Line*.

Kelly likes to dish the dirt, and his sometimes purple prose (lines like "The dream would beguile him, then waver in agony") may test the patience of some readers. But a respect for Bennett's achievements and the complexity of his psyche is evident, and the thoroughness of the research is commendable; the volume of personal material Kelly collected and the numerous conversations he had with Bennett himself make it unlikely that any future study will be more exhaustive, at least on a personal level. Nevertheless, the book has gone out of print. It was published by Doubleday in 1990 as a hardcover; there are sixteen pages of black-and-white photos, including some rare personal ones from the collection of Bennett's mother, Helen DiFiglia. A mass-market paperback edition was published by Kensington in 1991.

The Longest Line: Broadway's Most Singular Sensation: A Chorus Line by Gary Stevens and Alan George

This wide-format hardcover, released by Applause Theatre Book Publishers in 1995, is the only book on the show that qualifies as a "coffee table book." Written by a couple who may have been the show's biggest fans (they saw the Broadway production over seventy-five times between them, plus many more performances on tour and abroad, and also spearheaded the drive to raise funds to install the bronze commemorative *Chorus Line* plaque that hangs in the Shubert Theatre lobby today), it's a love letter to the show, done in the form of an oral history. The author's voices are heard only in the introductory material; otherwise, the format is a patchwork quilt of photos, many of them rare or unique, and quotations from the 125 people they interviewed.

As the title might suggest, the focus is more on the show's long Broadway run (with substantial information about the major touring companies as well) rather than the original workshop and rehearsal period, which had been so exhaustively covered in the earlier books; the Broadway replacements and touring performers receive more space and attention than the original cast. In addition to performers, the authors interviewed personnel from nearly every department and every aspect of the production, including musicians; production managers and stage managers; set, sound, lighting, and wardrobe personnel; Shubert Organization and theatre staff; photographers; marketing and advertising agencies; and so forth. The result is a highly entertaining and informative insider's guide to the workings

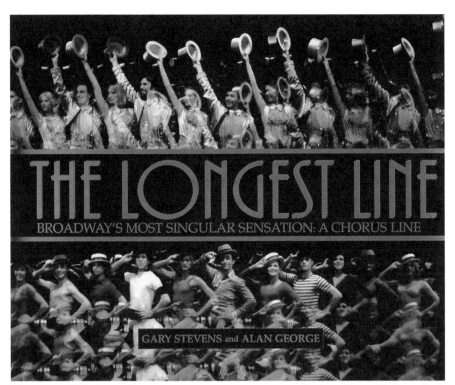

The cover of *The Longest Line*.   *Applause Theatre & Cinema Books*

of a hit Broadway show. There are also extensive appendices with facts, figures, and statistics, including a week-by-week rundown of the fifteen-year Broadway run complete with box-office sales figures. Especially notable are vivid, emotional reminiscences of both the legendary 3,389th performance and the events leading up to the closing of the show. The 256-page volume, now out of print, is printed on glossy paper, lavishly illustrated with black-and-white photos throughout, plus a four-page selection of color photographs. It's a must for hard-core fans of the show.

23

"But We Won't Forget"

A Chorus Line and the Plague

So many people from *A Chorus Line*, they had such a fantastic success that it was almost like they were handed their own deaths on a plate because they were all sleeping with each other and taking drugs and having a ball and nobody knew about AIDS—or not everybody did—and so they ended up, all of them, dying. It was out of just exuberant ignorance."

The above quote, spoken by gossip columnist Liz Smith to author Sean Egan for his book *Ponies & Rainbows*, may be an exaggeration and an oversimplification. Still, it would be impossible to overstate the enormity of the effect the AIDS crisis had on the *Chorus Line* community, and the larger worlds of theatre and dance, during the years the show was still running on Broadway, and ever since. That story is the very dark shadow hanging over the otherwise golden and triumphant history of the musical.

HIV was first discovered and identified in America about halfway through the fifteen-year run of the show, and it decimated the ranks of the musical's creators and performers. Director Michael Bennett died in July 1987, almost three years before the show ended its Broadway run. Jim Kirkwood and Nick Dante, coauthors of the book, also succumbed to the disease the year before and the year after the show closed, respectively, and the virus has claimed the lives of at least two members of the original cast, two from the film cast, and three from the first International Company, as well as countless touring and replacement dancers, crew, and staff members. Not only was the plague devastating to the friends, colleagues, and loved ones of those lost, but there are those who believe the development and future of the American musical as an art form was crippled by it, as nearly a whole generation of dancers and potential choreographers, as well as directors and writers, was ravaged, their careers and their lives cut short in their prime or even earlier.

And yet *A Chorus Line* kept on playing every night at the Shubert Theatre, new dancers always eager and ready to put on those iconic costumes, year after year through the 1980s—while the members of the Broadway community were more and more often spending their days at funerals and memorial services. The show became a living monument to a very recent but forever vanished time before sex became lethal, when dancers were hopeful and optimistic about the future, and chronic unemployment ("I need this job!") was the biggest and most common problem in most of their lives. It's the fact that it includes no mention of AIDS that dates *A Chorus Line* most decisively; it's probably no coincidence that it was in the early eighties that the producers decided to stop updating the cultural references in the show and let it remain suspended forever in 1975.

Alyce Gilbert, the beloved wardrobe mistress who stayed with *ACL* for its entire New York run, was interviewed by Barry Singer (for his book *Ever After*) at the tag sale following the production's final performance in the spring of 1990. She had brought fifteen years of costumes out of the basement at the Shubert so they could be tagged for sale, and said: "It was pulling the costumes out of the cave that really got to me. . . . All of them have many, many names inked into their collars. It's really the history of the show right there, and as I was laying them out I realized I recognized at least fifteen boys' names who were dead now. Young, healthy boys. It shocked me. I don't just remember their faces, you see, I remember their bodies."

Because the epidemic affected the lives of the show and its participants and fans so directly and so deeply, *ACL* became an early leader in fund-raising efforts and special events to draw attention to the crisis. One of the most memorable was a benefit at the Dorothy Chandler Pavilion in Los Angeles in 1988. Tommy Tune described it to Kevin Kelly: "The last half of the second act was a tribute to Michael. The stage went to black and we heard the beginning of *Chorus Line*. The lights came up on this big picture of him sitting on a stairway, smoking and smiling, his little feet, his little calves, his little legs showing. Then, standing there, on the line in the logo, the original cast. And there they were: old and young, thick and thin, creased and smooth. They'd been through the wars. But there they were in the same old costumes, on the same old line with Michael up above them . . . I . . . I had no idea I had not released my feelings. . . So many have died from AIDS, you get numb to it . . . Yes, yes, there's grief—and then you just go to work."

Another now-legendary event was the famous Actors' Fund Benefit for Equity Fights AIDS (EFA) during the show's last month on Broadway, a special performance initiated and organized by Kevin Neil McCready, who played Larry in the final Broadway company. Working with Tom Viola of EFA, McCready publicized the performance energetically, handing out flyers at the TKTS booth in Times Square and backstage at other Broadway theatres. The performance was on April 8, 1990, on what would have been Michael Bennett's forty-seventh birthday. Because the show's closing notice had recently been posted (the benefit was only made possible because it was extended for four weeks past the originally announced closing date of March 31), the performance became not only a passionate expression of dedication to the cause, but also a farewell celebration of *A Chorus Line* itself by the community of Broadway gypsies, to whom the show had always meant so much. Keith Bernardo, who was playing Don in the final cast, is quoted in *The Longest Line*: "That performance was the most incredible evening I've ever spent in the theatre. Everyone in the audience was throwing so much love to the people on the stage, who in turn were throwing the love to the audience. It felt like the reason I went into theatre. Nothing has ever come close to that." Jack Noseworthy (recently hired to play Mark) added: "To perform a show about gypsies for all the gypsies on

Broadway was absolutely the most thrilling performance in the entire ten weeks I ended up doing the show."

Fifteen years later came the 21st Annual Southland Theatre Artists Goodwill Event (S.T.A.G.E.), presented for three performances March 11–13, 2005, at the Luckman Fine Arts Complex on the campus of California State University Los Angeles. The longest-running annual AIDS benefit in the world, S.T.A.G.E. raised money for two Los Angeles AIDS charities. Each year the music of one or more great Broadway songwriters has been featured, and in 2005 they saluted two in a lavishly produced program entitled "Two on the Aisle." The first act presented the music of Harry Warren (*42nd Street*), and the second was devoted to Marvin Hamlisch, opening with a collage of scenes and numbers from *A Chorus Line*. A full lineup of seventeen dancers in the traditional costumes included original cast members Ron Kuhlman, Nancy Lane, Ronald Dennis, and Sammy Williams; Jane Lanier, who had played Cassie in several major regional productions, performed "The Music and the Mirror." Photos from the event attest to the fact that thirty years on, the originals still looked quite terrific in their dance clothes. Tonya Pinkins, Susan Anton, Patrick Cassidy, and Tyne Daly were among the many other celebrities who appeared on the program, as was Loretta Devine of the original cast of *Dreamgirls*. David Galligan directed the evening, with Gerald Sternbach as musical director. The fight continues.

24

"I Was in Ev'rything"

A *Chorus Line* in a Town Near You

B
ecause *A Chorus Line* was the biggest hit Broadway had ever seen, and for years the producers didn't want any competition for the New York production or the various touring companies, the stock and amateur rights to the show were not released until the summer of 1985—by which time the Broadway production had been running for ten years. The National, International, and Bus & Truck Companies had ended their long tours by that point, but the show continued to run at the Shubert, as it would for another five years. They could have waited until it closed, but a decision was made to open this new stream of potential revenue, partly because the show's creators wanted a round of regional productions to open before the release of the film version, set to premiere later that year. So in 1985, theatre groups, colleges, and school drama clubs that had been dreaming about getting a chance to put on their favorite musical for years finally got the opportunity.

Many companies jumped on it as soon as they could, and there was a great flurry of productions at all levels during the 1985–86 season, including three much-publicized and almost-simultaneous versions in the Chicago area. The frequency of local productions declined somewhat by the mid-1990s, but the show never really went out of style and has remained a staple of the musical theatre repertoire. The 2006 Broadway revival seems to have led to increased interest in the property, and regional revivals have multiplied over the past seven years.

Most of these productions are, on the surface, very similar. Being "Michael Bennett's *A Chorus Line*," the show is almost inextricably linked to his original staging; some of the choreography is even included in the dialogue and lyrics. The dances have become iconic, and the majority of productions duplicate the original steps and formations as closely as they can, if occasionally simplifying the more difficult moves for less highly trained dancers. Even those that use some new choreography will usually retain the original, familiar staging for the opening jazz combination and the finale—and the very difficult choreography for "The Music and the Mirror," so specifically tailored to Donna McKechnie's unique talents, has challenged countless Cassies.

This puts the show in an unusual position among musicals, as in recent years an attempt has been made to establish copyright protection for direction and cho-reography, and directors of regional productions of other shows have at times even been sued for stealing the original director's staging ideas. This never happens with *A Chorus Line*, since theatres licensing the show are automatically granted the rights to use the Bennett staging. But the choreography is especially complicated and difficult, so this has led to a relatively small contingent of choreographers, most of whom have experience performing in one or more of the Broadway productions or tours, being hired over and over again to choreograph, and often direct, regional versions. Baayork Lee and Mitzi Hamilton have each directed over forty companies of the show, and others like Donna Drake, Rudy Hogenmiller, and Stephen Nachamie have also staged multiple versions. Most of their productions have followed not only the choreography but also the original set, costume, and lighting designs as closely as the various venues allow. (Productions that depart substantially from the standard template, such as the 2009 version at LaGuardia High School or the 2012 production at the Fulton Theatre, both discussed below, are in a very small minority.)

In surveying the history of regional productions, one also finds the same names of dancers appearing again and again: many performers who have the right combination of talents for the show tend to find themselves specializing in it for a period of years, so there's a network of *ACL* alumni out there who all know each other and have done the show together in different combinations all over the country. This is partly because regional and summer stock theatres often have very short rehearsal periods, and the choreography for the show is complex; when given the choice, directors often cast actors who have done the show before and will remember the staging.

Every venue poses its own particular challenges, and the survey below will give the reader a sense of how the show has been fitted to theatres of different sizes and shapes. Several of the longest-established and most respected musical theatres in the nation, for example, are theatres in the round, a type of space that is especially problematic for a show whose staging is built on a line of dancers facing the audience and includes active use of mirrors. Nevertheless, directors and designers have come up with numerous different and creative solutions for staging *A Chorus Line* in such spaces. By now the show has been done everywhere from outdoor theatres seating over twelve thousand to small venues with stages too narrow to accommodate a line of seventeen dancers, necessitating cutting or combining some of the smaller roles—something else that different companies have approached in different ways. As Baayork Lee recently said, the late Michael Bennett told her: "I want you to be able to stage *A Chorus Line* on a flatbed truck. It's not the steps, it's not the choreography, it's the heart of the show I want you to convey."

ACL has never been a musical that relied on star casting, at any level. It's a show about chorus performers struggling to survive in a cutthroat business, and a production with famous faces would seem inappropriate, violating both the theme and the story. On rare occasion, a summer stock theatre will present a TV celebrity in the role of Zach (as did the Broadway revival, when Mario Lopez took over that role in the second year): since Zach is meant to be a famous director, casting a well-known actor in that role feels less wrong. But star casting of the other roles just isn't ever done (the producers of the 2013 London revival were actually criticized in some quarters for casting too well-known a performer as Cassie—a role that requires star presence if not a star name). So you won't see a litany of celebrity names here, though occasionally there will be mention of a prominent actor who did the show before going on to fame and fortune.

Sargent Aborn, the president of Tams-Witmark Music Library Inc., which licenses the show and controls the performance rights, estimates that there have been three thousand productions over the past thirty years, so the survey below makes no claim to comprehensiveness; apologies in advance if your favorite production, or the one you were in, is not listed here. An effort has been made to include most of the productions at the nation's major professional musical theatre venues, as well as a sampling of unusual or outstanding productions at non-Equity, amateur, college, and high school theatres. Because many of the organizations have presented the show more than once, the listing is alphabetical rather than chronological.

Analy High School, Sebastopol, CA, 1986

Our alphabetical survey of thirty years of regional productions begins appropriately enough with the first-ever high school production of the musical. Analy High, which consistently appears on lists of the best public high schools in the nation, is in the small town of Sebastopol, known for its apple blossoms. The show was codirected by the school's drama teacher, Amy Connolly, and Greg Victor, an aspiring dancer who had graduated four years earlier from the school; when a student there, like the teenage Michael Bennett, he had produced and directed his own musical revues. Victor (who later went on to a career as a Broadway stage manager) had learned the *Chorus Line* choreography by watching the show over a hundred times as an usher at the Curran Theatre in San Francisco, where the touring companies played several engagements and made him an unofficial company mascot; he remembers practicing the dances in the back of the house during performances.

The school was a bit short on boys who were interested in dancing, so Larry, Don, and Mark became female characters—though they wore male costumes in the finale, preserving the boy/girl formation in the section where the characters pair off. The opening number was shortened and simplified somewhat (following the structure of

Greg Victor teaches the "One" choreography to the cast of the first high school production, Analy High School, 1986.   *Courtesy Gregory Victor* the abridged version on the cast album), but the iconic choreography for the jazz combination was used. Rather than simplifying the choreography to "The Music and the Mirror," the willowy Cassie (Hiya Swanhuyser) added more high kicks and backbends (as had Ann Reinking on Broadway ten years earlier), which she executed with splendid aplomb. The sets and costumes closely followed the Broadway model, but some substantial liberties were taken with the text. Rather than being a solo for Paul, "Who Am I Anyway?" was divided up among several singers, and many of the solo lines in "And" and the Montage were also distributed differently than they are in the score. "What I Did for Love" was sung by Maggie (Joni Allen) rather than Diana, and surprisingly the group of dancers who got the job at the end of the evening was somewhat different than that specified in the text. Other cast members included Ethan Smith (Zach), Brett Gillen (Bobby), Jessica Rotnicki (Val), and Laura Dalrymple (Sheila).

Censorship necessitated the deletion of "adult language," with solutions including "Shoot, Richie!" and "T and A" (initials only). The references to homosexuality were omitted from Greg's (John Grech) monologue, which was rewritten to focus on his love of movies—but Paul (Brent Lindsay) got to deliver his story intact. With a female Mark, the "wet dream" sequence had to be cut, with the chorus chiming in after "Rose" had declared her affection for the anatomy textbook. (The production at the International Thespian Festival the very next year, with a cast of high school students from around the country, was allowed to do the unexpurgated show; see below.) Even in somewhat bowdlerized form, though, Analy did an admirable job of introducing the show to the high school market, with some outstanding acting and dance performances. Greg Victor reports that the number of tickets sold surpassed the population of the entire town, adding: "One of the things I was most proud of was that in this little town about a dozen of our high schoolers went on to have careers in the theatre (or TV or music). I know how much doing *ACL* meant to them as teens and I was proud that it gave them permission to pursue their dreams."

Arkansas Repertory Theatre, Little Rock, AR, 2006

Arkansas Rep's production of *A Chorus Line* was directed by the theatre's first artistic director, Cliff Fannin Baker, and managed to open on time despite the fact that he had a heart attack several days before the opening night. (He recovered well.) The production was billed as a celebration of the thirtieth anniversary of both the show and the venue, the state's largest nonprofit regional theatre, which was founded by Baker in 1976. The choreographer was Lynne Kurdziel-Formato, who staged the dances for the proscenium stage of the Rep's intimate MainStage theatre, which seats 385 patrons on three levels.

The cast included Kathryn Mowat Murphy, a red-headed dancer from New Zealand who was the go-to Cassie for American regional productions for several years around that time; the Arkansas production marked her fourth outing in the role. Critics Joy Ritchey and Max Brantley, collaborating on a review for the *Arkansas Times*, said of Murphy: "Her dancing is so refined and gorgeous that she

Paige Davis as Val at Austin Musical Theatre, 2000.   *Photo courtesy Scott Thompson*

should not be missed. She is, simply, stunning." Other cast members included Bob
Gaynor as Zach, Colleen Hawks as Val, Case Dillard as Bobby, Joi Chen as Connie,
Hollie Howard as Sheila, Stephen Baker as Mark, and Deborah Leamy as Maggie.

Austin Musical Theatre, Austin, TX, 2000

Jane Lanier and Luis Villabon recreated their well-traveled portrayals of Cassie
and Paul for this Texas production, staged at Austin's Paramount Theatre, which
featured a mix of local actors and New York imports. The company's producing
artistic director, Scott Thompson, staged a traditional mounting that also featured Tracy Powell as Sheila, Paul Hadobas as Zach, Christine Langner as Diana,
Kristopher Cussick as Mike, and Mindy Paige Davis as Val. (Davis would drop the
first name a year later when, as Paige Davis, she became the hostess of the reality
series *Trading Spaces*, a gig that made her a national TV celebrity. She would later
return to musical theatre as Charity in the revival tour of *Sweet Charity* and as a
replacement Roxie in the long-running Broadway revival of *Chicago*.) Reviewer
Michael Barnes of the *Austin American-Statesman* claimed this locally produced
Chorus Line was superior to the last six touring versions of the show that had passed
through town.

Beef and Boards Dinner Theatre, Indianapolis, IN, 1986

This long-established venue in Indianapolis, still operating successfully today, is
the last of what was once a chain of dinner playhouses; on its thrust stage, artistic
director Douglas E. Stark presented a version of *ACL* that is notable as the first
production of the show in which Laurie Gamache played Cassie. She had toured in

the show, mainly as Kristine, beginning in 1980 and had already appeared with the New York company as an understudy when she starred in this production near her family's Indiana home. She played opposite the theatre's frequent leading man, Doug Holmes, as Zach; William Alan Coats played Mike and also choreographed. The cast included Teresa Wolf (now a respected New York talent agent) as Sheila, Phillip H. Colglazier as Paul, Carol Lynn Worcell as Val, Michael Worcell as Bobby, Kimberly Nazarian as Diana, Julie Graves as Kristine, and Broadway vet Stephen Bourneuf as Al. As has been done on other small stages, a few of the smaller roles were cut/combined; most of the original choreography was used. When Gamache left the cast to return to the Broadway company, Carol Lynn Worcell moved up from Val to Cassie and was succeeded as Val by the assistant choreographer: Kathleen Marshall, renowned today as a Broadway director/choreographer.

Berkshire Theatre Group, Pittsfield, MA, 2012

This company, a reorganized version of the former Berkshire Theatre Festival, presented the show in the Colonial Theatre, a recently restored Broadway-sized venue with a proscenium stage. The production featured new designs: set by Gary English, costumes by David Murin, and lighting by Michael Chybowski. But the direction by Eric Hill was mostly traditional; according to Elyse Sommer on the website Curtain Up: "For young first-timers this is an opportunity . . . to see a legendary musical which, thanks to Gerry McIntyre's recreation of the original eye-popping choreography by Michael Bennett and Bob Avian, is as close as they can get to experiencing what their parents and grandparents saw when the show opened in 1975." The cast featured New York actors Noah Racey (Zach) and Nili Bassman (Cassie); they had performed together on Broadway in both *Curtains* and *Never Gonna Dance*. Others included Dana Winkle as Sheila, Ashley Arcement as Val, Neil Totton as Richie, Natalie Caruncho as Diana, Matthew Baumann as Mike, Sara Andreas as Judy, and Karley Willocks as Maggie. Steven Freeman conducted a thirteen-piece orchestra. Charles Giuliano, in a detailed response to the show for the website Berkshire Fine Arts, had a unique take on the material as "a paradigm for (Joe) Papp's Marxist theatre company." He opined that "The nature of a *Chorus Line* is its anonymity. There is an emphasis on group precision and the repression of the individual. It is intended that we view them as a flawless unit. By its very nature no individual is supposed to stand out or shine. They are the lumpen proletariat, the anonymous workers, who with frozen smiles flesh out those big Broadway musicals." He also reported that, the night he saw the show, the homosexual content "sent an offended, older male patron screaming out of the theatre in a disruptive manner." Maybe the show isn't dated after all.

Boulder's Dinner Theatre, Boulder, CO, 1985–86, 1988, 1994

An elegant 274-seat venue, BDT had been presenting musicals since 1977 when it snagged the rights to the Rocky Mountain regional premiere of *A Chorus Line* and presented one of the first professional non-Equity productions. The theatre's

The principal cast of the 1986 production at Boulder's Dinner Theatre, posed on the theatre's small thrust stage. The production used four extra cut dancers, not shown here, in the opening number.

artistic director, Ross Haley, and resident choreographer, Barbara Demaree, adapted the show to the theatre's small three-quarter thrust stage, which necessitated combining some of the smaller roles: the stage could not accommodate a line of seventeen dancers, so the number was reduced to fourteen, a practice later followed by other professional productions in intimate spaces.

The theatre used prerecorded and synthesized orchestral tracks rather than live musicians. Demaree choreographed new dances, utilizing the original choreography only for the opening jazz combination and "One." The production opened in the summer of 1985 to strong reviews and broke attendance records at the theatre; there followed several extensions and return engagements, with numerous cast changes, over the next three years. Several times, the production found itself in the local news, often over casting. The first Paul had to withdraw a couple weeks into the run when it was discovered he was actually a member of Actors' Equity Association and the union issued him a cease and desist order—an unfortunate episode that ironically resulted in additional publicity for the show. The role of Val was played by Lisa Frees Fairmont, who had represented Colorado the previous year in the Miss America pageant. Barb Reeves Kuepper, an actress who had been with the theatre for years before going on to international fame as a member of the vocal jazz group Rare Silk, returned home to play Maggie and later Diana. Janet Hayes Trow gave an especially memorable, layered performance as Sheila.

Several of the production's Cassies went on to big things. The first, Beth Swearingen, would make her Broadway debut in *Cats* and then go into the Broadway cast of *ACL* as Bebe. Her first replacement as Cassie in Boulder was Lise Simms, who departed on short notice to join an international touring company of the show, in which she would play Judy and Sheila alongside Donna McKechnie. Not wanting to leave BDT in the lurch, she recommended her sister, Joan Leslie Simms, to take her place. Joan knew the role, having just played Cassie in a college production at the University of Northern Colorado in Greeley, and jumped in with just a few days' rehearsal. A very young but elegant and commanding Cassie, she reprised the role in the production's revival two years later before moving to New York, where she has appeared in five Broadway shows to date under her married name, Joan Hess.

BDT brought back the show one more time in 1994, after having transitioned to a live orchestra. This time, the director and choreographer was Brian Kelly, who knew the show well, having played Mike on tour in the early 1980s. His version still used the reduced cast (the stage had not gotten any wider), but incorporated more of the original choreography. In the cast this time as Kristine: a young local ballet dancer named Amy Adams. Yes, *that* Amy Adams: she went on to a major film career, including five Academy Award nominations so far and a Golden Globe Award for the 2013 film *American Hustle*. Years later, she spoke of the experience to *Interview* magazine: "The one where I started, we waited tables and then we would get up and do *A Chorus Line*. The problem was, of course, that the show is performed without intermission, so when are people going to get their dessert? This was always a big problem! I was a really bad waitress, but I had the time of my life there."

Candlelight Dinner Theatre, Summit, IL, 1985, 1991

The trio of professional Chicago-area productions that were announced as soon as the stock rights to the show became available in 1985 (beginning with the Marriott Theatre and continuing with Drury Lane Oakbrook Terrace) concluded on September 26 of that year with the opening of the production at the Candlelight Dinner Theatre in Summit, directed by the theatre's artistic director, William Pullinsi. The choreographer was Rudy Hogenmiller, who had played Larry in the National Company briefly in 1977 (see Chapter 16), until Michael Bennett paid a visit and decided he was too young for the role. Eight years later, Hogenmiller found he didn't remember all of the choreography and needed guidance especially with "The Music and the Mirror," so the theatre flew him to New York where he worked for a couple days with Laureen Valuch Piper, a friend of his who was understudying in the show on Broadway at the time and whom he credited with helping him relearn the dances. (Hogenmiller would go on to choreograph, direct, and perform in several more productions of *ACL* in the Chicago area over the next twenty years.)

Like the Marriott Theatre, Candlelight was a theatre in the round. The square-shaped stage was in sections on lifts that could be raised or lowered mechanically to create leveled playing areas; this led to unique, dynamic staging solutions for several scenes. Scenic designer William B. Fosser figured out a way to incorporate the all-important mirrors, attaching them to the edge of the theatre's surround balcony, from which they reflected both the dancers and—as originally intended—sections of the audience.

Brian Lynch played Zach and Karen Frankel Jones was Cassie; Shannon Cochran, fresh from her performance as Judy at Drury Lane Oakbrook Terrace, this time played Sheila. Now suitably mature, Hogenmiller himself finally got to recreate the role of Larry. David Bedella won a Jeff Award for his performance as Paul, the only individual performer in any Chicago-area production of the show ever to be so honored. Nick Venden was the musical director. This version was generally considered the best of the three Chicago productions that year. It received glowing reviews; initially announced to run for three and a half months, it ran for six.

Pullinsi revived the production six years later with a new cast but with the Fosser set design and Venden repeating as musical director. James Harms was credited as co-choreographer with Hogenmiller, who did not perform in the show this time; they were honored with a Jeff Award for their work. The cast included Ann-Marie Rogers as Cassie, Larry Yando as Zach, Tedd Greenwood as Paul, Marie-Laurence Danvers as Diana, Susan Hart as Sheila, Michael Ian-Lerner as Bobby, and Mary Beth Dolan as Val. Kenny Ingram, who had played Richie in the regional premiere at the Marriott in 1985, repeated that role here.

Famed as the first dinner theatre in the nation, Candlelight closed its doors in 1997 after thirty-eight years. Changing tastes and new options for entertainment were chipping away at the audience for dinner theatres in general, and this once-popular form of entertainment seemed in danger of dying out as similar venues around the country also ceased operations—substantially reducing the number of opportunities for musical theatre performers.

Carousel Dinner Theatre, Akron, OH, 1985, 1994, 2005

The 1985 production was staged in the theatre's original building by director/choreographer Joseph Patton, who had loved *A Chorus Line* since seeing one of its earliest previews—with an audience including Lauren Bacall, Mary Martin, and Stephen Sondheim—at the Public Theater in April 1975 (he also attended the Broadway opening night six months later). The director was praised for his ingenuity in adapting the show for a theatre in the round with a very small, square playing area. This necessitated perhaps the smallest *ACL* cast on record; with only twelve dancers on the line, five roles were cut or combined: there was no Connie, Greg, Bebe, Al, or Kristine ("Sing!" was omitted). With a mere six days of rehearsal, Patton devised his own choreography for the unique space, and with his team came up with an innovative production design. Instead of tape or paint on the floor, "the line" was defined by light shining up from under the stage—and thus its orientation could be changed so that the line of dancers faced each of the four corners of the house at various points during the evening. The problem of the mirrors, always a challenge for in-the-round playhouses, got an especially inventive solution here, with an arrangement of one-way mirrors that were attached to the low ceiling and then pivoted down on hinges to surround Cassie (played by Blake Atherton) during her dance. With the stage lit from inside the circle, the mirrors closest to each section of seats became translucent; the audience looked through them to see Cassie and her reflections in the opposite mirrors. Zach was played by Dennis Edenfield, who had been a replacement Don on Broadway; the cast also included Urban Sanchez as Paul, Barbara Rhayne-Gordon as Diana, Lynn Paynter as Sheila, and Terry McLemore as Mike and dance captain.

By the time Carousel presented the show again, in 1994, it had a new physical plant: a thousand-seat proscenium house billed as the largest dinner theatre in the United States. Patton was again at the helm of this second production, and this time utilized most of the original Broadway choreography and a full lineup of seventeen dancers. Much of the cast had done the show before, on tour or in other regional productions, where they had been drilled on the minutest details of the traditional staging but not always the meaning or imagery behind it; Patton made a point of taking them back to the basics of the show and empowering them to make it their own. His assistant choreographer/dance captain, Timothy Kasper, also played Zach in the production, taking on a leadership role with the cast in rehearsal that translated productively to the onstage director/dancer relationship. Rita Rehn and James Beaumont, who had toured nationally as Diana and Mark, here graduated to the roles of Cassie and Paul, with Connie Baker as Sheila, John Fedele as Bobby, Debbie Hughson as Val, and Lori Lynch as Diana. As in 1985, Ron Lord was the musical director.

Carousel's final production of the show, in 2005, was directed by Donna Drake of the original Broadway company, who also recreated the original choreography. This version had only a week of rehearsal—but Drake was helped by the fact that all but two of the cast members had done the show before. Kathryn Mowat Murphy (Cassie) and Katie Cameron (Sheila) were seen in roles they have played to acclaim in numerous regional productions. Elena Gutierrez played Diana and Scottie Gage was Paul. Joseph Ledford, reviewing the show for the Wooster *Daily Record*, said, "Jessica Goldyn is sex appeal defined as the perky Val": the nineteen-year-old dancer would shortly be chosen for the same role in the Broadway revival, which opened the next year.

Casa Mañana, Fort Worth, TX, 1985, 1988, 2006

Casa Mañana was one of the first regional theatres to produce *A Chorus Line*, and their 1985 production was one of the earliest staged in the round. The cast included Tina Walsh as Cassie and Bud Franks as Zach, with Linda Dangcil as Diana, Mark T. Owens as Mike, Gail Pennington as Sheila, Marty Bongfeldt as Val, Nancy Drotning as Kristine, and Alann Estes as Maggie. The popular production was held over for an extra week, and the theatre brought the show back in 1988.

A true theatre in the round, Casa Mañana (constructed in 1958 and known as the "House of Tomorrow") has a large, circular stage with audience (capacity 1,805) equally distributed on all sides. In its first production of *ACL*, "the line" reconstituted itself repeatedly throughout the show, each time facing a different direction in order to give every section of the audience an opportunity to see the dancers' faces. There were scenes where, rather than standing on line, the characters sat on the floor around the edges of the stage and on ramps going through the audience, which facilitated more eye contact and connection between the characters than there is in more traditional proscenium stagings, though unfortunately the configuration did not allow for use of the all-important mirrors. The choreography included many of the original Bennett/Avian step combinations, reconfigured spatially; performed by a company of strong dancers, it looked excitingly expansive and energetic on the large, wide-open arena stage.

Casa Mañana produced the musical again in May 2006, but by then the organization had use of an alternate performing space with a proscenium stage: the Nancy Lee and Perry R. Bass Performance Hall, a two-thousand-seat venue built in 1998. The show played eight performances there and then moved to Richardson, Texas, for an additional five performances. This version was directed and choreographed by Kerry Casserly, who had played Kristine on Broadway and on tour. Cassie was played by Darcie Roberts, a Broadway veteran who had recently played the title role in the national tour of *Thoroughly Modern Millie*, and Zach was Eugene Fleming, possibly the first African American actor to play the role in a major production; his many appearances on Broadway had included a stint as Richie during the original run of *ACL*, as well as a featured role in *Fosse*. The Casa Mañana cast was also notable for including several actors who would shortly appear in the show's Broadway revival, which opened later that year. Chryssie Whitehead played Kristine, the same role in which she would open on Broadway; she went into the San Francisco tryout very soon after closing the show in Texas. Tommy Berklund (Greg) and Bryan Knowlton (Paul) would both go on to play those roles during the Broadway run, though not in the first cast. E. Clayton Cornelious was Richie, a part he would understudy on Broadway, and Jay Armstrong Johnson, who played Mark, would later reprise that role in the revival's first national tour.

Cherry County Playhouse, Muskegon, MI, 1993, 2001

The traditional summer stock company was founded in 1955 and began life in a tent in Traverse City; by 1993, it was based at the Frauenthal Center in Muskegon, a large proscenium house where both productions of *A Chorus Line* were staged. The group produced annual seasons of big musicals, usually with a star name or two in each cast.

The celebrity factor for the 2001 production of *ACL* was provided by the Zach, Peter Scolari (TV's *Bosom Buddies* and *Newhart*), who received name-above-the-title billing (extremely unusual for this show). Dennis Edenfield (who the next year was named producing artistic director of the theatre) reproduced the Bennett staging with the help of associate choreographer Amy Uhl, who also played Cassie. (Uhl had been Bebe on the Gordon Crowe tour in 1993–94.) The cast also included Stephen Nachamie as Paul, Julie Connors as Sheila, Kevin Ray as Mike, Leslie Goddard as Maggie, Peter Connelly as Bobby, Jerry Chapa as Don, and Julie Graves as Val. Musical director Antony Geralis conducted a ten-piece orchestra.

Like so many of the nation's large summer stock venues, the theatre was a casualty of changing economic times; it ceased operations after the 2003 summer season, when, according to their website: "It became clear that Muskegon,

Michigan could no longer sustain a professional equity theatre company and Cherry County could no longer afford the high costs associated with operating a 1750 seat theatre."

Downtown Cabaret Theatre, Bridgeport, CT, 1997

Dancer Mitzi Hamilton told the story of her body-enhancing plastic surgery at the second tape session in 1974 (see Chapter 1), and the character Val was based partly on her; she has recreated Bennett's direction and choreography for over forty productions. This Connecticut version was in an unusually intimate space, a dinner theatre where the audience was invited to bring their own food. Gina Philistine, known for her Bebe on tour, was Diana this time and was honored with the Connecticut Critics Circle Award for Outstanding Actress in a Musical. Peggy Taphorn played Cassie, and Jan Leigh Herndon was acclaimed for recreating her Sheila, previously seen on tour and on Broadway. Paul Clausen was Zach, Kendra Kassebaum was Val, and John Fedele was Bobby. Due to the small size of the stage, there were only fifteen dancers on the line, with no Don or Connie, but Alvin Klein in the *New York Times* suggested that the intimate setting brought to mind the show's original run at the 299-seat Newman Theatre, before the move to Broadway.

Drury Lane Evergreen Park, Chicago, IL, 1999

This theatre, which opened in 1958, was the first of a family of Chicago-area theatres founded by Tony DeSantis (which also included Drury Lane Oakbrook Terrace and Drury Lane North, later sold and renamed the Marriott Theatre: see below for their respective productions of *ACL*).

The Drury Lane Evergreen Park production was staged by the theatre's artistic director, Marc Robin. Like the Marriott Theatre and the Candlelight Dinner Theatre, both of which had previously done the show, Evergreen Park was a theatre in the round; *A Chorus Line* probably would have been done there sooner, but the twenty-five-foot-long stage was deemed too small to accommodate a line of seventeen dancers. Undaunted, Robin initiated a renovation in order to accommodate the show, expanding the stage and eliminating a hundred audience seats. He also had Zach continuously circle around the theatre, to enhance the dramatic tension. Thirteen years later, Robin would direct the show again at the Fulton Theatre in Pennsylvania (see below), where he got considerable attention by jettisoning the Bennett staging and the original designs completely and approaching the script as if it were a new show. At Drury Lane, however, he took a more traditional approach, which included hiring Rudy Hogenmiller to choreograph. Hogenmiller had a long history with the show, including the two highly acclaimed productions at the Candlelight Dinner Theatre (see above), and so he was by this time an expert not only on the original Michael Bennett/Bob Avian dances, but on how to adapt them for the round. Having also appeared onstage as Larry in the 1991 production at Candlelight, this time he graduated to the role of Zach. Cassie was played by Rachel Rockwell, who would go on to a career as a Chicago choreographer herself, including the 2010 production of *ACL* at the Marriott Theatre (see below). Tammy Mader, who had been Cassie three years earlier at Drury Lane Oakbrook Terrace, played Val; she too is now a busy choreographer/director.

Hogenmiller was to return to *A Chorus Line* yet again in 2003 when he directed, choreographed, and played Zach for a production at Theatre at the Center in Munster, Indiana. That same year, Drury Lane Evergreen Park, which had enjoyed some of its most productive and acclaimed seasons under Robin's direction, closed its doors after forty-five years.

Drury Lane Oakbrook Terrace, IL, 1985, 1996

Drury Lane Oakbrook Terrace was the second of three Chicago-area musical theatres to produce *ACL* as soon as they could when the rights were released in the summer of 1985; the opening there followed the regional premiere at Marriott's Lincolnshire (see below) and preceded the production at the Candlelight Dinner Theatre. Directed and choreographed by James Beaumont, who had toured in the show and understudied Larry, Mark, and Paul in the Broadway production, the Drury Lane version was the only one of the three to be presented on a large proscenium stage—the kind of space for which the show was originally intended—rather than in the round. Another of the family of Drury Lane theatres in the Chicago area originally founded by Tony DeSantis, Drury Lane Oakbrook Terrace had only opened its beautiful 971-seat theatre the year before. Its production of *A Chorus Line* received lukewarm reviews. *Chicago Tribune* critic Richard Christiansen cited sloppy dancing by several of the cast members, especially in the finale, as well as light cue problems and inadequate mirrors for the Cassie dance as contributing to a sense of letdown. Steven Breese played Zach and Nancy Hess was Cassie. Christiansen singled out two of the actors for praise: Rhae Ann Marie Theriault as Diana and Shannon Cochran as Judy. Cochran later recalled having moved to Chicago that year from Indianapolis with a bunch of actor/dancer friends, largely because they knew the regional rights to *A Chorus Line* were about to released; they had predicted (accurately) that there would be a spate of productions in the Chicago area and thus an unusual demand for dancers. The gamble paid off in Cochran's case: she went on to play Sheila in the Candlelight Dinner Theatre production later that year and has since developed a successful career as a serious actress with Chicago's renowned Steppenwolf Theatre Company.

Drury Lane presented the show again in 1996, receiving a much stronger critical response this time for a production codirected by Mitzi Hamilton and Gary Griffin. The producers added an intermission, which Christiansen, reviewing again, claimed made it hard for the show to regain momentum in its second half. Nevertheless, the technical production and the dancing were generally praised this time around, and the show was nominated for a Jeff Award for Best Production of a Musical. The cast featured Tammy Mader as Cassie and Tom Daugherty as Zach; others included Marci Caliendo (Diana), Tedd Greenwood (Paul), and Guy Adkins (Bobby).

Fifth Avenue Theatre, Seattle, WA, 2003, 2014

The Fifth Avenue is a large-scale Seattle venue that hosts some of the Broadway tours that swing through town as well as producing its own homegrown versions of classic shows. In recent years it has also earned a reputation as a top producer of new musicals, having premiered such properties as *Hairspray* and Disney's *Aladdin* before they went on to Broadway success. The 1926 building, with a Chinese-inspired décor, began as a vaudeville house and served as a movie theatre before closing down in the 1970s; it reemerged as a live theatre venue in 1980 after a $2.6 million renovation.

The 2003 production of *ACL* was produced in-house, with a few guest performers filling out a mostly local Seattle cast. The director/choreographer, Stephen Terrell, also Seattle based, had danced in the show on tour; ten years earlier he had directed it at the nearby Tacoma Actors Guild (see below). His assistant was Tim Johnson, who appropriately also appeared in the production as Larry, the assistant choreographer.

The role of Cassie was played by Jane Lanier, who had been featured on Broadway in the original cast of *Fosse*. The wife of Broadway actor John Rubinstein (the original Pippin), she had played Cassie twelve years earlier at the Paper Mill Playhouse; writing for TalkinBroadway.com, reviewer David-Edward Hughes said she was "certainly the most amazing dancer in the company." Hughes also felt that choreographer Terrell captured "the essence of Bennett's style and steps, without slavishly imitating them." The cast also included Doug Tompos as Zach, Taryn Darr as Val, Daniel Cruz Jr. as Paul, Maya R. S. Perkins as Diana, Tracy Powell as Sheila, and Kathryn Arnett as Maggie. W. Brent Sawyer conducted the orchestra.

A new production of *ACL* played the theatre in September 2014. David Bennett ("no relation") directed another mostly local cast, including Stephen Diaz as Paul, Trina Mills as Sheila, Gabriel Corey as Mike, Sarah Rose Davis as Maggie, Momoko Sugai as Connie, and Katrina Asmar as Diana. Taryn Darr repeated her Val from the 2003 production for the first week, and was then succeeded by Meaghan Foy; Andrew Palermo played Zach. Chryssie Whitehead gave a "lithe, impassioned portrayal of Cassie," according to Misha Berson in the *Seattle Times*. The original choreography was recreated by Kerry Casserly and associate choreographer Angelique Ilo, both veterans of the original Broadway run.

The Fulton Theatre, Lancaster, PA, 2013

Directed and choreographed by the Fulton's artistic director, Marc Robin, this version was touted as the first professional production of the show to "start from scratch," completely rethinking the staging and choreography. Rather than using Bennett's iconic dances, or even his overall design and staging concept, as a template, Robin discarded all the traditional visual elements and worked only from the score and script, as if it were a new musical that had never been staged before. The casting notices that went out before auditions cautioned applicants that the original staging would not be used, and that if they were "married to the original choreography, or a bit of a Chorus Line purist," they might want to choose to bypass this particular production. (Nevertheless, the cast Robin chose did include some dancers who had performed their roles in multiple traditional productions of the show, including Jessica Lee Goldyn as Cassie, Cary Michele Miller as Maggie, and Kevin Curtis as Richie.)

One of the intentions behind Robin's reinvention of the show was to make it more contemporary. Instead of the stage of a Broadway theatre, he set it in a rehearsal studio (set by William Mohney; lights by Paul Black). Before the show started, the audience could see the performers warming up through windows. Zach (Nathaniel Shaw) was an onstage presence interacting with the dancers most of the time, rather than an amplified voice from the back of the house. The costume designs by Anthony Lascoskie Jr. were completely new; Cassie wore black. Much of Robin's choreography was seen as more in the Bob Fosse than the Michael Bennett mode, with evocations of *Chicago* and *All That Jazz*; the cast in the finale even wore glittering black outfits with derby hats. For the dance variation at the end of "At the Ballet," a group of dancers came on in full classical ballet costumes; the new choreography for "The Music and the Mirror" included a pas de deux section for Cassie and Zach. Jillian Michaels, reviewing the show for LancasterOnline, found some of the added scenic elements distracting and felt that having Zach onstage reacting emotionally and sympathetically to the dancers' stories "weakens the tension between the dancers and the director and the whole structure of the show." (It will be recalled that Michael Bennett's adamant refusal to let Zach get emotionally involved was a key reason for actor Barry Bostwick's leaving the role during the second workshop; see Chapter 7.) But reviewers were largely enthusiastic and praised many of Robin's innovations: Marakay Rogers, on broadwayworld.com, said "Marc Robin is not a better choreographer than Michael Bennett, no. But his vision for this show is spot-on, reflecting his years as a dancer, and it will be a loss to this show if this choreography is not performed again." The cast included Brazilian actor Gabriel Malo as Paul, Marisa Rivera as Diana, Lauralyn McClelland as Sheila, Kristy Cavanaugh as Val, and Robbie Roby, who as Mike performed a tap solo in "I Can Do That."

Gateway Playhouse, Bellport, NY, 1990, 1999, 2009

In operation since 1950, Gateway is one of the oldest professional summer stock theatres in the United States; it is also known for its popular training program for young actors. The first few seasons focused on straight plays, including Shakespeare, Shaw, and Coward in addition to more recent Broadway favorites; around 1960, the theatre started programming musicals, which by the mid-eighties made up the entire mainstage repertoire. The theatre has extensive grounds and is known for its pool, which was the first in-ground swimming pool on Long Island; the Mainstage Theatre, built in 1962, is a five-hundred-seat house with a thirty-four-foot-high proscenium arch. It has been home to three productions of *A Chorus Line*.

The 1990 production was directed by Robert Longbottom and featured Eric Paeper as Paul. Like several other Gateway shows produced at about that time, it was subsequently sent out on an international tour. (For a brief period beginning in 1993, Gateway also operated the Candlewood Playhouse in New Fairfield, Connecticut: following a renovation, *A Chorus Line* was the first show they presented there.)

Paeper recreated Paul at Gateway in 1999, with Kevin Neil McCready (who had played Al and Larry on Broadway) in the role of Zach. This production was directed and choreographed by Mitzi Hamilton; the cast included Kendra Kassebaum (Val) and Angela Christian (Maggie), both of whom would shortly go on to major roles on Broadway. Others included Shannon Lee Jones (Cassie), Robert Tunstall (Bobby), John Flynn (Greg), and Cheyenne P. Gross, who also toured in the show using just the name "Cheyenne" (Mike). Kathryn Mowat Murphy, a frequent Cassie in regional productions, was Sheila this time and understudied Jones. Music director Fran Liebergall, who had been chosen by Marvin Hamlisch to be the show's very first pianist in 1975, led a ten-piece band.

Hamilton returned ten years later to direct Gateway's most recent mounting, along with costumer Jose Rivera, providing a set of Aldredge's original designs for the line. McCready also returned as Zach, with Kiira Schmidt as Cassie, Emily Jan Bender as Sheila, Yamil DeJesus as Paul, Melissa Manning as Val, and Kit Treece (who would shortly thereafter join the national tour in the role of Bobby) as Mark. Diana was played by Christine LaDuca, an actress whose name is eerily similar to that of a character in the show, Kristine DeLuca (just in case you're amused by that sort of thing).

As usual, Hamilton recreated the original Bennett staging, which by this time many of the show's fans knew by heart. Lee Davis, reviewing the show for the *East Hampton Press*, made a telling statement about the continuing appeal of the familiar: "The best musical about a musical ever written, and one of the three or four best musicals of all time, 'A Chorus Line' is to the musical theater what 'Casablanca' is to the screen. See it two or a score or a hundred times, know the dialogue word for word, the songs note for note and the dances move for move, and it still excites you and exhilarates you, breaks your heart, tingles your spine, and brings tears to your eyes as it does the first time around."

Geva Theatre Center, Rochester, NY, 2005

Mark Cuddy, the artistic director of Geva Theatre Center, Rochester's prime regional venue, made a last-minute change to his 2004–05 season lineup in order to include *A Chorus Line*; the Broadway revival had just been announced, and Cuddy wanted to do the show before regional rights were withdrawn. He directed the production himself, with the original choreography recreated by Danny Herman, who had played Mark and Mike during the Broadway run; Don Kot was the musical director. The venue seats 524 in a modified proscenium configuration with a wide stage apron.

Unlike most large-scale regional revivals, the designs were not based on the originals: set designer G. W. Mercier, costume designer Pamela Scofield and lighting designer Paul Monat gave the show a fresh look. The costumes for the "One"

Kurt Domoney as Bobby, Crista Moore as Cassie, E. Clayton Cornelious as Richie, Nicolette Hart as Val, and Tyce Diorio as Mike at Geva Theatre Center, 2005. The unusual design for the finale costumes is by Pamela Scofield.   *Photo by Ken A. Huth, HuthPhoto.com*

finale, all white and with the men in sleeveless vests without jackets or shirts, were particularly distinctive. The show was set in the present day, and some of the pop-cultural references in the script were updated: for example, Bobby sang "If Keanu Reeves could be a movie star, then I could be a movie star," substituting Reeves's name for the original Troy Donahue.

The cast featured two performers who were established favorites with Geva audiences: Remi Sandri as Zach and Crista Moore as Cassie. (Moore, known more for her singing than her dancing, had been nominated for a Tony Award for her leading role in the Broadway musical *Big*, and played Louise in the 1989 revival of *Gypsy* starring Tyne Daly.) Connie was played by Yuka Takara, who would shortly be chosen to play that role in the Broadway revival; E. Clayton Cornelious (Richie) and Kurt Domoney (Bobby) would also appear in that production, as understudies. Geva's Mike was Tyce Diorio of TV's *So You Think You Can Dance*; Diorio was not to be cast in the Broadway revival, though his audition for it would make for some of the more colorful sequences in the documentary film *Every Little Step* (see Chapter 21). Other cast members included Leslie Stevens (Sheila), Rocker Verastique (Larry), Nicolette Hart (Val), Ellyn Marsh (Diana), and Miguel A. Romero (Paul). Erin Crouch played Judy and went on several times as understudy to Moore as Cassie. The cast notably raised over $40,000 in post-show collections for Broadway Cares/Equity Fights AIDS (extremely high for a regional production), and the show broke the theatre's box-office record, earning over half a million dollars in ticket revenues.

The Grand Dinner Theatre, Anaheim, CA, 1985, 1988

The first-ever dinner theatre production of the show, in June 1985, was directed by Gene Nelson, the dancing star of such movie musicals as *Oklahoma!* (in which he played Will Parker). Nelson, who had gone on to a successful career as a TV director, had himself been directed by Michael Bennett, creating the role of Buddy Plummer in *Follies*. The production of *A Chorus Line* was produced by Frank Wyka, the managing director of the dinner theatre, and choreographed by Martie Ramm. Penelope Richards, who had played Sheila in the International Company, was cast as Cassie but hurt her back part way into the run and was replaced by Lisa Dryden, who had been playing Judy. The cast also included Lee Wilson as Kristine (a part she had played during the National Company's original Los Angeles engagement nine years earlier), Jim T. Ruttman as Bobby, and Glenn Shiroma as Paul. The show ran an impressive thirty-two weeks and was mounted again in 1988 at the four-hundred-seat venue, a part of the Grand Hotel, which had also presented the first dinner theatre productions of *Annie* and *42nd Street*. The theatre was profitable for over a decade but began to lose money in the early 1990s, so the management of the hotel decided to close it and reopen it as a dance hall featuring big bands; the final theatre production was *Camelot* in 1992.

International Thespian Festival, Muncie, IN, 1987

The International Thespian Society (ITS) is the association of official high school drama clubs around the world. In the summer of 1987, a unique production of *A Chorus Line* was presented at the Society's annual Festival, held on the campus of Ball State University. This "International Cast" production was a one-night-only presentation featuring a cast of high school students from all around the United States, and one from Canada. The ITS had produced a couple of other international-cast musicals earlier in the decade: *Godspell* (1980) and *Grease* (1982), both directed by Robert Johnson, at the time the theatre teacher at Niles West High School in Skokie, Illinois. These undertakings were expensive and considered risky at best, so there hadn't been one for several years, but Johnson had wanted to direct *A Chorus Line* ever since he attended a run-through of the original workshop production at the Public Theater in New York. When the rights were released, he found he couldn't help thinking about how perfect the musical would be as the centerpiece of the thespian conference. The ensemble nature of the show, and the fact that it's about young people, were pluses; the unique dynamic of a group of teen performers, some of the best from all over the country, coming together for a brief two-week rehearsal period and a single festive performance on the closing night of the conference, would reflect the all-or-nothing energy of the musical, with its story of dancers putting it all on the line for one shot at a job on Broadway. According to an article by James Palmarini in *Dramatics* (the ITS's monthly magazine), Johnson pitched the idea to the Society's directors, and they agreed. Auditions were announced in the magazine, and hopeful students submitted video auditions (on VHS tape; this was the eighties!) of themselves performing selections from the show. From these tapes the creative team invited eighty-eight students to

Kristine (Nikki Scrimizzi, right center) introduces herself in the teen production at the International Thespian Festival, 1987.   *Photo courtesy Amanda Watkins (shown at left as Cassie)*

try out in person. "Audition Workshops" were scheduled for the spring in five cities: Chicago, Denver, Atlanta, Los Angeles, and Philadelphia.

Amanda Watkins was a sixteen-year-old self-proclaimed "bun-head" at the time: having started ballet class at age three, she was already a member of a professional company in her home state of Georgia. A devoted fan of *A Chorus Line* (including the movie, which had come out less than two years earlier), she found out about the auditions from her drama teacher, sent in a tape, and was invited to try out. She had to ask for a weekend off from ballet rehearsals to go to the audition—angering her teacher, who dismissed musical theatre as frivolous and sarcastically asked whether the young dancer really thought she had any chance of getting a part. Undaunted, Amanda told her she felt confident she had a chance at Cassie. Never having been on an airplane before, she flew by herself to the auditions.

The weekend workshop was run by Johnson with choreographer Gretchen Witte Glader and musical director Sheri Owens. Mindful that they were dealing with teenagers, the team made a point of structuring the weekend as a learning experience, doing their best to keep the kids relaxed and encouraging them to have a good time getting to know one another, avoiding the cutthroat competitiveness that can make professional auditions so nerve-wracking. Still, the auditions mirrored the show itself to some degree, as the young actors were asked to introduce themselves and talk about their lives. As they sang and danced together—and learned how much they had in common—many of the kids felt they were having a *Chorus Line* experience of their very own, whether or not they got cast in the show.

That same sense of camaraderie was eventually shared with the young audience at the conference. Emens Auditorium seats almost three thousand—nearly twice as big as the largest Broadway theatres—and its huge stage accommodated twenty extra dancers (as opposed to the usual seven) in the opening number. The energy in the house, filled as it was with teenagers in love with musical theatre, was electric, and the pressure on the cast was enormous—but as Watkins (who was indeed cast as Cassie) put it: "When you're that young you don't know to be terrified." Many of the dancers remembered the experience as a formative one, which led to lifelong friendships; several of them majored in musical theatre together at Florida State University, and most have gone on to careers in the industry. The cast included Kyle Hall as Zach, Jennifer Fulton as Sheila, Tom Aaron as Bobby, Cydney Rosenbaum as Maggie, Kevin Covert as Larry, Michelle Dayan as Diana, and Jennise Canals as Bebe. Watkins made her Broadway debut in 1996 in the first revival of *Grease* and went on to perform in five more Broadway musicals; she is now a successful producer. She says that one-night *Chorus Line* changed her life: "It gave me a tremendous amount of confidence to have gotten that part; I don't think I would have had the nerve to move to New York and have a career in this business if it hadn't been for that experience."

LaGuardia High School of Music & Art and Performing Arts, New York, NY, 2009

Another outstanding teen production, this one had an ironically appropriate venue: after being immortalized, and none too flatteringly, in the *ACL* song "Nothing," it seemed only fitting that the original High School of Performing Arts—under its new name and in its new location near Lincoln Center—should finally stage its own production of the show. Whether or not the prototype for "Mr. Karp" was as bad as Diana Morales remembered, the school provided ample proof of the high quality of its twenty-first-century faculty and student body with a sleek and polished mounting of the musical. Director/choreographer Joey R. Smith provided all-new dances that looked every bit as difficult and challenging as Bennett and Avian's originals, and the well-honed teenage dancers (LaGuardia offers a dance major as well as voice and drama programs) were more than up to the challenge.

The wide stage accommodated about twenty extra dancers in the opening number (compared to seven in the Broadway original), divided into groups of six or seven rather than four; having over half the dancers onstage leave after the cut makes the scene impressively realistic. Smith's innovations included a mostly silent prologue in which Larry was seen giving instructions to a female assistant, then stretching until the dancers began coming on in groups of various sizes, handing him their dance cards and then commencing to learn the choreography. Cassie appeared with one of the last groups to arrive and was seen hugging Larry as an old friend. Finally the familiar piano intro was heard, and Zach proceeded to teach the steps; oddly, the routine that he taught, and that the dancers then repeated "facing away from the mirror," was a different combination from the one they later performed to the same music in their six groups.

Jeffrey Buchsbaum was both associate director and musical director. The student cast, which offered more ethnic diversity than usual for this show, included Leopold Manswell as Zach, Danielle Marie Gonzalez as Cassie, Lily Sondik as Sheila, Maurice Dawkins as Paul, India Carney as Diana, Mohammed Omari Ali as Larry, Yurina Kutsukake as Maggie, Pauline Chalamet as Val, and Paul Regan as Bobby. Alexzandra Sarmiento, who played Connie, was at the beginning of a long association with the role, which she would shortly repeat in the non-Equity tour, followed by Equity productions at the Pittsburgh Civic Light Opera and the Paper Mill Playhouse (see below) and finally the 2013 West End revival.

Las Palmas Theatre, Hollywood, CA, 1990

Playing a relatively small LA venue, this production opened about a month after the closing of the Broadway run; it featured Wayne Meledandri repeating the role of Paul, which he had played in New York. Cassie was portrayed by Janet Eilber, a distinguished actress and dancer and a rare case of the role being played by a performer whose background was primarily in modern dance (she had been a principal dancer with the Martha Graham Dance Company, which she now runs as artistic director). No stranger to musical theatre choreography, however, she had been featured in Bob Fosse's *Dancin'* and in performances with the American Dance Machine; she had also starred in movies like *Hard to Hold* (opposite rock star Rick Springfield) and the film adaptation of the stage hit *Whose Life Is It, Anyway?*

The Las Palmas production was codirected and choreographed by Steve Bellin and Danny Taylor, with a cast that also included Joseph Malone (Zach), Lynn Rose (Sheila), Suzanne Harrer (Val), Lloyd Gordon (Mike), and Elise Hernandez (Diana). The designs (the set was credited to "Gimmicks, Unlimited") mostly followed the Broadway originals. The show was produced by Stephen Rothman, William R. Greenblatt, and Symphony Pictures. Writing a guest column for the *Los Angeles Times*, Rothman lamented the premature closing of the show after eight weeks. The producers' goal had been to present an open-ended run of a top-notch production in a beautiful smaller venue that would approximate the intimate experience of seeing *ACL* in its original home, the Newman Theatre at the Public. (The Las Palmas Theatre has 380 seats.) But a cast of twenty-three actors and an orchestra of ten, all paid union scale, made the show too large to sustain in a house that size, despite good reviews. *ACL* has often broken box-office records and enjoyed unprecedented extended runs in regional houses, so this was a rare case of a production of the show being viewed as a financial failure. It has been successful at dinner theatres with similar seating capacities, but Equity permits lower salaries and more nonunion contracts for that type of venue; the Las Palmas production was on a contract comparable to those for large California institutions like the Mark Taper Forum and the Pasadena Playhouse. Rothman warned that the financial challenges of producing commercial theatre in mid-size Los Angeles theatres might be spelling the end of their viability, but *A Chorus Line* as a commercial property may just have been too big a show for this type of venue.

Lewis Family Playhouse, Rancho Cucamonga, CA, 2012

This beautiful theatre, owned and operated by the Southern California city of Rancho Cucamonga, presents several different performance series, including a community theatre group and the MainStreet Theatre Company, a professional children's theatre troupe. The 2012 production of *A Chorus Line* was the fourth annual presentation of their Broadway at the Gardens series, which produces a professional, non-Equity production of a large-scale adult musical each year. *ACL* was directed by Ron Kellum and codirected and choreographed by Hector Guerrero, who had directed the musical the previous year for the Woodstock Playhouse in upstate New York. Musical director David Lamoureux led a Broadway-sized orchestra. Guerrero recreated the original choreography for a cast that included Adrianna Rose Lyons as Cassie, Jason James as Zach, Kai Chubb as Sheila, Eric De Anda as Paul, Steven Rada as Mike, Cassandra Murphy as Diana, and Kristen Lamoureux as Judy. Reviewing the production for StageSceneLA.com, Steven Stanley wrote: "There are theaters—a lot of them in fact—that should never even attempt *A Chorus Line*. Fortunately, the Lewis Family Playhouse is not one of them, its current production's extraordinarily talented bunch of non-Equity performers coming astonishingly close to matching the caliber of the all-Equity Broadway National Tour which played the Ahmanson several years back. . . . The creative team of the upcoming 3-D Theatricals production would do well to check out the Rancho Cucamonga cast, who more than deserve their standing ovation." And indeed, the Equity productions at both 3-D Theatricals and Musical Theatre West the next year (see below for information on both) used several cast members from the Lewis Family Playhouse production, some in different roles; Theresa Murray was acclaimed for her performances as Kristine in all three productions.

Lyric Theatre of Oklahoma, Oklahoma City, OK, 1993, 2001, 2011

Lyric Theatre's 2011 production starred Natascia Diaz as Cassie, a role she had come close to getting in the Broadway revival—according to the documentary film *Every Little Step*, in which she is seen competing with Charlotte d'Amboise through an intense final callback session. Lyric's production was much less traditional than most. In an interview with Eric Webb of the *Oklahoma Gazette*, artistic director Michael Baron said: "When I asked David Marquez to direct it, I challenged him to make the show immediate and fresh. I wanted him to choreograph new dances in addition to re-creating the classic Michael Bennett choreography. There are also new takes on familiar monologues and an updating of the costuming so that the show is no longer clearly in 1975, but is more about the life of performers today." Marquez, who had worked with Diaz over a thirteen-year period on various projects, choreographed for her a completely new version of "The Music and the Mirror," which she performed in a sleeveless, salmon-colored minidress.

Both the University of Oklahoma and Oklahoma City University have strong musical theatre training programs, and Lyric's casting department draws heavily on their students and grads, mixing locals with imported Broadway veterans. The *ACL* cast featured Felipe Gonzalez Quillin as Paul, Robert Montano as Zach, Sasha Hutchings as Diana, and Eloise Kropp as Val. The show was presented on the huge stage of the five-level Civic Center Music Hall.

Lyric's previous production of *ACL* had been the last show the company presented in its prior home, the much smaller Kirkpatrick Theatre on the campus of Oklahoma City University. In that 2001 mounting, the role of Val was played by local favorite Lexi Windsor, who returned in 2011 as Sheila. The 2011 Connie, Hui Cha Poos, had an even longer history with the show, having played the same role in the company's first production back in 1993.

Mac-Haydn Theatre, Chatham, NY, 1986, 2008

Mac-Haydn Theatre was founded in 1969 by Lynne Haydn (who still runs it) and Linda MacNish. A traditional summer stock venue, it is located in the small town of Chatham, two and a half hours' drive from both New York City and Boston. The theatre in the round seats 350 patrons, with no seat farther than thirty feet from the stage. Their first production of *A Chorus Line*, in 1986, was directed by Patti D'Beck, who had been a dance captain for the Broadway company; her Zach was Dennis Edenfield, also a veteran of the New York production. Due to the very small size of the stage, the production combined and eliminated characters, with only thirteen dancers on the line; the cast included Cara Bujarsky as Cassie, Anne Allgood as Diana, future television star Paige Turco as Val, and Porfirio Figueroa as Paul.

The company produced the musical again in 2008, this time under the direction of Kevin Hill, whose adaptation of the choreography for the small space was described by reviewer J. Peter Bergman of *Berkshire Bright Focus* as "a miracle to behold." Like the 1986 production, this one added an intermission. The non-Equity cast notably included two sisters: Kelly L. Shook as Cassie and Karla Shook as Maggie, plus Tony Rivera as Zach. The reviewer singled out for praise Katy O'Donnell as Sheila, Juan Torres-Falcon as Paul, Lauren Palmieri as Diana, Colin Pritchard as Mike, and Jackey Good as Val.

Maine State Music Theatre, Brunswick, ME, 1997, 2012

The summer stock company performs in the Pickard Theatre on the campus of Bowdoin College, a large proscenium house complete with boxes, grand tier, and balcony. The 2012 production was directed by Donna Drake, a member of the original Broadway company, who has restaged the show more than a dozen times. No stranger to Maine State, she had directed *The Wiz* there the previous year. Michael Gorman, who has played Bobby and served as assistant choreographer and/or dance captain for numerous productions of the show over many years, worked with her as choreographer.

Rebecca Riker (Cassie) recreated the role she had played on the last leg of the Equity tour that followed the Broadway revival; Suzanna Dupree (Sheila) and Netanel Bellaishe (Mike) had taken part in the subsequent non-Equity tour. Bellaishe, a dancer from Israel, had achieved a measure of fame in his home country as a competitive dancer on reality TV. Selina Verastigui played Diana, Nicky Venditti was Paul, Kelly D. Felthous was Val, and Sean Bell was Bobby. Timothy Hughes, possibly the tallest dancer ever to appear in *A Chorus Line* at six feet six inches, was cast as Greg. Director Zach was played by Curt Dale Clark, who appropriately enough was shortly thereafter named the new artistic director of the theatre. The cast was enthusiastically reviewed, and in an interview with Bob Keyes in the *Portland Press Herald*, Drake called them her "dream line. I don't know how I got so lucky this time around. I got all of my first choices. No one turned down the gig."

Maltz Jupiter Theatre, Jupiter, FL, 1985, 1991, 2014

Josh Walden, who had been a swing in the Broadway revival, directed and choreographed the Florida venue's 2014 production, having previously staged the show for the Merry-Go-Round Playhouse and Theatre Memphis. Brian Ogilvie played Zach, with Elizabeth Earley reprising her Cassie from the Merry-Go-Round production four years earlier. Camden Gonzales (Diana) had recently played Bebe at Musical Theatre West in California (see below). The staging was mostly traditional, though scenic designer Michael Schweikhardt wrote a note for the theatre's website about his plans for the set, which involved extensive research into the backstage areas of Broadway theatres; the result was a more realistic and detailed environment, allowing the audience glimpses of the backs of flats and a bare brick wall upstage, rather than the traditional black velours. A sheer purple curtain provided an attractive backdrop for the finale. Cassie wore the classic red leotard and skirt, but Anna Christine Hillberry rethought the rehearsal clothes for many of the other characters. The production received a surprise review from critic Terry Teachout of the *Wall Street Journal*, who praised the high quality of the cast's acting: "Smaller parts like that of Bebe (pungently played by Michelle Petrucci) come across every bit as strongly as do the leads."

The Maltz Jupiter Theatre, the largest award-winning regional theatre in Florida, had first opened in 1979. The brainchild of movie star Burt Reynolds, who hails from the town, it was originally called the Burt Reynolds Dinner Theatre, and later the Burt Reynolds Jupiter Theatre; the venue housed an earlier mounting of *A Chorus Line* in 1985. That production was choreographed by T. Michael Reed, who won a Carbonell Award for his work; he had played Larry with the American cast that opened the original London run, later becoming dance captain for the Broadway company. After changing its name to Jupiter Theatre, the theatre presented the show again in 1991, with a cast that featured Robert Montano and Kerry Casserly.

The venue underwent several financial crises and changes in management before reemerging successfully in 2004. Rechristened after Milton and Tamar Maltz, board members and major donors who had made possible a major renovation, the remodeled facility is a state-of-the-art theatre seating 617, and one of Florida's best-equipped musical theatres.

Marriott Theatre, Lincolnshire, IL, 1985, 2010

When the regional rights to *A Chorus Line* were finally released by Tams-Witmark Music Library in 1985, ten years into the show's Broadway run, the professional musical theatre venues in the Chicago area competed in a mad dash to snag them. The winner was Marriott's Lincolnshire, which opened their production, the show's U.S. professional stock premiere, in June. The theatre is a part of the Marriott Lincolnshire resort in suburban Chicago; though not a dinner theatre, it offers dinner/show packages with two of the resort's restaurants. Under the leadership of artistic director Dyanne K. Earley and producer Kary M. Walker, the theatre developed a reputation as a proving ground for new musicals in addition to revivals of classic shows and frequent regional premieres. It seats approximately seven hundred, in the round.

The Marriott premiere of *A Chorus Line* was directed by Dominic Missimi, a high-profile Chicago director who taught acting at Northwestern University. The cast included several of his recent and current students, including Mark Hoebee as Don and Robyn Peterman as Bebe. Missimi's production was ahead of its time regarding nontraditional casting, with African American actors Don Franklin and Judith T. Smith playing Bobby and Sheila; ironically, though, they didn't have an Asian dancer for Connie (played by Michelle C. Kelly), nor were the Paul and Diana noticeably Latino (more common in those days than it is now). Lighting design was by John Williams, costumes by Nancy Missimi (wife of the director). The set design was by Jeffrey Harris, who found ways to incorporate some mirrors around a square stage that was bisected diagonally by the all-important white line. Richard Christiansen of the *Chicago Tribune* praised Missimi's blocking of the show for the arena setting: "In one striking case, this production even improves on Broadway."

The June 1985 opening at Marriott's Lincolnshire Theatre marked the show's first professional regional theatre production in the United States. Shown here are Ray Frewen as Zach (the unusual costume design is by Nancy Missimi) and Candace Tovar as Cassie.

Photo by Lisa Howe-Ebright

This happens when Cassie, Zach`s former love, pleads with him to let her return to the chorus. As they argue, those same chorus dancers she is praising are seen rehearsing in the Marriott`s theater lobby, and, as the argument heats up, the dancers advance down an aisle, singing their song of 'One' in a phalanx of comradeship and talent. Terrific." Bennett and Avian's choreography was adapted by Candace Tovar, who also played Cassie. An experienced gypsy, she had played the role on Broadway as an understudy, as well as serving as standby for Gwen Verdon in *Chicago*; she was one of the featured dancers in Bob Fosse's film *All That Jazz*.

It was twenty-five years before Marriott presented the show again. In September, 2010, an all-new production opened at the theatre, with costumer Nancy Missimi the only member of the creative team to return from the 1985 version. (Missimi's costumes, in bright, vivid colors, quoted Theoni Aldredge's originals in many details but did not recreate them as religiously as is often done; as Diana, for example, Pilar Millhollen wore a blue baseball shirt. The finale costumes were done in white and silver rather than the traditional champagne and gold.) The show was directed by Mark Lococo of the theatre faculty at Chicago's Loyola University and choreographed by renowned Chicago area director/choreographer Rachel Rockwell, who had been acclaimed for her own performance as Cassie in the 1999 production at Drury Lane Evergreen Park. The cast was made up primarily of Chicago talent, but imports included Mara Davi, playing Cassie after her breakout performance as Maggie in the Broadway revival, and Bryan Knowlton as Paul, a role he played as a replacement in that revival and has reprised in several regional companies. Like Marriott's previous production, this one had an African

Bryan Knowlton, center, as Paul in the finale, staged in the round at the Marriott Theatre, 2010.   *Photo by Peter Coombs*

American Sheila (Broadway veteran Anika Ellis); this time around, they did have an Asian American actress (Jastine Dumlao) to play Connie. For productions staged in the round, the question of how to incorporate mirrors is always a particular challenge. This one seems to have solved it especially well: as Scott Zacher of Chicago Theater Beat wrote in his review: "This arena staging may be in the round but the mirrors work even better than in a proscenium production. They may not suggest many more dancers than the cast itself but the recessed effect makes it look like we're seeing memories as much as moments here." The acclaimed production was nominated for five Jeff Awards.

Melody Top, Milwaukee, WI, 1985

Michael Bennett worked at the Melody Top early in his career; part of a chain of tent theatres, the beloved venue presented summer seasons of musicals and operettas beginning in 1963. The production of *A Chorus Line*, presented in their second-to-last season, featured Michaela Hughes as Cassie, P. J. Benjamin as Zach, Dwayne Chattman as Richie, Laura Soltis as Val, and David Loring as Paul. Directed by Sam Viverito, it joined the versions at Casa Mañana and Marriott's Lincolnshire as one of three major productions of the show staged in the round that summer. The cast was praised but the 2,156-seat space, with troubled acoustics, seems not to have been the most hospitable to this particular show. According to Tina Maples in *The Milwaukee Journal:* "Although Viverito alters the line—breaking it up, swinging it around or pivoting its members to give all sections of the audience some frontal views—the audience still gets overly long stretches of nothing but backsides, as in the roll call part of the show." Part of a fondly remembered and now mostly vanished species of summer stock theatre, the Melody Top ceased operations after the 1986 season.

Middleton Players Theatre, Middleton, WI, 2014

As the primary community theatre in this small city near Madison, the Middleton Players Theatre performs at the arts center at Middleton High School, and has a cooperative and mutually supportive relationship with the school. The company had traditionally presented one production a year, but their twenty-fourth season, which consisted of *RENT* and *A Chorus Line*, was the first to feature two full-scale musicals. *ACL* was codirected by Matthew Starika-Jolivet and Thomas J. Kasdorf, with choreography by Sarah Bartlett, who taught the original routines to a group of dancers with diverse levels of training and experience. The mostly local cast, which included several college students as well as two former Middleton residents living in New York who went back home to do the show, featured Jarrell Homesly as Richie, Stephanie Genito as Sheila, Kate Mann as Maggie, Eric Lloyd as Don, Britta Schlicht as Val, Andrew Lonsdale as Larry, and Marie McManama, a local singing teacher somewhat ironically cast as the tone-deaf Kristine. A young actor named Michael Costanzo was cast not as Mike Costa but in the role of Mark. Amy Ruth, a professional dancer originally from the area with fifteen years' experience as a Radio City Music Hall Rockette, was the Cassie. The next year, the theatre expanded its offerings again with its first three-show season, and appears to be entering its second quarter-century with bright prospects for future growth and success.

Montclair State University, Montclair, NJ, 2011

A large state school, Montclair has an impressive theatre department that is something of a well-kept secret on the national scene. Offering a BFA in musical theatre with unusually thorough training in dance, the school was able to field a strong enough student cast to present what Lori Sender, reviewing the production for newjerseynewsroom.com, called a "Broadway-caliber performance of *A Chorus Line*, starring 17 tremendously talented college kids, dance moves and voices to go head to head with any of those of the original cast members on Broadway from the 70's and 80's." It was directed by faculty member Clay James, coordinator of the BFA program, who had performed in the show professionally and taught the cast the original choreography. On the department's website, he wrote: "*A Chorus Line* represents a great learning experience for all students involved. We have a fast, four-week rehearsal period. The show is being presented without an intermission and without edits. It can be a grueling process, but the work we're putting in (including a Master-class via Skype with Priscilla Lopez, who originated the role of Diana on Broadway) will result in a great show." Jacob Seidman, the student who played Larry, told Stefanie Sears of the *Montclarion*: "My favorite part is Clay choreographing the original choreography. It's like learning a part of musical theater history." Zach was played by graduate student John Zisa, with junior Chris Cannon doing one performance. Cassie and Sheila received sophisticated, well-danced portrayals by Elish Conlon and Megan Elyse Fulmer, respectively, and Christian Castro was Paul.

Muhlenberg Summer Music Theatre, Allentown, PA, 2014

This summer stock season is an annual project of Muhlenberg College, a small four-year liberal arts school with a large and well-respected Theatre and Dance Department. The show was presented on the proscenium stage of the 392-seat Paul C. Empie Theatre, part of the campus's Baker Center for the Arts. The cast of students and new grads of the program performed under the auspices of director Charles Richter and choreographer Karen Dearborn, faculty members who, respectively, serve as the department's Director of Theatre and Chair of the Dance Program; the musical director was Michael Schnack. Dearborn was largely faithful to Bennett and Avian's original choreography but provided some new ideas of her own. During "The Music and the Mirror," at the point where the semicircle of mirrors usually descends from above, two male dancers dressed in black wheeled standing mirrors on from the wings. They then proceeded to dance the slow section of the number with Cassie (Emily Jeanne Phillips), who worked in some of the original moves while interacting with both men in a sort of pas de trois, including lifts and partner work. As the music accelerated at the point where the mirrors traditionally rise, the men departed, taking the mirrors with them, and Phillips performed the rest of the number alone in a version that mostly followed the original. The "One" finale also got a new look, with the dancers outfitted in glittering red costumes (with gold top hats) by designer Campbell Baird.

Municipal Opera Association of St. Louis, MO, 1981, 1982, 1985, 1989, 1997, 2002

Informally known as "the Muny," the St. Louis Municipal Opera is the largest musical theatre venue in the United States, with eleven thousand seats. Many of the nation's other big outdoor amphitheaters have extensive lawn seating behind the audience seats, but the Muny provides fixed seating for everyone. It first opened in 1917 and originally produced grand operas and operettas, but as the art form of American musical theatre developed, that repertoire gradually took over; the organization now produces an annual summer season usually consisting of seven large-scale musicals.

Many members of the original *ACL* team had histories with the Muny long before the show was created: Donna McKechnie reminisces memorably in her autobiography about doing *Call Me Madam* there in 1968 with that show's original star, Ethel Merman; Michael Bennett choreographed productions there during his days on the summer stock circuit; Nicholas Dante danced in several Muny productions in 1965; and Renee Baughman got her professional start at the theatre at age fifteen.

Besides producing its own mammoth outdoor productions of popular musicals, the Muny has often hosted touring productions—and even presented a week's worth of performances by the Broadway company of Bennett's *Seesaw*, which closed for a week in New York to make the journey to Missouri. It also offered a rare regional revival of Bennett's post-*ACL* Broadway show, *Ballroom*, starring Janis Paige and Forrest Tucker, in 1979.

A Chorus Line's first four appearances at the Muny were all touring companies. The 1981 engagement proved so popular that it was brought back the next summer as a replacement for a touring *Hello, Dolly!* that had closed prematurely; in both years, *ACL* played in August as the finale to the season. In 1985, Baayork Lee's tour starred Donna McKechnie in her return to the show after eight years and precipitated her return to the Broadway cast the following season. McKechnie was invited to return to the Muny in 1986 to star opposite Rex Smith in an unusual double bill of "The Diary of Adam and Eve" (one of the three one-act musicals that make up *The Apple Tree*) and *Joseph and the Amazing Technicolor Dreamcoat*. Another summer tour of *ACL*, again directed by Lee and starring McKechnie, played the MUNY in 1989.

The 1997 and 2002 productions, both directed by Mitzi Hamilton, were tailored specifically to the outdoor stage. Cassie was played by Laurie Gamache in

'97 and Jane Lanier in '02. Set designer Steve Gilliam devised a simple green art deco design to frame the traditionally bare stage space and provided "The Music and the Mirror" with seven twelve-foot-tall mirrors that had to be wheeled onto the stage by dancers, who continued to hold onto them throughout the number in case of wind.

Musical Theatre West, Long Beach, CA, 2013

An outgrowth of the Whittier Civic Light Opera, founded in 1952, Musical Theatre West has grown to be one of California's largest producers of professional musical theatre. In residence at La Mirada Theatre for the Performing Arts starting in 1977, the company moved twenty years later to the 1,074-seat Richard and Karen Carpenter Performing Arts Center on the campus of California State University. Under the leadership of executive director/producer Paul Garman, it produces a season of four musicals on the large proscenium stage, plus a reading series. The 2013 production of *A Chorus Line*, with a cast that included nine Equity and nineteen non-Equity actors, had traditional direction and choreography by Roger Castellano and musical direction by David Lamoureux. Lamoureux had also been musical director of the non-Equity production the previous year at the Lewis Family Playhouse (see above); his daughter Kristen, who had been Judy in that production, played Maggie this time, a role she had recently played for 3-D Productions in Fullerton. Theresa Murray played Kristine; Venny Carranza, playing her husband Al at MTW, had been Mike with 3-D Productions; Momoko Sugai was Connie at both 3-D and MTW, while Steven Rada moved from the ebullient Mike at the Lewis to the serious, sensitive Paul at MTW. Chryssie Whitehead, a California-based dancer who had wowed audiences as Kristine in the original cast of the 2006 Broadway revival, got her chance to dance Cassie this time around. Like the revival, MTW cast an African American actress, Sherisse Springer, as Sheila. Another black actor, Louis A. Williams Jr., played Larry; reviewing the show for StageandCinema.com, Tony Frankel singled Williams out as few performers in that role have ever been: "Far and away, my favorite actor of the night performs one of the smallest roles: Louis A. Williams as Larry, the director's assistant. Williams is not just magnetic and a kick-ass dancer, but captures the professionalism and discipline of one who would have such a job; he also shows a profound empathy with the auditioning dancers." Matthew Williams (no relation) was Bobby, Tory Trowbridge was Val, Chuck Saculla was Zach, and Ayme Olivo was Diana.

New Bedford Festival Theatre, New Bedford, MA, 2011

This professional non-Equity summer troupe performs at the Zeiterion Theatre and attracts actors from around the country. Though the company wasn't established until 1990, its founders, George Charbonneau and Armand Marchand, had hired New York choreographer Clay James to stage a previous production of *A Chorus Line* at the Zeiterion in 1985, the year the stock rights were first released.

The 2011 New Bedford production featured the original Broadway staging and choreography as recreated by Michael Susko. Scott Guthrie had a particular success as Zach; in an interview, he told Lorraine Lucciola of *South Coast Today* that he himself had put in "time on both sides of the (director's) table. Some directors and some auditions are open, free and there is communication between the director and the auditioning actors/dancers. Or, directors stay separate and apart from the actors, like Zach. Zach knows what he wants and how to get what he wants out of people in a seemingly socially unacceptable way. He's so attached to the role of director that he doesn't identify with the actors/dancers. There's a difference between a closed first and an open palm, and it's taken time for my skin to thicken and accept the notion of rejection."

Reviewing the production for the same publication, David B. Boyce later wrote: "Guthrie reveals Zach's professional demeanor, underscoring it with subtle elements of neurosis and self-doubt. It's a many-faceted performance that never rings false." The cast also included Sabra Michelle as Cassie, Michelle O'Bryan as Sheila, Lauren Gemelli as Diana, Eric B. Mota as Paul, Michael Peter Deeb as Mike, and Taavon Gamble as Richie. Caley Crawford, who had just graduated from the Boston Conservatory, played Val; she would shortly afterwards be tapped by Baayork Lee to go into the non-Equity national tour in the role of Cassie.

New York University, New York, NY, 1991, 2004

Just over a year after *A Chorus Line* ended its record-shattering fifteen-year run on Broadway, Greg Ganakas's New York University Summer Musical Theatre program presented what was billed as the first New York City revival of the show in the Frederick Loewe Theatre on West 4th Street, just a few blocks from the show's original home at the Public Theater. Ganakas directed the musical, and the original choreography and staging were recreated by Kerry Casserly, who had played several of the roles on tour and on Broadway (she was particularly well known for her Kristine). A School of Education benefit, the production had a brief limited run, but is remembered as a very special one by the participants; besides several NYU theatre students, the cast included professionals who had done the show all over the world, and for many of them it was an emotional reunion. Casserly herself played Cassie, alternating performances with two others in the role: Angelique Ilo (a Broadway Cassie and Judy) and Maria Laura Baccarini, who had played Cassie (in Italian) in a production in Italy. Another Italian, Barbara Tartaglia, who had been Bebe in that production, played Diana. Others included Nora Brennan (now a New York casting director) as Sheila, Billy Johnstone (who also assisted Casserly with the choreography) as Paul, Patrick Boyd as Don, Bethel Caram as Val, and Mark Robinson as Greg. Stephen Nachamie, then a sophomore at NYU, began his long association with the show playing Mark in this production. Dennis Wayne, a graduate of the High School of Performing Arts who had enjoyed a substantial career as a ballet dancer and choreographer, realized a longtime dream by playing Zach.

Another NYU production of the show was presented in the autumn of 2004 in the same theatre. NYU has numerous separate schools, departments, and divisions: this production was presented by the Steinhardt School of Education's Department of Music and Performing Arts Profession's Program in Vocal Performance. It was directed by Kari Nicolaisen, who taught the original Bennett staging.

North Carolina Theatre, Raleigh, NC, 1987, 1994, 2002, 2014

A professional Equity company focusing on big-scale musicals, this Raleigh institution has presented *ACL* four times during its thirty-year history; the 2014 mounting, staged in the Broadway-sized Raleigh Memorial Auditorium at the Duke Energy Center for the Performing Arts, was directed and choreographed by the ubiquitous Mitzi Hamilton, who had staged two of the company's earlier versions as well. It featured Jessica Lee Goldyn, Hamilton's Cassie from previous productions at the Paper Mill Playhouse, Theatre Under the Stars, and Paramount Theatre. She and her Zach (Nathaniel Shaw, a director and choreographer in real life as well) here returned to the original staging and choreography a year after playing the same roles in the very nontraditional production at the Fulton Theatre (see above). They were joined by Alexander Cruz, fully recovered from the injury that had sidelined his Paul during the recent run at the Surflight Theatre, also directed by Hamilton (see below), along with Tiffany Chalothorn in her fifth outing as Connie, Nick Varricchio as Mike, Alexandra Fassler as Diana, Rachel Schur as Val, and Brandon Rubendall as Al. Hilary Michael Thompson, who had played Kristine to Goldyn's Cassie at Stages St. Louis three years earlier and also toured in that role, graduated to Sheila this time. The theatre's programs include a conservatory that offers extensive training in musical theatre: the school's director of dance, Tito Hernandez, was appropriately cast as assistant choreographer Larry. James Dardenne's set design, from Hamilton's previous production at the Paper Mill Playhouse, appeared again here, with lighting by Craig Stelzenmuller. Edward G. Robinson was the musical director.

North Shore Music Theatre, Beverly, MA, 1986, 1998, 2010

Another in-the-round venue, the highly respected North Shore Music Theatre has done the show three times over the past thirty years. With a seating capacity of 1,800, the theatre, founded in 1954, became known as the largest regional theatre in New England. In 1986, Sam Viverito directed its first production of *ACL*. The role of Cassie was played by Marcia Albuquerque, a Brazilian dancer who three years earlier had played the part in Portuguese for the Sao Paulo premiere of the show. North Shore's next mounting, in 1998, was one of the dozens directed and choreographed by Mitzi Hamilton. Michael Danek, who had played Don on Broadway during the original run, was Zach, and Shannon Lee Jones was Cassie; Sachi Shimizu (Connie) and Jan Leigh Herndon (Sheila) had played those characters on Broadway, while Julie Graves (Val) and Donna Pompei (Diana) were recreating roles in which they had recently toured. Eric Paeper played Paul, while

Luis Villabon, who has made a specialty of Paul in numerous touring and regional productions, was Mike this time around. Valerie Gebert was the musical director.

In 2003, North Shore earned the distinction of premiering a new show that went on to Broadway success: David Bryan and Joe DiPietro's *Memphis: The Musical.* But two years later the building suffered a damaging fire and began a severe downward financial spiral; it closed its doors in 2009, seemingly for good. Later that year, however, the theatre was purchased by Bill Hanney, owner of a successful chain of cinemas; he brought in Evans Haile, a distinguished conductor who had previously served as producing artistic director of the Cape Playhouse, as the new artistic director. They reopened the renovated venue in 2010 and were able to turn things around, and the theatre has bounced back strongly.

Hanney and Haile brought back *A Chorus Line* in their very first season. This version was directed and choreographed by Mark Martino, who had played Zach in a 1996 national tour under the direction of Baayork Lee. His Zach and Cassie were the married team of Derek Hanson and Rebecca Riker. Hanson got more attention in the reviews than most Zachs; he was praised by more than one critic for the striking athleticism of his dancing and for his powerful presence and incisive acting choices. Martino used descending two-way mirrors for the opening number and "The Music and the Mirror"; other mirrors, surrounded by lights, sprang up from under the stage for the finale. The theatre's aisles were used as acting areas in some scenes, including the confrontation between Zach and Cassie (while the other dancers were on the stage rehearsing "One"); the ballet dancers who appear in the "background" during "At the Ballet" (the "ballet blaze") were also placed in the aisles, in red light. Kurt Domoney, who had understudied in the Broadway revival and played Bobby at both Geva Theatre Center and the Ogunquit Playhouse, was Martino's associate choreographer and dance captain, also playing those same roles onstage as Larry. Others included Jonathan Day as a particularly acrobatic Mike, Christopher Shin as an Asian American Mark, Delius Doherty as Richie, Katie Cameron as Sheila, Julie Kotarides as Diana, Cary Michele Miller as Maggie, and Leslie Flesner as Val.

Ogunquit Playhouse, Ogunquit, ME, 2009

A large New England summer stock venue, Ogunquit finally produced *A Chorus Line* in 2009 after several years of trying to get the rights. Their production opened shortly after the closing of the Broadway revival, and the executive artistic director, Bradford Kenney, arranged to rent the sets and costumes from that production; they also hired one of its leading ladies, Nadine Isenegger, who had been one of Charlotte d'Amboise's alternates as Cassie. Having played many Broadway performances opposite the Zach of media personality Mario Lopez, Isenegger found herself once again paired with a Latin TV heartthrob in that role: Lorenzo Lamas, popular star of *Falcon Crest, Renegade,* and *The Bold and the Beautiful.* Though not known for his dancing, Lamas had had a small role in the movie of *Grease* and had recorded one hit record, "Fools Like Me," a song from his 1984 film *Body Rock.* He had recently begun to explore musical theatre with appearances as El Gallo in *The*

Fantasticks at Casa Mañana and the King of Siam (opposite Broadway's Rachel de Benedet) in Ogunquit's 2007 production of *The King and I*. Though he reportedly acted the role of Zach effectively, he did not dance, appearing only briefly for a bow at the top of the finale. The production's cast also featured Leslie Flesner (Judy), Katie Cameron (Sheila), Megan Sikora (Val), Kurt Domoney (repeating his Bobby from the Geva production), Michael Biren (Mike), Thay Floyd (Richie), Christine LaDuca (Diana), and Felipe Quillin (Paul). Director Luis Villabon, known for playing Paul and assisting Baayork Lee on numerous tours and regional productions, reproduced the Bennett staging and choreography. The production and the theatre got a burst of unexpected publicity when former U.S. President George H. W. Bush and his wife Barbara attended a performance. They tried on a couple of the finale top hats and were a taught a few steps of the choreography in a friendly meet-and-greet with the cast and director following the show; a few days later, they invited the whole cast and crew to a joint birthday party at their home in Kennebunkport.

Olney Theatre Center, Olney, MD, 2013

Founded in 1938, the Olney has enjoyed a long reputation as an outstanding summer stock theatre. With a fourteen-acre campus that includes several performance spaces and support facilities, the Center has in recent years expanded its theatre season to run from April through October, focusing on twentieth-century American classics with a healthy percentage of musicals and a recently expanded focus on new works.

The 2013 production of *A Chorus Line* was directed by Stephen Nachamie, who has had a long association with the show, first as a performer (he played Mark, Mike, and Paul in various productions) and later as director and choreographer of several regional revivals. He remained faithful to the original choreography but meticulously reconfigured some of the staging (as well as the fly mirrors) for the tricky sightlines of the Center's New Mainstage Theatre, which has a wide stage with a partial thrust. The theatre imported elements of the innovative set that James Dardenne had designed for the previous season's production at the Paper Mill Playhouse (see below); the wall of mirrors flew in and out, and there was an impressive wall of lights that gave the finale an exciting new look; the costumes by Brad Musgrove were traditional, and lighting was by Andrew F. Griffin.

Carl Randolph played Zach, with Bryan Knowlton repeating his Paul, which he had played as replacement for Jason Tam in the Broadway revival, and assisting Nachamie as dance captain. Another alum of the revival cast, Michelle Aravena, was initially cast as Diana but moved to the role of Cassie shortly before opening when the originally announced Cassie had to withdraw due to an injury. Reviewer Charles Shubow of Broadwayworld.com referred to her performance of "The Music and the Mirror" as "goose-bump city." Jessica Vaccaro took over as Diana, and the cast also included Colleen Hayes as Sheila, Parker Drown as Bobby, and Jennifer Cordiner as Val. Kyle Schliefer incorporated some impressive tumbling moves into "I Can Do That," despite being substantially taller than most Mikes.

Speaking about the production later, Nachamie said he had made a point of including actors who hadn't done it before and had something unique to say. He said, "The hardest thing about directing the show is getting seventeen people in the same place with the same stakes," adding: "It's a show you can invest in, you can relish the experience and enjoy the experience. But it's not a show you can own. You have to live in the moment. There will never be a perfect production of the show because it's inherently theatrical and in the moment, and because it's a piece that shows our imperfections."

During the run, original Cassie Donna McKechnie visited the Center, where she performed a cabaret show entitled *Same Place, Another Time*. The Olney production of *A Chorus Line* was honored with the Helen Hayes Award (the Washington, D.C., area's version of the Tony) for Outstanding Resident Musical (in a tie with Signature Theatre/Ford's Theatre's *Hello, Dolly!*), and Vaccaro (also in a tie) was named Outstanding Actress in a Leading Role in a Resident Musical. Critic Peter Marks tweeted about the production: "I sort of thought I was over *A Chorus Line*. Stupid of me! Stephen Nachamie's production reminded me why you should never get over it."

Paper Mill Playhouse, Millburn, NJ, 1991, 2001, 2012

Unlike most of the nation's other large regional musical theatres, New Jersey's esteemed Paper Mill Playhouse did not snatch up the rights to *A Chorus Line* when they were first made available in the mid-1980s. The theatre is only a quick train ride from New York City's Penn Station, so it wouldn't have made sense to do the show there while it was still running on Broadway. But Paper Mill has now done three productions of the musical, the first of which opened in June 1991, slightly over a year after the Broadway run ended—and two weeks after the death of Nicholas Dante, coauthor of the show's book. That loss must have weighed poignantly on the shoulders of Eric Paeper, who was acclaimed for an especially sensitive performance as Paul, the character based on Dante. One of the many productions directed by Baayork Lee, this version also featured Michael Danek (who had played Don late in the Broadway run) as Zach, Jane Lanier as Cassie, Matt Zarley as Mike, and Jan Leigh Herndon as Sheila. The original designs were used; as a 1,200-seat venue with a Broadway-sized proscenium stage, Paper Mill was able to create an unusually close facsimile of the Broadway production.

The theatre presented the show again ten years later, in partnership with six other regional houses and producing organizations, including Theater of the Stars in Atlanta, the Pittsburgh Civic Light Opera, and the Starlight Theatre Association in Kansas City, Missouri. Again staged by Lee in the original designs, the production was something of an outgrowth of a national tour she had put together in 1996, with several holdovers from that tour's cast including Charlene Carr (Maggie), Cindy Marchionda (Diana), and Luis Villabon (Paul). Zach was played by Mark Bove (who had been a Mike on Broadway), and Cassie was Caitlin Carter, a striking blonde dancer with extensive Broadway credits including the dance revue *Swing* and the original cast of the long-running revival of *Chicago* (in which she played Mona and understudied Ann Reinking as Roxie). Nadine Isenegger played Val and understudied Cassie (a role she would go on to play in several future productions), while Kim Shriver, appearing in her ninth production of the show, was Sheila. Gregory Victor, who had codirected the first-ever high school production of *ACL* at Analy High School (see above), was the first assistant stage manager. The role of Mark was played by the fresh-faced Tim Federle, now known as the award-winning author of *Better Nate Than Ever* and other children's books about kids in the theatre. He reported being especially inspired when, during the run, the cast went to see Donna McKechnie's one-woman show, *Inside the Music*, which she performed at Paper Mill as a special event on October 2. (The dates of the run were September 5 to October 14, 2001, so this production is vividly remembered by the cast as the one that ran through the terrorist attacks of 9/11).

By the time Paper Mill revived *ACL* again in October 2012, the theatre was under the artistic direction of Mark S. Hoebee, who knew the show well, having played Don in the 1985 regional premiere at the Marriott Theatre in Illinois (see above) and Mike in the 1990 Visa tour. The 2012 Paper Mill version was staged by Mitzi Hamilton, who by that time had reproduced Bennett and Avian's choreography for over thirty-five productions of the show. This time she introduced a few innovations. The original designers were credited in the program alongside a new team. Costumer Gail Baldoni used most of Aldredge's classic costumes but designed new looks for a few of the characters, including Zach, who was all in black. Scenic designer James Dardenne's contributions were most evident in the finale, which featured an impressive wall of lights and a large tilted mirror that reflected the dancers from above.

Much of the audience interest, and press, for the production focused on Rachelle Rak, a veteran Broadway dancer who was finally getting her chance to play Sheila six years after her unsuccessful callback for that role in the Broadway revival, which had become one of the most riveting sequences in the documentary film *Every Little Step* (see Chapter 21); she proved magnificent in the part. Jessica Lee Goldyn as Cassie and Mike Cannon as Al were repeating roles they had played at the end of the revival's Broadway run; the production was a homecoming of sorts for Goldyn, a New Jersey native who had appeared at Paper Mill as a child in *Gypsy*. Martin Harvey, an alumnus of London's Royal Ballet Company, made a distinctive, British-accented Zach.

The opening night performance on October 7, 2012, was made especially memorable by a post-show tribute to Marvin Hamlisch, the show's composer, who had passed away that August. Immediately following the performance, Hamilton took the stage with Kelly Bishop, the original Sheila, for a brief spoken tribute to Hamlisch, following which part of the "One" finale was repeated with the cast joined by over fifty *Chorus Line* alumni, including original Broadway cast members and replacements, plus performers from the 2006 revival and numerous tours and regional productions. Heather Parcells (Judy in the revival) reported afterwards that, even at the rehearsal, all the dancers had immediately remembered the "One" choreography, no matter how long it had been since they had done the show. Hamlisch's widow, Terre Blair Hamlisch, was in attendance and told Playbill. com's Michael Gioia: "There is no doubt in my mind that today [Marvin] would be smiling from ear to ear and extraordinarily proud of this cast and what they did with this piece."

Pittsburgh Civic Light Opera, Pittsburgh, PA, 2001, 2012

Baayork Lee choreographed the 2006 Broadway revival of *ACL* and its 2008 touring version, as well as the two non-Equity tours that followed; when she directed the show for the Pittsburgh CLO in June 2012, she handpicked a top-flight cast, most of whom had been in one or another of those companies. Heather Parcells (Judy), Grant Turner (Zach), Bryan Knowlton (Paul), and Nadine Isenegger (Cassie) were recreating roles they had played on Broadway. Emily Fletcher (Sheila), Gabrielle Ruiz (Diana), Denis Lambert (Greg), Brandon Tyler (Larry), Kevin Curtis (Richie), and Hilary Michael Thompson (Kristine) were repeating from the Equity tour. Carleigh Bettiol, a standout dancer who had traveled to Japan as Cassie with the non-Equity tour, got her Equity card in Pittsburgh as Val; her long dark hair gave that character a new look. Other alums from the non-Equity tour included Eric Carsia (Don), Theo Lencicki (Al), Alexzandra Sarmiento (Connie), Jake Weinstein (Mark), and Hardy Weaver (Bobby). Shane Rhoades (Mike) and Gina Philistine (Bebe) had histories with their roles that went back even further. As Grant Turner told Sharon Eberson for a preopening interview in the *Pittsburgh Post-Gazette*, the short rehearsal period wasn't a problem because they had all done the show before. He said: "It's almost like we can go deeper because we all know the piece. . . . There's time to talk about things we never get to talk about that we couldn't do if it was the first time for everyone." Pittsburgh CLO had previously presented two tours of the show in the 1980s; a 2001 production, also directed by Lee, was shared with the Paper Mill Playhouse (see above).

Pittsburgh Playhouse/Pittsburgh Musical Theatre, Pittsburgh, PA, 1985, 2003, 2011

The Pittsburgh Playhouse has a complicated history, and its association with *A Chorus Line* has been unusually long and complex as well. A professional theatre since the 1930s, the space was taken over in the 1970s by Point Park College (now Point Park University), which ran a professional troupe, the Playhouse Theatre Company, there for many years, giving students the opportunity to take part in musicals alongside professional Equity actors from both Pennsylvania and New York. Under the general management and musical direction of Kenneth Gargaro, the Playhouse presented one of the first regional productions of the show in 1985; Pittsburgh native Danny Herman, who was then playing Mike on Broadway, took a leave from the New York production to direct and choreograph. The cast was made up primarily of students or recent graduates of Point Park, alongside five Equity actors. Pittsburgher Lenora Nemetz, a Broadway veteran with credits going back to stints in the original productions of *Cabaret* and *Chicago*, played Cassie. Nemetz has become almost legendary in the biz as the perennial Broadway understudy, to the point where her name is mentioned in that regard in a song from the hit musical *Nunsense* (and indeed her most recent Broadway engagement was playing Mazeppa and understudying Patti LuPone as Rose in the 2008 revival of Gypsy). She was joined by New York actor Michael Ragan as Zach. That 1985 Pittsburgh cast also included not one but two dancers who would go on to become Tony-winning Broadway choreographers and directors: Rob Davis (who later changed his name to Rob Ashford) as Paul and Kathleen Marshall as Val.

In 1992, Point Park discontinued the professional company (it was revived more recently with a focus on straight plays), but certain elements of it, led by Gargaro, regrouped to form Pittsburgh Musical Theatre, which was struggling financially when it produced its own *ACL* in 2003. Presented in the Byham Theatre in downtown Pittsburgh, the production had been scheduled for the previous fall but then cancelled due to lack of funds—after several of the cast members had already arrived in town to begin rehearsals. According to Christopher Rawson, writing for the *Pittsburgh Post-Gazette*, an energetic fund-raising campaign got it back on track for January, with Gargaro repeating as musical director. The cast this time included ten Equity actors, including the Cassie, Gina Philistine, who had toured extensively as Bebe. Tomé Cousin as Richie was repeating his role from the 1985 production, and Maura White, who had been in that cast as a cut dancer in the opening number, played Sheila, marking her eighth production of the show. Gavan Pamer, a Point Park grad, was the director/choreographer and also played Zach.

In the fall of 2011, Danny Herman again directed *A Chorus Line* on the Pittsburgh Playhouse stage, this time for a production by Point Park University's Conservatory Theatre Company. Composer Marvin Hamlisch was a master guest artist in residence at the university that year, teaching workshops on auditioning and film music; he also attended a rehearsal of the show. The all-student cast included Tyler Scherer as Zach, Lily Davis as Cassie, and Jerreme Rodriguez as Paul. Brandon Taylor (Mike), then a sophomore, has since begun a promising musical theatre career. On playing Mike, the role director Herman was known for, he told interviewer Kayleigh Smith for the Point Park website: "Danny, amazing as he is, let me play my Mike, or in other words, make it my own. And from then on out, I knew this was going to be such an incredible process. I will never forget this experience because of his love for us and his true commitment to not only putting on a great show but honestly caring that we come out as better dancers."

ReAct Theatre, Seattle, WA, 1998, 1999

The last production of the show staged in the Pacific Northwest during the twentieth century was a professional non-Equity mounting by ReAct Theatre, formerly known as Repertory Actors Workshop. It opened on August 7, 1998, at the Broadway Performance Hall in Seattle, which seats 295 audience members in a proscenium configuration (almost exactly the same size as the Newman Theatre at the Public, where *A Chorus Line* was first performed).

The show was directed by ReAct Theatre's founding artistic director, David Hsieh, whose goal was to recreate as much of the original staging and choreography as possible. To that end, he engaged a team of three choreographers who had worked on other local productions of the musical: Scot Charles Anderson (who was also cast as Zach), Brian Joe (who appeared in the opening number as Frank), and Audrey Fan (who played Val). He additionally arranged for the cast to have a couple of rehearsals with New York dancers Roxane Carrasco and Frank Kliegel, who had appeared in *ACL* on the road and on Broadway; they were passing through Seattle with a tour of another show and came in to help the cast refine their moves, and particularly to teach the original choreography for "The Music and the Mirror" to the production's Cassie, Crystal Dawn Munkers. The company also planned to rent the gold finale costumes that had been used in the 1985 movie version, but they arrived in poor condition and proved unusable for a stage production: designed for film, they had not been built to facilitate the all-important quick change, so a different set had to be rented from a costume house. In fact, this particular production required two sets of finale costumes, because one of Hsieh's innovations was to bring the cut dancers from the opening (increased in number from the usual seven to about a dozen) back onstage to double the line during the finale; these performers were also seen during the brief ballet sequence performed upstage during "At the Ballet."

Audrey Fan, also one of the production's choreographers, as Val at ReAct Theatre in Seattle, 1998.   *Courtesy David Hsieh*

Known as "Seattle's Multi-ethnic Philanthropic Theatre Company," ReAct's mission statement includes a commitment to nontraditional casting and creating opportunities for underserved artists. *A Chorus Line* was cast accordingly, with four African American and five Asian American actors featured on the line, as well as a woman playing Larry (changed to "Laurie") and a few cast members who did not have traditional dancer's physiques. Judy Turner was played by a black actress, and her line "My real name is Lana Turner" was changed to "My real name is Tina Turner." (Coincidentally, the actress's real name was Gina Turner!) That line change has been adopted by some larger-scale productions in recent years, but ReAct may have been the first to incorporate it. Even more actors got a chance to perform in ReAct's critically acclaimed production when it was brought back for a return engagement, with several cast changes, that opened in the same theatre on September 9, 1999.

Reagle Music Theatre, Waltham, MA, 1987, 1990, 1994, 2002, 2012

Originally called the Reagle Players, the company was formed in 1969 by executive producer Robert J. Eagle, who still runs it today. According to the theatre's website, Eagle, who has a background as a teacher and administrator in the area's public school system, "is a pioneer in blending talents of professional and amateur performers, creating a unique performing and learning environment for both, while increasing pleasure for Reagle audiences." With a mission to demonstrate that well-trained amateur actors from the local area can perform on the same high level as Equity guest artists with Broadway experience, the Reagle Music Theatre presents several large-scale musicals a year in the Robinson Auditorium at Waltham High School; the company has presented *A Chorus Line* five times.

The company's policy is to recreate original Broadway stagings closely whenever possible, including choreography and design elements. To that end, Eagle engaged actresses experienced in the role of Cassie to reproduce Bennett's staging for most of his productions. Laurie Gamache, whose long career with the show included Cassie in the final Broadway company, played that role in her own productions in Waltham in 1990, 1994, and 2002. Standing beside her on the line that last time was Dana Moore, who had first been Sheila to her Cassie on Broadway during the 1987–88 season. Zach was played by Russell Garrett—who later that year would play Greg in the production at the St. Louis Muny. The cast also included Bill Nagle as Mike and Susan Chebookian as Connie; a full orchestra was conducted by Robert Rucinski.

Gamache recently reminisced about a night during one of her productions there when the Bebe couldn't go on. There were no understudies, just one fourteen-year-old girl who was the swing, and she hadn't been rehearsed as Bebe and didn't know the harmonies for "At the Ballet." So Gamache herself put on black tights under her Cassie costume; after the line stepped back into the dark for the beginning of Sheila's verse of "At the Ballet," she ran into the wings, peeled off her Cassie leotard and tights, and put on a Bebe shirt; she then appeared onstage in the spotlight as Bebe for the second verse and sang the refrain with the Sheila and Maggie. Then, during the "ballet blaze," she slipped offstage and was replaced by the young swing, who (made up to look as much like Gamache as possible) played Bebe for the remainder of the show. As soon as she could get her costume changed, Gamache, having completed her do-it-yourself rescue, snuck back onto the line as Cassie!

In 2012, the director/choreographer was Leslie Woodies, a former ballerina who had toured as Cassie in both the National and International Companies and appeared on Broadway in the revival of *On Your Toes*. Now a faculty member at the Boston Conservatory, she directed a cast that included TV star Lorenzo Lamas in his second outing as Zach (he had previously played the part at the Ogunquit Playhouse; see above). Nancy Grossman, reviewing for Broadwayworld.com, said

Lamas "blends the harshness of Zach's process with moments of compassion." The cast that year also included Katie Clark as Cassie, Scott Abreu as Paul, Danielle Goldstein as Val, Aimee Doherty as Sheila, Matt Uriniak as Bobby, and Kerri Wilson as Diana; Dan Rodriguez was musical director.

Sacramento Light Opera Association, Sacramento, CA, 1999, 2010, 2014

One of the nation's largest producers of summer musicals, informally known as the Sacramento Music Circus, this is another of the major venues that have staged *A Chorus Line* in the round; the 1999 production was presented under a blue and green tent on a circular stage that revolved slowly during the show. It was directed and choreographed by David Thomé, who had played Don and Zach in the show extensively on tour and on Broadway, in collaboration with Kay Cole, the original Maggie. The Zach here was Blane Savage; he had played Don in the movie version fourteen years earlier. Other cast members included Kathi Gillmore as Cassie, Paula Leggett Chase as Sheila, Christopher Windom as Richie, Alec Timerman as Mike, Megan Sikora as Kristine, Luis Villabon as Paul, and Jennifer Cody as a non-Asian Connie.

In 2003, the company changed its name to California Musical Theatre and moved from the tent to a new permanent indoor space called the Wells Fargo Pavilion, built on the same site. They also began presenting some productions in a separate indoor proscenium space called the Community Center Theatre, where *ACL* made an appearance during the 2010 "Broadway Sacramento" season; this was actually a late stop on the national tour that followed the Broadway revival, with the husband and wife team of Derek Hanson and Rebecca Riker starring as Zach and Cassie.

An all-new production of the show opened in the summer of 2014 at the Wells Fargo Pavilion. It was directed by Stafford Arima, who knew the space well, having directed several previous shows there including *Ragtime* and *A Little Night Music*. He was able to make use of the dynamic capabilities of the Pavilion's mechanized circular stage, which can revolve in its entirety or be raised and lowered in sections. Choreography was by Randy Slovacek, who had played Mark on tour with Donna McKechnie in 1989.

In the cast were two dancers who had grown up on the Sacramento stage before going on to substantial careers. Kate Levering (Cassie) earned a Tony nomination as Peggy Sawyer in the Broadway revival of *42nd Street* before returning to California to pursue a successful career in TV. Standing beside her on the line as Sheila was her best friend from her Sacramento days, Jenifer Foote; she too had been in several Broadway shows, including *Rock of Ages* and *Dirty Rotten Scoundrels*, as well as the revival of *ACL*. Their Zach was Eric Sciotto, who coincidentally had appeared on Broadway with both women in the 2001 revival of *Annie Get Your Gun* and was a swing in the *ACL* revival. The supporting cast included Selina Michelle Verastigui as Diana and Xavier Cano as Paul.

Santa Barbara Civic Light Opera, Santa Barbara, CA, 1991, 1999

Santa Barbara's usual practice was to job in a few professional guest artists to perform with local actors, but, due to the unusual dance requirements of *A Chorus Line*, the company hired a cast of seventeen Equity members for their 1991 production, staged at the Lobero Theatre. One of the many productions of the show directed by Baayork Lee, it featured Scott Pearson, who had been Bobby in the original National Company in 1976 and subsequently played Zach in Australia and on Broadway; he recreated the latter role in Santa Barbara opposite the Cassie of Jani-K Walsh. The production was praised for its polish and professionalism, but received a surprising write-up in the *Los Angeles Times* from Philip Brandes, one of the few critics ever to write a scathing review of the show itself. He admired the production, but called the musical "pretentious as hell," and said: "These dancers' artistic ambitions may be on the line, but failure means only that they might have to make their way in the world without stardom, just like (gasp) the majority of the working population who are less than enamored with their means of livelihood. . . . There is a repellent undercurrent of self-absorption to these characters' obsession for success that seems wildly out of balance and dates the piece precisely in the most embarrassing sludge of the '70s mind-set. It's appropriate that the only props on the stage are mirrors." Each to his own taste.

The company produced the show again in 1999, this time at the Granada Theatre, directed and choreographed by Sam Viverito. The well-received production featured Christina Marie Norrup, who had toured as Judy, in the role of Cassie, plus Paul Hadobas as Zach, Kelli Fish as Val, Jill Lewis as Maggie, Laura Soltis as Sheila, Matt Kubicek as Bobby, and Cindy Marchionda as Diana. The theatre company filed for bankruptcy and ceased operations in 2001.

Seacoast Repertory Theatre, Portsmouth, NH, 2001, 2013

Seacoast Rep is a professional theatre located in a historic port city that is also a summer tourist community. Though small, it has produced acclaimed stagings of numerous large, complex musicals. Both of the Rep's productions of *A Chorus Line* were directed and choreographed by performers who had played major roles in the show on Broadway; each had the challenge of adapting the staging and choreography for the theatre's tiny thrust stage.

The 2001 production was directed by Laurie Gamache, who had already staged the show for the Reagle Players, where she also played Cassie; for Seacoast Rep, she directed Elizabeth Broadhurst in that role, with a cast made up primarily of college students, many of them from top musical theatre training programs. What made the experience unique for them was that *A Chorus Line* was presented in repertory with a production of *Hair*, and most of the cast appeared in both shows. The young performers had the opportunity to perform simultaneously two iconic musicals that had both opened at the Public Theater in New York before moving to Broadway, and which encapsulated, respectively, the experiences of American youth in the 1960s and 1970s.

When Seacoast Rep presented *ACL* again twelve years later, the director/ choreographer was Bryan Knowlton, who had played Paul extensively in regional productions and in the closing cast of the Broadway revival. A native of Portsmouth who had grown up on the Rep's stage, he was returning home to take his first stab at directing the show he had come to know so well. (Coincidentally, he would return again the next summer—to direct *Hair.*) He brought his Cassie with him: Michelle Aravena, who had played cut dancer Tricia ("I really need this job") and understudied several roles, not including Cassie, in the revival. (Knowlton and Aravena were to do the show together again several months later, playing Paul and Cassie at the Olney in Maryland: see above.) The cast included several New York performers in addition to locals. Craig Faulkner was Zach with Mary Page Nance as Sheila, Christine Dulong as Maggie, Alex Acevedo as Richie, Corinne Tork as Diana, Brian Swasey as Greg, and Michael Phillips as Paul. The small stage accommodated a line of fifteen; there was no Don or Connie. Set designer Jason Courson provided a row of three tall mirrors in large white frames, giving the set a slightly nontraditional look; the costumes by John Saunders were closer to the classic originals.

Seagle Music Colony, Schroon Lake, NY, 2004

Long known as "Opera Camp" among voice students in college and graduate programs around the country, Seagle Music Colony is a summer program for emerging singers that presents several operas a year, with the occasional musical added to the mix. Their 2004 production of the show was a rare instance of *A Chorus Line* being performed by a cast made up primarily of serious voice students, rather than dancers. The director/choreographer was Frank Bove, who also played Zach in the production; he had been on staff at the Colony for several years and was also director of the Virginia Ballet Theatre at the time. Having been an understudy in the first national tour, he taught the young cast as much as possible of the original staging. According to tenor Brandon Snook, who played Greg: "I found this quite humorous, since most of us were positively inept at the opening/ballet combination. I think that after rehearsing for 3 or so weeks, I was able to fake it well enough to not stand out in the dance combination, but the ballet for me was always rough. I'm sure there were a few in the audience who scratched their heads at some of the final seventeen (except for the characters of Cassie, Mike, and Larry, who were played by decent dancers). All in all, I think it was a wonderful production, obviously with great singing. . . . The 'Goodbye 12, Hello 13' remains one of the most enjoyable things I've performed on stage."

Reviewing the show for Poststar.com, Geraldine Freedman agreed that they pulled it off: "This chorus of would-be opera singers showed the capacity crowd that maybe not all of them would end up in classical music. Many showed a real flair with their lines or projected personality into their roles. Many seemed to have had dance training because they were comfortable with the routines. . . . Ryan Bowie as Richie was especially effective with his clear-edged voice, but he also had a lot of pizzazz as he covered the stage when he danced. . . . And Donata Cucinotta as Cassie sang and danced with great aplomb." Richard Kagey designed the set, which included a black-and-white umbrella for the finale; costumes were by Pat Seyller, and musical director Tony Kostecki accompanied at the piano.

Stages St. Louis, Kirkwood, MO, 1988, 2000, 2011

St. Louis is apparently one city that can't get enough of *A Chorus Line*: in addition to six summer runs between 1981 and 2002 at the eleven-thousand-seat Municipal Opera (see above), the show has had three hit productions at the much smaller Stages St. Louis under founding artistic director Michael Hamilton. It was the first show the theatre ever sold out, in 1988; it was brought back in 2000; and in 2011 it became the only show to get a third production by the company. All three were performed in the Robert G. Reim Theatre at the Kirkwood Community Center, an intimate space with a beautiful proscenium stage and a large apron. The narrow stage necessitated performing the show with a reduced cast: fifteen on the line instead of seventeen. Hamilton directed all three productions, also appearing onstage as Zach in the 1988 version. He claims a special affinity for *A Chorus Line*, which was the first show he ever saw on Broadway, shortly after moving to New York to pursue a career as a dancer.

For the 2000 production, Stephen Bourneuf adapted the original choreography for the small stage. A St. Louis native, Bourneuf had played Al on Broadway. He had made his Stages debut acting in the 1988 production and went on to direct and/or choreograph numerous shows there; in 2013, he would be named the theatre's associate artistic director. Peggy Taphorn, at the time already a veteran of four Broadway shows, played Cassie, and Yvonne Meyer was Sheila; Stephen Nachamie, who had played several of the roles on tour and would go on to direct his own productions of the show, including the award-winning version at the Olney Theatre Center in 2013 (see above), played Paul.

The most recent production, in 2011, was presented in celebration of the theatre company's twenty-fifth anniversary. This time the original choreography was restaged by veteran *ACL* performer Kim Shriver. The cast included David Elder (a favorite at Stages, where he had done *Cabaret* and *Crazy for You*) as Zach, Jessica Lee Goldyn as Cassie, Luke Wakeford as Bobby, William Carlos Angulo as Paul, Leonard Sullivan as Richie, Hilary Michael Thompson as Kristine, and Jeffrey Scott Stevens as Al (also getting to do Don's section of the Montage, since the character of Don, along with Connie, was cut from the production). Jessica Vaccaro (Diana) won that season's Kevin Kline Award for Best Supporting Actress in a Musical. Jill Slyter, a veteran Cassie from numerous touring and regional productions in the 1990s, filled in for an ailing Kimberley Wolff as Sheila at the press performance.

The Staples Players, Westport, CT, 1998, 2013

Founded in the 1950s by teacher Craig Matheson and a group of student actors that included Christopher Lloyd and Mariette Hartley, the Staples Players is the name of the drama program at Staples High School—a public school—and one of the most accomplished and acclaimed such programs in the United States. The progressive-minded program has given the students the opportunity to perform sophisticated shows like *Cabaret*, *The Laramie Project*, *Falsettos*, and *RENT*, some of which have been censored at other schools. The department's faculty offers extensive performing arts course work in addition to ambitious productions both during the school year and in the summer. The dance training is strong enough that they were able to present two student productions of *A Chorus Line* that utilized the original choreography, more than creditably danced by extraordinarily talented and well-prepared teens. Bradley Jones, an alumnus of the school who had gone on to play Greg on tour and on Broadway in the 1980s, returned to Staples to direct and choreograph the 1998 production; in 2013, he again recreated the choreography, assisted by Andrea Metchick; another alum, David Roth, now head of the drama program, directed. (Alisan Porter, who played Bebe in the Broadway revival, is also an alumna of the school.) The 2013 student cast included Will Smith (no relation to the movie star) as Zach, Cara McNiff as Sheila, Claire Smith as Cassie, and Tyler Jent as Mike; some of the other roles were double cast. Westport is not a particularly diverse community, so the school had a Caucasian actress playing

"Facing away from the mirror": a student cast, choreographed by Broadway veteran Bradley Jones, attacks the opening number. The Staples Players, 2013.   *Photo by Kerry Long*

Asian as Connie, and a blond Richie, whose famous line, "And I'm black," spoken at the end of his introduction, was changed to "And I'm straight." The faculty is well connected, and Broadway personalities are sometimes invited up to teach workshops; in the case of *A Chorus Line*, Baayork Lee and Laurie Gamache both visited with the cast, helping to coach the dances and sharing personal experiences and words of wisdom.

A dream came true for the students after Marvin Hamlisch's widow, Terre Blair Hamlisch, attended a matinee performance. She was so impressed and moved by what she saw that she returned to see the show again that night, and arranged for the cast to be invited to come down to New York to take part in an American Cancer Society benefit in honor of her husband. Entitled *One Centennial Sensation: A Tribute to Marvin Hamlisch*, the concert took place on June 3, 2013, the day after the late composer's sixty-ninth birthday, at the Hudson Theatre in the heart of the Broadway Theatre District. The young cast had the memorable experience of meeting the numerous Broadway stars who were taking part, including Bernadette Peters, Robert Klein, Lilla Crawford, Matthew Morrison, Lucie Arnaz, and Joel Grey. They performed excerpts from their production of *A Chorus Line* and backed up original star Donna McKechnie on her number. John Lloyd Young, the Tony-winning original star of *Jersey Boys*, joined the school's Diana Morales, Michelle Pauker, for a duet on "What I Did for Love." The young cast was thrilled to get their first taste of Broadway; it seemed likely that many of them would be back.

Surflight Theatre, Beach Haven, NJ, 1986, 1992, 2008, 2014

Mitzi Hamilton directed the 2014 production at this picturesque summer theatre, located on Long Beach Island off the Jersey Shore. Like the Downtown Cabaret, where she had directed one of her many previous productions (see above), Surflight has a proscenium stage that is too narrow to accommodate the full line of seventeen dancers, so the number was reduced to fifteen. The character of Don was cut, and his section of the Montage was given to Al. The other character deleted was Connie, usually cut in versions that use a reduced cast, but though some productions have given her lines to other characters, Hamilton cut the "Four foot ten" monologue entirely—along with the section of "Hello Twelve" that comes between the two sections of the speech—so that the end of Mark's monologue segued directly into Diana's lines setting up the song "Nothing."

With the help of assistant choreographer Jessica Lee Goldyn, Hamilton did a shrewd job of adapting the original choreography to fit a shallower stage space: for example, the vertical line of dancers that forms behind Richie at the end of "Gimme the Ball" was replaced by two side-by-side columns. The set used the original periaktoi concept, with the pieces rented from the Gateway Playhouse (another theatre where Hamilton had recently directed the show), but there were no additional mirrors to descend during Cassie's dance. Six of the actors were members of Equity, including Kevin Curtis, who had appeared in the recent national tour and several previous regional productions. Jena VanElslander, repeating a role she had played seven years earlier at the Arts Center of Coastal Carolina, was an appealing and dynamic Cassie.

The fifteen-member line in the production directed by Mitzi Hamilton at the Surflight Theatre, 2014. *Photo by Jerry Dalia*

Life imitated art a few days into the run when the Paul, Alexander Andy Cruz, injured his foot and required stitches. He put in a call to Joey Rosario, who had previously understudied him in the role on the non-Equity tour; with two days' notice, Rosario stepped in and gave an assured and moving performance.

The conductor and ten-piece orchestra were housed in an upstairs room adjoining the light booth: having experienced Hurricane Sandy less than two years earlier, the theatre's management decided expensive instruments couldn't be housed in an orchestra pit subject to flooding; the orchestral sound was routed through speakers that made it sound like it was coming from backstage.

Sadly, the show turned out to be the penultimate presentation by the beloved theatre; following a holiday production of *The Wizard of Oz*, the Surflight Theatre declared bankruptcy in February 2015 and closed up shop after sixty-five consecutive seasons.

Tacoma Actors Guild, Tacoma, WA, 1993

Under artistic director Bruce K. Sevy, Tacoma Actors Guild, known informally as TAG, opened its new space, Theatre on the Square, with a production of *A Chorus Line*; it was directed and choreographed by Stephen Terrell. The intimate 302-seat proscenium theatre has a surprisingly large stage, seventy-eight feet wide by forty-two feet deep, and a substantial orchestra pit to accommodate big musicals, which were popular with the theatre's subscribers. Paul Mitri was praised for his performance as Zach; a director in real life as well, he was one of the founders of the Seattle Shakespeare Festival. Kristie Dale Sanders played Sheila. Mayme Paul-Thompson and Lisa Estridge-Gray, who had done the show together the previous year at the University of Washington (see below) were reunited in this production: at the university, Estridge-Gray had played Cassie in a production choreographed and codirected by Paul-Thompson; at TAG, Paul-Thompson herself played Cassie, with Estridge-Gray (probably the first African American actress ever to play both roles) as a critically acclaimed Val.

3-D Theatricals, Fullerton, CA, 2012

This new Orange County company, presenting Broadway musicals on a large scale, was founded in 2009, at a time when many venerable civic light operas and summer stock companies were going out of business; it has brought renewed energy and opportunity to the Southern California musical theatre community. Executive producer/artistic director T. J. Dawson started the company and runs it with several members of his family; he directed the 2012 production of *A Chorus Line*, which played at Plummer Auditorium, a wide proscenium house with a Broadway-sized stage.

Michael Paternostro, whose physical resemblance to Michael Bennett was noted six years earlier when he played Greg in the Broadway revival, here got to play Bennett's avatar, director Zach. Broadway veteran Alexis A. Carra played Cassie, and the two were enthusiastically reviewed by critics. Writing for *Backstage*, Eric Marchese said: "Michael Paternostro captures Zach's driving perfectionism and laser-like curiosity about the people behind the faces of his would-be chorus line members. Alexis A. Carra's Cassie is a less defiant, more vulnerable take on the character than what is usually seen. She's heartbreakingly damaged, and Carra's notable work in the 'Music and the Mirror' scene depicts the fire burning beneath Cassie's newfound humility." The cast also included Tomasina Abate as Sheila, Robin De Lano as Diana, Adrianna Rose Lyons (who had recently played Cassie in the non-Equity production at the Lewis Family Playhouse) as Judy, Venny Carranza as Mike, and Kavin Panmeechao as Paul. Bebe was played by Hannah Jean Simmons, the daughter of the choreographer, Linda Love-Simmons, who had played the same role early in her career. Continuing with the family theme, Julie Lamoureux was the musical director and her daughter, Kristen—acclaimed for her perfect high note in "At the Ballet"—played Maggie.

Theatre Memphis, Memphis, TN, 1999, 2013

Theatre Memphis, one of the nation's largest and most acclaimed community theatres, produces a season of eleven plays and musicals on two stages. Though the performers are unpaid, the theatre allocates substantial resources for elaborate sets and costumes, and engages professional directors and choreographers, sometimes imported from New York. The 1999 production of *A Chorus Line* was directed by the ubiquitous Mitzi Hamilton and featured a young dancer who was still in high school at the time, Adam Lendermon, as Mark. Like many Memphis alums,

Lendermon went on to a professional career, including performing in two regional productions of *ACL* directed by Josh Walden. When Walden came to Memphis in 2013 to direct the show, Lendermon returned to his hometown as associate director/choreographer; Gary Beard was musical director. According to reviewer Christopher Blank in *The Memphis Commercial Appeal*: "Though the choreography and blocking strictly adhere to Michael Bennett's Tony-winning 1975 original, director Josh Walden (a cast member in the 2007 Broadway revival) didn't arrive with prepackaged characters in mind. The actors take the script personally; they play from the heart." Emma Crystal (Sheila) was considered a standout in a cast that included Leah Beth Bolton as Cassie, Chris Cotten as Zach, Justin G. Nelson as Richie, Bruce Huffman as Paul, and Lynden Lewis as Val. The opening night gala featured a presentation by original Cassie Donna McKechnie, who shared stories about the creation of the show with the theatre's patrons.

Timber Lake Playhouse, Mount Carroll, IL, 2013

When the Timber Lake Playhouse's executive director, James Beaudry, decided to present *A Chorus Line* as the opening production of the summer stock theatre's fifty-second season, he knew it would be one of the most challenging shows the company had ever taken on. But he had confidence in director/choreographer Will Taylor, who had choreographed *Guys and Dolls* and *Oklahoma!* for the theatre in previous seasons and knew the show well, having played Bobby for over a year in the Broadway revival. Taylor faithfully reproduced the original staging and choreography but made a couple of innovations, including omitting some of the musical underscoring—particularly in the "Alternatives" scene, for which he was going for a more contemporary and realistic tone. Since the theatre required that an intermission be added, he decided to place it after Larry takes the dancers offstage for a break, beginning the second act with Cassie's big scene with Zach. Geena Quintos, who had learned the show from Baayork Lee playing Connie on the recent non-Equity tour, recreated that role and served as Taylor's assistant choreographer. The mostly nonunion cast included two Equity guest artists: New York actors Kaolin Bass as Zach and Pilar Millhollen as Cassie. Though this was her first time as Cassie, Millhollen had a lot of experience with the show, having played Bebe (and

Pilar Millhollen as Cassie in Will Taylor's production at the Timber Lake Playhouse, 2013. *Photo by Loren Borja*

understudied Sheila) in the Equity revival tour and then Diana at the Marriott Theatre in Illinois (see above). The supporting cast included Lexie Plath as Sheila, Genna-Paige Kanago as Val, and Sawyer Smith as Bobby.

University of California, Los Angeles, Westwood, CA, 2012

Adjunct Professor Jeremy Mann directed the show for the UCLA Department of Theatre; it was presented in the Freud Playhouse on the campus of the huge public university. The cast was made up of undergraduates, mainly musical theatre majors, including senior Ian McQuown as Zach and sophomore Emma Degerstedt as Cassie. Degerstedt, who had only just turned twenty, might well have been considered too young to relate to the character, but she had a unique perspective on it. Having already completed a very successful career as a child actress, playing Maris on the Nickelodeon series *Unfabulous* and Kendra in the premiere production of Jason Robert Brown's musical *13*, she claimed in an interview with Daniel Boden for the *Daily Bruin*: "I have a character who I'm very similar to. I had a lot of success when I was younger. Then I had four or five years where I didn't have anything because I was in high school and I couldn't audition as much. It was really rough for me that I went through this awkward phase in my life where I just wasn't castable."

Choreographer Jane Lanier had played Cassie in several major regional productions, but choreographed a version of "The Music and the Mirror" for Degerstedt that, while it alluded frequently to the Bennett original, was quite different from the standard choreography.

University of Michigan School of Music, Ann Arbor, MI, 2004

The University of Michigan's BFA program in musical theatre, a division of the School of Music, has grown to become one of the largest and most respected in the nation, feeding a steady stream of well-trained double- and triple-threat performers into the Broadway community. The school's 2004 production of *ACL* had a cast made up completely of students in the BFA program and was notable for including an unusually high number of young performers who have since gone on to big jobs and successful careers in the industry. These include Whitney Bashor as Val (Broadway debut in *The Bridges of Madison County*; Off Broadway in *The Fantasticks*), Thomas Berklund as Greg (the role he would play again three years later as a replacement in the Broadway revival, under the name Tommy Berklund), Nick Blaemire as Al (composer/lyricist of the musical *Glory Days*, which premiered on Broadway the same season he made his Broadway debut as a performer in *Cry-Baby*), Anne Horak as Sheila (*Chicago*, *Young Frankenstein*, and *White Christmas* on Broadway; also played Judy in *ACL* at Music Theatre of Wichita), Chelsea Krombach as Maggie (Broadway in *Wicked* and the revival of *Promises, Promises*), Kate Loprest as Diana (five Broadway shows so far including *Xanadu*, *Hairspray*, and *First Date*), and Brian Spitulnik as Mike (*Chicago* on Broadway). Playing Roy in the opening number and understudying Mark and Richie was no less than Andrew

Kerry Casserly, right, works with the student cast at the University of Michigan, 2004.
Photo courtesy U-M School of Music, Theatre & Dance, Department of Musical Theatre

Keenan-Bolger, then a sophomore, who had already appeared on Broadway as a child actor in *Seussical: The Musical* and would return in *Newsies*. Alexis Sims played Cassie; musical director Cynthia Kortman Westphal conducted a nine-member orchestra. The traditional production was directed and choreographed by Kerry Casserly, who had played Kristine on Broadway in the eighties as well as touring as Kristine, Judy, Cassie, and Sheila; she was assisted by Billy Johnstone, who has also toured with the show. In her program note, Casserly said: "Most of the students at U of M have never seen the stage version of *A Chorus Line* and because of that they breathe new life, creativity, humor, reality, and a fresh depth into these 26 characters so many of us have come to know and love."

University of Washington School of Drama, Seattle, WA, 1992

Though it's a show about young people and much beloved of aspiring performers, *A Chorus Line* is a tricky undertaking for colleges, few of which offer the comprehensive dance training needed to prepare a cast for its requirements. The show has been done successfully at schools with large, high-powered musical theatre programs like those at UCLA and the University of Michigan (see above), but the 1992 production at the University of Washington may be the only version ever performed by graduate students on a competitive, classically oriented MFA Acting track—long known in Seattle as the Professional Actor Training Program, or PATP. The fourteen serious actors that entered that program in the fall of 1990 were, as usual, signed up for a jazz dance class as part of their rigorous curriculum;

they ended up receiving unusually high marks from the teacher, who even invited several of the male dancers in the class to take part in an off-campus recital he was choreographing. Some of the actors also had extensive musical theatre experience from their undergrad days. So the School of Drama chose *A Chorus Line* as one of three mainstage productions the class would perform as an ensemble during their second year in the program—along with Edward Bond's *The Sea* and Shakespeare's *The Merchant of Venice.*

Initial rumors were that the plan was to mount a "deconstruction of the story of *Chorus Line*"—which might have been in keeping with academic theatre aesthetics of the early nineties. However, once the directors were hired, it became clear that the production would be much more traditional. Jeff Caldwell, a grad student in the UW's opera directing program who also served as the PATP's singing teacher, codirected the musical with Mayme Paul-Thompson; each did double-duty, with Caldwell also credited as musical director and Paul-Thompson as choreographer. A highly respected Seattle-area choreographer who had played Val on tour, Paul-Thompson knew the show well; she used much of Bennett and Avian's original work, integrated with some of her own. Her innovations included simplifying some of the original steps to accommodate the cast's uneven abilities: there was no double pirouette in the opening jazz combination. All but one of the members of the class were cast in the show, to play Zach and twelve of the dancers on the line; the ensemble was filled out by undergrads (some of whom were more accomplished dancers) as Maggie, Connie, Bebe, Kristine, Mark, and Larry, plus the seven cut dancers in the opening. The production was staged in the 224-seat Meany Studio Theatre, very similar in size and configuration to the Public/Newman, the show's original home. Staff costumer Josie Gardner gave Lisa Estridge-Gray a standard Cassie outfit, but most of the others wore new designs; actor David Morden, pulling focus as the flamboyant Bobby, took the 1970s concept as far as it would go, devising his own bright blue, tie-dyed unitard, complete with headband.

Westchester Broadway Theatre, Elmsford, NY, 1991

A Chorus Line marked a milestone in the life of this now long-established suburban venue. It was the first production presented by the company in a brand new $4.5 million facility and under a new name (the theatre, in a different location, had existed since 1974 as An Evening Dinner Theatre). This was also the first professional regional mounting of the show in the New York area, opening less than a year after the closing of the Broadway production.

Westchester Broadway has a large thrust stage, with an audience of 449 seated on tiered tables on three sides and—unusual for a dinner theatre—all chairs directly facing the stage. The production of *ACL* was directed and choreographed by none other than a young Rob Marshall, already an alumnus of the show's touring company but not yet the phenomenally successful director of the film versions of *Chicago, Nine,* and *Into the Woods.* Cassie was played by Pamela Sousa, who had first done the role on Broadway in 1977. The cast also included Lauren Goler as

Sheila, Susan Santoro (the final Broadway Maggie) as Diana, Valerie Wright as Bebe, Randy Donaldson as Richie, and Christine Gradl as Maggie. In a generally positive review for the *New York Times*, Alvin Klein praised Marshall's ingenious adaptation of the staging for a thrust venue (the set design was by Michael Bottari and Ron Case) but complained about the insertion of an intermission, which he claimed made it hard for the show to regain momentum in its second half. This same criticism has been leveled at other revivals that also divided the piece into two acts—especially common in dinner theatres, where dessert must be served. The successful production ran for over three months.

Weston Playhouse, Weston, VT, 2014

This venerable summer venue, Vermont's oldest professional theatre, presented *A Chorus Line* as part of its seventy-eighth season. It was directed by the theatre's producing director, Malcolm Ewen, and choreographed by Michael Raine. Raine used the original choreography for "I Hope I Get It" and "One," though the latter was somewhat simplified and reconfigured to fit the theatre's narrow stage; despite the small size of the proscenium, the line included all seventeen characters. Innovations included having Mike (played by John Scacchetti) take off his jazz shoes and change into tap shoes (with the aid of a shoehorn) during the short monologue leading into "I Can Do That"; for once, the audience heard taps during the dance routine, like on the original cast album but unlike the actual Broadway production. At the climax of "At the Ballet," instead of revealing the whole ensemble in the famous "ballet blaze," Raine had Al and Kristine (Brandon Rubendall and Felicity Stiverson) appear alone, wearing different costumes, for a brief pas de deux. "The Music and the Mirror" had new choreography, though some of the classic signature moves were included; a major departure was that at the beginning of the final fast section, two of the male dancers, dressed in black, entered and danced the climactic measures with Cassie, though they exited a few bars before the end. (It will be recalled that a similar idea was tried and discarded during rehearsals for the original production; see Chapter 12.) Several of the performers had appeared in other recent *ACL* productions: David Grindrod (Bobby) had been Mark in the non-Equity tour; Tyler Jent (Mark), now a college student, was Mike for the Staples Players (see above) just over a year earlier; Tiffany Chalothorn was playing Connie for the fourth time, and Genna-Paige Kanago was repeating her Val from the Timber Lake Playhouse the previous summer; Sara Andreas (Cassie) had been Judy at Berkshire Theatre Group and Nikka Graff Lanzarone (Sheila) had been Bebe at the Paper Mill Playhouse. Broadway veteran Jim Raposa (*Cats*) played Zach.

Worth-Tyrrell Studios, Morristown, NJ, 1981–2012

In 1978, Brad Tyrrell and his wife Caroline Worth-Tyrrell moved the Ryan-Worth school of dance, which had been founded by Caroline's family in 1954, into the historic Woman's Club Building in Morristown and renamed it Worth-Tyrrell Studios; it operated there until the couple retired in 2012. With around 150 students enrolled each term, the Studio, which employed professional performers as teachers, offered classes in musical theatre and voice as well as ballet, tap, and jazz dance for kids of all ages, ranging from elementary through high school. There was also a program of productions to showcase the youngsters' work, including, for thirty years, an annual presentation of *A Chorus Line*. Photos and videos of the productions show casts, and actors, of various shapes and sizes; dance students would get a chance to be in the opening number at eleven or twelve and then, if they continued studying at the Studio, move up to roles on the line in subsequent years. There were usually more girls than boys, and the show would be adapted and fitted to the talent at hand.

Worth and Tyrrell were greatly beloved by generations of students, including Broadway performers who still credit them in their bios. One of these is Jessica Lee Goldyn, who did the show seven times at the Studio by the time she finished high school, playing various roles. (The *Chorus Line* documentary *Every Little Step* features a clip of her there, performing an acrobatic version of "I Can Do That" as a female Mike!) The experience served Goldyn well, as *A Chorus Line* has continued to be a major part of her life: She went on to play Val in the Broadway revival and has since played Cassie in no fewer than seven regional productions. Faithful to the Studio, she continued to go back to Morristown whenever she could to help with the choreography, teaching a new generation of kids eager to know what it was like to dance on Broadway—and proving that, just sometimes, dreams do come true.

Appendix One

A Chorus Timeline

Chronological List of Major Events in the History of the Show
(with thanks to AChorusLineLondon.com and *The Longest Line*)

January 1, 1974	Michael Bennett, Michon Peacock, and Tony Stevens meet to discuss a project for dancers
January 26, 1974	First Tape Session: Dancers meet at Nickolaus Exercise Center to talk about their lives
August 9, 1974	First Workshop begins
Late January, 1975	Second Workshop begins
April 16, 1975	First preview performance at the Public/Newman Theater
May 21, 1975	Opening Night at the Newman
June 3, 1975	Recording session for original cast album
July 13, 1975	Closing night at the Public (after 101 performances)
July 25, 1975	First preview performance on Broadway at the Shubert Theatre
September 18–October 13, 1975	Broadway musicians strike: Shuts down previews and delays opening
October 19, 1975	Opening Night at the Shubert
March 23, 1976	Tony Award nominations announced: twelve nominations
April 19, 1976	Tony Awards Ceremony and telecast: nine wins
May 3, 1976	Wins Pulitzer Prize for Drama
May 3, 1976	First performance of the International Company in Toronto, Canada
May 11, 1976	First performance of the National Company in San Francisco, California
July 1, 1976	National Company begins open-ended run in Los Angeles (to run a year and a half)
July 22, 1976	International Company (American cast) opens at the Drury Lane Theatre, London
December 4, 1976	Michael Bennett and Donna McKechnie are married in Paris
January 24, 1977	British cast takes over for American cast in London production
February 9, 1977	International Company opens in Baltimore on return to U.S.
February 12, 1977	Wins *London Evening Standard* Award for Best Musical
March 21, 1977	President and Mrs. Gerald Ford attend the Broadway production

April 7, 1977	L.A. Drama Critics Awards: five wins
May 24, 1977	Australian Company opens at Her Majesty's Theatre, Sydney
January 17, 1978	Gold Record Award, Columbia Records
March 31, 1979	London production closes
September 14, 1980	National Company ends its run, in Montreal
September 18, 1980	First performance of the Bus & Truck Company, in Schenectady, NY
January 30, 1981	Newly released Iran hostages attend the Broadway production
May 27, 1981	First sign-interpreted performance of a Broadway musical for hearing-impaired patrons
October 3, 1982	Bus & Truck Company closes in Pittsburgh
May 29, 1983	International Company closes in Chicago
September 29, 1983	Gala performance to mark 3,389th performance, becoming longest-running Broadway show in history
June 12, 1985	First American professional stock production opens at Marriott's Lincolnshire Theatre, Illinois
December 9, 1985	World premiere of the movie version at Radio City Music Hall
December 13, 1985	Wide release of the movie
September 1, 1986– May 16, 1987	Donna McKechnie's return engagement in the Broadway company
July 2, 1987	Michael Bennett dies in Tucson, Arizona (age forty-four)
August 10, 1987	5,000th performance on Broadway
December 28, 1987	Edward Kleban dies in New York (age forty-eight)
April 21, 1989	James Kirkwood dies in New York (age sixty-four)
February 21, 1990	Closing of Broadway production announced by producer Joseph Papp for March 31
April 28, 1990	Closing night on Broadway (6,137 performances) after final four-week extension
May 21, 1991	Nicholas Dante dies in New York (age forty-nine)
January 12, 2005	Forthcoming Broadway revival announced by producer John Breglio
July 23, 2006	Revival first preview in San Francisco (Curran Theatre)
August 14, 2006	Recording session for revival cast album
September 18, 2006	First preview of Broadway revival (Schoenfeld Theatre)
October 5, 2006	Revival opening night at the Schoenfeld
May 4, 2008	Revival tour opens in Denver (Buell Theatre)
August 17, 2008	Closing night at the Schoenfeld (759 performances)
September 6, 2008	Film *Every Little Step* premieres at Toronto International Film Festival
April 17, 2009	*Every Little Step* released in United States
August 6, 2012	Marvin Hamlisch dies in Los Angeles, California (age sixty-eight)
February 5, 2013	First performance of London revival (Palladium)
August 31, 2013	London closing performance at the Palladium

Appendix Two

Cast List (with all replacements) for Original Broadway Production, 1975–1990

Many actors alternated in and out of the show several times; they are listed in the order in which they first took over the role.

Role: Original Actor	Replacements	
Zach: Robert LuPone	Joe Bennett Eivind Harum* Kurt Johnson Clive Clerk Anthony Inneo	Scott Pearson Tim Millett David Thomé Steve Boockvor Randy Clements
Don: Ron Kuhlman	David Thomé Dennis Edenfield Michal Weir	Michael Danek Randy Clements Keith Bernardo*
Maggie: Kay Cole	Lauree Berger Donna Drake Christina Saffran Betty Lynd Marcia Lynn Watkins Pam Klinger	Ann Heinricher Dorothy (Tancredi) Dybisz Michele Pigliavento Susan Santoro*
Mike: Wayne Cilento	Don Correia Jim Litten Jeff Hyslop Buddy Balou Cary Scott Lowenstein Scott Wise Danny Herman	J. Richard Hart Charles McGowan Mark Bove Tommy Re Kelly Patterson Michael Gruber*
Connie: Baayork Lee	Lauren Kayahara Janet Wong Cynthia Carrillo Onrubia	Lauren Tom Lily-Lee Wong Sachi Shimizu*
Greg: Michel Stuart	Justin Ross Danny Weathers Ronald A. Navarre	Michael-Day Pitts Bradley Jones Doug Friedman*

Role: Original Actor	Replacements	
Cassie: Donna McKechnie	Ann Reinking	Deborah Henry
	Vicki Frederick	Wanda Richert
	Pamela Sousa	Angelique Ilo
	Cheryl Clark	Laurie Gamache*
Sheila: (Carole) Kelly Bishop	Kathrynann Wright	Jane Summerhays
	Bebe Neuwirth	Cynthia Fleming
	Susan Danielle*	Dana Moore
	Jan Leigh Herndon	
Bobby: Thommie Walsh	Christopher Chadman	Ronald Stafford
	Ron Kurowski*	Michael Gorman
	Tim Cassidy	Matt West
Bebe: Nancy Lane	Gillian Scalici	Tracy Shayne
	Karen Meister	Karen Ziemba
	Rene Ceballos	Beth Swearingen
	Pamela Ann Wilson	Christine Maglione*
	Karen Curlee	
Judy: Patricia Garland	Sandahl Bergman	Jannet (Horsley) Moranz
	Murphy Cross	Melissa Randel
	Victoria Tabaka	Trish Ramish
	Joanna Zercher	Cindi Klinger
	Angelique Ilo*	
Richie: Ronald Dennis	Winston DeWitt Hemsley	Kevin Chinn
	Edward Love	Reggie Phoenix
	Wellington Perkins	Eugene Fleming
	Larry G. Bailey	Gordon Owens*
	Carleton T. Jones	Bruce Anthony Davis
	Ralph Glenmore	Gregg Burge
Al: Don Percassi	Bill Nabel	Scott Plank
	John Mineo	Buddy Balou
	Ben Lokey	Mark Bove
	Jim Corti	Kevin Neil McCready
	Donn Simione	Tommy Re*
	James (Warren) Young	Charlie Marcus
	Jerry Colker	Stephen Bourneuf
Kristine: Renee Baughman	Cookie Vazquez	Kerry Casserly
	Deborah Geffner	Flynn McMichaels
	P. J. Mann	Cynthia Fleming*
	Christine Barker	
Val: Pamela Blair	Barbara Monte-Britton	Deborah Henry
	Karen Jablons	Joanna Zercher
	Mitzi Hamilton	DeLyse Lively-Mekka
	Gail Mae Ferguson	Wanda Richert
	Lois Englund	Diana Kavilis*
Mark: Cameron Mason	Paul Charles	Fraser Ellis
	Timothy Scott	Chris Marshall
	R. J. Peters	Gib Jones
	Timothy Wahrer	Andrew Grose
	Dennis Daniels	Matt Zarley
	Gregory Brock	Jack Noseworthy*
	Danny Herman	

Role: Original Actor	Replacements	
Paul: Sammy Williams	George Pesaturo	Tommy Aguilar
	Danny Ruvolo	Wayne Meledandri
	Rene Clemente	Drew Geraci*
	Timothy Wahrer	
Diana: Priscilla Lopez	Barbara Luna	Dorothy Tancredi
	Carole Schweid	Kay Cole
	Rebecca York	Roxann (Caballero) Biggs*
	Loida (Iglesias) Santos	Mercedes Perez
	Chris Bocchino	Denise DiRenzo
	Gay Marshall	Arminae Azarian
	Diane Fratantoni	
Larry: Clive Clerk (Wilson)	Jeff Weinberg	J. Richard Hart
	Adam Grammis	Scott Plank
	Paul Charles	Brad Jeffries
	R. J. Peters	Jim Litten
	T. Michael Reed	Danny Herman
	Michael-Day Pitts	Kevin Neil McCready*
	Donn Simione	

* Denotes final company/closing night cast, April 28, 1990

Appendix Three

Opening Cast Lists for the Second Broadway, National, International, and London Companies: 1976–1977

Role	Second Broadway company	National Company (San Francisco, Los Angeles)	International Company (Toronto, London opening)	Second London company (first British cast)
Zach	Joe Bennett	**Robert LuPone**	Eivind Harum	Jean-Pierre Cassel
Don	David Thome	**Ron Kuhlman**	Ronald Young	Lance Aston
Maggie	Lauree Berger	**Kay Cole**	Jean Fraser	Veronica Page
Mike	**Wayne Cilento**	Don Correia	Jeff Hyslop	Michael Howe
Connie	Lauren Kayahara	**Baayork Lee**	Jennifer Ann Lee	Cherry Gillespie
Greg	Justin Ross	**Michel Stuart**	Andy Keyser/Mark Dovey	Stephen Tate
Cassie	Ann Reinking	**Donna McKechnie**	Sandy Roveta	Petra Siniawski
Sheila	**Kelly Bishop**	Charlene Ryan	Jane Summerhays	Geraldine Gardner
Bobby	**Thomas J. Walsh**	Scott Pearson	Ron Kurowski	Leslie Meadows
Bebe	Gillian Scalici	**Nancy Lane**	Miriam Welch	Susan Claire
Judy	Sandahl Bergman	**Patricia Garland**	Yvette Mathews	Judy Gridley
Richie	Winston DeWitt Hemsley	**Ronald Dennis**	A. William Perkins	Ron Gayle
Al	Bill Nabel	**Don Percassi**	Steve Baumann	Jeffrey Shankley
Kristine	Cookie Vazquez	**Renee Baughman**	Christine Barker	Vicki Spencer
Val	Barbara Monte-Britton	**Pamela Blair**	Mitzi Hamilton	Linda Williams
Mark	**Cameron Mason**	Paul Charles	Timothy Scott	Peter Barry
Paul	George Pesaturo	**Sammy Williams**	Tommy Aguilar	Michael Staniforth
Diana	Barbara Luna/ Carol Schweid	**Priscilla Lopez**	Loida Iglesias	Diane Langton
Larry	**Clive Clerk**	Roy Smith	T. Michael Reed	Jack Gunn
Directed by:	*Michael Bennett*	*Michael Bennett*	*Michael Bennett*	*Michael Bennett*

Original cast members in **boldface**

Appendix Four

Opening Cast Lists for Touring Companies, 1980–1997

Role	Bus & Truck tour 1980	Robert L. Young Jr. tour 1985	Robert L. Young Jr. tour 1989
Zach	Eivind Harum	Anthony Inneo	Randy Clements
Don	Michal Weir	Randy Clements	Kelly Woodruff
Maggie	Jane Bodle	Pamela Blasetti	Joan O'Neill
Mike	Cary Scott Lowenstein	Jamie Torcellini	Jim Litten
Connie	Sachi Shimizu	Suzen Murakoshi	Zoie Lam
Greg	Bradley Jones	Robert Warners	Stanley Kramer
Cassie	Thia Fadel	Donna McKechnie	Donna McKechnie
Sheila	Jan Leigh Herndon	Rita O'Connor	Cilda Shaur
Bobby	John Salvatore	Michael Gorman	Matt West
Bebe	Kathleen Moore	Carole Schweid	Linda Griffin
Judy	Melissa Randel	Darlene Wilson	Darlene Wilson
Richie	Eugene Fleming	Reggie Phoenix	Carleton T. Jones
Al	Danny Rounds	William Frey	Chris Pelaez
Kristine	Laurie Gamache	Cilda Shaur	Rosemary Rado
Val	DeLyse Lively	Melinda Buckley	Vicki Bell
Mark	Brian Andrews	Alec Timerman	Randy Slovacek
Paul	Wayne Meledandri	Nicholas Dante	Porfirio
Diana	Alison Gertner	Lisa Leguillo	Anna Simonelli
Larry	Evan Pappas	Jeff Seibert	Paul Charles
Directed by:	Michael Bennett	Baayork Lee	Baayork Lee

Visa tour 1990	Gordon Crowe non-Equity tour 1993	Jon B. Platt Equity national tour 1996	Non-Equity national tour 1997
Randy Clements	Matthew Johnson	Mark Martino	Matthew T. Johnson
Frank Kliegel	Mike Krsul	David Alan Combs	Paul Buschman
Christine Gradl	Merete Muenter	Charlene Carr	Erin Malloy
Mark S. Hoebee	Denis Jones	Evan Marks	Matt Loehr
Melinda Cartwright	Marilyn Villamar	J. Elaine Marcos	Marilyn B. Villamar
Bradley Jones	Rudd Anderson	Timothy Kasper	Chris Lockamy
Laurie Gamache	Amy Spanger	Jill Slyter	Lori Melissa Marshburn
Gail Benedict	Kimberly Shriver	Michelle Bruckner	Kristen E. Gerding
Michael Gorman	John Fedele	John Salvatore	Robert Tunstall
Pamela Khoury	Amy Uhl	Gina Philistine	Petra Van Nuis
Paula Leggett	Patricia Reed	Christina Marie Norrup	Lili Calahan
Philip Michael Baskerville	Peter Innis	Randy Donaldson	Ra-Sean Holloway
Buddy Balou	Eric Klein	Kevin M. Burrows	Spencer T. Rowe
Michelle Michaels	Kimberly Rokosny	Rebecca Sherman	Erin Hunter
Julie Graves	Sara Smolen	Kimberly Dawn Neumann	Pattie Ford
John Scott	Edward Morand	Todd R. Smith	Seth Hampton
Porfirio	Luis Villabon	Luis Villabon	Eric Sciotto
Donna Pompei	Melissa Giattino	Cindy Marchionda	Michelle Scarpa
Dennis Daniels	Christopher James	James Hadley	Mark MacKay Lusk
Baayork Lee	*Lois Englund*	*Baayork Lee*	*Baayork Lee*

Appendix Five

Opening Cast Lists for the Broadway Revival, Tours, and London Revival, 2006–2013

Role	Broadway revival opening company	First National Company	NETworks non-Equity tour	American Theatre International non-Equity tour	West End (The Palladium) company
Zach	Michael Berresse	Michael Gruber	Ryan Steer	Jeremiah Ginn	John Partridge
Don	Brad Anderson	Derek Hanson	Eric Carsia	Pim Van Amerongen	Gary Watson
Maggie	Mara Davi	Hollie Howard	Karley Willocks	Bronwyn Tarboton	Vicki Lee Taylor
Mike	Jeffrey Schecter	Clyde Alves	Eric Mann	Michael Peter Deeb	Adam Salter
Connie	Yuka Takara	Jessica Wu	Cassandra Hlong	Geena Quintos	Alexzandra Sarmiento
Greg	Michael Paternostro	Denis Lambert	Justin Clynes	Jerreme Rodriguez	Andy Rees
Cassie	Charlotte d'Amboise	Nikki Snelson	Rylyn Juliano	Caley Crawford	Scarlett Strallen
Sheila	Deidre Goodwin	Emily Fletcher	Suzanna Dupree	Brooke Morrison	Leigh Zimmerman
Bobby	Ken Alan	Ian Liberto	Hardy Weaver	Jordan Haskins	Ed Currie
Bebe	Alisan Porter	Pilar Millhollen	Erica Cenci	Bonnie Kelly	Daisy Maywood
Judy	Heather Parcells	Stephanie Gibson	Julia Freyer	Erika Conaway	Lucy Jane Adcock
Richie	James T. Lane	Anthony Wayne	Mickey Junior-Ayer	Sharrod Williams	James T. Lane
Al	Tony Yazbeck	Colt Prattes	Paul Flanagan	Nick Varricchio	Simon Hardwick

Role	Broadway revival opening company	First National Company	NETworks non-Equity tour	American Theatre International non-Equity tour	West End (The Palladium) company
Kristine	Chryssie Whitehead	Jessica Latshaw	Ashley Klinger	Ashley Klinger	Frances Dee
Val	Jessica Lee Goldyn	Natalie Hall	Jessi Trauth	Aisling Halpin	Rebecca Herszenhorn
Mark	Paul McGill	Jay Armstrong Johnson	David Grindrod	Nick Raynor	Harry Francis
Paul	Jason Tam	Kevin Santos	Gaspare DiBlasi	Eddie Gutierrez	Gary Wood
Diana	Natalie Cortez	Gabrielle Ruiz	Gina Duci	LauRen Nicole Alaimo	Victoria Hamilton-Barritt
Larry	Tyler Hanes	John Carroll	Netanel Bellaishe	Matthew Couvillon	Alastair Postlethwaite
Directed by:	Bob Avian	Bob Avian	Baayork Lee	Baayork Lee	Bob Avian

Bibliography

Books

Bloom, Ken and Frank Vlastnik. *Broadway Musicals: The 101 Greatest Shows of All Time.* New York: Black Dog and Leventhal, 2010.

Carter, Diana. *Richard Attenborough's Chorus Line.* New York: Plume, 1985.

Chapin, Ted. *Everything was Possible: The Birth of the Musical "Follies."* New York: Applause Theatre & Cinema Books, 2005.

Egan, Sean. *Ponies and Rainbows: The Life of James Kirkwood.* Duncan, OK: BearManor Media, 2012.

Eichenbaum, Rose. *The Dancer Within: Intimate Conversations with Great Dancers.* Middletown, CT: Wesleyan University Press, 2008.

Epstein, Helen. *Joe Papp: An American Life.* New York: Little, Brown and Company, 1994.

Filichia, Peter. *Broadway Musical MVPs 1960–2010: The Most Valuable Players of the Past 50 Seasons.* Milwaukee, WI: Applause Theatre & Cinema Books, 2011.

Filichia, Peter. *Let's Put On a Musical! How to Choose the Right Show for Your School, Community or Professional Theater.* New York: Avon Books, 1993.

Flinn, Denny Martin. *Musical! A Grand Tour.* New York: Schirmer Books, 1997.

Flinn, Denny Martin. *What They Did for Love: The Untold Story Behind the Making of A Chorus Line.* New York: Bantam Books, 1989.

Gottfried, Martin. *Broadway Musicals.* New York: Harry N. Abrams, 1979.

Grubb, Kevin Boyd. *Razzle Dazzle: The Life and Work of Bob Fosse.* New York: St. Martin's Press, 1989.

Guernsey, Otis. *The Burns Mantle Yearbook: The Best Plays of 1974–75 (56th Year)* through *1977–78 (59th Year).* New York: Dodd, Mead, 1975–78.

Hamlisch, Marvin and Edward Kleban. *A Chorus Line: Vocal Score.* Milwaukee, WI: MPL Communications, 1975.

Hamlisch, Marvin, with Gerald Gardner. *The Way I Was.* New York: Charles Scribner's Sons, 1992.

Hoffman, Warren. *The Great White Way: Race and the Broadway Musical.* New Brunswick, NJ: Rutgers University Press, 2014.

Kantor, Michael and Laurence Maslon. *Broadway: The American Musical.* New York: Bulfinch Press, 2004.

Kelly, Kevin. *One Singular Sensation: The Michael Bennett Story.* New York: Doubleday, 1990.

Kirkwood, James. *Diary of a Mad Playwright*. New York: E.P. Dutton, 1989.

Kirkwood, James and Nicholas Dante, Marvin Hamlisch, Edward Kleban, and Michael Bennett. *A Chorus Line: The Book of the Musical*. New York: Applause Theatre & Cinema Books, 1995.

Lopez, Mario, with Steve Santagati. *Just Between Us*. New York: Celebra, 2014.

Mandelbaum, Ken. *A Chorus Line and the Musicals of Michael Bennett*. New York: St. Martin's Press, 1989.

McGilligan, Pat. *Backstory 3: Interviews with Screenwriters of the 1960s*. Berkeley: University of California Press, 1997.

McGovern, Dennis and Deborah Grace Winer. *Sing Out, Louise! 150 Stars of the Musical Theatre Remember 50 Years on Broadway*. New York: Schirmer Books, 1993.

McKechnie, Donna, with Greg Lawrence. *Time Steps: My Musical Comedy Life*. New York: Simon & Schuster, 2006.

Mordden, Ethan. *Anything Goes: A History of American Musical Theatre*. New York: Oxford University Press, 2013.

Mordden, Ethan. *Better Foot Forward: The History of American Musical Theatre*. New York: Viking, 1976.

Mordden, Ethan. *One More Kiss: The Broadway Musical in the 1970s*. New York: Palgrave Macmillan, 2003.

Shapiro, Eddie. *Nothing Like a Dame: Conversations with the Great Women of Musical Theater*. New York: Oxford University Press, 2014.

Singer, Barry. *Ever After: The Last Years of Musical Theater and Beyond*. New York: Applause Theatre & Cinema Books, 2004.

Stevens, Gary and Alan George. *The Longest Line: Broadway's Most Singular Sensation: A Chorus Line*. New York: Applause Books, 1995.

Stevenson, Isabelle. *The Tony Award: A Complete Listing of Winners and Nominees with a History of the American Theatre Wing*. New York, Crown Publishing, 1984.

Turan, Kenneth and Joseph Papp. *Free for All: Joe Papp, the Public, and the Greatest Theater Story Ever Told*. New York: Random House, 2009.

Viagas, Robert. *I'm the Greatest Star: Broadway's Top Musical Legends from 1900 to Today*. Milwaukee, WI: Hal Leonard, 2009.

Viagas, Robert and Baayork Lee and Thommie Walsh. *On the Line: The Creation of A Chorus Line*. New York: William Morrow, 1990.

Viagas, Robert and Louis Botto. *At This Theatre: 110 Years of Broadway Shows, Stories & Stars*. New York: Applause Theatre & Cinema Books, 2010.

Viagas, Robert (editor). *The Playbill Broadway Yearbook: June 2006–May 2007*. New York: Playbill Books, 2007.

White, Timothy R. *Blue-Collar Broadway: The Craft and Industry of American Theater*. Philadelphia, PA: University of Pennsylvania Press, 2015.

Willis, John. *Theatre World Volume 31 (1974–75) through Volume 46 (1989–90)*. New York: Crown Publishers, 1975–1991.

Willis, John and Ben Hodges. *Theatre World Volume 63 (2006–07) and Volume 64 (2007–2008)*. Milwaukee, WI: Applause Theatre & Cinema Books, 2008–09.

Websites

Internet Broadway Database ibdb.com
Internet Movie Database imdb.com
www.wikipedia.com
www.playbill.com
www.broadway.com
www.broadwayworld.com
www.backstage.com
www.stagesceneLA.com
www.youtube.com
www.achoruslinelondon.com
www.talkinbroadway.com

Articles

Barnes, Clive. "'A Chorus Line' Review." *New York Times*, October 20, 1975.

Barnes, Clive. "'A Chorus Line' Terrific to a '2nd Nighter's' Eye. *New York Post*, December 14, 1985.

Barnes, Clive. "A Tremendous 'Chorus Line' Arrives." *New York Times*, May 22, 1975.

Barnes, Clive. "'Chorus Line' with a New Cast, Still Hottest Ticket for a Reason." *New York Times*, December 18, 1976.

Barnes, Michael. "This 'Chorus Line' Has Plenty of Star Power." *Austin American-Statesman*, October 2008.

Berson, Misha. "'A Chorus Line' Showcases Up-and-Comers at Fifth Avenue." *Seattle Times*, September 12, 2014.

Billington, Michael. "*A Chorus Line*—Review." *The Guardian*, February 20, 2013.

Blank, Christopher. "Chorus Line Delivers, Dazzles." *Memphis Commercial Appeal*, March 14, 2013.

Boden, Daniel. "'A Chorus Line,' running at the Freud Playhouse, Mirrors Lives of UCLA Theater Students." *Daily Bruin*, May 23, 2012.

Boyce, David B. "Review: 'A Chorus Line' Raises the Bar." *South Coast Today*, August 3, 2011.

Brandes, Philip. "'A Chorus Line' Stepping High: The Santa Barbara Production Is Done with Professionalism and Style, but the Musical Stumbles in Some Places." *Los Angeles Times*, May 16, 1991.

Brantley, Ben. "From the Top: Five, Six, Seven, Eight!" *New York Times*, October 6, 2006.

Brantley, Ben. "The Eternal Ingénue Conducts a Tour of Her Life." *New York Times*, August 3, 2001.

Canby, Vincent. "Film: Attenborough's 'Chorus Line.'" *New York Times*, December 10, 1985.

Carroll, Kathleen. "Broadway's Hit 'A Chorus Line' Kicks Up Its Heels on Screen." *New York Daily News*, December 10, 1985.

Christiansen, Richard. "'A Chorus Line': Classic Musical Still Sparkles, Despite Drury Lane's Staging." *Chicago Tribune*, July 15, 1985.

Christiansen, Richard. "'Chorus Line' Suffers from Bad Break." *Chicago Tribune*, September 11, 1996.

Christiansen, Richard. "Newest 'Chorus Line' Still Sensational." *Chicago Tribune*, June 14, 1985.

Corry, John. "Fresh Faces Give Broadway a New Look." *New York Times*, February 27, 1981.

Davis, Lee. "'A Chorus Line' for the Ages at Gateway." *East Hampton Press*, September 22, 2009.

Denby, David. "*A Chorus Line* Film Review." *New York*, December 16, 1985.

D'Souza, Karen. "Dancers Take Flight in Broadway Hit's Remake, but Compelling Story Never Gets Off the Ground." *San Jose Mercury News*, August 4, 2006.

Eberson, Sharon. "Preview: Director of CLO's 'A Chorus Line' Says the Show 'Has Always Been Something to Aspire To.'" *Pittsburgh Post-Gazette*, June 14, 2012.

Gerard, Jeremy. "Why Michael Bennett Has Said Goodbye, for Now, to Broadway." *New York Times*, November 2, 1986.

Heilpern, John. "A Masterpiece Revived: One Singular Sensation." *New York Observer*, October 16, 2006.

Hernández, Lee. "Natalie Cortez—Preaching to the 'Chorus Line.'" *New York Daily News*, April 17, 2008.

Hitchings, Henry. "A Chorus Line, Palladium—Review." *London Evening Standard*, February 20, 2013.

Hurwitt, Robert. "'Chorus' Classic: Nearly Picture-Perfect Revival Creates That Singular Sensation of Great Dance and Music." *San Francisco Chronicle*, August 4, 2006.

Kabaker, Marion E., "Disappointment Turns Sweet for Dancer." *Chicago Tribune*, December 13, 1985.

Kalem, T. E. "Dance of Life." *Time*, June 2, 1975.

Keyes, Bob. "'A Chorus Line': One Singular Sensation." *Portland Press Herald*, June 7, 2012.

Klein, Alvin. "'Chorus Line' Opens a Theater." *New York Times*, February 24, 1991.

Klein, Alvin. "'Chorus Line' Remains Legend with Kick, Relating Stage Stories." *New York Times*, January 4, 1998.

Kroll, Jack. "The Kids on the Line." *Newsweek*, June 2, 1975.

Ledford, Joseph. "'Chorus Line' Definitely One Singular Sensation." *Daily Record* (Wooster, OH), June 5, 2005.

Lucciola, Lorraine. "For New Bedford Festival Theatre, 'A Chorus Line' Is Art Imitating Life." *South Coast Today*, July 23, 2011.

Maples, Tina. "'Chorus Line' Adapts Poorly to Melody Top." *Milwaukee Journal*, June 19, 1985.

Martinfield, Seán. "Review: 'A Chorus Line.'" *San Francisco Sentinel*, August 2, 2006.

McCarter, Jeremy. "Broadway Melody of 1975." *New York*, October 16, 2006.

McKinley, Jesse. "A Broadway Survivor Joins 'Chorus Line.'" *New York Times*, January 27, 2006.

McKinley, Jesse. "Revisiting Some Singular Sensations: 'A Chorus Line' Returns." *New York Times*, August 4, 2006.

Moore, Dick and Helaine Feldman. "Who Says It's the . . . End of the Line?" *Equity News*, May, 1990.

Moore, John. "'A Chorus Line' Rating: ***." *Denver Post*, May 10, 2008.

Palmarini, James. "One Thrilling Combination." *Dramatics*, October 1987.

Purves, Libby. "'A Chorus Line' Review." *London Times*, February 20, 2013.

Rawson, Christopher. "Veterans Kick Up Heels in 'Chorus Line.'" *Pittsburgh Post-Gazette*, January 11, 2003.

Reed, Rex. "Stage Magic's Fled from 'Chorus Line.'" *New York Post*, December 10, 1985.

Robertson, Campbell. "'A Chorus Line' Returns, as Do Regrets." *New York Times*, October 1, 2006.

Rooney, David. "Review: 'A Chorus Line.'" *Variety*, October 5, 2006.

Rothman, Stephen. "'A Chorus Line'—A Sad Lesson in Big-Squeeze Theater Economics." *Los Angeles Times*, July 9, 1990.

Scott, A. O. "What They Did for Work (Love, Too). *New York Times*, April 16, 2009.

Segal, Lewis. "Choreographer Jeffrey Hornaday Is on the Line." *Los Angeles Times*, December 16, 1985.

Smith, Liz. "'A Children's Crusade' May Save Theater." *New York Herald Tribune*, September 29, 1984.

Sutcliffe, Tom. "Numbers Up." *Time Out London*, July 23–29, 1976.

Teachout, Terry. "Seventeen Sensations." *Wall Street Journal*, January 23, 2014.

Thomas, Bob. "Jeffrey Hornaday Is Still a 'Gypsy.'" *Gainesville Sun*, January 8, 1986.

Uncredited, "Edward Kleban, 48, 'Chorus Line' Lyricist." *New York Times*, December 30, 1987.

Watt, Douglas. "Tell Me, Little Gypsy." *New York Daily News*, May 22, 1975.

Webb, Eric. "New Sensation." *Oklahoma Gazette*, August 2, 2011.

Weinraub, Bernard. "'A Chorus Line' Is Smashing in London." *New York Times*, July 26, 1976.

Wellard, Nancy K. "'A Chorus Line' Is a High-Energy Theater Treat." *Island Packet*, June 28, 2007.

Williams, Sally. "A Chorus Line: Behind the Scenes." *The Telegraph*, February 26, 2013.

Index

Page numbers in italics refer to illustrations.

THE FAQ SERIES

AC/DC FAQ
by Susan Masino
Backbeat Books
978-1-4803-9450-6 .... $24.99

Armageddon Films FAQ
by Dale Sherman
Applause Books
978-1-61713-119-6 .... $24.99

Lucille Ball FAQ
*by James Sheridan
and Barry Monush*
Applause Books
978-1-61774-082-4 .... $19.99

The Beach Boys FAQ
by Jon Stebbins
Backbeat Books
978-0-87930-987-9 .... $22.99

Black Sabbath FAQ
by Martin Popoff
Backbeat Books
978-0-87930-957-2 .... $19.99

Johnny Cash FAQ
by C. Eric Banister
Backbeat Books
978-1-4803-8540-5 .... $24.99

Eric Clapton FAQ
by David Bowling
Backbeat Books
978-1-61713-454-8 .... $22.99

Doctor Who FAQ
by Dave Thompson
Applause Books
978-1-55783-854-4 .... $22.99

The Doors FAQ
by Rich Weidman
Backbeat Books
978-1-61713-017-5 .... $24.99

The Eagles FAQ
by Andrew Vaughan
Backbeat Books
978-1-4803-8541-2 .... $24.99

Fab Four FAQ
*by Stuart Shea and
Robert Rodriguez*
Hal Leonard Books
978-1-4234-2138-2 .... $19.99

Fab Four FAQ 2.0
by Robert Rodriguez
Backbeat Books
978-0-87930-968-8 .... $19.99

Film Noir FAQ
by David J. Hogan
Applause Books
978-1-55783-855-1 .... $22.99

Football FAQ
by Dave Thompson
Backbeat Books
978-1-4950-0748-4 .... $24.99

The Grateful Dead FAQ
by Tony Sclafani
Backbeat Books
978-1-61713-086-1 .... $24.99

Prices, contents, and availability
subject to change without notice.

Jimi Hendrix FAQ
by Gary J. Jucha
Backbeat Books
978-1-61713-095-3 .... $22.99

Horror Films FAQ
by John Kenneth Muir
Applause Books
978-1-55783-950-3 .... $22.99

James Bond FAQ
by Tom DeMichael
Applause Books
978-1-55783-856-8 .... $22.99

Stephen King Films FAQ
by Scott Von Doviak
Applause Books
978-1-4803-5551-4 .... $24.99

KISS FAQ
by Dale Sherman
Backbeat Books
978-1-61713-091-5 .... $22.99

Led Zeppelin FAQ
by George Case
Backbeat Books
978-1-61713-025-0 .... $19.99

Modern Sci-Fi Films FAQ
by Tom DeMichael
Applause Books
978-1-4803-5061-8 .... $24.99

Morrissey FAQ
by D. McKinney
Backbeat Books
978-1-4803-9448-3 .... $24.99

Nirvana FAQ
by John D. Luerssen
Backbeat Books
978-1-61713-450-0.............$24.99

Pink Floyd FAQ
by Stuart Shea
Backbeat Books
978-0-87930-950-3...........$19.99

Elvis Films FAQ
by Paul Simpson
Applause Books
978-1-55783-858-2.............$24.99

Elvis Music FAQ
by Mike Eder
Backbeat Books
978-1-61713-049-6.............$24.99

Prog Rock FAQ
by Will Romano
Backbeat Books
978-1-61713-587-3..............$24.99

Pro Wrestling FAQ
by Brian Solomon
Backbeat Books
978-1-61713-599-6.............$29.99

Rush FAQ
by Max Mobley
Backbeat Books
978-1-61713-451-7................$24.99

Saturday Night Live FAQ
by Stephen Tropiano
Applause Books
978-1-55783-951-0.............$24.99

Prices, contents, and availability
subject to change without notice.

Seinfeld FAQ
by Nicholas Nigro
Applause Books
978-1-55783-857-5.............$24.99

Sherlock Holmes FAQ
by Dave Thompson
Applause Books
978-1-4803-3149-5.............$24.99

Soccer FAQ
by Dave Thompson
Backbeat Books
978-1-61713-598-9..............$24.99

The Sound of Music FAQ
by Barry Monush
Applause Books
978-1-4803-6043-3...........$27.99

South Park FAQ
by Dave Thompson
Applause Books
978-1-4803-5064-9..........$24.99

Bruce Springsteen FAQ
by John D. Luerssen
Backbeat Books
978-1-61713-093-9...............$22.99

Star Trek FAQ
(Unofficial and Unauthorized)
by Mark Clark
Applause Books
978-1-55783-792-9...............$19.99

Star Trek FAQ 2.0
(Unofficial and Unauthorized)
by Mark Clark
Applause Books
978-1-55783-793-6.............$22.99

Quentin Tarantino FAQ
by Dale Sherman
Applause Books
978-1-4803-5588-0..........$24.99

Three Stooges FAQ
by David J. Hogan
Applause Books
978-1-55783-788-2..............$22.99

U2 FAQ
by John D. Luerssen
Backbeat Books
978-0-87930-997-8...........$19.99

The Who FAQ
by Mike Segretto
Backbeat Books
978-1-4803-6103-4..........$24.99

The Wizard of Oz FAQ
by David J. Hogan
Applause Books
978-1-4803-5062-5...........$24.99

Neil Young FAQ
by Glen Boyd
Backbeat Books
978-1-61713-037-3................$19.99

HAL•LEONARD®
PERFORMING ARTS
PUBLISHING GROUP

FAQ.halleonardbooks.com

0515